Contemporary American
women poets

CONTEMPORARY AMERICAN WOMEN POETS

CONTEMPORARY AMERICAN WOMEN POETS

An A-to-Z Guide

Edited by Catherine Cucinella

Emmanuel S. Nelson, Advisory Editor

GREENWOOD PRESS
Westport, Connecticut • London

Library of Congress Cataloging-in-Publication Data

Contemporary American women poets : an A-to-Z guide / edited by Catherine Cucinella.
p. cm.
Includes bibliographical references and index.
ISBN 0-313-31783-6 (alk. paper)
1. American poetry—Women authors—Bio-bibliography—Dictionaries. 2. Women and literature—United States—History—20th century—Dictionaries. 3. American poetry—20th century—Bio-bibliography—Dictionaries. 4. Poets, American—20th century—Biography—Dictionaries. 5. Women poets, American—Biography—Dictionaries. 6. American poetry—Women authors—Dictionaries. 7. American poetry—20th century—Dictionaries. I. Cucinella, Catherine.
PS151.C665 2002
811'.54099287'03—dc21
[B] 2002067811

British Library Cataloguing in Publication Data is available.

Library of Congress Catalog Card Number: 2002067811
ISBN: 0-313-31783-6

First published in 2002

Greenwood Press, 88 Post Road West, Westport, CT 06881
An imprint of Greenwood Publishing Group, Inc.
www.greenwood.com

Printed in the United States of America

The paper used in this book complies with the Permanent Paper Standard issued by the National Information Standards Organization (Z39.48–1984).

10 9 8 7 6 5 4 3 2 1

CONTENTS

PREFACE

American women poets compose a significant part of an American poetic tradition; however, discussions regarding American poetry that include women focus on a very small group of American women poets. Unfortunately, this "elite" group of female poets then becomes representative of all American women poets. While troublesome in itself, this pattern proves particularly damaging for the contemporary female poet. Female poets writing today must not only struggle with or within a predominately male poetic tradition, but they must also negotiate and confront exclusive female or feminist expectations. This either/or paradigm seems to leave little room for the inclusiveness that prevails among contemporary American female poets.

Feminist efforts have "recovered" the works of earlier (pre-twentieth century) women poets, and much of this rediscovered work now shows up in anthologies. Furthermore, anthologies devoted to the works of specific groups of poets—Language poets, award winners, poets of color—also exist. This reference work, however, deals specifically with contemporary American women poets—well known and lesser known, women of color as well as white women—as it begins to fill a gap in our understanding of contemporary American poetry. This project also manifests limitations and politics of inclusion and exclusion. I do not suggest that this reference book is by any means complete or exhaustive. I view it as only one resource through which to identify and acknowledge the many women who have written and continue to write on American poetics.

This volume includes American women poets who published a significant part of their work from 1946 to the present and provides an important contribution to the study of American women poets during this time frame. It also continues the work of Denise Knight's *Nineteenth-Century American Women Writers: A Bio-Bibliographical Critical Sourcebook* (1997), Laurie Champion's *American Women Writers, 1900–1945: A Bio-Bibliographical Critical Sourcebook* (2000), and Laurie Champion and Rhonda Austin's *Contemporary American Women Fiction Writers: An*

A-to-Z Guide (2002). In an effort to avoid duplication, some poets do not appear in this volume, most notably Elizabeth Bishop.

The women included in *Contemporary American Women Poets* come from a variety of racial and ethnic backgrounds, and they both represent and inhabit multiple social and class positions. In addition, the seventy poets in this book write from and about all parts of the United States. These voices also include international accents as many of these women come from, write about, and understand countries outside of the borders of the United States. Thus, this volume acknowledges the global, cultural, and social influences in the poetry of contemporary American women poets.

All of the women included in this reference have received acclaim for their craft; however, some prove relatively unknown except by a small group of academics and/or poetry specialists. Regardless of the "fame" of each poet, each has added to a tradition of American poetry, and each continues to shape our understanding of that tradition. You will also find that I have included Muriel Rukeyser, although she died in 1980 and published her most important works much earlier than most of the poets in this volume. Rukeyser's poetry, however, looks beyond its own time and suggests the concerns manifest in the poetry of contemporary American women poets, such as the intersection of poetry and politics, the body and sexuality, memory and history. Anne Sexton has called Rukeyser "the mother of us all." You will find within these pages poets of renown such as Audre Lorde, Rita Dove, Maya Angelou, Adrienne Rich, Sylvia Plath, June Jordan, Sharon Olds, and Denise Levertov. You will also find poets just beginning to receive public recognition for their work and poets of long standing who have quietly claimed a space within American letters, such as Rae Armantrout, Lynn Emmanuel, Jane Shore, Natasha Sajé, Carla Harryman, Cathy Song, Carolyn Kizer, and Ruth Stone.

The format of this sourcebook is similar to that of other references Greenwood has published. Each entry begins with a section on the poet's biography, offers a detailed discussion of her major works and themes, followed by an overview of the critical commentary about the poet, and ends with a bibliography of works by the poet (listed chronologically by publication dates) and works about the poet (reviews, scholarly books and articles). Because many of these women also write in genres other than poetry, each contributor has, in the "Works by the Poet" section, identified the specific genre of each work; if no designation follows the citation then that work is a volume of poetry. In some cases, when the list of reviews and critical sources proves immense, I have provided a selected list.

Finally, I would like to acknowledge and thank the contributors to this project. Like the poets about whom they write, the contributors represent a diverse group of men and women, both inside and outside of academia. Their essays speak with various accents, and they manifest the spirit of the writer. Some of the contributors, poets themselves, write, publish, and perform their poetry throughout this country. In most cases, the writer of the entry conveys his or her own connection to and investment in a particular poet as well as his or her individual love of poetry. The depth of understanding, insight, and commitment that I found in each entry has touched my own spirit, and for that, I thank each and every contributor. Thank you to Renée R. Curry and Steven Gould Axelrod for helping me in the early stages of this project and, more importantly, for their expertise regarding, and love of, poetry, which they so generously share with me. I also thank Laurie Champion for her faith in my ability to take on this project. I give my personal thanks to Angela Oberle and Jen Silverwood for helping me through the crunch. *Muchas Gracias, mi amor*. I also thank the editors at Greenwood for their careful scrutiny with a special thank you to George Butler and Emmanuel Nelson. I offer my sincere gratitude to Penny Sippel, Senior Production Coordinator and Lori Ewen, Production Editor of this project.

I end this preface with a final thank you. I thank the women who write poetry. This volume salutes your craft, your perseverance, and your talent.

INTRODUCTION

On September 26, 2001, poet laureate Billy Collins told Terry Gross, host of National Public Radio's program *Fresh Air*, that crisis often generates a need for poetry. Collins's comments echo the sentiments expressed by Adrienne Rich in a 1995 conversation with Bill Moyers: "I see poetry in the United States as coming out of the stress points in our society . . . not only from those places, but certainly from those places—as if the stress in itself creates a search for language in which to probe and unravel what is going on" (338). Significantly, both Rich and Collins identify the importance of language in times of unrest and crisis, and they delineate a specific language, the language of poetry. In poetry, we find both words and images—language as image. In poetry, we find language striving to concretize abstractions into recognizable images, language striving to make the familiar uncanny in order to create new images, and language striving to reconfigure existing metaphors in order to deepen understanding, heighten awareness, and challenge complacency.

Indeed, in the introduction to *The Language of Life: A Festival of Poets*, Bill Moyers writes, "Poetry is news—news of the mind, news of the heart" (xii). Thus, poetry conveys a sense of the here and now through its use of figurative language, making one keenly aware of his or her physicality and bodily presence. This sense of immediacy arises from the "news" aspect of poetry and because figurative language draws on, depends upon, and calls upon the senses of the body, the mind, and the spirit. Therefore, poetry always seems to foreground a sense of immediacy as it demands engagement from the individual reader while it transforms experience into language, giving words and form both to individual and shared experiences.

Poets, of course, place great importance on poetry, and in their attempts to define poetry and its function in our world, poets seldom see it as a thing in and of itself. Instead, poets view poetry as a dynamic process possessing a myriad of possibilities. Rita Dove, poet laureate of the United States (1993–95), proclaims: "By making us stop for a moment, poetry gives us an opportunity to think about ourselves as human beings on this planet and what we mean to each other" (Moyers 110). Lawrence

Ferlinghetti calls poetry "prophecy"; Mary Oliver calls it a river filled with many voices (9); Naomi Shihab Nye calls poetry a conversation—with the world, with printed words, with oneself; Stanley Kunitz calls it "difficult," "solitary," and "life-enhancing"; and Jane Kenyon calls poetry "a safe place always, a refuge" (Moyers 321, 245, 219). Thus poetry pulses with energy, sometimes comforting, sometimes challenging, sometimes explaining, and, at all times, acknowledging the importance of language to each of us individually and to all of us collectively.

The women poets included in this reference recognize the role of language—specifically the significance of figurative language—in shaping the self, in situating the self in relation to others and to the world, and in sustaining the self in the face of tragedy, crisis, and stress. In his elaboration of poetry's role in the time of crisis, Collins foresees a change in the way contemporary poets and writers use metaphor after the American tragedy of September 11, 2001. For Collins, all comparisons now fail, yet poets do, and will continue to, find the metaphors necessary for American poetics. Specifically, American women poets, represented in the following pages, recognize the significance and importance of figurative language. Individually each poet utilizes the full range of this language. While some work with and redefine metaphor, others privilege metonymy—finding in this figure of speech a new range of possibilities. Some of these women challenge all the conventions of language, bending those conventions and stretching them to the limits of meaning and then extending, through startling metaphors, unsettling metonymic markers, and dizzying syntax, our understanding of the self and of the world.

These poets write within and of diverse and shifting, solid and fixed, promising and disappointing worlds. All write within a postmodern era, but not all these poets write a postmodern poetics. In fact, each living poet in this reference defies ultimate categorization as she continues to write, and her opus continues to grow and change, often reflecting larger political and social shifts as well as mirroring intimate and personal changes. The poems that these poets write and the poetics that they create imbue the personal with political, cultural, and social concerns as each poet makes the ordinary, the mundane, and the personal matter. In this respect, all these poets invoke the tenets of second wave feminism: "The personal is political."

I do not attempt to identify a canon of contemporary American women poets; rather, this volume contains a diverse group of poets representing a range of poetic styles, standpoints, and subject positions. Furthermore, I do not argue that all the voices represented by this volume write from a feminist perspective, although many do. Yet even among those who do write from within a feminist framework, no one feminism emerges, nor does one female voice emerge from among those who write from within a belief in women's voice. Instead, these women reveal the dangers of assuming a female voice even while they invoke that voice; thus their poetry presents the feminine as their poems challenge the category itself. The works of these poets represent a multivocal poetics that resonates with and echoes the many strains that construct American poetry.

While it proves tempting to argue for a female literary tradition, I find that instead I must posit traditions, in the plural, of female literary production because a single women's tradition denies the reality of contemporary American poetry written by women. However, traditions do exist within the field of contemporary American poetry written by women, but these traditions refuse the stasis of our traditional understandings of "literary tradition." The women who write poetry today reflect many traditions, and they often take their place in several simultaneously as their poetry refuses the restraints of any bounded tradition. Thus, these women reflect and construct traditions of lesbian poetry (Adrienne Rich, Olga Broumas), feminist poetry (Adrienne Rich, Ntozke Shange), Chicana poetry (Ana Castillo, Sandra Cisneros, Pat Mora), African American poetry (Audre Lorde, Nikki Giovanni, Wanda Coleman), Asian American poetry (Marilyn Chin, Jessica Hagedorn, Mitsuye Yamada), Native American poetry (Joy Harjo, Leslie Marmon Silko), immigrant poetry (Beatriz Badikian), love poetry, domestic poetry, nature poetry, political poetry (June Jordan, Jayne Cortez, Denise Levertov, Sonia Sanchez), and female poetry. These various traditions expand, change, reconfigure, and redefine as individual poets insist on crossing the boundaries of traditions as well as ignoring generic boundaries. For example, Lyn Heijinian collapses the boundaries between poetry and autobiography with *My Life*, and in this reference, she also redefines the autobiographical tradition through the volume's refusal to offer any unified subject. Leslie Marmon Silko ignores generic restrictions by presenting multigenre works that blend poetry and narrative fiction. Silko's *Storyteller* best exemplifies her commitment to utilizing all genres in her own "storytelling," and Ntozake Shange's *For Colored Girls Who Have Considered Suicide/When the Rainbow Is Enuf* combines poetry, music, dance, and drama. As these women experiment among and within genres, they often disregard existing traditions.

Yet, all writers, men and women, possess an awareness of an officially sanctioned literary tradition or canon. Poet Grace Schulman rightly points out that "tradition has a way of exerting its strongest hold on us when we are least aware of its presence" (168). Therefore, although many contemporary women poets intentionally write in reaction to or against the grain of literary tradition, many also carry into their poetry the influences of that tradition. Sharon Bryan further points out that "many women poets have begun their writing lives assuming that they were part of an ongoing tradition, and then gradually revised their sense of what that meant after reminders that the tradition didn't necessarily return the favor" (xiii). Many of the women in this volume learned early in their careers as poets that while they understood and had mastered the criteria of poetic tradition, that tradition, for the most part, excluded them. Speaking of her own relationship to the literary tradition, poet Martha Collins acknowledges that "a male tradition . . . drew [her] to literature" (32). She also suggests that "women readers confronting a primarily male tradition have often made up their own version of it. . . . And . . . that women have, in this way, influenced the shape of that tradition" (32). Consequently, both women readers and women writers continually engage in tradition/canon building. Poet Deborah Tall acknowledges an ironic debt to the literary tradition: "If we owe literary tradition anything, it's our conscious revision of it" (188). Tall echoes Rich's insistence that women poets must continually look back and re-see history and then revise traditional histories, mythologies, stories, and texts. Indeed, contemporary American women poets constantly revise established literary traditions through their engagement with those traditions, through their insistence on the importance of difference, through their redefinition of appropriate poetic subjects, their inclusion of the materiality of the body, and finally through the commitment to their craft.

Women poets, writing from the margins of established literary tradition, historically struggled for inclusion in the very tradition that ignored and scorned them. However, as individual women poets began to rediscover the work of earlier women poets, and as each poet became aware that she did not possess the lone female poetic voice, commonalities began to emerge, patterns began to configure, and conversations began to occur. I am astounded by the connections among the diverse group of women included in this reference. Many of these women acknowledge the influence of male poets on their poetry and on their careers, and many of these women poets point to female poets as influences: Emily Dickinson, Elizabeth Bishop, Adrienne Rich, June Jordan, Audre Lorde. While these poets may appear as "foremothers" to many of the poets writing today, many of those named continue to write, and younger poets do not seem intent on either "killing" or displacing these "foremothers"; instead, contemporary American women poets embrace these earlier poets; they celebrate them; they learn from them, and then they stand alongside them. Each woman represented in the following pages extends and expands an earlier poetics and in moving away from that earlier model reconfigures existing American poetics.

Themes and subjects appear and reappear as concerns with the everyday, the mundane, the routine, as well as the abstract, the lofty, the sublime, touch almost every poet in this volume. Subjects and themes involve death, life, family, home, travel, violence, nationalism, voice, silence, pain, love, heterosexual love, lesbian love, joy, disappointment, hope, frustration, the body, sexuality, sex, gender, politics, struggle, spirituality, creativity, nature, illness, mythmaking, history, aging, birth, motherhood, daughterhood, language, and poetry itself. The themes, concerns, and subjects that fill the poetry of these women, the images that they construct, and the forms that they utilize bespeak similarity and difference. Each poet writes from a specific location—a particular subjectivity and selfhood. However, even the work of individual poets demonstrates differences within as she confronts the intersections of her own particular gender, sexuality, class, race, ethnicity, and nationality.

I stress again that I cannot argue for a unified and fixed tradition that defines women's poetry. However, I can posit a shared love of words and a communal sense of craft among these female poets, and I hope that this reference book offers a starting point for understanding the various female voices that sound within contemporary American poetry.

WORKS CITED

Bryan, Sharon, ed. *Where We Stand: Women Poets on Literary Tradition.* New York: Norton, 1993.

Collins, Billy. *Fresh Air.* Host Terry Gross. National Public Radio. KPBS, San Diego, California, 26 Sept. 2001.

Collins, Martha. "Reclaiming the Oh." In *Where We Stand: Women Poets on Literary Tradition,* edited by Sharon Bryan. 28–30. New York: Norton, 1993.

Ferlinghetti, Lawrence. *MacLear News Hour.* Public Broadcasting System. KPBS, San Diego, California, 26 Oct. 2001.

Moyers, Bill. *The Language of Life: A Festival of Poets.* New York: Doubleday, 1995.

Oliver, Mary. *A Poetry Handbook.* San Diego, CA: Harcourt, 1994.

Schulman, Grace. "The Persistence of Tradition." In *Where We Stand: Women Poets on Literary Tradition,* edited by Sharon Bryan. 168–74. New York: Norton, 1993.

Tall, Deborah. "Terrible Perfection: In the Face of Tradition." In *Where We Stand: Women Poets on Literary Tradition,* edited by Sharon Bryan. 184–94. New York: Norton, 1993.

DIANE (FINK) ACKERMAN (1948–)

J. Elizabeth Clark

BIOGRAPHY

"I left the planet that bore me," Diane Ackerman writes in "Pluto." In one line—imaginative and lyrical, connecting science and art—the eclectic and prolific Ackerman exposes the essential elements in her first book, *The Planets: A Cosmic Pastoral* (1976), which would come to characterize her poetry, essays, and memoirs. What other imaginative assertion could one expect from a writer who comes from a family inspired by creativity and curiosity? Diane Ackerman was born on October 7, 1948, in Waukegan, Illinois, to Marsha Tischler Fink and Sam Fink, a shoe salesman who went on to run one of the first McDonald's franchises. Ackerman has shared in interviews that her grandfather was an inventor in his free time and a translator for gypsies immigrating to the United States; her aunt Frieda was a belly-dancer called Fatima up until her death at eighty-seven; and her mother, who loved to travel, designed and crafted many things throughout her life as a way to express her unfulfilled desire to be an architect.

In interviews, Ackerman often explains that she always wanted to be a writer. She was fascinated by the world and examined it through words. She left home for Boston University in 1966 where she planned to pursue a degree in literature and science. Transferring to Pennsylvania State University in 1967, she received her BA in English in 1970. She entered graduate school at Cornell University in 1971, receiving an MFA in 1973, an MA in 1976, and a PhD in 1978.

Her time at Cornell University provided her with the unique opportunity to explore her dual interests in literature and science, a fusion that defines her poetry and provides a critical distinction between her work and that of her contemporaries. Cornell was home to the legendary scientist Carl Sagan, author of *Contact*, who played a role on her doctoral dissertation committee and for whom Ackerman wrote poems in both *The Planets: A Cosmic Pastoral* and the recent *I Praise My Destroyer* (1998). While in school Ackerman worked with the Jet Propulsion Laboratory and participated in night watches for the space shuttle. At Cornell, Ackerman completed three books: *Poems*, which she wrote with Judy Bolz and Nancy Steele (1973), *The Planets: A Cosmic Pastoral* (1976), and *Wife of Light* (1978).

After graduate school, Ackerman worked in both academic and professional writing-related fields while maintaining a rigorous publishing schedule. From 1980 to 1983, she taught English at the University of Pittsburgh, Pennsylvania, and 1980 saw the beginning of her extensive work as an essayist with *Twilight of the Tenderfoot: A Western Memoir* and then another collection of poetry, *Lady Faustus* (1983). From 1984 to 1986, Ackerman directed the writers' program at Washington University in St. Louis, Missouri, where she served as writer-in-residence while also writing her memoir of flying, *On Extended Wings* (1985). From 1988 to 1994, she was a staff writer at *The New Yorker* magazine. In 1988, Ackerman completed the dramatic poem *Reverse Thunder*, which was followed by the enormously popular nonfiction book *A Natural History of the Senses* in 1991. In the next decade, Ackerman published nine more books, including two well-received poetry collections, *Jaguar of Sweet Laughter: New & Selected Poems* (1993) and *I Praise My Destroyer* (1998). She also has taught writing at Columbia, New York University, the College of William and Mary, and Ohio University. She currently lives in Ithaca, New York, where she is a visiting professor of English at Cornell University. For the past thirty years, Ackerman has shared her life, love, home, and writing with novelist husband Paul West.

Her essays about nature and human interaction have appeared in *Parade*, *National Geographic*, the *New York Times*, *The New Yorker*, and other journals. Three of her works have been transformed into stage and television productions, widening her already popular appeal. *On Extended Wings*, adapted for stage by Norma Jean Giffin, was performed in New York's William Redfield Theater in April 1987; *Reverse Thunder* was staged as a dramatic reading with music by Paul Goldstaub at the Old Dominion Literary Arts Festival in 1992; the most extensive production was a five-hour 1995 PBS *NOVA* production "Mystery of the Senses," hosted by Ackerman and based on *A Natural History of the Senses*.

MAJOR WORKS AND THEMES

"It's hard for me to keep science out of my writing," Ackerman told interviewer Dulcy Brainard in *Publisher's Weekly*. She continued, "A critic once said that airfoils, quasars, corpuscles aren't the proper form of art. But to agree ignores much of life's fascination and variety. Writing, which is my form of celebration and prayer, is also my way of inquiry" (62). Inquiry—into the worlds of emotion, science, human nature, history, and senses—is one way to define Ackerman's eclectic *oeuvre*. Historic figures such as Mexican nun Sor Juana Inés de la Cruz, nature, flying, astronomy, travel, spirituality, and love form the subjects for her poems and essays.

Ackerman's first book, *The Planets: A Cosmic Pastoral*, epitomizes her desire to fuse scientifically accurate information with beautiful language unfolded in a wide range of poetic forms and voices: science and nature meet poetic craft. Science, as an exploration of nature, provides the ultimate way for Ackerman to connect to the world in which she lives, and poetry is the vehicle through which Ackerman exposes that connection to her audience.

Nature provides the impetus for Ackerman, as scientist, explorer, adventurer, and poet, to interrogate the world around her. She continues this exploration of nature in

Lady Faustus and *Jaguar of Sweet Laughter*; however, the two later collections are also dominated by an interrogation of the everyday minutia of life. In all three collections, which are dominated by a poetic consideration of science and nature, Ackerman moves from the macro level of the universe to the micro level of plants and animals. In *Planets*, Ackerman travels through the universe in nine planet poems, one poem for Cape Canaveral, one for Comet Kohoutek, and two introductory poems. Similarly, the poems of *Lady Faustus* examine the natural world from above, inspired by Ackerman's experiences as a pilot, and from below in a scuba-diving poem, "A Fine, A Private Place." *Jaguar* moves between different natural locations: from the rainforest of the Amazon to the icebergs of Antarctica, to her backyard, to the planetary visions of her first collection. No topic, from contact lenses to penguins, escapes the examination of the poet naturalist. *Jaguar*, as a more sophisticated collection, also acknowledges the influence of a vast American literary tradition. Ackerman writes a "Letter to Wallace Stevens," a poem that both admires and critiques Sylvia Plath, and a poem set at the birthplace of Walt Whitman.

Wife of Light, which Ackerman has referred to as her "normal" poems, contains a more miscellaneous thematic approach. It, along with *Reverse Thunder* and *I Praise My Destroyer*, can be loosely categorized as love poems, another of Ackerman's prominent themes. They share Ackerman's celebratory love for the world and for the people who occupy it. While these three collections are not dominated by the same strong connection to science and nature as her previous volumes, Ackerman is never far from her muse. *Wife of Light* includes a poem about the origin of the mathematical number pi as well as poems about menstruation. *Reverse Thunder*, a dramatic poem, continues the theme of love as Ackerman imagines the life of Sor Juana Inés de la Cruz. While the historical facts of de la Cruz's life provide the background for the poem, Ackerman extends her poetic consideration of de la Cruz to include an imagined thematic treatment of love, passion, and creativity.

In many ways, each of Ackerman's previous collections served as previews for the poems she wrote in *I Praise My Destroyer*. Her most recently published collection (although another is forthcoming in 2002), this volume shows Ackerman at the height of her poetic power. Most generally a book of love poems, this collection intimately connects nature and love. While Ackerman revels in a celebration of daily life, she comes to acknowledge that the very science and nature she reveres in other poems can only lead to death. This new poetic consideration—one that heightens Ackerman's connection to a spiritual world as well—was brought on by the unexpected death of Carl Sagan. As the poet wrestles with love and death, she comes to the realization that death is an intimate part of the natural world she loves. The reconciliation in this collection comes in the space between poems such as "Natural Wonder" and "Tender Mercies" where the poet writes everything she has learned about the natural world, about science, and about love in one place.

Ackerman extends many of her stylistic practices and thematic explorations to prose as well. She combines journalism, science, and poetry to create a different kind of nonfiction. Her nine nonfiction books have received critical acclaim: *Twilight of the Tenderfoot: A Western Memoir* (1980); *On Extended Wings* (1985); *A Natural History of the Senses* (1991); *The Moon by Whale Light: And Other Adventures among Bats, Penguins, Crocodilians, and Whales* (1992); *The Rarest of the Rare: Vanishing Animals, Timeless Worlds* (1995); *A Natural History of Love* (1994); *A Slender Thread* (1997); *The Book of Love* (1998); and *Deep Play* (1999). She has also branched out to write three books for children: *Monk Seal Hideaway* (1995); *Bats: Shadows in the Night* (1997); and *The Senses of Animals* (2000).

Critics have commented on Ackerman's lush lyricism and her linguistic precision. John Taylor writes of *I Praise My Destroyer* that "Ackerman weaves intricate, colorful, often stunning linguistic tapestries" (182). The constant in her work—language and a powerful use of imagination to render the invisible visible—is often achieved as a juxtaposition of opposites. She uses precise scientific language against a beautifully wrought description; the language of objectivity rendered fully in the language of explanation. Ackerman is unusual among her contemporaries with her fusion of science and art, often considered binary oppositions in the twentieth century. Her celebration of the natural through a lyrically rich and well-crafted verse make her a feminist descendent of Wallace Stevens and Walt Whitman. She extends their celebration of nature into an interrogation of the natural. Science and poetry become two tools through which the natural world enters the reader's life. For Ackerman, science is another word for sensuality. Through the senses and a poetic and imaginative rendering, both reader and poet come to know the world and the universe more fully.

CRITICAL RECEPTION

Ackerman's copious publishing record is juxtaposed by her sparse critical reception. Taylor's review of *I Praise My Destroyer* is indicative of Ackerman's favorable critical reception in publications such as *Publisher's Weekly* and *Booklist.* In part because of Ackerman's prodigious, and multi-genre publishing career, however, she is sometimes the subject of highly negative reviews for her poetry, typified by Carolyn Kizer's review of *I Praise My Destroyer*: "Ackerman is a spirited and intelligent woman who has given us valuable information about endangered species and other matters. As a poet she is careless—including her grammar—and inclined to hyperbole. Poetry is more difficult than she seems to believe" (171).

Despite Kizer's concerns about Ackerman's work, Ackerman has received considerable critical reception, in the form of prizes and awards, for both her poetry and nonfiction writing. She has been recognized with the Art of Fact Award for Creative Nonfiction (2000); Amazon.com Top Ten List of Spirituality Books for *Deep Play* (1999); *New York Times Book Review* New and Noteworthy Book of the Year for *A Slender Thread* (1997); the "Literary Lion," from the New York Public Library (1994); *New York Times Book Review* New and Noteworthy Book of the Year for *Jaguar of Sweet Laughter: New and Selected Poems*, paperback edition (1993); *New York Times Book Review* Notable Book of the Year for *The Moon by Whale Light* (1992); the Wordsmith Award (1992); the National Book Critics Circle Award nomination for *Jaguar of Sweet Laughter: New and Selected Poems* (1991); *New York Times Book Review* Notable Book of the Year for both *Jaguar of Sweet Laughter: New and Selected Poems* and *A Natural History of the Senses* (1991); a Prix Médicis nomination for *A Natural History of the Senses* (1991); the Lowell Thomas Award (1990); a National Endowment for the Arts Creative Writing Fellowship (1986); the Peter I. B. Lavan Award from The Academy of American Poets (1985); a Pushcart Prize VIII (1984); the *Black Warrior Review* Poetry Prize (1981); a National Endowment for the Arts Creative Writing Fellowship (1976); and the Abbie Copps Poetry Prize (1974).

In addition to these literary awards, Ackerman has received other awards recognizing her work as a naturalist. She was recently honored in a manner truly fitting to her dual interests in science and poetry: a molecule, "dianeackerone," was named for her in 1999. She has also received the John Burroughs Nature Award (1997), was named a fellow in the Explorers Club (1997), received the Golden Nose Award from Olfactory Research Fund (1994), Regional Semi-Finalist status in the Journalist-in-Space Project (1986), and was named a Rockefeller Fellow in Humanities, Science and Technology (1974).

BIBLIOGRAPHY

Works by Diane Ackerman

Poems. With Judy Bolz and Nancy Steele. Ithaca, NY: Stone-Marrow, 1973.
The Planets: A Cosmic Pastoral. New York: Morrow, 1976.
Wife of Light. New York: Morrow, 1978.
Twilight of the Tenderfoot: A Western Memoir. New York: Morrow, 1980. (nonfiction)
Lady Faustus. New York: Morrow, 1983.
On Extended Wings. New York: Atheneum, 1985. (nonfiction)
Reverse Thunder. New York: Lumen, 1988.
A Natural History of the Senses. New York: Vintage Books, 1991. (nonfiction)
The Moon by Whale Light: And Other Adventures among Bats, Penguins, Crocodilians, and Whales. New York: Vintage Books, 1992. (nonfiction)
Jaguar of Sweet Laughter: New & Selected Poems. New York: Vintage Books, 1993.
A Natural History of Love. New York: Random House, 1994. (nonfiction)
Beyond the Map. Lithographs by Enid Mark. Wallingford, PA: ELM Press, 1995. (anthology)
Monk Seal Hideaway. New York: Crown Publishers, 1995. (juvenile nonfiction)
The Rarest of the Rare: Vanishing Animals, Timeless Worlds. New York: Random House, 1995. (nonfiction)
About Sylvia. Lithographs by Enid Mark. Wallingford, PA: ELM Press, 1996. (anthology)
Bats: Shadows in the Night. New York: Crown Publishers, 1997. (juvenile nonfiction)
A Slender Thread. New York: Random House, 1997. (nonfiction)
I Praise My Destroyer. New York: Random House, 1998.
The Book of Love. With Jeanne Mackin. New York: Norton, 1998.
Deep Play. New York: Random House, 1999. (nonfiction)
Senses of Animals: Poems. New York: Alfred Knopf, 2000. (children's)
Origami Bridges: Poems of Psychoanalysis and Fire. New York: Harper, 2002 (forthcoming)

Studies of Diane Ackerman

Adams, Barbara. "Diane Ackerman: Tight Focus in Small Places." *Writer's Digest* 77.9 (1997): 29.
Brainard, Dulcy. "Interview." *Publishers Weekly*, 1 Nov. 1991, 62.
Dillard, R.W.H. "Diane Ackerman." In *Contemporary Poets*, edited by Tracy Chevalier. Chicago: St. James, 1991: 4–5.
Doty, Mark. "Horsehair Sofas of the Antarctic: Diane Ackerman's Natural Histories." *Parnassus* 20.1 (1995): 264.
Gates, Barbara, and Ann B. Shteir. "Interview with Diane Ackerman." In *Natural Eloquence: Women Reinscribe Science*, edited by Barbara T. Gates and Ann B. Shteir. Madison: University of Wisconsin Press, 1997. 255–64.
Gossin, Pamela S. "Living Poetics, Enacting the Cosmos: Diane Ackerman's Popularization of Astronomy in *The Planets: A Cosmic Pastoral*." *Women's Studies* 26 (1997): 605–38.

Hubbarb, Kim, and Sam Mead. "Natural Woman." *People Weekly* 36.19 (1991): 105.

Kizer, Carolyn. Review of *I Praise My Destroyer*, by Diane Ackerman. *Michigan Quarterly Review* 39.1 (2000): 167–72.

Myers, Kathleen A. Review of *Reverse Thunder*, by Diane Ackerman. *Michigan Quarterly Review*. 29.3 (1990): 453.

Schultz, Robert. "Poetry and Knowledge." *The Hudson Review* 44.4 (1992): 667.

Seaman, Donna. "The Booklist Interview: Diane Ackerman." *Booklist*, 15 Feb. 1992, 1074.

———. Review of *I Praise My Destroyer*, by Diane Ackerman. *Booklist*, 15 March 1998, 1197.

Taylor, John. Review of *I Praise My Destroyer*, by Diane Ackerman. *Poetry* 173.2 (1998): 182.

Velsany, Kathleen. "A Conversation with Diane Ackerman." *Creative–Nonfiction* 3 (1995): 91–102.

AI (1947–)

Nikolas Huot

BIOGRAPHY

Florence Ai Ogawa was born October 21, 1947, in Albany, Texas, of an adulterous affair between her married mother and a Japanese man she met at a bus stop. Raised in Tucson, Arizona, in a strict Catholic household, Ai moved with her mother and stepfather to Los Angeles in 1958. Though she lived in Los Angeles for just three years, this brief period helped shape her life. When she was twelve years old and attending Catholic school, a writing assignment propelled her into the world of poetry. Pretending to be a martyr about to be fed to the lions, Ai had to write her last letters. Her work was so good that she was asked to read it in front of the class. Although she did not start writing poetry regularly for two more years, Ai's career as a poet began in that class in Los Angeles. She left Los Angeles in 1961 and returned to Tucson to complete high school and attend college. Ai graduated from the University of Arizona in 1969 with a BA in English/Oriental Studies. Through the poet Galway Kinnell, whom she met while an undergraduate and who became a mentor and friend, Ai pursued her education at the University of California at Irvine where she earned an MFA in 1971.

Toward her senior year as an undergraduate, Ai changed her surname from Florence Haynes (second stepfather's name) to Florence Anthony (first stepfather's name) because she thought it "sounded more poetic" ("Movies" 241). In 1969 she began to adopt the pen name Ai, which means "love" in Japanese. It was only in 1973, when Ai was twenty-six years old, that she learned of her Japanese ancestry. Ai legally took her biological father's surname and made her pen name her legal middle name; thus was born the poet Florence Ai Ogawa. The same year that she learned of her origins, Ai published her first collection of dramatic monologues, *Cruelty* (1973). Her second volume of poetry, *Killing Floor* (1979), was the 1978 Lamont Poetry Selection of the Academy of American Poets. Ai's third collection of dramatic monologues, *Sin* (1986), received the Before Columbus Foundation American Book Award in 1987.

Ai followed these successful volumes with the publication of *Fate* in 1991 and *Greed* in 1993. Her sixth collection of dramatic monologues, *Vice: New and Selected Poems* (1999), earned Ai the National Book Award for Poetry in 1999. In addition to awards, Ai has received numerous fellowships, including a Guggenheim (1975), Bunting (1975), National Endowment for the Arts (1978), Ingram Merrill (1983), and the St. Botolph Foundation grant (1986).

Currently a professor at Oklahoma State University at Stillwater, Ai has taught and served as visiting poet in such universities as State University of New York at Binghamton, Wayne State University, George Mason University, Arizona State University, and University of Colorado at Boulder. She is at the present time working on a memoir dealing largely with her Choctaw and Southern Cheyenne ancestors from her mother's side, who lived in Oklahoma, and on a collection of dramatic monologues.

MAJOR WORKS AND THEMES

Ai's poetry consists exclusively of dramatic monologues. This decision to concentrate on a sole form of poetry arose from Ai's first poetry teacher who instilled in her the belief that "the first person voice was always the stronger voice to use when writing" (Ackerson 8). Ai's dramatic monologues, however, serve not as vehicles for her own voice, but instead as vehicles for the voices of the poor, the rich, the famous, the unknown, and the dead, all who variously talk about relationships, sex, violence, love, and death. Using a traditional poetic style, Ai makes her poetry contemporary not only by the range of her topics but also by the personae and the language they use. Far from old-fashioned, Ai's monologues emerge as hard-hitting, graphic, and violent. As one critic put it: "Imagine a Browning monologue rewritten in the terse manner of Sam Shepard and you have a good idea of what an Ai poem sounds like" (Wojahn 38).

Cruelty, Ai's first collection of short monologues, deals mostly with the plight of anonymous men and women. The lives portrayed are of those who have no illusions about life and no ways of escaping the many cruelties that befall them. Whether the persona is detached or not from the cruel and depressive weight of life that falls on him or her, disillusion and frustration are found in every poem. In this collection, Ai uses such different voices as an unfulfilled wife ("Why Can't I Leave You?"), a killer ("The Hitchhiker"), a desolate man who must lie to his dying wife ("The Tenant Farmer"), an old prostitute ("Tired Old Whore"), a mother who mercilessly beats her daughter ("Child Beater"), and a disillusioned midwife who wishes a freeing death for her patient (The Country Midwife: A Day"). Through the desperation and disillusion of those personae, Ai explores relationships between men and women. In her monologues, Ai puts two individuals together in a desperate situation and, without judging or apologizing, discloses the inner thoughts of one character. As her personae are unlikely to lie to themselves, Ai presents the readers with the ugly facts in an unadulterated manner. Whether she deals with abortion, child abuse, rape, or domestic abuse, Ai remains unbiased and unburdened with social norms.

If *Cruelty* presents the lives of unnamed but fully characterized people, Ai introduces famous and infamous personae in her second collection, *Killing Floor*. Thus, the reader can read the thoughts of such historical figures as Leon Trotsky, Marilyn Monroe, Ira Hayes, Yukio Mishima, and Emiliano Zapata. Using mostly male voices in *Killing Floor* (*Cruelty* used female voices for the most part), Ai examines the same themes as in her previous work but from a different approach. Instead of showing her personae as devoid of hope and illusions, Ai portrays them as survivors, as people who learned to adapt to life's cruelties and look past the false hopes. In *Killing Floor*, Ai's personae perceive the pitfalls of their environments and conceive survival techniques to deal with their treacherous surroundings. Even when faced with imminent death, Ai's characters, such as Trotsky and Zapata, retain their visions and their fighting spirits. By using known historical characters as her voices, Ai also manages to move the private struggles into a public arena and, in a way, criticize "a social order which has become somehow anesthetized to human agony" (Forché, qtd. in Field 15).

As the title suggests, *Sin*, Ai's third book of monologues, deals with immoral behavior. For the most part, her characters, consciously or unconsciously, desperately yearn for power; this quest, however, leaves them corrupted and, too often, in a state of "physical and psychological crisis" (Wojahn 38). Whether Ai uses the voice of the Kennedy brothers, of Joseph McCarthy, of the Atlanta child murderer, of a priest, or of an American journalist in her monologues, her characters invariably "offer a kind of stammering, desperate testimony, last-ditch efforts at self-justification before acknowledging their damnation" (Wojahn 38). Most memorable in this collection are "The Priest's Confession," which deals with a clergyman's unrestrained desire for a sixteen-year-old; and "The Journalist," which takes the persona back to the time he took a picture of a self-immolating nun to whom he supplied the necessary matches.

In her successive volumes of poetry, Ai relies more and more on famous personae to explore moral corruption. *Fate* and *Greed* continue to expose the degradation and the vice of the American society. The themes predominantly discussed in these two books are sex, politics, religion, greed (for money, power, and sex), and how people pursue those things with a debasing obsession. In *Fate* and in *Greed*, Ai uses the inner voices of Mary Jo Kopechne, J. Edgar Hoover, Jack Ruby, James Dean, Elvis Presley, Alfred Hitchcock, Jimmy Hoffa, the Virgin Mary, and others. Far from rewriting an accurate history of these people, which she does not attempt to do, Ai prefers to write "fictionalized versions of people's lives" (Erb 30). As she explained to Lisa Erb in an interview: "I always try to be true to character. . . . Whatever character, I set up what I like to think are keys to the character at the beginning of the poem. . . . So I like to think that as long as I'm true to my vision of the character, it's all right" (30). Thus, Ai's monologues expose the American psyche more than the historical figures' states of mind.

In *Vice: New and Selected Poems*, Ai includes eighteen new and fifty-eight previously published monologues. Of those eighteen new monologues, the vast majority are taken directly from headlines. Ai writes of the police officer who committed suicide four days before receiving a medal of honor for rescuing people after the Oklahoma City bombing ("The Antihero"), of the women caught in a civil war who are raped and murdered ("Rwanda"), of President Clinton's affair ("Blood in the Water"), of a comatose patient raped by an aide ("Sleeping Beauty"), and of JonBenet Ramsey's murder ("False Witness"). In these monologues, Ai zeroes in on the American consciousness and, as in all her previous works, does not worry about social proprieties, for, as she exposes in her poetry, these conventions and "values" are responsible for the deplorable state of society.

CRITICAL RECEPTION

Despite the many awards received for her poetry, Ai's monologues have not always been well received by critics. Upon the publication of *Cruelty*, many critics found her choice of subjects appalling and often too explicit, violent, or pornographic. Some, however, managed to see beyond the violence and the sex. Eugene Redmond, for example, perceives Ai's poetry as a reflection of the poet's intelligence and her ability in making the reader aware of societal problems. Although deploring her lack of variety and "corny tacked-on endings," Redmond asserts that "the accolades and superlatives attending publication of Ai's poetry are deserved" (167).

Although criticisms have been kinder and often overshadowed by the praises since the publication of her first volume of poetry, not everyone appreciates Ai's monologues. After *Sin* was published, some critics saw the longer poems as weaker than the short ones, blaming Ai's seeming inability at "keeping the intensity going after two or three pages" (Field 15). Ai has also been accused of using sensationalism to convey her points, and David Wojahn claims that her "elliptical, expressionistic presentation never allows the [historical figures] to become anything but cartoons" (Wojahn 38). In fact, Wojahn believes that Ai is most effective as a poet when she "chooses speakers not based so directly on actual public figures" (38).

For the most part, however, most critics seem to agree that Ai's strengths lie in her ability to "render [the] male experiences as realistically as she does the female ones," in her expertise at "startl[ing] the mind and terrify[ing] the soul," in her "richness of detail and [her] narrative complexity," and in her mastery of the dramatic monologue form (Field 13, "Movies" 240, Wojahn 38). If some critics are uncomfortable with her unadulterated approaches to some controversial issues, none can dismiss Ai and her poetry.

BIBLIOGRAPHY

Works by Ai

Cruelty. Boston: Houghton Mifflin, 1973.
Killing Floor. Boston: Houghton Mifflin, 1979.
Sin. Boston: Houghton Mifflin, 1986.
Cruelty/Killing Floor. New York: Thunder's Mouth Press, 1987.
Fate: New Poems. Boston: Houghton Mifflin, 1991.
"Movies, Mom, Poetry, Sex and Death: A Self-Interview." *OnthebusI* 3–4.2–1 (1991): 240–48.
Greed. New York: Norton, 1993.
"Smoking Gun." *Callaloo* 17 (1994): 405–06. (short story)
Vice: New and Selected Poems. New York: Norton, 1999.

Studies of Ai

Ackerson, Duane. "Ai." In *Contemporary Women Poets*, edited by Pamela L. Shelton. Detroit, MI: St. James Press, 1998. 8–9.

Becker, Robin. "The Personal Is Political Is Postmodern." *American Poetry Review* 23.6 (1994): 23–26.

Dooley, Dale A. "Ai." In *American Women Writers*, edited by Carol Huard Green and Mary Grimley Mason. New York: Continuum, 1994. 7–9.

Erb, Lisa. "An Interview with Ai: Dancing with the Madness." *Manoa* 2.2 (1990): 22–40.

Field, C. Renee. "Ai." *Dictionary of Literary Biography* Vol. 120. Detroit, MI: Gale, 1992. 10–17.

Forché, Carolyn. Foreword to *Cruelty/Killing Floor*. New York: Thunder's Mouth Press, 1987.

Ingram, Claudia. "Writing the Crises: The Deployment of Abjection in Ai's Dramatic Monologues." *Lit* 8.2 (1997): 173–91.

Kilcup, Karen L. "Dialogues of the Self: Toward a Theory of (Re)Reading Ai." *Journal of Gender Studies* 7.1 (1998): 5–20.

Leavitt, Michele. "Ai's 'Go.' " *Explicator* 54.2 (1996): 126–27.

Moore, Lenard D. Review of *Vice*, by Ai. *Black Issues Book Review* 2.2 (2000): 44–45.

Redmond, Eugene. "Five Black Poets: History, Consciousness, Love, and Harshness." *Parnassus* 3.2 (1975): 153–72.

Wilson, Rob. "The Will to Transcendence in Contemporary Poet Ai." *Canadian Review of American Studies* 17.4 (1986): 437–448.

Wojahn, David. "Monologues in Three Tones." Review of *Sin*, by Ai. *New York Times* 8 June 1986, final ed., sec. 7, 38.

MAYA ANGELOU (1928–)

Sandra L. West

BIOGRAPHY

Marguerite Ann Johnson, later known as Maya Angelou, was born April 4, 1928, in St. Louis, Missouri. Her mother, Vivian Baxter, a carefree gambler, ran a boarding house, and her father, Bailey Johnson, served as a navy cook. Maya's older brother, Bailey Johnson, Jr., always very protective of her, referred to her using the possessive form of "My" and "Mya Sister." Thus Marguerite became Maya, meaning "mine."

Angelou's early life, unsettling, mobile, dramatic, did not change terribly as she grew older. In 1930 Vivian and Bailey Johnson divorced, and their children shuttled back and forth between each parent as well as between grandparents, moving from Missouri to Long Beach, California to Stamps, Arkansas. In St. Louis, eight-year-old Marguerite was sexually assaulted by her mother's boyfriend, resulting in the young victim's inability to speak for several years. The children then lived in Arkansas with their paternal grandmother, Anne Henderson. During her years of silence, Angelou read ravenously and wrote poetry. She embraced the works of William Shakespeare, Rudyard Kipling, and Edgar Allan Poe and devoured Harlem Renaissance writers Langston Hughes, W.E.B. DuBois, James Weldon Johnson, and Paul Laurence Dunbar.

Angelou graduated with honors from Lafayette County Training School in Arkansas in 1940, moved to San Francisco with her mother in 1941, and attended George Washington High School in California. At age fourteen, she accepted a scholarship to California Labor School in San Francisco to study drama and dance. In 1943 she moved to Los Angeles with her father but ran away and after living a month in a junkyard with other homeless children Angelou returned to her mother. In 1944 Angelou gave birth to a son, Guy Johnson, now a novelist. One year later the teenage mother graduated from Mission High School in San Francisco.

Nothing Angelou did was small, ordinary, or without grand flourish, and this trend continued. Raising her son alone, she worked as a bordello madam and prostitute before settling into marriage in 1950 with Tosh Angelos (she later changed Angelos to the more exotic Angelou). When the marital union dissolved in 1952, she secured scholarships to study dance with Pearl Primus and Martha Graham. During the 1950s Angelou appeared as a singer in New York's Village Vanguard and San Francisco's The Purple Onion. Angelou danced in *Porgy and Bess* from 1954 to 1955 in a twenty-two nation tour sponsored by the U.S. Department of State. After touring with the African American folk opera in France, Italy, Yugoslavia, and Egypt, Angelou returned to the states and resettled in California.

In Los Angeles, Angelou met novelist John Oliver Killens, and he suggested she relocate to New York, where she joined the Harlem Writers Guild in 1957, a collective Killens founded during the Harlem Renaissance years. She sang in New York nightclubs and at the famous Apollo Theatre on 125th Street and aligned herself with artistic friends such as jazz artists Abbey Lincoln and Max Roach, novelist Paule Marshall, and essayist James Baldwin. Her work with the writer's guild took solid form.

During the 1960s civil rights movement, Angelou found her place, both politically and culturally. She met Dr. Martin Luther King, Jr., and from 1959 to 1960, worked for the civil rights leader as Northern Coordinator for the Southern Christian Leadership Conference (SCLC). In 1960 she performed in an off-Broadway production, *The Blacks* by Jean Genet, wrote *Cabaret for Freedom* and performed in it with Godfrey Cambridge in an off-Broadway production to benefit the SCLC. In the early 1960s, Angelou relocated to Cairo, Egypt, with Vusumzi Make, a South African, Pan-African Congress (PAC) freedom fighter. She worked as an editor for *The Arab Observer*, an English-language weekly in Cairo from 1961 to 1962 until the relationship with Make dissolved. Angelou and her son then moved to Accra, Ghana, a place where she finally felt at home.

The Black Power Movement and Black Arts Movement (BAM) was in full swing in America by 1963, and the largest civil rights demonstration in history, the March on Washington, entered the annals of history. This historic year found Angelou teaching music and dance at the University of Ghana, Institute of African Studies in Legon-Accra, under the black nationalist regime of Kwame Nkrumah. She also worked for the Ghanian Broadcasting Corporation, as administrative assistant at the University of Ghana, performed in Bertolt Brecht's *Mother Courage* at the university, wrote feature articles for *African Review*, and freelanced for *Ghanian Times*. Angelou lived in Ghana until 1965. In 1966 Angelou wrote and studied cinematography in Sweden. The formal lessons served her well, for she is one of a few women admitted into the Director's Guild of America. She wrote the original screenplay and musical score for the film *Georgia, Georgia* (1972) and has appeared in, written, and produced numerous television programs ranging from sitcoms to dramas to documentaries.

In 1970 Angelou garnered national celebrity for the publication of *I Know Why the Caged Bird Sings*, the first volume of her five-book autobiography, which details her encounters with southern racism. *Caged Bird* received a National Book Award nomination. Her literary triumph resulted in a Yale University Fellowship, and she worked as writer-in-residence at the University of Kansas. The next year a volume of poetry, *Just Give Me a Cool Drink of Water 'Fore I Diiie* (1971), appeared and, in 1972, was nominated for a Pulitzer Prize. In 1973 she performed on Broadway in *Look Away*, for which she received a Tony Award nomination, married Paul de Feu, and published her second autobiographical novel, *Gather Together in My Name* (1974). In 1974 President Gerald Ford appointed Angelou to the Bicentennial Commission.

In 1975 Angelou received a Rockefeller Foundation Scholarship and published *Oh Pray My Wings Are Gonna Fit Me Well*, a collection of poetry. In 1976 she directed her first film, *All Day Long*, and published the third in her series of autobiographical novels, *Singin' and Swingin' and Gettin' Merry Like Christmas*. In 1977 President Jimmy Carter appointed Angelou to the Commission for International Woman of the Year, and in the same year, she was nominated for an Emmy for her portrayal of Nyo Boto in the television miniseries *Roots*. The following year she published her popular poetry collection *And Still I Rise* (1978).

The fourth installment in her autobiographical series, *The Heart of a Woman*, was published in 1981. During the 1980s Angelou narrated various programs on the humanities for Public Broadcasting System (PBS). In the subsequent years, she wrote one book after another: a poetry collection *Shaker, Why Don't You Sing?* (1983); her fifth autobiographical novel, *All God's Children Need Traveling Shoes* (1986); *Poems: Maya Angelou* (1986); and *Now Sheba Sings the Song*, illustrated by Tom Feelings (1987), a celebration of black womanhood.

A productive writer who can complete a book per year but can, reportedly, only work on one project at a time, Angelou is extremely focused. Her more recent works include the poetry collection *I Shall Not Be Moved* (1990); *Wouldn't Take Nothing for My Journey Now* (1993); poem "On the Pulse of Morning," which she read at the 1993 inauguration of President Bill Clinton; *The Complete Collected Poems of Maya Angelou* (1994); and a poem "A Brave and Startling Truth" (1995). Beside holding many honorary doctorate degrees, Angelou holds a lifetime chair as Z. Smith Reynolds Professor of American Studies at Wake Forest University in Winston-Salem, North Carolina.

MAJOR WORKS AND THEMES

Angelou has written poetry, plays, and screenplays, a cookbook, juvenile literature, and five autobiographical novels. Racism, courage, hope, sisterhood, self-worth, and sexuality compose her major themes. However, love and humanity emerge as the predominate concerns in Angelou's work. As a child, Angelou lived under racist Jim Crow laws. Crippling segregation, and the courage to rise above it, are also prevalent themes in her novels and poetry. In *I Know Why the Caged Bird Sings,* she writes of several painful childhood memories involving racism, and she employs the theme of racism through the devices of memory in both her prose and poetry. For example, the poem "The Calling of Names" chronicles the various names used to define African American people through the years—"colored," "nigger," "Negro," "black"—and examines the impact of each name upon the African American psyche. The poem identifies some of the names as woefully derogatory but suggests that the move "from Colored man to Negro" depicts pride in the classier sounding "Negro." However, the black man fails to understand why he has been named by someone else.

Angelou's monumental poem "And Still I Rise" (1978), a "historical indictment of racism" (Hitt 212), sounds an appeal for harmony, community, and civility across the racial divide. Despite all the degradation heaped upon the psyche of the black American, "still," the persona says, "like dust, I rise" (*And Still I Rise* 1). The "I" in this poem, as in the majority of Angelou's work, has the collective meaning "us" or "the black community." This poem emerges as a rallying cry of "have courage" to those black Americans suffering from racism in America. Angelou gets "high" on courage: "Courage—that's what we need. . . . Those of us who submitted or surrendered our ideas and dreams and identities to the 'leaders' must take back our rights, our identities, our responsibilities. . . . We have to confront ourselves. . . . We will have to say yea or nay—*and rise!*" (Kelley 25).

The inner strength, self-worth, and acknowledged sexuality of a black sisterhood are extremely important to Angelou. For example, the female narrator of the poem "Phenomenal Woman" (1994), symbolizing all black women, feels gorgeous and blessed with her natural attributes. As one who has made it through and continues to make it through life's challenges, Angelou, as woman and as poet, is fascinated with the art of survival, especially the domestic survival of women and of those women whom society deems "ugly" but who, all the same, walk "pretty." In Angelou's work, these sisters and mothers signify authentic women.

Angelou writes of self-worth and positive self-image because she has learned that in order to survive and flourish amid obstacles such as racism and sexism she must be "straight of back." Therefore, the body and body parts predominate in her autobiographical novels and poetry. This focus on the body represents and presents the love/hate relationship many black women have with their bodies in a society where beauty standards generate from white male mandates. Angelou's work does not deny black female sexuality; rather, both her prose and poetry celebrate it as "the diamonds between my thighs" (*Phenomenal Woman* 1). The speaker of "Phenomenal Woman" evokes the chorus of black sisters recognizing a collective as well as personal phenomenal womanhood. This poem has become a national and international poetic anthem for self-actualization, positive self-image, and liberated, courageous womanhood.

Angelou moves from black sisterhood back to racism in America and makes an appeal to the community and humanity of mankind in "On the Pulse of Morning," offering the melting pot that is America the chance "to place new steps of change" (The Inauguration, A14L). Angelou's poetic signature of short words and short lines changes in "On the Pulse of Morning." In this poem metaphors predominate. This poem also provides a look at another of Angelou's concerns—religion. The unwieldy "Pulse" is spotted with familiar words, terms, and phrases from tried and true sermons of Southern Baptist ministers and African American gospel songs. As one reads or listens to the poem, especially if privy to the black religious tradition or the Southern religious experience, one can hear the jubilee choir singing in the background. The use of African American folk idioms emerges as a strength in Angelou's poetry.

Angelou, a master of the autobiographical genre, says she is not afraid of looking back in order to write; she is "not afraid of ties (between past and present)." In fact, Angelou admits to cherishing these ties. Through autobiography, whether she frames the telling of the story in prose or poetry, she seeks always to examine the human condition, to study suffering, to offer words of encouragement, and to raise the art of survival to its highest level.

CRITICAL RECEPTION

Maya Angelou's poetic intentions may be noble, but her critics do not always deem them successful. Her novels tend to fare better than her poetry under critical scrutiny, but not always. While critic Selwyn R. Cudjoe touts *Caged Bird* as "powerful," he views the autobiographical novel *Gather Together in My Name* as difficult for the reader to believe. He writes that Angelou's explanation of her fall into prostitution rings hollow and that "the incidents of the book appear merely gathered together in the name of Maya Angelou" (29). Although appreciated as a "people's poet" for her clear, plain delivery of everyday issues, Angelou is often maligned for this very simplicity and for depicting an unexamined individual experience in her poetry.

Angelou's poetry does, however, garner favorable reviews. Reviewer Monica Stark aptly identifies the strength of "Phenomenal Woman": "You'll never again have to struggle to remember the words" (2). This poem, along with "And Still I Rise," is a womanist poem, although "Rise" more directly suggests the impact of racism and sexism upon black womanhood. "And Still I Rise," an anthem undemanding upon the tongue, simple to remember, with rich waves of repetition is eagerly, lovingly, and dramatically read at Women's Day celebrations and in black churches across America. However, some critics wonder if this poem has been perceived as too simple. Carol Gargan questions the author's "conviction." The problem with "And Still I Rise," explains Gargan, is that it is too "generalized" and that the metaphors are "trite" (404). Generalizations and metaphors, on the other hand, are what make Angelou's poetry accessible, especially in the black community about whom and to whom she writes. "And Still I Rise" presents a self-portrait of a black sisterhood, a liberating portrait with which black women can live and of which they can be proud.

Angelou knows how her people speak and to what they respond, and she writes in their language. Her "I" remains "We."

BIBLIOGRAPHY

Works by Maya Angelou

I Know Why the Caged Bird Sings. New York: Random House, 1970. (autobiography)
Just Give Me a Cool Drink of Water 'Fore I Diiie. New York: Random House, 1971.
Georgia, Georgia. Independent-Cinerama, 1972. (screenplay)
All Day Long. American Film Institute, 1974. (screenplay)
Gather Together in My Name. New York: Random House, 1974. (autobiography)
Oh Pray My Wings Are Gonna Fit Me Well. New York: Random House, 1975.
Singin' and Swingin' and Gettin' Merry Like Christmas. New York: Random House, 1976.
And Still I Rise. New York: Random House, 1978. (poem)
The Heart of a Woman. New York: Random House, 1981. (autobiography)
Shaker, Why Don't You Sing? New York: Random House, 1983.
All God's Children Need Traveling Shoes. New York: Random House, 1986. (autobiography)
Poems: Maya Angelou. New York: Bantam, 1986.
Now Sheba Sings the Song. Illustrated by Tom Feelings. New York: Random House, 1987.
I Shall Not Be Moved. New York: Random House, 1990.
On the Pulse of Morning. New York: Random House, 1993. (poem)
Wouldn't Take Nothing for My Journey Now. Hingham, MA: Wheeler, 1993. (essays)
Lessons in Living. New York: Random House, 1993.
The Complete Collected Poems of Maya Angelou. New York: Random House, 1994.
Phenomenal Woman: Four Poems Celebrating Women. New York: Random House, 1994.
A Brave and Startling Truth. New York: Random House, 1995. (poem)
Even the Stars Look Lonesome. New York: Random House, 1999. (essays)

Studies of Maya Angelou

Angaza, Maitefa. "A Precious Prism-Maya." *Black Issues Book Review* 3.2 (2001): 30–33.

Bloom, Harold, ed. *Maya Angelou's I Know Why the Caged Bird Sings*. New York: Chelsea House, 1995.

Cudjoe, Selwyn R. "Maya Angelou and the Autobiographical Statement." In *Black Women Writers (1950–1980): A Critical Evaluation*, edited by Mari Evans. New York: Anchor Books, 1984.

Elliot, Jeffrey M., ed. *Conversations with Maya Angelou*. Jackson: University Press of Mississippi, 1989.

Gargan, Carol. Review of *And Still I Rise*, by Maya Angelou. *Best Sellers* 38.12 (1979): 404.

Hitt, Greg. "Maya Angelou." In *Conversations with Maya Angelou*, edited by Jeffrey M. Elliot. Jackson: University Press of Mississippi, 1989. 205–13.

The Inauguration. "Maya Angelou: 'On the Pulse of Morning.' *New York Times*, 21 Jan. 1993, A14L.

Jelinek, Estelle C., ed. *Women's Autobiography: Essays in Criticism*. Bloomington: Indiana University Press, 1980. 180–205.

Kelley, Ken. "Interview with Maya Angelou." *Mother Jones* 30.3 (1995): 22–25.

King, Sarah E. *Maya Angelou: Greeting the Morning*. Brookfield, CT: Millbrook Press, 1994.

Lisandrelli, Elaine Silvinski. *Maya Angelou: More than a Poet*. Springfield, NJ: Enslow, 1996.

O'Neale, Sondra. "Reconstruction of the Composite Self: New Images of Black Women in Maya Angelou's Continuing Autobiography." In *Black Women Writers (1950–1980): A Critical Evaluation*, Edited by Mari Evans. New York: Anchor Books, 1984.

Pettit, Jayne. *Maya Angelou: Journey of the Heart*. New York: Lodestar Books, 1996.

Shapiro, Miles. *Maya Angelou*. New York: Chelsea House, 1994.

Spain, Valerie. *Meet Maya Angelou*. New York: Random House, 1994.

Stepto, R. B. "The Phenomenal Woman and the Severed Daughter." *Parnassus* 8.1 (1979): 312–20.

Williams, Mary E., ed. *Readings on Maya Angelou*. San Diego, CA: Greenhaven Press, 1997.

RAE (MARY) ARMANTROUT (1947–)

Christina J. Mar

BIOGRAPHY

In the late 1970s, Rae Armantrout published her first collection of poetry and quickly distinguished herself as one of the most innovative and challenging writers among those known as the Language Poets, a group of poets whose writing emphasizes the underlying processes and structures that imbue language with meaning. Armantrout spent her childhood and adolescence in San Diego, California. It was while living in San Diego that she gained her first significant exposure to twentieth-century poetry. Her seventh grade teacher gave her a copy of a poetry anthology containing the work of the modernist poets William Carlos Williams, T. S. Eliot, and Ezra Pound, authors with whom her writing would later be in dialogue. Had she never received this gift from her teacher, according to Armantrout, she likely would never have embarked on her career as a poet (Beckett 110).

Armantrout's mother's religiousness (she was a fundamentalist Methodist when Armantrout was a child, though she later became a Pentecostal) heavily informs Armantrout's interest in the construction of consciousness that appears as a theme throughout her poetry. After becoming an atheist at the age of twelve (a philosophical positioning that consequently alienated her from her mother), Armantrout then began to ponder existential questions rather than concerning herself with the relationship between the subject and God that had previously occupied her. Religious allusions nonetheless arise in a number of her poems ("The Garden" and "It"), though not as a means to assert religious teleology. Quite the contrary, Armantrout employs such religious references in order to examine origins or the myths of origins, specifically those of formations of the subject and its entrance into consciousness in relation to various and competing ideologies.

While she was living in the San Francisco Bay area and studying at the University of California, Berkeley during the 1970s, Armantrout first came into contact with other poets identified with the Language movement such as Ron Silliman, Lyn Hejinian, and Bob Perelman. While the aggressive critiques that this group of emergent Language Poets launched on each other's writing might seem to privilege masculinist valuations of confrontational engagement, she felt that the group's attitude was, relative to the dominant American culture of the time, nonetheless progressive in its treatment of gender. Additionally, those writers and that period added to the development of her keen critical perspective and powerful poetic voice. In fact, Armantrout wrote some of the poems included in her first collection, *Extremities* (1978), during this period, and these poems reflect the minimalism popular with other Language Poets with whom she was in close contact at the time.

Armantrout has since returned to San Diego, a place whose complex combination of open spaces and strong military presence parallel the tensions between limitation and abundance that is manifested throughout her poetry. She has been anthologized numerous times and continues to write, publishing her most recent collection, *Made to Seem*, in 1995. To her collections of poetry, Armantrout has added *True* (1998), a prose memoir. *Pretext*, another volume of poetry, was published in 2001. Armantrout currently teaches writing at the University of California, San Diego.

MAJOR WORKS AND THEMES

Implicit critiques of conventional language use, traditional narrative forms, and claims to objectivity underwrite all of Armantrout's poetry, with each collection adding further complicating layers to these themes. For example, her first collection of poems, *Extremities*, reveals, as the title clearly suggests, Armantrout's preference for tension and difference rather than the usual preference for synthesis and harmony that informs conventional poetic structures. In this collection, she first demonstrates her characteristic talent for creating incredibly incongruous images, such as that of a bouquet constructed of "doorknobs" and "nails." Armantrout often employs a single image in her poetry in order to produce multiple internal tensions, destabilizing traditional assumptions about what constitutes supposedly mutually exclusive categories, such as masculine and feminine, self and other, reality and fiction. Armantrout's skepticism toward singularity also manifests itself through her poetry's interrogation of closed narratives and any claims to absolute "Truth." By rewriting the familiar fairytale of Hansel and Gretel in "Generation," Armantrout subverts the authority of traditional narratives by refusing to end the tale with the expected familial reunion. Armantrout thus exposes the way that closed narratives homogenize the complexity of experience into a linear march toward resolution.

In *Precedence* (1985), Armantrout continues to challenge the power of received narratives, though she turns her critical gaze from the past as constituted in fairytales to the present as constructed through American commodity culture. She focuses her attention on the surfaces of American culture, or rather American culture as constituted by surfaces. Multiple allusions to department stores, fast-food restaurants, bumper stickers, and cartoon characters bubble up everywhere in this collection. Nonetheless, her treatment of what might otherwise be thought of as the waste of commodity culture, though skeptical, is far from dismissive. In fact, a careful critical analysis of the volume reveals a very serious commentary on the ways in which postmodern American commodity culture allows for a superficial sense of inclusiveness that elides the structural inequities imbedded in American society. For example, "Fiction" describes a black man, notably wearing a Union Jack tee shirt, yelling, "Do you have any idea what I mean?" (27). Images such as these signal how fetishization via commodification threatens to eclipse complex heterogeneous identities. *Made to Seem* similarly examines the effects of a culture that hinges on the production of glossy, prepackaged images for consumption (things "made to seem"). In this case, Armantrout's commentary concentrates less on the larger social ramifications of commodification and more on its effect on the internal formation of the subject who assimilates commodity culture into his or her consciousness as part of his or her identity. Armantrout thus troubles any simple equation between commodity culture and superficiality by suggesting commodity culture's import in constructing subjectivity.

The subversive quality of Armantrout's poetry not only resides in the way it undercuts familiar narratives but also in its reconstruction of new narratives that foster a plurality of possible meanings. The theme of revisionary myth making reveals Armantrout's project to be more than a negative one that simply rejects all forms of knowing. On the contrary, her poetry highlights the importance of situated knowledge, knowledge that does not make claims to objective truth but originates from socially constructed positions that may be multiple and conflicting. *Necromance* (1991) proves highly concerned with the way a subject's location allows for the production of different myths of identity ("Location," "Late Returns"). "Getting Warm" describes a woman who is "sewing, stringing holes together," evoking a particularly powerful image of feminine artistic production (*Necromance* 43). This image of feminine artistry intimates the necessity of producing new myths in response to traditional ones, a type of "necromancy," yet these myths prove openended and full of "holes," thereby resistant to constraints of teleology.

Armantrout's reference to embodied experience as a form of situated knowledge breaks down traditionally constructed binaries between knowledge and experience, mind and body. An interest in the body as the site through which experience is gained is first evidenced as a key idea in her first volume, *Extremities*. Armantrout returns to the theme of the body with added critical vigor in *The Invention of Hunger* (1979). The opening poem of the volume, "Natural History," insistently interrogates whether it is "the need or the system" that should be given primacy in determining hierarchical structures. This question is, in typical Armantrout style, poignantly never answered but left to trouble the idea of primary origins itself. These poems place that which is conventionally considered to be a natural expression of a basic bodily need for food within systems of power that shape and thus "invent" hunger. The friction that arises between notions of the body as "natural" and ideas of the body as socially constructed similarly play out in "You Float" and "Fiction." With *The Invention of Hunger*, Armantrout offers a highly critical view of the way the body and its needs are tied to an economy of desire in which the body is cited as the "natural" basis for the creation and perpetuation of structures of domination.

All of Armantrout's collections emphasize the impossibility of language to render singular, linear meaning. Several poems in each collection, particularly "Visibility" (*Made to Seem*) and "Mechanism" (*Necromance*), take into consideration whether language's inherent deceptiveness should be viewed with cynicism or with hope and pleasure. "Covers" explores the feeling of entrapment within systems of meaning that continually double back on themselves, infinitely self-reflexive and without an original referent. Nonetheless, other poems such as "Dusk" and "Necromance" (*Necromance*) suggest that language's inability to render a singular "truth" is actually a site of potential power, revealing the possibility of multiplicity and abundance. Such a visionary conception of the potential of nonlinear language is cultivated everywhere in Armantrout's poetic practice, a practice that offers threads of a narrative only partially disclosed, language that is always multidimensional and complex, and images that are at once hard-edged and shadowy.

CRITICAL RECEPTION

Although Armantrout remains ambivalent about the nature of categorization, she is generally associated and identifies with the Language movement in poetry. Indeed, many characteristics of her writing, such as her use of unconventional syntactical expression, phonetic play, and pastiche, would all seem to solidify her position among the Language poets. Furthermore, like others of the Language movement, Armantrout employs these techniques in order to flesh out the structures that underpin conventional language usage, especially the arbitrary relationship between words and referents or signifiers and signifieds.

Nonetheless, though her artistic roots may have begun in language-centered writing, there remain important aspects of her version of Language poetry that distinguish her from other poets of the genre. Michael Leddy astutely identifies this difference in noting Armantrout's production of "alternative views" or "counter-narratives." While suggesting the arbitrariness of language, her poetry does not seek to utterly dislodge meaning from language in a manner that would suggest the interchangeability of signifiers *ad infinitum*. Instead, her writing exists in perpetual tension with structural norms and hegemonic demands. As such, Leddy suggests Armantrout's poetry is as concerned with imposed limitations as it is with language play.

Given Armantrout's interest in situated knowledge, counternarrative, and traditionally feminine artistry, it is not surprising that critics such as Ann Vickery and Jeffrey Peterson align Armantrout with a specifically feminist viewpoint. In her reading of Armantrout's poetry alongside that of poet and novelist Fanny Howe, Vickery appropriately notices this feminist slant in Armantrout's recognition of an implicit violence in the structures of representation. Vickery suggests language is "burdened" by "the relations of social power determining who speaks," thereby marginalizing women's knowledge (55). Because language is always already imbedded in systems of domination and subordination, Armantrout's poetry, according to Vickery, attempts to ameliorate the violence of these structures by fostering dialogic interplay instead of seeking linear progression. Peterson likewise reads Armantrout's work as imbedded in a feminist orientation, citing Armantrout's rejection of empathetic writing that purports to be able to fully represent the other as demonstrative of her desire for ethical representation (102). Empathy, in this sense, is not simply a form of identification with the subject being written about, but it is also an elision of the specificity of that subject and of his or her experience. As always, Armantrout's work negotiates between identifying the larger mechanisms of social power and maintaining the distinctiveness of each subject.

BIBLIOGRAPHY

Works by Rae Armantrout

Extremities. Berkeley, CA: The Figures, 1978.
The Invention of Hunger. Berkeley, CA: Tuumba Press, 1979.

Precedence. Providence, RI: Burning Deck, 1985.
Necromance. Los Angeles: Sun and Moon Press, 1991.
Made to Seem. Los Angeles: Sun and Moon Press, 1995.
True. Berkeley, CA: Atelos Press, 1998. (a memoir)
Writing the Plot about Sets. Tucson, AZ: Chax Press, 1998.
Pretext. Los Angeles, CA: Green Integer, 2001.
Veil: New and Selected Poems. Hanover: Wesleyan University Press, 2001.

Studies of Rae Armantrout

Beckett, Tom, ed. *A Wild Salience: The Writing of Rae Armantrout*. Cleveland, OH: Burning Press, 1999.

Caze, Antoine. "Form as Freedom in the Poetry of the LANGUAGE Group." In *Freedom and Form: Essays in Contemporary American Poetry,* edited by Esther Giger and Agnieszka Salska. Lodz, Poland: Wydawnictwo Uniwersytetu Lodzkiego, 1998. 52–66.

Leddy, Michael. Review of *Made to Seem*, by Rae Armantrout. *World Literature Today* 70 (1996): 407.

———. "See Armantrout for Alternative View: Narrative and Counternarrative in the Poetry of Rae Armantrout." *Contemporary Literature* 35 (1994): 739–60.

Peterson, Jeffrey. "The Siren Song of the Singular: Armantrout, Oppen, and the Ethics of Representation." *Sagetrieb*. 12.3 (1993): 89–104.

Vickery, Ann. "Finding Grace: Modernity and the Ineffable in the Poetry of Rae Armantrout and Fanny Howe." In *A Wild Salience: The Writing of Rae Armantrout,* edited by Tom Beckett. Cleveland, OH: Burning Press, 1999. 55–74.

BEATRIZ BADIKIAN (1951–)

Tara Betts and Catherine Cucinella

BIOGRAPHY

Beatriz Badikian, poet, essayist, and fiction writer, was born March 24, 1951, in Buenos Aires, Argentina. Her father, George, born in Turkey, moved to Greece at the age of five, and Badikian's mother, Georgia, was born in Greece. The poet's parents emigrated to Argentina after World War II and in 1970 to the United States, finally settling in Chicago. In a personal interview, Badikian provides insight into her parents' motivation for coming to the United States: "Like all immigrants, my parents brought me here in their search for a better life. Unfortunately, that never materialized for them." Her parents returned to Greece in 1981. Badikian, however, remained in the Chicago area, earning her doctorate in creative writing from the University of Illinois at Chicago in 1994.

Badikian wrote her first poem, "Poema No. 1," in December 1968, shortly before she left Buenos Aries for the United States. Badikian's early work is in Spanish; however, after living in the United States for a few years, she began writing in English as well. Her volumes often include poems written in both languages. By 1980 Badikian declared herself a poet, submitted her work, and attended poetry readings and workshops. At a workshop led by Sandra Cisneros and Reggie Young, Badikian met many Chicago poets including Carlos Cumpian, the founder and publisher of MARCH/Abrazo Press. Cumpian later published Badikian's chapbook, *Akewa Is a Woman* (1983).

The poet's second volume, *Mapmaker* (1994), extends her doctoral thesis. In 1999 Badikian republished most of *Akewa Is a Woman* and *Mapmaker* as *Mapmaker Revisited: New and Selected Poems*. Her poems have appeared in numerous journals, newspapers, and textbooks including *Third Woman*, *Spoon River Quarterly*, *Pleiades*, and *La Raza*. Her poems have been translated and published in India, Greece, Mexico, Argentina, and Canada. In 1993 Badikian received a nomination for the Pushcart Prize. Badikian, an active and popular participant within Chicago's poetry circuit, teaches at Roosevelt University.

MAJOR WORKS AND THEMES

In her four volumes of poetry, Badikian draws from her own experiences: leaving Argentina, negotiating familial and romantic relationships, and developing a voice. These experiences underwrite and propel the poet's major themes: migration and immigration, comings and goings, memory and history, womanhood and selfhood. Badikian's poems tell of love, friendship, sisterhood, political repression, exile, travel, and loneliness, and they speak of poetry itself. These themes and subjects point to questions of identity and one's coming to be, and specifically for this poet, coming to be within the context of cultural duality.

Many of the poems in *Mapmaker Revisited* juxtapose memories of Argentina with lived realities in Chicago, and these poems shift between the landscapes of both Argentina and the United States. In "Ragdale Evenings," the speaker by-passes Chicago while dreaming of Buenos Aires, and in "We Are What We Dream," the speaker stands on a street in Buenos Aires caught between the romantic markers of Argentina (trumpets, guitars, coffee) and the political realities of the country (a black car that turns everyone into robots). The speaker, torn between watching and not watching, tells us "my blood is greek my bones argentine." Thus this poem bespeaks division, a disjunction between lived reality and desired imaginings and a split between knowing and a disavowal of that knowledge. This poem exemplifies Badikian's concern with negotiating an existence split between cultures, and it also furthers her concern with the tension that arises at the intersection of history, memory, and mythology. Badikian's poems, such as "A Revolutionary Love Poem" and "Un Poema Argentina," contrast her experiences in her Argentine homeland with the romanticized elements of South American culture (*Mapmaker Revisited*). In her poetry, Badikian insists on de-romanticizing perceptions of South America and on articulating the stories of exiles and migrants.

Badikian's poem "Migrants" delineates migrants not as conquerors, colonizers, "ramblers," "mountain climbers," "hunters," or "yachtsmen." Instead, the poem sees those who travel as merchants claiming the "charm of ports and harbors." Erik Kestler notes that "Migrants" suggests that "we only understand where we've been once the trip is over" (10). Thus Badikian's metaphor of cartographer functions on several levels, to map a journey both before and after the sojourn and to delineate boundaries (or more precisely in Badikian's work to establish relationships between subject positions). Marcus Casal addresses what he calls the "provocative metaphor" of the mapmaker. He reads Badikian's use of the mapmaker as something more than metaphor: "It is a guiding light, an organizing principle, and, ultimately, a revelatory gesture" (110). The cartographer invoked in *Mapmaker Revisited* delineates more than geographical boundaries.

The mapmaker of these poems negotiates through the five major sections of the volume: "Mapmaking," "Litanies of Exile and Return," "Love Letters," "Womanscapes," and "Calendarios." Each section exemplifies and furthers Badikian's major themes. Casal perceives each section as "a continent of the poetic realm" (110). Although this organization appears to delineate a rigid demarcation among subjects, the separation proves porous as themes occur and recur throughout the volume. The speakers in the various poems search for connections with home, with memory, with history, with lovers, with friends, with parents, with political causes, with landscapes, with words.

Relentless movement marks much of Badikian's work, and that movement serves as a unifying principle of her body of work and more blatantly her last volume, *Mapmaker Revisited.* In this volume, she writes about the geographical separation and emotional detachment between father and daughter in "Father Speaks," yet in "Elements for an Autobiographical Poem," she points to a father's belief that his daughter would have a political voice. These seemingly contradictory shifts or insistence on binary oppositions mark many of Badikian's poems. Indeed, her major themes often involve elements set in opposition (history/myth, exile/return, arrival/departure, lived lives/mythic vision). "Two Husbands" gives us conflicting views of the speaker's husband as well as offering insight into a female psychic negotiating emotional confusion. The speaker sees her husband as a comfort, a place of safety, and a place for rejuvenation, and she also sees him as "the string" that anchors "the flag to the mast." For Badikian, then, both safety and constraint mark the landscape of love.

Badikian also relies on archetypes in much of her work. Eratosthenes plotting his maps becomes a metaphor for how the narrator, presumably Badikian, plots her verse. Hermes, Penelope, Ariadne, and the woman warrior Akewa recur in her poems as images of strength. In "We Are Penelope," the speaker searches for a name for her daughter and looks to several women as models including Penelope, Antigone, Emma Goldman, and Anais Ninn. In his review of *Mapmaker Revisited*, Casal indicates this same fascination with naming in "A Night in the Village," as the women in the poem give name to the sky, and he links this naming directly to a feminist consciousness: "It is an act of naming that at once recognizes the archetypal order, the cartographic impulse, and the feminist consciousness" (111). Significantly, "A Night in the Village" links identity both to the act of naming and to an awareness of a continuum of shared female lives: "One night in the village we became all the women who've ever shared their lives" (*Mapmaker Revisited* 17). Perhaps these poems also acknowledge Badikian's own poetic muses and influences: Marge Piercy, Sonia Sanchez, Denise Levertov, and Sandra Cisneros.

Badikian writes in both Spanish and English, and the inclusion of poems written in both languages makes "visceral through language the world citizenship of the migrant" (Kestler 10). The inclusion of Spanish and English poems extends Badikian's major theme of identity construction in the face of a split or dual existence. However, Badikian not only uses the language of the poem, Spanish or English, to examine the importance of language to one's identity, but she also presents language as the subject of a poem. For example, "Teaching English as a Second Language" addresses the differences between Spanish and English. Drawing on her own experiences in the classroom—as both student and teacher—Badikian offers a sophisticated look at the troubling nature of language in general. In "Teaching English as a Second Language," the instructor reads works by Jacques Derrida and Paul De Man as her students labor over their assignments, and like her students, this teacher of English also wonders about difference in languages.

Badikian's early work, written almost exclusively in Spanish, and her more recent work, using both Spanish and English, share similar structures. They sound a strong and clear poetic voice that returns again and again to the themes of migration, travel, exile, home, and place, and the difficulty of discovering the self.

CRITICAL RECEPTION

Critical comment on Beatriz Badikian's poetry remains scarce, and to date, no sustained scholarly treatments of her work have yet emerged; however, reviewers write favorably about her work with *Mapmaker Revisited* garnering most of the critical attention. Reviewers use words such as "lyrical," "poignant," "ironic," "romantic," "realist," "honest," "political," "intimate," and "strong" to describe Badikian's poetic voice and the written utterances of that voice. The critical comment and reviews generally fall into the following broad categories: geography, migration, gender, and identity. While no single theoretical approach frames these discussions of Badikian's poetry, most reviewers identify the political, feminist, and multi-ethnic influences in her works. In addition, most praise her inclusion of nontranslated poems written in Spanish. John Barry identifies this lack of translation for the Spanish poems as one of *Mapmaker Revisited*'s virtues: "[These poems] simply exist on their own terms, directly and honestly" (B6). Margaret McColley argues that the Spanish poems point to the problematics of translation. By keeping the difficulties of translation in view, Badikian's poetry also makes visible the literal difficulties of traversing geographical and cultural landscapes.

In his review of *Mapmaker Revisited,* Marcus Casal stresses Badikian's success at exploring the "question of location and identity in a way that addresses the particular without losing sight of the broader horizon" (110). Casal examines the intersections of geographical and personal identities in this volume, and he finds that throughout the volume, the poems continually explore the mythic and the mundane, "the bodily and the political, as locations within a constantly unfolding map of the self" (112). Indeed, Badikian's poetry unsettles notions of travel, home, geography, and identity as it moves through various locations, sometimes providing a panoramic perspective of literal geography and sometimes offering intimate glimpses of personal landscapes. Her poetry sounds a particularly contemporary voice, one that acknowledges a global influence. Through her poems, Beatriz Badikian maps the intersections and crossroads of coming to be, and she marks this journey to selfhood as both a personal and social one.

BIBLIOGRAPHY

Works by Beatriz Badikian

Akewa Is a Woman. Chicago: MARCH/Abrazo Press, 1983.
Akewa Is a Woman and Other Poems. Chicago: MARCH/Abrazo Press, 1989.
Mapmaker. Chicago: Red Triangle Books, 1994.
Mapmaker Revisited: New and Selected Poems. Chicago: Gladsome Books, 1999.

Studies of Beatriz Badikian

Alessio, Carolyn. "Finding Their Directions: Chicago Poets Make Connections, Internal and External." *Chicago Tribune* final ed. 23 Jan. 2000: 2.
Barry, John. Review of *Mapmaker Revisited: New and Selected Poems*, by Beatriz Badikian. *La Raza* 6 Nov. 1999: B6.
Casal, Marcus. "The Poet as Cartographer." Review of *Mapmaker Revisited: New and Selected Poems*, by Beatriz Badikian. *FEMSPEC* 2.1 (2000): 110–12.
Kestler, Erik. "Arrivals, Departures and Blues: Two New Poetry Books." Review of *Sight Lines*,

by Charlotte Mandel, and *Mapmaker Revisited: New and Selected Poems*, by Beatriz Badikian. *The Independent Scholars Coalition Newsletter* 128.1 (2000): 15–17.

McColley, Margaret. Review of *Mapmaker Revisited*, by Beatriz Badikian. *IRIS*. 42 (2001): 68–69.

GWENDOLYN ELIZABETH BROOKS (1917–2000)

Seretha D. Williams

BIOGRAPHY

Gwendolyn Elizabeth Brooks, the first African American awarded the Pulitzer Prize for Poetry, was born to David and Keziah Brooks in Topeka, Kansas. Shortly after her birth in 1917, Brooks's family moved to the South Side of Chicago, Illinois. The setting and the people of the South Side serve as the backdrop and subject matter of much of her poetry. With the encouragement of her mother, Keziah, who predicted that Gwendolyn would be the "lady Paul Laurence Dunbar," Brooks, at the age of eleven, began to keep a notebook of her writings. As a thirteen-year-old, her first poem, "Eventide," was published in *American Childhood Magazine*. Soon after, Brooks met James Weldon Johnson and Langston Hughes, who urged her to read the modern poetry of T. S. Eliot, Ezra Pound, and e.e. cummings.

In 1934 Brooks began to contribute poems to the *Chicago Defender*'s weekly poetry column. She graduated from Wilson Junior College in 1936; two years later, she married Henry Blakely, a fellow aspiring poet. Brooks and Blakely raised two children: Henry Jr. and Nora. Brooks used her personal experiences as a mother and a wife to inform many of her earlier poems, as well as her only novel, *Maud Martha* (1953).

Brooks's vivid characterization of the people who inhabited the South Side in *A Street in Bronzeville* (1945), her first collection of poetry, brought her instant critical acclaim. She was awarded two Guggenheim Fellowships, selected as a fellow of the American Academy of Arts and Letters, and named one of *Mademoiselle* magazine's "Ten Young Women of the Year." In 1950 Brooks was awarded the Pulitzer Prize for *Annie Allen* (1949), her second volume of poetry. President John F. Kennedy invited her to read at the Library of Congress Poetry Festival in 1962, and in 1964, Brooks received the first of many honorary degrees, a Doctor of Humane Letters from Columbia College. Brooks has held teaching positions at Columbia College, Elmhurst College, Northeastern Illinois State College, Columbia University, The City College of New York, and the University of Wisconsin. In 1968 Brooks succeeded Carl Sandburg as the poet laureate of Illinois, a post that she held until her death in 2000.

One of the most significant milestones for Brooks occurred when she attended Fisk University's Second Black Writers Conference in 1967. During this conference, Brooks listened to the impassioned political speeches of young black authors such as Imamu Amiri Baraka (LeRoi Jones), John Henrik Clarke, and Ronald Milner, outspoken leaders of the burgeoning Black Arts movement. In *Report from Part One* (1972), Brooks's autobiography, Brooks describes both the personal and the spiritual impact of the conference: "I who have 'gone the gamut' from an almost angry rejection of my dark skin by some of my brainwashed brothers and sisters to a surprised queenhood in the new black sun—am qualified to enter at least the kindergarten of new consciousness now. New consciousness and trudge-toward-progress. I have hopes for myself" (86). Her next two poetry volumes, *In the Mecca* (1968) and *Riot* (1969), reflect a significant shift in tone, voice, intent, and audience. Although she had written about blacks and their lives, her audience had been primarily white. Now, she determined to write about blacks and to blacks.

Despite her poetic shift, Gwendolyn Brooks remains a poet whose work investigates the human condition and reveals that which makes us human. She was a prolific writer, publishing poetry for children, writing reviews for newspapers, giving young poets advice. In 1994 Brooks was selected by the National Endowment for the Humanities as the Jefferson Lecturer, the highest humanities award given by the federal government.

MAJOR WORKS AND THEMES

Brooks's early work reinterpreted the traditional forms of the sonnet and the ballad by experimenting with adaptations of conventional meter and rhyme. In her poetry, Spenserian and Chaucerian stanzas meld with blues rhythms and jazz refrains. Brooks fused the conventions of traditional poetry and prose with the folk elements of black life and oral tradition, creating a new genre of rhythmic improvisations and off-rhymes. She employed the conventions of traditional poetry to discuss the heroic lives of unconventional characters. Her poetry is truly an American art; she reinvented the Western canon by including the excluded voices of women and minorities in literary treatises on the human experience.

Moreover, the legacy of Gwendolyn Brooks's poetry and prose embraces the social and historical realities of Africans in America. Her language reveals the pain of black life and, by writing the poetry of that suffering, she offers America a prescription for healing. Brooks celebrated the human spirit that triumphs in spite of the human condition and interrogated the meaning of human existence by exploring the source of her own personal pain. Her major themes include exploitation, alienation, exile, and intraracial colorism. In her earlier poetry, Brooks presented her themes and subjects objectively; however, in her later poetry, she personalized the pain and introduced her subjective voice as narrator of that human suffering.

In *Annie Allen* Brooks explores both the tragedy and the triumph of urban life. Brooks's character Annie Allen, originally called Hester Allen, is described as an ordinary girl growing up in the inner city in the early 1900s. Despite Annie's ordinariness, Brooks uses elevated language and complex poetic structures to chronicle the life of this unremarkable woman. *Annie Allen* comprises three parts: "Notes from the Childhood and the Girlhood," "The Anniad," and "The Womanhood." The text is structured as a poem sequence with a narrative organizing thread, but the compressed diction makes the poetry in *Annie Allen* less accessible for nonacademic audiences. However, Claudia Tate suggests that the poetry of *Annie Allen* is not "merely cloaked in elaborate surface design, but rather, that the structural formats for the poems, in and of themselves, communicate discursive content about Annie's life (141). Brooks imagines a fictional world in which Annie Allen's mundane existence becomes heroic—worthy of epic portrayal.

Just as Annie Allen's ordinariness is celebrated, so is the ordinariness of all of Brooks's characters. She did not overlook the artistic value of the everyday, the commonplace. Instead, she insisted that the world is changed by this intrusion of ordinary personal art. Satin Legs Smith, who "looks into his mirror, loves himself," represents those individuals whose voices are drowned out by the noise of everyday life (*A Street in Bronzeville*). Satin Legs loves himself because he accepts the "bits of forgotten hate" and "all his skipped desserts" as a part of his "sculpture and art." Satin Legs dresses in silk, listens to the blues, dines at "Joe's Eats," and sips love from the "honey bowl" of a body "like summer earth." His art is not "Saint-Saens" or "Brahms," but it is art nevertheless. He fashions an individual art from life experience and communal memory. Brooks suggests that we are not unlike Satin Legs Smith; we are all attempting to find beauty in truth. Satin Legs Smith situates his narrative in the context of history and transforms himself through artistic interpretation. However, Brooks intimates that the quest for wholeness and personal truths requires more than history.

"The Life of Lincoln West" (*Family Pictures* 1970) illustrates Brooks's prescription for personal transformation. Human beings, in general, and blacks in particular, must become the "authors of their new ideas" and engage seriously the question of their identities. Lincoln West reinvents his identity by re-appropriating the derogatory remark of a white man who refers to him as "the real thing." He turns that statement into a positive attribute and, thus, is able to accept himself and to realize the value of his life. Once Lincoln accepts that he is "the real thing," he will have achieved a wholeness of spirit with which to combat the everyday trials of living. Brooks proposes that each body has its art and that it is only through the realization of this personal art that humans can appreciate the art of life.

Gwendolyn Brooks, like her characters, struggled with issues of color. In her autobiography, *Report from Part One*, she discusses the tribulations of growing up dark-skinned. As a result, color resounds as a recurring theme in Brooks's delineation of the human condition because it is the life text of her personal ambivalence to blackness. Throughout her poetry, she refers to the "high-yellows," "low-yellows," "bright girls," "caramel dolls," the "cream-colored," the "cream-yellows," as well as the "bronzy lads," the "daughters of dusk," the "sweet and chocolates," the "unembroidered browns," and the "cocoa straights." As author of her own narrative, she attempts to write through the tension of color and make peace with her skin. Thus, color functions as a symbolic quest for wholeness throughout Brooks's body of work. The historical referent and metaphor of color translates into a communal journey through which African Americans search for the sources of their self-hatred and resolve the tension of their existence. Brooks's text of color proposes a collective vision for African Americans and reclaims the humanity of people defined as "other."

Similarly, Brooks acknowledged the impact of color on gender. The usual context for her sermons on colorism is situated in the larger narrative of black male and female relationships. For instance, in "The Ballad of Chocolate Mabbie" (*A Street in Bronzeville*), Mabbie is described as being "cut from a chocolate bar," intimating sweetness and richness of flavor, that is, goodness. However, Willie Boone "wore like a jewel a lemon-hued lynx." The images of color that Brooks produced in her narratives often refer to edible items or precious stones. Generally, the dark-skinned women are described as food, and the light-skinned women are described as jewels. The dark-skinned women tend to be consumed by their ambivalence to color and also by the male characters in the narrative. "The Ballad of Pearl May Lee" and "Independent Man" (*A Street in Bronzeville*) exemplify Brooks's observation that light skin and white features are symbols of prestige and prizes for those women who possess them. Whereas light-skinned women are priceless jewels to be worn, dark skinned women are depicted as unadorned and, thus, worthless.

Brooks's controversial poem "The Mother" (*A Street in Bronzeville*) addresses a different issue of gender. Written as a dramatic monologue, "The Mother" depicts the inner turmoil of a woman who decides to abort her children. The mother determines that she and not the cruel world will kill her children; she assumes responsibility for their lives and for her actions. Brooks's objective posture does not judge the mother; instead, the poem presents the stark reality of some women who are faced with this tough decision. Brooks read this politically charged poem when she was invited by President Kennedy to speak at the Library of Congress in 1962.

"We Real Cool" (*The Bean Eaters* 1960), the most anthologized of Brooks's poems, is written in modern vernacular. Deliberately simple, this poem depicts the demise of naive youth who ultimately succumb to their environment. Through the poem's monosyllabic and three-beat lines, Brooks introduces to us the pool players, who in their own words, "Jazz June" and "die soon." Brooks laments the loss of youth while asserting the humanity of the seven at the Golden Shovel. The youths are not mere thugs; they are fun loving and full of life. Brooks insists that we hear their voices—the sounds of everyday existence in the city.

Gwendolyn Brooks's challenge to America is to "somehow find a still spot in the noise" of life. While her poetry features the real-life narratives of black people, her intention is to speak to all of America, all of humanity. In "The White Troops Had Their Orders but the Negroes Looked Like Men" (*A Street in Bronzeville*), Brooks asserts that the recognition of a common humanity contains the possibility for difference to coexist in the same spaces with sameness. Thus, in the world of Gwendolyn Brooks, the greatest feat of humanity is its ability to transform creatively its condition by becoming the author of its own situation.

CRITICAL RECEPTION

Critics often divide Gwendolyn Brooks's complex canon into two phases: the early poetry that experimented with language and form and the post-1967 poetry that revealed her increasing concern with political and social issues. Her early writing has been described as academic and objective while her later writing has been characterized as urban and subjective. Nevertheless, "at the nexus of Brooks's art lies a fundamental commitment to both the modernist aesthetics of art and the common ideal of social justice" (Mootry and Smith 1).

Although *Annie Allen* has been praised for its linguistic technicality and its modernist aesthetics, critics seldom critique this Pulitzer Prize winning collection. Indeed, in the preface to *Report from Part One*, Brooks acknowledges that while most African Americans applauded her efforts, inevitably, as poet Haki Madhubuti (don l. lee) asserts, *Annie Allen* is an important book written for whites and unread by blacks. The audience for much of Brooks's early writing was white.

In the late 1960s, Brooks's style shifted; instead of experimenting with traditional forms, she began to write free verse and to overtly critique the condition of blacks and women in the United States. However, her intent to document the truth of the human experience did not waver. Brooks's poetry gauged the social and political climate and responded with a doctrine of humanism that, from the beginning, informed her narratives. Scholar R. Baxter Miller proposes that Brooks's prescription for humanism heals the wounds inflicted by oppression and prejudice and elevates discussions of race to a plane on which all Americans can see the good in humankind.

Gwendolyn Brooks's writing has been compared to T. S. Eliot, Ezra Pound, Countee Cullen, Gertrude Stein, Margaret Walker, and Langston Hughes to name a few. Recent scholarship on Brooks situates her work in a feminist tradition. Critics such as Beverly Guy-Sheftall, Hortense Spillers, and Barbara Christian have begun to study the feminist implications of Brooks's character development, use of language, and social commentary; many of these essays have been collected in the seminal text by Maria Mootry and Gary Smith, *A Life Distilled: Gwendolyn Brooks, Her Poetry and Fiction* (1989).

BIBLIOGRAPHY

Works by Gwendolyn Elizabeth Brooks

A Street in Bronzeville. New York: Harper & Brothers, 1945.
Annie Allen. New York: Harper & Brothers, 1949.
Maud Martha. New York: Harper & Brothers, 1953. (novel)
Bronzeville Boys and Girls. New York: Harper & Brothers, 1956.
The Bean Eaters. New York: Harper & Brothers, 1960.
Selected Poems. New York: Harper, 1963.
We Real Cool. Detroit, MI: Broadside Press, 1966.
The Wall. Detroit, MI: Broadside Press, 1967.
In the Mecca. New York: Harper, 1968.
Riot. Detroit, MI: Broadside Press, 1969.
Family Pictures. Detroit, MI: Broadside Press, 1970.
The World of Gwendolyn Brooks. New York: Harper, 1971.
Aloneness. Detroit, MI: Broadside Press, 1971.
Black Steel: Joe Frazier and Muhammad Ali. Detroit, MI: Broadside Press, 1971. (special broadside)
Report from Part One. Detroit, MI: Broadside Press, 1972.
The Tiger Who Wore White Gloves, Or What You Are You Are. Chicago: Third World Press, 1974.
Beckonings. Detroit, MI: Broadside Press, 1975.
Primer for Blacks. Chicago: Black Position Press, 1980.
Young Poet's Primer. Chicago: Brooks Press, 1980.
To Disembark. Chicago: Third World Press, 1981.
Very Young Poets. Chicago: Brooks Press, 1983.
Mayor Harold Washington and Chicago, The I Will City. Chicago: Brooks Press, 1983.
The Near-Johannesburg Boy and Other Poems. Chicago: The David Company, 1986.

Blacks. Chicago: The David Company, 1987.
Report from Part Two. Chicago: The David Company, 1987.
Gottschalk and the Grande Tarantelle. Chicago: The David Company, 1988.
Winnie. Chicago: The David Company, 1988.

Studies of Gwendolyn Elizabeth Brooks

Axelrod, Steven Gould. "The Middle Generation and WWII: Jarrell, Shapiro, Brooks, Bishop, Lowell." *War, Literature, and the Arts* 11.1 (1999): 1–41.

Boyd, Melba Joyce. " 'Prophets for a New Day': The Cultural Activism of Margaret Danner, Margaret Burroughs, Gwendolyn Brooks, and Margaret Walker during the Black Arts Movement." *Revista Canaria de Estudios Ingleses* 37 (1998): 55–67.

Bresnahan, Roger J. Jiang. "The Cultural Predicaments of Ethnic Writers: Three Chicago Poets." *Midwestern Miscellany* 27 (1999): 36–46.

Callahan, John F. "Essential African: Gwendolyn Brooks and the Awakening to Audience." *North Dakota Quarterly* 55.4 (1987): 59–73.

Clark, Cheryl. "The Loss of Lyric Space and the Critique of Traditions in Gwendolyn Brooks's *In the Mecca*." *Kenyon Review* 17.1 (1995): 136–47.

Dawson, Emma Waters. "Vanishing Point: The Rejected Black Woman in the Poetry of Gwendolyn Brooks." *Obsidian II* 4.1 (1989): 1–11.

Flynn, Richard. "The Kindergarten of New Consciousness: Gwendolyn Brooks and the Social Construction of Childhood." *African American Review* 34 (2000): 483–99.

Greasley, Philip. "Gwendolyn Brooks at Eighty: A Retrospective." *Midamerica* 23 (1996): 124–35.

Grey, John. "Subversive Parody in the Early Poems of Gwendolyn Brooks." *South Central Review* 16.1 (1999): 44–56.

Hughes, Gertrude Reif. "Making It Really New: Hilda Doolittle, Gwendolyn Brooks, and The Feminist Potential of Poetry." *American Quarterly* 42 (1990): 375–401.

Kent, George. *A Life of Gwendolyn Brooks*. Lexington: University Press of Kentucky, 1990.

Lindberg, Kathryne V. "Whose Canon? Gwendolyn Brooks: Founder at the Center of the 'Margins.' " In *Gendered Modernisms: American Women Poets and Their Readers,* edited by Margaret Dickie and Thomas Travisano. Philadelphia: University of Pennsylvania Press, 1996. 283–311.

Maasa, Suzanne Hotte. "Gwendolyn Brooks." In *Contemporary African American Novelists: A Bio-Bibliographical Critical Sourcebook*, edited by Emmanuel S. Nelson. Westport, CT: Greenwood Press, 1999. 47–52

Melhem, D. H. "Cultural Challenge, Heroic Response: Gwendolyn Brooks and the New Black Poetry." In *Perspective of Black Popular Culture*, edited by Harry B. Shaw. Bowling Green, KY: Popular, 1990. 71–84.

———. *Gwendolyn Brooks: Poetry & the Heroic Voice*. Lexington: University Press of Kentucky, 1987.

Miller, R. Baxter, ed. *Black American Poets between Worlds, 1940–1960*. Knoxville: University of Tennessee Press, 1986.

Mootry, Maria K. " 'The Step of Iron Feet': Creative Practice in the War Sonnets of Melvin B. Tolson and Gwendolyn Brooks." In *Reading Race in American Poetry: "An Area of Act*," edited by Aldon Lynn Nielsen. Urbana: University of Illinois Press, 2000, 133–47.

———, and Gary Smith. *A Life Distilled: Gwendolyn Brooks, Her Poetry and Fiction*. Urbana: University of Illinois Press, 1989.

Saunders, Judith P. "The Love Song of Satin-Legs Smith: Gwendolyn Brooks Revisits Prufrock's Hell." *Papers on Literature and Language* 36.1 (2000): 3–18.

Schweik, Susan. *A Gulf So Deeply Cut: American Women Poets and the Second World War.* Madison: University of Wisconsin Press, 1991.

Shaw, Harry B. *Gwendolyn Brooks.* Boston: Twayne, 1980.

———. "Perceptions of Men in the Early Works of Gwendolyn Brooks." In *Black American Poets between Worlds, 1940–1960*, edited by R. Baxter Miller. Knoxville: University of Tennessee Press, 1986. 136–59.

Smethurst, James. "Hysterical Ties: Gwendolyn Brooks and the Rise of a 'High' Modernism." In *The New Red Negro: The Literary Left and African American Poetry, 1930–1946*, edited by James Smethurst. New York: Oxford University Press, 1999. 164–79.

Stanford, Ann Folwell. "An Epic with a Difference: Sexual Politics in Gwendolyn Brooks's 'The Anniad.' " *American Literature* 67.2 (1995): 283–301.

———. "Dialectics of Desire: War and the Resistive Voice in Gwendolyn Brooks's 'Negro Hero' and 'Gay Chaps at the Bar.' " *African American Review* 26 (1992): 197–211.

———. " 'Like a Narrow Banners for Some Gathering of War': Readers, Aesthetics, and Gwendolyn Brooks's 'The Sundays of Satin-Legs Smith.' " *College Literature* 17.2–3 (1990): 162–82.

Sullivan, James D. *On the Walls and in the Streets: American Poetry Broadsides from The 1960s.* Urbana: University of Illinois Press, 1997.

Tate, Claudia. "Anger So Flat: Gwendolyn Brooks's *Annie Allen.*" In *A Life Distilled: Gwendolyn Brooks, Her Poetry and Fiction*, edited by Maria K. Mootry and Gary Smith. Urbana: University of Illinois Press, 1989. 140–50.

Walther, Malin LaVon. "Re-Wrighting Native: Gwendolyn Brooks's Domestic Aesthetic in *Maude Martha.*" *Tulsa Studies* 13.1 (1994): 143–45.

Williams, Gladys Margaret. "Gwendolyn Brooks's Way with the Sonnet." *CLA Journal* 26 (1982): 215–40.

Wright, Stephen Caldwell, ed. *On Gwendolyn Brooks: Reliant Contemplation.* Ann Arbor: University of Michigan Press, 1996.

OLGA BROUMAS (1949–)

Darlene Cohn

BIOGRAPHY

Olga Broumas was born in Hermoupolis, Greece, on May 6, 1949, to Nicholas Constantine Broumas (a Greek army officer) and Claire Antonia (Pendeli) Broumas. She immigrated to the United States in 1967 on a Fulbright Scholarship. She received her BA in 1970 from the University of Pennsylvania and her MFA in 1973 from the University of Oregon. That same year she married Edward Bangs. They divorced in 1979.

Her career as an instructor began in 1972 at the University of Oregon where she was a professor of English and women's studies. Throughout her academic career, she taught at the University of Idaho (1978), at Goddard College in Vermont (1979–1981), at Freehand (a learning community she co-founded in Provincetown, Massachusetts, 1982–1987), and at Boston University (1988–1990). She has been the Fanny Hurst poet-in-residence at Brandeis University since 1990 and the director of creative writing there since 1992.

Her poetic career was officially launched in 1977, when she won the Yale Younger Poets Award for her book *Beginning with O* (1977). Since then, she has published nine books of poetry, including the most recent *Rave: Poems 1975–1999* (1999), a retrospective of her work. She has also been a very active collaborator and translator, working with Jane Miller and T. Begley on poetry and translations of the Greek writer Odysseas Elytis.

MAJOR WORKS AND THEMES

Broumas is known as a "lesbian" poet, although exactly what that means remains a matter of critical debate. In her 1983 study of several lesbian writers, including Broumas, Mary J. Carruthers offers a definition of "lesbian poetry": "[Lesbian poetry's] energy springs . . . from the perception that women together and in themselves have a power which is transformative, but in order to recover their power women need to move psychically and through metaphor to a place beyond the well-traveled routes of patriarchy and all its institutions, especially its linguistic and rhetorical ones" (294). Broumas's poetry embodies both this spirit and this challenge to the language of patriarchy. She feels the language of patriarchal society (whether that language be her native Greek or English) is insufficient—limited by its masculine images, metaphors, and sounds—to describe the experiences and relationships of women to each other and to the world. Broumas wants to move beyond the "well-traveled routes" of language to describe her own experiences (Hammond 36). For example, in *Beginning with O*'s "Artemis," she writes of lesbian love as a different kind of "alphabet" that cannot be decoded, which seems "to consist of vowels, beginning with O" (23). Broumas's identity as a lesbian informs all of her poetry because she wants to find the most clear, communicative, evocative language she can to describe her world from a woman's, and particularly a lesbian's, perspective. She feels that expanding language to accommodate these perspectives is both politically and aesthetically necessary (Hammond 36). She calls for women to create a "complex vocabulary" with "simple syntactical and grammatical structure" in order to communicate their experiences with greatest accuracy (37).

Just as she adapts language to her needs, Broumas takes the tools of male dominated culture—the classic stories and images of women in mythology, poetry, fairy tales, and music—and turns them over, re-appropriating them to make them useful and meaningful to women. For her project with artist Sandra McKee, called "Twelve Aspects of God," Broumas re-wrote Greek myths of gods and goddesses. These poems appear in *Beginning with O* and remain some of her most memorable. Also in *Beginning with O*, she revisits fairy tales such as "Beauty and the Beast," "Cinderella," "Sleeping Beauty," and "Rapunzel," re-writing them as powerful tales of contemporary women's lives. She lists Adrienne Rich, Anne Sexton, and Sappho among her influences, all women who have taken on the similar task of reclaiming the feminine voice in a world of masculine language and paradigms.

In her review of *Beginning with O*, Janet Beeler notes Broumas's thematic attention to the details of contemporary women's lives: "The words which fascinate [Broumas] suggest the range of her themes: salt, flesh, milk, mouth, blood, fire, bone, tongue, bread, knife, stone, breast. Her realm is the experience of womanhood unadorned" (46). Time and again, the poems return to water, to salt, to the tongue and their range of connotations. For example, in *Beginning with O*'s poem "The Knife and the Bread" Broumas writes of knives as instruments of cooking and also of murder. Food becomes discomforting because it reminds her that women are "food" to be devoured by men (*Rave* 51). Everything domestic and "innocent" becomes threatening and deadly to the woman. Similarly, in the poem "Lullaby," a lover's quilt is both "treacherous" and comforting like the body of a lover or the undertow of an ocean (*Rave* 64). In these ways, Broumas's poems are filled with the lyrical, sensual imagery and details of her existence as a woman.

But Broumas's interest in the lives of lesbians does not limit her topically to domestic and private subject matter. She is also interested in exposing the harshness of historical and current events, particularly as they relate to women. Broumas does not shy away from images of war and violence, both domestic and political. From this violence, though, she always brings the reader back to the possibility of love and joy and healing through human contact. For example, in "The Massacre," she writes of dead friends before her for whom she can only attempt to help "with their breath and my hands" (*Rave* 241).

Her poetry is stylistically adventurous, and Broumas experiments with new forms in every volume. In *Soie Sauvage* (1979), she omits almost all punctuation and syntactical line breaks. This writing, lyrical and natural, makes for interesting juxtapositions of meaning, but the poems' rhythms seem sometimes strained or hidden without the traditional "signposts" of written punctuation. She returns to using punctuation and more traditional line breaks in her next volume, *Pastoral Jazz* (1983). Some of her poems use short lines and short, regular poetic paragraphs of two and three lines each; others use longer lines and irregular, but longer poetic paragraphs. However, Broumas's work never lacks artistic composition because she is skilled at subtly using the form of the poem to add to its mood, tone, and meaning.

Academically, Broumas's interests rest in the play between the English and Greek languages, and she has done extensive translation work both alone and in collaboration with other writers. In the early 1990s, she did more collaborative work than solo projects. In addition to the project with artist Sandra McKee, Broumas published a prose poem titled *Black Holes, Black Stockings* in 1985, which she wrote with Jane Miller. In addition to translating Elytis, Begley and Broumas have written poetry together in the volumes *Sappho's Gymnasium* (1994), *Helen Groves* (1994), *Unfolding the Tablecloth of God* (1995), and *Ithaca: Little Summer in Winter* (1996). This collective work reinforces Broumas's approach to and philosophy of poetry—that it should be a medium of conversation between women.

CRITICAL RECEPTION

In 1977, when *Beginning with O* was published and Broumas's name became recognizable as the Yale Younger Poet, she was one of several lesbian writers struggling to use poetry and language to describe their experiences. Critics at the time read her poetry as fresh, daring, sexy, and original. In his introduction to *Beginning with O*, poet Stanley Kunitz writes: "I am struck by the directness and naturalness of the inflection, the ease of the controls, and the bright tangibility of the perceptions. This is a poetry that rests on the intimate authority and rightness of its sensory data . . . a poetry of sensations animated by a fierce and committed intelligence" (ix). However, Kunitz later admits "now and then I detect a note of stridency in her voice, a hint of doctrinal overkill" (xii), but this reservation obviously did not prevent him from choosing her as the Yale Younger Poet.

Since winning the Yale Younger Poets award, Broumas has remained a writer on the edge of the poetry world—perhaps intentionally. During her twenty-five-year career she has won a National Endowment for the Arts grant, a Guggenheim Fellowship, and the Witter Brynner Translation Grant. Her volumes receive some, but not a lot, of critical attention. Largely, critical writing about Broumas's work comes in the form of book reviews. Not many scholars are studying her work at the moment, although she clearly continues to write and publish with considerable regularity. When critics do include Broumas in scholarly studies, they usually do so in combination with other poets who have worked on themes similar to hers. Mary J. Carruthers's essay titled "The Revision of the Muse: Adrienne Rich, Audre Lorde, Judy Grahn, Olga Broumas" provides a good example of this practice. Carruthers explores lesbian poetry and cites Broumas as one of the prime players in this movement, along with the other writers listed in the article's title. Carruthers looks particularly at the importance of Greek language and mythology in Broumas's work. Critics generally appreciate Broumas's characteristically vivid language and stunning images, but they feel chilly about her collaborations. For example, Pamela Uschuk writes, in her review of *Sappho's Gymnasium*, "When the poems are working, they read like someone entranced, speaking in tongues, and the effects are dazzling. Other times, the poems are simply puzzling" (108). In reviewing *Rave*, Adrian Oktenberg notes, "I believe the collaborations mostly tend to drag her down, however much Broumas may enjoy the process. In particular, I don't think the union with T. Begley has been all that fruitful" (13). While all critics acknowledge her considerable talent, several also echo Kunitz's early concerns about her stridency by noting her poetry's "shrill," "self-conscious," and "pretentious" tendencies (Beeler; Russell). However, Broumas remains well regarded for being the breakthrough lesbian voice in contemporary American poetry, and she continues to stay true to her own voice and style by keeping a quiet but constant presence on the American poetry landscape.

BIBLIOGRAPHY

Works by Olga Broumas

Restlessness. Athens, Greece: Alvin Redman Hellas, 1967.

Beginning with O. New Haven, CT: Yale University Press, 1977.

Soie Sauvage. Port Townsend, WA: Copper Canyon Press, 1979.

If I yes. Seattle, WA: Watershed, 1980. (sound recording).

Pastoral Jazz. Port Townsend, WA: Copper Canyon Press, 1983.

Black Holes, Black Stockings. With Jane Miller. Middletown, CT: Wesleyan University Press, 1985.

What I Love: Poems by Odysseas Elytis. Port Townsend, WA: Copper Canyon Press, 1986. (translation)

The Little Mariner by Odysseas Elytis. Port Townsend, WA: Copper Canyon Press, 1988. (translation)

Perpetua. Port Townsend, WA: Copper Canyon Press, 1989.

Sappho's Gymnasium. With T. Begley. Port Townsend, WA: Copper Canyon Press, 1994.

Helen Groves. With T. Begley. Tucson, AZ: Kore Press, 1994.

Unfolding the Tablecloth of God. With T. Begley. Northport, AL: Red Hydra Press, 1995.

Open Papers by Odysseas Elytis. Port Townsend, WA: Copper Canyon Press, 1995. (translation with T. Begley).

Ithaca: Little Summer in Winter. With T. Begley. San Anselmo, CA: Radiolarian Press, 1996.

Eros, Eros, Eros: Selected and Last Poems by Odysseas Elytis. Port Townsend, WA: Copper Canyon Press, 1998. (translation)

Rave: Poems 1975–1999. Port Townsend, WA: Copper Canyon Press, 1999.

Olga Broumas: A Listeners Guide. Port Townsend, WA: Copper Canyon Press, 2000. (audio CD)

Studies of Olga Broumas

Anastasiadou, Anastasia. "An Amazon Twin in Public: Broumas's Resistance to Homogeneity in America." In *Nationalism and Sexuality: Crises of Identity*, edited by Domna Pastourmatzi. Tessaloniki, Greece: Aristotle University, 1996. 7–13.

Beeler, Janet. Review of *Beginning with O*, by Olga Broumas. *American Poetry Review* 8.1 (1979): 46.

Carruthers, Mary J. "The Revision of the Muse: Adrienne Rich, Audre Lorde, Judy Grahn, Olga Broumas." *Hudson Review* 36 (1983): 293–322.

Carter, Kate. "Olga Broumas." In *Contemporary Lesbian Writers of the United States: A Bio-Bibliographical Critical Sourcebook*, edited by Sandra Pollack and Denise Knight. Westport, CT: Greenwood, 1993. 89–93.

Cooksey, T. L. Review of *Open Papers*, by Olga Broumas. *Library Journal* 119.21 (1994): 91.

Hammond, Karla. "An Interview with Olga Broumas." *Northwest Review* 18.3 (1980): 32–45.

Horton, Diane. " 'Scarlet Liturgies': The Poetry of Olga Broumas." *North Dakota Quarterly* 55 (1987): 322–47.

Ingram, Claudia. "Sappho's Legacy: The Collaborative Testimony of Olga Broumas and T. Begley." *Tulsa Studies* 19.1 (2000): 105–20.

Kaganoff, Penny. Review of *Perpetua*, by Olga Broumas. *Publisher's Weekly* 25 Aug. 1989, 59.

Lynch, Doris. Review of *Perpetua*, by Olga Broumas. *Library Journal* 115.5 (1990): 94.

Myles, Eileen. "The Fruit Measures Itself." Review of *Sappho's Gymnasium*, by Olga Broumas and T. Begley. *Lambda Book Report* 4.9 (1995): 13.

Oktenberg, Adrian. "From Pain to Pleasure." Review of *Rave: Poems 1975–1999*, by Olga Broumas. *Women's Review of Books* 17.4 (2000): 13.

Rose, Ellen Cronan. "Through the Looking Glass: When Women Tell Fairy Tales." In *The Voyage In: Fictions of Female Development,* edited by Elizabeth Abel, Marianne Hirsch, and Elizabeth Langland. Hanover, NH: University Press of New England, 1983. 209–27.

Russell, Sue. "A Yale Younger Now Older: *Rave: Poems 1975–1999*." Review of *Rave: Poems 1975–1999*, by Olga Broumas. *Lambda Book Report* 8.6 (2000): 27.

Seaman, Donna. Review of *Rave: Poems, 1975–1999*, by Olga Broumas. *Booklist* 1 June 1999, 1782.

Selman, Robyn. Review of *Sappho's Gymnasium*, by Olga Broumas and T. Begley. *Village Voice* 40.6 (1995): 5.

Stenstrom, Christine. Review of *Sappho's Gymnasium*, by Olga Broumas and T. Begley. *Library Journal* 119.19 (1994): 70.

Uschuk, Pamela. Review of *Sappho's Gymnasium*, by Olga Broumas and T. Begley. *Parabola* 20.3 (1995): 108.

van Buren, Ann K. Review of *Rave: Poems 1975–1999*, by Olga Broumas. *Library Journal* 124.12 (1999): 93.

ANA CASTILLO (1953–)

Chris Ruíz-Velasco

BIOGRAPHY

Ana Castillo, the Chicana poet, novelist, short storywriter, and essayist, was born in Chicago, Illinois, on June 15, 1953. Her parents, Raymond Castillo and Raquel Rocha Castillo, were Mexican immigrants, and Castillo, along with her family, spoke Spanish in the home. Raised in Chicago, Castillo made her first visit to Mexico at the age of ten. This visit served to heighten Castillo's cultural and ethnic awareness, and the trope of journeys figures into much of her work. During her teenage years, she became involved in the nascent Chicano movement. Meanwhile, Castillo remained in Chicago where she attended and graduated from Jones's Commercial High School. She then attended Chicago City College for two years and entered Northeastern Illinois University in Chicago. She received a BA in 1975 with a major in art and a minor in secondary education.

After receiving her degree, Castillo relocated to Sonoma County, California. There she taught ethnic studies at Santa Rosa Junior College. She returned to Chicago and became writer in residence for the Illinois Art Council from 1977 through 1979. In 1977 Castillo began her publishing career with her first self-published chapbook *Otro Canto*. Castillo then became a Graduate Fellow in 1979 and earned an MA in Latin American and Caribbean studies from the social science division at the University of Chicago. Her only child, her son Marcel Ramón Herrera, was born in Evanston, Illinois, on September 21, 1983. During this period, Castillo continued to teach and to write, as well as to work as an activist. She held a Dissertation Fellowship in the Chicano studies department at the University of California at Santa Barbara between 1989 and 1990 and, in 1991, received a PhD in American studies from the University of Bremen in Germany.

MAJOR WORKS AND THEMES

Castillo claims to have written her first lines of poetry as a child on the playground, and she wrote these lines in response to the death of her paternal grandmother. Later during her involvement in the Chicano movement, Castillo continued to write, resulting in her first collection of poetry, *Otro Canto* (1977). With this publication, Castillo embarked on her career during which she has published extensively, one could say prodigiously, and in a variety of genres, including novels, short stories, and essays.

Otro Canto contains sixteen poems that appear in both English and Spanish. This linguistic mixture seems emblematic, not only of Castillo's work, but also of her themes and the issues with which she deals. In *Otro Canto*, Castillo focuses on important social issues within the Chicano movement, then just beginning to emerge. However, the poet also brings her voice to bear on deeply personal issues. The first poem in this volume, "i feel sad," offers a speculative examination of hopelessness and desperation. While Castillo would later write in the introduction to *My Father Was a Toltec* (1988) that her use of the lower case "i" in her early work signified a collective identity, the tone of this poem, and other poems, works to personalize that collective, creating a sense of intimacy. Other poems such as "A Christmas Carol: c. 1976," "Milagros," and "El Ser Mujer" also give voice to a bleak and desolate outlook. However, Castillo's work also displays rage and anger in such poems as "Mental Exercises," "Euthanasia," "Canción del Revolucionario," and "Desde Aztlan Hacia Anahuac." Importantly, already with her first work Castillo makes clear her concern for issues that focus on women of color. This last theme runs throughout Castillo's work, including her novels, essays, and interviews.

Castillo next published *The Invitation*, another chapbook, in 1979. This collection displays a shift from her earlier more overtly political poems, and she chooses, instead, to present nine erotic poems and prose poems. Such poems as "Despues de probar (la manzana)," and its English translation, "After tasting (the apple)," literally drip with sensuality and sexuality. In this volume, Castillo celebrates not just the female body, but also the dark female body, the body of Chicana women. In these poems, Castillo also breaks with traditional Chicano culture through her unashamed and unrepentant portrayal of Chicanas as sexual beings. In "Tango (de la Luna)" and "What Only Lovers" images of female bodies are lovingly rendered, while "Coffee Break" and "The Cavern" explicitly articulate female sexual desire. The imagery of music and dance appears throughout several of these poems, and this imagery reappears in later works including her novels such as *Sapagonia* (1990) and *Peel My Love Like an Onion* (1999).

Five years later, in 1984, Castillo published her third collection of verse, *Women Are Not Roses*. Considered her first complete book of poems, it contains selections from her two earlier chapbooks. *Women Are Not Roses*, like Castillo's melding of Spanish and English, brings together a number of the themes, concerns, and emotions found in her earlier work and integrates them into a work whose individual poems range across a wide field of expression. Thus, poems like "La Tristesse" or "And All Octobers Become One" seem to echo Castillo's earlier bleak vision found in her first collection; "An Idyll" articulates her rage; "Whole" makes use of Castillo's warm sensuous language in its celebration of womanhood. Despite this wide emotional range, Castillo's concerns regarding the position of women of color within the milieu she creates binds these poems together. This over-arching concern runs throughout each of the poems, and it provides *Women Are Not Roses* with a feeling of unity and cohesiveness.

Castillo's fourth volume of poetry, *My Father Was a Toltec: Poems*, first appeared in 1988, and a reissue that includes selections from previous works, *My Father Was a Toltec and Selected Poems*, followed in 1995. *My Father Was a Toltec* displays many of the same themes that Castillo had already explored. However, in this volume, Castillo begins to explore issues of masculinity, especially Latino masculinity and its relationship to, and power over, Latinas. Castillo divides *My Father Was a Toltec and Selected Poems* into several sections, including "The Toltec," "La Heredera," "Ixtacihuatle Died in Vain," "In My Country," as well as selections from *Women Are Not Roses*, *The Invitation*, *Otro Canto*, and a section entitled "Five Random Arrows," which contains five poems previously published elsewhere.

In the first section, "The Toltec," Castillo explores issues surrounding the Chicano family. Through the figure of "The Toltec," her father, Castillo meditates on childhood, poverty, masculinity, and the place of women within Chicano society. Like much of her work, in this collection Castillo conveys a sense of loss as well as a challenge to stereotypes of women and men, especially as they circulate within Chicano culture. Again, Castillo ranges across a variety of themes and emotions. Thus poems such as "The Toltec" or "For Ray" can seem celebratory or even nostalgic, while other poems such as "The Suede Coat," and "Red Wagons" focus on grinding poverty as seen through the eyes of a child. In this collection, Castillo also gives voice to her anger over racial tensions in poems such as "Dirty Mexican."

Castillo's most recent collection of poetry, *I Ask the Impossible*, was published in 2001. This collection, which spans some eleven years, seems like a continuation of many of the themes that Castillo has already articulated. While at first glance it may appear that Castillo offers more of the same fare, this collection, in fact, serves to more fully elaborate many of the ideas that have occupied her thoughts, her attention, and her writing.

CRITICAL RECEPTION

While Castillo has garnered a great deal of critical interest for her novels, her poetry has not received the same level of attention. Much work remains to be done on her poetry, and it offers a promising area for scholars to direct their work. Nevertheless, much of the scholarship that focuses on Castillo's novels does offer insights into her poetic work as well. This overlap occurs because Castillo's *oeuvre*—essays, novels, or poems—concentrates on those themes that interest her, and these themes arise in nearly all of her work.

Yet despite this oversight of her poetic work, Castillo enjoys considerable respect. According to Mary Louise Pratt, "Castillo is one of a generation of vital and talented women . . . who in the last ten years have undertaken to create not only rich and immensely variegated accounts of women's experience, but alternative visions of Chicano culture" (871). We especially see these alternate visions in Castillo's reconfiguration of, and challenge to, traditional Chicano gender roles and the ways in which these roles play out within the context of the family. Much of Castillo's work focuses on patriarchy and its effect on women, and much of her poetry forms an attack on patriarchy and its manifestation as machismo.

For Castillo, though, it is not enough to simply present the problems she sees inherent in traditional Chicano culture. In addition, she presents alternatives. Maria Gonzalez argues that Castillo "addresses the need to begin anew in the rearing of sons; in fact the rearing of sons like daughters is the only salvation for the world" (163). Clearly such an iconoclastic viewpoint flies in the face of the traditional culture of machismo found within Chicano society. Likewise, much of Castillo's work centers on explorations of gender roles within families and how machismo both informs and debilitates the family. Thus, much of Castillo's poetry revolves around the home. According to Carmela Delia Lanza, the home "is infused with political resistance" (66). The home, and all who inhabit it, become actors as Castillo attempts to stretch traditional Chicano roles and values to the point that they no longer hold.

Perhaps, however, Castillo's most radical move in this attempt to push these boundaries comes about in her reconfiguration of female desire. At the heart of this move lies Castillo's various reconfigured subjectivities for women. Thus Theresa Delgadillo argues that Castillo presents "a virtual catalog of the subjectivities, often in opposition to one another, in Chicana communities" (893). In these various subjectivities, Castillo both presents and challenges stereotypes as she seeks to redefine the positions of Chicanas. According to Debra A. Castillo, for Castillo "personal and cultural identity rest on the borderlines of a loss corresponding to an ambiguous surplus of stereotypical identities" (152). We see these stereotypical identities as they circulate within Castillo's poetry. Significantly, these stereotypes serve Castillo's work as a way of challenging the very representations and limitations that they offer. Thus, as a part of her attempts to tear down these stereotypes, Castillo works "to appropriate the erotic and its significance for the female speaker" (95). This use of the erotic helps Castillo's work go beyond ethnic and gender stereotypes and opens it up to a broader evaluation and exploration of the role of the Chicana within culture.

BIBLIOGRAPHY

Works by Ana Castillo

Otro Canto. Chicago: Alternativa Publications, 1977.
The Invitation. San Francisco, CA: La Raza Graphics, 1979.
Women Are Not Roses. Houston, TX: Arte Público Press, 1984.
The Mixquiahuala Letters. Binghamton, NY: Bilingual Press/Editorial Bilingue, 1986. (novel)
Esta puenta, mi espalda: voces de mujeres tercermundistas en los Estados Unidos. Ed. Cherríe Moraga and Ana Castillo. San Francisco, CA: ISM Press, 1988. (essays)
My Father Was a Toltec: Poems. Novato, CA: West End Press, 1988.
Sapagonia: (an anti-romance in 3/8 meter). Tempe, AZ: Bilingual Press/Editorial Bilingue, 1990. (novel)
The Sexuality of Latinas. Ed. Norma Alarcón, Ana Castillo, and Cherríe Moraga. Berkeley, CA: Third Woman Press, 1993. (essays)
So Far from God. New York: Norton, 1993. (novel)
Massacre of the Dreamers: Essays on Xicanisma. Albuquerque: University of New Mexico Press, 1994. (essays)
My Father Was a Toltec and Selected Poems 1973–1988. New York: Norton, 1995.
Goddess of the Americas/La Diosa de las Américas. Ed. Ana Castillo. New York: Riverhead Books, 1996. (essays)
Loverboys. New York: Norton, 1996. (novel)
Peel My Love Like an Onion. New York: Doubleday, 1999. (novel)
Mi Hija, Mi Hijo, el Águila, la Paloma: Un Canto Azteca. New York: Dutton, 2000. (children's book)
My Daughter, My Son, the Eagle, the Dove: An Aztec Chant. New York: Dutton, 2000. (children's book)
Carmen la Coja. New York: Vintage, 2001. (novel)
I Ask the Impossible. New York: Vintage, 2001.

Studies of Ana Castillo

Alarcon, Norma. "The Sardonic Powers of the Erotic in the Work of Ana Castillo." In *Breaking Boundaries: Latina Writing and Critical Readings*, edited by Asunción Horno-Delgado et al. Amherst: University of Massachusetts Press, 1989. 94–107.

Bennett, Tanya Long. "No Country to Call Home: A Study of Castillo's *Mixquiahuala Letters*." *Style* 30 (1996): 462–78.

Bus, Heiner. " 'I Too Was of the Small Corner of the World': The Cross-Cultural Experience in Ana Castillo's *The Mixquiahuala Letters* (1986)." *Americas Review* 3–4 (1993): 128–38.

Castillo, Debra A. "Borderliners: Federico Campbell and Ana Castillo." In *Reconfigured Spheres: Feminist Explorations of Literary Space*, edited by Margaret R. Higonnet and Joan Templeton. Amherst: University of Massachusetts Press, 147–70.

Curiel, Barbara Brinson. "Heteroglossia in Ana Castillo's *The Mixquiahuala Letters*." *Discurso* 7.1 (1990): 11–23.

Delgadillo, Theresa. "Forms of Chicana Feminist Resistance: Hybrid Spirituality in Ana Castillo's *So Far from God*." *Modern Fiction Studies* 4 (1998): 888–916.

Gomez-Vega, Ibis. "Debunking Myths: The Hero's Role in Ana Castillo's *Sapogonia*." *Americas Review* 1–2 (1994): 244–58.

Gonzalez, Maria. "Love and Conflict: Mexican American Women Writers as Daughters." In *Women of Color: Mother-Daughter Relationships in 20th–Century Literature*, edited by Elizabeth Brown-Guillory. Austin: University of Texas Press, 1996.

Lanza, Carmela Delia. "Hearing Voices: Women and Home and Ana Castillo's *So Far from God*." MELUS (1998): 65–79.

Milligan, Bryce. "An Interview with Ana Castillo." *South Central Review* 16.1 (1999): 19–29.

Pérez-Torres, Rafael. *Movements in Chicano Poetry: Against Myths, Against Margins*. Cambridge: Cambridge University Press, 1995.

Platt, Kamala. "Ecocritical Chicana Literature: Ana Castillo's *Virtual Realism*. In *Ecofeminist Literary Criticism: Theory, Interpretation, Pedagogy*, edited by Greta Gaard and Patrick D. Murphy. Urbana: University of Illinois Press, 1998. 139–57.

Pratt, Mary Louise. "Yo Soy la Malinche: Chicana Writers and the Poetics of Ethnonationalism." *Callaloo* 16 (1993): 859–73.

Quintana, Alvina E. "Ana Castillo's *The Mixquiahuala Letters*: The Novelist as Ethnographer." In *Criticism in the Borderlands: Studies in Chicano Literature, Culture, and Ideology*, edited by Héctor Calderón and José David Saldívar. Durham, NC: Duke University Press, 1991. 72–83.

Racz, Gregary J. "Two Bilingual Spanish-English Collections." *Literary Review* 41 (1997): 137–41.

Roland, Walter. "The Cultural Politics of Dislocation and Relocation in the Novels of Ana Castillo." *MELUS* 23 (1998): 81–97.

Saeta, Elsa. "Ana Castillo's *Sapogonia*: Narrative Point of View as a Study in Perception." *Confluencia* 10.1 (1994): 67–72.

Sánchez, Rosaura. "Reconstructing Chicana Identity." *American Literary History* 9 (1997): 350–63.

Seyda, Barbara. "Massacre of the Dreamers: An Interview with Ana Castillo." *Sojourner* 20.9 (1995): 16–17.

Toyosato, Mayumi. "Grounding Self and Action: Land, Community, and Survival in *I Rigoberta Menchu, No Telephone to Heaven*, and *So Far from God*." *Hispanic Journal* (1998): 295–311.

LORNA DEE CERVANTES (1954–)

Benay Blend

BIOGRAPHY

Lorna Dee Cervantes, political activist, feminist, and "Xicana" poet, spent her childhood in the barrio district of San Jose, California. Born in 1954, of Native-American and Mexican ancestry, Cervantes began writing at the age of eight, after being inspired by books that she found in houses that her mother cleaned for a living. Twelve years later, her poems were published in Mexican and America newspaper and literary reviews. Significantly, Cervantes's work gives voice to the otherwise invisible histories of Mexican Americans, especially Chicanas. It also relies on autobiographical material, a strategy that has caused tension in her family.

Personal experience as a woman of color and a Chicana writer influences the tone and style of Cervantes's poetry. She draws her inspiration from the culture of Xicanismo, a term for the indigenous people of the Americas who refuse to acknowledge what they consider imaginary borders. "Coffee," a poem written in 1998, for example, expresses her anger with Europeans' invasion of Azatlán, the mythical land of the Southwest claimed originally by the Mexican Indians. At the age of seventeen, while living in the San Francisco Bay area, Cervantes's participation in the "Teatro" movement taught her that poetry could express both her political activism as well as her personal experience as a Chicana poet. In addition, surrealism and music, especially the music of her brother, informs her writing so that it transcends political rhetoric. While this Xicano heritage provides her vision, Cervantes's struggle with language also informs her poetry. As assimilationists, her parents forbade Spanish to be spoken in the home. Much later, at the age of forty, an encounter with a Spanish-speaking woman in Texas revealed to Cervantes that, paradoxically and despite her indigenous features, her native tongue was foreign. In order to resolve this contradiction, Cervantes spent the next year and a half mastering Spanish.

In her first work, *Emplumada* (1981), Cervantes charts her growth from novice to accomplished Chicana poet. By challenging master narratives of Mexico and North

America with words taken from both, words weaving a web between two cultures, she creates something new. Her second collection, *From the Cables of Genocide* (1991), a complex exploration of the relationship between love, expression, and resistance, established Cervantes as a major voice in American literature. For her works that express a feminist Chicana re-reading of inherited knowledge, Cervantes has received numerous awards: two fellowship grants for poetry from the National Endowment for the Arts; a Colorado Council on the Arts and Humanities Fellowship; the American Book Award in 1981 for *Emplumada*; and *From the Cables of Genocide* received the Paterson Prize for Poetry and the Latino Literature Award.

Lorna Dee Cervantes has also founded a literary journal and a press, both entitled *Mango*, in order to publish Chicano/a writers. The recipient of a Lila-Wallace Readers Digest Fund Writers Award, Cervantes resides in Boulder, Colorado, where she is associate professor at the University of Colorado, Boulder.

MAJOR WORKS AND THEMES

Lorna Dee Cervantes's personal experience as a political activist, Chicana feminist, and more reverently, a "Xicana" poet, has guided the direction of her poetry. A central theme of her writing is cultural hybridity, or in Gloria Anzaldúa's terms, "the borderlands." A literal and figurative term, this concept, in her poem "Archeology," included in Ray Gonzalez's anthology *Touching the Fire*, by its very nature encourages the poet to locate within "grazing zebras of hieroglyphs" (36) a creative space for multiple points of view.

Cervantes expresses this multiplicity in *Emplumada*, a collection through which the poet weaves her feelings of alienation from both the dominant culture and her own. Estranged from ancient knowledge, "orphaned" from her Spanish language, she reflects in these poems on the irony of her native features that belie words that are "foreign, stumbling" on her tongue (41). She creates a third language, that of childhood and of dreams, the rhythm "of her own mythology" that offers a way out of cultural, bilingual confusion (21).

Feathers, plumage, and quills emerge as images that Marta Sánchez claims central to this collection. Because of its association with the feminine adjective meaning "feathered in plumage," as well as "*pluma*," which means "pen," *Emplumada* connotes the poet as lyrical artist who gathers feathers for quills that weave a graceful web. The image of feathers in *Emplumada*, as in other poems, Sánchez continues, also recalls Quetzalcoatl, a pre-Columbian god who represents the union of bird (flight) and snake (earth). Like this feathered serpent of Mexico's mythology, a figure that could move between material and spiritual terrain, Sánchez notes that Cervantes's poetry also deals with tension between utopia and reality (103), binaries that she resolves in her poetry.

Influenced by the Chicano cultural movement of the 1960s and 1970s, Cervantes began to question during those years the portrait of the so-called ideal Chicana drawn by Chicano cultural nationalists. In such poems as "Para un Revolution" and "You Cramp My Style, Baby," Cervantes explores how this stereotype reflected an ideology that equated Chicano cultural survival with glorification of traditional gender roles for women. Caught in a double-bind, restrained within her own and the dominant culture's patriarchal stereotypes, Cervantes strives to reformulate her heritage by claiming a new relationship between herself and the Chicano community. Wanting to participate equally with men in the Chicano movement, but also recognizing the need to present a unified front, Cervantes expresses her desire "Para un Revolution" in which women collaborate as more than producers and reproducers of the race. Thus, while the narrator needs to make her own voice rise above "the wail of the hijos" and "the chatter of dishes" (151) that drown out, too, the revolutionary message of her man, she does not want her desires heard at the expense of her "Hermano Raza" (*Infinite Divisions* edited by Tey Diana Rebolledo and Eliana Rivero 151–52).

Cervantes's authority to tell stories about herself and other Chicanas derives from the oral tradition of her community, "eloquent illiterates" that in "Visions of Mexico" she implies includes men as well as women (*Chicana Poetry* edited by Cordelia Candelaria 45). Nevertheless, she claims as her own the masculine privilege of committing her stories to writing; "there are songs in [her] head" that Cervantes gathers for "quills" (45) to rewrite racial as well as gender stereotypes from the position of the oppressed.

In other poems, too, Cervantes addresses how Chicanas reproduce and/or rebel against prevailing stereotypes. In *Emplumada*, "Beneath the Shadow of the Freeway" expresses Cervantes's interest in writing the protagonist's self as a product of multiple cultures yet shaped by a "women family," a world of communal relations very different from the public world of words (11). As a "Translator of Foreign Mail," the narrator negotiates between the dominant world, signified by the freeway that often destroys not only physical structures but cultural traditions, too, and the maternal, nurturing aspects of the grandmother's private world. Significantly, it is the elder woman who passes on comforting tradition (*Emplumada* 11). As Elizabeth Ordónez notes, quilting in this poem serves as a metaphor for mediating generational and gender difference, particularly as this patchwork, made from the remnants of the abusive grandfather's clothes, signifies how women transform even the worn leavings of their enemies into something satisfying and new (176). But Cervantes recognizes her grandmother's world as a limited one for women of her class. She knows, too, that her mother's acculturated, pragmatic generation no better suits her needs. To "trust" as her grandmother did, "only what [she] built" with her "own hands" (14), Cervantes turns to literature. Associating the written word with the male perspective, she uses it to her own advantage. By transforming her maternal legacy into an agrarian utopia with matriarchal implications, she inscribes her cultural identity by rewriting patterns of her grandmother's life without literally returning to the past.

As portrayed by Cervantes, the city is not a land of hope and opportunity. In "Bird Ave," Cervantes writes about those who live at the margins of urban culture, "model rambos" who survive on the edge in a barrio *(Chicana Creativity and Criticism* edited by Helen María Viramontes, and María Herrera-Sobek 53*)*. Reiterating her fascination with feathered creatures, Cervantes allies herself here not with those who escape by rising above their environment but instead with street "birds," "chicks," who, according to María Herrera-Sobek and Helena María Viramontes in their introduction to this poem, mold themselves into what they term "urban animal survivors" (5): "Cat-eyes and Mouse." Like those poems derived from the historical experience of a communal culture other than the dominant one, "Bird Ave" originates in a community of alienated women whose street talk and "righteous rage" revise stereotypes of the passive, timid Chicana.

As already shown, migration to the city challenges poets such as Cervantes to seek a new connection with the landscape. While her poem "Astro-no-mi" translates quite literally to "planet-not-mine," implying the Chicana's literal dispossession from the land as well as from academic disciplines like astronomy, it also celebrates how Cervantes can "wish [herself] into the sky" (*Chicana Creativity and Criticism* 48) through the venue of her literary imagination. Elsewhere in "Freeway 280" Cervantes writes of "new grasses," "wild mustard," and "old gardens" that survive along with the "*viejitas*" who come there to "gather greens" and thus preserve the old healing arts that are passing (Emplumada 39).

Just as the medicine woman uses her herbs in order to mediate between light and dark, Cervantes incorporates her power into words in order to expose social ills, a process that often leads to a healing transformation. Silence and overcoming it through testifying and remembering inform "Bananas" (I-V), a series of poems linking such themes as political and economic oppression, hunger, ecological issues, and racism in Estonia and Latin America (*Chicana Creativity and Criticism* 49). According to Diana Rebolledo, Chicanas borrow that notion of *testimonio*, or testimonial literature, which originally made "present" those who disappeared in Latin America but also functions within the cultures that have been silenced and erased (119). For Cervantes, as expressed in the title piece "From the Cables of Genocide," writing is a political struggle, "stories of old ways," signified by the Seven Sisters constellation, incorporated into Chumash creation stories (*From the Cables of Genocide* 44). This symbol, however, also has a dark side; in this case, it is the seven big oil companies of whose destructive power Cervantes's writing bears witness.

Even though writing often causes pain, it also has the power of healing. As a poet, Cervantes has the ability to fight social evils, as she does in "Poem for the Young White Man Who Asked Me How I, an Intelligent, Well-read Person Could Believe in the War Between Races" (*Emplumada* 53). In one sense, Cervantes longs for an aesthetic refuge where political oppression, racism, and poverty do not exist. But she knows that "in this country," for Chicanos, "there is war" (35), and so she is determined to confront reality. Just as a healer cures an ugly wound, however, confrontation brings relief, for as she affirms, in "Bananas" (V), "poetry is for the soul" (*Chicana Creativity and Criticism* 52), a form of magic that cures historical neglect by describing with dignity what has been regarded as unworthy of discussion.

Among recent writers, Cervantes uses her pen to transmit a sense of identity that is Chicana and deeply committed to social justice. As much as generational change looms large, Cervantes also acknowledges respect for the ways of elder women, attempting in particular to preserve communal and cultural tradition that would otherwise pass on. Moreover, while in *Emplumada*, as elsewhere, she incorporates the "sounds of blasting and muffled outrage" (36), Cervantes also stresses the curative powers of writing. As evidenced in her poems, the theme of writing often appears as mediator between individual and collective identity; gender and social affiliation; historical reality and lyrical, utopian desire—all binaries that arise out of Cervantes's dilemma of wanting to be an American poet without compromising her responsibility to the Chicano/a community.

CRITICAL RECEPTION

Contemporary scholarship of Lorna Dee Cervantes positions her within the Chicano renaissance of the past thirty years. Focusing on how Cervantes broadens the canon beyond *mestizaje* or *chicanismo* issues, Cordelia Candelaria calls attention to feminist issues and women's themes, such as domestic violence, that inform Cervantes's poetry (156). Urban scenes, too, Candelaria affirms, are a new arena that Cervantes adds to emerging Chicana writing. In her introduction to "Bird Ave" and "Astro-no-mia," Herrera-Sobek explores how feminist themes surface in Cervantes's portrayal of alienated female gang members who destroy traditional images of passive, retiring Chicanas (*Chicana Creativity and Criticism* 4). Castoffs from society, these tough young girls reinvent themselves in a space of their own and thus refuse to accept what their society dictates as their future.

Such streetwise Chicanas represent a realistic world. Laden with social problems, it counters Cervantes's desire for an idealized, utopian universe in which her voice speaks primarily as a visionary poet. According to Sánchez, these two conflicting positions, that of a poet's longing for a peaceful harmonious universe but the acknowledgment that such a universe can be brought about only by social revolution, form the central positions of Cervantes's poetry. These two perspectives, Sánchez adds, express Cervantes's dual identity: a poet who is also Chicana. Cervantes wavers between hoping that racial conflict can be reconciled through the beauty of her words and recognizing that her responsibility as a Chicana demands not lyrical verse but the power of political rhetoric (86).

Ordónez agrees with Sánchez. However, Ordónez places the "justification of political anger and aesthetic desire" that she finds in Cervantes's work within a postmodern framework (177). While Ordónez acknowledges the problems of locating ethnic women writers within any theory derived out of dominant discourse, she goes beyond stylistic questions to position Cervantes's poetry within a strategy that she claims has political overtones. Because it challenges tradition to find "other ways of knowing," Ordónez says she finds postmodernism particularly applicable to describe Cervantes's writing (176). Ordónez recognizes, as does Sanchéz, that, as outsiders, Chicana poets have less of the dominant literary tradition to give up and perhaps more of it to desire. Thus Ordónez builds on that tension in Cervantes's poetry previously discussed by Sanchéz. Reinventing her own belief system, Cervantes signifies, for Ordónez, a "Native postmodern woman artist" who, by weaving "stuff of her own dreams," "desire[s], destabilize[s], and interrogate[s]" patriarchal codes both within and outside her own culture (176, 183).

BIBLIOGRAPHY

Works by Lorna Dee Cervantes

Emplumada. Houston, TX: Arte Publico Press, 1981.

From the Cables of Genocide: Poems on Love and Hunger. Pittsburgh, PA: University of Pittsburgh Press, 1991.

Studies of Lorna Dee Cervantes

Binder, Wolfgang, ed. *Partial Autobiographies: Interview with Twenty Chicano Poets*. Erlangen, Germany: Verlag Palm and Enke Erlangen, 1985.

Candelaria, Cordelia. *Chicana Poetry: A Critical Introduction*. New York: Greenwood, 1986.

Gonzalez, Ray, ed. *Touching the Fire: Fifteen Poets of Today's Latino Renaissance*. New York: Doubleday, 1998.

Ordónez, Elizabeth. "Webs and Interrogations: Postmodernism, Gender, and Ethnicity in the Poetry of Cervantes and Cisneros." In *Chicana (W)rites on Word and Film,* edited by María Herrera-Sobek and Helena María Viramontes. Berkeley, CA: Third Woman Press, 1995. 171–185.

Robelledo, Tey Diana. *Women Singing in the Snow: A Cultural Analysis of Chicana Literature.* Albuquerque: University of New Mexico Press, 1995.

Robelledo, Tey Diana and Eliana S. Rivero, eds. *Infinite Divisions: An Anthology of Chicana Literature.* Tucson: University of Arizona Press, 1993.

Sánchez, Marta Ester. *Contemporary Chicana Poetry: A Critical Approach to an Emerging Literature.* Berkeley: University of California Press, 1985. 85–138.

Viramontes, Helen María, and María Herrera-Sobek, eds. *Chicana Creativity and Criticism: New Frontiers on American Literature.* Albuquerque: University of New Mexico Press, 1996.

MAXINE CHERNOFF (1952–)

Robert Archambeau

BIOGRAPHY

Since the publication of her first book, *The Last Aurochs*, in 1976, Maxine Chernoff has been remarkably active in a number of literary fields: she has written seven volumes of poetry and prose-poetry, two volumes of short stories, and three novels; she has had a distinguished career as the co-editor of the journal *New American Writing*; and she has taught both literature and creative writing at the university level. Born in Chicago on February 24, 1952, to Philip and Idell Hahn, she attended the University of Illinois, Chicago, from which she received her BA in 1972 and her MA in 1974. She married Arnold Chernoff in 1971 and was divorced a year later. In 1974 she married Paul Hoover, a poet, novelist, and editor. They have three children and live in the San Francisco Bay area.

Chernoff began her poetic career precociously: by 1979, at the age of twenty-seven, she had three collections of prose poetry to her name (*The Last Aurochs* [1976], *A Vegetable Emergency* [1977], and *Utopia TV Store* [1979]), as well as publications in such prestigious literary journals as *The Paris Review* and *The Partisan Review*. She was an active member of an experimentally inclined Chicago literary community that included Richard Friedman, Paul Hoover, and Michael Anania (who had been Chernoff's professor). She taught English at the University of Illinois, Chicago, conducted a poetry workshop at Columbia College, and was an editor for *OINK!*, an organization that published books of poetry and a little magazine. The name of the organization expresses some of the playfulness of the work then being written by Chernoff and her circle in Chicago, a playfulness informed by their reading of surrealist writers.

During the 1980s, Chernoff's work began to branch off in directions other than surrealism. While her 1985 collection of poems, *New Faces of 1952*, continued in the surrealist style of her earlier work, the 1986 book *Bop* showed Chernoff experimenting with short fiction, and 1987's *Japan* saw Chernoff writing in the neo-avant-garde style known as Language poetry. At this time, Chernoff's work began receiving public acclaim. *New Faces of 1952* won both the Carl Sandburg award and a PEN award, and *Bop* received the Friends of American Writers Fiction award and the LSU/Southern Review short fiction award. Chernoff became an active member of the Illinois Arts Council and Chicago's Poetry Center, continued her Columbia College workshop, and became a professor at Truman College. In the late 1980s, she also taught at the School of the Art Institute of Chicago, and in 1986, she began editing *New American Writing* with Paul Hoover.

In 1991, Chernoff's first novel, *Plain Grief*, appeared. It was indicative of the turn Chernoff's career was to take in the 1990s, when she began to emerge as a notable writer of fiction. While she continued to write poetry (including the small 1998 collection *Next Song*), Chernoff increasingly poured her creative energy into short stories (1993's *Signs of Devotion*) and novels (*American Heaven* in 1996 and *A Boy in Winter* in 1999). While her novels have been well reviewed in major publications, so far it is Chernoff's early work in poetry and prose poetry that has attracted the most attention from academic literary critics.

Chernoff moved to California in 1994 to direct the creative writing program at San Francisco State University, but her roots in the Midwest have remained strong: to date, all of her novels have been set in Chicago.

MAJOR WORKS AND THEMES

The European and Latin American surrealists, especially the Argentinean Julio Cortázar and the French-language poets Henri Michaux and Max Jacob, emerge as the most important influences behind Maxine Chernoff's works. From these writers Chernoff derives much of her comic energy, her understanding of the possibilities of word play, and her sense of poetry as an art that need not be mimetic. Like her surrealist models, Chernoff makes extensive use of the prose poem form, which dominates *The Last Aurochs, A Vegetable Emergency,* and *Utopia TV Store.*

Chernoff has said that the prose poem, with its lack of line breaks, syllabic patterning, and end rhyme, allows for increased concentration on dense metaphors, and many of her early prose poems take the form of extended metaphors. "Van Gogh's Ear," for example, uses the famously severed ear as a metaphor for art and the institutions that surround art (*Utopia TV Store*). Chernoff often quite elaborately extends metaphors, as in "Vanity, Wisconsin," which begins with the premise that vanity is a town and goes on to show how each element of the town—its fire department, its police, its festivals, the habits of its citizens—embodies that premise (*Utopia TV Store*). The technique has some affinities with seventeenth-century metaphysical poetry, with its extended metaphors or "conceits."

Chernoff likens another technique of metaphysical poetry, yoking of opposites or linkage of apparently incongruous elements, in a single poem to surrealism's unusual juxtapositions (Lehman 27), and she makes extensive use of such juxtapositions in her work. Sometimes the juxtapositions can be visually striking, as with the odd combinations of form and material in "Evolution of the Bridge," in which Chernoff depicts bridges made of feathers, pancakes, and rubber bands. More often, however, the yoking together of the incongruous in Chernoff's early writing involves a disparity between tone and situation. In the title prose poem of *A Vegetable Emergency*, for example, the narrator unearths a living human head in her garden, but she speaks in a deadpan tone at odds with her alarming circumstances.

Many of Chernoff's early prose poems share formal characteristics with pre-novelistic prose narratives like the fable or the parable. In *Utopia TV Store*, the characters in prose poems such as "The Sitting," "The Last Good Man," "Top Hand with a Gun," and "What the Dead Eat," for example, tend to be members of undifferentiated crowds rather than individuals and to be flat (or unchanging) rather than round (or seemingly capable of change). The narrators of many of these early prose poems often speak in the first person plural, "we," representing the voices of groups or communities rather than differentiated individuals.

While some of Chernoff's later poems and prose poems also follow this form, a new emphasis on first-person voice and autobiographical subject matter begins to appear in *New Faces of 1952*. The narrator of "The Color Red," for example, is recognizably autobiographical, and the prose poem tells a family history based closely on Chernoff's own family story of immigration and the Jewish-American experience. As in many of Chernoff's more autobiographical writings, the themes of motherhood and women's history loom large in "The Color Red," which, in contrast to earlier writings, eschews surrealistic techniques for an almost essayistic efficiency and clarity. Other poems and prose poems that pursue the autobiographical theme include "Wall Decorations"; the long, eight-part narrative "Machinery"; and the elegiac "For My Father."

In stark contrast to the autobiographical and semi-autobiographical works, another strand exists in Chernoff's poetry, a strand that uses language in a disjunctive and largely nonmimetic or nonreferential way. In such poems as "Isms" and "Token," from *Leap Year Day* (1990), and the twenty-six parts of *Japan*, Chernoff avoids storytelling, emphasizing the sounds of words and non-narrative methods of organization. While *Japan* may at first seem chaotic to a reader expecting statement or narrative, a different kind of order soon emerges. The titles of the poems, for example, are arranged alphabetically, one poem for each letter of the alphabet. Each poem has twenty-seven lines, and each poem begins with a word starting with the letter "s." The poems invite and reward an attentive reader's search for parallels, symmetries, and systems based on the properties of language, while at the same time being complex and contradictory enough to remain irreducible to simple formulas.

In the final analysis, Maxine Chernoff's most important contribution to American literature lies in her playful yet profound concern with language, a concern that permeates all of her work.

CRITICAL RECEPTION

Most critics writing about Chernoff's work focus on the formal qualities of her work and on the way her work challenges some of our commonplace assumptions about language and genre. Michel Delville, a Belgian critic with a strong background in the European surrealist writing so influential on Chernoff's prose poetry, writes about Chernoff's work in relation to surrealist traditions and techniques. He also examines her prose poetry as a combination of the techniques of narrative fiction and the metaphoric emphasis of lyric poetry. In "The Marginal Arts: Experimental Poetry and the Possibilities of Prose," Delville writes that for Chernoff the prose poem becomes "a compromise between the metaphorical density of the traditional lyric and the metonymic energy of the narrative mode" (114). When he examines the prose poem "Phantom Pain," he finds that it "reclaims for poetry the story telling functions of narrative fiction" (113) and that the potentially overwhelming density of its metaphors is "undermined by Chernoff's matter-of-fact tone and the 'fast-forward' effect conveyed by the narrative" (114).

The American critic Marjorie Perloff writes about a number of Chernoff's prose poems, identifying them as witty parables about the way language both communicates and fails to communicate. Perloff goes on to demonstrate that Chernoff's short stories also examine language as a flawed medium of communication. She finds Chernoff's stories superior to her prose poems in that they manage to place these language-oriented concerns in the context of ordinary life.

In addition to this critical concern with language in Chernoff's works, some attention has been paid to Chernoff as a distinctly midwestern writer. James Hurt argues that *Bop*, for example, is a rewriting of "perhaps the oldest and most durable" plot in Chicago fiction, "the immigrant adrift in the chaotic impersonality of the city" (110). This observation locates Chernoff in a lineage that includes Theodore Dreiser, Upton Sinclair, and Richard Wright, and in doing so brings to light another tradition, beyond that of European and Latin American surrealism, for Chernoff's writing.

BIBLIOGRAPHY

Works by Maxine Chernoff

The Last Aurochs. Iowa City, IA: Now Press, 1976.
A Vegetable Emergency. Venice, CA: Beyond Baroque Foundation, 1977.
Utopia TV Store. Chicago: Yellow Press, 1979.
New Faces of 1952. Ithaca, NY: Ithaca House, 1985.
Bop. Minneapolis, MN: Coffee House Press, 1986. (short stories)
Japan. Bolinas, CA: Avenue B, 1987.
Leap Year Day: New and Selected Poems. Chicago: Another Chicago Press, 1990.
Plain Grief. New York: Summit Books, 1991. (novel)
Signs of Devotion. New York: Simon and Schuster, 1993. (short stories)
American Heaven. Minneapolis, MN: Coffee House Press, 1996. (novel)
Next Song. Saratoga, CA: Instress, 1998.
A Boy in Winter. New York: Crown, 1999. (novel)

Studies of Maxine Chernoff

Delville, Michel. *The American Prose Poem: Poetic Form and the Boundaries of Genre.* Gainesville: University Press of Florida, 1998. 138–44.

———. "The Marginal Arts: Experimental Poetry and the Possibilities of Prose." In *Mechanics of the Mirage: Post-War American Poetry,* edited by Michel Delville and Christine Pagnoulle. Liège, Belgium: University of Liège Press, 2000. 107–22.

Hurt, James. *Writing Illinois: The Prairie, Lincoln and Chicago.* Urbana: University of Illinois Press, 1992. 109–12.

Lehman, David, ed. *Ecstatic Occasions, Expedient Forms: 85 Leading Poets Select and Comment on Their Poems.* Ann Arbor: University of Michigan Press, 1980. 26–30.

Perloff, Marjorie. "Fiction as Language Game: The Hermeneutic Parables of Lydia Davis and Maxine Chernoff." In *Breaking the Sequence: Women's Experimental Fiction,* edited by Ellen G. Friedman and Miriam Fuchs. Princeton: University of Princeton Press 1989. 199–214.

MARILYN CHIN (1955–)

Catherine Cucinella

BIOGRAPHY

Marilyn Chin, born Mei Ling in Hong Kong on January 14, 1955, identifies herself as a Chinese-American poet. Her family moved to the United States soon after her birth, and she grew up in Portland, Oregon. Chin's father, George, left his family when Chin was very young, and raised by her grandmother and mother, Rose, Chin asserts that she "was raised by a matriarchy" (Moyers 75). Chin attended the University of Massachusetts at Amherst, graduating in 1977 with a BA, and graduated from the University of Iowa in 1981 with an MFA.

In interviews and in her poem "How I Got That Name: an essay on assimilation," Chin explains that her father changed her name from Mei Ling to Marilyn because of his obsession with the blonde actress Marilyn Monroe (*The Phoenix Gone, the Terrace Empty* 16–18). For Chin, this name change marks her physical relocation to the United States, and it also signals the violence to self demanded by assimilation. Chin's poetry reflects and amplifies her early understanding of the cost of assimilation into white America for the immigrant. Consequently, she writes as a political poet and credits the influence of other political poets such as Adrienne Rich and June George. Like these poets, Chin sees poetry as a way to enact her activism, a commitment that she brings not only to her poetry but also into the classroom. As a professor in the MFA program at San Diego State University, California, Chin introduces her students to cross cultural genres, forms, and languages, and she insists that they recognize themselves as part of the larger global community.

Chin has published three volumes of poetry and co-edited an anthology of Asian American writing: *Dwarf Bamboo* (1987); *The Phoenix Gone, the Terrace Empty* (1994); *Rhapsody in Plain Yellow* (2002); and *Dissident Song: A Contemporary Asian American Anthology* (1991). Chin has received two National Endowment for the Arts Writing Fellowships (1984–85, 1991); the Mary Roberts Rhinehart Award (1983); a Stamford Stegner University Fellowship (1984–85); a MacDowell Colony Fellowship

(1987); a Yaddo Fellowship (1990–94); Josephine Miles Award, PEN (1994, 1995); and the Pushcart Prize (1994, 1995, 1997).

MAJOR WORKS AND THEMES

Marilyn Chin writes about assimilation—a major theme, that unifies her work. Chin tells Bill Moyers, "So much of my poetry is about assimilation—about fearing it and loathing it but also celebrating the wonderful magic of it" (69). However, as her poetic voice unravels the complexity of this process, she interweaves various other themes: loss, exile, cultural history, silence, family relationships, sadness, sacrifice, and gender. "How I Got That Name: An Essay on Assimilation" not only explains the poet's name, but the poem also details gender divisions—the father as "tomcat," "gambler," and "thug" and the mother relegated to the kitchen surrounded by "loving children." As its title indicates, this poem offers a litany on the markers, cost, and consequences of assimilation: confrontations with stereotypes, the yearning for China, negotiations with Western popular culture, the instability of a bicultural existence.

Chin's deep commitment to the poetry of activism propels most of her poetry, sometimes lending a blatant political overtone to a poem ("Beijing Spring" from *The Phoenix Gone*) and at other times, juxtaposing the political and the personal in startling ways ("A Portrait of the Nation, 1990–1991" and "Tienanmen, The Aftermath" from *The Phoenix Gone*). Matthew Rothschild writes of these poems: "Chin parks the reader at the busy intersection of love, sex, family, and politics" (49). *Dwarf Bamboo*, Chin's first volume, opens with a dedication to the Chinese revolutionary and poet Ai Qing, thus making clear the volume's political nature as do the titles of many of the poems: "We Are a Young Nation, Uncle," "Exile's Letter," "Love Poem from Nagasaki." As readers navigate through her poems, they soon realize that for Chin all issues become political.

Dwarf Bamboo consists of four sections: "The Parent Node," which emphasizes the Chinese immigrant's connection with his or her cultural heritage; "American Soil," which highlights the Chinese immigrant's experiences of dislocation and assimilation; "Late Spring," which privileges the world of Asian females; and "American Rain," which contains only two poems. Each section keeps in view the complexity of assimilation while simultaneously highlighting particular experiences with, reactions to, and consequences of negotiating between two cultures.

In his review of *Dwarf Bamboo*, Da Zheng calls "Late Spring" "the most compelling part of the book" and finds it "filled with women's anger, fury and hesitation" (174). In "Beauty, My Sisters, Is Not Regalia," the narrator speaks of her face "scarred with reticence," and she details how her mother sank into the sea while her father watched the sea but not his drowning wife. This same sea "swallows" the speaker disorienting and tumbling, and thus, the speaker struggles for focus—for voice. "Night Visit" tells of a woman desperate to remove the tattooed marigolds from her body before her marriage to a man above her caste. This poem bespeaks the fear of exposing a body unacceptably marked, as well as the need to conceal any female body deemed unacceptable. In "I Confess . . . ," the speaker admits to reading both Gaston Bachelard and "The Compassionate Buddha." The speaker addresses her mentor, Ai, reporting her progress as a scholar faithfully reading and writing, yet the narrator admits to feminine behavior, wearing make-up and giving her body to boys. The poem ends with the speaker wondering whether she should have listened to her mother and married a Chinese. Chin suggests the obstacles facing a woman hoping to maintain an intellectual life.

The Phoenix Gone, the Terrace Empty furthers Chin's concern with all aspects of assimilation. This volume particularly expresses a strong sense of history, nostalgia for the lost home, and passion for freedom. In his review of *The Phoenix Gone*, Da Zheng believes that the volume's opening poem, "Prelude," contains these key themes (186–87). In this poem, dedicated to Chin's mother, the speaker decries the loss of country, but she also suggests that knowing one's cultural history means holding one's country "within." The poet turns to her mother's favorite poem for comfort, safety, and home. Chin links this search and longing for home to the processes of cultural displacement and assimilation.

This volume offers a glimpse into the lives of those who cannot survive either the displacement or the acculturation in such poems as "Elegy for Chloe Nguyen," and the ten poems that compose "Homage to Diana Toy." The latter address the suicide of a young anorexic woman. In "Disorder" from this section, Chin writes of a young woman starving herself in the land of plenty: "The only truth you know now is your hunger." Chin tells Moyers, "Diana Toy is spiritually starved, which is what happens to many of us who appear on the shores of the promised land" (79). This sense of irony underscores many of the poems that compose *The Phoenix Gone, the Terrace Empty*: In "How I Got that Name," Chin notes the irony of bearing the name of one of whiteness's shining icons, Marilyn Monroe, and in "Turtle Soup," the speaker watches as the mother boils the life out of a turtle, the symbol of longevity.

Like *Dwarf Bamboo*, *The Phoenix Gone* makes bold political statements. Sarcasm seems to replace irony in "A Portrait of the Self as Nation, 1990–1991," as the speaker addresses the history of U.S. immigration—focusing on the Asian Exclusion Acts. As the title of the poem indicates politics and identity merge—making the personal always political. According to Da Zheng, "The poems in the section 'Beijing Spring: for the Chinese Democratic Movement' reflect the poet's bicultural status and psychological affiliation with the unyielding pro-democratic activists in China" (187). Chin's poems in this section often make clear the profound effect that the 1989 movement had on her as in "Tienanmen, The Aftermath" and "Beijing Spring." Chin's poetry gives personal voice to the politics of immigration, exile, cultural displacement, oppression, and assimilation without reducing those issues only to the personal.

CRITICAL RECEPTION

While Marilyn Chin's work has not garnered a large amount of critical attention, it has enjoyed favorable reviews. In his review of *Dwarf Bamboo*, George Uba calls Chin "a master ironist and satirist whose emotional amplitude allows her to bless even as she mocks," and he finds *Dwarf Bamboo* "a marvelous book" (125, 127). The reviewer for *Publisher's Weekly* echoes Uba's assessment: "Chin refuses to sacrifice her sensibility to cynicism . . . though at times she is willing to acknowledge bitterness, contempt or disappointment as her lot" (79). In her critical discussion of four Asian-American poets and their immigration poems, Mary Slowik identifies Chin's language as "tense, accusatory, bristling with irony" (226). Within the context of each review, this attention to Chin's language and tone emerges as positive, each reviewer seeing her poetry as "unsentimentally courageous" "deflating ideological pretensions with a well horned wit" (*Publishers Weekly* 79, Uba 125).

Critics and reviewers generally address the political nature of Chin's work and her ability to infuse the political with personal specificity and the feminist aspect of her poetry and its inclusion of a variety of female voices. Both these concerns remain intimately tied to Chin's thematic focus on the losses, griefs, and displacements that mark an immigrant experience. George Uba in "Versions of Identity in Post-Activist Asian American Poetry" and Mary Slowik in "Beyond Lot's Wife: The Immigration Poems of Marilyn Chin, Garrett Hong, Li-Young Lee, and David Mura" offer the most sustained treatment of Chin's work.

Uba situates Chin within a group of contemporary Asian American poets (David Mura and John Yau) who recognize the instability of identity and who use both the troubling nature of language and event to "approach identity and [renounce] its stability" (35). This critic argues that for Chin identity emerges as a possibility only through an acknowledgment of its partialities. Pointing to such poems as "The Landlord's Wife," "Untrimmed Mourning," "After My Last Paycheck from the Factory . . . ," "Repulse Bay," "A Chinaman's Chance," and "I Confess . . . ," in *Dwarf Bamboo*, Uba identifies the destabilizing factors on identity construction: history, ideology—the presence and absence of both. For Uba, Chin's poetry, along with the other poets he discusses, reveals "some of the depth, range, and sophistication of Asian American poetry today" as it recognizes and visualizes the "increasingly heterogeneous nature of Asian America" (47). Finally, Uba notes that while in some sense her poetry moves away from the concerns of Asian American poetics in the 1960s and 1970s, Chin's writing "ultimately refer[s] back" to that earlier tradition.

This notion of looking back frames Slowick's arguments regarding Chin's immigrant poems. Slowick sees as the central project of Chin, Hongo, Mura, and Lee, "as poets and as Asian American children of immigrants" confrontation with "the silence of their families head-on" (222). She further argues that these poets must look back to their cultural and familial narratives in order to develop a voice, one not isolated "but a family's voice discovering its own expression" (223). Specifically, Slowick identifies a cross-generational dialogue in the immigration poems of Chin. This critic offers the following poems as examples of Chin's negotiation with looking backward and forward, of her insistence on talking with and across generations, and to her commitment to voicing the political: "The Phoenix Gone, the Terrace Empty," "Exile's Letter: After the Failed Revolution," "Turtle Soup," and "Altar" (from *The Phoenix Gone, the Terrace Empty*). These poems deal with the losses and emptiness with which immigrants and their children must deal, and these poems also resonate "with the weight of a violent history and with the threat of the continued violence visited on women" (230–31). Despite the foreboding of these poems, Slowick identifies survival, celebration, and optimism—a testament to the power of poetry to engage in conversations "across and through the fissures of geography and time and grief" (241). Finally Zheng, in his review of *The Phoenix Gone*, expresses the passion and power of Chin's poetry: "[Chin] writes about banishment, yearning, and searching for destination; the tone may not always be sanguine, but the words echo incessantly" (189).

BIBLIOGRAPHY

Works by Marilyn Chin

The Selected Poems of Ai Qing. With Eugene Eoyang. Bloomington: Indiana University Press, 1982. (bilingual edition translation)

Dwarf Bamboo. New York: Greenfield Review Press, 1987.

Dissident Song: A Contemporary Asian American Anthology. With David Wong Louie. Santa Cruz, CA: Quarry West, 1991.

The Phoenix Gone, the Terrace Empty. Minneapolis, MN: Milkweed Editions, 1994.

Rhapsody in Plain Yellow. New York: Norton, 2002.

Studies of Marilyn Chin

Jordan, June. Review of *The Phoenix Gone, the Terrace Empty*, by Marilyn Chin. *Ms*, March-April 1994: 70–74.

Lynch, Doris, Review of *The Phoenix Gone, the Terrace Empty*, by Marilyn Chin. *Library Journal*, 15 Feb. 1994: 164.

Moyers, Bill. *The Language of Life: A Festival of Poets*. New York: Doubleday, 1995. 67–80.

Publishers Weekly. 28 Feb. 1994, 79.

Rothschild, Matthew. "A Feast of Poetry." Review of *The Phoenix Gone, the Terrace Empty*, by Marilyn Chin. *Progressive* 58.5 (1994): 48–52.

Slowik, Mary. "Beyond Lot's Wife: The Immigration Poems of Marilyn Chin, Garret Hongo, Li-Young Lee, and David Mura." *MELUS* 25.3–4 (2000): 221–42.

Speirs, Logan. Review of *Dwarf Bamboo*, by Marilyn Chin. *English Studies* 619 (1988): 431.

Svoboda, Theresa. "Try Bondage." Review of *Saturday Night at the Pahala Theatre*, by Lois-Ann Yamanka, *Joker, Joker, Deuce*, by Paul Beatty, *American Dreams*, by Sapphire, and *The Phoenix Gone, the Terrace Empty*, by Marilyn Chin. *Kenyon Review* 17.2 (1995): 157–61.

Uba, George. Review of *Dwarf Bamboo*, by Marilyn Chin. *MELUS* 15.1 (1988): 125–28.

———. "Versions of Identity in Post-Activist Asian American Poetry." In *Reading the Literatures of Asian America,* edited by Shirley Geok-lin Lim and Amy Ling. Philadelphia, PA: Temple University Press, 1992. 33–48.

Zheng, Da. Review of *Dwarf Bamboo*, by Marilyn Chin. *Amerasia Journal* 21.1–2 (1995): 173–75.

———. Review of *The Phoenix Gone, the Terrace Empty*, by Marilyn Chin. *Amerasia Journal* 24.2 (1998): 186–89.

SANDRA CISNEROS (1954–)

Lisa B. Day

BIOGRAPHY

As the only daughter of seven children born to an impoverished Mexican father and a Chicana mother, Sandra Cisneros has naturally coped with marginalization related to her gender, ethnicity, and class. Cisneros spent her childhood in Chicago barrios and in Mexico, where her father sporadically moved the family when he became homesick. Overcoming the financial limitations of her upbringing, Cisneros received her BA degree from Loyola University in 1976 and her MFA from the University of Iowa in 1978. In addition to her consistent publishing record of poetry, fiction, and essays, she has worked as a college recruiter for Loyola University; as an artist-in-residence in Vence, France; as a director of literary programs at Guadeloupe Cultural Arts Center in San Antonio, Texas; and as a guest professor at several colleges and universities. Cisneros has received many awards for her work, including two National Endowment for the Arts Fellowships, and a "genius grant" from the MacArthur Foundation. An activist for Chicano issues, Cisneros sponsors other Chicano writers, participates in political events, and promotes Tejano culture in San Antonio, where she caused quite a bit of local uproar in the historical district by painting her house neon purple to display her cultural heritage. A cigar smoker and the owner of several birds, cats, and dogs, Cisneros frequently identifies herself as "nobody's wife and nobody's mother."

MAJOR WORKS AND THEMES

Cisneros's subjects spring largely from her experiences growing up in the Chicago barrios and from forging her identity as an independent, single Chicana. *Bad Boys*, her first poetry collection published as a chapbook in 1980, contains the themes of cultural loyalty and social alienation seen throughout Cisneros's work. In her subsequent publications, Cisneros expands these themes to include a wider range of multi-ethnic concerns in America, including the themes of coming of age as an individual while maintaining a communal self within one's culture, having a place to call home, obtaining freedom from oppression through literacy, and accomplishing a dual identity as a marginalized citizen in America.

The poems in *Bad Boys* provide the catalyst for Cisneros's highly acclaimed novel *The House on Mango Street*, published in 1983. Written as a series of vignettes that have often been called prose poems, *The House on Mango Street* provides multiple perspectives of life in a Chicago barrio, giving each character a dynamic, nonstereotypical role in the neighborhood. The novel focuses on the experiences of Esperanza, the spunky adolescent main character who describes her life in present-tense verbs and simple, yet profound diction in cadences similar to fairy tales or jump-rope rhymes: "I make a story for my life, for each step my brown shoe takes" (109). The exuberant, yet cautious, attitude of Esperanza also appears in *Woman Hollering Creek*, a collection of short stories published in 1991. The stories illustrate episodes in Latin women's lives, loosely structured around legends that provide a foundation of strong female identity in Latino and Chicano culture.

Continuing the same cultural themes as in her fiction, Cisneros narrows her perspective in her poetry from third-person, a somewhat objective point of view, to a more personal, introspective voice in her poetry. In both *My Wicked Wicked Ways* (1987) and *Loose Woman* (1994), Cisneros boldly addresses the vicissitudes of adult female independence, mostly involving relationships with men. In her poetry, Cisneros focuses on feminist issues of independence, often metaphorically conveyed through sexual freedom. Cisneros unapologetically claims, "Poetry doesn't have anything to do with the public" (Prescott and Springen 60), and she compares the act of sex with writing, perhaps explaining why her poetic subjects often contain a significant amount of sexual content: "Like writing, you [have] to go beyond the guilt and shame to get to anything good" ("Guadalupe the Sex Goddess" 49). In *My Wicked Wicked Ways*, Cisneros explores feminine maturity and identity through sexual experiences in a section called "The Rodrigo Poems," providing the voices of several women involved with one rather roguish man. The poems are not antimale diatribes; rather, the character of Rodrigo provides the catalyst for these women not to depend on a man to achieve their sense of identity.

While Cisneros's language conveys a distinct sense of confidence, the tone is delicately juxtaposed with a sense of vulnerability. As a result of her poetic approach of directness, Cisneros often employs lively, sometimes explicit language when writing about sexuality. She explains, "I am obsessed with becoming a woman comfortable in her skin" ("Guadalupe the Sex Goddess" 50), and this obsession is obvious in *Loose Woman*, a collection of first-person poems published in 1994. These poems contain extremely personal subjects, as seen in her graphic descriptions of subjects such as menstruation ("that burgundy dollop," compared with the color of her lover's car) or the scene of a bedroom following a lover's departure ("My Nemesis Arrives After a Long Hiatus"). Even though Cisneros's poetry often seems directed toward the sexual element of a relationship, the tone inevitably conveys the painful healing process after a relationship falls apart. Yet, the stubbornly independent, resilient voice of the poems never takes itself too seriously, as seen in the title poem of the collection when she declares herself "the woman of myth and bullshit" and later calls herself "Pancha Villa" ("Loose Woman"). Regardless of the content, Cisneros always writes in vivid, specific language, and whenever the English language is not expressive enough for her, Cisneros intersperses Spanish, as in the poem "*Dulzura*": "I want you *juntito a mí*" (*Loose Woman* 27).

CRITICAL RECEPTION

Throughout her writing Cisneros blends form and content in a smooth, nearly conversational manner; as a result, her work proves difficult to classify into a specific genre. Her fiction, written in poetic language and rhythm, contains multiple points of view concerning Latino and Chicano culture in America. Her poetry, often written in narrative style, tends to focus on her personal experiences as a single, adult Chicana negotiating her independence against cultural stereotypes, patriarchal social norms, and personal demons related to interpersonal relationships.

Cisneros has received extensive critical acclaim for *House on Mango Street* for its form as well as its subject matter. Critics have resisted classifying the book into a particular genre, lauding its "brief voice vignettes" and calling it a series of prose poems instead of classifying it along traditional narrative standards of fiction (Muske 409; Phelan 221). Its reception in literary criticism focuses on its place as a *bildungsroman* within Chicano culture, along with its universal themes of female independence despite male manipulation and cultural oppression. Cisneros's writing has drawn comparisons with the work of Gloria Anzaldúa, Judith Ortiz Cofer, Flannery O'Connor, Adrienne Rich, Leslie Marmon Silko, Alice Walker, and Virginia Woolf, among others, placing her in a community of writers who raise concerns of race, class, or gender in nontraditional forms.

Multiculturalist critics examine Cisneros's work for its affirmation of Chicano culture (Doyle; Kanoza; Satz), informed by Cisneros's experiences with dislocation between America and Mexico and with her family's struggles with poverty (Yarbro-Bejarano 139). Cordelia Chávez Candelaria indicates that Cisneros's poetry expresses a "wild zone" in Chicana culture, focusing on her bold revisions of cultural stereotypes and legends (248). While most of the criticism on Cisneros's work emphasizes her skill with adolescent narrators, only a few critics have examined her work written from an adult point of view. Cisneros's work has also attracted attention for its articulation of the importance of space in a person's development, and her technique has been praised for its implicit critique of Gaston Bachelard's theories in his *Poetics of Space* (Gutierrez-Jones; Heredia; Herrera; Olivares).

As Cisneros's critical reception grows, more analysis needs to be done on her poetry, which has traditionally not garnered as much scholarly attention as her novels and short stories. Multicultural and feminist approaches seen in regard to Cisneros's expressions of group cultural loyalty in her fiction could be applied to the more personal subjects and perspectives within her poetry.

BIBLIOGRAPHY

Works by Sandra Cisneros

Bad Boys. San Jose, CA: Mango Press, 1980. (chapbook)
The House on Mango Street. New York: Vintage, 1983. (fiction)
My Wicked Wicked Ways. Bloomington, IN: Third Women Press, 1987.
Woman Hollering Creek and Other Stories. New York: Random House, 1991. (fiction)

Hairs: Pelitos. New York: Knopf, 1994. (juvenalia)
Loose Woman. New York: Knopf, 1994.
"Guadalupe the Sex Goddess." *Goddess of the Americas: Writings on the Virgin of Guadalupe*, edited by Ana Castillo. New York: Riverhead, 1996. 46–51. (essay)

Studies of Sandra Cisneros

Candelaria, Cordelia Chávez. "The 'Wild Zone': Thesis as Gloss in Chicana Literary Study." In *Feminisms: An Anthology of Literary Theory and Criticism*, edited by Robyn R. Warhol and Diane Price Herndl. New Brunswick, NJ: Rutgers University Press, 1997. 248–56.
Carbonell, Ana Maria. "From Llorona to Gritona: Coatlicue in Feminist Tales by Viramontes and Cisneros." *MELUS* 24.2 (1999): 53–74.
Carter, Nancy Corson. "Claiming the Bittersweet Matrix: Alice Walker, Sandra Cisneros, and Adrienne Rich." *Critique* 35.4 (1994): 195–204.
Doyle, Jacqueline. "More Room of Her Own: Sandra Cisneros's *The House on Mango Street*." *MELUS* 19.4 (1994): 5–35.
Grobman, Laurie. "The Cultural Past and Artistic Creation in Sandra Cisneros's *The House on Mango Street* and Judith Ortiz Cofer's *Silent Dancing*." *Confluencia* 11.1 (1995): 42–49.
Gutierrez-Jones, Leslie S. "Different Voices: The Re-Bildung of the Barrio in Sandra Cisneros's *The House on Mango Street*." In *Anxious Power: Reading, Writing, and Ambivalence in Narrative by Women*, edited by Carol J. Singley and Susan Elizabeth Sweeny. Albany: State University of New York Press, 1993. 295–312.
Heredia, Juanita. "Down These City Streets: Exploring Urban Space in 'El Bronx Remembered' and *The House on Mango Street*." *Mester* 22–23. (1993–94): 93–105.
Herrera, Andrea O'Reilly. " 'Chambers of Consciousness': Sandra Cisneros and the Development of the Self in the BIG House on Mango Street." *Bucknell Review* 39.1 (1995): 191–204.
Kanoza, Theresa. "Esperanza's Mango Street: Home for Keeps." *Notes on Contemporary Literature* 25.3 (1995): 9.
Karafilis, Maria. "Crossing the Borders of Genre: Revisions of the Bildungsroman in Sandra Cisneros's *The House on Mango Street* and Jamaica Kincaid's *Annie John*." *Journal of the Midwest Modern Language Association* 31.2 (1998): 63–78.
Kessler, Elizabeth A. "A Sociolinguistic Study of Male-Female Interaction in Cisneros' *The House on Mango Street*." *Conference of College Teachers of English Studies* 55 (1995): 10–17.
Kleing, Dianne. "Coming of Age in Novels by Rudolfo Anaya and Sandra Cisneros." *English Journal* 81.5 (1992): 21–26.
Kolmar, Wendy K. " 'Dialectics of Connectedness': Supernatural Elements in Novels by Bambara, Cisneros, Grahn, and Erdrich." In *Haunting the House of Fiction: Feminist Perspectives on Ghost Stories by American Women*, edited by Lynette Carpenter and Wendy K. Komar. Knoxville; University of Tennessee Press, 1991. 236–49.
Kuribayashi, Tomoko. "The Chicana Girl Writes Her Way In and Out: Space and Bilingualism in Sandra Cisneros's *The House on Mango Street*." In *Creating Safe Space: Violence and Women's Writing*, edited by Tomoko Kuribayashi and Julie Tharp. Albany: State University of New York Press, 1997. 165–77.
McCracken, Ellen Sandra. "Cisneros's *The House on Mango Street*: Community-Oriented Introspection and the Demystification of Patriarchal Violence." In *Breaking Boundaries: Latina Writing and Critical Readings*, edited by Asuncion Horno-Delgado et al. Amherst: University of Massachusetts Press, 1989. 62–71.

Miriam-Goldberg, Caryn. *Sandra Cisneros: Latina Writer and Activist.* Hillside, NJ: Enslow, 1998.

Mullen, Harryette Romell. " 'A Silence Between Us Like a Language': The Untranslatability of Experience in Sandra Cisneros' *Woman Hollering Creek.*" *MELUS* 21 (1996): 3–20.

Muske, Carol. Review of *My Wicked Wicked Ways*, by Sandra Cisneros. *Parnassus* 20.1 (1995): 409–23.

Olivares, Julian. "Sandra Cisneros' *The House on Mango Street* and *The Poetics of Space.*" *Americas Review* 3.4 (1987): 160–70.

Payant, Katherine. "Borderland Themes in Sandra Cisneros's *Woman Hollering Creek.*" In *The Immigrant Experience in North American Literature: Carving Out a Niche*, edited by Katherine B. Payant and Toby Rose. Westport, CT: Greenwood, 1999. 95–108.

Phelan, James. "Sandra Cisneros's *Woman Hollering Creek*: Narrative as Rhetoric and as Cultural Practice." *Narrative* 6.3 (1998): 221–35.

Prescott, Peter S., and Karen Springen. "Seven for Summer." *Newsweek* 3 June 1991: 60–63.

Rangil, Viviana. "Pro-Claiming a Space: The Poetry of Sandra Cisneros and Judith Ortiz Cofer." *MultiCultural Review* 9.3 (2000): 48–51.

Rodriguez Aranda, Pilar E. "On the Solitary Nature of Being Mexican, Female, Wicked and Thirty-Three: An Interview with Writer Sandra Cisneros." *Americas Review* 18.1 (1990): 64–80.

Rojas, Maythee G. "Cisneros's 'Terrible' Women: Recuperating the Erotic as a Feminist Source in 'Never Marry a Mexican' and 'Eyes of Zapata.' " *Frontiers* 20.3 (1999): 135–57.

Sanchez, Ruben. "Remembering Always to Come Back: The Child's Wished-For Escape and the Adult's Self-Empowered Return in Sandra Cisneros's *House on Mango Street.*" *Children's Literature* 23 (1995): 221–41.

Satz, Martha. "Return to One's House." *Southwest Review* 82.2 (1997): 166–85.

Spencer, Laura Gutierrez. "Fairy Tales and Opera: The Fate of the Heroine in the Work of Sandra Cisneros." In *Speaking the Other Self: American Woman Writers*, edited by Jeanne Campbell Reesman. Athens: University of Georgia Press, 1997. 278–87.

Sugiyama, Michelle Scalise. "Of Woman Bondage: The Eroticism of Feet in *The House on Mango Street.*" *Midwest Quarterly* 41.1 (1999): 9–20.

Szadziuk, Maria. "Culture as Transition: Becoming a Woman in Bi-Ethnic Space." *Mosaic* 32.3 (1999): 109–29.

Valdes, Maria Elena de. "The Critical Reception of Sandra Cisneros's *The House on Mango Street.*" In *Gender, Self, and Society*, edited by Renate von Bardeleben. Frankfurt, Germany: Peter Lang, 1993. 287–300.

———. "In Search of Identity in Cisneros' *The House on Mango Street.*" *Canadian Review of American Studies* 23.1 (1992): 55–72.

Yarbro-Bejarano, Yvonne. "Chicana Literature from a Chicano Feminist Perspective." In *Chicana Creativity and Criticism: Charting New Frontiers in American Literature*, edited by María Herrera-Sobek and Helena María Viramontes. Houston, TX: Arte Publico, 1988. 139–45.

AMY CLAMPITT (1920–1994)

Barbara Schwarz Wachal

BIOGRAPHY

A sense of restlessness pervaded Amy Clampitt's soul and, thus, colors all of her poetry. This restlessness led her, after her childhood on a small Iowa farm and her 1941 graduation from Grinnell College in Iowa, to graduate school at Columbia University in New York City; after only one year of study, however, she dropped out. Clampitt spent her early adult years working in support roles at the University of Oxford Press and later at the Audubon Society and in writing fiction that she neither liked nor published.

Clampitt often termed herself "a misfit," a state that she frequently traced to a childhood in which her family life was stable yet unhappy, one in which her father and grandfather turned every emotion into anger, and her mother similarly transformed all emotion into tears and guilt. Drawing on her family's tradition of Quakerism (and on her father's pacifism in particular), Clampitt found her own voice during the turbulent 1960s, a time of personal and artistic liberation for her. Although she had begun writing poetry some fifteen years after her graduation from college, it was not until the self-publication of her first volume, *Multitudes, Multitudes* (1974), that Clampitt overcame her self-avowed reluctance "to become a poet(ess)," as she often jokingly put it. This debut and subsequent publications met with wide critical acclaim. In 1987 Clampitt was presented a fellowship by the American Academy and Institute of Arts and Letters; she won the Lila Wallace-Reader's Digest Writer's Award in 1990; and in 1992, she was awarded a Guggenheim Genius Grant. She also taught English at a number of post-secondary schools, and she served as writer-in-residence at the University of Wisconsin, Milwaukee, at the College of William and Mary in Virginia, and at Amherst College in Massachusetts.

Throughout her career, Clampitt was known for her modesty and for her sense of personal playfulness. When readers presumed her to be in her late twenties or early thirties, rather than in her sixties and seventies, it was some time before she allowed a photograph of herself to be distributed, saying that she instead preferred to remain "mysterious." She married Columbia law professor Howard Korn in 1993; Amy Clampitt died of ovarian cancer in September 1994.

MAJOR WORKS AND THEMES

Amy Clampitt treats a number of themes in her poetry. Perhaps the most pervasive motif within her work is that of motion. Whether describing the swooping bird at the conclusion of the love poem "The Kingfisher" (*The Kingfisher* 1983), or recounting her own travels through Europe in *Westward* (1990), in letting the reader join her joyful observation of the prowling feline in "Bertie Goes Hunting" (*What the Light Was Like* 1985), or comparing Chekhov's journeys on the steps with her own grandfather's sojourns in "The Prairie," Clampitt seems determined to convince her readers that she is absolutely correct when she declares that "nothing stays put" (*Westward).* What, then, is the source of all this motion, and what is its goal? The source can best be attributed to what Clampitt understood as the inherent restlessness of the Midwest; the goal is the desire to ascertain and experience what is beyond time or space. Along the path between these two points, several themes emerge within the body of Clampitt's poetry.

For Amy Clampitt, her native Midwest bears far more significant connotations than simply that of the rugged, self-sufficient frontier. In many respects, this region represents the poet's Land of Sorrows. She once said that, in Iowa, "I was in the middle, and I didn't want to be there. I was conscious of that from as early as I can remember. . . . Nothing authentic was there. . . . Everything was derived from somewhere else" ("Out of the Depressed Middle" 6). Thus, "Voyages: An Homage to John Keats" and much of her other early poetry seek the authenticity and validation of European landscapes, form, and culture (*What the Light Was Like*). However, as she learns through the personal, imaginative, and intellectual travels recounted in this poetry, her sense of "an uncultivated childhood" is one not bounded by time or location; in effect, she comes to the realization that her uncomfortable fascination with the Midwest is in fact the basis of her true poetic voice. Nonetheless, Clampitt never overcame her heartland origins; her discomfort at facing westward was a traditional one that she shared with most of her fellow midwesterners, including Marianne Moore, to whom she is often compared. In her later poetry, Clampitt used this discomfort to her advantage, shifting her gaze toward the American (rather than the European) past as a way of approaching the authenticity she sought. The result is some of her best poetry, including "The Prairie," "Matoaka," and other poems collected in *Westward* and in *A Silence Opens* (1994). Indeed, by applying a historical approach and a critical eye to both the present and the past, Clampitt achieved a portrait of America that captures her native land's complexity and diversity with astonishing clarity.

One of the themes that emerges from this critique is Clampitt's abiding relationship with the natural world. Raised as a farm girl, she had an innate love for nature, for the birds and wildflowers, the streams and fields of crops that she knew from her earliest memories. *The Kingfisher* (1983) is organized around the elements of fire, water, earth, and air; within this collection, which addresses the issues of life and death, love and loss, and even (in "Hydrocarbon") politics, the language of nature is Clampitt's natural idiom. This language produces some of her most intimate and profound images, and it allows her to make connections among widely divergent objects and ideas. The connections Clampitt draws could easily be overlooked, but once she makes them, they seem perfectly logical and even obvious to the reader. For example, in "Discovery," the linkage of the playful manatees swimming in the warm stream to the astronauts aboard the morning's space shuttle launch plays not only on their physical proximity, but it also resonates with the notion of all of nature—both man and beast—existing arbitrarily at the whim of some higher power. The character of that power, whether manmade or divine, is for the reader to determine; Clampitt's goal is to raise the question in the reader's mind.

While she unabashedly, and sometimes romantically, appreciated the natural world around her, Clampitt always leaves her reader with a sense of a greater or lesser degree of isolation within nature. Nature and landscape provide a site of knowledge in her poetry, but unlike the Romantics, Clampitt cannot approach absolute truth via the natural world. Nature serves as a tool, not as an end product, within her art. While she had an exceptional talent for seeing and relating the subtleties within nature, she also treated her subject matter in an organic style: that is, as in nature, little goes to waste in the thought processes behind and within Clampitt's poetry. While others might discard the monotonous drip of water in a subway ("Times Square Water Music" *Archaic Figure*), broken refuse in the sand ("Beach Glass" *The Collected Poems*), or the nomads, drifters, and Ur-men who populate "The Prairie" as unsuitable subject matter for art, Clampitt takes notice of the insignificant and what she often termed "the strange and wonderful," developing them into telling and profound images of a larger reality.

Another of nature's truths permeates Clampitt's poetry: death. Clampitt treats death in several forms. The metaphorical death incurred within troubled love relationships is addressed in "The Kingfisher" and "A Hairline Fracture." The death of famous personages is the topic of "Voyages: An Homage to John Keats" and "The Dakota," the latter providing an exquisite expression of grief at the murder of John Lennon. More immediately, the death of loved ones also figures in Clampitt's poetry. "A Procession at Candlemas" describes the death of her mother; "What the Light Was Like" speculates on a friend's last moments in a storm at sea; "Urn-Burial and the Butterfly Migration" and "The Curfew" are based on the events of her beloved younger brother's death following an extended illness (*What the Light Was Like*). The most interesting example of Clampitt's treatment of death in her poetry occurs in *A Silence Opens*. She composes many of the poems collected in this volume after the diagnosis of the ovarian cancer that would eventually take her life. Yet in this volume, the poems dealing with death never sink into maudlin sentimentality; in Amy Clampitt's hands, death, no matter how sudden or protracted, easy or painful, emerges as simply a mode of transition.

In a sense, these poems can be read both as part of her critique of American life and, more importantly, as an assurance of transcendence between the temporal and the spiritual. In effect, the continuity and authenticity Clampitt sought as a midwesterner within American life is the same experience she extrapolates as a goal common to human experience overall. Her desire for a still and quiet place, whether as a displaced midwesterner or as a unique individual, is a desire that recognizes the realities of everyday life. Her Americanism is constantly under attack by the activity, clutter, and cultural noise of some two hundred years, just as any individual's physical and spiritual life is constantly under attack by natural and manmade ills. In her poems addressing death, Clampitt assures herself and her reader that neither the attacks nor even death itself are the point of life. Instead, the point is the sense of peace that comes only as a result of the calm of recognizing and accepting this anticipated transcendence. In the title poem "A Silence Opens," the silence referred to is that precise "stillness at the center," a stillness that surpasses both language and images, both life and death. It is the same stillness that serves as the absolute essence of poetry, not its absence or negation.

This very transcendence is, in fact, a running undercurrent throughout Clampitt's work. The silence that opens actually informs all of her writing: the edge-of-experience position it occupies is where both religious experience and Clampitt's poetry have their beginnings. Thus, the recognition of the mundane stands out in this silence, and is often presented to us in the language and imagery of nature. The voices of history, whether from ancient Greece or nineteenth-century Europe, from frontier America or the ever-changing immediacy of the here-and-now, speak within this silence, and Clampitt articulates these voices within her poems about love and about history and about what it means to be an American with a sometimes less-than-admirable legacy. The perception of death as a transition, rather than as an ending, speaks directly to her belief that there is something available beyond language or beyond mortal life. In all of these interwoven themes, Amy Clampitt addressed concerns, universal and timeless in their scope.

CRITICAL RECEPTION

Although her poetry received widespread acclaim from readers and critics alike, it is important to realize that Amy Clampitt was not always embraced by the literary community. Unable to sell her early poems to the small press (she once told an interviewer, "I guess I just don't write in a style that little magazines are used to accepting"), she was compelled to self-publish *Multitudes, Multitudes* in 1974. However, Howard Moss of *The Atlantic Monthly* was highly impressed with this debut collection, and Clampitt's works soon began appearing in major American publications. Her readership quickly grew with this increasing exposure, and critics and readers offered her a warm reception. Several facets of Amy Clampitt's poetic style are usually the subject of comment by both her defenders and her detractors.

Critics frequently point out similarities between a given poet's work and that of other writers. Most often, Clampitt's work has been compared to the poetry of Marianne Moore, Elizabeth Bishop, and Gerard Manley Hopkins, three of her own favorite writers. A cursory examination of Clampitt's verse makes the reason for these comparisons clear: her subject matter and tone recall Moore and Bishop; her style, which ranges from the romantic to the vernacular to the baroque, echoes the general language and form of Hopkins (although she is far less effusive). Critics, however, often praise Clampitt for her differences from these forebears, remarking that "since her ideas are of great complexity" the voice within her poetry is uniquely her own. Unlike her female predecessors, whom "the literary establishment has traditionally preferred to be coolly objective and restrained," Clampitt is frequently cited for her tendency to make sentimental connections between events and experiences in her own life to those of other people, but then to step beyond that feminine sentimentality to seek clusters of ideas that can provide a sense of universality. This tendency, which pressed her to test the boundaries of language and syntax in her quest for artistic and emotional transcendence, is precisely what the vast majority of contemporary critics praised most highly in her poetry.

A sense of urgency that seemed to compel Clampitt to push against virtually all conventional boundaries is also the trait with which critics often take issue when considering her poetry. As critic Willard Spiegelman notes, Clampitt's "over-richness" could be a problem, and certainly was not "to everyone's taste." In many respects, Clampitt's debt to T. S. Eliot—an influence that she recognized as implicitly foundational—disturbed those critics unfavorable to Clampitt for the same reasons they do not appreciate Eliot: Both poets often send their readers scurrying for the reference shelf to decode their dense verse that, in fact, deals with organic, universal truth by way of intricate syntax, difficult and obscure vocabulary, literary allusiveness, and scholarly apparatus. The challenges presented by these devices are usually cited as flaws by critics offering unfavorable assessments of Clampitt's poetry. Perhaps any perceived failing in Clampitt's poetry lies not in the poetry itself, but rather in the reader's inability to meet its challenge.

BIBLIOGRAPHY

Works by Amy Clampitt

Multitudes, Multitudes. New York: Washington Street Press, 1974.

The Kingfisher. New York: Knopf, 1983.

The Summer Solstice. New York: Sarabande Press, 1983.

A Homage to John Keats. New York: Sarabande Press, 1984.

What the Light Was Like. New York: Knopf, 1985.

Archaic Figure. New York: Knopf, 1987.

Manhattan: An Elegy, and Other Poems. Iowa City: University of Iowa Center for the Book, 1990.

Westward. New York: Knopf, 1990.

Predecessors, Et Cetera. Ann Arbor: University of Michigan Press, 1991. (essays)

A Silence Opens. New York: Knopf, 1994.

"Out of the Depressed Middle: The Imagination of Marguerite Young." In *Marguerite Young, Our Darling: Tributes and Essays*, edited by Miriam Fuchs. Normal, IL: Dalkey Archive Press, 1994. 5–8.

The Collected Poems of Amy Clampitt. New York: Knopf, 1997.

Studies of Amy Clampitt

Goodridge, Celeste. "Reimagining 'Empire's Westward Course': Amy Clampitt's *A Silence Opens.*" In *Women Poets of the Americas: Toward a Pan-American Gathering*, edited by Jacqueline Vaught Brogan and Cordelia Chávez Candelaria. Notre Dame, IN: University of Notre Dame Press, 1999. 159–75.

Goske, Daniel. "Hanoi, Buchenwald, Nueva York: (Trans)National Identities in Contemporary American Poetry." In *Negotiations of America's National Identity, vol. II*, edited by Roland Hagenbuchele and Josef Raab. Tubingen, Germany: Stauffenburg, 2000. 229–47.

Hosmer, Robert E., Jr. "Amy Clampitt: The Art of Poetry XLV." *Paris Review* 35.126 (1993): 76–109.

Howard, Richard. "The Hazardous Definition of Structure." *Parnassus* 11.1 (1983): 271–75.

Reprinted as "Amy Clampitt: 'The Hazardous Definition of Structures.' " In *American Women Poets*, edited by Harold Bloom. New York: Chelsea, 1986. 295–300.

Huesgen, Jan, and Robert W. Lewis. "An Interview with Amy Clampitt." *North Dakota Quarterly* 58.1 (1990): 119–28.

Salter, Mary Jo. "Foreword." *The Collected Poems of Amy Clampitt*. New York: Knopf, 1997. xiii-xxv.

Spiegleman, Wilard. "What to Make of an Augmented Thing." *Kenyon Review* 21.1 (1999): 172–81.

Weisman, Karen A. "Starving before the Actual: Amy Clampitt's Voyages: *A Homage to John Keats*." *Criticism* 36.1 (1996): 119–37.

Yenser, Pamela. "The Physical World of Amy Clampitt." *Iowa Woman* 6.3 (1986): 8–14.

KILLARNEY CLARY (1953–)

Richard Quinn

BIOGRAPHY

Killarney Clary, a poet of the western United States, writes prose poems and paints. As a child growing up in the Los Angeles suburb of Pasadena, California, Clary came to experience what she describes as "a mix of fear and security" amidst the quietude of suburban culture. She enrolled at the University of California, Irvine, as an art student and began exploring her relationship to the southern California of her youth. During a course in conceptual art, a teaching assistant encouraged Clary to try her hand at writing, leading to an MFA in creative writing (1977) following the completion of her BA in studio art (1975). It was at UC Irvine where Clary developed her signature poetic form.

While she worked toward her degree, the poet Charles Wright encouraged Clary to break lines only when a particular reason for doing so arose. This practice led to prose poems where margins alone limited line length. Clary's work came to reflect, in her words, a belief in the connection between "mundane form" and "experimental inside material." A subsequent workshop with John Ashbery led to the conjoining of close observation with poetic language, thereby merging Clary's talents in studio art with linguistic experimentation. Equally important for Clary's burgeoning career as a poet, Ashbery took notice of her abilities, leading to her inclusion in a 1981 *American Poetry Review* collection of new poets, introduced by Ashbery. Upon earning her degree, Clary took a job as a secretary at California State University in Los Angeles where she was exposed to the energies of diverse peoples. As she describes it, the "perfect, well-kept, quiet" of the suburbs had always made her "nervous," and once in the city, she began to explore new spaces and environments. This experience led to an even greater focus on place in her work.

In 1992 Clary returned to UC Irvine as a visiting instructor in the graduate writing workshop, and in 1994, she accepted an appointment as visiting poet at the Iowa Writer's Workshop. She received a Lannan Literary Fellowship in 1992, a Wurlitzer

Foundation Fellowship in 1996, and a Lannan Foundation Residency Award in 1999. She has served on a number of award panels, including the National Endowment for the Arts Poetry Awards in 1996 and the PEN West Poetry Award in 1999. In both 1990 and 1993, her work was selected for inclusion in Scribner's and Collier's *Best American Poetry* series. In addition to her three published books, her work has appeared in over twenty-five journals and anthologies. Currently, Clary lives in Los Angeles.

MAJOR WORKS AND THEMES

In a poem near the end of *By Common Salt* (1996), Clary queries her readers, "would you venture with me into the most treacherous ordinary?" (43). Consisting entirely of tightly woven, untitled prose poems, Clary's three volumes of poetry propel readers into the messiness of ordinary experiences. Her poems address relationships, the natural world, remorse, sadness, and momentary revelation in what might be described as a spatial language. While Clary constructs her poems from brief prose paragraphs, generating the appearance of narrative, the paragraphs consist of fragmentary phrases held together by only the frailest of connections. As such, the poems appear as a kind of pastiche, where recollection and the immediacy of perception blend together. In addition, many of Clary's poems, particularly in *By Common Salt*, barely fill half of the page, running from the left margin to the right margin but leaving the bottom half blank. As such, the physical density of the poem on the page mimics the internal density of the poetic language.

Yet unlike wholly experimental writing, Clary's mind still performs its role as an organizing force, and she writes most poems in the first person, albeit an "I" who faces the world tentatively. In her first two books, many poems deal with the narrator's personal relationships with family members, friends, and strangers alike, though in a unique way. The "you" in her poems is often impossible to discern. She talks to herself, to her readers, and to a mysterious second person singular simultaneously, as if all are in a room together. "Yesterday, when you went to New York," she writes in *Who Whispered Near Me* (1993), "everything you left here was white. . . . I try not to miss you" (41). She speaks to an absent beloved and to her readers through an internal monologue, as if she is in the audience for her poems. The narrator constantly sorts out her memories and her experiences through brief, disconnected language. The flatness of tone, reflected in nonsequiturs like those describing a departed friend, whiteness, and longing for another, appears throughout *Who Whispered Near Me*. Whether describing a deceased figure who haunts her, a group of strangers on the street, a childhood friend named Anne waiting for a ride, or her own mother driving her home, Clary remarks on those who populate her memories with a certain aloofness. Her poems rarely scream in anger, cry in sadness, or shout in protest. No matter the subject matter, Clary's poems are usually quiet.

In addition to poems about relationships, Clary also creates disjointed images of the visual world around her. Birds, trees, street life, and especially water surface throughout her work, though not as traditional poetic symbols. The visual world appears as the poet experiences it, always partial and subject to qualification. In other words, Clary's poems seek less to portray the world through a heightened, poetic language, than they reflect one individual's partial perception of an always shifting reality. As Clary writes in *Who Whispered Near Me*, people and objects transform themselves perpetually. As images shift, so do our understandings of them, whether they be visions of hurried insects, undulating flags, or Neil Armstrong bounding across the moon. Her poems plot these shifting images for us to see, and we get inklings of their significance to the narrator's mind, but the poems never convey a sense of total meaning.

By Common Salt carries *Who Whispered Near Me* one step further. The poems grow denser, and the organizing "I" more dissipated, but the themes remain the same. Poems about relationships intertwine with those about concrete, albeit fragmentary, experiences with the visual world. In one poem, a narrator describes driving from Los Angeles to Pasadena to see her dying mother, doing the Sunday crossword, then returning home. She looks out upon the "red sliver horizon" as she returns, remarking, "Out and away, in growing disorder, there is a great deal." But a great deal of what? Is the disorder in the streets of Los Angeles or in her heart? The poem suggests that the emotional impact of an ill mother can affect one's visual acuity, but so can all experiences described in Clary's work. As such, the poet concentrates less on the meaning of particular emotions and experiences than on the recording of images fleetingly understood. As in her previous books, Clary describes visions of nature and other people. Yet in this volume, she spends more time than in her previous books on the meanderings of her own mind, as if these thought processes themselves were images. She records snippets of dialogue from a gas station attendant, a radio announcer, and her mother, but this language appears not for its meaning but rather as an object within a particular landscape. Such a visual approach to language, emotion, and meaning creates difficulty for readers in that it requires a great deal of speculation regarding authorial intent, but it also ensures a compelling specificity of image.

CRITICAL RECEPTION

Printed commentary on Clary's work appears entirely in book reviews. The early American reviews celebrate her linguistic innovation and focus on careful observation. Robert Schultz describes her work as a "transcript of inner life" reflecting the "texture of dailiness" (142) while Susan Stewart comments on Clary's "strikingly original experiment in observation" and "consistent immediacy of attention conducted through the senses" (13). The most comprehensive reviewer of Clary's work is British poet Ian Gregson. His 1989 review of *Who Whispered Near Me* in the *Los Angeles Times Book Review*, virtually reprinted in the *Times Literary Supplement* (*TLS*) upon the book's publication in London, cites Clary's "diaristic voice and particularity" (3). Clary's "inquiry into the meaning of small, daily experiences" reflects a "transcendentalist sensibility," but her fragmentary language suggests that her sensibility is "balked by a modernist uncertainty" (9). Other than Gregson's accolades in *TLS*, Clary's work generally met with harsh criticism in London. In the *London Review of Books*, James Wood critiques the poems for the very reasons they were so celebrated in the United States, namely their "consistent evasiveness" (33). Rodney Pybus concentrates on the personal side of Clary's poems, calling them "sentimental and maundering" while arguing that they "find it difficult to see beyond I, I, I" (59). Kevan Johnson seconds Pybus, contending that at her worst, Clary is "the author of mere emotional doodling" (76). Despite such criticism, Clary's later work has met with increasing acclaim. Craig Watson's review of *By Common Salt* describes a poetic "I" less self-obsessed than Pybus discerns. "Clary's 'I,' " Watson writes, "repeatedly dissolves and reforms, moving in relationship to the so-called objects of narrative, but not necessarily subsumed by them" (23).

In a world dominated by cool irony, Clary's poems wrench readers into meaningful emotion. That some have found her work maudlin reflects how difficult it can be to engage readers immersed in a confessional culture with any language grounded in self-perception, even if that language functions far beyond the boundaries of lyric self-absorption. Clary's success as a poet depends on her abilities to take us beyond these boundaries into a world where individual expression suggests less about private revelation than about our shared environment. In seeing through her eyes, we see a much richer world.

BIBLIOGRAPHY

Works by Killarney Clary

By Me, By Any, Can and Can't Be Done. Santa Cruz, CA: Greenhouse Review Press, 1980.
Who Whispered Near Me. New York: Farrar, 1989; London: Bloodaxe, 1993.
By Common Salt. Oberlin, OH: Oberlin College Press, 1996.

Studies of Killarney Clary

Gregson, Ian. "Her Number Is Disconnected." Review of *Who Whispered Near Me*, by Killarney Clary. *Los Angeles Times*, 6 Aug. 1989, Book Review: 3+.
Johnson, Kevan. "Arguable Melodies." Review of *Who Whispered Near Me*, by Killarney Clary. *Poetry Review* 83.4 (1993): 74–76.
Pybus, Rodney. Review of *Who Whispered Near Me*, by Killarney Clary. *Stand Magazine* 35.2 (1994): 54–59.
Schultz, Robert. Review of *Who Whispered Near Me*, by Killarney Clary. *Hudson Review* 43 (1990): 142.
Stewart, Susan. "After the Ancients and After the Moderns: Eight Books." Review of *Who Whispered Near Me*, by Killarney Clary. *American Poetry* Review 20.4 (1991): 9–13.
Watson, Craig. "Terra Firma." Review of *By Common Salt*, by Killarney Clary. *American Book Review* 18.4 (1997): 23.
Wood, James. "Jihad." Review of *Who Whispered Near Me*, by Killarney Clary. *London Review of Books*, 5 Aug. 1993, 33.

LUCILLE CLIFTON (1936–)

Laurie Champion

BIOGRAPHY

Thelma Lucille Sayles Clifton was born on June 27, 1936, in Depew, New York, one of four children of Samuel L. Sayles, steel mill worker, and Thelma Moore Sayles, a laundress and homemaker. Clifton's parents encouraged their children to read by maintaining an abundance of books in their home. In 1953, at age sixteen, Clifton began studying drama at Howard University, in Washington D.C. There she met such African American intellectuals as Sterling A. Brown, A. B. Spellman, and Toni Morrison. In 1955 Clifton transferred to Fredonia State Teachers College in New York, where she acted and wrote poetry. In 1958 Clifton married Fred James Clifton. They had six children before his death in 1984.

Clifton won the 1969 YW-YMHA Poetry Discovery Award, which led to the publication of her first poetry collection, *Good Times* (1969). In 1970 Clifton made her debut as a writer of children's books with the publication of two picture verse books, *The Black BC's* and *Some of the Days of Everett Anderson* (1970). Clifton served as poet-in-residence at Choppin State College, Baltimore, from 1971 to 1974. She taught literature and creative writing at the University of California, Santa Cruz, from 1985 to 1989. Clifton was Poet Laureate of Maryland from 1979 to 1982. Clifton's poetry and children's books have received prestigious awards, including two Pulitzer Prize nominations; three grants from the National Endowment of the Arts; an Emmy Award from the American Academy of Television Arts and Sciences; a Juniper Prize; and a Coretta Scott King Award. She has also received honorary degrees from University of Maryland and Towson State University also in Maryland. Clifton has served as Distinguished Professor of Humanities at St. Mary's College in Maryland since 1989 and as visiting writer at Columbia University School of the Arts in New York since 1994.

MAJOR WORKS AND THEMES

Acclaimed as both a poet and an author of children's literature, Lucille Clifton has made significant contributions to both genres. In her poetry and her writings for children, Clifton explores African American history, culture, and society to celebrate African American heritage and identity.

Clifton's poems generally are short and precise. She uses simple, easy-to-understand language that dictates direct meaning. The simple, concrete words give Clifton's poems the illusion of spontaneity. The language of the poems works within Clifton's style to create powerful images that transcend literal meanings. Although Clifton's poetry is sometimes moralistic, it blends teaching with humor and subtly provides insights without pretentiousness. Along with her themes that celebrate black life and her terse writing style, one of Clifton's poetic signature traits is the exclusive use of lowercase letters.

The major energy of Clifton's poetry derives from her celebration of African American culture, society, and history. Her poetry, especially her early work, reveals ideas expressed in the Black Arts movement. For example, her collection of poetry *Good News about the Earth* (1972) is dedicated to victims of student protests in Orageburg, South Carolina, and in Jackson, Mississippi. "Heroes," the second section of *Good News about the Earth*, pays homage to distinguished African American political leaders and artists such as Malcolm X, Eldridge Cleaver, Angela Davis, Bobby Seale, and Richard Penniman (Little Richard). Exemplary of the subjects addressed in the collection is that of the poem "apology," in which the speaker thanks the Black Panthers for inspiring pride in her African American heritage.

Celebrations of African American identity blend with praise for women in many of Clifton's poems, including those that pay tribute to the status of being a woman, through references to female body functions and female body parts. For example, "homage to my hair" celebrates nappy hair that is able to touch a black man's mind. Privileging old age over youth, "homage to my hair" contradicts the attitude of the speaker of "the way it was," who straightens her hair and greases her legs in order to appear "a nice girl" (*Good News* 3).

In addition, many of the poems' titles reveal their tones of praise: "homage to my hips," "poem in praise of menstruation," "to my last period," and "poem to my uterus." "Homage to my hips" defies the popular conception that slim women are more appealing to men than women who are not slim. When the speaker celebrates that her hips have not been enslaved, she refers both to African American bondage and to the bondage of women who feel they must strive to meet socially prescribed definitions of beauty. The speaker praises her big hips for their power to cast spells on men and applauds their ability to gratify sexually both her black lover and herself.

"Poem in praise of menstruation" compares the menstruation cycle to the flow of a river. The poem includes biblical allusions, refers to nature, and lauds brave women. Connections between women and nature define the menstrual cycle as representative of a cycle of historical women that can be traced back to Eve. The poem suggests that the menstrual cycle shares affinities with nature and gives women power as a symbolic river that not only connects past, present, and future women, but also unites communities of women.

In "to my last period" and "poem to my uterus," the speaker reveals bittersweet memories of the end of specific developmental stages that produce physical changes for women. In "to my last period," the speaker directly addresses her personified menstruation. A eulogy to a woman's menstruation, the poem presents the speaker's joy that she has known her period for thirty-eight years and remembers it as beautiful. "Poem to my uterus," another eulogy, reveals a more disheartened speaker, who has lost her uterus due to a hysterectomy. The speaker acknowledges that the uterus has held both her living and her dead children and connects those children with the larger African American culture by referring to the uterus as "my black bag of desire" (*Quilting* 58). She wonders where both she and her uterus will venture without the other.

Similar to the poems in which the speaker bids farewell to bodily functions that cease at specific stages in life, some of Clifton's poems comment on developments in life marked by specific ages. The speaker acknowledges in "february 13, 1980" that she has transformed from a girl to a woman at the age of twenty-one. The "I" of the poem expresses gratitude to her mother for protecting her and giving her insights that have helped her to mature. The speaker praises her mother at another crossroad in life in "poem on my fortieth birthday to my mother who died young." Here, the speaker compares her present age with the age of her mother when she died. Using the trope of running to represent the life span, the speaker says she has almost arrived at the physical place where her mother tripped at age forty-four, and she expresses the hope that she will sustain the distance required by a marathon. However, the speaker acknowledges that she may fall before she completes the race. Similarly, in "we are running," the speaker compares life to a sprint and suggests that we are all being timed with the stopwatch. The speaker hopes that when we reach our goals they will meet our expectations.

In addition to her poetry, Clifton writes children's books. Her most acclaimed children's books are those that portray the character Everett Anderson, a small African American child who lives in an urban apartment with his mother. Some of the books in the Everett Anderson series incorporate verse. For example, *Some of the Days of Everett Anderson* contains nine poems; *Everett Anderson's Year* (1974) celebrates a year of Everett's life through verse, and *Everett Anderson's Christmas Coming* (1971) illustrates the days before Christmas through poems. Throughout her children's books, as in her poetry, Clifton celebrates life and claims an African American identity.

Clifton has made major contributions to the American literary scene, both as a poet and as an author of children's books. Her *oeuvre* describes hopes, fears, and struggles, and her poetry and prose help us to celebrate even the smallest triumphs.

CRITICAL RECEPTION

Although Lucille Clifton has published over ten volumes of poetry and won many prestigious awards for her writing, her works have received little critical attention. Her books have not been widely reviewed, but her work has been the subject of essays published in anthologies. Two essays about Clifton appear in *Black Women Writers: A Critical Evaluation (1950–1980)*, edited by Mari Evans: Haki Madhubuti's "Lucille Clifton: Warm Water, Greased Legs, and Dangerous Poetry" and Audrey T. McCluskey's "Tell the Good News." McCluskey offers a brief overview of Clifton's poetry and children's literature and notes the influence of Gwendolyn Brooks on Clifton's poetry. Madhubuti discusses the poems in *Good Times* and *An Ordinary Woman* (1974) as black nationalist poems. Similarly, Hank Lazer examines the ways

Clifton celebrates African American identity in her poetry and in her children's books. Mark Bernard White points out that Clifton's poetry acts as rhetoric with her uses of poetic devices such as hyperbaton, and he places these devices in the "African American communicative strategies such as signifyin,' call and response, and teaching by parable, metaphor, and example" (303). Rita Dove examines the form and style of Clifton's poems that allow her to speak quietly and gracefully her affirmation of African American identity.

As Lucille Clifton continues to prove her importance as a contemporary American poet, hopefully, her work will garner more critical attention. Critical scholarship on Clifton needs to address her treatment of gender, race, and ethnicity within social and cultural frameworks.

BIBLIOGRAPHY

Works by Lucille Clifton

Good Times: Poems. New York: Random House, 1969.

The Black BC's. New York: Dutton, 1970.

Some of the Days of Everett Anderson. Illustrated by Evaline Ness. New York: Holt, Rinehart & Winston, 1970. (children's fiction)

Everett Anderson's Christmas Coming. Illustrated by Jan Spivey Gilchrist. New York: Holt, Rinehart & Winston, 1971. (children's fiction)

Good News about the Earth: New Poems. New York: Random House, 1972.

Everett Anderson's Year. Illustrated by Ann Grifalconi. New York: Holt, Rinehart & Winston, 1974. (children's fiction)

An Ordinary Woman. New York: Random House, 1974.

Generations: A Memoir. New York: Random House, 1976.

Two-Headed Woman. Amherst: University of Massachusetts Press, 1980.

Good Woman: Poems and a Memoir, 1969–1980. Rochester, NY: BOA Editions, 1987.

Next: New Poems. Rochester, NY: BOA Editions, 1987.

Quilting: Poems 1987–1990. Rochester, NY: BOA Editions, 1991.

The Book of Light. Port Townsend, WA: Copper Canyon Press, 1993.

The Terrible Stories. Rochester, NY: BOA Editions, 1996.

Dear Creator: A Week of Poems for Young People and Their Teachers. Illustrated by Gail Gordon Carter. Garden City, NY: Doubleday, 1997.

Blessing the Boats: New and Selected Poems 1988–2000. Rochester, NY: BOA Editions, 2000.

Studies of Lucille Clifton

Anaporte-Easton, Jean. "Healing Our Wounds: The Direction of Difference in the Poetry of Lucille Clifton and Judith Johnson." *Mid-American Review* 14.2 (1994): 78–87.

Bryant, Thema. "A Conversation with Lucille Clifton." *Sage* 2.1 (1985): 52.

Dove, Rita, "Notes to the Earth: The Poems of Lucille Clifton." *Gettysburg Review* 1 (1988): 501–07.

Evans, Mari, ed. *Black Women Writers (1950–1980): A Critical Evaluation.* Garden City, NY: Anchor, 1984.

Hayes, Ned Dykstra. "Whole 'Altarity': Toward a Feminist A/Theology." *Divine Postmodern Conversations about the Other.* Lewisburg, PA: Bucknell University Press, 2000. 172–89.

Holladay, Hilary. " 'I Am Not Grown Away from You': Lucille Clifton's Elegies for Her Mother." *CLA Journal* 42 (1999): 430–44.

———. "Songs of Herself: Lucille Clifton's Poems about Womanhood." In *The Furious Flowering of African American Poetry*, edited by Joanne V. Gabbin. Charlottesville: University Press of Virginia, 1999. 281–97.

Hull, Akasha. "In Her Own Images: Lucille Clifton and the Bible." In *Dwelling in Possibility: Women Poets and Critics on Poetry,* edited by Yopie Prins and Maeer. Ithaca, NY: Cornell University Press, 1997. 273–95.

Johnson, Joyce. "The Theme of Celebration in Lucille Clifton's Poetry." *Pacific Coast Philology* 18 (1983): 70–76.

Jordan, Shirley, M. "Lucille Clifton." In *Broken Silences: Interviews with Black and White Women Writers*, edited by Shirley Jordan. New Brunswick, NJ: Rutgers University Press, 1993. 38–49.

Lazer, Hank. "Blackness Blessed: The Writings of Lucille Clifton." *Southern Review* 25 (1989): 760–70.

Madhubuti, Haki. "Lucille Clifton: Warm Water, Greased Legs, and Dangerous Poetry." In *Black Women Writers: A Critical Evaluation (1950–1980)*, edited by Mari Evans. Garden City, NY: Anchor, 1984. 150–60.

McCluskey, Audrey T. "Tell the Good News." In *Black Women Writers: A Critical Evaluation (1950–1980)*, edited by Mari Evans. Garden City, NY: Anchor, 1984. 139–49.

Ostriker, Alicia. "Kin and Kin: The Poetry of Lucille Clifton." *American Poetry Review* (Nov.-Dec. 1993): 41–48.

Rushing, Andrea Benton. "Lucille Clifton: A Changing Voice for Changing Times." In *Coming to Light: American Women Poets in the Twentieth Century*, edited by Diane Wood Middlebrook and Marilyn Yalom. Ann Arbor: University of Michigan Press, 1985. 214–22.

Wall, Cheryl A. "Shifting Legacies in Lucille Clifton's *Generations*." *Contemporary Literature* 40 (1999): 552–74.

Waniek, Marilyn Nelson. "Black Silence, Black Songs." *Callaloo* 6.1 (1983): 156–65.

White, Mark Bernard. "Sharing the Living Light: Rhetorical, Poetic, and Social Identity in Lucille Clifton." *CLA Journal* 40 (1997): 288–304.

WANDA COLEMAN (1946–)

Orathai Northern

BIOGRAPHY

Wanda Coleman writes urban Los Angeles into vivid poetry and prose. She was born and raised in Los Angeles, California, to George, who worked in advertising, and Lewana Evans, a seamstress. In an interview with Leland Hickman, Coleman reveals that her father's work in advertising and design influences her play with the spatial arrangements of her poems.

Coleman, twice married, has three children, Anthony and Tunisia by her first marriage, and later, Ian Wayne Grant. She has worked as a co-host of a radio show, scriptwriter for daytime soap operas (winning an Emmy for *Days of Our Lives*), Hollywood screenwriter, magazine editor of *Players*, medical transcriber, and billing clerk. Her local fame stems from her dramatic poetry readings at various venues.

Coleman's prolific writing career has produced ten books in multiple genres. In an interview with Tony Magistrale and Patricia Ferreira, Coleman reveals her influences: Charles Bukowski, Tillie Olsen, Ezra Pound, Edgar Allan Poe, Nathanael West, and Anton Chekhov (499). Three of Coleman's plays have been locally produced. Despite an inclination toward longer fiction, Coleman initially honed her poetry. Given time and energy constraints, negotiating work and family, she found poetry more amenable to her schedule. Coleman's poetry has been published in numerous periodicals, including *Bachy*, *Black American Literature Forum*, and *Callaloo*. Her first publication, *Art in the Court of the Blue Fag*, a chapbook of poems, appeared in 1977, followed by three poetry collections: *Mad Dog Black Lady* (1979), *Imagoes* (1983), and *Heavy Daughter Blues: Poems & Stories 1968–1986* (1987). Subsequently, a full collection of short stories, *A War of Eyes and Other Stories* appeared in 1988, followed in 1989 by *The Dicksboro Hotel*; *African Sleeping Sickness: Stories & Poems* (1990); *Hand Dance* (1993); and *American Sonnets* (1994). In 1996 *Native in a Strange Land: Trials & Tremors* gathered short essays, many previously published as columns in local periodicals. Her most recent poetry collection, *Bathwater Wine* (1998) received the 1999 Lenore Marshall Poetry Prize.

MAJOR WORKS AND THEMES

Wanda Coleman's ten books span the genres of poetry, short story, essay, drama, and novel. Her unabashed and unapologetic style probes the tribulations of the working class, the oppressive racist and sexist regimes, and the landscapes of daily living under brutal conditions. In her first three collections of poetry, Coleman depicts richly complex personae battling a system that works to marginalize them. Her work relentlessly portrays characters such as prostitutes, waitresses, and clerks hustling to eke out a living and struggling to articulate frustrations. Magistrale comments that "the dryness, the absence of pathos, the refusal of all idealism, and the indefatigable examination of black suffering" are characteristic forces throughout Coleman's poetry (541). For example, "A Black Woman's Hole," from *Mad Dog Black Lady*, meditates on a refuge created by and for black women as a necessary haven from "the world": "if the world know [about the hole] it would put her hole up for sale and turn her out" (21). In concise verse, Coleman captures the compression of daily struggle, the need to construct personal and private sanctuary. Moreover, the discovery of personal space would inevitably lead to the system's commodification of that space at the expense of a black woman's sense of sanity.

While Coleman portrays the frustrations of working class figures, predominantly black women, she asserts their power as well; to crib an old saying, "They make a way outta no way." Personae in Coleman's poetry sustain dignity and pride themselves in their initiative. Coleman's poem "I seat I mop I stink," offers a glimpse of the mundane and routine motions of motherhood; the speaker reels off, as if by rote, the catalogue of necessary activities to maintain order in a home and the well-being of children. She names a meticulous list of things already done, thereby giving a sense of domestic accomplishment; the poem ends with "faces washed and asses wiped," suggesting a glittering wink of satisfaction (*Imagoes* 112).

Magistrale also notes how Coleman's work embodies the sounds and rhythms particular to jazz and blues, hallmarks of black music (451). For instance in *Heavy Daughter Blues*, "Trouble on My Doorstep," "Variations on a Blues Motif," and "Blues for the Man on Sax" exemplify Coleman's invocation of jazz and blues. Her blues lyricism contributes to her stylistic prowess as well as affirming the resonance between blues and poetry as mediums of black expression.

In addition, Magistrale points out Coleman's emphasis on the disjunction between male and female communication (545). Despite Coleman's clear endorsement of feminist agendas, she grapples with where to locate women's collectivity. Magistrale further posits this frustration as "less a criticism of the individual women involved in a relationship than a comment on the restrictive patriarchal world surrounding these 'illicit' relationships" (549).

Coleman situates her work in the particular spaces of urban Los Angeles, examining how race, class, gender, and sexuality intersect in that space. Krista Comer, whose discussion of *Mad Dog Black Lady* applies to all of Coleman's work, emphasizes Coleman's attention to how bodies become raced and gendered in that geographical space. Comer discusses how those markings limit the spatial possibilities and circumscribe access within the Los Angeles context. Being marked as black and female leads to a heightened visibility in dominant culture where whiteness and maleness maintain a normative status. These layered indices of subjectivity afford Coleman a particular vantage point from which to record and depict her observations. Comer writes, "Coleman lays claim to multiple territories at once, and though none of them alone provides her an enabling logic from which to speak, deploying all of them at once permits her the last word" (366). Comer argues that such multiple interpellations enable Coleman's work to inform several discourses: "Coleman puts Watts on the literary map of both Southern California and African America and links California to black and western and feminist narratives" (373).

In her collection of short stories, *War of Eyes*, Coleman reworks her uncompromising black feminist voice and powerfully portrayed characters in a genre that allows her more space and extended use of dialogue than does her poetry. She manipulates this medium by fusing the prose with the poetry she practices, experimenting with punctuation and style. Landscapes resonate with and within her poetry: black working class men and women in urban Los Angeles dealing with the trials of living. This medium enables Coleman to construct larger frameworks of narratives such as dialogues within a living room, an office, or a job space. She wields this genre as concisely and controlled as her verse, depicting for instance, frustrated conversations grappling to name the unnameable, invoking images of shadows or inner screams.

Subsequent poetry collections, *African Sleeping Sickness* and *Hand Dance*, both published in the early 1990s, celebrate a collective black culture as well as the black body. In *Hand Dance*, "Talk about the Money" engages the intersections of money, power, and desire, and the poem ends by calling for a collective blackness that supports and encourages. "Buttah" exalts the beauty of the black body, marginalized in a society that privileges whiteness. "Essays on Language (2)" and "What It Means to Be Dark" meditate on the reality of how black bodies signify, are made hypervisible, and must necessarily endure. New personae appear in these later volumes of poetry, such as "the girl with cerebral palsy."

Coleman's most recent volume of poetry, *Bathwater Wine* (1998), offers reflections of a growing girl whose journey into adulthood is inflected by her urban upbringing and literary influences. In this collection, Coleman includes a series of poems invoking other poets and writers. Marilyn Hacker writes, "The book begins in the uncinematic working-class South Central of the poet's childhood in the sequences 'Dreamwalk' and 'Disclosures,' whose tutelary genius is the poet's father, a ring-damaged former boxer working the numbers and other hustles by day and as a 'maintenance engineer' in an office building by night" (45). Resonating with Comer's remarks on the particularity of the Los Angeles context in terms of race and gender in Coleman's first book of poetry, Hacker comments, "Reading through *Bathwater Wine* I get the sense of a chorus of Afro-Angeleno Trojan women speaking these poems, with different poems picking up the 'recitatif' " (47). The combination of black/working class/woman/Los Angeleno threads throughout Coleman's *oeuvre* and urgently challenges the audience to be attentive to, as well as active in, forces of change. Coleman is unabashedly political and unapologetically raw.

CRITICAL RECEPTION

Despite Coleman's prolific writing career spanning over twenty years, a dearth of critical attention to her work exists. Both Krista Comer and Tony Magistrale agree that Coleman's poetry has not received the attention that her work clearly inspires. Magistrale attributes Coleman's critical marginalization to the general neglect that the genre of poetry suffers in the African American literary canon (539). Moreover, that

Coleman's work reflects a strong feminist tone and portrays the underbelly of urban Los Angeles moves her further from more recognized poets. Magistrale praises Coleman's frank portrayals of figures of urban Los Angeles such as prostitutes, single mothers, and victims of sexual abuse (540).

Krista Comer situates Coleman within what she calls "the new female regionalism" to denote American western women writers from the 1970s. She argues that particular kinds of rigid regionalism—North/South, East/West—necessarily eclipse writers such as Coleman who disrupt the North/South dichotomy. This regional dichotomy has served as a literary template in the African American literary canon (particularly regarding narratives of the Civil War and black migration). Writers from the West whose works re-inscribe that dichotomy have been afforded a recognition that other western writers who utilize the western landscape have been denied (348).

Comer further argues that Coleman intervenes on how the West gets imagined as rural frontier dominated by the white male Symbolic, thus Coleman's urban LA-identified work serves as a productive place to reorient the West: "This sassy emplotment of Los Angeles geography maps an alternative moral economy onto spaces which otherwise do not feature black women in affirming ways that explore in non-depreciatory ways the historical sexualization of black women's bodies" (366). Coleman writes against the oppressive and marginalizing systems within the Los Angeles framework, clearing a discursive space to re-imagine the U.S. literary landscape and re-inscribe subjectivity into that terrain.

BIBLIOGRAPHY

Works by Wanda Coleman

Art in the Court of the Blue Fag. Santa Rosa, CA: Black Sparrow Press, 1977.

Mad Dog Black Lady. Santa Rosa, CA: Black Sparrow Press, 1979.

Imagoes. Santa Rosa, CA: Black Sparrow Press, 1983.

Heavy Daughter Blues: Poems & Stories 1968–1986. Santa Rosa, CA: Black Sparrow Press, 1987.

A War of Eyes and Other Stories. Santa Rosa, CA: Black Sparrow Press, 1988.

The Dicksboro Hotel. Santa Rosa, CA: Black Sparrow Press, 1989.

African Sleeping Sickness: Stories & Poems. Santa Rosa, CA: Black Sparrow Press, 1990.

Hand Dance. Santa Rosa, CA: Black Sparrow Press, 1993.

American Sonnets. Santa Rosa, CA: Black Sparrow Press, 1994.

Native in a Strange Land: Trials & Tremors. Santa Rosa, CA: Black Sparrow Press, 1996. (essays)

Bathwater Wine. Santa Rosa, CA: Black Sparrow Press, 1998.

Mambo Hips and Make Believe: A Novel. Santa Rosa, CA: Black Sparrow Press, 1999.

Studies of Wanda Coleman

Braverman, Kate. "Dancing in the Blood." Review of *Mad Dog Black Lady*, by Wanda Coleman. *Bachy* 15 (1979): 141.

Comer, Krista. "Revising Western Criticism through Wanda Coleman." *Western American Literature* 33.4 (1993): 157–83.

Durant, Celeste. "The Ms. Is a Connoisseur of Female Nudes." *Los Angeles Times*, 26 Nov. 1973, Sec. II: 1+.

Hacker, Marilyn. "1999 Lenore Marshall Poetry Prize." *The Nation*, 6 Dec. 1999, 44+.

Hickman, Leland. "Interview with Wanda Coleman: 'Ready to Feel the Leather.' " *Bachy* 16 (1980): 51–61.

Kessler, Stephen. Review of *Mad Dog Black Lady*, by Wanda Coleman. *Bachy* 15 (1979): 140–41.

Magistrale, Tony. "Doing Battle with the Wolf: A Critical Introduction to Wanda Coleman's Poetry." *Black American Literature Forum*. 23 (1989): 539–54.

———, and Patricia Ferreira. "Sweet Mama Tells Fortunes: An Interview with Wanda Coleman." *Black American Literature Forum*. 24 (1990): 491–507.

Moffet, Penelope. "Gutsy Poetry, from the 'Mad Dog Black Lady.' " Review of *Mad Dog Black Lady*, by Wanda Coleman. *Los Angeles Times*, 31 Jan. 1982, Calendar Sec., 3.

Prado, Holly. "In Verse." Review of *Imagoes*, by Wanda Coleman. *Los Angeles Times,* 13 Nov. 1983, Book Review, 9.

JAYNE CORTEZ (1936–)

Lisa B. Day

BIOGRAPHY

Separating Jayne Cortez's artistry from her life poses a nearly impossible task. Cortez absorbs every element of her surroundings, resulting in a vibrant, often surreal expression of what it means to form an independent identity despite barriers or oppressive forces. The middle child of three in a military family, Cortez was born in 1936 in Fort Huachuca, Arizona, and moved to San Diego, California, and later to Los Angeles, where she became accustomed to the urban lifestyle that has formed her life and informed her writing. Her parents' extensive jazz collection captivated her interest, and she began exploring diverse forms of artistic expression, including poetry, music, and visual arts at Manual Arts High School. Cortez briefly attended Compton Junior College, but because of financial difficulties, she left college to pursue independent routes (Melham 71). During this time, she worked in blue-collar jobs to make ends meet, including factory work and clerical positions (Brown 7).

As a young woman who paid attention to jazz and blues music for its form as well as its content, Cortez developed a personal goal to devote herself to her heritage through her artistic talent. Her mission combined the themes of political struggle and resistance with a celebratory theme focusing on the beauty of African American heritage (Brown 74). She co-founded the Watts Repertory Company, leading drama and writing workshops emphasizing social change. In 1963 Cortez decided to combine her artistic talents with her political intentions, and she moved to Mississippi, where she took an active role in the civil rights movement. In 1967 Cortez widened her geographic scope by carrying her social message to Brazil, Japan, Zimbabwe, and Europe. Cortez's work has received vast international attention, having been translated into twenty-eight different languages. She maintains her primary residence in New York City.

Cortez remains active in publishing her poetry, even forming her own publishing company, Bola Press, in 1972. She devotes herself to her work by encouraging other writers of color, lecturing and teaching at many universities, festivals, and conferences, dedicating most of her mature career to the performative element of her writing and music. In the 1970s Cortez became an integral voice in the Black Arts movement, often adding jazz-influenced music to her poetry readings and eventually recording albums with her musical group, the Firespitters. Her son, Denardo Coleman, plays drums for the band. In addition to her numerous American appearances, Cortez has performed and read her work at the Berlin Jazz Festival and at the United Nations World Conference on Women in Beijing, China. Her awards include fellowships from the National Endowment for the Arts and the New York Foundation for the Arts; the International African Festival Award; the American Book Award; and the Fannie Lou Hamer Award. She also co-founded the Organization of Women Writers of Africa.

MAJOR WORKS AND THEMES

Cortez's work displays a highly individualized voice speaking passionately about political subjects. As a young woman, Cortez began keeping a journal, a lifelong habit that shows its influence in her artistry as a poet and as a performer. Along with the personalized influence of her journalling, her writing shows the free style of expression found in jazz music. Cortez finds a holistic inspiration from jazz in its aesthetics of individual expression as well as its founding principles of creating a forum for revolution against ethnic oppression and subjugation. For Cortez, art is truly not for art's sake, as she consistently combines aesthetics with her own experience as well as the communal experiences of oppressed groups. Cortez places herself in the revolutionary tradition of the Black Aesthetic movement, combining the ideology of revolution with a keen sense of the materiality involved in oppression (Brown 68).

Cortez constantly weaves herself into her heritage by giving her predecessors a place in her poetry. Crediting "the old African praise poetry" as her influence, she pays homage to the revolutionary voices who preceded hers, indicating an awareness of her communal voice while simultaneously creating her own niche within the tradition (Nielsen 222). In her poetry collection *Mouth on Paper* (1977), Cortez shows her spontaneous style. In "For the Poets," Cortez often closes her lines with words like "ah," "huh," and "uh-unh" to punctuate the lines through sound, adding a performative quality to the poem. Cortez addresses many poems to her predecessors, including poets Christopher Okigbo and Henry Dumas; fourteen-year-old victim of police violence, Claude Reece, Jr.; performers Bessie Smith, Josephine Baker, Duke Ellington, Aretha Franklin, and Big Mama Thornton; and revolutionary students from Soweto. Within each of these tributes, Cortez speaks in a confident first-person voice, eager to make her own bold statement within the courageous tradition of her bold ancestors and peers. The speaker declares in "Give Me the Red on the Black of the Bullet": "I want to make a tornado." In all of her tribute poems, the characters range from victims to survivors, and the narrative voice of the poems uses their examples to offer hope for change instead of acceptance and passivity toward oppression (Christian 238).

Scarifications (1973) provides the neologism for Cortez's overall message: Through our mental and physical scars left from oppression, we define ourselves as individuals as well as part of a group and a specific place (Brown 68). In the poem "I Am New York City," Cortez's poetic persona identifies herself with "tobacco teeth," "legs apart," and "plaited ovaries." She then broadens her scope to describe her urban environment with its chaotic blend of suggestive and violent images. The speaker is surrounded by a "seance of peeping toms" and the "brown spit and soft tomatoes." She welcomes the shards of flesh in effect commanding the whole chaotic, often brutal scene to "never change never sleep never melt." Cortez leaves nothing out, no matter how disturbing it may be, effectively illustrating her poetic philosophy: "Everything in the world should be addressed by poets" (Melham 77).

Cortez initializes her contribution to the Black Aesthetic movement through her distinctly female perspective. Her work shows a woman's view of the violence of oppression, emphasizing the gender-based violence that occurs too regularly and is often ignored because of its painful reality. Cortez's poetry refuses to ignore the brutality, and her language is as graphic as the scene that it describes; as a result, Cortez matches the form of the poetry with its content (Brown 75). In the poem "If the Drum Is a Woman," Cortez personifies the drum in a fairly typical feminine metaphor, but she places her signature on the metaphor by directly addressing black men who play the drums and appealing to them to honor the drum instead of abusing it, emphasizing her plea through the refrain of "don't abuse your drum" (*Firespitter).* Cortez's language explicitly refers to different forms of abuse, from gun violence to verbal abuse, beatings, and rape. As a result, Cortez's speaker presents the woman's side of an important dialogue between black women and men, challenging men to take responsibility for their intracultural role in race relations. Overall, this poem exemplifies Cortez's entire mission: One should honor heritage, art, and all of humankind and make a commitment to take action against any negativity.

CRITICAL RECEPTION

Unquestionably, Cortez's poetry exposes "the realities of our world," forcing readers to acknowledge the brutal treatment of people toward each other (Christian 236), and to convey this chaotic social condition, she often employs graphic language and violent descriptions (Brown 73). While Karen Jackson Ford views Cortez's style as "excessive," a typically pejorative term in literary circles, this excess is what marks Cortez's undeniable place in contemporary poetry. Ford explains that Cortez "provides a literary link between the dignity and bitchiness of the earlier blues queens and the empowered voices of the later black feminist poets because she [is] able to deploy excess without being silenced by it" (220). An indication of her diverse poetic range, her writing has been compared with Amiri Baraka, bell hooks, Langston Hughes, June Jordan, Audre Lorde, Adrienne Rich, Ntozake Shange, and William Carlos Williams. Cortez is frequently credited for her role as a bridge between early jazz artists and post-structuralist poets (Crouch 99), and critics such as Aldon Lynn Nielsen even suggest that to understand Cortez, it is essential to study jazz, designating Cortez's work as part of a "jazz text" genre (232).

Perhaps because Cortez is a "blatantly political poet" (Christian 239) and because of what Cortez herself calls her "supersurrealism" (Melham 74), Cortez's work has often been neglected in anthology projects and in literary criticism. Her most popularly anthologized poem, "How Long Has Trane Been Gone," is a "relatively tame poem," reflecting the conservative bent of the canon (Brown 79). Kimberly N. Brown suggests that Cortez is not fully accepted into the canon because of her "aggressive" language and graphic subject matter (80). Another challenge within the criticism includes an accusation of homophobia in Cortez's earlier work, a misreading that Cortez believed that homosexuals could not be revolutionaries. However, as her later writing and social activism prove, her agenda is to expose the contradictions within immediate, mainstream society, and Cortez's poetry provides a revolutionary voice to expose these inconsistencies (Brown 77–78).

More attention should be paid to Cortez's contributions to American poetry not only for its aesthetic value as powerful examples of the development of American poetry, but also for its insistence on proving the black aesthetic is not monolithic and for demonstrating that American women's poetry is not always "ladylike" (Brown 70, 80). Stylistically, Cortez's work proves its beauty in its multisensory, often surreal form as well as its content to stop oppression of all people, regardless of the social constructions of race, class, and gender.

BIBLIOGRAPHY

Works by Jayne Cortez

Pissstained Stairs and the Monkey Man's Wares. New York: Phrase Text, 1969.
Festivals and Funerals. New York: Phrase Text, 1971.
Scarifications. New York: Bola Press, 1973.
Mouth on Paper. New York: Bola Press, 1977.
Firespitter. New York: Bola Press, 1982.
There It Is. New York: Bola Press, 1982.
Coagulations: New and Selected Poems. New York: Thunder's Mouth Press, 1984.
Poetic Magnetic. New York: Bola Press, 1991.
Somewhere in Advance of Nowhere. New York: Serpent's Tail/High Risk Books, 1996.

Studies of Jayne Cortez

Brown, Kimberly N. "Of Poststructuralist Fallout, Scarification, and Blood Poems." In *Other Sisterhoods: Literary Theory and U.S. Women of Color*, edited by Sandra Kumamoto Stanley. Urbana: University of Illinois Press, 1998. 63–85.
Christian, Barbara. "There It Is: The Poetry of Jayne Cortez." *Callaloo* 9 (1986): 235–39.
Crouch, Stanley. "Big Star Calling." *Yardbird Reader* 5 (1976): 99.
Ford, Karen Jackson. *Gender and the Poetics of Excess: Moments of Brocade*. Jackson: University Press of Mississippi, 1997. 216–21.
Melham, D. H. "A *MELUS* Profile and Interview: Jayne Cortez." *MELUS* 21.1 (1996): 71–79.
Nielsen, Aldon Lynn. *Black Chant: Languages of African-American Postmodernism*. Cambridge: Cambridge University Press, 1997.

TOI DERRICOTTE (1941–)

Monifa A. Love

BIOGRAPHY

This award-winning poet, educator, and activist has written four books of poetry and a memoir. Published extensively in journals, Toi Derricotte has contributed to diverse anthologies and hundreds of poetry projects. Her work has been hailed for its transgressive approaches to sexuality, motherhood, domestic violence, and the internalization of oppression.

Born Toinette Webster on April 12, 1941, in Hamtramck, Michigan, she was the only child of Benjamin and Antonia Baquet Webster. As a child, Derricotte played, helped out, and prayed over the dead in her grandparents' funeral parlor in nearby Detroit. Derricotte's father and paternal grandmother were powerful, exacting, and mercurial forces in Derricotte's life. Her parents divorced when Derricotte was an adolescent.

By Derricotte's accounts, her family's experiences with death, abuse, and the perplexities of racism, color, and middle-class values created an environment in which she felt fearful and alienated. Her Roman Catholic upbringing and schooling exacerbated these feelings. She began keeping a journal when she was ten, and her writing coincided with the breakdown of her parents' marriage and the death of her paternal grandmother. At fifteen, Derricotte shared her writing with an older, male cousin whom she viewed as open minded. He denounced her work as macabre. Although she did not stop writing, Derricotte did not share her work again until she was twenty-seven.

After her 1959 graduation from Catholic Girls' Central High School, Derricotte entered Michigan's Wayne State University where she planned to study psychology and earn a doctorate. Her studies were interrupted by pregnancy, marriage to artist Clarence Reese, and their considerable financial difficulties. Their son, Anthony, was born in 1962. They divorced in 1964. Derricotte graduated from Wayne State with a bachelor's degree in special education in 1965. In Detroit, she taught in the Manpower

Program from 1964–66 and at the Farand School for mentally retarded students from 1966–68. In 1967, she married Bruce Derricotte, and they moved to the East Coast.

In 1968, Derricotte began her involvement in writing workshops, publishing her first work in the *New York Quarterly* in 1972. She received the Pen and Brush Award from the New School for Social Research in 1973 for an untitled poetry manuscript and a prize from the Academy of American Poets in 1974 for "Unburying the Bird." She served as poet-in-residence for the New Jersey State Council on the Arts from 1974–88. Lotus Press published Derricotte's first collection, *The Empress of the Death House*, in 1978. *Natural Birth* appeared in 1983. Derricotte earned an MA in English and creative writing from New York University in 1984. Her third collection, *Captivity* (1989), is in its fourth printing. *Tender*, her latest collection, and *The Black Notebooks*, her memoir, were published in 1997.

Among her many awards, Derricotte has received two fellowships from the National Endowment for the Arts (1985 and 1990); the Lucille Memorial Award from the Poetry Society of America (1985); the Folger Shakespeare Library Award (1990); the Distinguished Pioneering of the Arts Award from the United Black Artists (1993); two Pushcart Prizes (1989 and 1998); the Anisfield-Wolf Book Award for nonfiction from The Cleveland Foundation (1998); the Paterson Poetry Prize (1998); and the Black Caucus of the American Library Association Award for nonfiction (1998).

Derricotte is professor of English at the University of Pittsburgh and has taught in the graduate creative writing programs at numerous universities and colleges. Along with poet Cornelius Eady, Derricotte founded Cave Canem, the historic workshop retreat for African American poets. In 1999–2000 she held the Delta Sigma Theta Endowed Chair in Poetry at Xavier University in Ohio.

MAJOR WORKS AND THEMES

Derricotte's 1995 contribution to the collection of poems and stories of African American women, *My Soul Is a Witness*, edited by Glora Wade-Gayles, "Litany for the Blessing of a House," begins with the Caller speculating on the meanings of a house. She then asks that the inhabitant of the house be blessed with sustenance, calm, joy, good arrivals and departures, spontaneity, relinquishments, resolution, courage, irrepressible truth, ripening, and renewal. The meanings of home serve as metaphors for Derricotte's poetry and the blessings as the characteristics of her espoused and practiced aesthetics.

In a 1991 interview with Charles Rowell, Derricotte described her mission to develop work that pried open the world and that turned her inside out (654). Derricotte's body of work attests to her appetite for deep investigation as she vehemently explores cultural taboos, political prohibitions, and her own guarded spaces. In addition, Derricotte changes her poetic language from one volume of poetry to the next. In *Conversations with the World*, Derricotte explains that her different approaches reflect her desire to balance the exploration of a central idea with her ongoing discovery and "underlayering" (Davidson 42). She asserts that when she becomes too comfortable and begins to sense that she knows what she is doing "it all falls apart" (42).

The Empress of the Death House, a volatile first collection, depicts a speaker racing to take flight. By identifying both herself and her grandmother as the empress, Derricotte binds herself to a powerful, androgynous ancestral figure and asserts her ability as a poet to combat the myriad forces that would suffocate her. Inspired by the work of Sylvia Plath, the life and death of Anne Sexton, and the social consciousness poems of the Black Arts movement, Derricotte delivers a flurry of intense images and Ginsberg-like gaps over which the reader must leap in this raucous hymn to self-determination and resurrection.

"The Mirror Poems," from *Empress*, serves as the preamble to Derricotte's exploration of spectatorship and identity. The mult-part poem begins with the desire to "break the glass" and to see the "transparent thing" that emerges from that destruction and concludes with the recognition that sight does not guarantee insight (17, 22). In her exploration of the maddening and invalidating power of mirrors, Derricotte plays with references to Snow White, the Lady of the Lake, and Ophelia. Thus, dalliances with the tropes of master narratives emerge in much of Derricotte's work.

However, home and life compose the subject of *Natural Birth*. In this book-length, Whitmanian discourse on the birth of her son, the poet describes childbearing with its uncertainties, humiliations, upheaval, pain, and transformation. Her personal tumult serves as a metaphor for our own struggles to exist naturally in the world—vulnerable without sedation. In "Birth, Death and *Captivity*," Hilda Raz applauds Derricotte's blurring of "the boundaries between body, mind, mother and infant and child, woman and women and community, metaphor and history" (175). *Natural Birth* opens with Derricotte's journey to a maternity home where there is no room for her. This link with the Virgin Mary infuses the physical and emotional discussions of parturition with a religious subtext while subverting another master narrative. Instead of viewing Jesus's crucifixion as an act that saved the world, Derricotte suggests rather that the pain of childbirth is the source of salvation and ought to be sufficient for permanent global deliverance (45). "Maternity," "10:29," and "Transition" mark Derricotte's disappearance into a "wider whole of nothing," where she truly realizes her existence (44). In "Delivery" Derricotte shifts from husky prose-poem stanzas to lean tunnel-like stanzas punctuated, as Calvin Hernton notes, "by the white spaces of breathing" (*Sexual Mountain* 120). "In Knowledge of Young Boys," a beautiful yet unsentimental lullaby rings with the trauma of what came before and celebrates the arrival of mother and son and the provisional home both find in birth.

Memory organizes Derricotte's next volume, *Captivity*. Working with the filamentary nature of recollection, Derricotte composed slender and electric poems for this volume. Beginning slowly the collection gains speed and complexity as Derricotte digs deeper into how we can possibly live remembering what we do. The poems in this volume explore the common borders shared by captivity, retrospection, seduction, and resistance. "The Minks" brings these themes together with startling simplicity. The poem describes the minks that Derricotte's uncle attempts to domesticate, and the description evokes images of a slaver as the cages emerge as an array of housing projects as well as the interior spaces of a slaver. This blending of past and present questions all memories of domestication. In the poem, Derricotte reports her uncle's harsh treatment of the animals, her benevolence toward them, the animals' disquietude, the tranquilized behavior of the young, the minks' useless resistance, infanticide, and the minks' value as "the sweetest cargo" of pelts (4). The poem ends with the uncle showing off the furs to company as he blows across the pelts to expose the "shining underlife" (4). The poem interrogates the need to make captive that which captivates, and it asks what memories keep us "wild," set on freedom. Derricotte eerily links

"The Minks" to the final poem, "A Note on My Son's Face." The poems share vocabulary, imagery, and underlying questions about the imprisonment of cultural memory and history.

Combing elements of each of Derricotte's preceding works, *Tender* continues the poet's unflinching word play. With another nod to Whitman, Derricotte explores her most tender lovers, including herself, and she moves deeper into the possibilities she created in "The Minks." She looks at the sale of human beings, examining the "tender"—the easily crushed and consumed. Derricotte looks at the bruises caused by espousals of love. The seven-part, nonlinear collection also reads as an offering to Derricotte's experiences at Elmina Castle, the fort and holding pen for enslaved persons along Africa's Gold Coast. In "Beneath Elmina" Derricotte describes a six-inch opening through which "our ancestors were pushed" (7). The narrow space, thought to prohibit rebellion and escape, accommodated the size of malnourished bodies. The unconventional six-inch width of *Tender* aligns with the narrow openings described in "Beneath Elmina," and the volume's dimensions ask us to consider it a portal through which Death comes and goes.

Portions of Derricotte's award-winning prose work, *The Black Notebooks*, have been reprinted in numerous anthologies and journals, and the *New York Times* selected it as a notable book of the year. In October 2000, Philippe Moreua translated the book, and it bears the Fanon-like title *Noire la couleur de ma peau blanche* (Diron Editions du Félin). The product of twenty-plus years of journal writing, this work demonstrates Derricotte's relentless pursuit of expiation and release from the tyrannies of radical politics.

CRITICAL RECEPTION

For Jon Woodson, "Derricotte's poetry springs from the unique social conditions with which she has engaged in a life-long psychic and artistic struggle: as an African American woman who looks white . . . whose every expression generates controversy" (87). James W. Richardson, Jr., outlines two problems regarding the critical analysis of Derricotte's work. First, she complicates "the myth of monolithic blackness with poems that speak into consciousness obscure, unconventional black bodies." Second, in a charged poststructural climate, Derricotte's poems strike out against "depersonalized bodies," "esoteric discourse," and "hyperbolic identity politics" with "her own complex, quirky vision—a vision both concrete and abstract, both quotidian and phantasmagoric" (210). When, as Keith Gilyard has stated, "Derricotte has experienced self-doubt about being real enough" how does the critic resist his or her own self-doubt in the face of her work (194)?

Although reviewers have praised each of Derricotte's works, they offer the most unambiguous and uniformly positive response to *Natural Birth*. Many critics, particularly male reviewers, found *Natural Birth* to be a tour de force with the collection's mix of unbridled energy, control, and ground breaking approach to childbirth. *Captivity* and *Tender*, with their dramatic shifts in language and style, have received a number of ambivalent reviews.

Susan Schultz describes Derricotte's *Captivity* as being "short on aesthetics, long on pain" (18). She finds Derricotte's work to be "raw" and "artless," more "enjambed prose" than "poetry" (19), and she argues that Derricotte fails to "show us how language—attenuated, sometimes broken—can help us to communicate almost despite ourselves" (22). Hilda Raz, an admirer of Derricotte's first two collections, criticizes the "mainstream" technique of *Captivity*, and this critic strikes at Derricotte's seeming ignorance of experiences of women outside of Derricotte's "light-skinned progenitors" (178). Raz ends her review with an appeal to Derricotte "to write poems of reconciliation and protest that include a wider definition of female sexuality and experience" (179). In his *Washington Post* review of *Tender*, Jabari Asim finds that in Derricotte's best poems "repetition and enjambment create a shattering whirlwind of feelings and images, which can be heard as the poetic equivalent of John Coltrane's sheets of sounds" (X09). Asim also comments on Derricotte's "finely wrought conceits" and uncharacteristic distancing that diminished the sensory and emotional pleasures of the text.

Calvin Hernton, who provided one of the earliest studies of Derricotte's work, places the poet in the context of the "formidable phalanx of the conscious-raising activities of the 1960s" (*Sexual Mountain* 119). He views Derricotte's works as "the poetry of liberation and testament" in a tradition critic Chanta Haywood terms "prophesying daughters." Hernton's poignant effective criticism calls for further consideration of Derricotte as a liberation theology poet.

BIBLIOGRAPHY

Works by Toi Derricotte

The Empress of the Death House. East Lansing, MI: Lotus Press, 1978.
Natural Birth. Trumansburg, NY: Crossing Press, 1983.
Captivity. Pittsburgh, PA: University of Pittsburgh Press, 1989.
Tender. Pittsburgh, PA: University of Pittsburgh Press, 1997.
The Black Notebooks: An Interior Journey. New York: Norton, 1997. (prose)

Studies of Toi Derricotte

Asim, Jabari. Review of *Tender*, by Toi Derricotte. *Washington Post*, 25 Jan. 1998, X09.
Boyd, M. J. "Out of the Poetry Ghetto—The Life Art Struggles of Small Black Publishing Houses." *The Black Scholar* 16.4 (1985): 12–24.
Caudell, Robin M. "Where Poets Explore Their Pain While Others Beware the Dog." *American Visions* 14.5 (1999): 30–32.
Davidson, Phebe. *Conversations with the World: American Women Poets and Their Work*. Pasadena, CA: Trilogy, 1998. 37–61.
Gilbert, Roger. "Dialogues of Self and Soul." *Michigan Quarterly Review* 39.1 (2000): 146–166.
Gilyard, Keith. "Kinship and Theory." *American Literary History* 11.1 (1999): 187–95.
Hernton, Calvin. *The Sexual Mountain and Black Women Writers: Adventures in Literature, and Real Life*. New York: Anchor, 1987. 119–55.
———. "The Tradition." *Parnassus* 12 (1985): 518–50.
Raz, Hilda. "Birth, Death, and *Captivity*." *Kenyon Review* 13.2 (1991): 175–79.
Richardson, James M., Jr. "Toi Derricotte." *The Oxford Companion to African American Literature*. New York: Oxford University Press, 1997.
Rowe, Monica Dyer. "Recent and Relevant Collections of Poetry." *American Visions* 13.1 (1998): 30–31.
Rowell, Charles H. "Beyond Our Lives: An Interview with Toi Derricotte." *Callaloo* 14.3 (1991): 654–64.

Schultz, Susan. "A Warning and an Appeal." *American Book Review* 13.2 (1991): 17.

Wade-Gayles. *My Soul Is a Witness: African-American Women's Spirituality*. New York: Beacon, 1996.

Weaver, Afaa Michael. "Cave Canem: A Few Thoughts on African-American Poetic Form—An E-mail Discussion." *Obsidian II* 13.1–2: (1998): 83–97.

Woodson, Jon. "Toi Derricotte." In *Contemporary Women Poets*, edited by Pamela L. Shelton. Detroit, MI: St. James Press, 1998. 86–87.

DEBORAH DIGGES (1950–)

Jacqueline A. K. McLean

BIOGRAPHY

Deborah Digges is a poet, memoirist, and teacher. Born on February 6, 1950, she is one of six daughters as well as the sixth of ten children born to Dutch immigrant parents. Everett D. and Geneva Sugarbaker raised Deborah and her siblings on an apple orchard in Jefferson City, Missouri. Despite her childhood's idyllic setting, Digges did not experience an escapist existence. The Sugarbakers exposed their large family to the realities of life and death very early on. Geneva, a former nurse, and Everett, an oncologist, allowed Deborah and her sisters to participate in his laboratory experiments. He also took them on his hospital rounds. One of Digges's most moving poems, "Laws of Falling Bodies," depicts a very young Deborah accompanying her father as he visits his female patients (*Vesper Sparrows* 9).

The family was a structured and deeply religious one, adhering closely to the teachings of the Southern Baptist Church. Adolescence brought out the rebel in Digges. During her teenage years, she railed against her traditional upbringing, eventually flunking out of the Christian college her parents insisted she attend. In 1969, at age nineteen, Deborah married Vietnam Air Force pilot Charles Digges with whom she had one son. They divorced in 1980, and Digges moved to California to complete her BA at the University of California, Riverside. Five years later, in 1985, Digges married Stanley Plumly, with whom she also had a son. They divorced in 1993.

Deborah Digges holds an MA from the University of Missouri and an MFA from the Iowa Writers Workshop. She has received grants for her writing from the Ingram Merrill Foundation, the John Simon Guggenheim Foundation, and the National Endowment for the Arts. Digges has taught in the graduate writing divisions of New York, Boston, and Columbia universities. Digges is currently associate professor of English at Tufts University and lives in Amherst, Massachusetts.

MAJOR WORKS AND THEMES

Vesper Sparrows (1996) won the Delmore Schwartz Memorial Poetry Prize from New York University. With her first book of poetry, published when Digges was thirty-six, she grounded herself as a promising poet and an heir to the Romantic tradition. Hers is a graceful and often melancholic lyric voice that remains free of sentimentality and easy resolution. Family narrative and intimate confession are hallmarks of Digges's writing; these are balanced by or set against historical allusion, textual reference, and connections to the natural world. With each book, Digges's technique has become progressively more syntactically and imagistically complex. She creates dense networks of allusion and a learned intellectual framework. Yet it is with her first book that Digges exhibited what became an abiding interest in linking the ordinary, mundane elements of our lives with the mythic and the extraordinary. In "Faith-falling," for example, the speaker mythologizes falls of all kinds, juxtaposing her son's gently imagined falls from a playground horse with her friend's somber "fall" through radiation treatments, as well as the expert falls of the Great Wallendas—circus tight-rope walkers—and lastly, the terrifying fear of falling during a hazardous plane flight in which the speaker takes strange comfort in the fact that "On earth you can say good-bye" (*Late in the Millennium* 44).

Throughout her work, Digges explores and opens up more formal possibilities for free verse. Most of her poems manifest uneven line length as she tends toward longer, loose lines. She may break up a poem into regular stanzas, but increasingly, she writes long, expansive, single stanzas. Digges is a poet of gravitas: measured, weighty cadences characterize her poetry. In his review of *Rough Music* (1995), David Baker notes that her poems, despite their free shape, traditionally "bear a distinctly formal inflection, a kind of rhetorical dignity" (200). The opening to "Laws of Falling Bodies" exemplifies Baker's point: "My father taught me how strong the body is" (*Vesper Sparrows* 9).

Both the syllabic and the sestina recur in Digges's work. Whereas *Vesper Sparrows* includes the traditional sestina "In Exile," with her adaptation of the form in "Rock, Scissors, Paper," included in *Rough Music*, she manifests the craft and confidence of the mature poet. "Rock, Scissors, Paper" is a sprung sestina modeled after the taxonomy scale of seven end-words and not six. Each stanza contains fourteen lines, and Digges uses the end-words in every other line. "Rock, Scissors, Paper" not only exemplifies her formal complexity as a poet but also attests to the intensified role of allusion in her work. At least half of the poem consists of quotes from a diverse array of sources including Charles Darwin, Karl Marx, and Sigmund and Anna Freud.

Though Digges's networks of allusion are complex, they are always readable. When it comes to place, Digges tends toward navigable places—landscapes to be managed on foot—and recurrent time in her poetry is that of childhood. In *Late in the Millennium* (1989), Digges looks back in detail at moments from this formative period, at points drawing upon the imagery of the natural world to describe her emotions; at other points, she looks to myth or to the marvels of ordinary existence. Often, Digges's poems gain in power precisely because the directions in which they head prove so unexpected. For example, "The Rockettes" recalls her mother's experience dancing with this legendary troupe to earn a little extra money after working a day job as a nurse. This same woman dances in the family's Missouri home with her six daughters.

In this poem, as in so many of Digges's poems, the present experience is significant because it carries with it the weight of the past.

Though all of Digges's books prominently place the presence of various family members, her father, whom she draws as darkly heroic but also as very human, emerges as the formative member. In "Apples" (*Rough Music*), he resurfaces as an old man on his hospital bed, patiently attentive to his daughter's gesture—she has brought him apples and lays them in his hands, an homage to his love of the orchards that were a part of Deborah's childhood, orchards that attested to the continuance of life in the face of death.

Childhood is a recurrent trope in Digges's poetry, but her return to the past is rarely sentimental. Rather, in these flights across time, Digges often explores what is most painful—most raw in herself and in all of us—without flinching from difficult truths: a man's faithlessness but also her own ("Brooms," *Rough Music*); the realization that one might live a whole lifetime without realizing the worst about oneself ("Gypsy Moths," *Rough Music*). "For the Daughters of Hannah Bible Class of Tipton, Missouri's Women's Prison: Mother's Day, 1959," the opening poem to *Vesper Sparrows*, recounts Digges's childhood visit to a woman's prison on Mother's Day 1959 where she pictures the female inmates as they once must have been—carefree and young.

In short, Deborah Digges is a poet of great range. The voices of the poems consistently belong to her, yet she exists in many guises and in many ages. The lyric speaker is multifaceted and ranges confidently through time. The speaker is alternately—and sometimes simultaneously—a child, a lover, a mother, a citizen of the modern and often difficult world. Digges's two sons resonate throughout the poetry. Although the poems recognize the sons' importance as individuals, the poems inevitably imagine them in relation to their mother's story or in connection with a larger human story ("Ancestral Lights," *Vesper Sparrows*). We see them newly born, as small children, and later as difficult adolescents. Ultimately, Digges compels her reader to imagine a time when these boys will grow away from the speaker. One somber note that courses through the poetry is the fear that her sons will forget her, or that they will remember her in ways she would prefer they did not ("For the Lost Adolescent," *Rough Music*). At points, she frames herself with the conscious hope that her sons will remember her in a particular way ("Stealing Lilacs in the Cemetery," *Vesper Sparrows*). In such poems as the whimsical "We're Making Stars" (*Vesper Sparrows*) and "The Little Book of Hand Shadows" (*Rough Music*), we see the playfulness and joy that comes with motherhood. So, too, Digges is honest about—though opaque in her muted presentation of—the difficulties involved in raising sons on her own or with the help of the more transient father figures who pass in and out of all their lives.

In places Digges's own woundedness becomes unflinchingly evident. If relationships are an ongoing trope in her work, the most difficult of these is that between man and woman. Yet the hunger for love—the promise it holds out to the self—does not diminish. In *Vesper Sparrows*, Digges makes a brave beginning as she explores love's failure in spite of all that was shared. Lyricising memories of her air force pilot ex-husband flying home at three A.M. smelling of other lands, she is able to retain the beauty of these remembered moments despite the difficult present of shuttling a child back and forth after the divorce ("The Alphabet of the Air").

By the time Digges writes about love in *Rough Music*, the reader feels he or she is being allowed to enter a very raw emotional space in which the speaker—despite her ability to philosophize—is hurting. Baker identifies a broken relationship as "the central, suppressed narrative" of the book and finds "loss inscribed onto every gesture and detail" (201). Such an appraisal may sound harsh, and yet the embodiment of such dark and lonely feeling emerges as neither bitter nor self-pitying. Instead, the poems strive toward understanding of self and others, and they move toward strength. Mark Doty praised *Rough Music* as "a fierce, headlong book, so exhilarating that even its darkest notes shine with a strange joy" (*Rough Music*, promotional copy). The speaker has not had an easy time of it, yet this speaker is recognizably that of Digges's previous books, a woman who can find grace in simple things and is able to cherish and remember love in spite of its inevitable loss or leave-taking.

Rough Music embodies Digges's maturity as a poet able to sustain manifold contradictions. Here, she depicts pain without self-pity or blame, and here, she maps out the geography for joy in simple, concrete acts, such as sweeping. "Broom," one poem among many, captures the ebullience of a particular moment and captures, too, the intricate, wondrous natural world as it seeps into the nooks and crannies of the human. All the while, Digges's poetry remains peculiarly aware—and makes the reader peculiarly aware—of the odd things we make and cherish, whether clothespin dolls, brooms, English china, children, or love.

CRITICAL RECEPTION

Currently, the scholarship on Deborah Digges's work consists almost exclusively of book reviews. The conversation concentrates in three areas: Digges's development as a poet whose work continues to show promise and innovation; the growing precision and simultaneous complexity of a difficult, learned style; and the range of her strongly and clearly autobiographical subject matter. It, therefore, comes as no surprise that her memoir, *Fugitive Spring* (1992), was also favorably reviewed and received. *Publishers Weekly* calls it an "evocative . . . memoir . . . filled with childlike wonder at life's simple pleasures" (59).

Speaking in greater detail of Digges's development as a poet, reviewers uniformly agree upon Digges's considerable growth since her fine first book *Vesper Sparrows* appeared in 1986. Despite the feeling of belatedness that pervades the time of this book, with its attention to her own childhood and to nature, *Late in the Millennium* is recognized as the most hopeful of Digges's three collections. *Rough Music* is clearly identified as her darkest work but also the most stunning for the complexity of syntax and the depth and maturity of ideas.

*Kenyon Review*er David Baker concisely summarizes Digges's evolution: "While she did not always project the personal or familiar impulses of [*Vesper Sparrows*] into wider spheres of connective consequence, she was already gifted with a moving Romantic melancholy. . . . Her 1989 volume, *Late in the Millennium*, demonstrated a poet for whom family narrative and intimate disclosure had become forcefully balanced by historical or social attachments" (200).

With the publication of *Rough Music*, Baker names Digges "a powerful, fully realized writer" who writes of the lonely, dark, and mournful aspects of her life with great power and intensity (200–01). Mark Doty believes that in *Rough Music*, Digges writes "a poetry we've never heard before" (*Rough Music*, promotional copy). In part, Digges's power comes from her ability to link together disparate emotions and ideas.

Though Digges has manifested this ability in her early works, in *Rough Music*, she is at her finest. Again, in his review of *Rough Music*, Baker writes, "Digges's new book is exacting and forceful; its demands on itself are severe and yet its rewards are the large kind won from the ordeals of difficult fate" (202).

Though reviewers of Digges's work consistently attend to the darkening of voice and tone—a darkening that is at times almost bitter—between the first book and the third, not one sees disillusionment. Rather, Digges is praised for her severity; for her learned patterns of allusion; and for the raw directness of her lyric voice.

BIBLIOGRAPHY

Works by Deborah Digges

Late in the Millennium. New York: Knopf, 1989.
Fugitive Spring: Coming of Age in the '50s and '60s. New York: Knopf, 1992. (memoir).
Rough Music. New York: Knopf, 1995.
Vesper Sparrows. Pittsburgh, PA: Carnegie Mellon University Press, 1996.
Stardust Lounge. New York: Doubleday, 2001. (memoir).

Studies of Deborah Digges

Baker, David. Review of *Rough Music*, by Deborah Digges. *Kenyon Review* (1996): 200–202.
Green, John. "*The Stardust Lounge*: Stories from a Boy's Adolescence." *Booklist*, 15 May 2001, 1726.
Review of *Fugitive Spring*, by Deborah Digges. *Los Angeles Times Book Review*, 25 July 1993, 12.
Review of *Fugitive Spring*, by Deborah Digges. *Chicago Tribune*, 29 Aug. 1993, 2863.
Review of *Fugitive Spring*, by Deborah Digges. *Publishers Weekly*, 15 Nov. 1991, 59.
Review of *Late in the Millennium*, by Deborah Digges. *Publishers Weekly*, 12 Oct. 1989, 48.
Review of *Rough Music*, by Deborah Digges. *Publishers Weekly*, 31 July 1995, 74–75.
Review of *Rough Music*, by Deborah Digges. *Yale Review* (April 1996): 160–83.
Whitehouse, Anna. Review of *Fugitive Spring*, by Deborah Digges. *New York Times*, 23 Feb. 1992, 20.

DIANE DI PRIMA (1934–)

Timothy Gray

BIOGRAPHY

Born to Italian American parents at "the lower end of the middle class" (Waldman 45) in 1934, Diane di Prima rose from the streets of Brooklyn to become one of the most prolific writers of the Beat Generation. Taking courage from John Keats, another literary aspirant from the underclass whose letters she had been perusing at the Brooklyn Public Library, she decided at age fourteen to become a poet, frustrating her parents and their dreams of cultural assimilation. That same year, she entered Hunter High School, where poets Audre Lorde and Joyce Johnson (née Glassman) were classmates. Upon graduation, she entered Swarthmore College to major in physics. In the middle of her sophomore year, she dropped out of college and dropped in on a burgeoning bohemian scene in lower Manhattan.

While living in a series of apartments (or "pads") on the Lower East Side and other bohemian neighborhoods, di Prima cultivated friendships with key figures in the literary and artistic worlds, including Allen Ginsberg, LeRoi Jones, and Lawrence Ferlinghetti, the latter of whom wrote the introduction to her first collection of verse, *This Kind of Bird Flies Backward* (1958). In addition to writing poetry, di Prima managed avant-garde stage productions at the Living Theatre and the Poets Theatre, and co-edited one of the most influential newsletters of the day, *The Floating Bear*. With her first husband, Alan Marlowe, she established the Poets Press, which published the first volumes of poetry by Lorde, David Henderson, and other emerging figures on the New York scene.

Di Prima moved around quite a bit throughout the 1960s. She made several trips to the West Coast and eventually left her native city, living for a time in three upstate locations, including Timothy Leary's commune in Millbrook, New York. In 1967 she crossed the country in a Volkswagen bus on a reading tour. Parting ways with Marlowe the following year, she moved to San Francisco, where she took part in the "free city" movement and wrote the politically charged *Revolutionary Letters* (1971), a volume she dedicated to Bob Dylan. By the end of the 1960s, this mother of five children (by four different men) had become a leading voice of the hippie movement.

In the 1970s, di Prima was chosen to participate in the Poet-in-the-Schools program sponsored by the National Endowment for the Arts. During her seven-year tenure, she ranged far and wide throughout the interior west, from Indian reservations in Arizona to reform schools in Minnesota, bringing literature to those with little access to books and teaching a population others had claimed could not be taught. In the 1980s, she continued to immerse herself in nontraditional education, founding a program in poetics at New College of California and leading classes at the San Francisco Institute of Magical and Healing Arts. Fiercely independent, she eventually broke ranks with these institutions and now teaches privately.

During the 1990s di Prima oversaw the publication of two major works: *Pieces of a Song: Selected Poems* (1990), and *Loba* (1998), a book-length poem she has published in stages since the early 1970s. A devoted student of Buddhism, she lives with her long-time partner, Sheppard Powell, in San Francisco.

MAJOR WORKS AND THEMES

Di Prima's special brand of streetwise moxie is on full display in her early work. In "More or Less Love Poems," she combines the compact wisdom of Buddhist aphorism with the kind of backhanded compliments traded back and forth in barroom conversation. "In case you put me down I put you down" (*Pieces of a Song* 9), runs a typical refrain. "The Passionate Hipster to His Chick," an update of a Christopher Marlowe poem, playfully evokes a scenario of shepherds and nymphs cavorting in an urban pastoral. But di Prima's artfulness never fully concealed the frustration she felt as a woman writer in a male-dominated milieu. In "Short Note on the Sparseness of Language," she calibrates the effectiveness of Beat lingo while taking stock of her precarious living situation. "Wow" means one thing to a woman after an erotic night of rolling around on the "mattressrags" in an unkempt pad, but the word has quite a different flavor on the day she is "put down" by her lover. "Wow man oh wow," she utters dejectedly, picking up her comb and two books and "cutting" the scene (*Dinners and Nightmares* 108).

Because she refrains from romanticism and caricature, di Prima provides an unusually vivid depiction of Beat and hippie life. Her poems about childbirth and abortion ("Song for Baby-O, Unborn," "Brass Furnace Going Out," "Moon Mattress," "Four Takes in a Pregnant Spring," "I Get My Period, September 1964") are particularly hard hitting, as are the poems that rebuke inconstant hippie men ("November," "Zero," "Chronology," "Seattle Song"). Like many women writers of her era, di Prima did double duty as a domestic caretaker. In one coldwater flat after another, it was she who cooked the meals, paid the rent, and took care of the kids. She also participated in legendary sexual orgies, the most famous of which involved Ginsberg and Jack Kerouac. As the prose pieces in *Dinners and Nightmares* (1961) and *Memoirs of a Beatnik* (1969) illustrate, she was a guiding force in an atmosphere otherwise given over to languor, selfishness, and despair. That she still had the energy to sustain a writing life speaks not only to her ambition but also to her resourcefulness.

In 1965 di Prima and Marlowe were forced out of their Lower East Side apartment. After some deliberation, they decided to move their growing family and their printing press upstate. In "First Snow, Kerhonkson," the poet comes to realize that the life she knew in New York bohemia has disappeared for good, with the recent deaths of close friends Freddie Herko and Frank O'Hara and the general dispersal of those who got married and moved away from the downtown scene. The best that she can do is to make peace with the white silence of her new surroundings. Other poems from this time chronicle her earnest and initially clumsy attempts to commune with rural America. In the aptly titled "Biology Lesson," the city slicker takes measure of the abundant life that thrives in "noisy" upstate nights and exclaims, "They were dead wrong about no spontaneous generation" (*Kerhonkson Journal*). At other times, di Prima seems to have had some fun with her experiment. She even posed with Marlowe and two of her children in a bonnet and old peasant dress for a daguerreotype-style photograph (reproduced as the frontispiece to *Kerhonkson Journal, 1966* [1971]), offering up a slightly campy version of the American homesteading experience. But no amount of posturing could deflect the very real change she was undergoing. "Oh it is very like being a pioneer," she admits in "Spring Song for the Equinox," "but it is also slightly boring" (*Selected Poems* 152). As she muses in "The Bus Ride," she felt as though she was now living on the edge of the world.

It was the cross-country reading tour in 1967, more than anything else, that helped di Prima transform herself from a street-tough Beat poet to natural hippie poet. Traveling with her husband, two of her three children, two puppies, and an ex-Marine named "Zen," she zigzagged across the country, reading at a discotheque in Buffalo, an all-black art gallery in Pittsburgh, a concert hall in Chicago (where she performed *The Calculus of Variation* [1972] with the avant-garde jazz musicians of the Art Ensemble of Chicago), and at scores of other venues in out-of-the-way places. The extended family camped and cooked out of their Volkswagen bus, getting in touch with the land and its people, and riding a "wave of excitement" that crested as they moved westward. Di Prima remembers that tie-dye shirts and experimental forms of rock music marked their entry into a new cultural frontier on the eve of the Summer of Love. On the West Coast, she met dropped-out professors and stayed with Janis Joplin on the eve of her debut at the Monterey Pop Festival. Unfortunately, some old problems followed the poet on her long, strange trip. In the curiously titled "Poem in Praise of My Husband (Taos,)" she chastises Marlowe for constantly interrupting her scheduled writing periods to discuss mundane matters like insurance policies and broken carburetors (*Selected Poems: 1956–75*). Apparently, she was still the first person called upon whenever a domestic situation looked like it might unravel.

These frustrations notwithstanding, di Prima pressed on, taking care of her children and countless others, in the years to come. She gave traditional domesticity the heave-ho in "Poem of Refusals" and "These Days," but she also trumpeted the simple joys of motherhood (*Pieces of a Song: Selected Poems*). She matured in other ways, as well. For instance, the strident tone of her political poetry was mitigated by the Buddhist teachings she was receiving at the San Francisco and Tassajara Zen centers. In "Tassajara" (*Pieces of a Song*) di Prima speaks of the pulverizing power of the American west, a land in which even Buddha is lost. Bodhidharma, a monk who began the eastward transmission of Buddhism from India centuries ago, might indeed face a formidable challenge in a land where tricksters like Coyote lie in wait, but in the end, the poet implies that wily survival skills and saintly compassion need not be regarded as mutually exclusive traits.

Di Prima's own capacity for compassion was enhanced during her stint as Poet-in-the-Schools. Making her way through the interior west, she was profoundly affected by the people she met—kids in reform schools, Indians on reservations, and rednecks in bars—the kind of people that Beats such as Kerouac and Neal Cassady tended to rush by in their frenetic coast-to-coast travels. As it happened, di Prima discovered that the basic education she was paid to provide was returned to her in full. She held on to her street-tough moxie, to be sure, but she also learned about a different brand of toughness required of those who make their way in a harsh land. The result was a hip variety of Americana, for in di Prima's most powerful poems ("Brief Wyoming Meditation," "Sixth Notebook Incantation," "Wyoming Series") and prose statements (the Waldman interview, "Light / And Keats"), the hardscrabble intensity of poor westerners and the beatific vision of hipsters come to a powerful point of confluence.

Loba, begun in 1971, is di Prima's most ambitious work. This long poem about a female wolf takes the landscape of the west as its starting point, but it proceeds to cobble together goddess traditions from around the world in an effort to portray the "feralness of the core of woman" ("Tapestry" 22). The best sections are infused with the scrappy spirit of di Prima's early work. One section calls forth all the "lost moon sisters" wandering from Avenue A in New York to Fillmore Street in San Francisco for a show of solidarity (*Loba* 3). Another section places the Loba in a redneck bar, where she dances and cavorts easily with rough-hewn customers. The ring of fur around her ankles is the only thing that betrays the Loba's identity, and in the end, we are left wondering whether di Prima has become the wolf, or the wolf has become the poet. The middle sections of *Loba*, many of them plagued with esoteric jottings influenced by the alchemical traditions di Prima studied during the late 1970s and early 1980s, are not nearly as winning. Far better are the later sections discussing the tribulations of old age. No myths remain for this older, ample woman, di Prima writes dispiritingly at one juncture, though her readers know better than to believe her.

Full of unbridled spirit and compassion, di Prima has ranged far from her Brooklyn roots in a quest for a more meaningful life. Her poetry is a roadmap of that journey and of her efforts to make postwar America a more inclusive and equitable society.

CRITICAL RECEPTION

Hailed in recent Beat anthologies as the archetype of the female Beat, di Prima is renowned for her lifestyle as much as for her work. With her long hair and black clothing, she certainly cut a striking figure in the New York underground. Unfortunately, too many critics tend to linger on this image, disregarding the significant contributions she has made as a poet and as a spokesperson for women of the counterculture.

In the past twenty years, only George Butterick and Blossom Kirschenbaum have published sustained critical analyses of di Prima's work. Butterick's biographical essay serves primarily to orient the general reader. While he sometimes falls prey to caricaturizing tendencies, Butterick offers cogent commentary on the sadness that crept into di Prima's work in the early 1960s, when her frustration with irresponsible men began to take its toll. Kirschenbaum takes a somewhat different tack, maintaining that, despite her nonconformist ways, di Prima stayed true to her Italian heritage by generously accommodating members of an extended family under one roof. Though her "poems flaunt defiance of family," Kirschenbaum argues, they "enlarg[e] the circle of quasi-family" until it becomes "the Human Family" (57, 66). Brief examinations by Brenda Knight, Michael Davidson, and Maria Damon have sought primarily to align her work with the nascent feminist movement of the 1960s.

Di Prima's later life and work have yet to receive their due from critics (except perhaps from Carol Tonkinson, who tracks her encounter with Buddhism). My own recently completed essay concentrates on the poet's travels in the American west, beginning in 1965, when she left New York to live in various rural locations and in San Francisco (Gray, "A Place Where Your Nature Meets Mine"). In time, I hope that others will agree that di Prima belongs in the company of Terry Tempest Williams, Gretel Ehrlich, and other women writers who have enhanced our understanding of the cultural geography west of the Rockies.

BIBLIOGRAPHY

Works by Diane di Prima

This Kind of Bird Flies Backward. New York: Totem Press, 1958.

Dinners and Nightmares. New York: Corinth Books 1961. San Francisco: Last Gasp, 1998.

The New Handbook of Heaven. San Francisco: Auerhahn Press, 1963.

Earthsong: Poems 1957–1959. New York: Poets Press 1968.

Hotel Albert: Poems. New York: Poets Press, 1968.

Memoirs of a Beatnik. New York: Traveller's Companion, 1969. San Francisco: Last Gasp, 1988.

Kerhonkson Journal, 1966. Berkeley, CA: Oyez, 1971.

Revolutionary Letters. San Francisco: City Lights, 1971.

The Calculus of Variation. San Francisco: Privately printed, 1972.

Freddie Poems. Point Reyes, CA: Eidolon Editions, 1974.

Selected Poems 1956–1975. Plainfield, VT: North Atlantic, 1975.

"Light / And Keats." In *Talking Poetics from Naropa Institute: Annals of the Jack Kerouac School of Disembodied Poetics,* edited by Anne Waldman. Boulder, CO: Shambhala, 1978. (lecture)

Loba: Parts I-VIII. Berkeley, CA: Wingbow, 1978.

Pieces of a Song: Selected Poems. San Francisco: City Lights, 1990.

"Diane di Prima." In *Beneath a Single Moon: Buddhism in Contemporary American Poetry*, edited by Kent Johnson and Craig Paulenich. Boston: Shambhala, 1991. 56–61. (autobiographical statement and five poems)

Seminary Poems. Point Reyes, CA: Floating Island, 1991.

Loba. New York: Penguin 1998.

Recollections of My Life as a Woman: The New York Years. New York: Viking, 2001. (autobiography)

Studies of Diane di Prima

Butterick, George F. "Diane di Prima." In *The Beats: Literary Bohemians in Postwar America*, edited by Ann Charters. *Dictionary of Literary Biography*. Vol. 16. Detroit, MI: Gale Research, 1983. 149–60.

Damon, Maria. "Victors of Catastrophe: Beat Occlusions." In *Beat Culture and the New America, 1950–1965*, edited by Lisa Phillips. New York: Whitney Museum of American Art, 1985. 141–49.

Davidson, Michael. "Appropriations: Women and the San Francisco Renaissance." In *The San*

Francisco Renaissance: Poetics and Community at Mid-century. New York: Cambridge University Press, 1989. 172–99.

Gray, Timothy. " 'A Place Where Your Nature Meets Mine': Diane di Prima in the West." (unpublished essay)

Kirschenbaum, Blossom S. "Diane di Prima: Extending La Famiglia." *MELUS* 14.3–4 (1987): 53–67.

Knight, Brenda. "Diane di Prima: Poet Priestess." In *Women of the Beat Generation: The Writers, Artists and Muses at the Heart of a Revolution*. Berkeley, CA: Conari Press, 1996. 123–40.

Tonkinson, Carol, ed. "Diane di Prima." In *Big Sky Mind: Buddhism and the Beat Generation*. New York: Riverhead, 1995. 139–60.

Waldman, Anne. "Interview with Diane di Prima." *Rocky Ledge* 7 (1981): 35–49.

RITA DOVE (1952–)

Jana Evans Braziel

BIOGRAPHY

Born in 1952 in Akron, Ohio, to Ray A. Dove and Elvira Elizabeth Hord, parents who exposed their daughter to music and literature, Rita Dove distinguished herself early as a voracious reader, precocious child, and promising writer. Exposure to literature in childhood allowed Dove's mind to grow and her imagination to thrive. In 1970 Dove graduated from high school (in the top one hundred seniors nationally) and visited the White House as a President Scholar. Enrolled at Miami University, Ohio, as a National Achievement Scholar, Dove graduated *summa cum laude*, *Phi Beta Kappa*, and *Phi Kappa Phi* with a BA in English in 1973. In 1974 she studied at the Universität Tübingen, Germany, as a Fulbright Scholar; from 1975 to 1977, Dove studied creative writing at the University of Iowa, where she graduated with an MFA in 1977. While in Iowa, Dove met Fred Viebahn, a German Fulbright Fellow in the International Writing Program, whom she married in 1979.

Early in her career, Dove won accolades for her poetry. She was awarded a National Endowment for the Arts (NEA) Fellowship in 1978 and two years later published *The Yellow House on the Corner* (1980). Dove taught creative writing at Arizona State University from 1981 to 1989. She is currently Commonwealth Professor of English at the University of Virginia, where she has taught since 1989.

In 1982 Dove was awarded the Portia Pittman Fellowship from the National Endowment for the Humanities as writer-in-residence at Tuskegee Institute, and she published the chapbook *Mandolin*. In 1983 Dove gave birth to her daughter Aviva Dove-Viebahn and, in the same year, published *Museum*. Lauded as a new poet, Dove won a Guggenheim Foundation Fellowship (1983–84). In 1985 Dove chaired the NEA Poetry Panel and published *Fifth Sunday* (short stories).

In 1986 Dove established herself critically with the publication of *Thomas and Beulah* (winner of the 1987 Pulitzer Prize), a volume tracing the Great Migration North through her grandparents' lives. Dove's *The Other Side of the House* (limited edition) was published in 1988, and the following year, Dove received a second NEA Fellowship. Dove published *Grace Notes* in 1989 and the novel *Through the Ivory Gate* in 1992. Dove continued to distinguish herself as a poet and, in 1993, was honored as poet laureate of the United States, serving as poet laureate and poetry consultant to the Library of Congress from 1993 to 1995. During her laureate tenure, Dove published *The Darker Face of the Earth* (1994, a modern Oedipus drama set in antebellum South Carolina) and *Mother Love* (1995). Both fuse classical mythology with American sensibility. Dove's laureate lectures were published as *The Poet's World* in 1995. Dove served as chair for the Poetry Jury for the 1997 Pulitzer Prize.

Setting poetry to music, Dove wrote the song cycle *Seven for Luck* (John Williams wrote the score) in 1998—performed at Tanglewood by Cynthia Haymon (soprano) and the Boston Symphony Orchestra. In 1999 Dove published *On the Bus with Rosa Parks* (nominated for the 2000 National Book Critics Circle Award). From 1999 to 2000, Dove served again as consultant in poetry to the Library of Congress.

MAJOR WORKS AND THEMES

Dove's poetry is universal, yet particular in its images, voices, and themes. As Dove notes, "We've come to believe that being 'universal' is to transcend difference—again, the incredible trauma of difference in modern society has made us yearn for conformity. Why can't we find the universal in those differences?" (Steffen 176–77). Myriad themes circulate in Dove's poetic universe: history, myth, music, art, literature, reading, autobiography, and African American experience.

Dove is immensely concerned with history and has, as the lyrical persona in "Maple Valley Branch Library, 1967" states, "studied history for its rhapsody of dates" (*On the Bus* 33). Indeed history and memory are central to Dove's œuvre; other poetic themes cannot be disentangled from these preoccupations. Historical figures in Dove's poems include Liu Sheng; Prince Ching of Chung Shan (western Han Dynasty), who died in 113 BCE; and his wife Tou Wan ("Tou Wan Speaks to Her Husband, Liu Sheng" *Museum*); Dominican dictator Rafael Trujillo, who ordered the massacre of over 20,000 Haitian cane laborers in 1937 ("Parsley" *Museum*); important African American heroes such as the abolitionist "David Walker (1785–1830)" (*Yellow House*); the intellectual Benjamin Banneker ("Banneker"), the first black American to create an almanac; the civil rights heroine Rosa Parks (*On the Bus*); and the lesser known Claudette Colvin ("Claudette Colvin Goes to Work" *On the Bus*), who, like Parks, refused to give up her seat on a segregated, southern bus.

Other historical figures in Dove's poetry include writers and, frequently, literary characters, such as Don L. Lee, a "black arts" movement writer ("Upon Meeting Don L. Lee, In a Dream" *Yellow House*); medieval Italian poet Boccaccio (in "Boccaccio: The Plague Years" *Museum*) and his idealized lover Fiammetta (in "Fiammetta Breaks Her Peace" *Museum*); and the German poet Hölderlin ("Reading Hölderlin on the Patio with the Aid of a Dictionary" *Museum*). Dove's poetry also includes religious figures such as "Catherine of Alexandria" (*Museum*) and "Catherine of Sienna" (*Museum*); St. Paul ("On the Road to Damascus" *Grace Notes*); and St. Veronica ("On Veronica" *On the Bus*), who mopped Christ's brow. Mythological figures—Nestor, the old Aegean soldier in Homer's *Iliad* and *Odyssey* ("Nestor's Bathtub" *Yellow House*), and the Gorgon "Medusa" (*Grace Notes*)—also populate her poems. (Creative fusions of Greek myth and American experience are also seen in Dove's play *The Darker Face of the Earth* and *Mother Love*.)

Dove's historical figures include archaeological relics ("The Venus of Willendorf" *On the Bus*), as well as artists and musicians: the German artist Christian Schad (1894–1982), whose painting "Agosta the Winged Man and Rasha the Black Dove" becomes the title of Dove's poem (*Museum*); the American artist Ivan Albright, whose painting "Into the World There Came a Foul Called Ida" is imagined in "There Came a Soul" (*On the Bus*); and the musicians Robert Schumann ("Robert Schumann, Or: Musical Genius Begins with Affliction" *Yellow House*) and Billie Holiday in "Canary" (*Grace Notes*).

Dove is also concerned with history's "underside," lives eclipsed by time and unknown to posterity. She writes "poor man's history" ("The Gorge" *Grace Notes* 63). Speaking to Stan Rubin and Judith Kitchen, Dove says her imagination plumbs "the underside of the story, not to tell the big historical events, but in fact to talk about things which no one will remember" (156). She is "interested in the thoughts, the things which were concerning these small people, these nobodies in the course of history" (161).

The "underside" is prominent in poems about African American and autobiographical experience. Dove's poems capture unsung heroes of African American experience. Poems in *Yellow House* (third section) speak to the hardships and hopes of lives under slavery. "Belinda's Petition" evokes the language of the Declaration of Independence in its appeal for abolition. "The House Slave" recounts the lament of one who witnesses the plight of field slaves. In "Pamela," Dove portrays a woman fleeing slavery to find freedom in the North. An anonymous slave considers flight in "The Slave's Critique of Practical Reason," but rejects it as impossible, and escapes only into daydreams, thoughts, and imagination. In "Kentucky, 1833" (a poetic monologue set in the year the British abolished slavery in the West Indies), a slave laments words he cannot read that "would change our lives" (*Yellow House* 45).

Dove historicizes the Great Migration through her maternal grandparents' lives in *Thomas and Beulah*. In these poems—told from the dual perspectives of first Thomas and then Beulah—history and autobiography are intimately interwoven. Dove explains that history must be understood "through the family around the table" (Moyers 124). She further notes "how grand historical events can be happening around us but we remember them only in relation to what was happening to us as individuals at that particular moment" (124). Poems such as "The Event," "The Zeppelin Factory," and "Wingfoot Lake (Independence Day, 1964)," create a poetic matrix in which the personal histories of Thomas and Beulah intersect with U.S. political history. In poems such as "Saints" (*Grace Notes*), Dove returns to religion, but the saints she canonizes are everyday women shelling blackeyed peas, growing fat, and going to church.

Dove addresses the civil rights movement through the personal and public life of Rosa Parks in *On the Bus*. She traces Parks's persona from unknown domestic worker in the segregated South ("Sit Back, Relax") to courageous activist ("Rosa") and later as national hero ("In the Lobby of the Warner Theatre, Washington, D.C.," a poem about Parks's attendance at *Amistad*'s premiere). In poems such as "The Situation is Intolerable" and "The Enactment," Dove explores racism and political mobilization, respectively. Poems such as "Climbing In" and "QE2 Transatlantic Crossing. Third Day" situate Dove within this history—first as child and later as woman and accomplished poet.

Another important theme in Dove's poetic *œuvre* is autobiography. "Adolescence-I," "Adolescence-II," and "Adolescence-III" (*Yellow House*) capture metamorphosis from child to adult; "The Boast" and "First Kiss" explore early experiences with intimacy and erotic feelings. "The Fifth Grade Autobiography" (*Grace Notes*) reveals a moment in Dove's childhood fishing with her grandparents and older brother. In the poem, she intimately remembers her late grandfather who "smelled of lemons" (8). In "Buckeye" Dove remembers kicking and lobbing buckeyes as weapons in childhood battles.

Poems in "My Father's Telescope" (*Museum*, third section) also explore the terrains of childhood and family. "Grape Sherbet" explores a Memorial Day barbecue—her father grilling, children playing, and later, eating sherbet. "Roses" shows the father teaching his daughter how to capture and kill Japanese beetles. In "Centipede," the father takes the girl, after a storm, down into the basement where the fuse box is located and surprises her by showing her a centipede. "My Father's Telescope" shows the father futilely constructing a wood telescope, failing, and vowing to buy one next Christmas. In "Anti-Father," Dove disputes the things her father has taught her. The section concludes with "A Father Out Walking on the Lawn." Dove's father appears again in "Flash Cards" (*Grace Notes*): After reading *The Life of Lincoln*, he quizzes his daughter over mathematics. Dove portrays her mother in "My Mother Enters the Work Force" (*On the Bus*).

Thomas and Beulah records Dove's maternal grandparents' lives as they migrate from the South (Tennessee for Thomas; Georgia for Beulah) northward to Akron, Ohio. The first section, "Mandolin," is shown through Thomas's eyes. Dove's grandparents reappear in "Sunday Night at Grandfather's" (*Museum*), "Summit Beach, 1921" (*Grace Notes*), and "The Fifth Grade Autobiography" (*Grace Notes*).

If *Thomas and Beulah* fuses history and autobiography, Dove's *Mother Love* interweaves mythology and autobiography. In *Mother Love*, Dove adapts the myth of Demeter, Persephone, and Hades (most notably in "Persephone, Falling," "The Narcissus Flower," "Persephone Abducted," "Demeter Mourning," "Persephone in Hell," and "Demeter Waiting") to probe the mother-daughter bond. Though not directly autobiographical, the sentiments and intimate expressions are. The mother-daughter relationship is further explored in "After Reading *Mickey in the Night Kitchen* for the Third Time before Bed." In the poem, the daughter playfully and innocently explores her body, demanding to compare with her mother. "Genetic Expedition" also explores bodily intimacy—through difference, not similarity—between mother and daughter.

CRITICAL RECEPTION

Despite Dove's stature and critical acclaim, her work has received relatively little critical attention. Dove's poetry volumes have been widely reviewed, and many interviews with Dove about her work have been published; however, only a score or more articles addressing her poetry have been published in academic journals. Helen Vendler, one of Dove's earliest and most sustained critics, has published substantial analyses of Dove's poetry in her two monographs *The Given and the Made* and *Soul Says*, as well as in articles and reviews. To date, only one book-length study of Dove's work has been undertaken: Therese Steffen's *Crossing Color: Transcultural Space and Place in Rita Dove's Poetry, Fiction, and Drama*. Dominant themes in the scholarship include Dove's use of the lyrical voice and her aesthetic innovation; race, language, and African American experience; memory and historical revision; and transcultural poetics. Minor themes include Dove's reassembling of myth and literature and the role of gender in her poetry.

Vendler, a critic of lyric poetry, places Dove within the lyrical tradition in which experience is abstracted. Vendler's approach—though not eschewing a thematic discussion—is primarily formalist. Vendler argues that Dove "looks for a hard, angular surface to her poem" and that she is "disjunctive" rather than "meditative" ("The Black Dove" 146). Vendler also discusses the important themes of "family history, love, politics, and motherhood," but these themes, she insists, are geometrically stylized ("The Black Dove" 157). In several articles, Vendler explores Dove's treatment of blackness and her poetic reach "beyond blackness." Vendler examines the particularities of Dove's identity as expressed lyrically, yet she also explores Dove's universalism.

Thematically, other critics share Vendler's focus on African American experience. Houston Baker examines how race informs—but also how race is "poetically transformed" through—Dove's poetry. Race, gender, and class are interrogated in Ekaterini Georgoudaki's study of African American women poets (Rita Dove, Maya Angelou, Gwendolyn Brooks, Nikki Giovanni, and Audre Lorde). Patricia Wallace explores the representation of minority cultures by Dove, Lorna Dee Cervantes, and Cathy Song. Kirkland Jones discusses the role of vernacular speech in the poetry of Dove and Yusef Komunyakaa. Ekaterini Georgoudaki and Kevin Stein analyze Dove's focus on history's "underside."

Several critics (Georgoudaki, Rampersad, Stein, Steffen, and Vendler) explore Dove's "cross-cultural poetics" that speaks to African American experience but also transcends the particularities of personal identity, moving toward the global or universal. Stein examines Dove's historical diversity and the myriad voices woven into her poems. Arnold Rampersad focuses on Dove's humanist vision and her poetic innovation in exploring difference.

For Steffen, Dove writes literature that crosses cultures, races, languages, geography, nationalities, and genres. Steffen argues that Dove's poetry (with its multiple references to the Italian Renaissance, Germanic Romanticism, ancient Greece, ancient China, and modern America, to name only a few of the sites her poetry tours) is global, cross-cultural, universal. In *Crossing Color*, Steffen analyzes Dove's poetry through its "transcultural spaces," and thus, follows the lead of Dove in *The Poet's World*.

In more narrowly focused analyses, Robert McDowell explores Dove's mythic synthesis; Peter Erickson addresses Dove's Shakespeare poems and Emily Cook and Maria Proitsaki explore gender in *Thomas and Beulah* and *Mother Love*, respectively. Alison Booth, Stephen Cushman, and Lotta Lofgren (a discussion edited by Mark Edmundson) have also written about *Mother Love*.

BIBLIOGRAPHY

Works by Rita Dove

Ten Poems. Lisbon, IA: Penumbra Press, 1977.
Oedipus Rex: A Black Tragedy. Washington, D.C.: Library of Congress, 1980.
The Only Dark Spot in the Sky. Tempe, AZ: Porch Publications, 1980.

The Yellow House on the Corner. Pittsburgh, PA: Carnegie-Mellon University Press, 1980.
Mandolin. Athens: Ohio Review Poetry Series, 1982.
Museum. Pittsburgh, PA: Carnegie-Mellon University Press, 1983.
Fifth Sunday. Charlottesville: University Press of Virginia, 1985. (short stories)
Thomas and Beulah. Pittsburgh, PA: Carnegie-Mellon University Press, 1986.
The Other Side of the House. Photographs by Tamarra Kaida. Tempe, AZ: Pyracantha Press, 1988.
Grace Notes. New York: Norton, 1989.
Through the Ivory Gate. New York: Pantheon Books, 1992. (novel)
Lady Freedom among Us. Westburke, VT: Janus Press, 1993.
Selected Poems. New York: Pantheon, 1993.
The Darker Face of the Earth: A Verse Play in Fourteen Scenes. Brownsville, OR: Story Line Press, 1994.
Mother Love: Poems. New York: Norton, 1995.
The Poet's World. Washington, DC: Library of Congress, 1995. (poet laureate lectures)
On the Bus with Rosa Parks: Poems. New York: Norton, 1999.

Studies of Rita Dove

Baker, Houston A. "Rita Dove, *Grace Notes*." *Black American Literature Forum* 24 (1990): 574–77.
Booth, Alison. "Abduction and Other Severe Pleasures: Rita Dove's *Mother Love*." *Callaloo* 19 (1996): 125–30.
Cook, Emily Walker. " 'But She Won't Set Foot / In His Turtle Dove Nash': Gender Roles and Gender Symbolism in Rita Dove's *Thomas and Beulah*." *College Language Association Journal* 38 (1995): 322–30.
Cushman, Stephen. "And the Dove Returned." *Callaloo* 19 (1996): 131–34
Edmundson, Mark, ed. "Rita Dove's *Mother Love*: A Discussion." *Callaloo* 19 (1996): 123–42.
Erickson, Peter. "Rita Dove's Shakespeares." In *Transforming Shakespeare: Contemporary Women's Re-Visions in Literature and Performance*, edited by Marianne Novy. New York: St. Martin's, 1999. 87–101.
———. "Rita Dove's Two Shakespeare Poems." *Shakespeare and the Classroom* 4.2 (Fall 1996): 53–55.
Georgoudaki, Ekaterini. *Race, Gender, and Class Perspectives in the Works of Maya Angelou, Gwendolyn Brooks, Rita Dove, Nikki Giovanni, and Audre Lorde*. Thessaloniki, Greece: Aristotle University of Thessaloniki, 1991.
———. "Rita Dove: Crossing Boundaries." *Callaloo* 14 (1991): 419–33.
Jones, Kirkland C. "Folk Idiom in the Literary Expression of Two African American Authors: Rita Dove and Yusef Komunyakaa." In *Language and Literature in the African American Imagination*, edited by Belay Carol Aisha Blackshire. Westport, CT: Greenwood, 1992. 149–65.
Kitchen, Judith, Stan Sanvel Rubin, and Earl G. Ingersoll, eds. "A Conversation with Rita Dove." *Black American Literature Forum* 20 (1986): 227–40. Reprinted in *The Post-Confessionals*. Albany: State University of New York, 1989. 151–66.
Lofgren, Lotta. "Partial Horror: Fragmentation and Healing in Rita Dove's *Mother Love*." *Callaloo* 19 (1996): 135–42.
"Maryse Condé and Rita Dove." Special Issue of *Callaloo* 14 (1991): 347–438.
McDowell, Robert. "The Assembling Vision of Rita Dove." *Callaloo* 9 (1986): 61–70. Reprinted in *Conversant Essays: Contemporary Poets on Poetry*, edited by James McCorkle. Detroit, MI: Wayne State University Press, 1990. 294–302.

Moyers, Bill, ed. "Rita Dove." In *The Language of Life: A Festival of Poets*. New York: Doubleday, 1995. 109–28.

Proitsaki, Maria. "Seasonal and Seasonable Motherhood in Dove's *Mother Love*." In *Women, Creators of Culture*, edited by Ekaterini Georgoudaki and Domna Pastourmatzi. Thessaloniki, Greece: Hellenic Association of American Studies, 1997. 145–52.

Rampersad, Arnold. "The Poems of Rita Dove." *Callaloo* 9 (1986): 52–60.

Steffen, Therese. *Crossing Color: Transcultural Space and Place in Rita Dove's Poetry, Fiction, and Drama*. Oxford: Oxford University Press, 2001.

Stein, Kevin. "Lives in Motion: Multiple Perspectives in Rita Dove's Poetry." *Mississippi Review* 23.3 (1995): 51–79.

Steinman, Lisa M. "Dialogues between History and Dream." *Michigan Quarterly Review* 26 (1987): 428–38.

Van Dyne, Susan R. "Siting the Poet: Rita Dove's Refiguring of Traditions." In *Women Poets of the Americas: Toward a Pan-American Gathering*, edited by Jacqueline Vaught Brogan and Cordelia Chávez Candelaria. Notre Dame, IN: University of Notre Dame Press, 1999. 68–87.

Vendler, Helen. "The Black Dove: Rita Dove, Poet Laureate." In *Soul Says*. Cambridge: Belknap Press, 1995. 156–66.

———. "Blackness and Beyond Blackness." *Times Literary Supplement*, 18 Feb. 1994, 11–13.

———. "A Dissonant Triad." *Parnassus* 16 (1991): 391–404. Reprinted in *Soul Says*. Cambridge: Belknap Press, 1995. 141–55.

———. "Rita Dove: Identity Markers." *Callaloo* 17.2 (1994): 381–98. Reprinted in *The Given and the Made: Strategies of Poetic Definition*. Cambridge: Harvard University Press, 1995. 59–88.

Wallace, Patricia. "Divided Loyalties: Literal and Literary in the Poetry of Lorna Dee Cervantes, Cathy Song and Rita Dove." *MELUS* 18.3 (1993): 3–19.

LYNN EMANUEL (1943–)

Michael Dittman

BIOGRAPHY

Born into an artistic Mt. Kisco, New York, family, Lynn Emanuel was exposed to professional artists at a very young age. Her father was a visual artist and many of her aunts and uncles were painters, sculptors, dancers, and choreographers. Today, Emanuel is a frequent grant and award winner as well as frequent conference instructor and guest of honor. Her work has been featured in the *Pushcart Prize Anthology* and *Best American Poetry* in 1994, 1995, and 1998. Her book *The Dig* received the National Poetry Series Award, selected by Gerald Stein. Her work has appeared in a variety of collections and journals, including *New American Poets of the '90s*, the *American Poetry Review*, *Ploughshares*, *Parnassus*, *Michigan Quarterly Review*, *Antioch Review*, *Georgia Review*, *Prairie Schooner*, and the *Kenyon Review*. Emanuel has been a poetry editor for the *Pushcart Prize Anthology*, worked for and received a grant from the National Endowment for the Arts, and is a judge for the James Laughlin Award from the Academy of American Poets. She has taught at the Bread Loaf Writers Conference and the Bennington Writers Workshops. In addition to her teaching and writing, Emanuel keeps a busy performance schedule. Currently she lives in Pittsburgh, Pennsylvania, with her husband, paleontologist Jeffery Schwartz. Emanuel, a professor of English, heads the writing program at the University of Pittsburgh.

MAJOR WORKS AND THEMES

Thematically, Emanuel appeals to the idea of rebirth, of movement, and of re-creating the self. Emanuel often describes this collaborative act of meaning making in terms of a birth process. In the poem "Stone Soup" from *The Dig* (1992), it is a baby who literally wills herself into being, inventing a mother, father, and life of her own. Stylistically, Lynn Emanuel's work is concerned not just with the presentation of the final product of the poem but also with exposing the process that a poet goes through in creating a piece of poetry. Her poem "Homage to Sharon Stone" goes beyond a mere tribute piece (*Then, Suddenly—*). The persona of Emanuel herself pushes its way into the poem by naming herself, admitting to playing the role "of someone writing a book," a role that she takes seriously. Emanuel exposes the writing process by dealing with extra-literary moments.

In her first books, such as *Hotel Fiesta* (1984) and *The Dig*, Emanual seems fascinated by the way the reader works alongside the author to develop meaning. In speaking about her poem "Inventing Father in Las Vegas" in *Hotel Fiesta*, Emanuel makes it clear that she sees the poem as not only an exercise in the author trying to invent a life for her father beyond what she knows first hand, but as an invitation to the reader as well to work with her in inventing a life and world for the man described in the poem.

In her more recent short prose piece "What Is American about American Poetry?" (2000) written exclusively for the Poetry Society of America's website, Emanuel implies a connection between her creation of poetry and her father's creation of objects upon a turning wheel: "Once, wanting to feel that effervescence more deeply, inside me, in my body, I held the tip of my finger to the turning wheel. I watched myself ground down, I watched myself disappear behind the little safety glass window that automatically locked into place over the wheel." Yet even with these words, Emanuel hedges the truth. In her work, the poet seems in search of a voice, seeking to create herself within the confines of her work, which manifests as not a grinding down, but rather as a building up.

Emanuel has suggested that her books, especially *The Dig*, are as much about the act of writing as they are about embodying a meaning within the text. Emanuel claims in an interview with Camille Domangue that the "drama" of *The Dig* is not within the narration of the work, but in the drama "between a reader and a writer, although the writer in this book is becoming an increasingly tenuous entity"(3). Instead of asking the reader to read the poem and to extract some meaning or image from it, through repetition and addresses directed at the reader, Emanuel coerces the reader into helping to create the poem. Emanuel enacts this coercion by introducing and making evident the very structure of the poem and its existence as a created artifact. In the "Coda" section of *The Dig*, Emanuel takes a risk by including a section that proves challenging, not only in form, but in subject as well. "Coda" attempts to describe, in a form somewhere between straight prose broken into line breaks and prose poetry, why and how Emanuel created and included the preceding poems. As the most overtly "created" section of the book, "Coda" proves unsettling to many readers and critics. In it the author speaks directly to the reader, blatantly stating that these poems contain themes "dealt with more directly elsewhere." This literary move, although by no means innovative (Emanuel claims that she was inspired by Italo Calvino's similar use of structure) runs the risk of alienating readers more comfortable with more traditional lyrical forms of poetry. Addressing the reader from within the poem can also push readers away by creating a cynicism with readers less likely to make an emotional investment in the reading of the poem because of the "gimmick." Emanuel, in an *American Poetry Review* interview with Eliot Wilson, defends her use of repetition both in words and in settings by claiming this repetition is purposeful: She repeats words and setting from poem to poem and from book to book to create a sense of claustrophobia for the reader. The claustrophobia, she believes, will further disquiet the reader, making the poem more obvious as a created object and alienating the created voice found within the poems even more. For example, the opening poem of *The Dig*, "Stone Soup," contains the repetition of the phrase "she invents." The phrase proves telling as it not only alludes to the character in the narrative poem but also to Emanuel's creative process, and finally to the reader's task of inventing a persona for the poet-speaker of not only "Stone Soup" but for the entire book as well. *The Dig* relies upon these monuments, where the use of repetition forces the reader into understanding not only the reading of the poem as a creative experience but also juxtapostioning that creation with the acknowledged subject of the poem.

Emanuel's work not only exposes the workings of the poem, but it also attempts to explain her belief that the poem creates the reader's image of the author just as surely as the writer creates the poem. In her most recent book, *Then, Suddenly—* (1999), Emanuel continues this theme, pushing it to a new level. This collection, more than the others, leaves the reader feeling like a voyeur. *Then, Suddenly—* is a book of growth and breaking away. At times the characters seem to have broken away from their creator, and through the asides where she addresses the reader directly, Emanuel seems to be trying to break away from playing the role of creator.

CRITICAL RECEPTION

Eliot Wilson, in the *American Poetry Review*, calls Emanuel a "disturbing poet . . . in the very best way. Even [her] earlier poems work to disrupt and subvert the reader's expectations" (29). Because Emanuel is a contemporary poet, her work has, as yet, received limited critical attention. No full-length study of her work is available. Criticism appears in journals and within the context of book reviews. Emanuel's work deals mostly with form rather than a more overtly political content; therefore, critics bring attention to her stylistic obsession with the construction of language and theme. While Cynthia Hogue in her review of Emanuel's *Then, Suddenly—* suggests that the poet's greatest debt is to poets of the New York School, such as John Ashbery and Kenneth Koch, in her work, Emanuel makes more appeals to Gertrude Stein, Walt Whitman, and the New York poet John O'Hara. Emanuel's strength as a poet comes not from her role as a narrative poet or as a storyteller within the confines of a prose poem; rather, her strength emerges from her role as a lyrical observer.

BIBLIOGRAPHY

Works by Lynn Emanuel

Oblique Light. Pittsburgh, PA: Slow Loris Press, 1979.

Hotel Fiesta. Athens: University of Georgia Press, 1984.

The Technology of Love. Omaha, NE: Abattoir Editions, 1988.

The Dig: Poems. Urbana: University of Illinois Press, 1992.

"The Politics of the Paragraph." *Critical Quarterly* 37 (1995): 118–119. (essay)

Then, Suddenly—. Pittsburgh, PA: University of Pittsburgh Press, 1999.

"What Is American about American Poetry." *Poetry Society of America*, 9 Sept. 2000, <http://www.poetrysociety.org/emanuel.html>. (essay)

Studies of Lynn Emanuel

Domangue, Camille. "Ordinary Objects: An Interview with Lynn Emanuel." *AWP Chronicle* (Sept. 1997): 1–9.

Hogue, Cynthia. "Poetry, Politics and Postmodernism." *Women's Review of Books* 17 (2000): 20–22.

Leavitt, Michele. "Frying Trout While Drunk (Poem)." *Explicator* 53.1(1994): 62–64.

Pope, Deborah. "Everybody's Story." Review of *The Dig*, by Lynn Emanuel. *Southern Review* 29 (1993): 820.

Wilson, Eliot. "Then, Suddenly—: An Interview." *American Poetry Review* 29.3 (2000): 29–32.

CAROLYN FORCHÉ (1950–)

Shanna Flaschka

BIOGRAPHY

Carolyn Forché, a self-described "poet of witness," was born in Detroit, Michigan. She is the eldest of seven children, all of whom were born between 1950 and 1961. Her father was a tool-and-die maker while her mother took care of the children at home. The family remained in Detroit until 1955, when they moved to Farmington Township, Michigan.

As a child, Forché cultivated her writing skills through various stories, essays, and poems. Nevertheless, she planned to be a physician and spent most of her adolescence working as a nurse's aid in hospitals, a clinic, and a nursing home. However, due to the social climate at the time, women were rarely admitted to medical school, so Forché eventually returned to creative expression. She earned a degree in international relations and creative writing from Michigan State University (1972), and an MFA from Bowling Green State University (1975), and then entered the teaching profession. Over the course of several years, she has taught at a number of universities, including the University of Virginia and University of California, Los Angeles.

Forché began teaching at San Diego State University in 1975, where she met Maya Flakoll Gross, the daughter of Salvadorian poet Claribel Alegría, who introduced Forché to Alegría's poetry. This meeting initiated Forché's commitment to an English translation of Alegría. In 1976 she won the Yale Series of Younger Poets Award for her first collection of poetry, *Gathering the Tribes*, subsequently published by Yale University Press in the same year. A year later, she began her work on translations of Alegría's *Flores del Volcan*.

Shortly after returning from Mallorca, Spain, where she worked closely with Alegría, Forché was visited by Alegría's nephew, Leonel Gomez Vides. He convinced Forché to use her recently awarded Guggenheim Fellowship to travel to El Salvador, in order to translate the poetry of Alegría and to learn about the condition of the country. Forché utilized her early interest in medicine as she worked in rural Salvadoran hospitals and clinics for nearly two years. She witnessed countless political and social atrocities in her work with local citizens and with Alegría. Because of these experiences, Forché became a human rights advocate and an outspoken activist against social and political repression worldwide.

Emerging from her tenure in Central America, Forché published her second collection of poems, *The Country Between Us* (1981), which received the Lamont Poetry Selection Award for 1981. A year later, Forché published her translation of Alegría's poetry, *Flowers from the Volcano* (1982). She subsequently returned to El Salvador, this time as a journalist for Amnesty International. In 1984 she married Harry Mattison, a photographer whom she had met in El Salvador in 1980. Forché and Mattison worked together in Beirut, Lebanon, and South Africa. The couple lived in Paris for a year when their son was born and then moved to the United States, where they have been living since.

Forché published her most recent volume of poetry, *The Angel of History*, in 1994. This collection, though different stylistically from her previous publications, continues her thematic expression of the cruel and dehumanizing effects of political oppression throughout the world.

Carolyn Forché, currently living in Bethesda, Maryland, with her husband and son, is a professor in the Master of Fine Arts Program in Poetry at George Mason University in Virginia. Her poems have been published in over fourteen languages, and she continues to speak out on behalf of human rights at various events throughout the world.

MAJOR WORKS AND THEMES

In the foreword to *Gathering the Tribes*, Stanley Kunitz introduced kinship as "the theme that preoccupies Carolyn Forché" [xi]. In fact, Forché's seminal collection serves as almost a *bildungsroman* in verse, in which the growth she experiences throughout the course of the volume illuminates the relationship between kinship and the poet's ability to grow. *Tribes* is thus effectively a microcosm of the whole body of Forché's work. In the first poem, "The Morning Baking," for example, Forché presents the metaphoric severing of her birth cord through the death of her kin. The reader's introduction to Forché comes at the precise moment the artist first recognizes she is both alone and part of a greater whole. By the last poem, "White Wings They Never Grow Weary," she has entered the wonderment of her own woman/motherhood in awe that "there will ever be milk in her." Throughout the collection, a clear trajectory of both emotional and spiritual growth emerges, as the poet discovers the pleasure ("Kalaloch") and pain ("Alfansa") of life's experiences, as well as a sense of her own mortality ("Plain Song").

Likewise, Forché provides a clear sense of growth from one collection of poetry to the next. The poems in *Tribes*, written in Forché's youth, prove simple and accessible, almost procedural. *The Country Between Us* manifests as somewhat more complex, as the poet examines her own apprehension of the atrocities she has witnessed. The topics in this work are more adult and represent the larger issues that become apparent when one is forced to look outside his or her understanding of the world. *The Angel of History*, presented almost as an epic, is Forché's most complex work to date.

But as Kunitz noted, kinship is the glue that binds Forché's poems one to the other. Writing of her dead grandmother, Forché confronts her own heritage as personified in the form of an old Slavic woman. In "Burning the Tomato Worms," for instance,

Forché shoulders the quotidian tasks of her ancestors, even though she was born thousands of miles from her family's homeland (*Gathering the Tribes*). She shifts between first- and third-person narrative, thus becoming her grandmother's voice while, at the same time, recognizing her own voice and continuing the sentence begun at her family's inception.

Although Forché places herself squarely in southern Michigan at times, her poems point to an inference that setting is less important than character. For instance, in "Tomato Worms" she works "the same fields" as those worked by her distant Uzbek relatives. Though her fields are in Michigan, she gradually becomes her own grandmother through the course of the first section of poems. In "In Early Night," she refers to being wrapped in "sheep leather" and makes reference to her own "round Slovak face" (*Gathering the Tribes*). The experiences she relates in her poetry, then, need not be spoken out loud with her family, but are understood as ancestral rites of passage.

The vivid kinship motifs begin to fade in *The Country Between Us* and *The Angel of History*, but Forché's borderless connection of herself with a people and land remains distinct. With increasing adroitness, Forché internalizes the cultures she visits, to transplant them into her history and kin. One poem in particular from *The Angel of History*, "The Garden Shukkei-en," shows the poet reversing her own identity to enable a deeper empathic connection with the Japanese for the tragedy of their World War II devastation ("Do Americans think of us?"). This transposition strongly echoes the manner in which Forché becomes a medium for Claribel Alegría in "The Island," from *The Country Between Us*. Here, Forché moves beyond mere witness and becomes Alegría's inverse image, voicing the elder poet's wisdom to Forché herself.

Another pertinent aspect of Forché's poetry is that it resonates with political activism and awareness. *Gathering the Tribes*, published before her trip to El Salvador, foreshadows her interest in cultural consciousness. All three poetry collections are riddled with references to her Slovak heritage, but when juxtaposed to her Salvadoran poems in *The Country Between Us*, Forché begins to present the universality of human oppression. In "On Returning to Detroit," Forché watches the dawn "coming into Detroit but like Bratislava." The observations she makes of her various fellow passengers on the train seamlessly illustrate the relativity of grief and the inherent commonality of the human experience.

The Angel of History continues the moral examination begun in *Country*, but on a much broader level. With the eyes of a woman who has, by this point in her life, seen much more of the world than most people ever do, Forché writes of the devastation caused by humans to each other throughout the twentieth century. In her essay "El Salvador: An Aide-Mémoire," Forché writes, "I have been told that a poet should be of his or her time. It is my feeling that the twentieth-century human condition demands a poetry of witness. . . . If I did not wish to make poetry of what I had seen, what is it I thought poetry was?" (257). It is precisely as a "poet of witness" that Forché should best be considered, for such a title explains her adeptness in juggling the themes of kinship and cultural awareness. Forché's work makes clear that she has served as the eyes of each reader since her first poem.

CRITICAL RECEPTION

Although no books have yet been published that exclusively study Carolyn Forché's work, there are many critics who point to Forché as a notable example of a "political" poet in the contemporary canon. It is customary for a study of contemporary American poetry to contain a reference to Forché's poem "The Colonel"—which concerns a dinner at a high-ranking officer's house in El Salvador attended by Forché—in order to classify the type of poetry by which Forché is known. This move becomes both ironic and unfortunate because, as Forché has noted in interviews, she did not originally intend "The Colonel" as a poem, but rather as a documentation of the event itself.

In his foreword to *Gathering the Tribes*, Kunitz writes, "Carolyn Forché's poems give an illusion of artlessness because they spring from the simplest and deepest human feelings, from an earthling's awareness of the systemic pulse of creation" (xii). Yet other critics, when reviewing Forché's second two books, write that her poetry's simplicity is in itself an illusion. Mary DeShazer, for example, when explicating "The Colonel," noted that "the poet's terse opening lines" actually highlight the "incongruities between the 'civilities' of the colonel's family life and the atrocities for which he is responsible." DeShazer elaborates that underneath the simple prose and staccato rhythm of the piece "is an ominous note, struck vividly in Forché's juxtaposition of the ordinary and the horrific" (286).

Yet not all critics have been as generous. When *Gathering the Tribes* was released, the poet Hayden Carruth wrote in a *New York Times* book review that he did not much like the book. Likewise, although *The Country Between Us* received praise from Robert Pinsky and Larry Levis in the *American Poetry Review* and from Terrence Diggory in the periodical *Salmagundi*, other critics wrote reviews that were less sympathetic. These conflicting reviews indicate that Forché produces a disturbing poetics that bears further critical examination.

BIBLIOGRAPHY

Works by Carolyn Forché

Gathering the Tribes. New Haven, CT: Yale University Press, 1976.

The Colonel. St. Paul, MN: Biel Press, 1981.

The Country Between Us. Port Townsend, WA: The Copper Canyon Press, 1981.

"El Salvador: An *Aide-Memoire*." *American Poetry Review* (July-August 1981): 3–7. (essay)

Flowers from the Volcano. Pittsburgh, PA: University of Pittsburgh Press, 1982. (translation of the poetry of Claribel Alegrìa)

The Selected Poems of Robert Desnos. With William Kulik. New York: Ecco, 1991. (translation)

Against Forgetting: Twentieth-Century Poetry of Witness, ed. New York: Newton, 1993. (anthology)

The Angel of History. New York: Harper, 1994.

Sorrow. Willimantic, CT: Curbstone Press, 1999. (translation of the poetry of Claribel Alegrìa)

Studies of Carolyn Forché

Arsenault, Joseph, and Tony Brinkley. "Traumatized Words, Tress, A Farmhouse: In Response to *The Angel of History*." *Sagetrieb* 16.3 (1997): 103–14.

Balkaian, Peter. "Carolyn Forché and The Poetry of Witness: Another View." *Agni* 40 (1994): 186–93.

Carruth, Hayden. Review of *The Country Between Us*, by Carolyn Forché. *New York Times Book Review* 8 August 1976: 12.

DeShazer, Mary K. " 'Lust for a Working Tomorrow': U.S. Women's Poetry of Solidarity and Struggle." *A Poetics of Resistance: Women Writing in El Salvador, South Africa, and the United States*. Ann Arbor: The University of Michigan Press, 1994.

Diggory, Terrence. "Witnesses and Seers." *Salmagundi* (Fall 1983): 112–24.

Greer, Michael. "Politicizing the Modern: Carolyn Forché in El Salvador and America." *Centennial Review* 30.2 (1986): 160–80.

Gregory, Eileen. "Poetry and Survival: H.D. and Carolyn Forché." In *H.D. and Poets After*, edited by Donna Krolik Hollenberg. Iowa City: University of Iowa Press, 2000. 266–81.

Helle, Anita. "Elegy as History: Three Women Poets 'By the Century's Deathbed.' " *South Atlantic Review* 61.2 (1996): 51–68.

Levis, Larry. "War as Parable and War as Fact: Herbert and Forché." *American Poetry* 12.1 (1983): 6–12.

Mann, John. "Carolyn Forché: Poetry and Survival." *American Poetry* 3.3 (1986): 51–69.

Mitchell, Nora, and Emily Skoler. "History, Death, Politics, Despair." *New England Review* 17.2 (1995): 67–81.

Montenegro, David. "Carolyn Forché: An Interview." *American Poetry Review* 17.6 (1988): 35–40.

———. *Points of Departure: International Writers on Writing and Politics*. Ann Arbor: University of Michigan Press, 1991.

Moyers, Bill. *The Language of Life: A Festival of Poets*. New York: Doubleday, 1995. 129–41.

Rea, Paul, W. "An Interview with Carolyn Forché." *High Plains Literary Review* 2.2 (1987): 150–64.

———. "The Poet as Witness: Carolyn Forché's Powerful Pleas from El Salvador." *Confluencia* 2.2 (1987): 93–99.

Smith, Lenora. "Carolyn Forché: Poet of Witness." In *Essays on Women Poets and Writers*, edited by Sheila Roberts and Yvonne Pacheco Tevis. San Bernardino, CA: Borgo, 1993. 15–28.

Stone, Carole. "Elegy as Political Expression in Women's Poetry: Akmatova, Levertov, Forché." *College-Literature* 18.1 (1991): 14–91.

Strawser, Amy K. *Imaging the Body in Contemporary Women's Poetry: Helga Novak, Ursula Krechel, Carolyn Forché, Nikki Giovanni, Amy Kepple Strawser*. New York: Peter Lang, 1999.

Taft-Kaufman, Jill. "Jill Taft-Kaufman Talks with Carolyn Forché." *Text and Performance Quarterly* 10.1 (1990): 61–70.

KATHLEEN FRASER (1937–)

Deborah M. Mix

BIOGRAPHY

Born in Tulsa, Oklahoma, Kathleen Fraser grew up in Colorado and Southern California. After earning a BA in English literature at Occidental College in California, she moved to New York City in 1959, where she started writing poetry in evening workshops with Stanley Kunitz and Kenneth Koch and publishing in magazines (her first publication appeared in *Poetry* in 1963) and small press journals in the early 1960s.

Fraser received recognition for her work beginning in the mid-1960s, including the New School's Frank O'Hara Poetry Prize and the NEW Young Writers Discovery Award, both in 1964. Her first book of poetry, *Change of Address*, appeared in 1968. After spending two years teaching at the Iowa School of Writers Workshop and one year as a poet-in-residence at Reed College, Fraser moved to San Francisco with her son David (born in 1966). She taught at San Francisco State University from 1972–92, winning a National Endowment for the Arts Fellowship in 1978 and a Guggenheim Fellowship in 1981. While at San Francisco State, Fraser directed the Poetry Center and founded the American Poetry Archives.

In addition to her work as a teacher, poet, and critic, Fraser's personal and scholarly interests led her to co-found (with Beverly Dahlen, Frances Jaffer, Susan Gevirtz, Rachel Blau DuPlessis, and Carolyn Burke) the feminist journal *HOW(ever)* in 1983. Designed to redress the absence of women from discussion of modernist and contemporary innovative writing and poetics, *HOW(ever)* ran until 1991. In 1998 this journal was resurrected, with Fraser's participation, as the online journal *HOW2*.

Today, Fraser divides her year between San Francisco and Rome. Fraser resigned from San Francisco State in 1992 to concentrate on her own writing and editorial projects, and she continues to play an active role in both poetic and academic communities.

MAJOR WORKS AND THEMES

Fraser's earliest work as a poet was shaped by second-wave feminism and her investigation of gender's relationship to language, identity, and tradition. Most of Fraser's early teachers and poetic models were male, and she found herself troubled by the absence of women's voices from literary canons. Her early role models, most notably Wallace Stevens and George Oppen, were finally joined by Barbara Guest, whom she met while living in New York, and together they stand as what Peter Quartermain calls in his introduction to *il cuore: the heart* (1997) "her three great permission-givers" (xii), those poets whose form, content, and poetic philosophies pushed her toward a more experimental approach to reading and poetry. Even as her work developed, though, Fraser continued to seek more female role models. She reflects on her desire to uncover female tradition in her essay "The Tradition of Marginality" (1989), writing of a desire "to locate a poetics on our own terms" through a "different kind of attentiveness: it wasn't the witty polish of posturing of 'great lines,' but a listening attitude, an attending to unconscious connections, a backing off of the performing ego to allow the mysteries of language to come forward and resonate more fully" (24, 25). Much of her early poetry reflects this investigative focus, both in form and content. These early works are closely linked to her New York School roots and mark only the beginning of her investigations of the relationship between gender, identity, and language.

During the 1970s, Fraser began using her journals as a primary source for her poetry, as a way to explore this "different kind of attentiveness." For Fraser, journal writing offered a release from narrative structure since, as Suzanne Juhasz notes in her 1984 essay on Fraser, "The Journal as Source," a journal's "dailiness, wherein the events of the domestic and interpersonal life occur, is by definition never a conclusion, always a process" (16). Fraser's 1978 collection, *New Shoes*, reflects her growing interest in feminist exploration. Linda A. Taylor notes that "the poems imagine a female self-empowerment through dismantling and reconstruction of [the] 'text' of a woman" (342). In these poems, Fraser seeks to uncover and dismantle the patriarchal myths that women have internalized, setting loose a "flood" of women's language (*New Shoes* 37).

Fraser has always viewed poetry as a vehicle of radical ideas; in *Feminist Poetics* (1983), she calls poetry a venue in which a woman writer "can resist making a commodity and can push against or extend the formal directives of literature shaped by a poetics largely developed out of the experiences and pleasure principles of men writing" (7). Her 1980 volume *Each Next* uses the genre-busting form of prose poems to further experiment with issues of authority. In one prose poem, "Talking to Myself Talking to You," she muses, "in fact, there seems to be no systematic plan to the bits and pieces of me. Only this listening, trying to catch up, questioning everything, yet "no answer surfaces" (29). Increasingly influenced by the works of French feminists, Fraser began considering whether a feminine discourse might exist and what it might look like. In *Something (even human voices)* (1984), Fraser extends this consideration, again through prose poems, continuing her investigation of the links between gender and language, and these pieces reflect the kinds of sensual excesses of detail often associated with *jouissance*.

By 1987, in *Notes Preceding Trust*, Fraser seems to have concluded that a feminine discourse does in fact exist, and she locates such a discourse within a tradition of women's innovative writing, which she was helping to uncover at the time through her work with *HOW(ever)*. As with the two preceding volumes, *Notes* also bends genre with the use of both prose and poetry forms, and Fraser also begins to experiment with accident and chance, as when a typographical error transforms "boundary" into "boundayr." In "Faulty Copying" (originally published in 1994 as "This Phrasing Unreliable Except as Here" and reprinted in *Translating the Unspeakable*, 2000), Fraser explains that such "involuntary errors" "gave me a kind of freedom to interrogate a wider terrain than I'd imagined at the beginning" (*Translating* 81). Thus an accidental error becomes a window into the arbitrary nature of any boundary. Other poems, such as "La La at the Cinque Fernando, Paris" (written in 1988 and included in *il cuore*), and "Giotto: ARENA" (in *when new time folds up*, 1993) also reflect Fraser's willingness to use chance and error as entries into the unexpected. Fraser writes in an explanatory noted for "La La" that the protagonist's "private matrix thus evolves from her own fragmented story" (*il cuore* 1997).

Poems such as "La La" also reveal Fraser's interest in essentially arbitrary forms (matrices, errata, etc.) as structures that limit meaning both prophylactically (to prevent overwhelming the reader with undifferentiated material) and politically (to challenge readers to envision what remains unwritten). In *when new time folds up* (1993), she questions representationality, comparing the act of reading to an archaeological dig in which one tries to make sense of discovered fragments, interpreting the pottery shards as metonyms for an entire culture. Likewise, in reading a poem, she remarks that while we know what the words on the page *are*, we know "not, in retrospect, what was intended" (11). She also continues to investigate the ways in which poetic form works to enact just such limitations and the ways in which altering form might alter the boundaries. In her essay "Line. On the Line. Lining Up" (1988), she sees breaking the traditional poetic form as essential to breaking with other traditional social and political structures: "Resistance is an ongoing condition-of-being for most women poets . . . because what wants to be said and who wants saying can't be expressed with appropriate tonal or spatial complexity in the confident firm assertions cheered on by witty end-rhymes or taut lines matching with left-margin precision down the page" (166).

Fraser's work as a critic and editor has done much to uncover a tradition of women writers who refused "confident firm assertions . . . witty end-rhymes [and] taut lines" in favor of "the *necessity* behind the pursuit of innovation" (*Translating* 3). Her essays have treated the work of writers such as Emily Dickinson, Mina Loy, Lorine Niedecker, Barbara Guest, and Susan Howe with insight and care that has surely helped to secure their visibility within Anglo American literary traditions. Though she is frequently associated with the school of poetry called Language Writing, Fraser is ambivalent about such a classification. In "Partial Local Coherence" (1982), she writes that while feminists share similar interests in deconstructing language as a means to deconstructing "the dominant and turgid mainstream" (both aesthetic and material), "for a writer whose awareness has been tuned by the growing need to claim her own history and present tense, Language Writing's directives are often encountered—if not intended—as the newest covenant" ("Partial" 135). Still, she remains a part of the Language Writing community, frequently appearing at conferences and panels with Language Writers and publishing in Language Writers periodicals. Fraser continues to experiment with the intersections of gender, genre, and language, writing in her

1995 volume, *WING*, "itself the wing not static by frayed, layered, fettered, furling" (72).

CRITICAL RECEPTION

Despite her substantial publishing record, relatively few assessments of Fraser's work have appeared over the years. Linda Kinnahan has published the most substantial studies of Fraser's work, first in a 1992 essay in *Contemporary Literature* (under the name Linda A Taylor) and later in her book *Poetics of the Feminine.* Despite her poetry's feminist bent, early attention to Fraser's writing by feminist critics was likely hindered by a preference for "experiential" poetic style among feminist poets and critics. Experimental work was, too often, dismissed by women writers and scholars as inattentive to gender concerns. These are precisely the issues Fraser considers in her essays collected in *Translating the Unspeakable*; many of these essays take her own work and experiences as an innovative poet as an object of study. Fraser's essays and recovery work are frequently cited by scholars of both modernist and contemporary innovative poetry by women.

Fraser has earned unequivocal praise for her work as editor-in-chief of *HOW(ever)*, with many critics finding the journal a watershed moment in studies of feminist, modernist, and experimental literature. A new study of women and American language poetry, by Ann Vickery, devotes a chapter to Fraser's editorial work and its effects on both poetic and scholarly communities. Fraser had finally begun to receive more widespread critical attention with the publication of her volumes of selected poems and her collected essays.

BIBLIOGRAPHY

Works by Kathleen Fraser

Change of Address. San Francisco: Kayak, 1968.

In Defiance (of the Rains). Prints by Judy Starbuck. San Francisco: Kayak, 1969.

Little Noises from Lucas Street. Urbana, IL: Penumbra, 1972.

What I Want. New York: Harper, 1974.

Magritte Series. Willits, CA: Tuunba Press, 1977.

New Shoes. New York: Harper, 1978.

Each Next, Narratives. Berkeley, CA: The Figures, 1980.

"Partial Local Coherence: Regions with Illustrations: Some Notes in Language Writing." *Ironwood* 10: 2 (1982): 120–137. Reprinted in *Translating the Unspeakable: Poetry and the Innovative Necessity.* Tuscaloosa: University of Alabama Press, 2000. 63–76 (essays)

Feminist Poetics. Editor with Judy Frankel. San Francisco: San Francisco University Press, 1983. (anthology of critical essays)

HOW(ever). 1983–1991. www.departments.bucknell.edu/stadler_center/how2/intro.html (archived online)

Something (even human voices) in the foreground, a lake. Berkeley, CA: Kelsey Street Press, 1984.

boundayr. Limited edition with aquatints by Sam Francis. San Francisco: Lapis Press, 1987.

Notes Preceding Trust. San Francisco: Lapis Press, 1987.

"Line. On the Line. Lining up. Lined with. Between the Lines. Bottom Line." In *The Line in Postmodern Poetry*, edited by Henry Sayre and Robert Frank. Urbana, IL: University of Illinois Press, 1988. 152–74. Reprinted in *Translating the Unspeakable: Poetry and the Innovative Necessity*. Tuscaloosa: University of Alabam Press, 2000. 141–60. (essay)

"The Tradition of Marginality." *Frontiers* 10.3 (1989): Reprinted in *Translating the Unspeakable: Poetry and the Innovative Necessity*. Tuscaloosa: University of Alabama Press, 2000. 25–38. (essays)

when new time folds up. Minneapolis, MN: Chax Press, 1993.

WING. Mill Valley, CA: EM Press, 1995.

il cuore: the heart, Selected Poems 1970–1995. Hanover, NH: Wesleyan/New England University Press, 1997.

how2. www.departments.bucknell.edu/stadler_center/how2. (online journal)

Translating the Unspeakable: Poetry and the Innovative Necessity. Tuscaloosa: University of Alabama Press, 2000. (essays)

Studies of Kathleen Fraser

Hogue, Cynthia. " 'I Am Not of that Feather': Kathleen Fraser's Postmodernist Poetics." In *H.D. and Poets After*, edited by Donna Krolik Hollenberg. Iowa City: University of Iowa Press, 2000. 172–83.

———. "Infectious Ecstasy: Toward a Poetics of Performative Transformation." In *Women Poets of the Americas: Toward a Pan-American Gathering*, edited by Jacqueline Vaught Brogan and Cordelia Chávez Candelaria. Notre Dame, IN: University of Notre Dame Press, 1999.

———. "An Interview with Kathleen Fraser." *Contemporary Literature* 39 (1998): 1–26.

Juhasz, Suzanne. "The Journal as Source and Model for Feminist Art: The Example of Kathleen Fraser." *Frontiers* 8.3 (1984): 16–20.

Kinnahan, Linda. *Poetics of the Feminine*. New York: Cambridge University Press, 1994.

Quartermain, Peter. Introduction. *Il cuore: the heart: Selected Poems 1970–1995*, by Kathleen Fraser. Hanover, NH: Wesleyan/New England University Press, 1997. xi-xiii.

Taylor, Linda A. " 'A Seizure of Voice': Language Innovation and a Feminist Poetics in the Works of Kathleen Fraser." *Contemporary Literature* 33 (1992): 337–72.

Vickery, Ann. "Kathleen Fraser's Feminist Alternative: *HOW(ever)*." In *Leaving Lines of Gender*. Hanover, NH: Wesleyan/New England University Press, 2000. 88–100.

ALICE FULTON (1952–)

Ernest J. Smith

BIOGRAPHY

Alice Fulton was born on January 25, 1952, in Troy, New York, where she lived until she was in her early twenties. She earned a BA in creative writing from Empire State College in Albany, New York, graduating in 1978, and in 1992, an MFA from Cornell, where she studied with the poet A. R. Ammons, whom she frequently notes as an influence. In an interview with Alec Marsh, Fulton mentions reading poetry as a high school student in anthologies belonging to her sister, an English major, and being enchanted with poetry's language. Emily Dickinson was an early and continuing influence, one that Fulton discusses in her essay "Her Moment of Brocade: The Reconstruction of Emily Dickinson," included in *Feeling as a Foreign Language* (1999), a collection of Fulton's nonfiction.

Fulton says she began reading contemporary poetry in the mid-1970s, as an undergraduate, when she also attended a poetry conference at Amherst College, Massachusetts, where she heard Adrienne Rich and other feminist poets read their works. Fulton's postmodern feminist strain, one of several notable features in her work, has drawn serious analysis from contemporary scholars. In the late 1970s, Fulton received fellowships at the MacDowell Colony, Yaddo, and the Millay Colony and, by the early eighties, had won several poetry prizes, including the Emily Dickinson Award, and awards from the Academy of American Poets and The Poetry Society of America. After holding visiting appointments on various campuses, Fulton joined the faculty at the University of Michigan, where she has taught ever since. In 1980 she married Hank DeLeo, a painter whose work has appeared on the covers of most of Fulton's books.

Fulton's first collection, *Dance Script with Electric Ballerina* (1983), won the Associated Writing Programs Award, and the noted poet Mark Strand selected her next volume, *Palladium* (1986), for inclusion in the 1985 National Poetry Series. *Palladium* later won the Society of Midland Authors Award. By the time of her third volume,

Powers of Congress (1990), Fulton had won Guggenheim and Ingram Merrill fellowships and was publishing regularly in the best literary magazines, such as *The Paris Review*, *Poetry*, and *Grand Street*. Subsequently, Fulton received the coveted and prestigious MacArthur Foundation award in 1991, which provided time for her to complete her fourth collection, *Sensual Math* (1995), a book that may well come to be seen as one of the most significant individual volumes of the 1990s. Her most recent collection is titled *Felt* (2001).

In addition to the poetry, much of Fulton's nonfiction has been collected in *Feeling as a Foreign Language*. Along with the Dickinson essay and Fulton's important early examination of her own poetry in "To Organize a Waterfall," the book includes two essays on what Fulton has come to call her "fractal verse." Fulton's short story "Queen Wintergreen" appeared in *The Best American Short Stories, 1993*, and the story "Happy Dust" won the 1997 editor's prize from the *Missouri Review*. Her poetry has been set to music by the contemporary composer William Bolcom, and she collaborated with Bolcom on the song cycle "Turbulence: A Romance," which premiered at the Walker Art Center in Minneapolis in 1997.

MAJOR WORKS AND THEMES

Fulton's poetry delights in the exuberance of language, its intellectual, aural, and emotional registers intermingling in a work that employs all available levels of diction and association. A delight in the unexpected emerges as a recurring theme and technique in Fulton, the use of a word, phrase, or voice that can shift a poem into a new key, or that can wittily comment on itself. In "Point of Purchase," the longest poem in *Powers of Congress*, she includes a variety of handwritten marginal critiques of her poem, from four individual, imagined readers, seeming to parody both the workshop method and contemporary critical theory. At one point, the poem even uses the margin comments to quote a negative review of an earlier volume, where a reviewer compared Fulton's language to a woman who draws attention to herself by wearing too much make-up. But these comments running alongside the typeset poem are more than parodic. In her long essay "To Organize a Waterfall," she describes how the poem is akin to polyphonic music, the imagined readers' scribbled comments responding to the voice of a somewhat abrasive speaker in the poem proper. The speaker is a woman sculptor and pool player, and her opinions, language, and range of diction clearly exasperate the readers who write in the margins, readers including a contemporary Marxist theorist and a naïve reader who responds in a purely personal, subjective fashion. Fulton claims that the poem simultaneously "describes (and argues with) my aesthetic in oblique fashion," and "speaks to Marxist-poststructuralist, reader response, reception, and feminist ideologies" (*Feeling* 202, 206).

Another significant theme in Fulton's work is the dialectic between the individual and culture, both historically constructed aspects of culture and contemporary, popular culture. In "Some Cool," from *Sensual Math*, Fulton invokes Elvis Presley to explore the relationship of an adoring audience with a cultural icon in decline, while at the same time providing a vivid, detailed description of pigs on their way to the slaughterhouse. An Elvis cookbook titled "Are You Hungry Tonight?" provides the connection between the two. The poem exemplifies how Fulton mixes humor with a serious exploration of cultural touchstones such as Presley. In her interview with Barbara Petoskey, Fulton observes that Elvis Presley was primarily a cultural construct, completely mediated by either television or film. Elvis reappears in *Sensual Math* in a poem titled "Elvis from the Waist Up," part of the sequence "My Last TV Campaign," a dramatic monologue spoken from the perspective of an advertising man coming briefly out of retirement.

In the *Sensual Math's* final long poem, "Give: A Sequence Reimagining Daphne and Apollo," Fulton works with the ancient myth of Daphne and Apollo, recasting Elvis and Frank Sinatra as Cupid and Apollo. In the myth, Cupid's arrows cause Apollo to desire Daphne but Daphne to despise Apollo. Ultimately, Daphne is turned into a tree. As Fulton explains in an interview: "In my retelling, Cupid sends Apollo and Daphne two 'hit' records, which take the place of arrows. By listening, Apollo and Daphne are permeated with Cupid's wishes" (Petoskey 27). But in her treatment of Daphne, Fulton returns to a theme running throughout both *Sensual Math* and earlier volumes: the position of women in culture. In an interview with Cristanne Miller, Fulton discusses her treatment of Daphne in a feminist context: "Myths reflect the largest beliefs and patterns of a given culture. So I was trying to write culture as it is, not as it should be. Misogyny and the subjugation of women are worldwide phenomena" ("Interview" 593). At the same time, Fulton expresses hope that her rewriting of the myth offers Daphne greater hope and more possibilities. Citing lines from Dickinson and Marianne Moore, Fulton's Daphne "has the traits of an electron, dark matter, light, a dolphin" (Petoskey 28).

Another innovation in Fulton's poetry, and one that she has discussed in several interviews, is the use of ungendered speakers. Refusing to affix a gender to a speaker whom a reader might conventionally expect to be male is another way Fulton works to challenge culturally constructed assumptions. In *Sensual Math*, the poem "Echo Location" uses the pronoun "it," which Fulton describes as "freeing . . . the pronoun takes on a spectrum of associations" ("Interview" 590). Other elements of Fulton's feminism prove similarly oblique. In "To Organize a Waterfall," she uses the opening poem from *Powers of Congress*, "Cascade Experiment," as an example. The poem mentions several species of lizards composed of only females as an instance of what the poem calls "truths we don't suspect." These solely female species have existed for centuries, but because of the assumption that males are part of all species, they went unnoticed. Fulton cites the inclusion of this fact about the lizard species as one of her "feminist strategies," typically "embedded because I believe linguistic structures are most powerful when least evident" (*Feeling* 185).

Fulton contends in the interview with Miller that the traditional approach to lyric poetry is to privilege voice, narrative, and autobiography, with a limited range of emotions. While a few poems from her first two collections could be described as including some of these elements, her later poetry attempts to work against them. *Dance Script with Electric Ballerina* includes poems about growing up and about parents, such as "From Our Mary to Me," "The Gone Years," and "The Perpetual Light." Several poems use quatrains, or more irregular stanza shapes, but all employ a consistent left-hand margin. There are even two fourteen-line poems, but without rhyme or a regular meter. The title poem, "Dance Script with Electric Ballerina," is something of an early *ars poetica* for Fulton. In it, she uses dancing and other media as metaphors for poetic composition. *Palladium* has a more overarching structure, each of its sections playing off a different definition of the word "palladium." Fulton describes the poems in this volume as having a "polyphonic texture," using the musical effect of counterpoint (*Feeling* 201). Various speakers and voices intermingle in *Pal-*

ladium, their language demonstrating Fulton's assertion that "I don't agree that the language of verse falls neatly into binary registers of diction" (*Feeling* 50).

While "Point of Purchase" and other poems in both *Powers of Congress* and *Palladium* extended Fulton's range and established her as one of the major voices in contemporary American poetry, it was *Sensual Math* that most clearly marked Fulton's work as postmodern, somewhere between, as she has said, the experiments of Language poetry and more mainstream verse. Certainly Fulton's abstraction and focus on language is a postmodern tendency, but the foregrounding of language is a strain in American poetry that can be traced back through John Ashbery and others to the avant-garde element in Wallace Stevens. Fulton's various levels of diction may also recall Ashbery, but the attention paid by her poetry to issues of gender, social and cultural construction, contemporary literary theory, and the approach of the sciences to reality all stamp her poetry as unique. One of the most useful discussions of her technique is her own essay "Of Formal, Free, and Fractal Verse: Singing the Body Eclectic," where she draws analogies between an approach to free verse poetry and both quantum physics and the "fractal" theory of the mathematician Benoit Mandelbrot. Fractal theory discerns a formal yet varied structure within apparent chaos. Examples would be a head of broccoli, a coastline, or a ridged beach at low tide. For Fulton, fractal form affords a new means of engaging poetry not governed by regular rules of prosody: "The poem will contain an infinite regression of details, a nesting of pattern within pattern . . . digression, interruption, fragmentation and lack of continuity will be regarded as formal functions rather than lapses into formlessness" (*Feeling* 58). Along with "To Organize a Waterfall," this essay offers a key to understanding Fulton's poetic method.

CRITICAL RECEPTION

Fulton's poetry has been well received by reviewers and critics, with each volume being widely reviewed. Reviewers of *Dance Script with Electric Ballerina* praised her first book's "unpredictability," "tremendous energy and imagination," "striking combinations of imagery," and "interplay of divine mystery and scientific fact, of nature and art, of the primitive and the civilized" (Alice Fulton's home page). Reviewing *Palladium* in the *Georgia Review*, Peter Stitt commented that "Fulton's style has so much texture, thanks to her images and to her use of words, and that texture places a palpable surface on the abstract construct of the poem" (803). Other reviewers were more guarded, or even catty. Calvin Bedient, writing in *The Sewanee Review*, found the poems in *Palladium* "high-spirited, but a bit egoistic and noisy. . . . I look forward to her years of middle-age sag, when her energy will be easier to bear" (143). Lynn Keller addresses the tone of such reviews in her scholarly essay on Fulton in *American Literature*: "The disapproving tone of many reviews indicates how much the heterogeneity of her diction, the polysemy of her line breaks and phrasing, the multiple voices, the playful and digressive movement, and the showy mixture of high and low culture in the poetry all violate norms for contemporary lyric" (312). Keller's essay addresses all of these aspects of Fulton's poetry up through *Sensual Math*, along with the way in which the poems are influenced by "theories of contemporary science" (315). The other important scholarly piece on Fulton, Cristanne Miller's " 'The Erogenous Cusp,' or Intersections of Space and Gender in Alice Fulton's Poetry," appeared in the 1994 book *Feminist Measures: Soundings in Poetry and Theory*, a collection of writing on various contemporary women poets by different critics. Miller's essay deals with Fulton's first three collections and focuses on the poet's ungendered speakers, various registers of language, resistance to theories of essentialism regarding the theme of identity in women's poetry, and use of "the epistemological framework of quantum mechanics to address poststructuralist and feminist concerns" (317).

Powers of Congress and *Sensual Math* drew more extensive reviews. The poet Eavan Boland, reviewing *Powers of Congress* for *Partisan Review*, characterized Fulton as "an ambitious, powerful poet . . . a thematic gambler of the best sort" (317). Stephen Yenser's review of *Sensual Math* in the *Yale Review* typifies the sort of praise garnered by Fulton's important fourth volume: "Ebullient, breathtakingly fluent, prolific, yet somehow always exact, she writes poems that teem with exotic terms and recherche facts yet also accommodate the multifarious postmodern world" (161). Fulton has characterized her work as "an exploration of mind," a poetry concerned with both experience and ideas (Miller, "Interview" 606). Her work is engaging, intellectual, often whimsical or humorous, and consistently challenging and surprising. At the opening of a new century, Fulton has established herself as one of contemporary American poetry's major voices.

BIBLIOGRAPHY

Works by Alice Fulton

Anchors of Light. Oneonta, NY: Swamp Press, 1979.
Dance Script with Electric Ballerina. Philadelphia: University of Pennsylvania Press, 1983.
Palladium. Urbana: University of Illinois Press, 1986.
Powers of Congress. Boston: David R. Godine, 1990.
Sensual Math. New York: Norton, 1995.
Feeling as a Foreign Language. Minneapolis, MN: Graywolf Press, 1999. (prose)
Felt. New York: Norton, 2001.

Studies of Alice Fulton

Alice Fulton's home page: http://www-personal.umich.edu/~slippage/afhome.html.
Bedient, Calvin. "The Wild Bird of Creation." Review of *Palladium*, by Alice Fulton. *The Sewanee Review* 96 (1988): 137–49.
Boland, Eavan. "In Perspective." Review of *Powers of Congress*, by Alice Fulton. *Partisan Review* 60 (1993): 316–21.
Keller, Lynn. "The 'Then Some Inbetween': Alice Fulton's Feminist Experimentalism." *American Literature* 71 (1999): 311–40.
Marsh, Alec. "A Conversation with Alice Fulton." *TriQuarterly* 98 (1996–97): 22–39.
Miller, Cristanne. " 'The Erogenous Cusp': or Intersections of Science and Gender in Alice Fulton's Poetry." In *Feminist Measures: Soundings in Poetry and Theory*, edited by Lynn Keller and Cristanne Miller. Ann Arbor: University of Michigan Press, 1994. 317–43.
———. "An Interview with Alice Fulton." *Contemporary Literature* 38 (1997): 585–615.
Petoskey, Barbara A. "An Interview with Alice Fulton." *AWP Chronicle* 30.6 (1998): 24–29.
Snodgrass, W. D. Introduction. *Dance Script with Electric Ballerina*, by Alice Fulton. Philadelphia: University of Pennsylvania Press, 1983. xi-xv.

Stitt, Peter. "To Enlighten, To Embody." Review of *Palladium*, by Alice Fulton. *Georgia Review* 41 (1987): 800–03.

Yenser, Stephen. "Poetry in Review." Review of *Sensual Math*, by Alice Fulton. *Yale Review* 83.2 (1995): 147–67.

TESS GALLAGHER (1943–)

Robert Miltner

BIOGRAPHY

The eldest of five children, Tess Gallagher was born on July 21, 1943, in Port Angeles, Washington, on the Olympic Peninsula. Her father, Leslie Bond, was a logger, longshoreman, and fisherman and her mother, Georgia Bond, a teacher-turned-logger, thus Gallagher's writing explores the lives of the working class in the Pacific Northwest. Drawn initially to a career as a journalist, she was a reporter at age sixteen for the *Port Angeles Daily News*; while working her way through the University of Washington, she enrolled in the last writing class taught by Theodore Roethke, which initiated her interest in poetry. Gallagher received a BA in English in 1968 from the University of Washington, studied with David Wagoner and Mark Strand for her MA in English in 1970 from the same institution, attended the University of Iowa Writers Workshop, and graduated with an MFA from the University of Iowa in 1974. In May 1989, she was awarded an honorary doctorate in humane letters from Whitman College in Washington.

In 1963 Tess Gallagher married sculptor Lawrence Gallagher, though the marriage ended in 1968; in 1974 she married poet Michael Burkard, but the couple divorced in 1977. In the same year, Gallagher met short story writer and poet Raymond Carver, and they began living together in 1979. As a result of their partnership, Carver began to write more poetry, while Gallagher began to write more fiction, leading to her two short story collections, *The Lover of Horses and Other Stories* (1987) and *At the Owl Woman Saloon* (1997). In Carver, Gallagher found her ideal partner or "soul barnacle," for they taught together at Syracuse University and collaborated on a screenplay, *Dostoevsky* (1985); the couple married in 1988 just prior to Carver's untimely death from cancer.

During her career, Tess Gallagher taught creative writing at a variety of colleges: St. Lawrence University, New York, 1974–75; Kirkland College in New York, 1975–77; University of Montana, 1977–78; University of Arizona, 1979–80; Syracuse University, 1980–90, where she also coordinated the creative writing program. Since 1990 Gallagher has largely devoted herself to writing, lecturing, and giving readings, though she taught as writer-in-residence at Whitman College in 1997 and at the Stadler Poetry Center at Bucknell University, in Pennsylvania in 1998.

MAJOR WORKS AND THEMES

Poet, short story writer, screenplay writer, essayist, memoirist, translator, Tess Gallagher, a diverse and prolific writer, has produced some twenty books during her career. Her poetry is characterized by its use of journalistic and narrative objectivity balanced against both its musicality and its empathetic sense of astonishment. In her fiction, she lets the language develop appropriate both to character and situation, and her plots tend toward traditional narrative lines as she explores the everyday lives of average working people.

Gallagher's early poetry from the 1970s was concerned with many of the women's issues of the era, especially what it means to be a woman and a poet, typical of the "doubles" that populate *Instructions to the Double* (1976). DeVillo Sloan, writing in *Dictionary of Literary Biography*, divides the early poems in this book into two groups, the confessional narratives, such as "Breats" or "Black Money," and the poems that consider the relationship between language and identity, such as "Beginning to Say No" or "When You Speak to Me" in which Gallagher considers the fever that is "inside the words we say" (25).

In the first part of *Under Stars* (1978), Gallagher writes seventeen poems in response to her visit to the Irish Republic and Northern Ireland while on a grant from the National Endowment for the Arts; these poems reflect the effects of violence, as in "Disappearances in the Guarded Sector" and in "The Ballad of Ballymote," the latter telling the story of a woman whose father was shot while eating dinner; when the poet asks the woman what she is cooking, she hauntingly replies, "Cabbage and bones." The eleven poems in the second half of the book explore Gallagher's family history. For example, in "3 A.M. Kitchen: My Father Talking," she captures the flat working class cadence of her father, told in his voice, and in "My Mother Remembers that She Was Beautiful," Gallagher contemplates the changing relations of mothers and daughters as they age.

Drawing from her Pacific Northwest background, Gallagher presents blue-collar figures with depth and dignity while acknowledging the frustrations of the working-to-keep-even lifestyle. The Olympic Peninsula, represented as lush and giving, provides the setting for many of Gallagher's poems in *Willingly* (1984), such as "Boat Ride," a moving elegy for her father. In an interview with Nicholas O'Connell, Gallagher discussed the "spiritual nearness" one finds on the Olympic Peninsula, which tells visitors to slow down and pay attention. In "Woodcutting on Lost Mountain," Gallagher narrates a day spent cutting firewood with her brother and her niece, "a logger's daughter, just like me," listening to his talk about how the boom days of logging are done; cut against this narrative, however, is her refrain about how the next day a log pile will collapse on him and he will barely escape with his life.

In order to write the poems included in *Moon Crossing Bridge* (1992), poems that grieve over the death of partner and husband Raymond Carver, Gallagher told Jay Woodruff that it was almost as if she "had to reform language to be able to say the kinds of things I had to say in that book of mourning" (63), thus continuing the focus on language evident in *Instructions to the Double*. In her essay "The Poem as a Reservoir for Grief," she states that a poem allows a writer to have "strictly private access" to "one's particular grief and thereby transform that grief" (104), which she accomplishes in "Red Poppy," "Black Pudding," and others in the collection.

Her more recent work, the new poems published in England in *My Black Horse: New and Selected Poems* (1995), demonstrates a sense of balance, as in the silver and gold bracelets in "Two Bracelets," or the sense, expressed in "Don't Wipe Your Madness Off Me," of openness, of the "other miracle" of being "a woman who doesn't love sorrow." Though many of her early poems tended toward the lyric mode, her poetry has become consistently more narrative; what has evolved is Gallagher's use of what, in "Again: Some Thoughts on the Narrative Impulse in Contemporary Poetry," she calls the lyric-narrative impulse, wherein lyric poems have become more dependent on narrative, anecdotal strategies, merging both the "poetic *persona* and the poet's own autobiography" into a concurrence of "an interior (emotional progression) and an exterior (plot) narrative" in which the poet's imagination becomes the hero of the poem (71, 74). In *Portable Kisses* (1978), which began as limited edition chapbook in 1978, expanding to a full-length collection in the 1990s, Gallagher makes the kisses the heroes of each incidental poem, evident in such titles as "Stubborn Kiss," and "The Kiss Gets a New Bonnet." Ron McFarland, writing in *Dictionary of Literary Biography*, calls the poems in this collection "delightfully capricious and upbeat" (15).

Gallagher's extended development of the narrative may be partly due to her having published two critically praised books of short stories, *The Lover of Horses* and *At the Owl Woman Saloon*. Many of the stories in *The Lover of Horses* are tales of flawed or failed marriages, while the stories in *At the Owl Woman Saloon* detail the rootlessness of working-class characters in Pacific Northwest small towns. Offering a new direction for her narrative talent, Gallagher's fiction has been praised by John Clute in *Times Literary Supplement* for her tight, revelatory endings in which the final words of each story "transform mute lives into significance, recoup solitary existences" (803).

CRITICAL RECEPTION

Tess Gallagher's work has earned her numerous awards and recognitions, including fellowships from the National Endowment for the Arts in 1977 for poetry and in 1987 for fiction, a Guggenheim Fellowship in 1979, and a Lyndhurst Foundation Fellowship in 1994. Her first full-length book of poetry, *Instructions to the Double*, won the Elliston Award for the best book published by a small press in 1976; *Moon Crossing Bridge* was selected for the Notable Books list by the American Library Association in 1993, and *At the Owl Woman Saloon* appeared on the *New York Times* Notable Books list in 1997.

De Villo Sloan calls Gallagher's *Instructions to the Double* her "most influential collection" (3) while praising her poems for their "consistent emphasis on morality" (4). Peter Stitt, in *Georgia Review*, sees Gallagher as "a sophisticated stylist, able to use rhetorical devices as a poem demands" (628). In a review of *Willingly* for the *New York Times Book Review*, William Logan notes Gallagher's growing use of the lyric-narrative, observing how "her poems have become minor fictions, with beginnings, middles, and ends" (9). Writing in *Parnassus*, Vicki Karp praises Gallagher's poetry for the way in which it "moves inch by inch, stopping all the time in order to allow an image or the lush cadence of a word to resonate" (415). The abstract nature of words, enriched by the concrete nature of the image, commingle in Gallagher's poetry, as they do in the best poetry, yet it is the abstract, observes Bin Ramke in *The Bloomsbury Review*, "which allows her to write her poems, allows her to escape the pain of her own past and enter the greater pain of the present tense of art" (28). In her emotional and philosophical poems, Tess Gallagher explores relationships between self and family, grief and gift, endowing the lives of working class people from rural America with a sense of justice, hope, and importance.

BIBLIOGRAPHY

Works by Tess Gallagher

Stepping Outside. Lisbon, IA: Penumbra, 1974.

Instructions to the Double. Port Townsend, WA: Graywolf, 1976.

On Your Own. Port Townsend, WA: Graywolf, 1978.

Portable Kisses. Seattle, WA: Sea Pen, 1978; enlarged editions, Santa Barbara, CA: Capra Press, 1992 1994; Newcastle upon Tyne, UK: Bloodaxe, 1996.

Under Stars. Port Townsend, WA: Graywolf, 1978.

Willingly. Port Townsend, WA: Graywolf, 1984.

Dostoevsky: A Screenplay. With Raymond Carver. Santa Barbara, CA: Capra Press, 1985.

A Concert of Tenses: Essays on Poetry. Ann Arbor: University of Michigan Press, 1986.

Amplitude: New and Selected Poems. St. Paul, MN: Graywolf, 1987.

The Lover of Horses and Other Stories. St. Paul, MN: Graywolf, 1987. (short stories)

Carver Country. With Bob Adelman. New York: Scribners, 1990; London: Pan, 1991.

Moon Crossing Bridge. St. Paul, MN: Graywolf, 1992.

Owl-Spirit Dwelling: A Poem. Illustrated by Marilyn Maricle. Portland, OR: Task House, 1993.

The Valentine Elegies. Drawings by Carl Darn. Fairfax, CA: Jungle Garden, 1993.

My Black Horse: New and Selected Poems. Newcastle upon Tyne, UK: Bloodaxe, 1995.

At the Owl Woman Saloon. New York: Scribners, 1997. (short stories)

She Who Is Untouched by Fire. Walla Walla, WA: Whitman College Book Arts Press, 1997.

Soul Barnacles. Ann Arbor: University of Michigan Press, 2000. (memoir)

Studies of Tess Gallagher

Bond, Georgia. "The Pure Place." In *Sleeping with One Eye Open: Women Writers and the Art of Survival*, edited by Marilyn Kallet and Judith Ortiz Cofer. Athens: University of Georgia Press, 1999. 167–83.

Clute, John. "Survivor's Stories." *Times Literary Supplement*, 21–27 July 1989, 803.

Karp, Vicki. "Two Poets: Several Worlds Apiece." *Parnassus* 12–13.2,1 (1985): 407–21.

Logan, William. "Poets Elegant, Familiar, Challenging." *New York Times Book Review*, 26 Aug. 1984, 13–14.

McFarland, Ronald E. *Tess Gallagher*. Boise, ID: Boise State University, 1995.

———. "Tess Gallagher." *Dictionary of Literary Biography: Twentieth-Century American Western Writers*. Farmington Hills, MI: Gale, 1999.

Moffett, Penelope. "An Interview with Tess Gallagher." *Poets & Writers Magazine* 16 (1988): 19–22.

O'Connell, Nicholas. "Tess Gallagher." In *At the Field's End: Interviews with 20 Pacific Northwest Writers*. Seattle: Madrona, 1987. 154–77.

Ramke, Bin. "The Confident Smile of the Living." *The Bloomsbury Review* 10.1 (1990): 7, 28.

Sloan, De Villo. "Tess Gallagher." *Dictionary of Literary Biography American Poets since WWII*. Farmington Hills, MI: Gale, 1992.

Stitt, Peter. "Objective Subjectivities." *Georgia Review* 38.3 (1984): 628–38.

Woodruff, Jay, ed. "Tess Gallagher." *A Piece of Work: Five Writers Discuss Their Revisions*. Iowa City: University of Iowa Press, 1993. 53–98.

AMY GERSTLER (1956–)

Amy Moorman Robbins

BIOGRAPHY

A California native, Amy Gerstler, born in San Diego, California, in 1956, attended Pitzer College in Claremont, where she studied acting and psychology. Her first book of poetry, *Yonder*, was published by Little Caesar Press in Los Angeles in 1981. Over the next several years, she followed this volume with several more collections of poetry, all of which were published by small California presses and received little or no critical attention. With the appearance of *The True Bride* (1986), Gerstler began to attract more notice from critics and received several favorable reviews for the collection. Her subsequent book, *Bitter Angel* (1990), was widely reviewed and won the National Book Critics Circle Award for poetry in 1991. Gerstler's *Crown of Weeds*, published by the Penguin Poets series in 1997, garnered the California Book Award in 1998. Her poetry has been anthologized in *Best American Poetry 1988*, *1990*, and *1992*, and in the Norton Anthology series' *Postmodern American Poetry* (1994), the most widely consulted anthology on the genre.

An art critic and journalist as well as a poet, Gerstler has contributed monthly reviews to *Artforum* magazine and has collaborated with visual artists Megan Williams and Gail Swanlund, as well as with her sister, choreographer Tina Gerstler. Also a writer of fiction, Gerstler won second prize in *Mademoiselle* magazine's fiction contest in 1987. In 1989 she collaborated with visual artist Alexis Smith on an art installation and accompanying artists' book, both entitled *Past Lives*. The installation, composed of a collection of schoolroom chairs from the 1950s surrounded by phrases and fragments of biographies displayed on the walls, first opened at the Santa Monica Museum of Art. In December 1990, it traveled to the Josh Baer Gallery in New York where it received excellent reviews, one critic calling it "an uncommonly engaging installation . . . a wonderful three-dimensional poem about . . . the enigma of destiny" (Johnson 133).

Gerstler has served as co-editor of the Los Angeles-based literary magazine *SNAP* and has taught English and Creative Writing at Otis Art Institute, University of California, Los Angeles extension, and the University of California, Irvine. She currently teaches in the graduate writing program at Antioch University, Los Angeles, and serves as a graduate adviser at Art Center College of Design in Pasadena. Her most recent book of poetry, *Medicine*, was published by the Penguin Poets series in 2000.

MAJOR WORKS AND THEMES

On the book jacket of *Bitter Angel*, poet Jorie Graham calls Amy Gerstler "a quintessentially postmodern poet," and critics frequently discuss Gerstler as a "quintessentially Los Angeles poet" as well (Goldstein 725). In locating Gerstler in postmodernism, Laurence Goldstein and other critics have cited Gerstler's use of the prose poem, the abundance of surreal imagery in her poetry, her compression of language (inviting frequent comparison with Emily Dickinson), and her work involving comic re-vision of popular American culture. "Della's Modesty" exemplifies her treatment of American culture (*Bitter Angel* 43–47). In this poem, Gerstler culls quotes from several of Erle Stanley Gardner's Perry Mason novels, juxtaposing fragments of Della Street's speech against quotes from Havelock Ellis's *Psychology of Sex* and pieces of other famous writings on the subject of human behavior and sexuality. With the infusion of her own poetry, the result is a witty collage speaking to the construction and function of female modesty in popular American ideology. Other examples of Gerstler's fresh approach to cultural icons include her send-up of Nancy Drew in "An Unexpected Adventure" (*Bitter Angel* 42) and, in the same volume, her allusion to the classical figure of the siren, a creature with "teeth in places you'd never suspect" (3). In each of these cases, a distinctly feminist wit informs the poetry, though "feminism" is not a word that comes up in Gerstler criticism.

Gerstler employs the device of dramatic voice in much of her work, which allows the poet to distance her authorial self from the poetry and thereby avoid what has become—in postmodern times—the perceived trap of the lyric "I." According to Molly Bendall, "Gerstler can easily play the role of confessor or of someone recounting his/her testimonies, and . . . she can play the guru, the spiritual advisor, the (postmodern) analyst" (500), among other roles. Through these voices, Gerstler conveys her own or the characters' surreal, often comic visions of everyday life, while simultaneously inviting the reader to deconstruct the proffered personae. Commenting on Gerstler's fusion of compressed language with dramatic persona in "Dear Boy George" (*The True Bride* 63), a poem in the form of a young fan's letter to the pop icon, critic Sven Birkerts terms the effect "strokes on the graph of the interior—they are the believable transcriptions of its hectic reality" (177). Thus, the scattered consciousness of the letter-writer becomes the subject of the poem, compelling speculation about the social context in which that consciousness resides.

Another example of Gerstler's use of dramatic voice appears in her well-known "The True Bride"(*The True Bride* 45–46). In this prose poem, the male speaker reveals that he feels a strong attraction toward sick or invalid women and proceeds to lovingly describe the impaired physical condition of Elaine, his primary fetish-object. Later in the poem, the speaker details his fantasy of "an army of true brides like her, hobbling women" (46), and the vivid Dali-esque imagery of frail and stumbling women crossing a desert to lure men is both disturbing and weirdly humorous. Here, as in "Dear Boy George," the subject of the poem is the consciousness—in this case compellingly perverse—of the speaker which, coupled with the intense visual imagery, aptly demonstrates Birkerts's point that Gerstler's work often blends "humor and unease" (178).

In his introduction to *The True Bride*, Tom Clark links Gerstler's artistic vision to John Keats's definition of negative capability, pointing out that the poet aims "to create a white and blameless paradise wherein our visions, terrors and desires merge together in the purity of our imagining them"(i). Yet, it is important to note that all terrors and desires are not equal in Gerstler's work. Frequent themes include preoccupation with death and the afterlife ("Since You've Been Gone," "Repose," "This Explains Everything," and "Loomings" from *True Bride*); women's sexual and life experience ("Christine," "Drifter," "Night Sweats," and "I Fall to Pieces" from *True Bride*); and, later in her work, grief over the loss of a loved one ("Recipe for Resurrection," "To My Brother," "Miasma," and "Colorlessness" from *Crown of Weeds*). However, Gerstler's trademark of surprising metaphors and acute comedic vision temper the genuine pathos of many of these poems; in fact, these various elements work in delicate balance to form distinctly original ruminations on what would otherwise be commonplace subject matter. In the words of Goldstein, Gerstler "internalizes the abundance and converts it to autonomous images fit for enumeration as an imaginary city of words," succeeding ultimately in a "ceaseless reinvention of the imaginary" (728, 729). It seems fair to say that Amy Gerstler's poetry succeeds both as the work of a technically gifted, postmodern "poet's poet" and also as the product of a poet deeply interested in and intrigued by the human condition.

CRITICAL RECEPTION

Gerstler's earliest critics placed her firmly in postmodernism, and to date, that judgment remains uncontested. In 1989 Birkerts used *The True Bride* to re-examine the definition of "prose poetry," pointing out that Gerstler is comfortable enough with both lineated and prose forms to "make us think of these forms in terms of option rather than stricture" (178). Gerstler's formal skills have been highly praised, with Goldstein writing that "the poems [of *Bitter Angel*] are disciplined by an extraordinary knowledge of lyric and narrative strategies" (730) and Thomas Disch terming the language of *Crown of Weeds* "concise" and "zesty," "after the fashion of May Swenson," adding that her metaphors "zip by like freeway traffic" (502). David Shapiro writes in *American Poetry Review* that he is impressed by Gerstler's "poetry of naked devices" (42), calling her prose poems "humorous . . . immediate and imagistic" (43).

However, feminist criticism of Amy Gerstler remains noticeably absent, and thematic or content-oriented discussions tend to focus on Gerstler's attention to perceived universalisms such as "savage pursuit of redemption through suffering," "man's inhumanity to man," and "the difficulty of love" (Review of *Nerve Storm* 69; Shapiro 43). Here it becomes evident that her poetry deserves further attention, as much work remains to be done regarding Gerstler's portrayals of women (especially those offered through the eyes of often seemingly-obsessive male speakers); her treatment of homophobia ("Molly" in *The True Bride*); her images of children and childhood sexuality ("Elementary School," "Impressions of the Midwest," and "Alice and Lewis" from *The True Bride*); and the pervasive themes of illness and disease, among others.

Finally, whereas Birkerts, Goldstein, and others have praised Gerstler for her wit and originality, others have termed her poetry at times "formulaic and contrived" (Review of *Nerve Storm* 69) or "glib, 'breezy' " (Muratori 152). However, some of this unfavorable critique may have more to do with general discomfort with post-modern irreverence, as the critic who describes parts of *Nerve Storm* as "formulaic" laments at the end of the same review that Gerstler "frequently leav[es] readers uncertain of the poet's intentions" (Review of *Nerve Storm* 69). In the current moment, this assessment might be taken as positive rather than negative criticism.

BIBLIOGRAPHY

Works by Amy Gerstler

Yonder. Los Angeles: Little Caesar Press, 1981.
Christy's Alpine Inn. Los Angeles: Sherwood Press, 1982.
Early Heaven. San Francisco: Ouija Madness Press, 1984.
Martine's Mouth. Los Angeles: Illuminati, 1985.
The True Bride. Santa Monica, CA: Lapis Press, 1986.
Primitive Man. New York: Hanuman Books, 1987.
Past Lives. With Alexis Smith. Santa Monica, CA: Santa Monica Museum of Art, 1989.
Bitter Angel. San Francisco: North Point Press, 1990.
January. Berkeley, CA: Moe's Books, 1991. (broadside)
Nerve Storm. New York: Penguin, 1993.
Crown of Weeds. New York: Penguin, 1997.
Georganne Deen. With Michael Duncan. Santa Monica, CA: Smart Art Press, 1997.
Medicine. New York: Penguin, 2000.

Studies of Amy Gerstler

Bendall, Molly. Review of *Crown of Weeds*, by Amy Gerstler. *Antioch Review* 55 (1997): 501.
Birkerts, Sven. "Prose [Poetry]." *Parnassus* 15 (1989): 163–84.
Clark, Tom. Introduction. *The True Bride*. Santa Monica, CA: Lapis Press, 1986.
Disch, Thomas M. "Poetry Roundup." *Hudson Review* 50 (1997): 499–507.
Goldstein, Laurence. "Looking for Authenticity in Los Angeles." *Michigan Quarterly Review* 30 (1991): 717–31.
Gorham, Sarah. "Drive for Ascension." *American Book Review* (Jan.-Mar. 1991): 27–29.
Johnson, Ken. Review of *Past Lives*, by Amy Gerstler. *Art in America* (March 1991): 133.
Larson, Kay. "Dying Light." Review of *Past Lives*, by Amy Gerstler. *New York Magazine*, 7 Jan. 1991, 50–51.
Lynch, Doris. Review of *Nerve Storm*, by Amy Gerstler. *Library Journal*, 15 Sept. 1993, 80.
Muratori, Fred. "Ambiguity Isn't What It Used to Be—Or Is It?" *Georgia Review* 52 (1998): 142–60.
Review of *Bitter Angel*, by Amy Gerstler. *Publishers Weekly*, 25 Dec. 1989, 54–55.
Review of *Bitter Angel*, by Amy Gerstler. *Voice Literary Supplement* 82 (1990): 7–8.
Review of *Nerve Storm*, by Amy Gerstler. *Publishers Weekly*, 18 Oct. 1993, 69.
Review of *Past Lives*, by Amy Gerstler. *Arts Magazine* (March 1991): 100.
Shapiro, David. Review of *Bitter Angel*, by Amy Gerstler. *American Poetry Review* 20 (1991): 42–44.

NIKKI GIOVANNI (1943–)

J. Elizabeth Clark

BIOGRAPHY

Yolande Cornelia Giovanni, Jr., was born on June 7, 1943, in Knoxville, Tennessee, to Yolande and Jones "Gus" Giovanni. The family moved to Cincinnati, Ohio, where Giovanni attended elementary and middle school. However, her roots remained in Knoxville. She returned to the South to live with her maternal grandparents, Emma Louvenia and John Brown Watson and to attend Austin High School in Knoxville. During high school, Giovanni's grandparents expected her to participate in community, activist, and religious organizations as part of her civic education.

Family and connections to kin are central issues in Giovanni's writing. Much of her success in later life stems from the support she received at home from her parents and grandparents. The Watson family was highly respected in Knoxville. Giovanni's grandfather, John Watson, was a graduate of Fisk University who taught Latin at Austin High School. Both he and his wife were active in the church and community. His second wife, Louvenia, worked for the National Association for the Advancement of Colored People, the Colored Women's Federated Club, and the church. Importantly, she set a clear example for the young Giovanni about women's and individuals' rights.

In 1960 Giovanni followed the family tradition by attending college. Education was a high priority for the Giovanni/Watsons. Both her mother and her father attended Knoxville College. Louvenia and John encouraged Giovanni to apply for early entrance to Fisk University in Nashville, Tennessee. With their help and that of two influential teachers, Giovanni entered college one year early, in 1960. However, she was "dismissed" in 1961 after her first term because she failed to obtain the dean's permission to visit her grandparents for Thanksgiving.

Giovanni believed she had made the right decision to visit her grandparents; her grandfather died in April 1962. After his death, she returned to Cincinnati, working at Walgreen's and taking classes at the University of Cincinnati. During this time, she was acutely aware of the struggle for civil rights unfolding around her. In 1964 she re-entered Fisk, working on the literary magazine and re-establishing the Student Nonviolent Coordinating Committee (SNCC) Chapter at Fisk. She graduated in 1967 with honors in history and organized the first Cincinnati Black Arts Festival in the same year.

Following in her mother's footsteps, Giovanni attended the University of Pennsylvania's School of Social Work with a Ford Foundation Fellowship for one semester but quickly realized that she wanted to go in another direction. After her success with the Black Arts Festival, she realized that she could best explore and express her politics and the articulation of a strong black, female identity through writing. Giovanni followed this initial impulse, to link literature and politics, throughout her career. At the festival, she had her first contact with the Black Arts movement, led by Amiri Baraka (then LeRoi Jones). While she became involved on a personal level with many of the key participants in this movement, and while her work mirrored many of the same goals—radically political poems that promoted consciousness about black rights, social equality, and black identity—she maintained her distance from the group as a whole because of its patriarchal structure.

In 1968 she attended the funeral of Martin Luther King, Jr., and then moved to New York City to study writing at Columbia University's School of Fine Arts. Her writing and the mostly white critics and students at Columbia were not an easy match for her. Giovanni left the program angry with the ignorant reactions to her work; subsequently, she published the enormously successful *Black Feeling, Black Talk* (1968) and established her literary career independent of a formal degree. *Black Judgement* (1968) and *Re:Creation* (1970) quickly followed.

Giovanni gave birth to her son, Thomas Watson Giovanni on August 31, 1969, an event that widened the focus of Giovanni's work to include writing for children. During the 1970s, Giovanni was active publishing poetry; her first book of autobiographical essays, *Gemini* (1971); an anthology, and books for children. In 1970 she established NikTom, Ltd., a communications company through which she also released several records, including the critically acclaimed 1971, *Truth Is on Its Way, The Way I Feel* (1975), *Legacies* (1976), and *The Reason I Like Chocolate* (1976). A fervent public speaker, she regularly traveled to give readings and lectures, including a 1972 reading at Lincoln Center and a 1973 reading at New York's Philharmonic Hall.

In 1978 she published the popular *Cotton Candy on a Rainy Day*. In the same year, after her father suffered a stroke, she moved home until 1987 to help, bearing most of the household and financial responsibilities. In 1983 she published *Those Who Ride the Night Winds*. The mid-1980s, while Giovanni worked as a visiting professor of English at Ohio State University, were filled with controversy. TransAfrica, a group started by activist Randall Robinson in 1977 to raise awareness about global policies affecting countries like South Africa, blacklisted Giovanni because of her opposition to the boycott of South Africa, and she received many death and bomb threats. Characteristically, Giovanni responded by actively publishing and teaching.

From 1985–87 she taught at the College of Mount Saint Joseph on-the-Ohio. Since 1987 Giovanni has lived in Virginia, working at Virginia Polytechnic Institute and State University where she is a Distinguished Professor. The late 1980s and 1990s saw the publication of several more books, including three books of poetry, two books of essays, three anthologies, a book of poems for children, and four children's books.

Her most recent works include *Love Poems* (1997) and *Blues: For All the Changes* (1999).

Giovanni's work has been widely acclaimed. Considered one of the most prominent African American poets, her work has traveled extensively to the people through her books of poetry and widely anthologized poems. In 1987 the Public Broadcasting System produced a special about Giovanni and her work entitled *Spirit to Spirit.* In addition to her popularity, Giovanni has received many awards for her work, including grants from the Ford Foundation (1967); the National Foundation of the Arts (1968); Harlem Council of the Arts (1969); a highest achievement award from *Mademoiselle* for *Truth Is on Its Way* (1971); a National Association of Radio and Television Announcers Award for Best Spoken Word Album for *Truth Is on Its Way* (1972); an American Library Association Award for *My House* (1973). Giovanni holds honorary doctorates from Wilberforce University (1974), Ripon University (1976), University of Maryland (1977), Smith College (1978), College of Mount St. Joseph (1985), Fisk University (1988), Indiana University (1989), and Otterbein College (1992). She has also won Woman of the Year Award from the Cincinnati YMCA (1983), Outstanding Woman of Tennessee Award (1985), entry into the Ohio Women's Hall of Fame (1985), the Post-Corbett Award (1986), and the Ohioana Library Award for *Sacred Cows . . . and Other Edibles* (1988).

MAJOR WORKS AND THEMES

In *Sacred Cows . . . and Other Edibles* (1988), Giovanni muses about the inspiration and impetus to write. Often accused by critics of writing angry poetry, she asserts in *Cows* that rage fuels good writing: "Rage is to writers what water is to fish. A laid-back writer is like an orgasmic prostitute—an anomaly—something that doesn't quite fit" (31). Giovanni's early work rages in response to a rising black, revolutionary consciousness in the United States. Following in the tradition of the Black Arts movement (but working independently of its patriarchal leadership) and inspired by the rise of the Black Panthers and the assassination of Martin Luther King, Jr., her first three collections of poems, *Black Feeling, Black Talk, Black Judgement*, and *Re:Creation*, were revolutionary, militant, unyielding, and accusatory. Her poems sought to portray the black experience against the background of white complacency. In *Black Judgement*'s "Nikka Rosa," she writes of whites that "they never understand Black love is Black wealth" (10). As Virginia Fowler comments in her biography, *Nikki Giovanni*, the poet "lays claim to her exclusive right to determine the meaning of her life and inscribes the centrality of family and love in that life," defying white critics who might portray her childhood and life as hard, unhappy, and loveless (1).

Giovanni's thematic concerns become more introspective, although the earlier volumes of poetry have their own reflective, personal poems, in the 1970s with the birth of her son. *Spin a Soft Black Song* (1971), *Ego-Tripping* (1973), and *Vacation Time* (1980) are collections of poems for children. *My House* (1972) and *The Women and the Men* (1975) present personal poems revolving around matters of family. At the same time, however, Giovanni continued to politicize the issue of gender, first presented in *Re:Creation*, a compelling theme present in all of her poetry. Additionally, the poems of the 1970s were marked by loneliness, reflections on a revolution and its outcomes, and unrealized dreams. *Those Who Ride the Night Winds*, with dedications to black American heroes and heroines, marked a return to overtly political poems and a new experimentation with a lineless form that uses ellipses to separate groups of words.

In addition to poetry, Giovanni has also written several books of autobiographical essays. In each, Giovanni has at stake control regarding interpretation of her work; she does not want her work co-opted and misinterpreted by racial or gendered assumptions. *Gemini*, *Sacred Cows . . . and Other Edibles*, and *Racism 101* (1994), lifecraft books, reveal Giovanni's motivations and aesthetics for writing in the context of her life's story. In *Racism 101*, Giovanni explains her theory of poetry, something that has guided all of her work: "Poetry, to me, is the association of disassociated ideas. I like clear simple images, clear simple metaphors, making clear simple statements about not-so-clear, not-so-simple human beings" (175).

Giovanni's work brings a new critical consciousness about black female identity into all of her poems. In all of her work, she challenges the racial and gender status quo, providing a poetry guided by a fervent political aesthetic. In *The Women and the Men*, Giovanni writes, "i used to dream radical dreams" ("Revolutionary Dreams" 11). Through her poetry, Giovanni still dreams radical dreams of a society more equal for all; Giovanni opens the door to dialogue about race and gender through her critical, political poetry.

CRITICAL RECEPTION

Like any prominent poet, Nikki Giovanni has had her supporters and her detractors. As noted earlier, she left Columbia University because she felt that the white professors and peers were unable to understand her work, and indeed, misinterpretations based on both race and gender have guided some of the critical responses to Giovanni's work. For example, Giovanni's biographer, Virginia Fowler, notes that Kalamu Ya Salaam, critic for *Black World*, wrote in response to the themes of loneliness and single motherhood in *My House*: "I betcha Nikki wanted to be married" (15). Such strange responses are far from unusual; in addition to sexist male commentary, Giovanni has faced derisive commentary based on her exploration of black identity, being accused of using the people in her populist zeal (Fowler *Nikki Giovanni* 15). In addition to criticism unequal to the task of considering Giovanni fully as a black female poet, with attention to the dually important aspects of her subject position, Giovanni has been at the center of the debate between politics and aesthetics in poetry. At times dismissed for her politics, she is revered by other reviewers for the very same political aesthetic.

Other critical commentary focuses on Giovanni's place in literary history as a prominent black poet. Martha Cook's "Nikki Giovanni: Place and Sense of Place in Her Poetry" and Margaret B. McDowell's "Groundwork for a More Comprehensive Criticism of Nikki Giovanni" typify this critical approach. Cook writes of Giovanni's poems that "they develop universal themes, such as coming to terms with the past and with the future. . . . These themes mark her work as a contribution to the canon not just of Southern poetry, of black poetry, of feminist poetry, but also of contemporary American poetry" (299). The most useful biographical literary study comes from Fowler, with whom Giovanni worked closely in the production of the book *Nikki Giovanni* (1992) and *Conversations with Nikki Giovanni* (1992).

While critical commentary is difficult to summarize because of the polarized reactions to Giovanni's work, one of the most interesting published responses to her work comes from Susan M. Kochman in the article "What Happens When a High School Censors: A Teacher Details Her Year-Long Censorship Battle Involving a Poem by Nikki Giovanni." Kochman chronicles her use of "Woman Poem" in a high school English class. One day she was summoned to the principal's office where she met with the assistant superintendent, the supervisor of secondary education, the principal, the English department chair, and another colleague using the same textbook. The administration deemed the 1994 *Literature and Society* text "vulgar" because of Giovanni's poem. Kochman and her colleague were instructed to "return to [their] classes to take the students' books" (58). During the year-long battle that ensued, Kochman was unable to convince the school that the work was important and legitimate for student study.

Giovanni found the political nature of this controversy over her useful. Giovanni wrote letters and supported Kochman in her battle against the school district. In a letter to Kochman, Giovanni observed that the struggle between Kochman and her colleague and the school district was one that harkened back to ancient Greece: the fear of the powerful when teachers expose young minds to radical knowledge (62).

BIBLIOGRAPHY

Works by Nikki Giovanni

Black Feeling, Black Talk. Privately printed, 1968.

Black Judgement. Privately printed, 1968.

Black Feeling, Black Talk/Black Judgement. New York: Morrow, 1970.

Night Comes Softly: Anthology of Black Female Voices. Privately printed, 1970.

Re:Creation. Detroit, MI: Broadside Press, 1970.

Gemini: An Extended Autobiographical Statement on My First Twenty-Five Years of Being a Black Poet. New York: Bobbs-Merrill, 1971.

Spin a Soft Black Song. New York: Hill and Wang, 1971.

Truth Is on Its Way. With the New York Community Choir. Benny Diggs, director. Right On Records, 1971.

My House. New York: Morrow, 1972.

A Dialogue: James Baldwin and Nikki Giovanni. New York: J. B. Lippincott, 1973.

Ego-Tripping and Other Poems for Young People. New York: Lawrence Hill, 1973.

Like a Ripple on a Pond. With The New York Community Choir. Benny Diggs, director. Niktom Records. Distributed by Atlantic Recording Corporation, 1973.

A Poetic Equation: Conversations between Nikki Giovanni and Margaret Walker. Washington, D.C.: Howard University Press, 1974.

The Way I Feel. With music composed by Arif Mardin. Niktom Records. Distributed by Atlantic Recording Corporation, 1975.

The Women and the Men. New York: Morrow, 1975.

Legacies. Folkways Records FL 9798, 1976.

The Reason I Like Chocolate. Folkways Records FC 7775, 1976.

Cotton Candy on a Rainy Day. New York: Morrow, 1978.

Cotton Candy on a Rainy Day. Folkways Records FL 9756, 1978.

Vacation Time: Poems for Children. New York: Morrow, 1980.

A Poetic Equation: Conversations between Nikki Giovanni and Margaret Walker. Washington, D.C.: Howard University Press, 1983.

Those Who Ride the Night Winds. New York: Morrow, 1983.

Spin a Soft Black Song. New York: Hill and Wang, 1985.

Sacred Cows . . . and Other Edibles. New York: Morrow, 1988.
Appalachian Elders: A Warm Hearth Sampler. Blacksburg, VA: Pocahontas Press, 1991.
Grandmothers: A Multicultural Anthology of Poems, Reminiscences, and Short Stories about the Keepers of Our Traditions. New York: Henry Holt, 1994.
Knoxville, Tennessee. New York: Scholastic Books, 1994.
Racism 101. New York: Morrow, 1994.
The Genie in the Jar. New York: Henry Holt, 1996.
Selected Poems of Nikki Giovanni. New York: William Morrow, 1996.
Shimmy Shimmy Shimmy Like My Sister Kate. New York: Henry Holt, 1996.
The Sun Is So Quiet. New York: Henry Holt, 1996.
Love Poems. New York: William Morrow, 1997.
Blues: For All the Changes. New York: William Morrow, 1999.
Grandfathers: Reminiscences, Poems, Recipes, and Photos of the Keepers of Our Tradition. New York: Henry Holt, 1999.

Studies of Nikki Giovanni

Boldridge, Effie J. "Windmills or Giants? The Quixotic Motif and Vision in the Poetry of Nikki Giovanni." *Griot* 14.1 (1995): 18–25.
Brooks, A. Russell. "Power and Morality as Imperatives for Nikki Giovanni and James Baldwin: A View of a Dialogue." In *James Baldwin: A Critical Evaluation*, edited by Therman B. O'Daniel. Washington, D.C: Howard University Press, 1977: 205–09
Cook, Martha. "Nikki Giovanni: Place and Sense of Place in Her Poetry." In *Southern Women Writers: The New Generation*, edited by Tonette Bond Inge. Tuscaloosa: University of Alabama Press, 1990: 279–300.
Cook, William W. "The Black Arts Poets." *The Columbia History of American Poetry*, edited by Jay Parini and Brett Millier. New York: Columbia University Press, 1993: 674–706.
Elder, Arlene. "A MELUS Interview: Nikki Giovanni." *MELUS* 9.3 (1982): 61–75.
Fowler, Virginia C. *Nikki Giovanni*. New York: Twayne, 1992.
———, ed. *Conversations with Nikki Giovanni*. Jackson: University Press of Mississippi, 1992.
Giddings, Paula. "Nikki Giovanni: Taking a Chance on Feeling." In *Black Women Writers (1950–1980): A Critical Evaluation*, edited by Mari Evans. Garden City, NY: Anchor-Doubleday, 1984. 211–17.
Harris, William J. "Sweet Soft Essence of Possibility: The Poetry of Nikki Giovanni." In *Black Women Writers (1950–1980): A Critical Evaluation*, edited by Mari Evans. Garden City, NY: Doubleday, 1984. 218–28.
Kochman, Susan M. "What Happens When a High School Censors: A Teacher Details Her Year-Long Censorship Battle Involving a Poem by Nikki Giovanni." *English Journal* 86.2 (1997): 58–62.
McDowell, Margaret B. "Groundwork for a More Comprehensive Criticism of Nikki Giovanni." In *Belief vs. Theory in Black American Literary Criticism*, edited by Joe Weixlmann and Chester J. Fontenot. Greenwood, FL: Penkevill, 1986. 135–60.
Reid, Calvin. "Nikki Giovanni: Three Decades on the Edge." *Publishers Weekly*, 28 June 1999, 46–47.
Spirit to Spirit. Directed by Mirra Banks. Produced by Perrin Ireland. PBS Television, 1987. Videocassette.
Tate, Claudia. "Nikki Giovanni." In *Black Women Writers at Work*, edited by Claudia Tate. New York: Continuum, 1983. 60–78.

LOUISE GLÜCK (1943–)

Marie C. Paretti

BIOGRAPHY

With a career that spans more than three decades and has produced eight volumes of poetry and one of prose to date, Louise Glück is one of the major figures in contemporary American poetry. Her work appears in numerous anthologies, from the *Norton Anthology of Modern American Poetry* to *The Best American Poetry* series. She has earned a long list of awards and prizes, including the National Book Critics Circle Award and the Melville Can Award for *The Triumph of Achilles* (1985); the 1993 Pulitzer Prize for *The Wild Iris* (1992); the William Carlos Williams Award; two Guggenheim Fellowships, and the PEN/Martha Albrand Award for First Nonfiction for her collection of essays, *Proofs and Theories: Essays on Poetry* (1994).

The older of two sisters, Glück was born in New York City in 1943. Twice divorced, most recently from writer John Darrow, Glück has one son, Noah. These men, along with her parents and sisters, figure prominently in her poetry. Her father, the only son of Hungarian immigrants, was a businessman who longed to be a writer. Her mother, a graduate of Wellesley, valued creativity and became, according to Glück, her primary reader during adolescence. Under her parents' tutelage, Glück encountered the stories of Greek mythology, history, and the English canon at a young age, providing an important ground for her later work.

At the same time that family life provided a fertile intellectual and creative environment for Glück, tragedy marked her childhood. The family's first child, a daughter, died before Glück was born, triggering a haunting sense of grief and loss that surfaces repeatedly in Glück's poetry. As a teenager, Glück's drive for perfection and control led to anorexia and eventually to psychoanalysis. Though she initially resisted the latter, fearing, she explains, that her doctor would "make me so well, so whole, I'd never write again" (*Proofs* 12), the experience had the opposite effect, teaching her to distance herself from psychological turmoil so that she could then transform it. She explains, "I cultivated a capacity to study images and patterns of speech, to see, as objectively as possible, what ideas they embodied" (*Proofs* 12). This careful, objective distance makes itself felt across her poetry, creating a surface of restraint around even the fiercest emotions.

At eighteen, instead of going to college, Glück began to study poetry under Leonie Adams at the School of General Studies at Columbia University in New York. Two years later, she turned to Stanley Kunitz, also at Columbia. She studied with Kunitz for five years, who became an important mentor to the young poet. Eventually, Glück became the teacher, and like psychoanalysis, teaching has become an important dimension of her own work. She calls it, in *Proofs and Theories*, "the prescription for lassitude" (17) that often helps sustain her through periods of creative silence. She continues to teach at Williams College in northwestern Massachusetts and currently makes her home in Cambridge.

MAJOR WORKS AND THEMES

The first and last poems in Glück's 1990 volume, *Ararat*, begin with the same phrase: "Long ago I was wounded" (15, 68); one senses, reading her work, that this fact frames not only that volume but also all of her work. Wounds—the death of a firstborn child, anorexia, failed relationships, sibling rivalry, a parent's death, divorce—form the foundation from which Glück's poetry arises. Birth, her work insists, thrusts us into a world of relationships where women, especially, must defiantly guard the inner self and continually struggle to find a voice.

Family life emerges as one persistent locus of this struggle. Many of the poems in *Firstborn* (1968), *The House on Marshland* (1975), *Descending Figure* (1980), and *Ararat*, in particular, probe the painful connections between parent and child: the silence of a distant father, the ache of an older child always striving for perfection, the tensions of a mother caught by competing demands. Most painful, perhaps, are poems such as "Lost Love" (*Ararat*) and the title sequence of *Descending Figure*, where the speaker grapples with the absent older sister who died in childhood. In "Lost Love," for example, the living child is locked in an unwinnable contest with her dead sister, who has become a "magnet" (27), pulling their mother's attention into the grave. A similar sibling rivalry haunts poems where the speaker examines the relationship with her younger sister. In "Paradise" (*Ararat*), for example, a young girl shakes with grief and anger at the profound loss she feels when a second child claims her parents' attention.

If family relationships are one key site of struggle, erotic relationships are the other. With brutal frankness, poems like "Grandmother" and "Aphrodite," from *Descending Figure*, or "Mock Orange" and "Marathon," from *The Triumph of Achilles* (1985), examine the pain and silence women experience through love and marriage. At times, the silence is almost tender, as in "Grandmother," where the husband's kiss gently covers his wife's lips; more common, though, is the violence of "Mock Orange," where the speaker feels her lover's kiss as an act of domination and responds with overt hatred. Such tensions permeate Glück's work, including the Pulitzer Prize winning *The Wild Iris* (1992). At the center of the volume's extended dialogue among a poetic gardener/speaker, the flowers in her garden, and the voice of God, we find Adam and Eve, the speaker and her husband, who have "exhausted each other" (3) in their constant struggle. That struggle culminates in *Meadowlands* (1996), which chronicles the dissolution of a marriage, paralleling the dissolution of Glück's marriage to Darrow.

While Glück's work draws heavily on her lived experiences, it is by no means confessional. Despite their intensely personal subjects, these poems are often emotionally restrained and distant, prompting responses such as Calvin Bedient's, who describes Glück's work as "full of a snow-maiden's dry-ice kisses" ("Man Is" 214). In part, this distance comes from Glück's use of Greek and Biblical mythology to transform the personal into the mythic. Myths appear throughout Glück's work, from early poems such as "Gretel in Darkness" and "The Magi" in *The House on Marshland*, to the sections of *Descending Figure* titled "The Garden" and "Lamentations." *The Wild Iris* and *Meadowlands*, her most extended transformations, use, respectively, the garden of Eden and the story of Ulysses and Penelope to frame the struggles of a contemporary woman grappling with her marriage and her world. This mythic sensibility lends both power and impersonality to Glück's poems, so that while her work is always painfully intimate, it is never strictly personal.

What is most powerful in Glück's work, however, is not simply the struggle, nor the transformation of the personal into the mythic, but the responses of each speaker, echoed forcefully in the form and texture of each poem. In the face of every wound, Glück and her speakers respond with a stony silence, a sense of brooding isolation that acts as both a weapon and a barrier, particularly in her first five volumes. Thus in "Aphrodite," a woman becomes a statue "with her thighs cemented shut" (*First Four* 141) to guard herself sexually and emotionally against the men who come and go; in *Ararat*, the speaker responds to the wounds of "long ago" by becoming hardened and empty of all emotion. The most often-quoted articulation of this response appears in the sequence "Dedication to Hunger" (*Descending Figure* 1980). Taking as its emblem anorexia, "The Deviation" (part 4) expresses the speaker's desire to strip her body of all ornament and achieve a pure, stark, controlled perfection—the same perfection, the poem notes, that the poet feels as she records her words on the page.

In *Proofs and Theories* (1994), Glück explains her spare style further, stressing her distrust of what she calls "the cult of exhaustive detail" (74), where "the ratio of words to meaning favors words" (82). She highlights instead her love of "what is implicit or present in outline . . . white space . . . the telling omission" (29), repeatedly emphasizing the power of silence. Particularly early in her career, Glück treats poems as "words inscribed in rock or caught in amber" (128), hard, sharp, and unforgiving. Images of stone and rock abound as her speakers bear their grief in stoic, sometimes bitter, silence. The resulting poetry, stripped down like the anorexic's body, distrusts any embellishment, relying primarily on harsh nouns and verbs, words of only one or two syllables, short sentences and strophes and even shorter lines, simple syntax, and terse phrasing. Throughout her first five volumes, the poet resembles nothing so much as the speaker of "Brooding Likeness," who, like the bull who marks her birth sign, stands with head lowered against the world, making life into "one controlled act of revenge" (*Triumph* 7).

Though her poetry retains its characteristic spareness, Glück's more recent volumes have begun to shift as she seeks what she describes as "a level of contact" (*Proofs* 128) absent in her earlier work. One result is that the later volumes function, if not strictly as long poems, as clearly united sequences. She has always included short sequences in her work, but beginning with *Ararat*, Glück began extending those sequences to the entire volume. Though many consider *Ararat* her coldest volume, it has a strong sense of unity because it traces the ways in which a father's death affects the wife and daughters he leaves behind. The connections between these poems, and between their speakers, create a new wholeness in Glück's work that, despite its cold surface, begins to move toward that elusive contact. Both *The Wild Iris* and *Meadowlands* continue this pattern, shaping explicit dialogues between speakers; in *The Wild Iris*, God, the poet/gardener, and the flowers all attempt to address one another, though in this case, the intended audience never seems to hear. So, too, in *Meadowlands*, do the couple and their child (both mythic and modern), accuse, reprove, and plead with one another. Her most recent book, *Vita Nova* (1999), returns to a single, dominant voice, but still the volume functions as a whole, chronicling the speaker's return from an ending (presumably the end of the marriage in *Meadowlands*) to find a new voice and a new life. Though still stark, these more recent poems have begun to soften at the edges; these are poems that, like the white lilies in the final poem of *The Wild Iris*, experience death only to "release . . . splendor" (63).

CRITICAL RECEPTION

Critical responses to Glück's work have varied widely, ranging from early reviewers such as Greg Kuzma, who faults Glück for failing to provide sufficient narrative context and for putting too much cold distance between reader and poem, to more laudatory ones such as Kate Daniels, who celebrates "the lapidary nature of Glück's language, as if each beautifully enunciated word, each elegantly constructed line, had been chiseled in stone" (848). At the center of many of these commentaries is the rock-hard character of Glück's style—Aphrodite with "her thighs cemented shut"—that provides the power of all Glück's work, even in her more open, lyrical volumes.

Although Glück's work has been widely reviewed, few longer critical studies have emerged thus far. Much of the extended analysis that does exist relies strongly on a feminist critical approach. In exploring both theme and style, for instance, critics invariably turn to the metaphor of anorexia from "Dedication to Hunger." Lynn Keller, Elizabeth Dodd, and Lynne McMahon, for example, all argue in varying ways that Glück's textual austerity stems from the anorexic impulse, reflecting the poet's sense of fundamental incompatibility between female eroticism and the demands of art. Keller describes Glück's work as a poetry of "renunciation" (125) that struggles to rid itself of female sensuality; Dodd terms it "personal classicism" in which "the voice of the self is muted by an amplified sense of the mythic, the archetypal," (149) allowing Glück to address personal, that is, female, subject matter without being disparaged by the male establishment as "feminine" and therefore not "universal."

This attention to feminist issues has been less true of responses to *The Wild Iris*. Both Allen Hoey and Helen Vendler, for example, develop complex analyses of the more abstract, spiritual dimension of Glück's work. Vendler, in particular, describes Glück (in earlier volumes as well as in *The Wild Iris*) as "a voice not of social prophecy, but of spiritual prophecy" ("Flower" 16). Similarly, Hoey probes the nature of truth and explores the religious impulse in these poems. With *Meadowlands* and *Vita Nova*, however, reviewers have returned to the woman at the heart of these poems, though as Kate Daniels notes, in this newest volume "[we see] at last the whole woman . . . Glück turn[s] her steely will and fierce discipline to the maintenance of the solitary self" (848), letting her own voice rise, whole, out of the struggle.

BIBLIOGRAPHY

Works by Louise Glück

Firstborn. New York: Ecco, 1968.
The House on Marshland. New York: Ecco, 1975.
Descending Figure. New York: Ecco, 1980.
The Triumph of Achilles. New York: Ecco, 1985.
Ararat. New York: Ecco, 1990.
The Wild Iris. New York: Ecco, 1992.
Proofs and Theories: Essays on Poetry. New York: Ecco, 1994.
The First Four Books. New York: Ecco, 1995.
Meadowlands. New York: Ecco, 1996.
Vita Nova. New York: Ecco, 1999.

Studies of Louise Glück

Bedient, Calvin. "Birth, Not Death, Is the Hard Loss." Review of *Descending Figure*, by Louise Glück. *Parnassus* 9.1 (1981): 168–86.

———. " 'Man Is Altogether Desire'?" Review of *Ararat*, by Louise Glück, *Human Wishes*, by Robert Hass, and *The Want Bone* by Robert Pinsky. *Salmagundi* 90–91 (1991): 212–30.

Berger, Charles. "Poetry Chronicle: Amy Clampitt, Louise Glück, Mark Strand." *Raritan* 10.3 (1991): 119–33.

Bond, Bruce. "The Unfinished Child: Contradictory Desire in Glück's *Ararat*." *New England Review and Bread Loaf Quarterly* 14.1 (1991): 216–23.

Bonds, Diane S. "Entering Language in Louise Glück's *The House on Marshland*: A Feminist Reading." *Contemporary Literature* 31 (1990): 58–75.

Burt, Steve. "The Dark Garbage with the Garbage." *PN Review* 25.3 (1999): 31–35.

Costello, Bonnie. "*Meadowlands*: Trustworthy Speakers." *PN Review* 25.6 (1999): 14–19.

Cramer, Steven. "Four True Voices of Feeling." *Poetry* 157.2 (1990): 101–06.

Daniels, Kate. "Bombs in Their Bosoms." *Southern Review* 35 (1999): 846–56.

Dodd, Elizabeth. *The Veiled Mirror and the Woman Poet: H. D., Louise Bogan, Elizabeth Bishop, and Louise Glück.* Columbia: University of Missouri Press, 1992. 149–96.

Farmer, Jonathan. "An Interview with Louise Glück." *The Writer's Chronicle* 33.1 (2000): 18–25.

George, E. Laurie. "The 'harsher figure' of *Descending Figure*: Louise Glück's 'Dive into the Wreck.' " *Women's Studies* 17.3 (1990): 235–47.

Gordon, Emily. "Above an Abyss." *The Nation* 262.17 (1996): 28–30.

Hoey, Allen. "Between Truth and Meaning." *American Poetry Review* 26.1 (1997): 37–47.

Keller, Lynn. " 'Free /of Blossom and Subterfuge': Louise Glück and the Language of Renunciation." In *World, Self, Poem: Essays on Contemporary Poetry from the 'Jubilation of Poets,'* " edited by Leonard M. Trawick. Kent, OH: Kent State University Press, 1990. 120–29.

Kitchen, Judith. "The Woods Around It." *Georgia Review* 47.1 (1993): 145–59.

Kuzma, Greg. "Rock Bottom: Louise Glück and the Poetry of Dispassion." *Midwest Quarterly* 24 (1983): 468–81.

Longenbach, James. "Louise Glück's Nine Lives." *Southwest Review* 84.2 (1999): 184–98.

Matson, Suzanne. "Without Relation: Family and Freedom in the Poetry of Louise Glück." *Mid-American Review* 14.2 (1994): 88–109.

McMahon, Lynne. "The Sexual Swamp: Female Erotics and the Masculine Art." *Southern Review* 28 (1992): 333–52.

Miklitsch, Robert. "Assembling a Landscape: The Poetry of Louise Glück." *The Hollins Critic* 19.4 (1982): 1–13.

Morton, Colleen. Review of *The Wild Iris*, by Louise Glück. *Mid-American Review* 14.2 (1994): 179–86.

Muske, Carol. "Wild Iris." *American Poetry Review* 20.1 (1993): 52–54.

Pettingell, Phoebe. Review of *The Wild Iris*, by Louise Glück. *Yale Review* 80 (1992): 111–17.

Raffel, Burton. "The Poetry of Louise Glück." *Literary Review* 31.3 (1988): 261–73.

Seshadri, Vijay. "The Woe That Is in Marriage." *The New Yorker*, 13 May 1996, 93–94.

Vendler, Helen. "Flower Power: Louise Glück's *The Wild Iris*." In *Soul Says: On Recent Poetry.* edited by Helen Vendler. Cambridge: Harvard University Press, 1995. 16–22.

———. "The Poetry of Louise Glück." *New Republic* 178.24 (1978): 34–37.

Yenser, Stephen. "Wild Plots." *Partisan Review* 61 (1994): 350–55.

JORIE GRAHAM (1950–)

Robert Miltner

BIOGRAPHY

Born in New York City in 1950, Jorie Graham was raised in Rome, Italy, by her mother, Beverly Stoll Pepper, an artist, and her father, Curtis, a *Newsweek* bureau chief. After studying philosophy at the Sorbonne, she returned to New York to take her BFA degree in film making from New York University in 1973. After working briefly in television, she entered the Writers' Workshop at the University of Iowa, receiving her MFA in creative writing in 1978. In 1983 she married poet Brendan Galvin, and the couple has one daughter, Emily. As a result of growing up in Europe, then returning to America as a young woman, Graham's multilingualism has affected her careful attention to sounds, meanings, cadences, and nuances of language.

Between 1978 and 1983, Graham taught at Murray State University, Kentucky, Humbolt State University, California, and Columbia University, New York before settling in at the Writers Workshops at the University of Iowa in 1983. Her first book, *Hybrids of Plants and of Ghosts* (1980), won the Great Lakes Colleges Association Award in 1981, setting up a series of recognitions and awards that include a Guggenheim; a National Endowment for the Arts Grant; a Whiting Award; a MacArthur Foundation Grant; a Lavan Award; and a Morton Zabel Award. She was selected by David Lehman to edit *The Best American Poetry 1990*, writing the introduction, which operates as her artist's statement detailing her theory regarding poetry. Yet it was the Pulitzer Prize for Poetry for *The Dream of the Unified Field: Poems, 1974–1994* in 1995 that brought Graham the widest public recognition and led to her appointment as Boyalston Professor at Harvard University in 1998. Artistically, Graham extended her range through interdisciplinary collaboration when, in 1998, she wrote poems in response to the photographs of Jeannette Montgomery Barron, published as *Photographs and Poems*, and generating the core of the work that became her 2000 publication, *Swarm*.

MAJOR WORKS AND THEMES

"Poetry," writes Jorie Graham in her Introduction to *The Best American Poetry of 1990*, "describes, enacts, is compelled by those movements of supreme passion, insight or knowledge that are physical yet intuitive, that render us whole, *inspired.* Among verbal events . . . poetry tends to leap, to try to move more vertically: astonishment, rapture, vertigo—the seduction of the infinite and the abyss" (xviii). The intuitive, vertical leap toward astonishment seems a shorthand description of Graham's poetry. Open to fluidity and flux, she seeks, through her typographical, spatial, and visual experiments, to identify relationships rather than sequences, putting the focus on the progress of the mind opening in the work rather than on the closed product, for, as Graham believes, when we experience "a breakdown of syntax's dependence on closure, we witness an opening up of the present-tense terrain of the poem, a privileging of delay and digression over progress" (Introduction xx). Thus her poetry employs an open form that resists closure, seeking divergence rather than convergence, suggesting an intellectual skepticism typical of the postmodern condition.

Graham's influences are predominately modernist, especially the work of Wallace Stevens, so that her poetry risks the difficulty of exploring a philosophical and intellectual discourse with the self. The dichotomous results engage her in the constant discovery of the dualities and polarities of life, of the creative and destructive tensions that exist between spirit and flesh, the real and the mythical, stillness and motion, organization and errancy, linearity and spontaneity, the interior and exterior existence. Stylistically, Graham's poetry is characterized by an interplay of long sentence units and short, strung fragments that seem spun out of the innate logic of each individual poem, giving her poems a kind of visual urgency and conversational immediacy.

Graham's first two books demonstrate her use of short line. *Hybrids of Plants and Ghosts*, which derived its title from Nietzsche's characterization of human beings, began with her keeping a journal, as revealed in its casual fragmented style and its general dispensation of closure. *Erosion* (1983) explores accountability or moral experience, both real and imagined. This dichotomy is evident in the poem "Reading Plato" in which Graham describes a fisherman friend who ties flies in the winter for use in the summer, creating a body, from the fly's image in the maker's mind as he attempts to make the ideal into the real.

The End of Beauty (1987) marked a new direction in Graham's poetry. Less dependent upon linearity, these poems break into long lines, sentences, fragments, or abrupt clauses. The introduction of random numerical sectioning suggests arbitrary organization of diffuse content, as if form is an intrusion on content rather than its collaborator. Graham's poetry challenges readers on new levels in this volume, as the poems become shaped more by sentence than stanza, more by collage than continuation, more by consequence than closure. Offering seemingly unrelated fragments that seem intuitively to be pieces of a larger collage, at times, the poet offers a kind of "cloze" reading, which requires readers to participate in the poem by filling in a blank. The reader's response thus completes Graham's sentences, extending beyond the poet's inability to express the difficult. Similarities can be seen with the Language poetry movement, especially in Graham's use of the sentence as a measure equivalent to the poetic line, as in "Self-Portrait a Both of Parties," which includes "3 Wanting to be true, at the heart of things but true" (14).

In her metaphysical sequence of poems, *Region of Unlikeness* (1991), Graham explores the tensions between existence and death, openness and shape, continuity and closure, indeterminacy and constancy. *Region of Unlikeness* moves forward from Graham's earlier works in its attempt to connect together these polarities through intersections in time and space, however disparate or oddly juxtaposed.

In its form and conception, the philosophical *Materialism: Poems* (1993) shows the influence of the kind of more spacious form attempted by Czeslaw Milosz in *Unattainable Earth*, one in which the poet intersperses texts written by other writers, which in Graham's case includes sources as disparate as Jonathan Edwards, Plato, Audubon, Emerson, Whitman, Francis Bacon, Wittgenstein, and Dante. The duality Graham explores in *Materialism* is the tension that results from the universal difficulty in perceiving and communicating the real, in how art is an attempt to express in some concrete way what humans experience through the senses. Evidence of this exploration is seen in "Notes in the Reality of Self," as the poet wonders, "Is there a new way of looking . . . ?" A selection of poems representing Graham's first five books and spanning twenty-two years, *The Dream of a Unified Field: Selected Poems 1974–1994*, earned Jorie Graham the Pulitzer Prize for Poetry in 1996.

After achieving critical acclaim, Graham set forth again artistically in *The Errancy* (1997), a book that takes its title from the medieval idea that to err is a way of learning from mistakes and miscues, as a way of discovery and movement, of proceeding even without a theory. This volume extends a process-orientation that has characterized Graham's poetry throughout her career, though in *Errancy*, discovery learning is offered as the only valid method in a postmodern era devoid of a dominant set of cultural values and beliefs upon which one can rely. The polarities engaged in this book consider both how learning has its limits and how it pushes its own definition to find new limits. Through her foray into content, Graham discovers guardian angels and new beginnings, reflected in the seven aubades, which function as constants in a world given to flux.

With *Swarm*, Graham returns to a short line, to fragments and phrases, in a book-length sequence of poems. Her poetic image of a swarm of ideas, like insects buzzing around one's head, echoes William Butler Yeats's gyre or Ezra Pound's vortex as metaphors for the creative act. The sixteen "underneath" poems suggest thematically what is below the surface, under the swarm, what is hidden and is in need of revelation, which is the goal of the poet's quest while leaping toward astonishment and rapture.

CRITICAL RECEPTION

Dave Smith in *American Poetry Review* calls *Hybrids of Plants and Ghosts* "as promising a first book as any recently published," due to Graham's "sustained control and a music not like anyone else's among us" (36–37). Peyton Brien, writing in *Dictionary of Literary Biography*, calls Graham a poet who is "at the forefront of the effort to revitalize and redefine American poetry" by writing "deeply searching and skillfully wrought poems that emerge from her firsthand, academic experience of art, literature, history, and religious thought" (96).

Brian Henry, writing in *Antioch Review*, places Graham squarely in the American poetic tradition by "introducing Dickinson's abrupt syntax and cadences into the sprawling Whitman line" (283), which is evident in her use of syntactical disjunction, unpredictable lineation, and special disturbance. She has, he observes further, "a penchant for stylistic innovation while pursuing important subject matter and demonstrating intellectual and emotional energy" (293).

Scholar Helen Vendler, reviewing for the *New York Review of Books*, praises the way in which Graham moves beyond the linear story line and seeks to connect through what Vendler calls a "coil," so that resemblances spiral and interlace, prompting Vendler to note that "deciphering the coiled sequencing of memory on different planes is the artist's task—finding (or inventing) likenesses in a region of unlikeness" (55). Thus, Vendler praises the intricacies of Graham's poems, the richly textured and interconnected lines that generate the tensions made evident through the juxtapositions of "unlikeness" of the yoked ideas.

In the *Kenyon Review*, David Baker sees Graham as "a challenging and important poet," noting how he "can think of no other current American poet who has employed and exposed the actual mechanics of narrative, of form, of strategic inquiry more fully than she has" (164), an effect that Graham achieves through bringing together such diverse fields of study as philosophy, science, art, and history. "If anyone can unify the disjoined fields of contemporary discourse," adds Baker, "I think it might be Jorie Graham" (165). Graham's poetry demonstrates the return to modernist difficulty at the end of the postmodern era. By posting dichotomous and contradictory impulses at the heart of her poetry, Graham reflects the challenge of the postmodern artist: the exploration of the irrational through the rationality of language.

BIBLIOGRAPHY

Works by Jorie Graham

Hybrids of Plants and Ghosts. Princeton, NJ: Princeton University Press, 1980.
Erosion. Princeton, NJ: Princeton University Press, 1983.
The End of Beauty. Hopewell, NY: Ecco, 1987.
The Best of American Poetry 1990. Edited with David Lehman. New York: Scribners, 1991.
Region of Unlikeness. Hopewell, NY: Ecco, 1991.
Materialism: Poems. Hopewell, NY: Ecco, 1993.
The Dream of the Unified Field: Poems 1974–1994. Hopewell, NY: Ecco, 1995.
The Hiding Place. Washington, D.C.: Library of Congress, 1995. (audio recording).
Earth Took of Earth: 100 Great Poems of the English Language. Editor. Hopewell, NY: Ecco, 1996.
The Errancy. Hopewell, NY: Ecco, 1997.
Photographs and Poems. With Jeannette Montgomery Barron. Zurich: Scalo, 1998.
Swarm. New York: Ecco, 2000.

Studies of Jorie Graham

Baker, David. "The Push of Reading." *Kenyon Review* 16.4 (1994): 161–76.
Brien, Peyton. "Jorie Graham." *Dictionary of Literary Biography: American Poets since World War II*. Farmington Hills, MI: Gale Research, 1992.
Gardner, Thomas. *Regions of Unlikeness: Explaining Contemporary Poetry*. Lincoln: University of Nebraska Press, 1999. 168–237.
Henry, Brian. "Exquisite Disjunctions, Exquisite Arrangements: Jorie Graham's "Strangeness of Strategy." *Antioch Review* 56.3 (1998): 281–93.
Oakes, Elizabeth. "To 'Hold Them in Solution Unsolved': The Ethics of Wholeness in Four Contemporary Poems." *Real* 25.1 (2000): 49–59.

Smith, David. "Some Recent American Poetry: Come All Ye Fair and Tender Ladies." *American Poetry Review* 11.1 (1982): 36–46.

Spiegleman, Willard. "Jorie Graham's 'New Way of Looking.' " *Salmagundi* 120 (1998): 244–75.

Vendler, Helen. "Mapping the Air." *New York Review of Books*, 21 Nov. 1991, 50–56.

———. *The Breaking of Style: Hopkins, Heaney, Graham*. Cambridge: Harvard University Press, 1995. 71–97.

———. *The Given and the Made: Strategies of Poetic Redefinition*. Cambridge: Harvard University Press, 1995. 89–132.

MARILYN HACKER (1942–)

Renée R. Curry

BIOGRAPHY

Marilyn Hacker was born on November 27, 1942, to Jewish immigrant parents, Albert Abraham Hacker and Hilda Rosengarten Hacker. Raised and educated in New York City, she ultimately attained her BA degree from New York University. This poet began writing poetry when she was in elementary school, and even then, her choice of quatrains demonstrated her interest in fixed forms. For Marilyn Hacker, the reading of poetry is synonymous with the writing of poetry, and she has been an avid reader, especially of women writers such as Adrienne Rich, Audre Lorde, and Judy Grahn whom she names as influences on her work.

Hacker's thirteen-year marriage to African American novelist and gay man, Samuel R. Delaney, produced one daughter, Iva Alyxander Hacker-Delaney, about whom and to whom Hacker often writes. Marilyn Hacker has won the Discovery/The Nation Award; the Lamont Poetry Book Award; the National Book Award; the Lambda Literary Award for Lesbian Poetry; and the Lenore Marshall Poetry Prize. Hacker has edited literary magazines including *13th Moon*, *Kenyon Review*, and an issue of *Ploughshares*. She is the current director of the master's program in creative writing and literature at the City College of New York and lives in New York City and Paris.

MAJOR WORKS AND THEMES

Marilyn Hacker has been writing poetry for over three decades. Her first book, *The Terrible Children* (1967), has been followed by nine subsequent books of poetry. The major themes of the poetry include lesbian lives, women's various relationships with other women, women writers' relationships to forms, frank lyrical portrayals of women's bodies, aging, cancer, and death. In 1974 she published *Presentation Piece*, won the National Book Award, and made herself known for the graphic images of sexual love that would become one of her trademarks. The book contains a number of fixed forms including the masterful sonnet sequence "A Christmas Crown," as well as villanelles and sestinas.

The language of sexual love continues in another of Hacker's well-praised books, *Love, Death, and the Changing of the Seasons* (1986). In this book, she writes vividly of the unspeakable love of lesbians. The poems often deliver a desire for cunnilingus as well as a sense of humor about sexual fantasy, masturbation, and dependency. Hacker creates a tension in this poetry by juxtaposing the stunning against the ordinary. The book, a chronicle of sonnets, depicts the development of a love relationship between two lesbians. Throughout the sonnets, Hacker takes her time with the details of the relationship. She shows the mundane events, the wild moments, the deep-seated emotions, the blinding love, the intolerable dependence as well as the stark loneliness of an ended relationship. She captures with exacting detail the excruciating highs and lows of falling into love, being in love, and being rejected. Throughout these sonnets, we read ourselves, our emotions, our fallibilities, our idiosyncrasies, our melodramas, our fantasies, and our strengths as loving human beings. Hacker makes us live through the tumultuousness of ourselves in love again.

In *Selected Poems 1965–1990* (1994), Marilyn Hacker writes about women and their various abilities and inabilities to connect with one another. She does not generalize about their capacities for nurturance; but instead, she examines the precise relationships between and among women that sometimes make them strained. In particular, she explores the relationship among her mother-in-law, herself, and her daughter as one that has lasted for more than two-thirds of the poet's life and as one about which she is always wishing for change. The sense of time that has lapsed during the formation of this relationship is one that becomes profoundly important in Hacker's 1994 book *Winter Numbers.* At fifty-two years old, Hacker considers the significance of time as well as time's implications regarding the deaths of individuals and the deaths of relationships. The opening poem of this book, "Against Elegies," praises the splendid sixty-five-year-olds who have weathered the world with their eccentricities, generosity, and anecdotes. In "One More Car Poem for Julie," she notices a "tough old lady," and expresses a desire to be like her. Likewise, in "Year's End," she praises the woman warrior that was Audre Lorde, but she also bemoans the fact of Lorde's early death from cancer.

In *Selected Poems*, Hacker tackles not only age, but also the sheer impact of the role that numbers come to play in one's midlife. Her concern is for the truths about life, love, and dying that permeate the particular numbers. For instance, in "Days of 1987," one relishes in the youthful ability to make love "nine times." In "Letter to a Wound," after having taken a younger lover, the narrator wonders whether she has not become a casualty of a twenty-five-year-old's developmental issues. The sonnet sequence "Cancer Winter" reveals numbers that measure what breast cancer does to a woman and her body. The "I" of the poem physically weighs less after her breasts have been removed. She craves hearing the stories of women who have lived into their eighties after having beat breast cancer. The "I" fantasizes about when her breasts were only twenty-five years old, and the poet comments in the twelfth sonnet of this sequence on the difficulty of getting numbers to sound lyrical and rhythmic in poetry. The journey throughout this book of poetry is toward looking beneath the numbers and the specificity toward a meaning about life as we age.

Marilyn Hacker's most recent book of poetry, *Squares and Courtyards* (2000), continues some of the same themes about aging, but in this collection, she has decided that the persistence of existence is reflected in the words she puts to paper. Because she is aging and surviving an illness herself, Hacker feels deeply connected to other people in similar situations. Thus, in "Invocation," she names all the women she knows who are currently living with disease and counting their days and years of survival. Hacker is deeply attuned to the emotions associated with death and not only the emotions of the aging. In "Grief," a poem dedicated to her daughter, Hacker chronicles her daughter's feelings upon learning that a twenty-year-old best friend has died in a car accident.

The poet wants to get the ailments, diseases, deaths, and their associative details correct. She thus includes dates; ages; and names of streets, medicines, medical procedures, and diseases, as well as names of complex emotional combinations in the poetry. In the title poem "Squares and Courtyards," she finds herself in an emotional state both "confused and grateful" that she explores throughout this sestina; she also understands that the precision she seeks in this book is related to the fact that each dying person could use an entire lexicon of his or her own to describe the life that was led. Her purpose in this book is to find a language that can precisely account for variances in life in the face of aging and death. Like the graphic, frank, and vivid detail and language that Marilyn Hacker brought to her early poems, she brings the same attributes to her study and exploration of aging, disease, and death. The poems are neither morbid nor obsessive in their insistence on attention to growing older; rather, they are meticulous in their consideration of the language needed to reveal the complexities of aging.

Hacker's life work has been about attending to the language that does yet exist, the language that will help us to know, to understand, and to care throughout our lives.

CRITICAL RECEPTION

Marilyn Hacker's works have been well received throughout her life, and we have come to expect each book of her poetry to expand the ideas that she has taught us to contemplate. Numerous contemporary writers have reviewed her work and have discerned within it profoundly brilliant feminist meditations.

Numerous essays have detailed her work and her importance to feminism, formalism, and gay and lesbian literature. Nancy Honiker analyzes Hacker's forms in terms of their ability to deliver a sense of freedom to ideas (94). Lynn Keller discusses the same forms in terms of the political constraints and freedoms afforded gays and lesbians in this era (260). Clearly, Marilyn Hacker is an extremely well-respected poet both for her brave content and her well-crafted *oeuvre*. We can only hope that Hacker continues to write new languages for us to contemplate as she continues to age, live, and love right in front of us.

BIBLIOGRAPHY

Works by Marilyn Hacker

The Terrible Children. New York: Samuel R. Delaney (privately published) 1967.
Presentation Piece. New York: Viking Press, 1974.
Separations. New York: Knopf, 1976.
Taking Notice. New York: Knopf, 1980.

Assumptions. New York: Knopf, 1985.
Love, Death, and the Changing of the Seasons. New York: Norton, 1986.
Going Back to the River. New York: Random House, 1990.
The Hang Glider's Daughter. London: Onlywomen Press, 1990.
Selected Poems 1965–1990. New York: Norton, 1994.
Winter Numbers. New York: Norton, 1994.
Squares and Courtyards. New York: Norton, 2000.

Studies of Marilyn Hacker

Augustine, Jane. "Marilyn Hacker." In *Contemporary Poets,* edited by Thomas Riggs. 6th ed. Farmington Hills, MI: St James Press, 1996.

Barrington, Judith. Review of *Love, Death, and the Changing of the Seasons*, by Marilyn Hacker. *13th Moon* 9.1–2 (1991): 136–38.

Finch, Annie. "An Interview on Form." *American Poetry Review* 25.3 (1996): 23–27.

Foy, John. "The Marriage of Logic and Desire: Some Reflections on Form (Anthony Hecht, Donald Justice, Edgar Bowers, Marilyn Hacker, Mark Jarman, Rebel Angels)" *Parnassus* 23.1–2 (1998): 8–25.

French, Marilyn. "Laura, Stella and Ray." *Nation,* 1 Nov. 1986, 242–47.

Gardiner, Suzanne. "Marilyn Hacker." In *Contemporary Lesbian Writers of the United States: A Bio-Bibliographical Critical Sourcebook*, edited by Sandra Pollock, Denise D. Knight, and Tucker Pamela Farley. Westport, CT: Greenwood Press, 1993: 258–68.

Hammond, Karla. "An Interview with Marilyn Hacker." *Frontiers* 5.3 (1980): 22–27.

Hanifan, Jill. Review of *Going Back to the River*, by Marilyn Hacker. *13th Moon* 9.1–2 (1991): 139–43.

Honicker, Nancy. "Marilyn Hacker's *Love, Death and the Changing of the Seasons*: Writing/ Living within Formal Constraints." In *Freedom and Form: Essays in Contemporary American Poetry*, edited by Esther Giger and Salska Agnieszka. Lodz, Poland: Wydawnictwo Uniwersytetut Lodzkiego, 1998. 94–103.

Johnson, Judith. "Poetics: A Conversation with Marilyn Hacker." *13th Moon* 9.1–2 (1991): 8–10.

Keller, Lynn. "Measured Feet 'In Gender-Bender Shoes': The Politics of Poetic Form in Marilyn Hacker's *Love, Death, and the Changing of the Seasons*." In *Feminist Measures: Soundings in Poetry and Theory,* edited by Lynn Keller and Christanne Miller. Ann Arbor: University of Michigan Press, 1994. 260–86.

Kumin, Maxine. 'The Lenore Marshall Poetry Prize: Review of Marilyn Hacker's Poetry." *Nation,* 18 Dec. 1995, 800–02.

Ocampo, Rafael. "About Marilyn Hacker." *Ploughshares* 22.1 (1996): 195–200.

Oles, Carole. S. "Mother Wit." *Nation,* 27 April 1985, 506–09.

Saner, Reg. "Studying Interior Architecture by Keyhole: Four Poets." *Denver Quarterly* 20.1 (1985): 107–17.

JESSICA TARAHATA HAGEDORN (1949–)

Nikolas Huot

BIOGRAPHY

Born and raised in Manila, Philippines, Jessica Tarahata Hagedorn grew up in a house where literature and art were omnipresent and where writing poetry was strongly encouraged. In the early 1960s, Hagedorn's family immigrated to the United States and settled in San Francisco. Shortly after her arrival, Hagedorn's poetry caught the attention of artist Kenneth Rexroth, who played a major role in her artistic development. Rexroth not only continued to encourage Hagedorn's artistic expression but subsequently published her first poems in 1973, grouped under the title "The Death of Anna May Wong," and introduced her to the vibrant artistic life of 1970s San Francisco. In 1975 Hagedorn published her first collection of poems, *Dangerous Music*, and formed a band, The West Coast Gangster Choir, of which she was the lead singer and lyricist.

Late in 1977 Hagedorn moved to New York City in order to pursue her interest in the performing arts. There, she performed and collaborated with fellow writers Ntozake Shange and Thulani Davis on *Where the Mississippi Meets the Amazon*, a series of poems set to music, produced by Joseph Papp's Public Theater in 1978. Later that same year, Hagedorn wrote and performed *Mango Tango*, a solo piece with live music. Many other plays and multimedia theater pieces have followed since then. Although busy performing and writing plays, Hagedorn continued to write poetry. In 1981 she published *Pet Food & Tropical Apparitions*, a collection of prose and poetry.

A prolific writer, Hagedorn never restricted herself to a single genre or medium. After writing poetry, songs, and plays, Hagedorn produced a first novel in 1990, *Dogeaters*, greatly praised by critics, earning a National Book Award nomination. In 1998 Hagedorn adapted her first novel for the stage and received a Kesselring Prize honorable mention in 2000 for its New York City production. Nominated for the *Irish Times* International Fiction prize, her second novel, *The Gangster of Love* (1996), was also received enthusiastically by critics and reviewers. Other than the novel, Hagedorn has pursued other genres by writing short fiction, essays, reviews, and screenplays.

In between novels, Hagedorn published her third collection of poetry, *Danger and Beauty* (1993), which she dedicated to the memory of Kenneth Rexroth, and edited the groundbreaking *Charlie Chan Is Dead: An Anthology of Contemporary Asian-American Fiction* (1995). Her most recent projects include *Burning Heart: A Portrait of the Philippines* (1999), a book on the Philippines with photojournalist Marissa Roth, and *The Pink Palace*, a series of short animated films about the adventures of a sixteen-year-old Filipina in San Francisco.

Besides writing and performing, Hagedorn has also taught at Columbia University and at New York University. Among grants and awards she has received are the Lila Wallace-*Reader's Digest* Fund Writer's Award in 1994; the National Endowment for the Arts Creative Writing Fellowship in 1995; the Sundance Theater Lab Fellowship in 1997; and the NEA-TCG Theatre Residency Fellowship in 1998. Still living in New York, Jessica Hagedorn is currently writing her third novel and completing a documentary entitled *Excuse Me . . . Are You Pilipino?* with filmmaker Angel Velasco-Shaw.

MAJOR WORKS AND THEMES

Danger and Beauty contains selections of her previous books of poems and prose as well as new and unpublished writings. Organizing her poems and short pieces of prose chronologically, Hagedorn shares with the reader her "ongoing personal and artistic explorations and discoveries, both playful and deadly serious" (*Danger* xi). Playfully and seriously, Hagedorn explores what it means to be female and Filipino in the United States. Leaving the Philippines behind her, yet unable to part from it, Hagedorn tries to make a life for herself in a country where "they ask me if i'm puerto rican" ("Song for My Father"). Unabashed and straightforward, the pieces included in *Danger and Beauty* explore the formation of an immigrant's identity amidst the sexism and racism present in the United States; *Danger and Beauty* presents an amalgam of Filipino roots and urban American experiences that never fully blends. As the titles of some of her works suggest ("The Death of Anna May Wong," "Ming the Merciless," and *Charlie Chan Is Dead*, for example), Hagedorn attempts to destroy the persisting stereotypes of Asian Americans as a nonthreatening and conforming people: "We don't complain. We endure humiliation. We are almost inhumane in our patience. *We never get angry*" (*Charlie Chan* xxiii). As Hagedorn discusses the shortcomings of America, she presents, at the same time, a critical picture of the Philippines, a country full of corruption that blindly accepts the image of the United States presented in Hollywood movies.

In "The Death of Anna May Wong" (1973), Hagedorn begins to examine her identity as a Filipino-American writer. The poems present Hagedorn as she arrives in San Francisco and tries to make sense of her new surroundings, completely different than what she had expected. "The Death of Anna May Wong" expresses the disillusion Hagedorn faces in America as the "mythologized Hollywood universe" loses its sheen and its appeal and exposes a certain "longing for what was precious and left behind in the Philippines" (*Charlie Chan* xxiii, *Danger* x). Hagedorn realizes quite early that as a woman of color in the United States, she is relegated to the ranks of the voiceless and powerless: "her name is nada" ("Canto de Nada"). In "Filipino Boogie," Hagedorn recounts how she received a Dale Evans cowgirl skirt for Christmas and how she cut it up in small pieces. Even at that young age, Hagedorn knows that her lot is cast not with the cowboys but with the Indians. Even if she were to adopt American values and internalize the belief that white Americans were superior, she still would suffer marginalization and be considered an untrustworthy member of the "yellow peril."

Greatly influenced by rock 'n' roll music and by her first return to the Philippines, the poems of *Dangerous Music* continue to paint the life of a woman of color in the United States. As the main lyricist for her rock band, Hagedorn increasingly developed a poetry that was "more rhythmic" and "meant to be 'performed' " (*Danger* x). In her first published collection of prose and poetry, music seems to pervade the lives of Hagedorn's characters. Whether it is part of the background, as in "Seeing You Again Makes Me Wanna Wash the Dishes," has an uncontrollable power over someone, as in "Sorcery" and "Canto Negro," or takes one away from pain, as in "Solea," music always plays a major role in Hagedorn's and her characters' lives. Hagedorn also explores in her poetry how music brings people together. In "Something about You," the songs generated by African Americans, Latinos, and Asian Americans come together and express a common experience: a remedy against sorrow. Other than music, the image of the Philippines recurs quite often in *Dangerous Music*. In "Song for My Father," Hagedorn recounts her return to a Philippines under martial law and the violence and corruption she finds there. Despite the desperate picture she paints of her native country, she finds herself unable to leave it completely behind and to dismiss it as inconsequential for her present life in America; haunted by the Philippines, Hagedorn writes that occasionally "i even forget english" ("Song for My Father").

Hagedorn's second collection of prose and poetry, *Pet Food & Tropical Apparitions*, and the previously unpublished works of "New York Peep Show" present a voice that "has hardened, become more dissonant and fierce" (*Danger* xi). The poems in these two collections reflect this angrier voice as Hagedorn discusses the plight of the Filipina immigrant ("Motown / Smokey Robinson"), the state of affairs in the Philippines ("The Song of Bullets"), and the stereotypes surrounding Asians in America ("Ming the Merciless"). Increasingly in *Pet Food & Tropical Apparitions* and "New York Peep Show," Hagedorn writes about how other races and cultures have been and are treated in the United States and the world. The postcolonial voice that had emerged in a few poems in *Dangerous Music* reaches its more powerful pitch in such poems as "The Mummy," "I Went All the Way out Here Looking for You, Bob Marley," and "The Leopard." Still present in her later poetry are the importance and the power of music; a music, however, that is more revolutionary. As Hagedorn indicates in "The Song of Bullets," this rage and defiance are not about to efface since she vows to "stay angry" as long as oppression is present.

CRITICAL RECEPTION

If Hagedorn's poetry has not been showered by the same attention and praises as her two novels, it still has been, for the most part, well received by critics. In most cases, reviewers seem to agree that the rhythm and musicality of her poems prove Hagedorn's strongest point: "She knows the power and betrayal of words and through them she plucks a rhythm to sustain the performance poet who must be seen and heard" (Ancheta 198). Her consistent style of poetry as performance does not always create a consistent quality, however, something that Caryn James deplores in his review. Arlene Stone, agreeing with James's assertion in her review of *Pet Food & Tropical Apparitions*, writes that Hagedorn's poetry "here and there gets into a prosy basement" and that, on occasions, "the title is better than the poem" (6). Overall, though, the boldness and creativity of the poet seem to salvage Hagedorn's poetry. Critics praise her honesty and passion, as well as the realistic portrayal of recent immigrants' experiences in the United States.

BIBLIOGRAPHY

Works by Jessica Tarahata Hagedorn

Chiquita Banana. Third World Women. San Francisco: Third World Communications, 1972. 118–127. (play)

"The Death of Anna May Wong." In *Four Young Women: Poems by Jessica Tarahata Hagedorn, Alice Karle, Barbara Szerlip, and Carol Tinker*, edited by Kenneth Rexroth. New York: McGraw-Hill, 1973. 3–43.

Dangerous Music: The Poetry and Prose of Jessica Hagedorn. San Francisco: Momo's Press, 1975.

Mango Tango. Public Theater: New York, 1978. (performance piece)

Where the Mississippi Meets the Amazon. With Thulani Nkabinda and Ntozake Shange. Directed by Oz Scott. Public Theater: New York, 1978. (play)

Pet Food & Tropical Apparitions. San Francisco: Momo's Press, 1981.

Tenement Lover: no palm trees in new york city. 1981. Reprinted in *Between Worlds: Contemporary Asian-American Plays*, edited by Misha Berson. New York: Theatre Communications Group, 1990. 81–90.

Teenytown. With Laurie Carlos and Robbie McCauley. Franklin Furnace, New York, 1987. (play)

Holy Food. Directed by Christina Yao. Magic Theater, San Francisco, 1989. (play)

Dogeaters. New York: Pantheon, 1990. (novel)

Kiss Kiss Kill Kill. 1992. (screenplay)

Two Stories by Jessica Hagedorn. Minneapolis, MN: Coffee House Press, 1992.

Danger and Beauty. New York: Penguin, 1993. (poetry and prose)

Airport Music. With Han Ong. Berkeley Repertory Theatre, Oakland, California, 1994. (play)

Fresh Kill. Directed by Shu Lea Cheang. ITVS, Channel 4/Strand Releasing, 1994. (screenplay)

Visions of a Daughter, Foretold. With Paloma Hagedorn Woo. Milwaukee, WI: Woodland Pattern Book Center and Light and Dust Books, 1994.

Charlie Chan Is Dead: An Anthology of Contemporary Asian American Fiction. New York: Penguin, 1995.

The Gangster of Love. Boston: Houghton, 1996. (novel)

Dogeaters. Directed by Michael Greif. La Jolla Playhouse, San Diego, California, 1998; Directed by Michael Greif. Public Theater, New York, 2001. (play)

Burning Heart: A Portrait of the Philippines. With Marissa Roth. New York: Rizzoli International Publications, 1999. (essays)

"Music for Gangsters and (Other) Chameleons." In *Stars Don't Stand Still in the Sky: Music and Myth*, edited by Karen Kelly and Evelyn McDonnell. New York: New York University Press, 1999. 252–59. (essays)

Silent Movie. In *The NuyorAsian Anthology: Asian American Writings on New York City*, edited by Alvin Eng. Philadelphia, PA: Temple University Press, 1999. 233–42. (play)

The Pink Palace. Directed by Jessica Hagedorn and John Woo. 2000. (screenplay)

Studies of Jessica Tarahata Hagedorn

Ancheta, Shirley. Review of *Danger and Beauty*, by Jessica Hagedorn. *Amerasia Journal* 20.1 (1994): 197–202.

Birkets, Sven. " 'In Our House There Were No Chinese Things.' " Review of *Charlie Chan Is Dead*, ed. Jessica Hagedorn. *New York Times*, 19 Dec. 1993, final ed., sec. 7: 17.

Bonetti, Kay. "An Interview with Jessica Hagedorn." *Missouri Review* 18.1 (1995): 90–113.

De-Manuel, Maria Teresa. "Jessica Hagedorn's *Dogeaters*: A Feminist Reading." *Likha* 12.2 (1990–1991): 10–32.

Doyle, Jacqueline. " 'A Love Letter to My Motherland': Maternal Discourses in Jessica Hagedorn's *Dogeaters*." *Hitting Critical Mass: A Journal of Asian-American Cultural Criticism* 4.2 (1997): 1–25.

Evangelista, Susan. "Jessica Hagedorn and Manila Magic." *MELUS* 18.4 (1993): 41–52.

———. "Jessica Hagedorn: Pinay Poet." *Philippine Studies* 35.4 (1987): 475–87.

Gelb, Hal. Review of *Airport Music*, by Jessica Hagedorn and Han Ong. *The Nation*, 26 Sep. 1994, 323–24.

Gonzalez, N.V.M. Review of *Dogeaters*, by Jessica Hagedorn. *Amerasia Journal* 17.1 (1991): 189–92.

James, Caryn. "Manila Pop." Review of *Danger and Beauty*, by Jessica Hagedorn. *New York Times Book Review*, 14 Mar. 1983, 12.

Mackey, Mary. "The Restless Heart of a Poet." Review of *Danger and Beauty*, by Jessica Hagedorn. *San Francisco Chronicle*, 28 Feb. 1993, Sunday Review: 3.

Meer, Ameena. "Jessica Hagedorn." *BOMB* 34 (1991): 43–45.

Pearlman, Mickey. "Jessica Hagedorn." In *Listen to Their Voices: Twenty Interviews with Women Who Write*, edited by Mickey Pearlman. New York: Norton, 1993. 134–42.

Ramraj, Ruby S. "Jessica Tarahata Hagedorn." In *Asian American Novelists: A Bio-Bibliographical Critical Sourcebook*, edited by Emmanuel S. Nelson. Westport, CT: Greenwood, 2000. 110–16.

San Juan, E., Jr. "Transforming Identity in Postcolonial Narrative: An Approach to the Novels of Jessica Hagedorn." *Post-Identity* 1.2 (1998): 5–28.

Stone, Arlene. Review of *Pet Food & Tropical Apparitions*, by Jessica Hagedorn. *American Book Review* 4.6 (1982): 6.

Winn, Steven. " 'Airport Music' Sings of Immigrant Cultural Disconnections." *San Francisco Chronicle*, 9 June 1994, E4.

JOY HARJO (1951–)

Monika Giacoppe

BIOGRAPHY

The thematic preoccupations of Joy Harjo's poetry may be traced back to her roots in the cultural and geographic landscapes that make up the American Southwest. Born to Allen W. and Wynema (Baker) Foster in Tulsa, Oklahoma, in 1951, and a lifelong member of the Muscogee tribe, Harjo was confronted early on with the legacy of the violent conquest of the Americas, the blessing and the curse of living surrounded by the stolen land. Harjo has battled that history of despair with a lifetime commitment to artistic expression. From the Institute of American Indian Arts in Santa Fe, New Mexico, where she studied dance, Harjo went on to the University of New Mexico, where she began writing at age twenty-two. The influence and friendship of other Native writers, perhaps most particularly Leslie Marmon Silko, has nurtured Harjo's writing since those early years. In 1976 she graduated from the University of New Mexico's Creative Writing Program; by that time, she had published a first chapbook, *The Last Song*, in 1975. The poems from *Last Song* were reprinted in her next collection, *What Moon Drove Me to This?* which appeared in 1980, shortly after her 1978 completion of an MFA at the University of Iowa's Writers' Workshop. (Both of those collections are now out of print.)

Harjo has extensive experience teaching literature and creative writing at institutions including the Institute of American Indian Arts, Arizona State University, the University of Colorado, the University of Arizona, and a visiting professorship at the University of Montana, while maintaining a busy schedule of publishing, readings, and conducting workshops. Her third book, *She Had Some Horses*, appeared in 1983, followed by a collaboration with photographer Steven Strom, *Secrets from the Center of the World*, in 1989. Harjo won wide praise and several awards, including the Poetry Society of America's William Carlos Williams Award, for *In Mad Love and War* (1990), and has continued to attract a growing audience with *The Woman Who Fell from the Sky* (1994) and *A Map to the Next World* (2000). Her creative endeavors have not been limited to poetry, however. Harjo has also written screenplays and co-edited with Gloria Bird an anthology of Native women's writing, *Reinventing the Enemy's Language* (1997). Among her current projects is a band, "Poetic Justice," with whom she produced a compact disc entitled *Letter from the End of the Twentieth Century* in 1997. A book for children, *The Good Luck Cat*, also appeared in 2000. The mother of a son and daughter, Phil and Rainy Dawn, Harjo is also now a grandmother whose family plays an important role in her poetry.

MAJOR WORKS AND THEMES

Although Harjo's style has evolved since the publication of her first chapbook, *The Last Song*, in 1975, the thematic core of her work remains steadily centered on Native American history and traditions. Harjo writes with compassion and solidarity of those who have been pushed to the margins by the dominant Anglo American culture, and her mixed-race heritage has given rise to a preoccupation with memory, landscape, travel, transformation, solidarity, and the value of life. That value is enhanced by the power of love, which Harjo has called "the strongest force in this world" (*Woman Who Fell* 30). Love, in all its many forms, is a frequent subject of Harjo's poetry. Poems such as "A Hard Rain," "Summer Night," "City of Fire," and "Crossing Water" (*Mad Love*) celebrate erotic or romantic passion, while others explore a more maternal or grandmotherly affection ("Rainy Dawn," "Bleed Through," from *Mad Love*, "The Naming," from *Woman Who Fell*). Still others, such as "Letter from the End of the Twentieth Century," from *Woman Who Fell* promote love as a redemptive force.

Many of Harjo's most famous poems invoke and celebrate Native traditions and history or probe the conditions of life in Native America today. They thus range from joyous celebrations of complete spiritual integrity, in poems such as "Eagle Poem" (*Mad Love*) and "Vision," "Remember," and "One Cedar Tree" (*She Had Some Horses*), to the decay of such belief systems when juxtaposed with racism, urban poverty, alcoholism, and despair. The "Deer Dancer" (*Mad Love*) who appears on a cold winter's night to the hardcore regulars in a downtown bar is "the end of beauty," "the myth slipped down through dreamtime" (5–6) offering the potential of redemption. "Anchorage" (*She Had Some Horses*) depicts the spirit worlds surrounding the Alaskan city, where the bustle continues, heedless of "those who were never meant to survive" (15). This juxtaposition is further explored in "The Woman Who Fell From the Sky," which alternates between Native creation stories and a contemporary cityscape.

Cities are important locations in Harjo's poetry, as is clear from poems including "Anchorage," "New Orleans," and "The Woman Hanging from the Thirteenth Floor Window" (*She Had Some Horses*), as well as "Song for the Deer and Myself to Return On," "Deer Dancer," "Climbing the Streets of Worcester, Mass.," in *Mad Love*. The poet survives an armed robbery in Los Angeles in "twins meet up with monsters in the glittering city," (*Map*) a poem that echoes the warnings about random urban violence found in "Letter from the End of the Twentieth Century" and in the comments following "A Postcolonial Tale" (*The Woman Who Fell*).

Yet grace remains possible, typically discovered in the southwestern landscapes sacred to several Native peoples, but occasionally even "in a truck stop along Highway 80," as in the poem "Grace," from *Mad Love* (1). Nonetheless, it is to the southwestern desert landscape that Harjo returns: As the speaker in *Secrets from the Center of the*

World, she sees herself "more beautiful than [she] could ever believe" (52). A product of the earth's own dreaming, she stands to admire the landscape that holds everything of importance in the world. This theme of identification with a living landscape is expressed with special strength in several poems in *She Had Some Horses*. Most notable among these are perhaps "Vision," describing the redemptive power of a rainbow that seems to open the door to another world, and "Remember," which reminds readers that the "plants, trees, animal life" are "alive poems" (40). In "Skeleton of White," the poet is "memory alive," part of this "web of motion" (31), while the ground that "goes on talking" (19) in "For Alva Benson, and for Those Who Have Learned to Speak," is evidence that the repetition of the acts of everyday living can bring about this miracle of continuity through the collapse of time. Many of the poems in *Map to the Next World* further elaborate this theme. "Ceremony" insists that humans must "live with integrity in this system," (58), while the poem "humans aren't the only makers of poetry" affirms that all living creatures experience the creative urge.

Such powerful affirmations of connectedness lead to expressions of solidarity and the desire for social justice in all of Harjo's books, but this drive may be felt most strongly in *In Mad Love and War*, which includes testimonial poems about Jacqueline Peters, a civil rights worker lynched in California in 1986 ("Strange Fruit"), and Anna Mae Aquash, a Native activist whose suspicious death on the Pine Ridge Reservation in South Dakota in 1976 has never been fully investigated ("For Anna Mae Pictou Aquash, Whose Spirit Is Present Here and in the Dappled Stars [for we remember the story and must tell it again so we may all live]"). This concern is further developed in *Map to the Next World*, where poems such as "Protocol" remark upon the cultural common ground shared by Natives from Hawaii and the mainland.

Animating these broader themes are figures that recur throughout Harjo's work, including the moon, an image that resonates both with the beauty of the natural world and with a sense of female power. But it is her horses, most markedly present in her first three works, and especially in the enigmatic and often-cited "She Had Some Horses," that have incited the greatest curiosity. Harjo refers to the horses as "very sensitive and finely tuned spirits of the psyche," with "strength running through them" (Coltelli, *The Spiral of Memory* 28). Noni Daylight, a struggling young Native woman described by some critics as Harjo's poetic "otherself," is a frequent presence in her earlier poems but does not appear in the more recent works, where Harjo's attention to music, especially jazz, is more prominent. Music has always been present in Harjo's poetry, but it becomes the major element in poems such as "Blue Elliptic," "Bird," and "Healing Animal," in *In Mad Love and War*. Perhaps the most outstanding feature of Joy Harjo's poetry is its exhortation to all of us to seek out and appreciate the presence of healing beauty in a violent, chaotic, often hostile world. Like the trickster crows who appear so often in her poetry, Harjo, too, finds scraps of the sacred in unlikely places. As she says in "The Path to the Milky Way Leads Through Los Angeles," (*Map*) "like crow I collect the shine of anything beautiful I can find" (45).

CRITICAL RECEPTION

Joy Harjo has been identified as an important Native American, feminist voice since the beginning of her publishing career. John Scarry's characterization of her is typical: "Joy Harjo is clearly a highly political and feminist Native American, but she is even more the poet of myth and the subconscious" (288). Andrew Wiget sees "the identification of Self with Other as a strategy for both poetic and personal self-realization" as the driving force behind her work, an identification that includes "the extension of self into the world's body, or conversely, of the incorporation of all experiences and persons into self" (186–87). As early as 1987, Patricia Clark Smith and Paula Gunn Allen asserted that "the primacy of travel in her works probably makes her . . . the most typical of contemporary American Indian writers" (174); the same essay praises her "strong home base" and "acute sense of the red earth" (175). While white feminists have embraced her work, most critical studies have placed it specifically within the context of Native literature. Mary Leen sees Harjo the poet taking on the role of storyteller, "promot[ing] survival in the resurrection of memory, myth, and struggles," through work that is "vital and regenerative" (1). Nancy Lang notes that "within expected structural and narrative formats of contemporary poetry, her poems also frequently resonate with the distinctive chanting rhythms and pause breaks associated with traditional Native American oralities" (41). Scarry takes an unusual step in comparing Harjo to male writers of the Anglo and Irish traditions. Finding similarities between Harjo's "Deer Dancer" and "The Second Coming" by William Butler Yeats, Scarry affirms that "Harjo, as much as Yeats, is able to survive in the larger culture while still breathing deeply of her native air. In a hostile place that has denied her dreams and often done its best to destroy the dreamer, she has responded by giving back to the larger culture values and insights it never realized it had lost" (291).

BIBLIOGRAPHY

Works by Joy Harjo

The Last Song. Las Cruces, NM: Puerto Del Sol Press, 1975.

What Moon Drove Me To This? New York: I. Reed Books, 1980.

She Had Some Horses. New York: Thunder's Mouth Press, 1983.

Secrets from the Center of the World. Photographs by Steven Strom. Tucson: University of Arizona Press, 1989.

In Mad Love and War. Middletown, CT: Wesleyan University Press, 1990.

"Writing with the Sun." In *Where We Stand: Women Poets on Literary Tradition*, edited by Sharon Bryan. New York: Norton, 1993: 70–74. (essay)

The Woman Who Fell from the Sky. New York: Norton, 1994.

Letter from the End of the Twentieth Century. Compact disc with the band Poetic Justice. Silver Wave Records, 1997.

Reinventing the Enemy's Language: Contemporary Native Women's Writings of North America, edited by Joy Harjo and Gloria Bird. New York: Norton, 1997. (literary collection)

The Good Luck Cat. New York: Harcourt, 2000. (children's fiction.)

A Map to the Next World: Poetry and Tales. New York: Norton, 2000.

Studies of Joy Harjo

Allen, Paula Gunn, and Patricia Clark Smith. "Earthy Relations, Carnal Knowledge: Southwestern American Indian Women Writers and Landscape." In *The Desert Is No Lady: Southwestern Landscapes in Women's Writing and Art,* edited by Vera Norwood and Janice Monk. New Haven, CT: Yale University Press, 1987. 174–96.

Coltelli, Laura, ed. *The Spiral of Memory: Interviews/Joy Harjo*. Ann Arbor: University of Michigan Press, 1996.

Goodman, Jenny. "Politics and the Personal Lyric in the Poetry of Joy Harjo and C. D. Wright." *MELUS* 19.2 (1994): 35–55.

Gould, Janice. "An Interview with Joy Harjo." *Western American Literature* 35.2 (2000): 131–42.

Lang, Nancy. " 'Twin Gods Bending Over': Joy Harjo and Poetic Memory." *MELUS* 18.3 (1993): 41–49.

Leen, Mary. "An Art of Saying: Joy Harjo's Poetry and the Survival of Storytelling." *American Indian Quarterly* 19.1 (1995): 1–16.

Perreault, Jeanne. "New Dreaming: Joy Harjo, Wendy Rose, Leslie Marmon Silko." In *Deferring A Dream: Literary Sub-Versions of the American Columbiad*, edited by Gert Buelens and Ernst Rudin. Basel, Switzerland: Birkhäuser Verlag, 1994.120–36.

Scarry, John. "Representing Real Worlds: The Evolving Poetry of Joy Harjo." *World Literature Today* 66.2 (1992): 286–91.

Smith, Stephanie Izarek. "An Interview with Joy Harjo." *Poets & Writers Magazine* 21.4 (1993): 23–27.

Wiget, Andrew. "Nightriding with Noni Daylight: The Many Horse Songs of Joy Harjo." In *Native American Literatures*, edited by Laura Coltelli. Pisa, Italy: Servisio Editoriale Universitario, 1989. 185–96.

CARLA HARRYMAN (1952–)

Deborah M. Mix

BIOGRAPHY

Born in 1952, Carla Harryman grew up in Orange, California. In the 1970s she moved to San Francisco, where she became involved with a community of writers we now know as Language poets. From the early days of Language poetry, Harryman contributed to the gradual formulation of theories and practices of this movement. She co-founded the Poets Theater in the San Francisco Bay area in 1978 as a venue for experimental drama (it closed in 1984).

Working across generic boundaries, Harryman is perhaps best known for her fusions of poetry with drama, and several of her plays have been staged. *Memory Play* was presented at the LAB, an interdisciplinary artists' organization in San Francisco, in 1994, and "Fish Speech" was performed as part of the Public Broadcasting System miniseries *The United States of Poetry* (1996). Harryman has also directed numerous plays and, in 1994–95, appeared in an operatic version of Max Ernst's *A Little Girl Dreams of Taking the Veil*. In addition to numerous books, Harryman has published extensively in magazines and journals, particularly those known for their interest in innovative writing, including *New American Writing*, *This*, *Avec*, and *Poetics Journal*.

Harryman also has been active in academia, teaching at the University of California, San Diego; Detroit Institute of the Arts, and Wayne State University in Detroit, Michigan. She currently lives in the Detroit area with her husband Barrett Watten and their son, Asa.

MAJOR WORKS AND THEMES

Carla Harryman, always uneasy with generic definitions, prefers to explore and cross boundaries rather than adhere to them. Though she is usually classified as a poet, her works consistently blur generic categories. As she told Megan Simpson in a 1996 interview, Harryman is "ambivalent" about being classified as a poet: "I'm exploring genre. [My] writing partakes of poetry in addition to prose narrative, discursive writing, theater. . . . A lot of my writing is prose or looks like combinations of poetry and prose" (514–15). Her earliest publications, including *Percentage* (1979), *Under the Bridge* (1980), and *Property* (1982) attest to this ambivalence. Each of the volumes features a pastiche of generic forms, ranging from traditional verse forms to narrative plays. In "Obstacle," in *Percentage*, Harryman writes of "heavenly distortion" that unsettles knowledge and claims of authority. Other pieces in the volume investigate issues of communication and understanding; "Percentage" seems at first to be a conversation between "D" and "E" but seeming nonsequiturs and nonresponsive answers reveal that each speaker is in fact caught up in a different conversation, only seemingly to connect to the other. Thus, Harryman zeroes in on her other major preoccupation as a writer and theoretician: the power of narrative to shape reality. Because the speakers in "Percentage" are so deeply involved in their own "stories," they hear other narratives only as part of their own, reading all stimuli as a seamless and chimeric "whole."

Under the Bridge continues Harryman's explorations of parataxis and imperfect communication. Many of the pieces in this collection center on what appears as fragments of conversations, often one-sided ones. In "In Front," the speaker attempts to explain his or her approach to communication: "I DID NOT MEAN ANYTHING." Harryman's suspicion about communicating appears located both in a sense of distrust in language to "mean what we say" and in a sense of distrust of an audience's reception of those words and ideas. Yet at the same time, these paradoxes, such as knots with slashes, insist on preserving both the possibility of connection (the knot) and the simultaneous futility of such efforts (the slash). With *Property*, Harryman moves toward deconstruction of other false certainties. The titles of the pieces in the volume—"Property," "Possession," "Privacy," "The Master Mind," and "Acting"—point to Harryman's interest in ideas of authority and boundaries. A speaker in "Property" informs his listeners, "The shape of the story ought to be that of a spiral of doubt."

Paradoxes, as the idea of maintaining a story that moves forward (or inward) even as it self-destructs, remain hallmarks of Harryman's work. In *The Middle* (1983), she approaches issues of meaning, or lack thereof, from numerous directions. As Bob Perelman notes in his study of the work, "*The Middle* in its 25 pages contains excerpts acknowledged to be from Freud, Wittgenstein, Robert Creely, Larry Eigner, Bernadette Mayer, Harryman's other writing, as well as numerous instances borrowing from other texts that are folded into Harryman's own words" (307), all strategies that confound attempts to tease a coherent narrative, or even a coherent subjectivity, from the text. What is surface and what is depth are never clear. At one point, a speaker ruminates on one man's name: "In any case, a little banal name, a name that says something, that is not easily forgotten." There is at once no depth, only banality, and inscrutable depth (saying something, not forgetting) paradoxically attached to a name of some kind. Frequently, figures in Harryman's work are caught up in massive efforts to "discover" meaning. Later in *The Middle*, a young woman discovers a sodden matchbook with a map of the world on it, and after speculating about the matchbook's origins, concludes that it was left deliberately for her as a clue to her mother's origins. Thus, even though she has highlighted the myriad possible narratives that could be behind the matchbook's appearance, she still selects one in which she chooses to believe. As Harryman writes in her 1985 essay "Toy Boats," "I choose to distribute narrative rather than deny it (*There Never Was a Rose* 2). She argues that narrative is necessary—it is the way in which humans situate themselves in the world. By "distributing" narrative, then, Harryman extends invitations to her readers to participate in her playful experimentations as equals, just as children might play together with "toy boats."

This sense of playfulness is part of Harryman's ludic deconstruction, and she often turns her deconstructive impulse toward issues of relationships and reception. In *Vice* (1987) Harryman writes, "I do not write with inner truth. Writing is a demonstration of the influence of relationships" (54). The ways in which these relationships (self to others, self to self, self to environment, self to memory) influence thinking have occupied Harryman throughout her work. One way that this concern manifests itself is through questions about what readers expect from literature and how those expectations influence their reading experiences. Harryman often approaches these questions through scenarios in which a character in the piece (often the narrator) views a particular work of visual art. In the title piece of the collection *In the Mode of* (1991), the speaker begins in a gallery, standing in front of an Emile Nolde painting and analyzing his/her response (Harryman carefully avoids assigning a gendered identity to this speaker). When another character enters the narrative and asks the speaker his/her opinion of the painting, the speaker responds by acknowledging that the painting looks different when viewed as a woman and looks different yet again if viewed as a man. In addition to considering how gender inflects reception, Harryman goes further, examining the ways in which sexual desire, physical surroundings, and contact with others might shape response. Through such strategies, she directly challenges the position of the artist as authority, as conveyor of truth. She simultaneously dislocates the reader's authority by pointing to the ways readers/viewers can never produce a definitive reading because their minds and bodies are always shaping the moment of reception, making each reading always already new.

Harryman is also concerned with the ways in which impermanence and plasticity shape the process of writing. In a short piece in *Animal Instincts* (1989) entitled "My Story," Harryman writes, "Speaking in a state of fidelity to the subject, living flesh though it may be, is similar to assuming one has acquired the song of birth through the ritual of repeating of the names and gestures of newborn infants" (32). Such an assertion, with its radical questioning of subjectivity, pushes against the simple assertion of the piece's title. On the one hand, the title suggests that not only is there a story to be told but that there is also a self to claim that story. On the other hand, the opening sentence asserts that any attempt to put that "living flesh" into language is impossible. Again while a "self" may be temporarily available to construct a story, this identity and its narratives are fluid and unstable. "Narrative is neither an oppressor to be obliterated nor the validating force of all literary impulse," Harryman argues (*There Never Was a Rose* 5).

Writing in her preface to *There Never Was a Rose Without a Thorn* (1995), a collection of new and previously published works, Harryman describes her work as "hybrid writings staged . . . between fiction and theory, the domestic and history, abstractions and androgyny, the rational and nonrational, the creator and her artifact" (1). Harryman's attention to hybridity and impermanence, to the imaginary lines between the creative and the critical, to paradox and play continues to shape her work, "Fish Speech," which is clearly a playful rewriting of originary stories: "In the beginning, there was no apoliticized moment of the absolute and no political critiques" (128). *The Words* (1999), a novel of sorts that leaps off of Jean-Paul Sartre's *The*

Words and Carl Sandburg's *Rootabega Stories*, immediately blurs generic boundaries (philosophy and fiction) and issues of authority (Sartre's imagined ideal of the autonomous self) and creativity. Yet even as Harryman tests the limits of language and identity, she holds fast to the promise of liberatory creativity: "And what we mean when we say this is: that our *apriori* knowledge and magical thinking have fused, and their union has left us in doubt as to the source of our questions" (75). Harryman's feminist experimentations continue to push her and her readers toward reclamation of what she calls in her 1998 essay of the same name "Wild Mothers": "A wild mother may be someone who exploits the site of her own imagined and imaginary autonomy. . . . The wild part comes from the imagination, which can create a formulation, a form of something that was once uncertain and in taking form unsettles the presumptions that held the uncertainty in a proper proprietary relationship to commonplace social presumptions about mothers and child rearing" (688).

CRITICAL RECEPTION

Like many experimental writers (particularly experimental *women* writers), Harryman and her work have remained far from the critical mainstream. Few studies of her work have been published, and most of the existing considerations of her work have been penned by other poets also associated with Language writing. Bob Perelman's 1987 essay, "Facing the Surface," comments on Harryman's deconstruction of meaning, a trait commonly associated with Language writing, but he also notes that her assertion that " 'There is not one meaning' . . . [is] a far different slogan than 'There is no meaning.' . . . For Harryman, the page is precisely obvious, full of the words it displays, with nothing underneath" (311). Leslie Scalapino offers a similar assessment in her analysis of *The Words* (still in manuscript when Scalapino was writing): "Carla creates paragraphs . . . designating hierarchy of objects in which the basis of hierarchy and comparison itself is extended to emptiness" (37), but Scalapino notes, it is this "unmapped terrain" in which sensation begins to occur (38). Many critics note that Harryman's writing requires and rewards substantial readerly participation. Gail Scott notes in her commentary on *There Never Was a Rose Without a Thorn* that the relationship between reader and writer is akin to dancing and "the remarkable consequence of this dance is that one becomes acutely aware of actually being in the process of thinking; aware of thinking in ways one has not before" (145). All of Harryman's critics note that her deconstructive experiments are always underpinned by a feminist impulse. Harryman admits, "We want our students and children to live in a different world" (Simpson 532).

BIBLIOGRAPHY

Works by Carla Harryman

Percentage. Berkeley, CA: Tuumba Press, 1979.
Under the Bridge. Oakland, CA: This Press, 1980.
Property. Berkeley, CA: Tuumba Press, 1982.
The Middle. San Francisco: Gaz, 1983.
Vice. Elmwood, CT: Poets & Poets Press, 1987.
Animal Instincts. Oakland, CA: This Press, 1989.

In the Mode Of. La Laguna, Canary Islands: Zasterle Press, 1991.
Memory Play. Oakland, CA: O Books, 1994.
Rubble: Variations: Screen Play Text for Abigail Child. Elmwood, CT: Poets & Poets Press, 1994.
There Never Was a Rose Without a Thorn. San Francisco: City Lights Press, 1995.
"Fish Speech," In *The United States of Poetry,* edited by Joshua Blum, Bob Holman, and Mark Pellington. New York: Harry N. Abrams, 1996. 128–29.
"Wild Mothers." In *Moving Border*, edited by Margaret Sloan. Jersey City, NJ: Talisman House, 1998. 688–94.
The Words: After Carl Sandburg's Rootabega Stories and Jean-Paul Sartre. Berkeley, CA: O Books, 1999.

Studies of Carla Harryman

Brito, Manuel. *A Suite of Voices: Interviews with Contemporary American Poets.* Santa Brigada, Spain: Kadle Books, 1992.
Perelman, Bob. "Facing the Surface: Representations of Representation." *North Dakota Quarterly* 55 (1987): 301–11.
Scalapino, Leslie. "Objects in the Terrifying Tense Longing from Taking Place." In *A Poetics of Criticism*, edited by Juliana Spahr, Mark Wallace, Kristin Prevallet, and Pam Rehm. Buffalo, NY: Leave Books, 1994. 37–42.
Scott, Gail. "Elixir for Thinking: Carla Harryman's *There Never Was a Rose Without a Thorn.*" *West Coast Line* 31.2 (1997): 144–48.
Simpson, Megan. "An Interview with Carla Harryman." *Contemporary Literature* 37 (1996): 511–32.
Wright, Laura. "Play in the Works of Carla Harryman." *Revista Canaria de Estudios Ingleses* 37 (1998): 173–86.

LYN HEJINIAN (1941–)

Richard Quinn

BIOGRAPHY

Lyn Hejinian requires more of readers than most contemporary poets. Born in Alameda, California, in 1941 to Chaffee Earl Hall, Jr., a high school teacher and aspiring writer, and Carolyn Frances Erskine, a homemaker, Hejinian developed her syntactically complex style in the 1970s as a founding member of the Language school. Married to John Hejinian in 1961, she gave birth to two children, Paul in 1964 and Anna in 1966, before earning a BA from Harvard in 1968. Upon her graduation, Hejinian returned to California where she was later divorced in 1972. She left San Francisco for the countryside in 1973, only to move back to the Bay area five years later, marrying saxophonist and composer Larry Ochs in 1977. The previous year, Hejinian founded Tuumba Press and began publishing her own experimental work while seeking out other like-minded poets. In consort with Rae Armantrout, Carla Harryman, Bob Perelman, Barrett Watten, Ron Silliman, and others, Hejinian began formulating theoretically complex statements on the relationship between language, identity, and social justice. These statements on the importance of nonstandard language in combating oppressive social hierarchies formed the basis for a new collaborative poetics and the group's ultimate identification as the Language school.

Self-publishing her first chapbook, *The gRReat adventure*, in 1972, Hejinian has published over fifteen full-length works of poetry and fiction, along with countless essays and translations of Russian poetry. Her work as a translator of Leningrad poet Arkadii Dragomoshchenko came about as the result of a 1983 trip to Russia with Ochs who was touring the country with the Rova Saxophone Quartet. Her friendship with Dragomoshchenko led to a return trip in 1989 with poets Michael Davidson, Silliman, and Watten, resulting in the collaborative work, *Leningrad: American Writers in the Soviet Union* (1991). These trips would prompt an enlarged global perspective in Hejinian's work and an even greater engagement with postmodern discourses on the dissolution of national identity. Her most recent book, *The Language of Inquiry* (2000), collects her most significant essays including "The Rejection of Closure" and "Two Stein Talks." A visiting poet at the Iowa Writer's Workshop in 1998, Hejinian continues to live and work in California.

MAJOR WORKS AND THEMES

Lyn Hejinian's poetry illustrates the inseparability of form, content, and technique. While her poems often explore the brand of personal experiences found in traditional lyric poems, they do so less as a means of presenting those experiences than as a method of exploring the functions of poetic language. Consequently, the focus in reading Hejinian's work is more on the materiality of words than on the world those words depict. In other words, the structure and language of the poems are often their content. This technique stems from Hejinian's belief, influenced by postmodern theory, that contemporary poetry should foreground the processes of its creation. Such beliefs are grounded in the idea that language determines and precedes, rather than accurately reflects, an already present reality.

Hejinian's major books of poetry include *Writing Is an Aid to Memory* (1978), *My Life* (1980), *The Cell* (1992), *Oxota* (1991), and *The Cold of Poetry* ((1994). This latter text, a compilation of many of Hejinian's more obscure books such as *Gesualdo* (1978) and *Redo* (1984), illustrates her early interest in engaging readers as active participants in the construction of meaning. As in much of her work, her poems here consist of a disjointed narration where gaps between sentences invite readers to construct meaningful semantic links. She writes in "Ground," section two of *The Cold of Poetry*, "Between buildings a lot of hazel brown. An iron spout and the curious thumb part." Interpretive questions abound. Is hazel brown the color of a smoggy sky, a field of dry grass, a garbage dump? Is the iron spout attached to one of the buildings, spewing hazel brown water? And what is curious about the thumb part? What is the thumb part, a piece of the spout or building? Readers must perform much of the labor here, calling upon associative rather than metaphoric semantic possibilities. The syntactical linkage of words and sentences provides little help, offering only the raw materials for many possible meanings.

My Life, easily Hejinian's most widely read and critically studied work, epitomizes her writing practice. Originally written in 1978 when Hejinian was thirty-seven, the book consisted of thirty-seven chapters of thirty-seven sentences each. Rewritten eight years later in her forty-fifth year, Hejinian added eight new chapters and supplemented the previous chapters with eight additional sentences. While the book might be considered an autobiography, its refusal to speak from or converge upon a unified subject position represents a revision of the autobiographical tradition. The text seeks less to articulate the momentous points in an individual's life than to mine the seemingly insignificant experiences autobiographical writing often excludes. That such experiences can only be uncovered through linguistic experimentation marks one of Hejinian's dominant themes. Her writing becomes a politics at this point, where the restrictions of standard poetic or autobiographical language reflect larger restrictions on the individual self.

Like much of Hejinian's work, *My Life* also critiques the chronological modalities of the traditional lyric and autobiographical writing. While the text may be divided into forty-five sections of forty-five sentences reflecting forty-five years of the poet's life, sections do not unfold chronologically, with section one expressing year one and so forth. Rather, Hejinian adopts a synchronic approach, where all experiences exist simultaneously in memory. In section eleven, for example, Hejinian recalls a childhood moment when "Every child wanted to be blackboard monitor in order to clap the chalk erasers at the end of the day," but she quickly moves into an adult consideration of infinity as an expression of sexual desire. Through disjointed language, where moments collide without regard to linear development, Hejinian seeks to more accurately recount life as a combination of alinear individual experiences. Childhood memories and inarticulate desires merge in the mind. In short, much of Hejinian's poetry argues that the standard language of the lyric and of autobiography tidies up the real messiness of experience in service of a false linearity. An easily understandable language suggests an easily understandable life, and life, Hejinian's work explains, is not so easy.

CRITICAL RECEPTION

Despite her presence outside the mainstream of American poetry, Hejinian's work has been widely celebrated for its innovative approach to language and meaning. Some of this criticism comes from fellow Language school poets and affiliated writers such as Barrett Watten, Michael Davidson, Bob Perelman, and Rae Armantrout, providing further evidence of the collaborative nature of contemporary experimental poetry. Perhaps the greatest focus in Hejinian criticism is on the link between her language and a radical politics. Armantrout, Juliana Spahr, and Hilary Clark, for example, have drawn attention to the rebellious feminism of Hejinian's work. As Clark argues in her essay "The Mnemonics of Autobiography," Hejinian's *My Life*, in its "loving inclusion and accumulation of detail" suggests that "women's autobiography can overturn dominant principles of decorum, of exclusion and selection" central to the language of authority (329). Similarly, Spahr contends in "Resignifying Autobiography" that with Hejinian's writing, "gender is not stable, not an absolute" (144). In dismantling linguistic barriers, her critics argue, Hejinian's writing challenges gender and other social barriers as well.

Others focus on the ways in which Hejinian's texts ask readers to work beyond their preconceived notions of the poetic text. In Stephen Radcliffe's words, "Hejinian's work forces us to re-examine what it means to read a text" through its "constant and disarmingly sudden shifts in syntax and substance" (41). This brand of text, what Craig Dworkin calls, "the kind of challenging and rewarding writing that is the hallmark of the avant-garde" attacks gentile definitions of poetic expression directly (58). "Autobiographical narrative, postmodern montage, and expressionist lyricism" merge, in Christopher Beach's words, yet refuse to converge into a particular genre (61). While Hejinian appears frequently on lists of contemporary poets, her critics recognize that it is exceedingly difficult to categorize much of Hejinian's work. For example, despite its name, *Oxota: A Short Russian Novel* reads much like poetry while *My Life*, defined by many as poetry, reads frequently like fiction or nonfiction.

In general, Hejinian's critics suggest that her brand of complex writing, whether we call it poetry or something else, counteracts reader passivity and encourages the critical mind. In engaging with Hejinian's texts, readers are forced to reconsider the ways in which the world gets constructed, thereby undermining the kind of passive subjectivity subscribed to by profiteers and quietists. In placing such demands on readers, Hejinian's work reflects a real belief in the active, rebellious, and thoughtful individual as central to both poetry and a more progressive, just planet.

BIBLIOGRAPHY

Works by Lyn Hejinian

The gRReat Adventure. [S.I.:s.n], 1972.
A Thought Is the Bride of What Thinking. Willits, CA: Tuumba, 1976.
A Mask of Motion. Providence, RI: Burning Deck, 1977.
Gesualdo. Willits, CA: Tuumba, 1978.
Writing Is an Aid to Memory. Berkeley, CA: The Figures, 1978; Los Angeles: Sun & Moon, 1996.
My Life. Providence, RI: Burning Deck, 1980. Expanded ed. Los Angeles: Sun & Moon, 1987.
The Guard. Willits, CA: Tuumba, 1984.
Redo. Grenada, MS: Salt-Works, 1984.
Individuals: A Book of Twenty-four Poems Written Individually in the Fall of 1986. With Kit Robinson. Tucson, AZ: Chax, 1988.
The Hunt. La Laguna, Canary Islands: Zasterle, 1991.
Leningrad: American Writers in the Soviet Union. With Michael Davidson, Ron Silliman, Barrett Watten. San Francisco: Mercury House, 1991.
Oxota: A Short Russian Novel. Great Barrington, MA: The Figures, 1991.
The Cell. Los Angeles: Sun & Moon, 1992.
The Cold of Poetry. Los Angeles: Sun & Moon, 1994.
Sight. With Leslie Scalapino. Washington, D.C.: Edge Books, 1999.
Happily. Sausalito, CA: Post-Apollo, 2000.
The Language of Inquiry. Berkeley: University of California Press, 2000. (essays)

Studies of Lyn Hejinian

Altieri, Charles. "Lyn Hejinian and the Possibilities of Postmodernism in Poetry." In *Women Poets of the Americas: Toward a Pan-American Gathering*, edited by Jacqueline Vaught Brogan and Cordelia Chávez Candelaria. Notre Dame, IN: University of Notre Dame Press, 1999. 146–55.
Armantrout, Rae. "Feminist Poetics and the Meaning of Clarity." *Sagetrieb* 11 (1992): 7–16. Reprinted in *Artifice & Indeterminacy: An Anthology of New Poetics*, edited by Christopher Beach. Tuscaloosa: University of Alabama Press, 1998. 287–96.
———. "Lyn Hejinian." In *Postmodern Fiction: A Bio-Bibliographical Guide*, edited by Larry McCaffery. Westport, CT: Greenwood, 1986. 400–03.
Beach, Christopher. "Poetic Positionings: Stephen Dobyns and Lyn Hejinian in Cultural Context." *Contemporary Literature* 38 (1997): 44–77.
Bernstein, Charles. "Hejinian's Notes." In *Content's Dream*. Los Angeles: Sun & Moon, 1986. 284–85.
Caze, Antoine. "Form as Freedom in the Poetry of the LANGUAGE Group." In *Freedom and Form: Essays in Contemporary American Poetry*, edited by Esther Giger and Agnieszka Salska. Lodz, Poland: Wydawnictwo Uniwersytetu Lodzkiego, 1998. 52–66.
Clark, Hilary. "The Mnemonics of Autobiography: Lyn Hejinian's *My Life*." *Biography* 14 (1991): 315–35.
Davidson, Michael. "Approaching the Fin de Siecle." In *The San Francisco Renaissance: Poetics and Community at Mid-Century*. New York: Cambridge University Press, 1989. 200–18.

Dworkin, Craig. "Penelope Reworking the Twill: Patchwork, Writing, and Lyn Hejinian's *My Life*." *Contemporary Literature* 36 (1995): 58–81.

Georgeson, Alison. "An Interview with Lyn Hejinian." *Southern Review* 27.3 (1994): 285–94.

Greer, Michael. "Ideology and Theory in Recent Experimental Writing of, the Naming of 'Language Poetry.' " *Boundary 2* 16 (1989): 335–55.

Jarraway, David R. "My Life through the Eighties: The Exemplary LANGUAGE of Lyn Hejinian." *Contemporary Literature* 33 (1992): 319–36.

McCaffery, Larry, and Brian McHale. "A Local Strangeness: An Interview with Lyn Hejinian." In *Some Other Fluency: Interviews with Innovative American Authors*, edited by Larry McCaffery. Philadelphia: University of Pennsylvania Press, 1996. 121–45.

McHale, Brian. "Telling Stories Again: On the Replenishment of Narrative in the Postmodernist Long Poem." *Yearbook of English Studies* 30 (2000): 250–62.

Perelman, Bob. "Parataxis and Narrative: The New Sentence in Theory and Practice." In *The Marginalization of Poetry: Language Writing and Literary History*. Princeton, NJ: Princeton University Press, 1996. Reprinted in *Artifice & Indeterminacy: An Anthology of New Poetics*, edited by Christopher Beach. Tuscaloosa: University of Alabama Press, 1998. 24–48.

Perloff, Marjorie. "The Return of the (Numerical) Repressed." In *Radical Artifice: Writing Poetry in the Age of Media*. Chicago: University of Chicago Press, 1991. 162–70.

———. "The Word as Such: L=A=N=G=U=A=G=E Poetry in the Eighties." *American Poetry Review* (May-June 1984): 15–22.

Quartermain, Peter. "Syllable as Music: Lyn Hejinian's *Writing Is an Aid to Memory*." *Sagetrieb* 11 (1992): 17–31.

Ratcliffe, Stephen. "Private Eye/Public Work." *American Poetry* 4 (Spring 1987): 40–48.

———. "Two Hejinian Talks: 'Writing/One's Life' and 'Writing/Re:Memory.' " *Temblor* 6 (1987): 141–47.

Spahr, Juliana. "Lyn Hejinian." *Dictionary of Literary Biography, Vol. 165: American Poets Since World War II, Fourth Series*, edited by Joseph Conte. Farmington Hills, MI: The Gale Group, 1996. 102–07.

———. "Resignifying Autobiography: Lyn Hejinian's My Life." *American Literature* 68:1 (1996): 139–59.

Waldrop, Rosemarie. "Chinese Windmills Turn Horizontally: On Lyn Hejinian." *Temblor* 10 (1989): 219–22.

Watten, Barrett. "The World in the Work: Toward a Psychology of Form." In *Total Syntax* Carbondale: Southern Illinois University Press, 1985. 146–49.

SUSAN HOWE (1937–)

Maria Elena Caballero-Robb

BIOGRAPHY

The poetry of Susan Howe, born in 1937 in Boston, Massachusetts, to Mary Manning Howe, an Irish actress and playwright, and Mark DeWolfe Howe, a Harvard law professor, was influenced by both her parents. Discouraged by her father from pursuing her interests in history, politics, and law, Howe became an apprentice actor at the Gate Theater in Dublin. This early training in drama both as an actress and as an assistant stage designer is reflected in the dramatic sections of her poems, as in *The Liberties* (1980). Her father's admonition against pursuing a career in history or the law may have contributed to her later interest in and critique of historical discourses.

Returning to the United States, Howe worked in theater in New York before going to the Boston Museum School of Fine Arts, where she majored in painting and graduated in 1961. In 1964 she returned to New York where she was influenced by a number of experimental artists, including John Cage, Robert Morris, Ellsworth Kelly, Andy Warhol, and Richard Serra. The influence of avant-garde art, with its use of collage, mixed media, and found materials, can be seen in practices that pervade both her critical and poetic work. In the late 1960s, she began with creating "art books" using assemblages of words juxtaposed with a drawing or a page of pencil marks. This practice prefigured her radical use of the page to create textual/graphic hybrids.

Closely associated with the late 1970s and 1980s Language poetry movement, Howe's poetry and scholarship are considered language-based and experimental. The subjects and locations of her work range from her interest in the editorial issues surrounding Emily Dickinson, to the marginalization of liminal figures such as Anne Hutchinson and Mary Rowlandson in early American history, to Jonathan Swift's Irish residency in *The Liberties*.

In 1985 Howe was one of ten American poets at the New Poetics Colloquium in Vancouver, British Columbia, returning in 1987 as visiting artist-in-residence. In 1988 she was named a Butler Fellow in the Department of English at State University of

New York, Buffalo. In 1980 Howe received the Before Columbus Foundation American Book Award for *Secret History of the Dividing Line* (1978). In 1987 she received the same honor for *My Emily Dickinson* (1985). In 1997 Howe donated her papers and recordings of her WBAI (New York) radio show in the late 1970s to the special collections at the Mandeville Library at University of California, San Diego. The papers include manuscripts, journals, and correspondence with Lyn Hejinian, John Taggert, George Butterick, and others.

MAJOR WORKS AND THEMES

Among Susan Howe's principle thematic concerns are history and historical discourses and the silencing of dissenters and the disfranchised. She views poetic attempts to remedy the historical violence done to the muffled of translated voices as necessarily incomplete, fragmented reconstitutions of lost voices—such as that of Dickinson, of Mary Rowlandson, those of female converts in the Puritan conversion narratives, or those of the invisible casualties of U.S. wars. For Howe, the role of the poet is to sift through the overlapping, mutually contradictory historical narratives for traces of alternative versions, told from the subject positions of the voiceless. In *The Europe of Trusts* (1990), she expresses a desire to give voice to those overlooked in historical discourses. For Howe, history is a wilderness of language from which silenced casualties must be redeemed.

Like the Language writers with whom she is associated, Howe self-consciously rejects the notion of the poet as unproblematic witness and recorder of experience. Rather than view the poet as a privileged voice or seer, whose experience is translated into verse (as in the contemporary mainstream first-person lyric), Howe's work suggests a model of poetic production in which the poet works with a tissue of previous texts, weaving poetry out of the "Wilderness of words." Thus poetry is not original, unique, transparent speech communicating to a reader the poet's inspired meditation or experience of nature or the world around him or her; instead poetry refracts and recycles the already-used language and discourse at the poets' disposal, such that "poetry is never a personal possession" ("Some Notes"). The tenuous relationship between language and language user—not to say the relationship between historical narrative and the Real—is underscored by Howe's use of fragmented syntax. The syntactic, even phonemic, fragmentation of Howe's work has been compared to stammering or stuttering: the appearance of cryptic lines of words, syllables, and characters with few syntactic guideposts for the reader dramatizes the difficulty of reconstituting ghostly voices as well as the dissolution of the language-using self that poststructuralism has so well documented.

This de-authorized poetics accounts for Howe's poetic techniques, including parataxis (or nonhierarchical syntax), ellipsis, puns and other word play, fragmentation, and collage. Howe's poetry often features a dramatic visual layout with a liberal use of white space. Drawing on her training as a painter—and echoing the Russian formalist Victor Schlovsky's principle of defamiliarization, as well as the tradition of field composition—Howe lays lines of text across the page diagonally, upside down, or radiating out from a center point, to create a textual graphic. "First I was a painter," she writes, "so for me words shimmer. Each one has an aura. Lines are laid on the field of a page, so many washes of watercolor" (Frank and Sayre 209). In her early art books, from the late 1960s, Howe used sketchbooks to juxtapose pictures and collections of words: "The words were usually lists of names. Often the names of birds, flowers, or weather patterns, but I relied on some flash association between the words and the pictures" (Keller 5). This extra-textual visual dimension of her poetics (as in the long poems "Thorow" and "Scattering as Behavior Toward Risk" in *Singularities* [1990], in *Frame Structures* [1996], and in *The Nonconformist's Memorial* [1993]) results in an unparaphraseable poetry that deliberately and productively alienates the reader. In this practice, Howe has affinities with Dickinson's self-published handwritten poems whose iconoclastic graphic dimensions Howe investigates in *My Emily Dickinson.* Howe's poems' distinctive presentation evokes tangled thickets of language—in some cases, complete with editorial marks such as carets, strikeouts, and underscoring. This formal feature visually echoes the hybrid visual-textual sign systems of maps and illustrates one of her thematic concerns, namely the incursion of Anglo American newcomers into supposedly "undiscovered" regions inhabited by Native Americans in the colonial and early national periods.

Susan Howe's poems can be seen as collages incorporating fragments of history, autobiography, family history, travel narratives, and literary history. Her long poem *Secret History of the Dividing Line*, for example, a meditation on boundaries, invisible limits, and hidden schisms, uses as one of its source texts William Byrd's eighteenth-century journal of the exploration of the Virginia wilderness. Her 1996 volume *Frame Structures,* which collects "Secret History" and three other early long poems, juxtaposes biographical sketches with memoir, disjointed literary allusions, and a history of the founding of Buffalo. The texture of fragmented historicity may appear in the form of unmarked quotations, or archaic-sounding phrases that are in fact Howe's own writing. Her sampling from historical documents real and imagined can be traced to her use of visual echoes in her early practice as a painter, in which she "made a copy in the painting of some part of another painting" (Keller 3). Proper names and place names, likewise, tantalizingly signal a historical "trace," yet their presence underscores the impossibility of reaching their origins, or of escaping the mediation of historical narrative; for while the capitalized names of historical actors and places appear deictic, their referents remain elusive.

Howe's critical work *My Emily Dickinson* is an important contribution to Dickinson scholarship as well as a radical contribution to U.S. literary history. In this volume, Howe discusses the manuscript versions of Emily Dickinson's poems and the delimited critical horizons of Dickinson scholarship and editing and of literary historiography. As with her project of resurrecting the translated voices of women's conversion narratives in *The Birth-Mark: Unsettling the Wilderness in American Literary History* (1993), her approach to the Dickinson materials emerges as a "radical conservative" attempt to exfoliate Dickinson's "antinomian" writing from beneath layers of conservative editorial interference and regularizing print conventions. Howe argues that print translations obscured the originality of Dickinson's punctuation, lineation, orthography, and her use of the page as the site of a radically graphic poetics that constituted her principled resistance to the burgeoning print culture of the nineteenth century.

CRITICAL RECEPTION

Included in virtually every anthology of Language poetry, Susan Howe is also considered an important contributor to feminist studies and U.S. literary historiography. Her work has been seen to resonate with contemporary critical theory, including that of Walter Benjamin, Julia Kristeva, and Michel Serres. While Howe is categorized as a Language writer, the label insufficiently accounts for all the features of her work, particularly the emphasis in her historical investigations on transcendence and the mystical. These features superficially contravene the language movement's stated commitments to reject the late Romantic poetry's tendency to stage the dramas of the individual subject in the "expressivist" mold of most contemporary mainstream poetry, in favor of a variegated, polyvocal, indeterminate poetry of "discourses" that short-circuits the ideological reproduction through the vectors of "common-sense" speech. Peter Quartermain, for example, argues that Howe's 1991 book *Singularities* reflects a tension between a desire to redeem the lost voices of history and the critical understanding that authentic origins can never be recuperated, or a conflict "between her desire for the secure, the stable, and the defined, and her apprehension of them as essentially false"(183). Perloff among others differs, arguing, "For Howe, origins cannot be known" ("Language Poetry"). Howe's innovative use of the page in the tradition of field composition, as well as her use of syntactic and semantic fragmentation, have been credited with engaging postmodern poetry's project of renovating the relationship between author and reader, by compelling unprecedented interactions between reader and text. Her transgeneric critical prose is seen in the tradition of other poets' literary historical/critical work, such as William Carlos Williams's *In the American Grain* or Charles Olson's *Call Me Ishmael*. Both *The Birth-mark* and *My Emily Dickinson* have been praised as radical renovations of literary critical writing that offer feminist revisionist approaches to literary history.

BIBLIOGRAPHY

Works by Susan Howe

Hinge Picture. New York: Telephone Books, 1974.
The Western Borders. Berkeley, CA: Tuumba Press, 1976.
Secret History of the Dividing Line. New York: Telephone Books, 1978.
Cabbage Gardens. Chicago, Fathom Press, 1979.
The Liberties. Guilford, CT: Loon Books, 1980.
Pythagorean Silence. New York: Montemora Foundation, 1982.
Defenestration of Prague. New York: The Kulchur Foundation, 1983.
My Emily Dickinson. Berkeley, CA: North Atlantic Books, 1985. (literary criticism)
"Women and Their Effect in the Distance." *Ironwood*. 28 (1986): 58–91. (criticism)
Articulation of Sound Forms in Time. Windsor, VT: Awede, 1987.
"Some Notes on Visual Intentionality in Emily Dickinson." *However* 3.4 (1988).<http://scc01.rutgers.edu/however/print_archive/alertsvole3no4.html>
A Bibliography of the King's Book, or, Eikon Basilike. Providence, RI and Berkeley, CA: Paradigm Press, 1989.
The Europe of Trusts: Selected Poems. Los Angeles: Sun & Moon Press, 1990.
Singularities. Middletown, CT: Wesleyan University Press, 1990.
Incloser. Sante Fe, NM: Weaselsleeves Press, 1992. (literary criticism)
The Birth-Mark: Unsettling the Wilderness in American Literary History. Middletown, CT: Wesleyan University Press, 1993. (literary criticism)
The Nonconformist's Memorial: Poems by Susan Howe. New York: New Directions, 1993.
Frame Structures: Early Poems, 1974–1978. New York: New Directions, 1996.

Pierce-Arrow. New York: New Directions, 1999.
Bed-Hangings. New York: Granary Books, 2001.

Studies of Susan Howe

Adamson, Gregory Dale. "Serres Translates Howe." *SubStance* 26.2 (1997): 110–24.

Dworkin, Craig Douglas. " 'Waging Political Babble': Susan Howe's Visual Prosody and the Politics of Noise." *Word & Image* 12 (1996): 389–405.

Foster, Edward Halsey. *Postmodern Poetry: The Talisman Interviews*. Hoboken, NJ: Talisman House, 1994.

Frank, Robert J., and Henry M. Sayre. *The Line in Postmodern Poetry*. Urbana: University of Illinois Press, 1988.

Hogue, Cynthia. "Infectious Ecstasy: Toward a Poetics of Performative4 Transformation." In *Women Poets of the Americas: Toward a Pan-American Gathering*, edited by Jacqueline Vaught Brogan and Cordelia Chávez Candelaria. Notre Dame, IN: University of Notre Dame Press, 51–67.

Keller, Lynn. "An Interview with Susan Howe." *Contemporary Literature* 36.1 (1995): 1–34.

Ma, Ming-Qian. "Articulating the Inarticulate: Singularities and the Counter-Method in Susan Howe." *Contemporary Literature* 36.3 (1995): 466–89.

———. "Poetry as History Revised: Susan Howe's 'Scattering as Behavior toward Risk.' " *American Literary History* 6.4 (1994): 716–37.

Marsh, Nicky. " 'Out of My Texts I Am Not What I Play': Politics and Self in the Poetry of Susan Howe." *College Literature* 24.3 (1997): 124–37.

McGann, Jerome. "Composition as Explanation." In *Cultural Artifacts and the Production of Meaning: The Page, the Image, the Body*, edited by Margaret J. M. Ezell and Katherine O'Brien O'Keefe. Ann Arbor: University of Michigan Press, 1997. 252.

Nanes, Erika. "The Reviser in the Word Forest: Susan Howe and the American Typology of Wilderness." *Journal x* 2.1 (1997): 19–34.

Naylor, Paul. *Poetic Investigations: Singing the Holes in History*. Evanston, IL: Northwestern University Press, 1999.

Nicholls, Peter. "Unsettling the Wilderness: Susan Howe and American History." *Contemporary Literature* 37.4 (1996): 586–601.

Palatella, John. "An End of Abstraction: An Essay on Susan Howe's Historicism." *Denver Quarterly* 29.3 (1995): 74–97.

Perloff, Marjorie. "Canon and Loaded Gun: Feminist Poetics and the Avant-Garde." *Stanford Literature Review* 4.1 (1987): 23–46.

———. " 'Collision and Collusion with History' ": The Narrative Lyric of Susan Howe." *Contemporary Literature* 30.4 (1989): 518–33.

———. "Language Poetry and the Lyric Subject: Ron Silliman's Albany and Susan Howe's Buffalo." *Critical Inquiry* 25.3 (1999): 405–35.

Quartermain, Peter. *Disjunctive Poetics: From Gertrude Stein and Louis Zukofsky to Susan Howe*. Cambridge: Cambridge University Press, 1992.

Reinfeld, Linda. *Language Poetry: Writing as Rescue*. Baton Rouge: Louisiana State University Press, 1992.

Vicery, Ann. "The Quiet Rupture: Susan Howe's *The Liberties* and the Feminine Marginalia of Literary History." *Southerly* 57.1 (1997): 91–102.

Williams, Megan. "Howe Not to Erase(Her): A Poetics of Posterity in Susan Howe's 'Melville's Marginalia.' " *Contemporary Literature* 38.1 (1997): 106–33.

JUNE JORDAN (1936–2002)

Samiya A. Bashir

BIOGRAPHY

Poet, essayist, novelist, political activist, and professor June Jordan was born in Harlem on July 9, 1936, and raised in the notoriously tough Bedford-Stuyvesant section of Brooklyn, New York. Determined to get the best education for their only child, Jordan's parents pulled her from public schools and sent her to boarding school in what she called the "completely white universe" at Midwood High School, then to the exclusive prep school environment of the Northfield School for Girls in Massachusetts. Although she was challenged as an outsider in an alien environment away from home, it was at Northfield that Jordan discovered her love for poetry.

By all accounts, including her own, Jordan was raised in a dysfunctional home, but one that encouraged her quest for knowledge from an early age. Her parents, Mildred and Granville Jordan, were both Jamaican immigrants with high ambitions for their only child. Her father, a night-shift postal worker, raised Jordan like the son he always wanted. He was a strict disciplinarian and was relentlessly tough on his daughter both emotionally and physically. "Regardless of any particulars about me," Jordan recalls in *Soldier: A Poet's Childhood* (2000), "he was convinced that a 'Negro' parent had to produce a child who could become a virtual white man and, therefore, possess dignity and power." Jordan's mother, who worked outside of the home as a nurse, looked past her husband's violent temper and often failed to protect her daughter from his rage. By the time Jordan went to boarding school, she had learned lessons in violence, power, and control that continue to inform her work.

Jordan enrolled at Barnard College, New York, in 1953, where she met and soon married Michael Meyer, a fellow student. After they were married, Jordan transferred her studies to the University of Chicago where her new husband completed his graduate degree. After his graduation, Jordan went back to Barnard where she completed her studies in 1956. In 1958 Jordan gave birth to her only child, Christopher David Meyer. Jordan and Meyer, an interracial couple during the civil rights movement of the 1950s and 1960s, found it difficult to negotiate their marriage within the social and legal restraints of their time. Their 1965 divorce left Jordan to tackle the new terrain of working, single motherhood.

Her first book, *Who Look at Me* (1969), is a long poem, initially intended for children, which began with a publisher who requested that Jordan step in to complete a project Langston Hughes was working on before he died in 1967. In what would prove to be signature Jordan style, she completely reconceived the project and made it her own. Jordan continued to write and publish poetry and children's literature while taking on a number of teaching jobs to support her family. Jordan taught at the City University of New York and Sarah Lawrence in Bronxville, New York. She was a tenured professor at the State University of New York, Stony Brook before taking her current position as a professor of African American Studies at the University of California, Berkeley, where she founded and served as the director of the Poetry for the People program, which celebrated its tenth anniversary in 2001. Jordan died of breast cancer in 2002.

MAJOR WORKS AND THEMES

Soldier, Jordan's twenty-sixth book, marked her as one of the most widely published African American writers in history. An autobiography of the poet as a child, from her earliest memory, until she leaves home for boarding school, the book also marks a return of focus to her first love: children. Jordan does not short-change the child's perspective with nostalgia or self-consciously imbued adult perceptions. She presents a self-aware young person who confronts life as it comes, taking the good with the bad and attempting to carve a place for herself into the world she has been given.

Her first novel, *His Own Where* (1971), a book for young readers, celebrated as the first novel written entirely in black English, won a nomination for the 1971 National Book Award amidst a storm of controversy over issues of language and racial diversity in schools. Never a stranger to controversy, Jordan learned from her father the warrior-like tactics that she would employ in her work to ensure a platform for the traditionally voiceless, including those whom she has called the world's largest oppressed group: children.

After *His Own Where*, Jordan continued to write children's books including *Dry Victories* (1972); *Fannie Lou Hamer* (1972), a biography on the legendary civil rights activist; *New Life: New Room* (1975); and *Kimako's Story* (1981), based on the life of Kimako Jones, poet Amiri Baraka's sister, who lost her life tragically early. In her children's literature, Jordan speaks to young readers in clear, accessible language, emphasizing awareness of the world around them and teaching survival skills to prepare them to live in an often hostile society, while also remaining dedicated to the celebration of love and beauty in even the most desolate situations.

With *Civil Wars: Observations from the Front Lines of America* (1981), a collection of letters, essays, and speeches that address political issues effecting the most marginalized in society with a conscious understanding of the impact that oppression of the few has on the many, Jordan became the first published African American woman essayist. Extensively anthologized, Jordan's work is unapologetically political in nature. In poems such as "Jim Crow: The Sequel," Jordan uses her poetry as a call to action for her readers to stand up and take notice. She actively works to engage and inspire her readers to step outside of their comfort zone and demand justice.

The crux of Jordan's political belief holds love as the greatest political action. In *Naming Our Destiny* (1989), *Living Room* (1985), *Passion* (1980), and *Things That I Do in the Dark* (1977), Jordan liberally peppers her overtly political work with poetry regaling the glory of love in all its forms, not the least of which is romantic love. Critic Peter Erickson warns, "Those who come to June Jordan's poetry because of her reputation as a strictly political poet will be surprised at the large number of love poems and of her constant recourse to this genre" (223).

Adrienne Rich, in her foreword to *Haruko/Love Poems* (1994), states, "[Jordan's] poems are extraordinarily tonal, sensuous, capturing moments or ways of being which might make love—in many dimensions—more possible, more revolution-directed." Jordan's love poetry is the ultimate political act of the woman Minnie Bruce Pratt dubbed the "Warrior Poet." Jordan lays herself prostrate, holds a steady spotlight on her own very human vulnerability, her need for intimacy, for physical touch, for sexual excitement, for even "an absolutely one to one a seven-day kiss" ("Alla Tha's All Right, but," *Passion*).

Jordan works within the tradition of many African American artists who came before her, making her statement by using a variety of platforms. Her work is not only literary, but it also reflects an oral tradition intricately linked to the transmission of information, education, history, and current events and then carries that oral tradition through the gates of the American literary canon. Jordan has also translated her oral grounding into writing for the stage in productions from New York to San Francisco.

Arising from the meeting points of the civil rights and Black Nationalist movements, the women's movement, the lesbian and gay rights movements, and global human rights movements, Jordan's work has always insisted that everyone is worthy. A fiercely independent spirit, Jordan was known and respected by each of the varying movements and artistic schools of the 1960s, 1970s, and 1980s, but she never allowed herself, or her work, to be confined to any one doctrine. M. J. Boyd observed that Jordan's work takes "the initiative to identify the restrictions of the reactions of the cultural separatists," (226) while forcing a re-examination of the high cost of such social isolation.

Jordan was a "tough girl" long before Girl Power (that ubiquitous 90s catch phrase for all things supposedly empowering for girls and women); her take-no-mess gumption—Jordan's distinctive brand of strength—is packed into every page like a gift. The "high" and "low" culture infiltration of Jordan's politics and poetics speaks to her efforts. Her work can be found simultaneously in the *Norton Anthology of Modern Poetry*, the *New York Times*, *Ms.*, *Transition*, *The Progressive* (where she remained a regular columnist until her death), and *Vibe*, the magazine of hip hop culture.

In her most widely anthologized poem, "Poem About My Rights," a scathing indictment of the individual oppression of women and the systematic oppression of Third World countries by the world's superpowers, Jordan examines the meeting place of the social movements that shaped her work. "Jordan's political poetry is, at its best, the opposite of polemic," observes Marilyn Hacker. "It is not written with a preconceived, predigested agenda of ideas and images. Rather, the process of composition is, or reproduces, the process of discovering how events are connected, how oppressions are analogous, how lives interpenetrate" (135).

If "Poem About My Rights" cemented Jordan's reputation as, in the words of Alice Walker, "the universal poet," then *Technical Difficulties* (1992) and *Affirmative Acts*

(1998)—two hard-hitting collections of essays that address national and global political issues, as well as intensely personal issues including her long fight with breast cancer—solidified her as, in the words of former editor and long-time friend Toni Morrison, "our premiere Black woman essayist." Jordan treats women's suffering in Kosovo and Tehran with the same delicate understanding and passionate empathy as she does women, children, and men fighting racism, classism, sexism, and homophobia in her own San Francisco Bay area neighborhood.

Poetry remains the lover to whom Jordan consistently returns as she weaves her poetic language and syntax throughout her essays. As a professor, her courses focused on poetry from a world perspective. Jordan continued her dogged dedication not only to her craft, but to teaching, criticizing, sharing, and publicizing of the work and the message of poetry—and the lives of poets—at home and abroad.

CRITICAL RECEPTION

Jordan has the adverse distinction of being one of the most widely revered contemporary American poets among both poets and readers, while concurrently being virtually ignored by the commercial mainstream. Although she has more books in print than almost any other contemporary African American poet, her volumes can rarely be found on shelves at the major bookstores. Critical writing about her work suggests that the reason for this oversight is that her work is often *too* effective, and that Jordan is considered a far greater threat than more widely celebrated radical thinkers. Jordan's danger lies in her absolute accessibility and refusal to rely on rhetorical crutches to convey her message.

David Baker celebrates Jordan as one of the few American poets "who have been . . . willing to take on other people's troubles" (155). Saundra Towns observes her struggle, through her life and work, to "successfully maintain a sense of spiritual wholeness and the vision of a shared humanity, while relentlessly engaging a brutal and often brutalizing reality" (601). Jordan's critique is not meant to preach to the converted, hers is no elite-minded art for art's sake. Jordan writes to inform, educate, and entertain the masses, "the people" to whom she so often refers in a way that, without patronization, claims the vernacular as a beloved first language.

Hacker finds Jordan's "fluid, speech-become-aria quality" effective because it "fixes the poems in the reader's memory," and makes "even those on the most serious subjects, paradoxically fun to read" (136). Amy Alexander observes that "June Jordan has a prolific intellect and a vast reservoir of extraordinary and broad-based knowledge, yet her writing maintains its solid grounding in everyday experience" (7). The popular reception of Jordan's work is of equal or greater importance to both the poet and her work, than its reception by critics and academicians. However, it is just that crossover, that balance of exacting craft and global popular accessibility, that positions Jordan as one of contemporary literature's truest poets for the people.

BIBLIOGRAPHY

Works by June Jordan

Who Look at Me. New York: Thomas Y. Crowell, 1969. (poem for children)
SoulScript: Afro-American Poetry. Garden City, NY: Doubleday/Zenith, 1970. (anthology)

The Voice of the Children. New York: Holt, Rinehart & Winston, 1970. (anthology)
His Own Where. New York: Thomas Y. Crowell, 1971. (novel)
Some Changes. New York: Dutton, 1971.
Dry Victories. New York: Holt, Rinehart & Winston, 1972. (children)
Fannie Lou Hamer. New York: Thomas Y. Crowell, 1972. (children)
New Days: Poems of Exile & Return. New York: Emerson Hall, 1974.
New Life: New Room. New York: Thomas Y. Crowell, 1975. (children's poetry)
Things That I Do in the Dark: Selected Poetry. New York: Random House, 1977.
Passion: New Poems, 1977–1980. Boston: Beacon Press, 1980.
Civil Wars: Observations from the Front Lines of America. Boston: Beacon Press, 1981. (essays)
Kimako's Story. Boston: Houghton Mifflin, 1981. (children)
Living Room. New York: Thunder's Mouth Press, 1985.
On Call: New Political Essays. Boston: South End Press, 1985.
Lyrical Campaigns. London: Virago Press, 1989. (essays)
Moving Towards Home. London: Virago Press, 1989. (essays)
Naming Our Destiny: New and Selected Poems. New York: Thunder's Mouth Press, 1989.
Technical Difficulties: African American Notes on the State of the Union. New York: Pantheon, 1992. (essays)
Haruko/Love Poems. New York: Serpent's Tail/High Risk, 1994.
I Was Looking at the Ceiling and Then I Saw the Sky. New York: Scribner, 1995. (libretto)
Kissing God Goodbye: Poems. New York: Anchor Books, 1997.
Affirmative Acts: Political Essays. New York: Anchor Books, 1998.
Soldier: A Poet's Childhood. New York: Basic Books, 2000. (autobiography)

Studies of June Jordan

Alexander, Amy. *Fifty Black Women Who Changed America*. New York: Birch Lane Press, 1999.
Baker, David. "Probable Reason, Possible Joy," *Kenyon Review* (1992): 152–57.
Bashir, Samiya A. "June Jordan's True Grit." *Black Issues Book Review* 2.5 (2000): 32–36.
Bloom, Harold. *Black American Women Poets and Dramatists*. New York: Chelsea House, 1995.
Boyd, M. J. "The Whitman Awakening in June Jordan's Poetry." *Obsidian* 2–3 (1981): 226–28.
Brogan, Jacqueline Vaught. "From Warrior to Womanist: The Development of June Jordan's Poetry." In *Speaking the Other Self: American Women Writers*, edited by Jeanne Campbell Reesman. Athens: University of Georgia Press, 1997. 198–209.
———. "Planets on the Table: from Wallace Stevens and Elizabeth Bishop to Adrienne Rich and June Jordan." *Wallace Stevens Journal* (1995): 255–78.
Erickson, Peter. "The Love Poetry of June Jordan." *Callaloo* 9.1 (1986): 221–34.
Hacker, Marilyn. "Provoking Engagement." *The Nation*, 29 Jan. 1990, 135–39.
Harjo, Joy. "An Interview with June Jordan." *High Planes Literary Review*. 3.2 (1988): 60–76.
MacPhail, Scott. "June Jordan and the New Black Intellectuals." *African American Review* 33.1 (1999): 57–71.
Mullaney, Janet Palmer, ed. *Truthtellers of the Times: Interviews with Contemporary Women Poets*. Ann Arbor: University of Michigan Press, 1998.
Pratt, Minnie Bruce. "Warrior Poet." *Lambda Book Report* (July 2000): 22.
Rich, Adrienne. "The Hermit's Scream." In *What Is Found There: Notebooks on Poetry and Politics*. New York: Norton, 1993.
Rothschild, Matthew. "A Feast of Poetry." Review of *City of Coughing and Dead Radiators*,

by Martin Espada, Review of *Poetry Like Bread: An Anthology of Political Poems*, ed. by Martin Espada, Review of *The Phoenix Gone, the Terrace Empty*, by Marilyn Chin, Review of *Neon Vernacular*, by Yusef Komunyakaa, Review of *Cosmopolitan Greetings: Poems 1986–1992*, by Allen Ginsberg, Review of *Haruko/Love Poems*, by June Jordan. *Progressive* 58.5 (1994): 48–52.

Splawn, P. Jane. "New World Consciousness in the Poetry of Ntozake Shange and June Jordan: Two African-American Women's Responses to Expansionism in the Third World." *CLA Journal* 39 (1996): 417–31.

Towns, Saundra. "June Jordan: An Overview." In *Contemporary Poets*, edited by Thomas Riggs. Detroit: St. James Press, 2001. 601–02.

JANE KENYON (1947–1995)

Jessica Allen

BIOGRAPHY

In her short life, Jane Kenyon wrote poetry, worked as a translator, contributed newspaper columns to her local daily, and gave talks and lectures at the occasional conference. Born in 1947, she spent the first twenty-some years of her life in Ann Arbor, Michigan, including earning her BA and MA degrees from the university there. While a student at the University of Michigan, Kenyon not only received the Avery and Julia Hopwood Award for poetry, but she also met poet and Michigan professor Donald Hall. In 1972, after Kenyon received her master's degree, the pair married and moved to Eagle Pond Farm, Hall's ancestral home in New Hampshire.

This transition proved most fruitful to Kenyon's work; she explained to Bill Moyers in a 1993 interview that when she moved to New England, she "had absolutely unstructured time . . . so [she] really began to work seriously as [a] poet" (224). She published her first book shortly after arriving in New Hampshire, and Hall was her first reader, harshest critic, and most ardent supporter throughout her life. She spent her days gardening, writing and reading voluminously, attending the church where Hall was a deacon, and enjoying the small New England community in which she lived. Bill Moyers filmed and interviewed Kenyon and Hall for the prize-winning documentary "A Life Together" for the Public Broadcasting System in 1993.

In 1994, after Kenyon nursed Hall through his bout with liver cancer and mourned the losses of her mother-in-law and father, doctors diagnosed Kenyon with leukemia. Despite intense treatments and bone marrow transplants, she died at her home in New Hampshire on April 22, 1995.

Her most famous remembrance remains Hall's book of poetry, *Without* (1998), published a few years after her death. It details Hall's responses to Kenyon's fifteen-month struggle with leukemia and the aftermath of her death, as well as portrays much of their life together. In "Midsummer Letter," one of the many letter-poems throughout the book addressed to Kenyon, Hall visits her grave and reads the headstone inscribed with words Kenyon wrote for Hall's death—an event both believed would precede her own; it reads, in part, "I Believe in the Miracles of Art" (56).

MAJOR WORKS AND THEMES

Three themes—nature, religion, and depression—appear again and again throughout the four books published in Kenyon's lifetime, *From Room to Room* (1978), *The Boat of Quiet Hours* (1986), *Let Evening Come* (1990), and *Constance* (1993), and the two published posthumously, *Otherwise: New and Selected Poems* (1996) and *A Hundred White Daffodils* (1999). Her poetry reveals a powerful talent for observation, a deep capacity for feeling, and the desire to persevere and to survive all that she suffered.

To understand the poetry of Jane Kenyon, one must understand the extent to which her personal life informed her writing life. She was a poet of observation and of the senses; as she experienced her life, so she wrote her poetry. Cleaning the kitchen floor and finding a stray hair led to a meditation on the women who preceded her in the New Hampshire farmhouse in "Finding a Long Gray Hair." Watching beavers move beneath a frozen pond caused her to meditate upon thoughts moving through the mind in "The Beaver Pool in December," and seeing an icicle penetrate a snowdrift conjured images of other violence in "Bright Sun after a Heavy Snow." In lyric poem after lyric poem, Kenyon used nature as a springboard for her thoughts about religion, depression, community, and redemption.

Kenyon published her first book, *From Room to Room*, shortly after moving to New Hampshire, and the book is full of commentary about the New England landscape. As her other books came out, critics named her a New England poet, despite her Midwestern upbringing. An avid gardener and fond of long walks, Kenyon found her source in nature. She delighted in describing her available landscape throughout all the seasons, as well as the foibles of animals on neighboring farms. In these poems, Kenyon begins with a description of an animal or the landscape, a generality that she discusses for two or so stanzas, and ends with a specific conclusion about human nature or life—as if the act of regarding the natural world allowed her to draw this conclusion.

In her later books, especially *Let Evening Come* and *Constance*, her conclusions and thoughts are more religious in scope. She returned to Christianity by attending the local church, and she often co-opted the language of prayer in her work. Some of the poems from *Let Evening Come* have been incorporated into various religious services, including the title poem, and William Bolcom set many of the poems in this volume to music for song and piano in *Briefly It Enters* to memorialize soprano Tatiana Troyanos.

Kenyon's religious poetry is moral in tone but never didactic. She makes sure that readers understand that this way of living works for her and her only, and she seeks to share her lessons, not to extol them. Each poem constantly reminds us of her humanity; we see a woman making the best out of her situations, sometimes failing, often succeeding. All her books contain poems about daily acts, from dieting to taking afternoon naps to running errands; reality is her starting point although she frequently shifts her attention to metaphysics and religion.

Constance, the last book published in her lifetime, is her most religious book. It begins with an epigraph from Psalm 139, and the prayer's themes of darkness and light, of suffering and redemption through religious awakening reverberate throughout the poems in this volume. Here, rushing water is a sign of "benevolence," and giving a dog a biscuit is compared to giving the sacrament in "Biscuit." Kenyon tried to find solace in daily acts and scenes to settle herself amidst the turmoil of death, sickness, and trauma surrounding her.

Her last book also contains "Having It Out with Melancholy," a nine-part poem dealing exclusively with her depression, a theme she introduced in her second book, *The Boat of Quiet Hours* (1986). Kenyon suffered from this disease throughout her adult life, as did Hall, and she joked on National Public Radio's *Fresh Air Program* about their struggles with mental illness by saying, "We try to arrange for one of us to be manic and the other depressed at the same time . . . if someone took the two of us and shook us up in a brown paper bag and turned us out, there would really be one complete human being." She claimed in Part 1 of "Having It Out with Melancholy" that depression "taught [her] to live without gratitude"; her body of work, however, proves otherwise. In her darkest moments, the world held no pleasure for her, and she moved through life as if a member of the walking dead, a feeling she details in numerous poems. When the medication worked or the fog lifted, she regained the lost gratitude and felt the immense pull of life surrounding her. Her poems show that despite odds and circumstances that might have dictated otherwise, she did in fact learn to feel and express gratitude. As Kenyon wrote in "Happiness," the opening poem in *Otherwise*, "there's just no accounting for happiness."

Most critics agree that she wrote best about herself, her perceptions and experiences, and less well in the poems that explore others. According to Adrian Oktenberg in a review of *Otherwise* in *Women's Review of Books*, Kenyon writes "a poetry based on privilege. . . . [She was] a woman with privacy, with the leisure to sleep away the afternoon," to tend her beloved garden, and to take long walks with Hall (28). In *Constance*, she explored life from different perspectives, including that of a wounded soldier in the Civil War and of a woman struggling in poverty, and Kenyon achieved more success here than in previous works. Indeed, Paul Breslin, in a review of *Otherwise* in *Poetry*, states that Kenyon had "the gift Aristotle thought was unteachable and the surest sign of genius: the swift perception of likeness amid difference" (229). These poems, as well as the new poems represented in *Otherwise*, show a shift in Kenyon's subject matter from the previous personal and private to the more universal and public. Her early death prevented us from seeing this shift achieve its true fruition.

Although Kenyon will be remembered first and foremost for her poetry, she also translated a volume of Anna Akhmatova's poetry from the Russian with Vera Sandomirsky Dunham and wrote the occasional prose piece for her local paper, *The Concord Monitor*, in New Hampshire. *A Hundred White Daffodils*, published in 1999, collects much of her other writings, mostly newspaper columns, some interviews she gave, and the Akhmatova translations. Again, we see the repetition and exploration of themes familiar from her poetry: gardening and the outdoors, the importance of Christianity and religion in her life, her daily struggles and small blessings.

CRITICAL RECEPTION

Perhaps more important than Kenyon's critical reception is her loyal readership. Her plain, unadorned style and vivid imagery attracted and held readers, as did her simple themes. She spoke to lovers of nature, those affected by depression directly or indirectly, and people struggling to find something sacred in a world that was often cruel, and these readers responded in kind by devouring her poetry. However, she was not without critical accolades. In 1995 Kenyon became New Hampshire's poet laureate, a position Hall held from 1984–1989. She received a Guggenheim Fellowship from 1992–93, and she was a National Endowment for the Arts Fellow in 1981. Anthologies and magazines including the *Best American Poetry* series, *Poetry*, *The New Yorker*, and *Atlantic Monthly* regularly published her work.

Critics praise her perspicacity, the tightly structured lyrical and musical aspects of her poems, and the poems' voices that provide glimpses into the psyche and the heart. One of her most ardent supporters, Carol Muske, notes that Kenyon had the ability to "capture truth at its familiar New England slant" (13) in a *New York Times Book Review* of *The Boat of Quiet Hours*. Kenyon's emphasis on New England, the subtle, almost quiet, style of her poetry, and its revelations all point to the influence of two other New England poets, Emily Dickinson and Robert Frost.

Critics also compare Kenyon's work to that of John Keats and Sylvia Plath. Kenyon read Keats passionately, deriving the title of her second book, *The Boat of Quiet Hours*, from his poem "Endymion" and often reworked his "Ode to Autumn" in her own particular style. In his entry on Kenyon in *Contemporary Women Poets*, Gary Roberts calls Kenyon a "Keatsian poet," a term meant to describe both her connection to Keats and her type of "philosophically minded pastoral poetry" (196). As for the Plath-Kenyon comparison, critics realize that it stems from similar subject matter and not from technique. Although both described their bouts with depression in great detail, Plath let her dark demons overwhelm both her life and her poetry. Kenyon, in contrast, struggled for redemption in her existence and in her work, and she sought to find the light, whether religious or natural, that would let her "fall into [her] life again," as she wrote in the poem "Back."

Since her death, the critical attention to her work continues to match the public response. The *New York Times* named *Otherwise* one of the Notable Books of the Year in 1997. Her poems receive acclaim and inclusion in anthologies, and poet-friends, namely Sharon Olds, Robert Bly, Maxine Kumin, and Galway Kinnell, dedicate poems and books to her life and memory. The Milne Special Collections and Archives Department at the University of New Hampshire's Dimond Library maintains an Internet website about her life with Hall. Scholars and writers gathered in her honor at the University of New Hampshire and the annual Jane Kenyon Conference at Bellarmine College in Louisville, Kentucky, and the New Hampshire Writers Project remembers her through the Jane Kenyon Fund by bestowing a cash award to a New England poet biannually.

BIBLIOGRAPHY

Works by Jane Kenyon

From Room to Room. Cambridge, MA: Alice James Poetry Cooperative, 1978.

Twenty Poems of Anna Akhmatova. Translator, with Vera Sandomirsky Dunham. St. Paul, MN: Eighties Press/Ally Press, 1985.

The Boat of Quiet Hours. St. Paul, MN: Graywolf Press, 1986.

Let Evening Come. St. Paul, MN: Graywolf Press, 1990.

Constance. St. Paul, MN: Graywolf Press, 1993.

Otherwise: New & Selected Poems. St. Paul, MN: Graywolf Press, 1996.
A Hundred White Daffodils. St. Paul, MN: Graywolf Press, 1999. (essays, interviews, and other writings)

Studies of Jane Kenyon

"A Life Together." *Bill Moyers' Journal*. PBS. WNET, New York, 17 Dec. 1993.
"A Tribute to Jane Kenyon 1947–1995." *Columbia* 26 (1996): 154–81.
Barber, David. Review of *Constance*, by Jane Kenyon. *Poetry* (June 1994): 161–65.
Breslin, Paul. Review of *Otherwise: New and Selected Poems*, by Jane Kenyon. *Poetry* (July 1997): 226–40.
Germain, Edward. "Jane Kenyon." In *Contemporary Poets*, edited by Thomas Rigs. 6th ed. New York: St. James Press, 1996. 576–78.
Hall, Donald. *Without*. Boston: Mariner Books, 1998.
Kuhar, Lawrence. "Optical Allusions and Personal Voices in Jane Kenyon's Poetry." In *"Bright Unequivocal Eye": Poems, Papers and Remembrances from the First Jane Kenyon Conference*, edited by Bert G. Hornback. New York: Peter Lang, 2000. 127–28.
Mattison, Alice. " 'Let It Grow in the Dark Like a Mushroom': Writing with Jane Kenyon." *Michigan Quarterly Review* 39.1 (2000): 121–37.
Moyers, Bill. *The Language of Life: A Festival of Poets*. New York: Doubleday, 1995. 219–38.
Muske, Carol. "In the Heart of the Heart of the Country." Review of *Otherwise: New and Selected Poems*, by Jane Kenyon. *New York Times Book Review*, 5 Jan. 1997, 12–16.
———. "Reading Their Signals." Review of *The Boat of Quiet Hours*, by Jane Kenyon. *New York Times Book Review*, 21 June 1987, 13–16.
Neff, Lavonne. "An Appetite for the Sun." *Books & Culture* (Jan./Feb. 1997): 22–24.
Oktenberg, Adrian. Review of *Otherwise: New and Selected Poems*, by Jane Kenyon. *Women's Review of Books*, 1 July 1997, 27–28.
Roberts, Gary. "Jane Kenyon." In *Contemporary Women Poets*, edited by Pamela L. Shelton. Detroit, MI: St. James Press, 1998. 196–97.

CAROLYN KIZER (1925–)

Deborah Phelps

BIOGRAPHY

Carolyn Kizer, considered one of the most technically virtuosic American poets writing today, is celebrated both for her translations and "imitations" of ancient Asian poetry and for her own contemporary work. Kizer was born in Spokane, Washington, where her parents—a lawyer and a biology professor, turned housewife—were deeply involved in community affairs and where their home served as a salon for various westward traveling intellectual and artistic figures of the Depression era. Both parents instilled in Kizer a love of literature; her father became a patron of the poet Vachel Lindsay for a time in Kizer's early childhood. Kizer, raised in Los Angeles, graduated from Sarah Lawrence College in New York in 1945, and attended graduate school at Columbia University and the University of Washington.

Although Kizer published her first poem in the *New Yorker* in 1942 at age seventeen, she did not begin to seriously prepare for a career in poetry until 1955. Divorced and once again living in Washington, Kizer enrolled in Theodore Roethke's poetry workshop at the University of Washington. From Roethke, Kizer learned the poetic techniques that would forever shape her own work: strict attention to form, risk-taking subject matter, and an unsentimental yet personal voice. In 1959 Kizer helped start the journal *Poetry Northwest*, which she edited until 1965.

Kizer's first major collection, *The Ungrateful Garden*, appeared in 1961, followed by *Knock Upon Silence* in 1965. When these two volumes quickly went out of print, Kizer brought together new work with older, more famous poems in *Midnight Was My Cry: New and Selected Poems* (1971) and *Mermaids in the Basement: Poems for Women* (1984). *Yin: New Poems* (1984) won the 1985 Pulitzer Prize for poetry. A book of Asian translations, *Carrying Over: Translations from Many Tongues* (1985), was followed by new work in *The Nearness of You: Poems for Men* (1986). A volume of selected poems, *Harping On: Poems 1985–1995*, was published in 1996. Kizer compiled her essays in two volumes: *Proses: Essays on Poets and Poetry* (1994) and

Picking and Choosing: Essays on Prose (1995). She also edited *The Essential Clare* (1992) and *100 Great Poems by Women* (1992). Kizer taught at numerous universities and poetry workshops, she served as the first director of the literature program for the National Endowment of the Arts (1966–70), and she held the position of Chancellor of the Academy of American Poets (1990–98). Kizer currently lives in Sonoma, California.

MAJOR WORKS AND THEMES

Kizer's poetry is difficult to categorize. In her long career, she has embraced both classical metric forms and experimented with Eastern syllabics. Her early volumes show the influence of her mentor Roethke in their vivid, highly formulaic verses that mingle nature with family relationships. In her later work, Kizer more frequently combines poems of formal prosody with those of free verse. Critics often classify her as a poet of "women's subjects," most famously for her feminist satire "Pro Femina" and for her poems about women's relationships with men in myth, history, and contemporary society.

The Ungrateful Garden (1961) introduces readers to Kizer's strikingly unromantic nature imagery. To Kizer nature is wild and detached from man, although man forces an interaction with nature. In "The Blue Heron," Kizer, mourning her mother's death, uses nature as an image of her loss; the heron does not represent her mother, but rather it represents her mother's inevitable departure from the daughter's life. In "An Intruder," another poem featuring her mother, Kizer's mother rescues a bat trapped by a cat. Kizer effectively undercuts the possible sentimentality of this narrative when she reveals the bat as lice-ridden.

Kizer's first book of poems in "the Japanese mode" hints at the poet's interest in Asian poetry, but in her second volume, *Knock Upon Silence* (1965), Kizer devotes the bulk of the text to translations and "imitations" of Chinese poetry. Kizer translates poems from the ancient Chinese poets Tu Fu and Po Chu-I. The real impact of this volume emerges in Kizer's use of Asian forms to create a new, modern narrative poetry. For example, she writes "A Month in Summer," the tale of a failed love relationship in the Japanese haibun, a mix of haiku and prose. The use of Asian syllabics has the expected effect of shortening Kizer's lines and pruning her verbiage, providing a contrast to poems in more elaborate Western metrical forms.

Despite the predominantly Asian tone of the book, "Pro Femina," a Juvenalian satire written in Roman hexameter, serves as the centerpiece of *Knock Upon Silence*. The three parts of "Pro Femina" refer loosely to the position of women in modern society and to women writers. This poem, a feminist polemic, appeared shortly after Adrienne Rich's "Snapshots of a Daughter-in-law" and Sylvia Plath's *Ariel*, but Kizer's poem anticipated the second wave of the Women's Movement. In "Pro Femina" Kizer, in a voice reminiscent of eighteenth-century Augustan poets Alexander Pope and John Dryden, archly rails against society's silencing of women.

"Pro Femina" takes aim at a patriarchal culture that severely circumscribes female lives and achievements, particularly in literature. Kizer describes how most women writers throughout history have been unmarried and childless as society made it difficult for women to achieve fulfillment in both family and career. In describing the pallid women poets of the past, Kizer recalls Virginia Woolf's "angel in the house," the archetypal female sacrifice to patriarchy, and Kizer warns her readers against challenging male literary authority even today. Although the poem's comedic complaint paints a dismal picture for women past and present, it ends hopefully, looking to a future where women and men can live together equally, and where women can have the conventional loves of wife and mother while writing freely.

With the publication of *Mermaids in the Basement: Poems for Women* (1984), Kizer added a fourth section to the collection's reprint of "Pro Femina," "Fanny" written in the voice of the American wife of Robert Louis Stevenson, Fanny. Kizer situates Fanny in Samoa recording in her diary the daily life of house world in the bewildering topics. While her husband writes every morning, Fanny works at her recalcitrant gardens, struggles with the climate, and nurses her various physical ailments. Kizer's portrait of Fanny as a strong, resilient woman is heroic as we recognize her as one of the censored and self-censoring—literary women described in earlier sections of "Pro Femina." When the hardworking Fanny has time to take up her diary, she sometimes finds it altered; her critical statements crossed out by "someone." She, however, knows the culprit. When her husband slights her American nationality, Fanny records the slight "hoping" that he will read the entry and regret his comments. Chillingly, after this entry comes the note "This will be erased." Kizer ends the poem at Robert Louis Stevenson's death with Fanny plotting her escape from her island of difficult domesticity to live "wild" as a free woman.

Mermaids in the Basement reprises a number of Kizer's more popular earlier works concerning women: "A Month in Summer," "The Great Blue Heron," and "The Intruder," as well as new works from *Yin: New Poems* (1984) such as "Fanny," "A Muse," and poems for her daughter and female friends. "A Muse," a prose memoir, again recalls Kizer's mother. "A Muse" shows her mother as a vibrant woman whose intellectual and creative potential was blunted by a traditional marriage to a difficult man. Kizer realizes her mother channeled her frustrated ambitions into nurturing Kizer's own artistic potential, and she writes with sensitivity of her adolescent resentment of her mother's anxious care and how her mother's death freed her as a poet. Nevertherless, Kizer admits that every poem is written still "for her."

As its title suggests, *Yin* continues Kizer's experimentations with Asian poetic forms. Although only "Three for Tu Fu" and "After Basho" are directly imitative of Asian syllabics, several poems with contemporary themes—"Race Relations," "Postcards from Rotterdam," and "Antique Father"—borrow from them as a break from Kizer's more typical long, regularly metered stanzas. "Threatening Letters," another variant prose poem, speaks in the voice of a woman to her ex-husband concerning his possible disclosures regarding their life together in his autobiography. In her warning to the man to keep her out of his book, the woman rehashes the petty irritants of their discarded marriage, providing a vivid picture of post-marital strife. With its run-on sentences and inconsistent punctuation and spelling, "Threatening Letters," proves effective as a document of pure rage, capturing the woman's well-worn resentments and also, surprisingly, her wish, hidden just beneath her anger, that her ex-husband *not* forget her.

"Afternoon Happiness," written in Kizer's familiar hexameters, provides a striking contrast to "Threatening Letters." Wondering if only suffering can yield poetry, Kizer declares herself *too* happy in a relationship to produce a good poem. Kizer reviews her life and finds nothing about which to complain as even thoughts of her ex-husband have lost their ability to wound. Loath to commemorate her love "in light verse," she toys with creating sadness by imagining the loved one's death or by picking a fight, but these machinations ring false. She concludes by giving the poem up to its true subject, happiness. "Afternoon Happiness" ultimately finishes as light verse with the intricacies of her tightly controlled stanzas and rhyme scheme providing the poem's strongest anchor.

Relationships between men and women are rarely this happy in Kizer's world. From the early "A Month in Summer" through "Pro Femina" and "Threatening Letters," Kizer portrays a feminist love/hate stance toward male friends, colleagues, lovers, and most significantly, her father. "My Good Father" and "Thrall" emerge as companion pieces that flesh out the portrait of Kizer's father seen peripherally in her earlier prose work "A Muse." "My Good Father" places the authoritarian figure of "A Muse" center stage, outlining Kizer's childhood façade of quiet obedience to a demanding yet, at heart, benevolent man. The adult Kizer warms to the memory of her father as a good and loving man though unable to show his child his deeper self. "Thrall" covers similar ground although the keynote here remains Kizer's simmering resentment of the stern patriarch she "almost" forgives in "My Good Father."

The Nearness of You: Poems for Men (1986) contains loving poems to her mentor Theodore Roethke and to fellow poets. In "Amusing Our Daughters," Kizer revels in the family of (mostly male) poet-friends that she has assembled through the years. As the final poem in this volume, "Final Meeting," her elegy to James Wright—Kizer's classmate in Roethke's poetry workshop—ends the collection on a tender note. "Final Meeting" recounts Kizer's last hospital visit to Wright for which she dressed extravagantly in order to dazzle the dying man's spirits one last time.

One cannot overestimate the impact of Roethke's 1955 poetry workshop on Kizer as she mentions his legacy in nearly every interview and published essay on her writing. In her second collection of essays *Picking and Choosing: Essays on Prose* (1995), Kizer includes a lengthy homage to Roethke, describing his teaching style, personality, and the lasting effect on her work—specifically, the male poet's tough editing of his students' work: pruning all adjectives, cutting a line from each stanza, and calling for different verse forms. Kizer's own varied use of poetic forms and condensation of expression clearly reveals Roethke's stamp. He also shaped her poetic taste. Roethke, Kizer notes, encouraged his students to appreciate specific poets, but he did not encourage his students to imitate these poets, and he especially discouraged the workshop members from imitating *him*. Roethke's most lasting gift to Kizer was perhaps his teaching method: his preference for workshops open to everyone regardless of literary background, the cutting of "good" but unnecessary lines from a poem, and the value of memorization.

Kizer's latest collection, *Harping On: Poems 1985-1995* (1996), brings together a decade of new work that reinforces her reputation as the master of poetic form. Here she uses pantoums, sonnets, imitations of Chinese lyrics, and light verse, among other forms, to comment on the travesties of twentieth-century society and on the impact of personal events. Beginning with "An American Beauty," a moving account of a close friend's death from breast cancer, and concluding with "The Valley of the Fallen," a poem recalling the human toll of the Spanish Civil War, Kizer indicates that the personal is, ultimately, political.

Harping On raises the question regarding Kizer's decision to wait ten years to publish a new collection of poems. As her publishing history shows, Kizer routinely follows up a new collection with a volume of "selected" poems. Cooper Canyon released Kizer's newest offering *Cool, Calm & Collected* in 2000.

CRITICAL RECEPTION

Carolyn Kizer's poetry has been generally well received from the beginning of her career. Critics nearly always praise her technical accomplishments but frequently have less confidence in her work's rhetorical power of content. Dabney Stuart in his review of *Knock Upon Silence* feels that Kizer's "imitations" of Tu Fu, while technically interesting, lack an emotional understanding of Asian poetry. Stuart also opines that Kizer's "Eastern attitudes" are at odds with the "Western aggressiveness" of "Pro Femina." Helen Fowler's review of the same books praises Kizer's Asian poetry for producing "a really modern narrative poem" but judges Juvenalian satire as an uninspiring rhetorical resource for "Pro Femina." Richard Howard criticizes Kizer's rendering of nature in her first two books as inferior to Roethke's, but he called the myth-based "Columns and Caryatids" "magnificent" in its depiction of female identity. However, this critic finds "Pro Femina" a mixed effort: "poetry, of a fruitfully damaged, unresolved and nearly inescapable order" ("Carolyn Kizer" 114).

Several critics express regret that the technical finish in "Pro Femina" seems to succeed at the expense of the emotional impact of the poem. Both Patricia Hampl and Diane Wakoski fault the lack of authority in the satiric mode as opposed to the more personal lyric. In *Mermaids in the Basement* and *The Nearness of You*, Hampl praises the more openly emotional poems "Thrall" and "A Muse," as she believes their forms do not obscure or undercut content as much as they do in the less successful Japanese haibun "A Month in Summer." Wakoski, writing for a leftist feminist publication, doubts Kizer's overall "stance of feminism." This critic finds Kizer's devotion to form an inadequate response to the chaos of modern life and considers that Kizer would have been "happier in medieval Provence . . . having no other purpose but to entertain the rich, the courtiers, the people in power" (7). Wakoski concludes that Kizer succeeds mainly as a chronicler of family life and personal relationships identifying her as "a poet of occasion, of person, and personality" (7).

Alice Fulton, in a review of Kizer's career, praises Kizer's "irreverent, unromantic stance" and singles out "Fanny" as a particularly valuable view into an obscure woman's life. Initially, Fulton also had doubts about Kizer's feminism in *Mermaids in the Basement*, but she finds that Kizer looks at men just as "ambivalently" in *The Nearness of You.* Fulton writes that Kizer's "wordplay, puns, extended conceits recalls seventeenth-century aesthetics" and "marvel[s] at Kizer's technical skill and inventiveness" (374). Clearly Kizer holds an important place in American poetics.

BIBLIOGRAPHY

Works by Carolyn Kizer

The Ungrateful Garden. Bloomington: University of Indiana Press, 1961.

Knock Upon Silence. Seattle: University of Washington Press, 1965.

Midnight Was My Cry: New and Selected Poems. New York: Doubleday, 1971.

Mermaids in the Basement: Poems for Women. Port Townsend, WA: Cooper Canyon Press, 1984.

Yin: New Poems. Brockport, NY: BOA Editions, 1984.

Carrying Over: Translations from Many Tongues. New York: Ecco Press, 1985.

The Nearness of You: Poems for Men. Port Townsend, WA: Cooper Canyon Press, 1986.

The Essential Clare. Ed. New York: Ecco Press, 1992.
100 Great Poems by Women. New York: Ecco Press, 1992.
Proses: Essays on Poets and Poetry. Cheney: Eastern Washington University Press, 1994.
Picking and Choosing: Essays on Prose. Port Townsend, WA: Copper Canyon Press, 1995.
Harping On: Poems 1985–1995. Port Townsend, WA: Copper Canyon Press, 1996.
Cool, Calm, & Collected. Port Townsend, WA: Copper Canyon Press, 2000.

Studies of Carolyn Kizer

Corradino, Dolfph. Review of *The Nearness of You*, by Carolyn Kizer. *Western American Literature* 4 (1988): 371.

Finch, Annie, Johanna Keller, and Candance McClelland, eds. *Carolyn Kizer: Perspectives on Her Life and Work*. Fort Lee, NJ: CarvanKerry Press, 2001.

Fowler, Helen. "More about 'Approach' Authors." *Approach* 59 (1966): 30–36.

Fulton, Alice. "Main Things." *Poetry* 4 (1988): 372–77.

Hampl, Patricia. "Women Who Say What They Mean." Review of *Mermaids in the Basement* and *Yin*, by Carolyn Kizer. *New York Times Book Review*, 25 Nov. 1984, 36.

Howard, Richard. "Carolyn Kizer." *Tri-Quarterly* 7 (1966): 109–17.

———. "Pursuits and Followings." Review of *Midnight Was My Cry*, by Carolyn Kizer. *Poetry* 5 (1972): 296–303.

Jarman, Mark, "Generations and Contemporaries." *Hudson Review* 2 (1985): 327–42.

Libby, Anthony. "Fathers and Daughters and Mothers and Poets." Review of *The Nearness of You: Poems for Men*, by Carolyn Kizer. *New York Times Book Review*, 22 Mar. 1987, 23.

Rigsbee, David, ed. *An Answering Music: On the Poetry of Carolyn Kizer*. Boston: Ford, Brown, 1989.

Stitt, Peter. "The Typical Poem." Review of *Yin*, by Carolyn Kizer. *Kenyon Review* 4 (1986): 128–33.

Stuart, Dabney. "Weights and Measures." *Shenandoah* 2 (1966): 91–102.

Wakoski, Diane. "Poets in Our Time." Review of *The Nearness of You: Poems for Men*, by Carolyn Kizer. *Women's Review of Books*, 12 Sept. 1987, 7.

MAXINE KUMIN (1925–)

Claudia Milstead

BIOGRAPHY

Maxine Kumin, a celebrated poet, has also written successful short stories, novels, essays, and children's books. Now in her seventies, she continues to write from the 200-acre horse farm in Warner, New Hampshire, that she and her husband have owned since 1963 and that became their permanent home in 1976. Recently recovered from an equestrian accident, Kumin travels frequently to accept awards or to read her work.

Born Maxine Winokur in Philadelphia, Pennsylvania, to Reform Jewish parents, she was the daughter of a pawnbroker. Kumin has always loved animals and remembers befriending the horses that pulled garbage wagons through the neighborhood where she grew up. Swimming was another passion. In mastering the Australian crawl as a child, Kumin says, she learned how to "achieve maximum thrust with minimum exertion" (*Always* 40), a practice she later applied to writing poetry. At eighteen, she was invited to join Billy Rose's Aquacade, a traveling show that performed synchronized swim routines, but her father refused to let her go.

Kumin earned a BA in 1946 and an MA in 1948, both from Radcliffe. Her first published poem was a four-liner in *The Christian Science Monitor*, written three months before her third child was born. In 1957 she enrolled in a poetry workshop taught by John Holmes at the Boston Center for Adult Education, where she met another young housewife named Anne Sexton. They read and critiqued each other's poetry, often talking for hours on the telephone, and collaborated on four children's books. Their friendship remained close until Sexton's 1974 suicide. Kumin and her husband Victor, a retired chemical engineer, have been married since 1946. They are the parents of two daughters and a son.

Kumin won the 1973 Pulitzer Prize in poetry for *Up Country: Poems of New England* (1972), which contains "Woodchucks," one of her best-known poems. Beginning in 1981, Kumin served one year as poetry consultant to the Library of Congress, a position renamed poet laureate of the United States. She was the twenty-sixth consultant in poetry and the fifth woman to hold the post since its creation in 1936. Convinced that women and minorities were not being given adequate consideration in the world of serious poetry, Kumin organized readings and lunches during her tenure as consultant to bring attention to women and minority poets.

In November 1980, just after her appointment as consultant, but before she took office, Kumin participated in the Library of Congress' Council of Scholars symposium on creativity. She sharply criticized a fellow participant, violinist Yehudi Menuhin, for his characterization of the creative urges of men and women. In his paper "Creativity in the Arts," Menuhin said that men's creative urges are a need "to strike out, to build roads—roads anywhere and nowhere in particular" while women's are a compulsion "to plough and till over and over again the same plot of earth, from time to time attracting a male to ensure its fertility and, if she has captivated him, defending it together, or alone, against other male depredations" (Darling F6). Kumin called these comments "a dangerous, sexist stereotyping" (Darling F6; Bird and Krebs B6). Menuhin, who was surprised to learn that his comments were offensive, said he regretted being characterized as "a male chauvinist pig" (Bird and Krebs B6). Kumin also took exception to the fact that she was one of only two women among the twenty-three members appointed to the council, and the only woman to attend the meeting. She remarked that she felt as though she had "stumbled into a stag club and ought to leap out of a cake" (B6). In 1998 Kumin resigned from the Academy of American Poets in support of charges that the organization was biased along race and gender lines. Refusing to accept her resignation, as well as others that followed, the academy began to revise its structure to include more women and minorities.

Kumin suffered a life-threatening accident at her New Hampshire farm on July 21, 1998, at age seventy-three. A skilled horsewoman, Kumin was training for a carriage-driving competition when a logging truck spooked her horse Deuteronomy, causing her to be thrown from the carriage. Although the horse carefully avoided stepping on her, the 350-pound carriage rolled over the right side of her body, breaking eleven ribs, puncturing a lung, and fracturing two vertebrae, in addition to causing other injuries. Kumin spent three months in a restraint called a "halo" that kept her head stationary while the vertebrae healed. Miraculously, Kumin not only survived but achieved nearly total recovery, and in less than a year, she was teaching a poetry class in Florida.

As she travels across the country reading her poems and being interviewed by newspaper reporters, Kumin frequently remarks that "you can't make a living writing poetry in this country, but you can make something of a living by going around and being a poet" (Knaff A16). She refers to the activity that provides a poet's living as "pobiz" (for "poetry business") and in fact calls her New Hampshire property "PoBiz Farm," implying that the farm is made possible by the business of being a poet. In her pursuit of pobiz, Kumin has served as visiting professor of poetry at colleges and universities across the country, including Claremont, Washington University, Florida International University, Columbia, Massachusetts Institute of Technology, and Princeton, where one of her poetry students was David Duchovny, later an actor.

Although known for her direct, no-nonsense approach to life as well as poetry, Kumin is supportive and nurturing of other poets, especially those not yet well known. A self-described atheist, Kumin nonetheless frequently calls herself an evangelist for poetry, a label she continues to earn as she travels across the country, talking about being a poet.

MAJOR WORKS AND THEMES

Kumin explores in her poems the world around her, a world inhabited not only by people, but also the dogs, horses, visiting ewes, and wildlife on and around her farm. Virtually every facet of her life, every significant and ordinary memory, has become the subject of Kumin's poems—a morning swim, the memory of her father's feet, Anne Sexton, vegetarianism, feeding time at the farm—but perhaps the clearest note is Kumin's unmistakable concern for animals. Wesley McNair finds Kumin's animal poems "important both in defining her nature poetry and in the uniqueness of her poetic vision" (122).

This note is particularly evident in *Up Country: Poems of New England*, which is pure Kumin. These poems display her unconditional love of animals, her keen eye for rural New England, and her unsentimental reverence for farm routine. All of these themes come together in "For a Shetland Pony Brood Mare Who Died in Her Barren Year," which ends with the titular pony lying dead in the sunshine after experiencing a false pregnancy. In "Woodchucks," Kumin uses the human propensity for violence to forge an unforgettable link between the garden-devouring rodents and the Jews of the Holocaust. This poem of woodchucks and Jews, both objects of hatred, exemplifies Kumin's philosophy: "To write about the monstrous sense of alienation the poet feels in this culture of polarized hatreds is a way of staying sane" (*Always* 144).

Kumin has written numerous essays on the poetic process, generously sharing herself with aspiring poets and other readers. Collected, these essays serve as companion texts to her poems but also as slices of her life because, for Kumin, no separation between her writing and her living exists. In *To Make a Prairie: Essays on Poets, Poetry, and Country Living* (1979; its title is taken from Emily Dickinson's poem #1755), Kumin comments on many of her own poems, her friendship with Anne Sexton, the work of other poets, and her relationship with animals. Several interviews with Kumin are also included. The more recent essays in *Always Beginning: Essays on a Life in Poetry* (2000) provide an update on Kumin's human and animal families.

Characteristically both unsentimental and moving, *Inside the Halo and Beyond: The Anatomy of a Recovery* (2000) is the story of Kumin's 1998 accident and recovery. Kumin's daughter Judith, who urged her to tell the story, brought a laptop computer to the hospital and transcribed the first draft as her mother dictated. This memoir, like Kumin's poems and essays, weaves together the varied elements of a woman's life.

The Long Marriage (2001), Kumin's first book of poems since her accident, focuses on the relationships of a woman's life and includes poems about her long marriage as well as poems about political and social causes. This volume investigates the poet's relationship to these causes, to her horse farm in New Hampshire, and with her own body. Finally, *The Long Marriage* is about poetry itself.

CRITICAL RECEPTION

Critically acclaimed, Kumin has won virtually every award available to poets, including the Pulitzer Prize, and she has granted numerous interviews to journalists and scholars. When Emily Grosholz, a poet who teaches at Pennsylvania State University, sought out critical commentary on Kumin's poems, however, she learned that no one had written a book on Kumin. To correct the deficiency, she edited and published *Telling the Barn Swallow: Poets on the Poetry of Maxine Kumin* (1997). Grosholz characterizes Kumin's poems as "hopeful without being sentimental, formal without being contrived, and deliberative without being doctrinaire," while holding a perspective that "is at once cosmopolitan and local, urban and rustic, human and female" (ix).

In the prize-winning *Upcountry: Poems of New England*, according to reviewer Ralph Mills, Jr., Kumin displays "a capacity for *seeing* that places [her] in a direct line from the greenhouse poems of Roethke" and that depicts "humanity in the midst of nature"(222). She is compared to Robert Frost because of her keen observations of rural New England and to Anne Sexton and Sylvia Plath because of the confessional nature of her poems. Kumin's place in American poetry remains uniquely her own, however, as a nurturer of budding poets and a clear, compelling voice of reason and compassion.

BIBLIOGRAPHY

Works by Maxine Kumin

Halfway. New York: Holt, Rinehart and Winston, 1961.

The Privilege. New York: Harper, 1965.

Through Dooms of Love. New York: Harper, 1965. Republished as *A Daughter and Her Loves*. London: Gollancz/Hamilton, 1965. (novel)

The Passions of Uxport. New York: Harper, 1968. Also published as *The Keeper of His Beasts*. New York: Harper, 1968; Westport, CT: Greenwood Press, 1975. (novel)

The Nightmare Factory. New York: Harper, 1970.

The Abduction. New York: Harper, 1971. (novel)

Up Country: Poems of New England. New York: Harper, 1972.

The Designated Heir. New York: Viking Press, 1974.

House, Bridge, Fountain, Gate. New York: Viking Press, 1975.

The Retrieval System. New York: Viking Press and Penguin Books, 1978.

To Make a Prairie: Essays on Poets, Poetry, and Country Living. Ann Arbor: University of Michigan Press, 1979.

Our Ground Time Here Will Be Brief: New and Selected Poems. New York: Viking Press and Penguin Books, 1982.

Why Can't We Live Together Like Civilized Human Beings? New York: Viking Press, 1982. (short stories)

The Long Approach: Poems. New York: Viking Press and Penguin Books, 1985.

In Deep: Country Essays. New York: Viking Penguin, 1987.

Nurture: Poems. New York: Viking Penguin, 1989.

Looking for Luck: Poems. New York: Norton, 1992.

Women, Animals, and Vegetables: Essays and Stories. New York: Norton, 1994.

Connecting the Dots. New York: Norton, 1996.

Selected Poems, 1960–1990. New York: Norton, 1997.

Quit Monks or Die! Ashland, OR: Story Line Press, 1999. (novel)

Always Beginning: Essays on a Life in Poetry. Port Townsend, WA: Copper Canyon Press, 2000.

Inside the Halo and Beyond: The Anatomy of a Recovery. New York: Norton, 2000. (memoir)

The Long Marriage. New York: Norton, 2001.

Studies of Maxine Kumin

Bird, David, and Albin Krebs. "Symposium Becomes a Battleground of the Sexes." *New York Times*, 21 Nov. 1980, B6.

Booth, Philip. "Maxine Kumin's Survival." *American Poetry Review* 7.6 (1978): 18–19.
Cramer, Jeffrey S. "Peaceable Island: A Conversation with Maxine Kumin and Victor Kumin." *New Letters* 66.3 (2000): 60–79.
Darling, Lynn. "In Search of the Wild Muse." *Washington Post*, 21 Nov. 1980, F6.
Estess, Sybil P. "Past Halfway: *The Retrieval System* by Maxine Kumin." *Iowa Review* 10.4 (1979): 99–109.
George, Diana Hume. "Itinerary of an Obsession: Maxine Kumin's Poems to Anne Sexton." In *Original Essays on the Poems of Anne Sexton*, edited by Francis Bixler. Conway: University of Central Arkansas Press, 1988. 243–66.
———. " 'Keeping Our Working Distance': Maxine Kumin's Poetry of Loss and Survival." In *Aging and Gender in Literature: Studies in Creativity*, Edited by Anne M. Wyatt-Brown and Janice Rossen. Charlottesville: University Press of Virginia, 1993. 314–38.
Grosholz, Emily, ed. *Telling the Barn Swallow: Poets on the Poetry of Maxine Kumin*. Hanover, NH: University Press of New England, 1997.
Knaff, Devorah L. "Kumin Finds Rhymes and Reasons to Be a Poet." *Press-Enterprise*, 2 Feb. 1996, A16.
McNair, Wesley. "Kumin's Animal Confederates." In *Telling the Barn Swallow: Poets on the Poetry of Maxine Kumin,* edited by Emily Grosholz. Hanover, NH: University Press of New England, 1997. 122–34.
Mills, Ralph, Jr. "In the Fields of Imagination (MacLeish, Eberhart, Levertov, Kumin)." *Parnassus* 1 (1973): 211–24.
Myers, George, Jr. "Resignations, Fallout Highlight Strife within Poets Academy." *Columbus Dispatch*, 10 Dec. 1998, final ed., 7G.
Ratiner, Steven. "Maxine Kumin: New Life in the Barn." *Christian Science Monitor*, 13 May 1992, 16.
Selby, Holly. "Portfolio." *Baltimore Sun*, 6 Aug. 2000, final ed.: 10F.

DENISE LEVERTOV (1923–1997)

Lynn Domina

BIOGRAPHY

Denise Levertov was born in Ilford, Essex, England, of a Welsh mother and a Russian Jewish father who converted to Christianity and became an Anglican priest. Levertov and her sister, Olga, were home schooled, although they had tutors for French, art, and music. During World War II, Levertov worked as a nurse in London—like other English women, she might otherwise have been drafted to work in a munitions factory. In 1947 she married American writer Mitchell Goodman; they had one son, Nikolai Gregor, and were divorced in 1972. In 1948 Levertov moved with Goodman to the United States; she became an American citizen in 1955.

Levertov began writing poetry as a girl. When she was twelve, she sent some of her poems to T. S. Eliot, who responded with a lengthy and encouraging letter. Her first book, *The Double Image* (1946), was published before she left England. After emigrating to America, she published her poems in many collections that sometimes appeared as frequently as every year. She taught at a number of American colleges and universities, including Vassar, Berkeley, Tufts, Brandeis, and Stanford, which houses the majority of her manuscripts. She earned a number of prestigious awards, including the Shelley Memorial Award, a Guggenheim Fellowship, the Lenore Marshall Poetry Prize, and the Robert Frost Medal.

Especially during the 1960s and 1970s, Levertov devoted much of her time to political causes. She engaged in both the anti-Vietnam War and antinuclear movements and in 1965 co-founded Writers and Artists Protest Against the War in Vietnam. She participated in several antiwar demonstrations and, as a result, was occasionally arrested for civil disobedience. Later in her life, her political activism became less public, primarily because the imminent danger of nuclear destruction appeared to decrease, but she remained committed to liberal issues.

After retiring from teaching in 1992, Levertov moved to Seattle, Washington, where her son lived. She died there in 1997 from complications of lymphoma.

MAJOR WORKS AND THEMES

Most of Levertov's poetry is clearly within the lyric mode, with her major concerns and subjects including nature and its relation to the human world, religion and the idea of belief, and justice and injustice within the political realm. Her feminist consciousness generally informs much of her work. While nature, religion, and feminism can seem to be discrete topics, and while as a result her audience may at times seem segmented, Levertov's major ideas are, in fact, well integrated in her work. That is, she drew her ideas of justice from her religious beliefs, and her respect for nature informed her political choices. While her concerns evolved over the course of her career, these shifts become more a matter of emphasis than abrupt change.

Levertov's first book, *The Double Image*, was published in England only two years before she emigrated to the United States. The lyrical and often formal style characteristic of British neo-romanticism popular in England at the time marks this volume. In the decade between publication of *The Double Image* and her next collection, *Here and Now* (1956), Levertov systematically attended to the distinctions between British and American speech patterns. While she continued to read such European poets as Rilke and Hopkins, she also paid conscious attention to the particularly American voice of William Carlos Williams, whose work had a profound influence on her own. By the time *With Eyes at the Back of Our Heads* (1960) was published a few years later, readers and critics considered her an unequivocally American poet.

As the 1960s progressed and the United States witnessed dramatic shifts in many of its cultural assumptions, Levertov's work begins to reflect what she viewed as her responsibilities as a citizen. Much of her work of this time, in the collections *The Sorrow Dance* (1967) and *Relearning the Alphabet* (1970), for example, serve as an overt response to the war in Vietnam, and the tone of her poems grows pessimistic, at times nearly despairing. As in much poetry of social protest, Levertov's themes in this work are direct, even didactic. At this point, she emerges most prominently as an antiwar poet. As the war in Vietnam ended, Levertov did not immediately cease from writing politically engaged poetry, however, since the cold war appeared in other territories, especially Central America. Her "A Speech: For Antidraft Rally, D.C., March 22, 1980," collected in *Candles in Babylon* (1982), expresses her discouragement, even disgust, with draft-age men and women who support the idea of fighting for one's country but who disregard history and politics to such an extent that they collapse all enemies of the United States into the category "Communist" and confuse Korea with Vietnam. A crucial piece in *A Door in the Hive* (1989), "El Salvador: Requiem and Invocation," a libretto, honors Archbishop Oscar Romero, assassinated as he said mass at the cathedral in San Salvador, and four American women, also murdered because of their work for justice and their work on behalf of the poor in El Salvador.

Although religious—or at least spiritual—motifs had previously been present in Levertov's poems, she did not call herself a believing Christian until the early 1980s, when she wrote "Mass for St. Thomas Didymus," or Doubting Thomas, which appears in *Candles in Babylon*. She began writing the poem as an exercise in structure, noting that musicians have composed masses for centuries. The poem's sections mirror the elements of a mass—the kyrie, Gloria, credo, sanctus, benedictus, and agnus dei; by the time she completed the entire poem, Levertov found herself a believer. Several additional poems in *Candles in Babylon* and in most of her subsequent collections take various Biblical characters as their subject, often exploring the notion of belief. She is most sympathetic to those who desire belief yet acknowledge doubt. Her final collection, *This Great Unknowing* (1999), published posthumously, integrates many of her themes as it also attempts to reconcile the poet's knowledge that she had entered the last phase of her life.

Levertov also published collections of essays intermittently throughout her career. These essays frequently address elements of poetic craft, especially the rhythm and lineation; in "Some Notes on Organic Form" and "On the Function of the Line," both published in *New and Selected Essays* (1992), she distinguishes the type of poetry she writes, organic, from free verse and discusses the factors a poet considers in creating effective lineation outside of metrical forms. Several of her essays are also appreciations of other poets, such as William Carlos Williams and Robert Duncan, who influenced her own work and who often also found a place in her circle of friends.

CRITICAL RECEPTION

From the moment she published an early poem in *Poetry Quarterly* in 1940, Levertov received an enthusiastic response from critics and other poets, including Kenneth Rexroth. Her early work has been praised for its clarity, precision, and tone. Because of her interest in "organic form" and her belief that the poetic line should reflect a unit of breath, that the line is primarily a rhythmic device, Levertov has been classified with the Black Mountain poets, although she was never formally affiliated with the school.

As Levertov's work became more politically engaged, her critical reception grew mixed. Although political poetry is a welcome aspect of many national traditions, American critics have consistently resisted the legitimacy of this genre. Because political poetry in the United States is often characterized as too direct, as too didactic, as bad prose chopped up into lines, and because Levertov's aesthetic encouraged her toward accessible poetry, her work has been particularly open to these charges. On the other hand, she, too, has said that she does not consider work such as "A Speech: For Antidraft Rally, D.C., March 22, 1980" to be, absolutely, poetry, but she included it in a collection of poetry because of numerous requests from readers. Because it is composed in lines, this piece, for example, is not prose, is not an essay, yet neither does it adhere to the qualities Levertov would presumably have set out for herself as necessary to a poem. In a sense, then, Levertov would agree with her critics who argue that not all of her political work is actually poetry, although she would likely disagree about what specifically does constitute a poem. However, other critics defend Levertov's work of this period by pointing to canonical American poetry, such as Williams's *Paterson*, that also incorporates passages of prose.

Since the second wave of feminism during the 1960s and 1970s, critics interested specifically in questions of gender within literature have also analyzed Levertov's work. In her groundbreaking book, *Stealing the Language*, Alicia Suskin Ostriker discusses Levertov within a group of women poets whose work reveals a divided consciousness or identity. Ostriker suggests that Levertov is among the most optimistic and least enraged of these poets, though Levertov's feminist poetry is at times angry, especially during the period of the Vietnam War. In her poems, Ostriker argues, Levertov acknowledges that in contemporary Western culture, women are expected to be nurturing, but Levertov also implies that women experience many emotions that could be contrary to nurturant behavior (78–80).

Levertov's later work garnered much more unequivocal praise than did her work before 1980. While evidence of a deep spirituality can be found in her early, as well as her later, work, her poems became particularly popular with liberal Christians after her own conversion. For example, *Sojourners* and *Christianity in Literature*, as well as more conventional literary periodicals, published interviews with Levertov, and she was asked to speak at retreat centers and conferences on religion and literature. Few recent interviews or articles entirely ignore the question of Levertov's religious perspectives.

In addition to increasingly prominent reviews of her books, Levertov's work received substantial attention from academic literary scholars during the last two decades of the twentieth century and is likely to continue receiving such attention. These academic articles, dissertations, and books cover the range of Levertov's work, although individual scholars tend to focus on specific aspects of it. While reviews aim to be evaluative, the more academic articles focus on the meanings and effects of Levertov's work; they assume the evaluative process has already occurred and, in that sense, demonstrate that Levertov has achieved a position in the literary canon.

BIBLIOGRAPHY

Works by Denise Levertov

The Double Image. London: The Crest Press, 1946.
Here and Now. Pocket Poets Ser. 6. San Francisco: City Lights, 1956.
5 Poems. [n.p.]: The White Rabbit Press, 1958.
Overland to the Islands. Highlands, NC: Jonathan Williams, 1958.
With Eyes at the Back of Our Heads. New York: New Directions, 1960.
The Jacob's Ladder. New York: New Directions, 1961.
O Taste and See. New York: New Directions, 1964.
The Sorrow Dance. New York: New Directions, 1967.
The Cold Spring & Other Poems. New York: New Directions, 1968.
In the Night. New York: Albondocani Press, 1968.
Three Poems. Mount Horeb, WI: Perishable Press, 1968.
A Tree Telling of Orpheus. Los Angeles: Black Sparrow Press, 1968.
Embroideries. Los Angeles: Black Sparrow Press, 1969.
Selected Poems of Guillevic. New York: New Directions, 1969. (translations)
A New Year's Garland for My Students. Mount Horeb, WI: Perishable Press, 1970.
Relearning the Alphabet. New York: New Directions, 1970.
Summer Poems 1969. Berkeley, CA: Oyez, 1970.
To Stay Alive. New York: New Directions, 1971.
Footprints. New York: New Directions, 1972.
Conversation in Moscow. [n.p.]: Hovey St. Press, 1973.
The Poet in the World. New York: New Directions, 1973. (essays)
The Freeing of the Dust. New York: New Directions, 1975.
Chekov on the West Heath. Andes, NY: Woolmer/Brotherson, 1977.
Modulations for Solo Voice. San Francisco: Five Trees Press, 1977.
Life in the Forest. New York: New Directions, 1978.
Collected Earlier Poems, 1940–1960. New York: New Directions, 1979.
Light Up the Cave. New York: New Directions, 1981. (essays)

Mass for the Day of St. Thomas Didymus. Concord, NH: William B. Ewert, 1981.
Pig Dreams: Scenes from the Life of Sylvia. Woodstock, VT: Countryman Press, 1981.
Wanderer's Daysong. Port Townsend, WA: Copper Canyon Press, 1981.
Candles in Babylon. New York: New Directions, 1982.
El Salvador: Requiem and Invocation. Boston: Back Bay Chorale, 1983.
Poems 1960–1967. New York: New Directions, 1983.
Oblique Prayers: New Poems with Fourteen Translations from Jean Joubert. New York: New Directions, 1984.
Selected Poems. Newcastle upon Tyne, UK: Bloodaxe Books, 1986.
Breathing the Water. New York: New Directions, 1987.
A Door in the Hive. New York: New Directions, 1989.
Evening Train. New York: New Directions, 1992.
New and Selected Essays. New York: New Directions, 1992.
Tesserae: Memories & Suppositions. New York: New Directions, 1995. (prose)
Sands of the Well. New York: New Directions, 1996.
The Life Around Us: Selected Poems on Ecological Themes. New York: New Directions, 1997.
The Stream & the Sapphire: Selected Poems on Religious Themes. New York: New Directions, 1997.
This Great Unknowing: Last Poems. New York: New Directions, 1999.

Studies of Denise Levertov

Brooker, Jewel Spears, ed. *Conversations with Denise Levertov*. Jackson: University of Mississippi Press, 1998.
Edler, John. *Imagining the Earth: Poetry and the Vision of Nature*. Urbana: University of Illinois Press, 1985.
Felstiner, John. "Poetry and Political Experience: Denise Levertov." In *Coming to Light: American Women Poets in the Twentieth Century*, edited by Diane Wood Middlebrook and Marilyn Yalom. Ann Arbor: University of Michigan Press, 1985. 138–44.
Gelpi, Albert, ed. *Denise Levertov: Selected Criticism*. Ann Arbor: University of Michigan Press, 1993.
Marten, Harry. *Understanding Denise Levertov*. Columbia: University of South Carolina Press, 1988.
Mersmann, James F. *Out of Vietnam Vortex: A Study of Poets and Poetry Against the War*. Lawrence: University Press of Kansas, 1974.
Mills, Ralph J., Jr. *Cry of the Human: Essays on Contemporary American Poetry*. Urbana: University of Illinois Press, 1981.
Nelson, Cary. *Our Last First Poets: Vision and History in Contemporary American Poetry*. Urbana: University of Illinois Press, 1981.
Ostriker, Alicia Suskin. *Stealing the Language: The Emergence of Women's Poetry in America*. Boston: Beacon Press, 1986.
Wagner, Linda Welshimer. *Denise Levertov*. New York: Twayne, 1967.
———, ed. *Denise Levertov: In Her Own Province*. New York: New Directions, 1979.

PHYLLIS LEVIN (1954–)

Barbara Schwarz Wachal

BIOGRAPHY

Phyllis Levin was born in 1954. She began writing poetry at the age of twelve, providing her with "an alarmingly large manuscript of poems" to present to her first professor of poetry in college. While her style has changed and matured over the years since her youthful attempts at verse, Levin admits that she often returns to her early habits, particularly that of employing meter and form when writing in first-person voice. More than a matter of pure stylistics, she states that she has adopted this technique for a very practical reason: "I needed—and continue to need—formal elements in order to create a ritualized experience, . . . to enter an altered state, a heightened relation to the temporal." This usage of form and rhythm serves to satisfy a deep personal need of the poet: "For me, embracing form is embracing fate. . . . [It is part of] a constant struggle to come as close as possible to the impossible." By employing formal poetic devices, Levin frames the elements of this struggle with the impossible in her verse, ritualizing the everyday and imposing order upon experience.

Levin received her MA at Johns Hopkins University in Baltimore, Maryland, in 1977; she has taught in the Creative Writing program in the English department at the University of Maryland, and she currently teaches creative writing at Hofstra University, New York. Levin has received a number of awards and honors, including service as a 1996 Resident Fellow, Yaddo, a working community of writers, composers, and visual artists in Saratoga Springs, New York; the Fulbright Scholar Award to Slovenia, 1994–95; recognition as a finalist, The Rome Prize for 1991–92, American Academy and Institute of Arts and Letters; winner of 1988 Norma Farber First Book Award from the Poetry Society of America; and service as a Resident Fellow, The MacDowell Colony, on five occasions. She has been the recipient of the Ingram Merrill Foundation Grant and is the holder of the Amy Lowell Poetry Traveling Scholarship. She has also served on numerous editorial and advisory boards in literature and the arts, including the editorial board of *Boulevard*; guest editor, *Correo*

Latino; advisory editor, *The Plum Review*; and board member, The International Artists' Museum, New York Center.

MAJOR WORKS AND THEMES

A theme found throughout Phyllis Levin's poetry is the aforementioned search for finality and definition. Whether considering the women at Christ's tomb in "The Third Day" or the abstract concept of infinity in "Mercury," Levin struggles to achieve "wholeness and completion." In "The Third Day," the poet shares the women's confusion on the first Easter morning; significantly, it is the absence of Jesus's body that creates their consternation. To be complete, the drama should have ended with the women performing the appropriate burial rituals; however, the scene they encounter forces them to acknowledge that the impossible is indeed real. A metaphysical wholeness and completion are the result, but the concept is one with which the women and the poet must grapple. Similarly, "Mercury" confronts the poet with the inexplicability of scientific concepts that cannot be explained rationally. How can a number be beyond naming or calculation? How can a metal be liquid yet solid, shattered to fragments yet restored to a homogeneous whole? By choosing these two examples, Levin approaches the wholeness she seeks; yet even these do not satisfy when she considers them in the wider context of her father's basement hideaway. Levin arguably comes closest to this wholeness in "The Afterimage." In this poem, at the climactic dark night of the soul, it is the afterimage of vision that is evoked; the poem is awash in its own self-knowledge. Although the poem is about loss, Levin asserts the self as a beacon that effectively occasions the afterimage; it is this sense of self that illuminates the darkness and allows the poet to glimpse completion and wholeness.

Levin's concern with finality is a highly personal one. While many poets employ the first-person narrative voice, Levin moves beyond the device and convinces the reader that her poems are, indeed, autobiographical. When she writes in "Planting Roses" about her father digging up a beehive in the garden, the speaker runs away while the father shields his child, "Taking the stings so I could flee." The strict meter and careful wording reveal that this is not a fleeting story from the imagination but rather a lived, remembered event from her past. Even in relating this memory, though, Levin focuses on the fact that in her dreams she seeks only closure to the event. Because she is convinced that the bees sought her, not him, even the narrator's unconscious thoughts turn toward accepting her own punishment, rather than allowing her father to serve as intermediary. Whether we read the poem as a factual account or as a metaphor of some other context in which the father protected his daughter, the poet's concern remains: Cosmic justice has not been served by his intervention, thus the story lacks a sense of finality.

Loneliness and sadness, at times nearly verging on despair, emerge as themes in the development of Phyllis Levin's work. This sensibility is most evident in her most recent volume, *Mercury* (2001). In the title poem, she recalls playing with a vial of the metal found on her father's desk, fascinated with the liquid/solid and its ability to divide and reform. Significantly, it is not the mercury that draws her attention when she first enters the basement room; instead, the young girl first engages with dry volumes of Kafka and the classics, only later opening the tube, knowing that it is a clandestine act. Levin consoles herself with the notion of the mercury itself, which can be divided and restored virtually *ad infinitum*. For the girl, her father represents these same qualities. The fact that he possesses the tube of mercury reveals to her that he had a past life, perhaps one involving experiments in a field whose pursuit he abandoned; yet he recalls and draws for her the mathematical sign for infinity (both a sign and a concept that can, by definition, have no completion), demonstrating that he has not totally lost touch with that past life. The poet is content until her father asks her a question revealing his own mortality, indicating that he is, in fact, subject to the same inability to achieve the perfection that she seeks in her world. The realization that his separation from her cannot be restored as simply as can the fragmentation of the mercury shakes the speaker's world: "His question altered everything," she writes in an understatement of her despair.

Similarly, in "Intervals in August," Levin speaks of the emptiness of the soul, which she feels at the very time when the earth and Nature are at their fullest. In "Futile Exercise," she expresses the inability of a survivor of one who has committed suicide to reconcile the various realities that made up the dead man's life. It is incomprehensible to the speaker that the hands that helped and healed her could not heal themselves but instead resorted to pulling the trigger of the suicide weapon. Levin knows that this most final of all acts is not final at all, but rather is only the beginning of the conundrum for those left behind to mourn the victim. Once again, the lack of finality, of completion, remains to haunt both poet and reader.

CRITICAL RECEPTION

Phyllis Levin's poetry has been widely accepted by readers, but there have been few formal reviews of her work. Her poems have appeared in many journals and anthologies, including *The New Yorker*, *The Nation*, *The Atlantic*, *The Paris Review*, *Partisan Review*, *Grand Street*, *The New Criterion*, *Antioch Review*, *Poets of the New Formalism*, *Burning Bright: An Anthology of Sacred Poetry*, and *The Best American Poetry 1989*. Levin also enjoys an international readership, having had her poems translated and published in Peru, Argentina, Slovenia, Poland, Russia, Hungary, and Israel.

James McCorkle compares Phyllis Levin's poetry favorably with that of Elizabeth Bishop. He points out that both possess a sharp eye for detail. For both, the act of writing is sacramental. "To consider writing as sacramental," McCorkle writes, "is to understand one's obligation to writing and to find in writing the supplementary or displaced object of devotion and grace. . . . This is not a poetry of skepticism . . . but a poetry of difficulty" (260). In Levin's case, particularly, it is a poetry that belies the struggles inherent in her consideration of her subjects. McCorkle points out that Levin shares Bishop's metaphysical proclivities.

Elizabeth Macklin, too, identifies metaphysical renderings in Levin's work and is particularly impressed with the poet's abilities with language in relation to ideologies. In her assessment, "Meditation on A and The" (*Mercury*) shows the poet moving away from her concerns with completion and actually reveling in "the joys of the indefinite, the liberty inherent in indecision." Macklin argues that what begins as an experiment with the language—a playful toying with the notions of indefinite and definite articles, "a" and "the"—takes on metaphysical overtones, "suddenly and bizarrely" confronting the day of the earth's creation. As Macklin points out, once Levin has defined "definite" to her own satisfaction, she seems to be willing to retreat somewhat and to consider "the" (definite) day in which "a" (indefinite) world was formed.

Compared to Levin's earlier works, this consideration marks a revolutionary shift in her poetic sensibility: the nebulous, indefinable day is accepted as a given, as is the indefinite world that should logically be empirically explicable. This shift in attitude may have begun as word play, but the final poem in *Mercury*, the "Meditation," leaves readers to speculate on Levin's future perspectives on the nature of the human condition.

BIBLIOGRAPHY

Works by Phyllis Levin

Temples and Fields. Athens: University of Georgia Press, 1988.

"Embracing Fate." In *A Formal Feeling Comes: Poems in Form by Contemporary Women*, edited by Annie Finch. Brownsville, OR: Story Line Press, 1994. 147–151. (essay)

The Afterimage. Port Townsend, WA: Copper Beech Press, 1995.

Mercury. New York: Penguin Books, 2001.

Studies of Phyllis Levin

Macklin, Elizabeth. "It's a Woman's Prerogative to Change Her Mind." In *By Herself: Women Reclaim Poetry*, edited by Molly McQuade. St. Paul, MN: Graywolf Press, 2000. 9–30.

McCorkle, James. "Elizabeth Bishop's Embracing Gaze: Her Influence on the Poetry of Sandra McPherson, Phillis Levin, and Jorie Graham." In *"In Worcester, Massachusetts": Essays on Elizabeth Bishop, from the 1997 Elizabeth Bishop Conference at WPI*, edited by Laura Jehn Menides and Angela G. Dorenkamp. New York: Peter Lang, 1999. 259–70.

AUDRE LORDE (1934–1992)

Deborah M. Mix

BIOGRAPHY

Born in 1934 to West Indian immigrants, Audre Lorde grew up in New York City. Lorde did not begin speaking until she was four years old and, even then, tended to express herself primarily by quoting poems she had read. After graduating from high school, Lorde left home, putting herself through college, earning her BA from Hunter College, and graduate school, earning an MA in Library Science from Columbia University. After graduation, she accepted a library position at the City University of New York, where she remained for several years.

After the dissolution of a short-lived interracial marriage that resulted in two children (a boy and a girl), Lorde turned her focus to creative writing and left her librarian position to teach writing at several universities, first at Tougaloo College in Mississippi and later at John Jay and Hunter colleges in New York. She also allied herself with the lesbian community, fashioning a highly political position for herself. Her politics and her writing were inseparable, and she produced and advocated an activist aesthetic, particularly for black and lesbian writers. Lorde worked tirelessly to raise consciousness about racism, sexism, and classism in America; she was particularly vocal about the blindness she saw plaguing U.S. feminist and lesbian communities, and she was also involved in speaking about South African apartheid's effects on women, an issue she discussed in her 1986 *Apartheid USA*.

Diagnosed with breast cancer in 1978, Lorde underwent a modified radical mastectomy and continued to battle against the metastasizing cancer until she succumbed to it in 1992. During the years in which she fought against cancer, Lorde left the United States and spent much of her time in Germany, seeking alternative cancer treatments, and in St. Croix, a community and environment she found more restful. Throughout her years of declining health, she remained actively involved in politics locally and internationally, playing a founding role in Sisterhood in Support of Sisters in South Africa (SISA), an organization speaking out against apartheid.

Throughout her career, Lorde was invited to lecture throughout the United States, Europe, Australia, and New Zealand, and she received numerous awards. She also devoted a great deal of time and energy to developing publication venues for work by feminists and women of color, most notably Kitchen Table Press. In 1991 she was named the first woman poet laureate of New York State. Lorde lost her battle with cancer in 1992, dying in St. Croix. Shortly before her death, she changed her name to Gamda Adisa, "Warrior—She Who Makes Her Meaning Known" (Keating, "Audre Lorde" 285). In all her work—her writing, her political activism, her motherhood, and her sisterhood—Lorde lived out her assertion that "I am a Black, Lesbian, Feminist, warrior, poet, mother doing my work" (Rowell 92).

MAJOR WORKS AND THEMES

Lorde's books of poetry have established her reputation as a highly political writer, one unafraid to speak truth to power, pointing out the ravages of racism, classism, misogyny, and homophobia in American society. Highly autobiographical, many of her poems grew from journal entries and remain deeply personal in communicating Lorde's own hopes, fears, and desires. It is through poetry, Lorde believed, that change can best be expressed. She told interviewer Charles H. Rowell in 1991 that "poetry is a way of articulating and bringing together the energies of difference within [various] communities so those energies can be used by me and others to better do what must be done" (86).

In her first book, *The First Cities* (1968), Lorde includes a poem entitled "Suffer the Children," in which she addresses the cultural pressures that threaten to bury America's girls, wondering how they are so easily lost. She considers how we might prevent these losses and who might be able "to read the legends written beneath their skin" (n.p.). In *New York Head Shop and Museum* (1974), Lorde returns again to this theme of lost (or nearly lost) daughters, questioning the interplay of poverty, racism, drugs, and education (particularly the lack of opportunities afforded to poor children and children of color) in their lives. Poems such as "My Daughter the Junkie on a Train" and "Blackstudies" deal unflinchingly with these issues. These poems provide a clear sense of Lorde's primary concerns—the fate of young women, the possible futures, and the desperate need for change. But Lorde also holds out hope in these early poems, arguing that if we can recognize the dangers, we can intervene.

Lorde's seventh and eighth books, *Between Our Selves* (1976) and *The Black Unicorn* (1978), marked a turning point in her career as these books received wide recognition for their efforts to create a voice simultaneously African, communal, feminist, personal, and prophetic. In these works, she looks not only at the present and toward the future, but also to the past as a source of strength and identity. Lorde dedicated *Between Our Selves* to "the embattled!" and recalls both images of halcyon nostalgia (such as the scent of ripening fruits) and quotidian struggle (such as the crushing darkness of nightmares). She refuses to settle on either side of the dividing line, always searching for ways to complicate it further as she marks the realities of the Black Diaspora. In his review of *The Black Unicorn*, Robert Stepto praises the uniqueness and clarity of her voice, particularly in terms of its orality and its links to African traditions. In "From the House of Yemenjá" (*The Black Unicorn*), the poet speaks to her ancestors, "mother I need your blackness now" (7). Lorde considered *The Black*

Unicorn an integrated and whole text, and she later refused to excerpt from it in her *Chosen Poems—Old and New* (1982).

Between *The Black Unicorn* and *Our Dead Behind Us* (1986), Lorde did not publish any new books of poetry (though *Chosen Poems* appeared during this period). Instead, she turned her energies toward prose works, publishing *The Cancer Journals* (1980), *Zami: A New Spelling of My Name* (1982), and *Sister Outsider* (1984) as well as two pamphlets. Lorde, never shy in making public her own struggles with cancer, chose to publish a record of her illness, beginning with the publication of *The Cancer Journals*. In this work, Lorde focuses on the need for breast cancer survivors to unite, despite their differences, as a way to support one another in their struggles. She chronicles her own deliberations about whether or not to wear a prosthesis (she fears doing so only contributes to the invisibility of breast cancer in American culture) and considers the disease from "A Black Lesbian Feminist Experience," as she puts it in one chapter title. Most strikingly, Lorde discusses her process of coming to grips with her own mortality: "once I face death as a life process, what is there possibly left for me to fear? Who can ever really have power over me again?" (61). When she learned the cancer had metastasized to her liver six years later, she wrote about her battle in *A Burst of Light* (1988) and in many poems published posthumously in *The Marvelous Arithmetics of Distance* (1993). In all of these poems, she deals with her illness with a combination of awe, fierceness, and humor. In the poems in *The Marvelous Arithmetics* (published posthumously), Lorde addresses the process of learning how to die in poems such as "Today Is Not the Day," "Legacy—Hers," and "Restoration—A Memorial 9/18/91." In "Restoration," she writes of "learning to laugh again" as she approaches the end of her life (41).

Zami, arguably Lorde's best-known work, spawned its own critical industry (ironically, however, *Zami* was rejected by over a dozen commercial presses before she found a publisher in the small independent Crossing Press). Lorde called *Zami* a "biomythography," a neologism that comes closest to capturing the generic hybridity of the work. A combination of autobiography, history, fiction, and myth, *Zami*'s episodic form concentrates on the roles of both real and mythic women in Lorde's life ("I am writing a book about the unfolding of my life and loves" 190). The work's title comes from a West Indian word that she translates as "*women who work together as friends and lovers*" (255), and it highlights Lorde's belief that women, particularly women in communities, have an extraordinary power to create both individual and social change. This word and its definition also highlight Lorde's desire to connect her own lesbianism to a long history of women-oriented women, particularly in the West Indian culture from which her family comes. Thus she "clear[s] an important path in Aframerican literature: freeing the idea of lesbianism from the closet of 'white decadence' " (Chinosole 386). In the book, Lorde demonstrates how the various women she encountered in her life helped her to create, as the subtitle suggests, "a new spelling" of her own identity, and she suggests the potential for women to create similar changes in other ways. The book also chronicles her awakening to the realities of racism, sexism, and homophobia and her development of strategies with which to do battle against these forces.

Sister Outsider, a collection of essays, addresses many of the same issues, often from a similarly personal point of view. The collection's title highlights Lorde's desire to be both insider ("sister") and outsider, connected and isolated. For Lorde, the ability to connect across differences provides the key to rupturing destructive social patterns. Thus, she seeks to maintain that liminal position at all times. In a 1991 interview, Lorde identified two essays in the volume, "Poetry Is Not a Luxury" and "Eye to Eye: Black Women, Hatred, and Anger," that serve as the core pieces of her prose writing (Rowell 91). In both of these essays, she discusses her own anger and alienation and the challenges of channeling that frustration into constructive action. For Lorde, that action began through the language of poetry. In "Poetry Is Not a Luxury," Lorde argues that, for women in particular, poetry offers a means to reconnect with our own reserves of creativity and power, which will then allow us to move into action to create radical and daring change. Lorde explains, "Poetry is not only dream and vision; it is the skeleton architecture of our lives. . . . Poetry coins the language to express and charter . . . revolutionary demand, the implementation of . . . freedom" (38). In "Eye to Eye," Lorde continues this line of reasoning, focusing on understanding and writing into one's own anger as a means to self-empowerment. It is only through examining, accepting, and moving beyond anger to love, Lorde explains, that black women can begin to band together in love, rather than viewing one another with suspicion or fear. She calls on black women to "establish authority over our own definition, provide an attentive concern and expectation of growth. . . . I have to learn to love myself before I can love you or accept your loving. You have to learn to love yourself before you can love me or accept my loving" (173–74). Working together, Lorde says, is the only way that black women can change not only their own self-perceptions but also the prejudices and attitudes of others.

In 1986 Lorde returned to publishing poetry with *Our Dead Behind Us*, her first book published with a major commercial press. Many of these poems invoke "martyred" women such as Eleanor Roosevelt, Indira Gandhi, and Eleanor Bumpurs (an elderly black woman shot to death by NYC police officers during an eviction proceeding); mythic women such as warrior queen Mmanthatisi and Rainbow Serpent woman Aido Hwedo; and imagined everyday women. This volume is driven by what Gloria T. Hull characterizes as a "devastating fury" and blistering irony (162). In this collection, Lorde calls readers to account for their complacency in the face of world suffering ("Soho Cinema"), to approach problems in new ways ("The Art of Response"), and to recognize the intertwined nature of sexism, homophobia, and racism ("Sisters in Arms").

As Lorde continued her fight against cancer, she remained deeply committed to issues of social justice and political action, as her work attests. "Audre Lorde: A Special Section," devoted to Lorde in the journal *Callaloo* (1991), includes a range of her work—both previously published as well as new poems, a speech, essays, and an interview. Even as she won greater public acclaim for her work, Lorde refused to compromise her principles. Upon winning the Bill Whitehead Memorial Award from the Triangle Group of the American Booksellers' Association in 1990, Lorde commented in her acceptance speech that she would accept the award (for her work in gay and lesbian publishing) but would refuse the prize money because the Triangle Group included no gays or lesbians of color ("What Is at Stake" in "Audre Lorde: A Special Section" 65–66). Lorde also published a scathing assessment of U.S. participation in the post-Hurricane Hugo cleanup in the Virgin Islands ("Of Generators and Survival—*Hugo* Letters" in "Audre Lorde: A Special Section" 72–82), remarking upon the condescension to and cruelly politicized treatment of St. Croix's people. Her poetry retained its unstinting clarity, political passion, and scathing humor throughout these years, with poems such as "Jessehelms" and "Women on Trains" reminding readers of the need to " 'stand and fight' " together ("Women on Trains" in "Audre Lorde: A Special Section" 54), not in spite of but because of our differences.

Lorde's too short career is marked by her concern for creating community and respecting differences. She writes, "As we arm ourselves with ourselves and each other, we can stand toe to toe inside that rigorous loving and begin to speak the impossible . . . to one another. Eventually, if we speak the truth to each other, it will become unavoidable to ourselves" (*Sister Outsider* 175).

CRITICAL RECEPTION

Though Lorde published a substantial body of poetry during her life, most critical discussions of her work tend to focus on *Zami*, a work that has emerged as a central text in conversations not only about black female identity but also about gay and lesbian identity. Studies of *Zami* tend to cluster around either the work's status as a groundbreaking text or around Lorde's use of feminist mythography. Early studies, such as those by Barbara Christian and Barbara Smith, concentrate on *Zami*'s contribution to the growing body of African American women writers' work. Smith's essay, "The Truth that Never Hurts," locates *Zami* within a new strain of black women's writings that address black lesbian experience. She is particularly complimentary of *Zami* because, she explains, "It is not a horror story, although it reveals the difficulties of Black Lesbian experience. It is not a fable, although it reveals the joys of a life committed to women" (241). Erin Carlston's "*Zami* and the Politics of Plural Identity" makes a similar claim, noting that the " 'impure' and non-static" identity Lorde constructs offers an effective challenge to simplistic identity constructions (233). In *The Safe Sea of Women*, Bonnie Zimmerman also holds up *Zami* as a model of the "more complex search for the source and meaning of identity" lesbian writers of color must undertake (199), a search that leads to a disruption of dominant lesbian feminist discourses. Other discussions of *Zami* tend to concentrate on Lorde's deployment of feminist mythmaking and maternal images. Chinosole's essay, "Audre Lorde and Matrilineal Diaspora," traces Lorde's use of her mother's roots to define herself, an argument Claudine Raynaud also develops in her essay on *Zami*. AnaLouise Keating, who has published extensively on *Zami*, argues in several essays that Lorde's use of feminist and maternal myth extends beyond the creation of individual identity to the construction of a collective and potentially transformational identity.

But while there are myriad studies of *Zami*, Lorde's other works have received only scant attention. Gloria T. Hull, in her study of Lorde's 1986 *Our Dead Behind Us*, theorizes that many critics have eschewed Lorde's other works because of her "moral and political vision combined with her demanding style" (166). Lorde refuses to let her readers off the hook when it comes to facing issues of discrimination and culpability, and her forcefulness may be off-putting to some. Hull quotes several reviews of Lorde's poetry that accuse her of trying to make the reader feel guilty or left out, none of which concede that Lorde may have particular political aims in doing so (such as bringing about recognition and even discomfort with a reader's own privileges) but only grouse about their own discomfort in the face of her honest and unflinching words (Hull 166–69). For these reasons, Lorde is often grouped with other unrepentantly political and confrontational feminist poets such as Adrienne Rich and Gloria

Anzaldúa in critical discussions of her work. The few studies of Lorde's poetry tend to concentrate on its political messages, particularly as they intersect with identity construction. In her discussion of *Our Dead Behind Us*, Hull notes that "almost as soon as [Lorde] achieves a place of connection, she becomes uneasy at the comfortableness . . . and proceeds to rub athwart the smooth grain to find the roughness and the slant she needs to maintain her difference-defined, complexly constructed self" (155–56). Other critics note Lorde's attention to approaching history as something that moves both forward and backward, and as something that can be a reservoir from which we can draw or a moat in which we can drown. Lorde wrote in her 1990 foreword to *Wild Women in the Whirlwind*, "Black women who follow us need to know that other Black women have fought and survived the same Black woman-hatred . . . that we wished to share, with passion and with beauty, the questions as well as the strengths that we learned throughout those struggles. And not all our songs are mourning" (xii).

BIBLIOGRAPHY

Works by Audre Lorde

The First Cities. New York: Poets Press, 1968.
Poetry Workshop. Providence, RI: Hellcoal Press, 1969.
Cables to Rage. London: Paul Brennan, 1970.
From a Land Where Other People Live. Detroit, MI: Broadside Press, 1973.
Alvin. Detroit, MI: Glass Bell Press, 1974.
New York Head Shop and Museum. Detroit, MI: Broadside Press, 1974.
Between Our Selves. Point Reyes, CA: Eidolon Editions, 1976.
Coal. New York: Norton, 1976.
The Black Unicorn. New York: Norton, 1978.
The Cancer Journals. Argyle, NY: Spinsters Ink, 1980. Reprinted in San Francisco: Aunt Lute, 1997. (essays)
Chosen Poems—Old and New. New York: Norton, 1982.
Zami: A New Spelling of My Name. Watertown, MA: Persephone Press, 1982. (biomythography)
Sister Outsider: Essays and Speeches. Trumansburg, NY: Crossing Press, 1984.
Apartheid USA. New York: Kitchen Table/Women of Color Press, 1986. (pamphlet)
Our Dead Behind Us: Poems. New York: Norton, 1986.
A Burst of Light. Ithaca, NY: Firebrand Books, 1988.
"Foreword." In *Wild Women in the Whirlwind: Afra-American Culture and the Contemporary Literary Renaissance,* edited by Joanne M. Braxton and Andrée Nicola McLaughlin. New Brunswick, NJ: Rutgers University Press, 1990. xi-xiii.
Need: A Chorale for Black Women's Voices. Latham, NY: Kitchen Table/Women of Color Press, 1990.
The Marvelous Arithmetics of Distance: Poems 1987–1992. New York: Norton, 1993.
Collected Poems of Audre Lorde. New York: Norton, 1997.

Studies of Audre Lorde

Ahmed, Sara. "Embodying Strangers." In *Body Matters: Feminism, Textuality, Corporeality,* edited by Avril Horner and Angela Keane. Manchester, NY: Manchester University Press, 2000. 85–96. Distributed in the U.S. by St. Martin's, 2000.
Alexander, Elizabeth. " 'Coming Out Blackened and Whole': Fragmentation and Reintegration

in Audre Lorde's *Zami* and *The Cancer Journals*." *American Literary History* 6 (1994): 695–715.

"Audre Lorde: A Special Section." *Callaloo* 14.1 (1991): 39–95.

Avi-Ram, Amitai F. "*Apo Koinou* in Audre Lorde and the Moderns: Defining the Differences." *Callaloo* 9.1 (1986): 193–208.

Birkle, Carmen. *Women's Stories of the Looking Glass: Autobiographical Reflections and Self-Representations in the Poetry of Sylvia Plath, Adrienne Rich, and Audre Lorde*. Munich, Germany: Fink, 1996.

Braxton, Joanne M., and Andrée Nicola McLaughlin, eds. *Wild Women in the Whirlwind: Afra-American Culture and the Contemporary Literary Renaissance*. New Brunswick, NJ: Rutgers University Press, 1990.

Carlston, Erin G. "*Zami* and the Politics of Plural Identity." In *Sexual Practice, Textual Theory: Lesbian Cultural Criticism*, edited by Susan J. Wolfe and Julia Penelope. Cambridge: Blackwell, 1993. 226–36.

Carr, Brenda. " 'A Woman Speaks . . . I Am Woman and Not White': Politics of Voice, Tactical Essentialism, and Cultural Intervention in Audre Lorde's Activist Poetics and Practice." In *Race-ing Representation: Voice, History, and Sexuality*, edited by Kostas Myrsiades and Linda Myrsiades. Lanham, MD: Rowman & Littlefield, 1998. 119–40.

Chinosole. "Audre Lorde and Matrilineal Diaspora: 'moving history beyond nightmare into structures for the future. . . . ' " In *Wild Women in the Whirlwind: Afra-American Culture and the Contemporary Literary Renaissance,* edited by Joanne M. Braxton and Andrée Nicola McLaughlin. New Brunswick, NJ: Rutgers University Press, 1990. 379–94.

Christian, Barbara. "No More Buried Lives: The Theme of Lesbianism in Audre Lorde's *Zami*, Gloria Naylor's *The Women of Brewster Place*, Ntozake Shange's *Sassafras, Cypress, and Indigo*, and Alice Walker's *The Color Purple*." In *Black Feminist Criticism: Perspectives on Black Women Writers*. New York: Pergamon Press, 1985.

DeHernandez, Jennifer Browdy. "Mothering the Self: Writing the Lesbian Sublime in Audre Lorde's *Zami* and Gloria Anzaldúa's *Borderlands/La Frontera*." In *Other Sisterhoods: Literary Theory and U.S. Women of Color*, edited by Sandra Kumamoto Stanley. Urbana: University of Illinois Press, 1998. 244–62.

Dhairyam, Sagri. " 'Artifacts for Survival': Remapping the Contours of Poetry with Audre Lorde." *Feminist Studies* 18 (1992): 229–56.

Georgoudaki, Ekaterini. *Race, Gender, and Class Perspectives in the Works of Maya Angelou, Gwendolyn Brooks, Rita Dove, Nikki Giovanni, and Audre Lorde*. Thessaloniki, Greece: University of Thessaloniki, 1991.

Ginzberg, Ruth. "Audre Lorde's (Nonessentialist) Lesbian Eros." *Hypatia* 7.4 (1992): 73–90.

Harper, Margaret Mills. "First Principles and Last Things: Death and the Poetry of Eavan Boland and Audre Lorde." In *Representing Ireland: Gender, Class, Nationality*, edited by Susan Shaw Sailer. Gainesville: University Press of Florida, 1997. 181–93.

Holland, Sharon P. "To Touch the Mother's C(o)untry: Siting Audre Lorde's Erotics." In *Lesbian Erotics*, edited by Karla Jay. New York: New York University Press, 1995. 212–26.

———. " 'Which me will survive?': Audre Lorde and the Development of a Black Feminist Ideology." *Critical Matrix* 1 (1988): 1–30.

Hubert, Susan J. " 'A Whole New Poetry Beginning Here': The Poetics/Politics of Adrienne Rich and Audre Lorde." *Revista Canaria de Estudios Ingleses* 37 (1998): 101–10.

Hull, Gloria T. "Living on the Line: Audre Lorde and *Our Dead Behind Us*." In *Changing Our Own Words: Essays on Criticism, Theory, and Writing by Black Women*, edited by Cheryl A. Wall. New Brunswick, NJ: Rutgers University Press, 1989. 150–72.

Hunt, Patricia. " 'Free to Do Something Wild': History and the Ancestor in Jazz." *LIT* 6.1–2 (1995): 47–62.

Keating, AnaLouise. "Audre Lorde (1934–1992)." In *Contemporary African American Novel-*

ists: A Bio-Bibliographical Critical Sourcebook, edited by Emmanuel S. Nelson. Westport, CT: Greenwood Press, 1999. 284–88.

———. "(De)Centering the Margins?: Identity Politics and Tactical (Re)Naming." In *Other Sisterhoods: Literary Theory and U.S. Women of Color*, edited by Sandra Kumamoto Stanley. Urbana: University of Illinois Press, 1998. 23–43.

———. "Making 'Our Shattered Faces Whole': The Black Goddess and Audre Lorde's Revision of Patriarchal Myth." *Frontiers* 13 (1992): 20–33.

———. "Myth Smashers, Myth Makers: (Re)Visionary Techniques in the Works of Paula Gunn Allen, Gloria Anzaldúa, and Audre Lorde." In *Critical Essays: Gay and Lesbian Writers of Color*, edited by Emmanuel S. Nelson. New York: Haworth, 1993. 73–95.

———. "Reading 'Through the Eyes of the Other': Self, Identity, and the Other in the Works of Paula Gunn Allen, Gloria Anzaldúa, and Audre Lorde." *Readerly Writerly Texts: Essays on Literature, Literary Textual Criticism, and Pedagogy* 1.1 (1993): 161–86.

———. *Women Reading Women Writing: Self-invention in Paula Gunn Allen, Gloria Anzaldúa, and Audre Lorde*. Philadelphia, PA, Temple University Press, 1996.

Kimmich, Allison. "Writing the Body: From Abject to Subject." *A-B* 13 (1998): 223–34.

King, Katie. "Audre Lorde's Lacquered Layerings: The Lesbian Bar as a Site of Literary Production." In *Lesbian Criticism: Literary and Cultural Readings*, edited by Sally Munt. New York: Columbia University Press, 1992. 51–74.

Lauter, Estella. "Re-Visioning Creativity: Audre Lorde's Refiguration of Eros as the Black Mother Within." In *Writing the Woman Artist: Essays on Poetics, Politics, and Portraiture*, edited by Suzanne W. Jones. Philadelphia: University of Pennsylvania Press, 1991. 398–418.

McDowell, Margaret. "The Black Woman as Artist and Critic: Four Versions." *Kentucky Review* 7.1 (1987): 19–41.

Olson, Lester C. "Liabilities of Language: Audre Lorde Reclaiming Difference." *Quarterly Journal of Speech* 84 (1998): 448–70.

———. "On the Margins of Rhetoric: Audre Lorde Transforming Silence into Language and Action." *Quarterly Journal of Speech* 83 (1997): 49–70.

Perrault, Jeanne. " 'That the pain not be wasted': Audre Lorde and the Written Self." *A-B* 4.1 (1988): 1–16.

Provost, Kara. "Becoming Afrikete: The Trickster in the Work of Audre Lorde." *MELUS* 20.4 (1995): 45–59.

Raynaud, Claudine. " 'A Nutmeg Nestled Inside Its Covering of Mace': Audre Lorde's *Zami*." In *Life/Lines: Theorizing Women's Autobiography*, edited by Bella Brodzki and Celeste Schenck. Ithaca, NY: Cornell University Press, 1988. 221–42.

Rowell, Charles H. "Above the Wind: An Interview with Audre Lorde." *Callaloo* 14.1 (1991): 83–95.

Smith, Barbara. "The Truth That Never Hurts: Black Lesbians in the 1980s. In *Wild Women in the Whirlwind: Afra-American Culture and the Contemporary Literary Renaissance*, edited by Joanne M. Braxton and Andrée Nicola McLaughlin. New Brunswick, NJ: Rutgers University Press, 1990. 213–45.

Steele, Cassie Premo. "Leading from 'You' and 'I' to 'We': Contemporary American Women's Poetry of Witness." *Leadership Journal* 2.2 (1998): 67–80.

———. *We Heal from Memory: Sexton, Lorde, Anzaldúa, and the Poetry of Witness*. New York: Palgrave, 2000.

Stepto, Robert B. "The Phenomenal Woman and the Severed Daughter." Review of *And Still I Rise* and Audre Lorde's *The Black Unicorn*, by Maya Angelou. *Parnassus* 8.1 (1979): 314–17.

Upton, Elaine Maria. "Audre Lorde (1934–1992)." In *Contemporary Lesbian Writers of the United States: A Bio-Bibliographical Critical Sourcebook*, edited by Sandra Pollack and Denise D. Knight. Westport, CT: Greenwood, 1993. 316–24.

Wallace, Kathleen R. " 'All Things Natural Are Strange': Audre Lorde, Urban Nature, and Cultural Place." In *The Nature of Cities: Ecocriticism and Urban Environments*, edited by Michael Bennett and David W. Teague. Tucson: University of Arizona Press, 1999. 55–76.

Wilson, Anna. "Audre Lorde and the African-American Tradition: When the Family Is Not Enough." In *New Lesbian Criticism: Literary and Cultural Readings*. New York: Columbia University Press, 1992. 75–93.

———. "Rites/Rights of Canonization: Audre Lorde as Icon." In *Women Poets of the Americas: Toward a Pan-American Gathering*, edited by Jacqueline Vaught Brogan and Cordelia Chávez Candelaria. Notre Dame, IN: University of Notre Dame Press, 1999. 17–33.

Worsham, Fabian Clements. "The Poetics of Matrilineage: Mothers and Daughters in the Poetry of African American Women, 1965–1985." In *Women of Color: Mother-Daughter Relationships in 20th-Century Literature*, edited by Elizabeth Brown Guillory. Austin: University of Texas Press, 1996. 177–231.

Zimmerman, Bonnie. *The Safe Sea of Women: Lesbian Fiction 1969–1989*. Boston: Beacon, 1990.

HEATHER MCHUGH (1948–)

Joelle Biele

BIOGRAPHY

Born in California, Heather McHugh grew up as the middle child of John Laurence McHugh and Eileen Francesca Smallwood in rural Virginia. McHugh started writing poetry as a small child, and at age five, she completed her first book of poems, complete with cardboard cover and ribbon ties. She entered Harvard University at sixteen, and two years later, she became a member of Robert Lowell's graduate poetry seminar and had her first poem, "Divorce," published in *The New Yorker*. While at Harvard, she married and divorced and then completed her degree in 1970. From Harvard, McHugh went to the University of Denver for a master's degree and then on to fellowships from the National Endowment for the Arts, the Provincetown Fine Arts Work Center, and the McDowell Colony. In 1977 her first book, *Dangers*, the winner of the Houghton Mifflin Poetry Prize, appeared.

Poet, translator, and essayist, McHugh has published regularly since *Dangers*. Her work in different genres often comes collectively, as in 1981 when her second book, *A World of Difference*, appeared with her translation of Jean Follain, *D'Apres Tout*. These books were followed by two books of poems, *To the Quick* (1987) and *Shades* (1988), and a translation of Bulgarian poet Blaga Dimitrova's *Because the Sea Is Black* (1989), with her husband Nikolai Popov. In 1993 she collected her essays on Yoruba poetry, Rainer Maria Rilke, Emily Dickinson, and Paul Celan for *Broken English: Poetry and Partiality*, and in 1994, she published new and selected poems in the award-winning volume, *Hinge & Sign: Poems 1968–1993*. Her most recent book of poems is *The Father of the Predicaments* (1999).

McHugh has spent her career as a teacher, first at the State University of New York, Binghamton, and then at the University of Washington, Seattle, as the McMillan Distinguished Writer-in-Residence. She has held this position for the last sixteen years while also teaching at Warren Wilson College and holding visiting appointments at such schools as the Iowa Writers' Workshop, Columbia University, and the University of California, Berkeley, in addition to participating in the Breadloaf Writers' Conference. McHugh has received numerous fellowships and prizes, including a second National Endowment for the Arts grant; a Guggenheim; a Rockefeller Foundation grant; and a Lila Wallace/Reader's Digest Writing Award. The last five years have seen her elected a chancellor at the Academy of American Poets and a fellow at the American Academy of Arts and Sciences. She spends her time between homes in Seattle and Eastport, Maine.

MAJOR WORKS AND THEMES

McHugh's first two volumes, *Dangers* and *A World of Difference*, introduce some of her major themes, the nature of the self, language, and the body. Poems such as "Ozone," "Blue Streak," "Hag," "Language Lesson 1976," and "Outcry" tackle these themes with wit. These are tightly written lyrics that move by association, particularly revamped clichés and etymologies. The poems build through parallel structure, taking a phrase, turning it over, and saying it back. The repetition of "hold" and "doubletalk" in "Language Lesson 1976" from *A World of Difference* leads to the poem's climax. "Hold" had been defined earlier in the poem as "forget," and at the end of the poem, the speaker asks that she never be held (39). This doubletalk is part of McHugh's approach to poetry, to find the unexpected in everyday phrases in order to unsettle a passive approach to language. "My whole work is to catch the word by surprise," McHugh has said, "sneaking up on language, sneaking up on the world as it lurks in words" (qtd. in Bock 12). From Latin to slang, she will mix words for the contrasts that they create. It is not unusual, as in "Meaning Business," to find "gizmos," "jeremiads," "glee," "apropos," "bailiwick," "inkling," and "sou" all in one stanza (*A World of Difference* 11). Linda Gregerson points out that McHugh "loves the thingness of words, their heft, their shimmy, their slickness and burn" (3).

To the Quick and *Shades* followed *A World of Difference*. These volumes continue to explore the ego and language while incorporating themes on loss. Peter Harris has linked these poems to Emily Dickinson for the amount of pressure they put on language as they voice "pain, loss, anger, wonder, amusement, and despair" (274). Like Dickinson, McHugh pokes at comfortable notions of the self with humor, as in *To the Quick's* "20–200 on 747" and *Shades*' "ID" and "Spilled." In "20–200 on 747," the speaker sits on an airplane when a fellow traveler, Phil Fenstermacher, asks what she writes about. The glib response is a riff on business, family, and nothing, which returns the traveler to his snack tray. This kind of wordplay is typical of McHugh's poems and can be found in other poems such as the comical opening stanza of "I Knew I'd Sing" in *To the Quick*. The wordplay leads to serious conclusions, generally with the self reflecting back on itself. In "20–200 on 747" the speaker later thinks she hears Mr. Fenstermacher ("window-maker" in German) ask, whose flight they are on, whose story is "this," and in whose words is it told? These questions prompt her to look at her glasses. "They're a sight" (4). This arc—rejecting what is seen, in this case Fenstermacher, to finally sympathizing with it by recognizing some fallibility of the self—is typical of McHugh's poetry.

Lost love and lost friends become major concerns in these mid-career poems. Emotional directness had been uncommon in McHugh's work, since like Dickinson, she generally comes to her subject by way of the slant. McHugh continues to use words and phrases as jumping points for her subjects. Ruminating over a word such as "in" can lead to a reflection on a relationship, as in "The Trouble with 'In' " from *To the Quick.* The speaker begins by contemplating different phrases in which "in" figures prominently. Thinking about the word leads her to consider "love" and typical questions people ask about relationships. McHugh repeats words throughout the poem in different contexts, building to the poem's conclusion about a particular relationship's end. When the beloved makes a casual remark, the speaker announces, "I knew the idiom: it meant So long" (39). Less prominent than the loss of love is the death of friends. "What Hell Is" proves unique in that it creates its own definition, instead of playing with received ones. As she tends to a friend dying of AIDS, the speaker discusses his illness with his family. As his condition worsens, they speak to him less and less. He becomes a word, sits in the living room, hell in a reclining chair (*To the Quick* 8). Poems such as "What Could Hold Us," "To the Quick," and "The Ghost" from *To the Quick* and "Inflation," "Earthmoving Malediction," and "Unspeakable" from *Shades* are also part of this group.

McHugh's most recent work appears in *Hinge & Sign* and *The Father of the Predicaments.* These poems continue their consideration of mortality, self, and language. The death of a friend is her subject again in poems such as "Not a Prayer" and "For Raya" from *The Father of the Predicaments* and egotism and poetry in "What He Thought" from *Hinge & Sign.* Playful poems such as "Qua Qua Qua" and "The Size of Spokane" celebrate everyday pleasures such as watching a "philosophical" duck in a pond or a child that "isn't cute" follow a shaft of light (*The Father of the Predicaments* 75, *Hinge & Sign* 36). These poems muse over sex in "Coming" and isolation in "Auto" (*Hinge & Sign*). They continue to explore "the hazy edge of the comprehensible" that was the subject of her first books (Wakefield M10). McHugh's use of form facilitates this probing. Using an iambic line, parallel structure, and rhyme, McHugh plays with syntactic disruptions to reawaken one's relationship with language. Therefore, like Dickinson, her lines often work against expectations, particularly in where they break and where they go after that break. This approach to grammar gives her poems a constant sense of surprise and openness, and it is what makes them distinctive in contemporary poetry.

In addition to poetry, McHugh, an active translator and essayist, has written extensively on poets she admires. These poets include Celan, Dickinson, and Rilke, in addition to Samuel Beckett, Emile Cioran, and Robert Creeley, all of whom McHugh cites as influences on her work. Her criticism also shows a deconstructionist approach. She has translated Celan, Jean Follain, and Blaga Dimitrova and is currently working on a translation of Euripides' *Cyclops.*

CRITICAL RECEPTION

McHugh is known as a poet's poet. This label bears out in that comment on her poetry appears almost exclusively in book reviews and in the pages of literary journals. In addition, many of these pieces are written by fellow poets. Since the outset of McHugh's career, reviewers divide over McHugh's love of wordplay and puns. While many were taken by her witty use of language in her early poems, some felt they were only about their musicality (Seidman 14). Those who admired the poems praised their celebration of the ordinary, their wry irony, and their "recognition of human weakness" (Weigl 174). Since midcareer, McHugh's playfulness has been regularly noted. Her work has been characterized as delightful, inventive, and challenging for its "intellectual sassiness" and "tender sensuality" (McClatchy 34). McHugh is a poet, former poet laureate Robert Hass writes, "for whom wit is a form of spiritual survival" (12).

BIBLIOGRAPHY

Works by Heather McHugh

Dangers. Boston: Houghton, 1977.

D'Apres Tout: Poems by Jean Follain. Princeton, NJ: Princeton University Press, 1981. (translation)

A World of Difference. Boston: Houghton, 1981.

To the Quick. Middletown, CT: Wesleyan University Press, 1987.

From 20,000 Feet. Dallas, TX: Northouse & Northouse, 1988. (broadside)

Shades. Middletown, CT: Wesleyan University Press, 1988.

Because the Sea Is Black: Poems by Blaga Dimitrova. With Nikolai B. Popov. Middletown, CT: Wesleyan University Press, 1989. (translation)

Broken English: Poetry and Partiality. Hanover, NH: University Press of New England, 1993. (essays)

Hinge & Sign: Poems 1968–1993. Hanover, NH: Wesleyan University Press and University Press of New England, 1994.

The Father of the Predicaments. Hanover, NH: Wesleyan University Press and University Press of New England, 1999.

107 Poems by Paul Celan. With Nikolai B. Popov. Hanover, NH: University Press of New England, 2000. (translation)

Studies of Heather McHugh

Bock, Paula. "Playful, Profound and Profane: Heather McHugh Leads Northwest Poetry Out of the Woods." *Seattle Times*, 28 May 2000, Pacific Northwest 12+.

Corn, Alfred. "Poems and Personality." Review of *Dangers*, by Heather McHugh. *New York Times Book Review*, 3 July 1977, 7+.

Davies, Lindsay. "Translating Jean Follain: Heather McHugh's D'apres tout." *Translation Review* 28 (1998): 35–39.

Dobyns, Stephen. "McHugh at Mid-Career." Review of *Hinge & Sign*, by Heather McHugh. *New England Review* 17 (1995): 166–70.

George, Lynell. "Poetic Justice: Heather McHugh and David St. John Have Labored in Obscurity on the West Coast, But Not Any Longer." *Los Angeles Times*, 11 Nov 1994, E1+.

Gregerson, Linda. "Among the Wordstruck." Review of *Hinge & Sign*, by Heather McHugh. *New York Times Book Review*, 23 Oct 1994, 3.

Harris, Peter. "Four Salvers Salvaging: New Work by Voight, Olds, Dove, and McHugh." Review of *To the Quick*, by Heather McHugh. *Virginia Quarterly* 64 (1998): 262–76.

Hass, Robert. "Poet's Choice: Heather McHugh." *Washington Post Book World*, 10 Oct 1999, 12.

Jackson, Richard. "Doubling the Difference." In *Acts of Mind: Conversations with Contemporary American Poets*. Birmingham: University of Alabama Press, 1983: 93–100.

Kirby, David. "Books in Brief: Fiction & Poetry." Review of *The Father of the Predicaments*, by Heather McHugh. *New York Times Book Review*, 30 Jan 2000, 17.

Kitchen, Judith. "Fourteen Ways of Looking at Selecteds." Review of *Hinge & Sign*, by Heather McHugh. *Georgia Review* 49 (1994): 501–22.

McClatchy, J.D. “Wars at Home and Abroad.” Review of *Shades*, by Heather McHugh. *New York Times Book Review*, 17 Apr. 1988, 34.

Milburn, Michael. “The Habit of Affection.” *Ploughshares* 11.4 (1985): 59–77.

Murphy, Bruce. “Book Reviews.” Review of *Hinge & Sign*, by Heather McHugh. *Poetry* 166.3 (1995): 170–73.

Palatella, John. “Brokenglish.” *Denver Quarterly* 31.1 (1996): 68–78.

Satterfield, Jane. “Books: Poetry Collections.” Review of *The Father of the Predicaments*, by Heather McHugh. *Antioch Review* 58 (2000): 247.

Seidman, Hugh. “Four Poets.” Review of *A World of Difference*, by Heather McHugh. *New York Times Book Review*, 13 Sept. 1981, 14.

Stumpf, Thomas A. “Three Prize Winners.” Review of *Dangers*, by Heather McHugh. *Chicago Review* 30.2 (1978): 127–33.

Turner, Alberta. “Poetry 1981: Review Essay.” Review of *A World of Difference*, by Heather McHugh. *Field: Contemporary Poetry and Poetics* 26.1 (1982): 68–76.

Wakefield, Richard. “Poet McHugh Has a Refreshing Way with Words.” Review of *The Father of the Predicaments*, by Heather McHugh. *Seattle Times*, 31 Oct. 1999, M10.

Weigel, Bruce. “A World of Difference.” *Poet Lore* 76.3 (1981): 170–74.

Weiner, Joshua. “Hinge & Sign: Poems 1968–1993.” *Boston Review* 19.5 (1994): 38.

Yenser, Stephen. “Poetry in Review.” Review of *The Father of the Predicaments*, by Heather McHugh. *The Yale Review* 88.1 (2000): 171–96.

SANDRA MCPHERSON (1943–)

Anett Jessop

BIOGRAPHY

By the date of her birth, August 2, 1943, Sandra McPherson's adoption had been arranged. Her birth mother, Joyce Turney Todd, was a young San Jose State University student majoring in mathematics and her birth father, John Todd, was preparing to ship off to the South Pacific. The details surrounding her birth and the whereabouts of her birth family remained hidden until she was already an acclaimed poet. McPherson was raised in San Jose, California, where her adoptive father, Walter McPherson, coached basketball at San Jose State. Her mother, Frances Gibson McPherson, introduced her daughter to reading at an early age. Throughout her childhood, McPherson enjoyed writing, drawing, painting, and handwork. In her entry for the *Contemporary Authors Autobiography Series* (23: 215–234), she portrays her childhood as one carefully proctored by parents and extended family members and as inspired by the natural world around her.

Much of the McPhersons' family life centered around the Presbyterian church. McPherson describes herself as having been "devout and studious." As she matured, she was confronted with church injunctions: against sexual curiosity, interracial relationships, and jazz. During high school, writing poetry afforded her a harbor against the pressures to conform. McPherson writes, "Creation of art has, I think, always been for me a counterpoint to destructive dogma" (219). Nevertheless, spirituality remains a dominant and pervasive theme in McPherson's work, with Biblical references and revised myths as part of her poetics.

McPherson first attended Westmont College then transferred to San Jose State, where she earned her BA degree. English professor Roberta Holloway became an important mentor and inspiration during her undergraduate years. McPherson began graduate work at the University of Washington, where she studied with David Wagoner and Elizabeth Bishop. Her schooling was cut short when her family's financial support stopped after a disagreement. In 1966 McPherson married fellow graduate student and poet Henry Carlile and gave birth in February 1967 to their daughter, Phoebe. The family moved from Seattle to Portland when Carlile accepted a teaching appointment in the English department at Portland State University. During these years, the challenges of parenthood were complicated by the gradual diagnosis of their daughter's Asperger's Syndrome autism.

In 1970 Indiana University Press published her first book of poems, *Elegies for the Hot Season*. Her second collection, *Radiation* (1973), received attention from Marvin Bell and Donald Justice, who invited her to teach at the Iowa Writers' Workshop (1974–76 and 1978–80). Her third volume, *The Year of Our Birth* (1978), was nominated for the National Book Award. In 1981 McPherson served as Roberta Holloway Lecturer at the University of California, Berkeley. It was then she researched her birth family using Berkeley's Bancroft Library. After an exchange of letters, McPherson met her birth parents and sister. The reunion was warmhearted, and she discovered that the Todds had followed her career for years and owned a complete collection of her books.

Ecco Press brought out *Patron Happiness* in 1983 and *Streamers* in 1988. McPherson was divorced in 1985 and, in the same year, was hired to teach in the English department at the University of California, Davis. She moved to Davis with her daughter and her partner Walter Pavlich, a poet she had met in Portland and whom she married in 1995. At Davis, McPherson developed courses exploring poetry through the themes of love and desire and in the context of Western, Eastern, and African spiritual traditions. She has an abiding interest in the blues and has made several trips to Chicago to hear and talk with musicians. This research directed *The God of Indeterminacy* (1993). McPherson is also an avid collector of antiques and African American quilts.

In 1996 Wesleyan University Press published *Edge Effect: Trails and Portrayals* and *The Spaces Between Birds: Mother/Daughter Poems 1967–1995*, poetic exchanges between McPherson and her daughter and meditations on the effect of Asperger's Syndrome in their lives. In 1999, she founded Swan Scythe Press and established a chapbook series. Her most recent collection, *A Visit to Civilization*, was published by Wesleyan University Press in 2002.

Additional honors include two grants from the Ingram Merrill Foundation, three National Endowment for the Arts fellowships, a Guggenheim Foundation Fellowship, and an award from the American Academy and Institute of Arts and Letters.

MAJOR WORKS AND THEMES

Sandra McPherson has published nine books of poetry and nine chapbooks. She writes about the traditional concerns of women writers of the past: childhood, love and marriage, children, the home and garden. While McPherson came of age, artistically, in the 1970s, she did not choose to address the larger social and political concerns of many writers of that decade. However, she continues to probe significant identities in the feminist domain: the role of woman as artist, the recovery of foremothers, tensions within social roles: daughter, wife, mother, teacher. She authorizes women's lives in poems highlighting pregnancy, labor, birth, motherhood, single parenthood ("Pregnancy," "Labor," "Lament, with Flesh and Blood," "On Being Told 'You Have Stars in your Eyes' "). Her particular resistance to the status quo, socially and aesthetically, has been to give voice and recognition to the "outsider" artist: the self-taught, mentally or emotionally handicapped, often anonymous poets, painters, blues musicians, and quiltmakers on the cultural margins.

McPherson is variously labeled a naturalist poet, not referring so much to the philosophy of naturalism as to her practice of careful observation when recording her environment. She looks for model truths in the vegetal and animal worlds, for instances of domination and survival, cycles and successions ("Fringecups," "The Mouse"). She often draws human parallels from the behaviors and social order of animals ("Lions," "Gnawing the Breast"). Where naturalism, per se, would deny a supernatural reality, McPherson's interest in the material, the world of things, enlarges to invite intimations of the unseen from spiritual traditions ranging from the Judeo-Christian to Haitian Voodoo and Yoruba. Events in the lives of insects, animals, even plants can be endowed with biblical proportion and significance ("Roofrat," "Yellow Sand Verbena"). In the end, McPherson articulates the many means to discover or place ourselves within the larger environmental order, in order to recover from our divorce from the natural, by learning to observe carefully, to find beauty in the landscape, to discover life lessons and spiritual meanings in regeneration.

For much of her career, McPherson has written in and through the elegiac. Her early poems are firmly grounded in the romantic tradition; under the influence of blues music, the convention is pushed so that the poems become less constrained and more conversant. The poems in her first book, *Elegies for the Hot Season*, are carefully crafted, serious meditations on life, love, death and the sacrifices that bridge the stations. True to the elegiac tradition, McPherson searches beyond immediate sadness and disappointment for consolations: sometimes in the realm of the aesthetic, sometimes in the knowledge that deaths, particularly in the animal and plant kingdoms, are never conclusive when viewed in the large design. In the volume's title poem, for example, the systematic killings of garden pests are remembered (the stomping of snails at night by the speaker's father and the torching of caterpillar nests by a neighbor). The event is evaluated in an interchange of perspectives: The childish memory registers an arresting image and a strong emotional response (a fanciful apocalypse of revenge brought on by the flowers); the poet's eye locates beauty ("The snail-pebbled lawns glimmer with slime trails"); the elegiac impulse seeks meaning in pattern, analogy, and the cycles of renewal in nature. Axiomatically, the "slow-brained" pests will return in the "next hot season." *Elegies* records other small infractions by humans upon the natural world ("Poppies," "Foetal Pig") and in our own domestic realm ("Keeping House," "The Wedding").

In a 1973 essay for *Field* journal, entitled "The Working Line," McPherson questions verse forms and the role of the individual line. Her next two collections, *Radiation* and *The Year of Our Birth*, contain poems that are more formally adventurous, both in their use of traditional structures, such as the sestina ("In a Garden"), triolet ("Triolet"), and sonnet ("Three Hard Sonnets"), and experimentation with the stanza and varying line lengths ("Collapsars" and "Senility"). While McPherson is consistently praised in reviews for her finely crafted poems, her relationship to prosody remains organic and intuitive. Two decades later, she asserted: "Home's in the meter, the pen's in a landscape" ("Ode to Early Work" *Edge Effect: Trails and Portrayals*).

In *The Year of Our Birth*, she continues to riddle the question of home and origins in poems such as "1943" and "January Apples." *Patron Happiness* answers some of the queries of personal identity with poems recording McPherson's reunion with her birth family. In the same gesture of retrieval, she offers a tribute to two of her poetic foremothers: "For Elizabeth Bishop" and "A Poem for My Teacher" (Roberta Holloway). A third artistic progenitor is acknowledged in her next book, *Streamers*, in the poem "At the Grave of Hazel Hall." The poet/critic J. D. McClatchy remarks upon her choice of Hazel Hall, "a minor turn-of-the-century Oregon poet, crippled and eventually blind" and speculates upon McPherson's empathy for Hall's "sorrowful life and the needlework incongruities of her art" (40).

McPherson's preoccupation with the "outsider" manifests with more force in *Streamers* and *The God of Indeterminacy*. In *Indeterminacy*, McPherson's research into the blues tradition and the history of African American quiltmaking generates poems that examine the ways people tell sad stories in the lyrics and mode of their music ("Some Metaphysics of Junior Wells") or sew the rags of their lives into comforters ("Quilt of Rights"). In her brief preface, she states that the collection "is about aesthetics, even metaphysics, as manifested in some often unlooked-at *corners* of culture in America and more distant places." McPherson suggests that these individuals are somehow divinely inspired to their work, and that the god of their engagement is as flawed, indeterminate but not, thereby, unworthy of praise, as they. She scores versions of her own life's blues in "Harmonies for the Alienation of My Daughter" and "Bad Mother Blues." She further commemorates and commiserates the relationship with her autistic daughter in *The Spaces Between Birds* (1996).

The "outsider" theme is most fully conceptualized in *Edge Effect: Trails and Portrayals*. In the book's two sections, the first sociological and the second ecological, McPherson conjoins examples of the notably unconventional and wild. Her intention, explained in an endnote, is to link "the poetics of outdoor natural history and the artistic discoveries of self-taught, 'Outsider,' or folk painters and sculptors" (81). Her politics, as such, is a call to uphold, even legitimate, the art of the untrained, handicapped, unqualified ("Outsider: Minnie Evans," "Justin McCarthy, Naive"). She locates their authenticity and greatness in "longing," something skill and polish veil or destroy. In the "Trails" section, McPherson enlists that same untutored and avid vision to travel through Pacific coast landscapes ("Coastscape and Mr. Begley"). The Japanese aesthetic shibui, the quality of aged beauty, offers her a principle with which to contain the enormous variety of matter and growth ("Research Trail, Cold Canyon, November"). She imports a poetics of the plain, using short imagistic stanzas, to describe the ways in which the wide world is also intensely private ("Waiting for Lesser Duckweed: On a Proposal of Issa's").

McPherson's *A Visit to Civilization* re-sounds William Carlos Williams's poetic credo, "No ideas but in things." Poems such as "Toy Soldier," "Jeffrey Dahmer's Boots," and "Material Theology" begin with objects that teach about history, that encourage reminiscing and association, that may even inventory a life ("Diary with Fishhooks"). *Civilization* records examples of social and material commerce: how people trade lessons and belongings. Exchanges have value when both parties are satisfied by the prospect of the object's "reuse." Even when an object is damaged, "new planes [are] revealed by the breakage" ("Brokenness: A Month's Diary").

CRITICAL RECEPTION

Sandra McPherson's work has been variously identified and anthologized under the following rubrics: contemporary women's voices, Western and Northwestern American writers, environmental, even devotional. In 1973 she was profiled in the feminist anthologies *Rising Tides: 20th Century American Women Poets* and *No More Masks!* Other sample collections include *Book of Birth* and *Mother Songs*. Most of the critical commentary on McPherson's work have appeared in reviews in poetry journals, such as *American Poetry Review*, *Poetry*, and *Gettysburg Review*. J. D. McClatchy characterizes hers as a "private voice," not in search of political or social truths but, rather, "domestic and emotional mysteries" (40). McPherson remains a committed practitioner in the tradition of her teacher Elizabeth Bishop: a master of the carefully crafted, descriptive, contemplative lyric. McClatchy calls McPherson "one of the very best of her generation" (40).

BIBLIOGRAPHY

Works by Sandra McPherson

Elegies for the Hot Season. Bloomington: Indiana University Press, 1970.
Radiation. New York: Ecco Press, 1973.
"The Working Line." *Field* 8 (1973): 54–60. (essay)
The Year of Our Birth. New York: Ecco Press, 1978.
Sensing. Hanover, NH: Meadow Press, 1980. (chapbook)
Patron Happiness. New York: Ecco Press, 1983.
Floralia. Illustrated by Claire Van Vliet. West Burke,VT: Trace Editions/Janus Press, 1985. (chapbook)
Pheasant Flower. Missoula, MT: Owl Creek, 1985. (chapbook)
Responsibility for Blue. Denton, TX: Trilobite, 1985. (chapbook)
Eve. London: Gefn Press, 1987. (chapbook)
At the Grave of Hazel Hall. Sweden, ME: Ives Street, 1988. (chapbook)
Streamers. New York: Ecco Press, 1988.
Designating Duet. West Burke, VT: Janus Press, 1989. (chapbook)
The God of Indeterminacy. Chicago: University of Illinois Press, 1993.
The Spaces Between Birds: Mother/Daughter Poems 1967–1995. Hanover, NH: Wesleyan University Press, 1996.
Edge Effect: Trails and Portrayals. Hanover, NH: Wesleyan University Press, 1996.
Beauty in Use. West Burke, VT: Janus Press, 1997. (chapbook)
A Visit to Civilization. Hanover, NH: Wesleyan University Press, 2002.

Studies of Sandra McPherson

Baressi, Dorothy. "*The Spaces Between Birds*." *Gettysburg Review* 10.1 (1997): 163–66.
Brown-Davidson, Terri. "The Belabored Scene, The Subtlest Detail: How Craft Affects Heat in the Poetry of Sharon Olds and Sandra McPherson." *The Hollins Critic* 29.1 (1992): 1–10.
Lasher, Susan. "The Poet as Curator." *Parnassus* 19.2 (1994): 174–94.
Matson, Suzanne. "Flowery Codes: Sandra McPherson's Poetics of Gender and Naturalism." *Denver Quarterly* 28.2 (1993): 86–92.
McClatchy, J. D. "Masks and Passions." *Poetry* 154.1 (1989): 40–43.
McMahon, Lynne. "Female Erotics: Paralysis and Passion." *American Poetry Review* 20.3 (1991): 9–19.
Ullman, Leslie. "*Edge Effect: Trails and Portrayals* and *The Spaces Between Birds: Mother / Daughter Poems 1967–1995*." *Poetry* 169.5 (1997): 341–45.

PAT MORA (1942–)

Kathlyn A. Barros

BIOGRAPHY

Pat Mora was born on January 19, 1942, in El Paso, Texas, into a family whose roots in the Southwestern "borderlands" go back to the Mexican Revolution. Mora's connection to this land affects much of her work in very powerful ways, and although she now divides her time between Santa Fe, New Mexico, and the northern Kentucky and Cincinnati areas, her work remains imbued with the imagery of the desert and of the people of the borderlands.

Mora attended Texas Western College, receiving her BA in 1963 and her MA from the University of El Paso in 1967. She has served as an educator, a museum director, as an administrator at the University of Texas, El Paso, and as a radio host. Mora also speaks at various conferences and educational institutions. In addition, Mora advocated for the induction of a national "Day of the Children/Day of Books—*El Día de los niños/Día de los libros*." Mora's accomplishments have garnered many honors and awards including the Creative Writing Award from the National Association for Chicano Studies (1983); Women Artists and Writers of the Southwest Poetry Award (1984); four Southwest Book Awards from Border Regional Library; named to the El Paso Herald-Post Writers Hall of Fame (1998); awarded the Pellicer-Frost 1999 Binational Poetry Award; awarded the Premio Aztlán Literature Award; in 1997, with illustrator, Raul Colon, received the Tomás Rivera Mexican American Children's Book Award for the children's book *Tomás and the Library Lady*.

MAJOR WORKS AND THEMES

Pat Mora's work addresses the connection between personal, familial, and communal identities, and a connection to the land. Mora discusses Chicano/Latino mythologies in her work. Her work also focuses on the domestic sphere and offers a valuable critique of the social and political juncture of Latina womanhood within the still predominantly patriarchal structure of Latina/o literature. She began her writing career by writing poetry, later writing children's stories and then a novel. This move indicates Mora's desire, as a writer, to be accessible to a wider audience. In her book of essays, *Nepantla: Essays from the Land in the Middle* (1993), Mora writes in a directive and teacherly voice and expresses her concern that Chicana/o (and especially Chicana) works establish as wide an audience as possible.

Mora focuses on poetry as a healing power, and she draws upon certain female archetypes to dispense this healing process: for example, the grandmother/matriarch, as in the "Abuelita" in the poem "Abuelita Magic," who embodies the elements of "learned wisdom, ritual, solutions springing from the land," (*Nepantla* 126); and the "indigenous healer," as in the *curandera/bruja*, who "uses the familiar for healing" (*Nepantla* 127). Mora uses the stories of the past to call upon a sense of the familiar as a way of healing cultural wounds. Mora's sense of using "elements of commonality with her listeners: the importance of family, the retelling of familiar tales," is important because it allows her to take "familiar" stories and then retell them in such a way as to deconstruct them just enough so that they can be re-viewed with a critical eye (*Nepantla* 127). The primary value that Mora sees in communicating with the reader through these tales is the recuperation of a lost sense of history. With this goal in mind, Mora casts herself in the role of the *curandera*/healer.

CRITICAL RECEPTION

Mora approaches many of the same themes (such as communal mythology and identity formation through a specific tie to a place) in her poetry and in her novel, *House of Houses* (1997). In this novel, Mora takes the opportunity to write in a style evocative of a literature of the Americas (magical realism) and to go into greater detail in the telling of what is ultimately a version of the oral tradition of passing on (family) history through rich imagery and first-person narrative. Mora writes herself into existence as a writer through the story of her family. The "characters" who play the key roles in her story are her Aunt Lobo and her father; these are parental figures whose role is to define Mora's family history by framing their "memories" retold at the kitchen table, the heart of the home.

In the poetry collection *Agua Santa/Holy Water* (1995), Mora plays with the notion of myth in a decidedly postmodern way by altering the A-L-T-A-R-E-D women of Chicano mythology, in the "Cuarteto Mexicano: Talk Show Interviews with Coatlicue the Aztec Goddess, Malinche the Maligned, The Virgen of Guadalupe and La Llorona: The Wailer." These four icons of Latina womanhood speak out in "talk show interviews," dispensing their advice and admonitions for women, rewriting their own myths and thus recuperating their space within the communal sphere. Mora, by focusing on the mythology surrounding these women, complicates the notion of myth. Like the *curandera/bruja*, (healer/witch) these mythical women are both lauded and reviled even as they redeem what Tey Diana Rebolledo calls the "Nahuatl dualities and negative and positive aspects of the folk legends" (94). Coatlicue, in "Coatlicue's Rules: Advice from an Aztec Goddess," proclaims that men created her by writing not only her story but also by writing the stories of Eve, Malinche, Guadalupe, and Llorona" (*Agua Santa/Holy Water*, 63). These mythical women exist as integral parts of community formation in that they give birth (literally) to history. Figures such as Malinche,

La Llorona, La Virgen de Guadalupe, and the *curandera/bruja* are presented as symbols for the ultimate reconciliation of the various disparate and problematic mythological identities partitioned out to Latinas.

From Malinche, who is "no virgin," to La Virgen de Guadalupe, Mora's concern with portraying "mythic women" in a new light stems both from a personal and a political desire to refigure marginalized figures. In an interview with Tey Diana Rebolledo in *This Is about Vision: Interviews with Southwestern Writers*, Pat Mora talks about her aunt "Lobo," her mother's half-sister, as a figure who played a vital part in the creation and re-creation of family mythology for Mora. Lobo appears in several literary incarnations throughout Mora's *oeuvre*, and Lobo is a vital part of Mora's vision of the strong woman character who is maternal yet also the "witch." Mora tenderly evokes "mythic women" in her work as a way of refiguring them back into a larger community, a larger sense of history.

By mining the past for familiar tales, Mora establishes a sense of shared history and a sense of community; from the communal, she moves to the individual and to the private. Her concerns are with and for the people who inhabit a harsh barren landscape. Within this landscape, a symbolic and literal place of death and rebirth, Mora brings forth the tales and symbols from a shared past and, like the *curandera*, heals.

BIBLIOGRAPHY

Works by Pat Mora

Chants. Houston, TX: Arte Publico Press, 1984.

Borders. Houston, TX: Arte Publico Press, 1986.

Communion. Houston, TX: Arte Publico Press, 1991.

Nepantla: Essays from the Land in the Middle. Albuquerque: University of New Mexico Press, 1993.

Agua Santa/Holy Water. Boston: Beacon Press, 1995.

Confetti: Poems for Children. New York: Lee & Low Books, 1996.

Aunt Carmen's Book of Practical Saints. Boston: Beacon Press, 1997.

House of Houses. Boston: Beacon Press, 1997. (novel/memoir)

Tomás and the Library Lady. New York: Knopf, 1997. (children's book)

My Own True Name: New and Selected Poems for Young Adults 1984–1999. Houston, TX: Piñata Books, 2000.

Studies of Pat Mora

Barrera, Rosalinda B. "Profile: Pat Mora, Fiction/Nonfiction Writer and Poet." *Language Arts* 75 (1998): 221–28.

Hurado, Aida. "Sitios y Lenguas: Chicanas Theorize Feminisms." *Hypatia* 13 (1998): 134–160.

Murphy, Patrick D. "Conserving Natural and Cultural Diversity: The Prose and Poetry of Pat Mora." *MELUS* 21.1 (1996): 59–69.

———. "Ecofeminism and Postmodernism—Agency, Transformation, and Future Possibilities." *NWSA* 9 (1997): 48–59.

Rebolledo, Tey Diana. "Pat Mora: Interview by Tey Diana Rebolledo." *This Is about Vision: Interviews with Southwestern Writers*, edited by William Balarssi, John F. Crawford, and Anne O. Eysturoy. Albuquerque: University of New Mexico Press, 1990. 129–39.

———. *Women Singing in the Snow: A Cultural Analysis of Chicana Literature*. Tucson: University of Arizona Press, 1995.

Rosenmeier, Rosamond. "Three Poets: Three Feminist Worlds." *Sojourner* 17 (1992): 39–41.

Torres, Lourdes. "Chicana Writers Explore the Land in the Middle." *Sojourner* 19 (1994): 10–12.

CHERRÍE MORAGA (1952–)

Sharon L. Barnes

BIOGRAPHY

Considered one of the founders of the Chicana literary tradition in the United States, Cherríe Moraga is a native Californian whose writing style and issues articulate the politics of the deepest preoccupations of her personal and artistic life, speaking to Chicanas, lesbians, mestizaje, feminists, and indigenous peoples. Moraga was born on September 25, 1952 in Whittier, California, to a Chicana mother, Elvira Moraga, and an Anglo father, Joseph Lawrence. As a young girl, Moraga liked to draw and play music, but because she was a poor reader, she connected to stories more through her sister's retelling of literature and her mother's and aunts' "premier" storytelling than through direct reading. The large, extended family, including cousins, aunts, uncles, friends, and caretakers, revolved around her mother's family, especially Moraga's grandmother, who lived in the San Gabriel Valley for many years. Despite her father's presence, Moraga situates herself in the cultural community of Chicanos, including the linguistic and cultural mix of Spanish and English, which appears as a dominant theme in much of her writing.

In high school, Moraga received some recognition for her writing, enough to earn a scholarship to a private college in Hollywood, where she received a BA in English in 1974. Moraga took some college writing classes but found the experience of being at the progressive school with people dedicated to their art more significant than her actual writing instruction. Teaching high school English for two years after earning her BA, and taking a writing class through the Women's Building in Los Angeles convinced Moraga to seriously investigate the prospect of becoming a creative writer. By her own account, coming out as a lesbian during this period significantly influenced her writing, which had, up to that point, been hiding "secrets" about her identity (Umpierre 55). When her writing group responded to her newly found voice with a classist critique of her vocabulary and the homophobic suggestion that she should not identify her lovers as female, Moraga's determination to write in her own voice increased. Interested in becoming more public about her lesbian identity, Moraga decided in 1977 to move to San Francisco and devote a year to creative writing.

Living in the highly politicized atmosphere of San Francisco of the 1970s opened Moraga's eyes to the race and class differences that influence both creative and political enterprise. She frequently describes an encounter with Judy Grahn's poem "A Woman Is Talking to Death" as a significant awakening for her, influencing her desire to write with an authentic voice, one that represented her race, class, and sexuality. Grahn's poem also gave Moraga motivation to continue seeking her voice as a Chicana lesbian. Personal encouragement from Grahn, along with a successful reading at a woman's coffeehouse in 1977, convinced Moraga that she could pursue a writing career.

She entered San Francisco State University to work on a master's degree in feminist writings, pursuing creative writing and studying feminist literature. She met many other women writers of color, including Gloria Anzaldúa, who solicited Moraga's help collecting work for a manuscript addressing the experience of women writers of color. The collection became Moraga's master's thesis as well as a ground-breaking piece of feminist literature, marking the emergence of a documented radical feminist tradition among women of color. *This Bridge Called My Back*—originally published in 1981 by Persephone Press—was republished in 1983 by the Kitchen Table Women of Color Press, which Moraga helped found. The experience of working on *This Bridge,* which won The Before Columbus Foundation American Book Award, had a profound impact on Moraga, as it had on many of its subsequent readers, making her more open to the connections between women of color yet also more sensitive to the specificity of her experience as a Chicana lesbian-feminist. After its publication, Moraga moved to the East Coast, where she lived in Boston and then New York, as she worked and organized with other feminists of color, including Anzaldúa, Audre Lorde, Barbara Smith, Alma Gómez, and Mariana Romo-Carmona. In 1983 Kitchen Table produced *Cuentos: Stories by Latinas,* the first anthology to collect creative writing by Latina feminists and co-edited by Moraga, Gómez, and Romo-Carmona. Moraga was also busy collecting her own poetic and critical writings, publishing them in 1983 as *Loving in the War Years: (lo que nunca pasó por sus labios),* translated as "What Never Passed Her Lips." Moraga moved from *Loving in the War Years* to working in the theater, hoping to find greater freedom to move from a mostly autobiographical authorial position to one that could give voice to the many members of her community, particularly women struggling with sexual freedom and independence. First as a fellow at the MacDowell Arts Colony in New Hampshire in 1982, then under the auspices of a playwright residency at INTAR (Hispanic-American Arts Center) in New York City, and later in San Francisco at the Brava! Theater Center (1990–96), Moraga wrote several plays set in the Los Angeles Chicano community and also taught playwriting and poetry in community and academic settings. She taught writing and theater in Chicano Studies at the University of California, Berkeley, from 1986–91, publishing *The Lost Generation*, a typical mix of poetry and prose, in 1993. Currently teaching creative writing at Stanford University, Moraga is busy writing and raising her son Rafael Angel Moraga, whose conception and premature birth form the subject of her most recent published work, *Waiting in the Wings: Portrait of a Queer Motherhood* (1997).

MAJOR WORKS AND THEMES

As contributor and co-editor to three groundbreaking collections—*This Bridge Called My Back, Cuentos: Stories by Latinas*, and the lesser known *The Sexuality of Latinas*—Moraga has made a crucial contribution to the tradition of writing by radical women of color in the United States. These works demonstrate many of the themes that dominate her other creative work, combined in poetry, journals, plays, essays, and sketches: her commitment to spreading the words and work of feminists of color, including expressing her experience as a Chicana lesbian; breaking the silence about sexuality and women's experience in the Chicano community; and exploring *mestiza/* indigenous consciousness.

A major preoccupation of most of Moraga's writing—almost all a mix of Spanish and English, genres—beginning with her earliest collection of poetry, sketches, and essays, *Loving in the War Years*, has been her unflinching, critical self-examination of her identity as a lesbian of mixed racial heritage from a working class background. The final essay written for her first volume, "A Long Line of Vendidas," is considered a significant contribution to Chicana lesbian/feminist theory. Through sketches of memories, prose, and journal entries, Moraga explores the repression of Chicana sexuality and male supremacy in Chicano cultures and calls for an acknowledged woman-centered commitment among Chicanas, regardless of sexual orientation. Her early poem "For the Color of My Mother" in *This Bridge* marks her growing awareness of and commitment to the connections between women of color that dominate much of her work as writer and editor. Her articulation of this precise cultural position includes her privileged status as a light-skinned, college educated woman who has mastered the language of the dominant culture, as in the often anthologized essay, "La Güerra" (the fair-skinned girl or woman). "Feed the Mexican Back into Her" poetically explores this theme as played out in her relations to other women of color (*Loving in the War Years*).

Moraga's plays have been the first to articulate the pain of sexual repression and violence suffered at the hands of Chicano men invested in a masculinist sense of superiority. *Giving Up the Ghost* (1986) presents three Chicana characters who direct monologues in which they explore how their sexual identities have been sculpted by their communities. Making visual, as well as audible, the experience of Chicana women, Moraga challenges audiences and the Chicano theater to open to women's words and pain. One of the characters, a young woman named Corky, recounts her rape experience screaming "He made me a hole!" (29). She also articulates a fear of betrayal by women, exploring in "Loving in the War Years," "Loving on the Run," and "You Upset the Whole System of This Place" the complexity of attraction and fear of being both female and queer. Poems from *The Last Generation*, "En Route para Los Angeles," "The Grass, Not Greener," "They Was Girls Together," and "La Ofrenda" maintain this focus, examining difficult choices between loved ones and "home" communities that are omnipresent in a *mestiza* consciousness.

The experience of Chicanos as indigenous people also occupies Moraga's poetry, and in a prose section from *The Last Generation*, she articulates her sense of Chicanos as a disappearing tribe that she envisions, can survive and rise as a new people, connecting the *indigenistas* of Euro-defined Mexico with their U.S. familia and calling for the redefinition of America (61). This cultural consciousness, combined with a focus on the physical environment—the endangered land is connected to endangered peoples—dominates the work, as Moraga forges a female-centered "Queer Aztlan." In "I Was Not Supposed to Remember," Moraga connects her "thoroughly hybrid" identity to the land, claiming she was not supposed to remember being the daughter of an Indian somebody somewhere. Aztlán America, in "Codex Xerí: El Momento Historico," is one in which the female scribe articulates the "Chicano Codex" of exploitation of indigenous lands and peoples; even as she waits in hope and anticipation of destruction and potential rebirth; the Codex-Makers remove their white masks, wait, and watch.

CRITICAL RECEPTION

Moraga's political and literary activism emerge as major contributions to the rise and growth of a Chicana literary tradition and in its growing wider recognition in feminist, Chicano, and mainstream culture. Immediately embraced by lesbian and feminist readers and critics after the publication of *This Bridge*, Moraga's work has been less well received by the Chicano community. Reviewing Latina lesbian literature for the *Lambda Book Report*, Terri de la Pena describes her experience of encountering *This Bridge* in 1981: "Their pathbreaking book convinced me—as nothing else could—that other Chicana lesbian feminist writers did exist" (12). Breaking the silence surrounding sexuality and the Chicana has alienated some sexist and/or homophobic Chicano communities, particularly in the theater. *Shadow of a Man*, premiering in 1990, marked a turning of critical attention to Moraga's work as a playwright among mainstream and Chicano culture alike. In 1996 David DeRose recognized her as "empowering a wider and more representative cross-section of the Chicano community" (77) than her male counterparts, particularly in her portrayal of Chicana women's struggles with sexuality within the largely sexist traditional Chicano community.

In her published works, Moraga's poetry often commingles with essays, journal entries, and sketches, all connecting personal with political reflection, earning her wide appreciation among audiences of color, who find her work a celebration of *mestiza* consciousness through form as well as content (de la Tierra 22). Some reviewers, however, have remarked on the mixture of English and Spanish with less comfort, finding it alienating to the exclusively English speaking/reading audience. While the fiercely political commitment to speaking from her experience and identity in Moraga's poetry has led mainstream reviewers to terms such as "polemical," more progressive reviewers, especially feminists, have responded with great appreciation. Paula Moya notes that Moraga has been "crucial to the production, the dissemination, and the theoretical understanding of literature by Chicanas and other women of color in the United States" (270). Yvonne Yarbro-Bejarano, a careful and insightful reader of Moraga's work, notes that although often considered polemical by feminist, Chicano, and mainstream critics alike, critics also see Moraga as courageous in her expressions of taboo identity ("Cherríe Moraga"165).

BIBLIOGRAPHY

Works by Cherríe Moraga

Cuentos: Stories by Latinas. Ed. Cherríe Moraga, Alma Gómez, and Mariana Romo-Carmona. Latham, NY: Kitchen Table/Women of Color Press, 1983.

Loving in the War Years: (lo que nunca pasó por sus labios). Boston: South End, 1983.

This Bridge Called My Back: Writings by Radical Women of Color. Ed. Cherríe Moraga and Gloria Anzaldúa. Watertown, MA: Persephone Press, 1981. 2nd ed. Latham, NY: Kitchen Table/Women of Color Press, 1983.

Giving Up the Ghost: Teatro in Two Acts. Los Angeles: West End Press, 1986.

Esta puente, mi espalda: voces de mujeres tercermundistas en los Estados Unidos. Ed. Cherríe Moraga and Ana Castillo. San Francisco: Ism Press, 1988.

The Last Generation. Boston: South End Press, 1993.

The Sexuality of Latinas. Ed. Cherríe Moraga, Norma Alarcon, and Ana Castillo. Berkeley, CA: Third Woman Press, 1993.

Shadow of a Man. Albuquerque, NM: West End Press, 1993.

Heroes and Saints and Other Plays: Giving Up the Ghost, Shadow of a Man, Heroes and Saints. Albuquerque, NM: West End Press, 1994.

Waiting in the Wings: Portrait of a Queer Motherhood. Ithaca, NY: Firebrand Books, 1997.

Studies of Cherríe Moraga

Alarcón, Norma. "Interview with Cherríe Moraga." *Third Woman* 3.1–2 (1986): 127–134.

———. "Making Familia from Scratch: Split Subjectivities in the Work of Helena Maria Viramontes and Cherríe Moraga." In *Chicana Creativity and Criticism: Charting New Frontiers in American Literature,* edited by Maria Hererra-Sobek and Helena Maria Viramontes. Houston, TX: Arte Publico, 1988. 147–159.

Blake, Debra J. "Unsettling Identities: Transitive Subjectivity in Cherrie Moraga's *Loving in the War Years.*" *A/B* 12.1 (1997): 71–89.

de la Pena, Terri. "Of Cursors and Kitchen Tables." *off our backs* 24.6 (1994): 10–11.

de la Tierra, Tatiana. "Birth-Smell." *Lesbian Review of Books* 4.4 (1998): 22.

DeRose, David J. "Cherríe Moraga: Mapping Aztlan." *American Theatre* 13 (1996): 76–78.

Kevane, Bridget, and Juanita Heredia. "City of Desire: An Interview with Cherríe Moraga." In *Latina Self-Portraits: Interviews with Contemporary Women Writers*, edited by Bridget Kevane and Juanita Heredia. Albuquerque: University of New Mexico Press, 2000. 97–108.

Moya, Paula. "Cherríe Moraga." In *Encyclopedia of Feminist Literary Theory*, edited by Elizabeth Kowaleski-Wallace. New York: Garland, 1997.

Romero, Lora. " 'When Something Goes Queer': Familiarity, Formalism, and Minority Intellectuals in the 1980s." *Yale Journal of Criticism* 6.1 (1993): 121–41.

Rosenberg, Lou. "The House of Difference: Gender, Culture, and the Subject-in-Process on The American Stage." In *Critical Essays: Gay and Lesbian Writers of Color*, edited by Emmanuel S. Nelson. New York: Haworth, 1993. 97–110.

Sternbach, Nancy Saporta. " 'A Deep Racial Memory of Love': The Chicana Feminism of Cherríe Moraga." In *Breaking Boundaries: Latina Writing and Critical Readings*, edited by Asunción Horno-Delgado, et al. Amherst: University of Massachusetts Press, 1989. 48–61.

Szadziuk, Maria. "Culture As Transition: Becoming a Woman in Bi-ethnic Space." *Mosaic* 32.3 (1999): 109–29.

Umpierre, Luz Maria. "With Cherríe Moraga." *Americas Review* 14.2 (1986): 54–67.

Ward, Skye. "Cherríe Moraga." In *Contemporary Lesbian Writers of the United States: A Bio-Bibliographical Sourcebook*, edited by Sandra Pollack and Denise D. Knight. Westport, CT: Greenwood Press, 1993.

Weatherston, Rosemary. "An Interview with Cherríe Moraga: Queer Reservations; or, Art, Identity, and Politics in the 1990s." In *Queer Frontiers: Millennial Geographies, Genders, and Generations*, edited by Joseph A. Boone, et al. Madison: University of Wisconsin Press, 2000. 64–83.

Wiley, Catherine. "Teatro Chicano and the Seduction of Nostalgia." *MELUS* 23.1 (1998): 99–115.

Worthen, W. B. "Staging America: The Subject of History in Chicano/a Theatre." *Theatre Journal* 49 (1997): 101–20.

Yarbro-Bejarano, Yvonne. "Cherríe Moraga." *Dictionary of Literary Biography, Vol. 82: Chicano Writers*. Detroit, MI: Gale, 1989.

———. "Cherríe Moraga's *Giving Up the Ghost:* The Representation of Female Desire." *Third Woman* 3.1–2 (1986): 113–20.

———. "Cherríe Moraga's 'Shadow of a Man': Touching the Wound in Order to Heal." In *Acting Out: Feminist Performances*, edited by Lynda Hart and Peggy Phelan. Ann Arbor: University of Michigan Press, 1993. 85–104.

———. "Chicana Literature from a Chicana Feminist Perspective." In *Chicana Creativity and Criticism: Charting New Frontiers in American Literature,* edited by Maria Hererra-Sobek and Helena Maria Viramontes. Houston, TX: Arte Publico, 1988. 139–45.

———. "Deconstructing the Lesbian Body: Cherríe Moraga's *Loving in the War Years*." In *Chicana Lesbians: The Girls Our Mothers Warned Us About,* edited by Carla Trujillo. Berkeley, CA: Third Woman Press, 1991. 143–55.

MARILYN NELSON WANIEK (1946–)

Kathrine Varnes

BIOGRAPHY

Marilyn Nelson, in characteristic matter-of-fact modesty, attributes most of her successes to her parents and other relations. Born in Cleveland, Ohio, Nelson spent much of her early life zigzagging across the country as the daughter of Melvin, a pilot in the U.S. Air Force, and Johnnie Nelson, a teacher. Together with her two siblings, the family moved a total of ten times. Perhaps this constant moving instilled in Nelson a wanderlust reflected in the many places she has lived, even as an adult. With a BA from the University of California, Davis (1968), an MA from the University of Pennsylvania (1970), and a PhD in Ethnic Studies from the University of Minnesota (1979), Nelson has taught at a dozen academic institutions, including Universität Hamburg in Germany and the Université Paul Valery in France during a Fulbright Teaching Fellowship, but most of her time since 1978 has been spent at the University of Connecticut, where she is a professor of Aframerican and American Ethnic Literature, and poetry writing. While books prior to 1995 were published under her previously married name of Nelson Waniek, her later titles have appeared solely under Nelson. She has two children with her second husband Roger Wildenfeld.

Since her first book *For the Body* was published in 1978, Nelson has received numerous enviable distinctions, including a National Endowment for the Arts Creative Writing Fellowship, a Yaddo residency, and two Pushcart Prizes. Two of her books were selected as National Book Award finalists in poetry—*The Homeplace* (1990), which also won the 1992 Annisfield-Wolf Award, and *The Fields of Praise* (1997), which also won the 1999 Poet's Prize and was a finalist for the 1998 Lenore Marshall Poetry Prize—and the PEN Winship Award. In addition to six books of poetry, she has translated from Danish (with Patricia Espeland) two books of Halfden Rasmussen's children's verse; served on the editorial boards of *Heavenly Muse*, *Callaloo*, and *MELUS*; published over a dozen reviews and essays; and had poems reprinted in over twenty anthologies and popular magazines, most notably *The Morrow Anthology of*

Younger American Poets, *Sound and Sense*, *Early Ripening*, *A Formal Feeling Comes*, *No More Masks* (2nd edition), *African-American Voices*, two Breadloaf anthologies, *Cosmopolitan* and *Essence*.

MAJOR WORKS AND THEMES

Marilyn Nelson's new and collected volume of work, *The Fields of Praise*, shows what even the most casual reader of her poetry will notice: Each of her volumes has its own overarching subject, such as motherhood, ancestral heritage, or faith under duress, which animates that particular volume. It is these themes that preoccupy this poet—family, history, and faith—rather than the history of her publication that determine the ordering of poems in this collection under four headings: "Mama and Daddy," "Homeplace," "Hermitage," and "Still Faith." She pins down these topics with research, experiential knowledge, clear thinking, and a remarkable ear for music in formal as well as free verse. Grounded in specificity, Nelson's poetry enlivens the past, bringing it into a startlingly real present, in part, through her reinvention of biblical and historical figures with contemporary idiom. In the nine-page "I Dream the Book of Jonah," from her second book, *Mama's Promises* (1985), Nelson blends the story of blues man Mississippi John Hurt, with that of the prophet, incorporating blues lyric patterns and familiar phrases such as "Trouble on my mind," and comparing the whale that swallows Jonah (Hurt) to a "freight train" (42). Besides writing about figures such as Hurt or the Tuskegee Airmen, Nelson also offers series or long poems that focus on lesser-known persons, such as her own ancestors, her friend and monk-priest Abba Jacob, or, in the case of a crown of sonnets, the first minister of a church who, according to a note from Nelson, "was known as a slave to preach to mules" (*Fields* 202). In this sense, she not only personalizes what might otherwise seem to be the dusty books of history, but she also asserts the importance of these lives and their struggles to her contemporary readers. There is a noble didactic purpose here on top of the poetry's beauty, something most obvious in her collection of poems conveying the life of George Washington Carver *Carver: A Life in Poems* (2001), which, while surely sophisticated enough for adults, is written for (and marketed toward) adolescent readers.

Her first two books, *For the Body* and *Mama's Promises*, are written primarily in a spare, free verse line that takes up familial conflict, loss, and poignant portraits of neighbors, friends, and others, including an unexpected picture of Emily Dickinson. Nelson draws her images and metaphors from the everyday, but in unanticipated ways—describing fall in "The Leaves Are Losing the War" as a time when "young girls' breasts are private" and boys' hands (rather than their minds) had forgotten about them (67). Even so, in *Mama's Promises*, Nelson's lines fatten a bit, just as her goal broadens to write from her maternal experience understood in the context of all mothers and mother gods. These poems have a fantastical, mythical quality, as in "Levitation with Baby" in which the speaker delays traipsing off with the Muse in order to take care of her baby, only to see her half-dressed neighbor rising over his rooftop with the Muse instead, or, as in "Confessional Poem," in which the speaker divulges a friend's fantasy to visit a lonely neighborhood mother and dance for her until she and her children laugh and join in.

In *The Homeplace* (1990), Nelson reaches as far back as her great-great-Grandmother Diverne's sale into slavery to shape stories from her family into poems.

The collection of poems offers snapshots of an African American family and the surrounding communities—the clouded affair between Diverne and "Marse Taylor," her son Pomp's business successes and seven children, the police chief Skullbuster Wright's inexplicably brutal attack on Pomp's son Rufus, and the six narrative poems of her father's experience as a Tuskegee Airman. *The Homeplace* reflects a heightened engagement with recognized form, as seen in "The Ballad of Aunt Geneva," the rhyming pentameter quatrains of "Diverne's Waltz," the villanelle "Daughters, 1900," and the four sonnets "Balance," "Annunciation," "Chosen," and "Chopin." Another poem, "Sisters," from her chapbook of sonnets, *Partial Truth* (1992), humorously illustrates Nelson's reworking of these forms for her own purposes. Most of the poem expresses the speaker's inability to understand women's cruelties to each other, then shifts the diction in the last line, explaining in perfect pentameter that she was too refined "to call a heifer out, and whup her ass" (reprinted. in *Fields* 68).

Nelson's poems grapple with big questions, problems of racism, of loss, of love, of evil, in such a way that welcomes rather than lectures her readers, something attributable to her adaptability. She is as at home in vernacular as she is versed in religious and scholarly learning, conversant in several languages, at ease in intricate formal as well as free verse. An equally flexible and generous thinker, Nelson offers an unflinching yet ultimately redemptive vision—recuperative when things are most bleak. Redemption runs through all of her books but is most apparent in *The Fields of Praise* and *Magnificat* (1994), which collects most of her Abba Jacob poems and her meditations on spiritual questions. While the poems in the last section of *Fields* are perhaps the most grim (the scientific torturing of animals is the subject of her translation of Thorkild Bjørnvig's Danish poem "Ape-Gods"; she scrutinizes the nature of evil in a series of sonnets; she conveys Hecuba's despair over the loss of her daughter in "The Death of Polyxena," a translation from Euripides), their placement under the subheading "Still Faith" insists on stubborn hope. Indeed, the volume's final poem, "Minor Miracle" illustrates Nelson's tendency to favor redemption when it describes a white truck driver who, after nearly clipping two African American bicyclists, calls out a racial insult. The poem's miracle occurs when the driver returns to apologize, albeit with a kind of awkward aggression. The poem, like much of her work, suggests that, no, the world isn't perfect, but neither is it void of the miraculous.

CRITICAL RECEPTION

Marilyn Nelson has received praise in diverse publications, including laudatory reviews in the *African American Review*, the *Women's Review of Books*, *Parnassus*, and the *Hudson Review*. Her ability with tone has been favorably compared to that of Anne Sexton (Ingebretsen) and her musical finesse with that of Gwendolyn Brooks (Gardinier). In addition, well-regarded poets such as R. S. Gwynn and Marilyn Hacker have found much to admire in both her technical and imaginative powers, or, as Miller Williams summed up, "her poems are well-wrought, and they say things that matter" (179).

A feature noted by nearly all her reviewers is her balancing of difficult materials with a wry humor, what Michael Weaver calls her "whimsy and philosophical glance" (505). This balance garners attention for most of her books. Anne West Ramirez, for instance, praises the "mysticism and humor" of the Abba Jacob poems, while James

Cotter reports that in "The pilot's story-telling voices dance off the page with heroism and humor" (512, 347). Likewise, Leslie Ullman describes "a humor that offers a healing perspective on hard facts even as it refuses to disguise them" (183). Under the same category of balance, Betty Adcock offers unreserved praise for *The Homeplace*, particularly for Nelson's knack for understatement (140).

Perhaps because Nelson moves so seamlessly between free verse and formal traditions, some reviewers will favor one or another section of poetry, but often this either/or judgment reflects an aesthetic preference in the reviewer rather than a flaw in the work. As Ullman explains it, Nelson's broad aesthetics "suggest that her own background as an African-American poet is a rich patchwork of traditions, and that her clearly organic sense of self and family history has moved her neither to embrace nor eschew current Formalist concerns" (182). For a poet with such a wide appeal, artistic patchwork may be the most apt metaphor, especially for Marilyn Nelson, who also spends a fair amount of time making real quilts out of cloth.

BIBLIOGRAPHY

Works by Marilyn Nelson Waniek

For the Body. Baton Rouge: Louisiana State University Press, 1978.

Hundreds of Hens. With Pamela Espeland. Minneapolis: Black Willow, 1983.

The Cat Walked through the Casserole and Other Poems for Children. With Pamela Espeland. Minneapolis: Carolrhoda, 1984.

Mama's Promises. Baton Rouge: Louisiana State University Press, 1985.

The Homeplace. Baton Rouge: Louisiana State University Press, 1990.

Partial Truth. Wellington, CT: The Kutenai Press, 1992. (chapbook)

Magnificat. Baton Rouge: Louisiana State University Press, 1994.

The Fields of Praise. Baton Rouge: Louisiana State University Press, 1997.

"Hecuba." *Euripides I*. Translation. The Penn Greek Drama Series. Philadelphia: University of Pennsylvania Press, 1997.

Carver: A Life in Poems. Chicago: Front Street Press, 2001.

Studies of Marilyn Nelson Waniek

Adcock, Betty. Review of *The Homeplace*, by Marilyn Nelson. *Obsidian II* 7.1–2 (1992): 137–43.

Cotter, James Finn. "The Truth of Poetry" *Hudson Review* 44 (1991): 343–50.

Dyer Rowe, Monica. Review of *The Fields of Praise: New and Selected Poems*, by Marilyn Nelson. *American Visions* 13 (1998): 30.

Gardinier, Suzanne. "Bootleg, Jackleg Medicine: Curing as Only Generations Can (Thylias Moss, Marilyn Waniek Nelson)." Review of *The Homeplace*, by Marilyn Nelson. *Parnassus* 17.1 (1992): 65–78.

Gwynn, R. S. Review of *The Fields of Praise: New and Selected Poems*, by Marilyn Nelson. *Hudson Review* 51 (1998): 257–64.

Hacker, Marilyn. Review of *The Fields of Praise: New and Selected Poems*, by Marilyn Nelson. *Women's Review of Books* 15.8 (1998): 17–18.

Ingebretsen, Edward J. Review of *The Fields of Praise*, by Marilyn Nelson. *America*, 25 Apr. 1998, 27–28.

Kitchen, Judith. "I Gotta Use Words." Review of *The Fields of Praise: New and Selected Poems*, by Marilyn Nelson. *Georgia Review* 51.4 (1997): 756–72.

Lattimore, Richard. Review of *For the Body*, by Marilyn Nelson. *Hudson Review* 32 (1979): 448.

Monaghan, Pat. Review of *Magnificat*, by Marilyn Nelson. *Booklist*, 1 Sept. 1994, 20.

Ramirez, Anne West. Review of *The Fields of Praise: New and Selected Poems*, by Marilyn Nelson. *Christianity and Literature* 47 (1998): 510–13.

Sofield, David. Review of *Magnificat*, by Marilyn Nelson. *America*, 13 Jan. 1996, 16+.

Ullman, Leslie. Review of *The Homeplace*, by Marilyn Nelson. *Kenyon Review* 13.2 (1991): 181–85.

Weaver, Michael S. Review of *Magnificat*, by Marilyn Nelson. *African American Review* 30 (1996): 504–06.

Williams, Miller. Review of *The Fields of Praise: New and Selected Poems*, by Marilyn Nelson. *African American Review* 33.1 (1999): 179–81.

Wiman, Christian. "An Idea of Order." *Poetry* 173.3 (1999): 241.

———. Review of *The Homeplace*, by Marilyn Nelson. *Shenandoah* 42 (1992): 100.

NAOMI SHIHAB NYE (1952–)

Persis M. Karim

BIOGRAPHY

To identify Naomi Shihab Nye as an "Arab American poet" would be far too limiting a label for such a versatile and prolific writer. However, neglecting to mention Nye's Palestinian background overlooks a significant aspect of her life and the way it has shaped her as a writer. Nye was born in St. Louis, Missouri, in 1952 to a Palestinian father and an American mother, and she became aware at an early age of her difference. The recognition that her parents originated from two entirely different cultures helped her develop what she has described as a kind of "bicultural instinct": "Even before I had been to the Middle East, I remember being conscious that part of me was from somewhere else entirely. It could stand back and separate itself" (Milligan 31). Although she spent most of her childhood in St. Louis, Nye's family moved to Palestine when she was fourteen years old. While her father served as editor of the *Jerusalem Times*, the Shihab family resided in the West Bank village of Singil for two years (the village where her father grew up and which was, in the 1960s, considered part of Jordan).

This two-year period in Palestine and her attendance at Quaker and Armenian schools, where the curriculum was in Arabic, Armenian, and English, made her acutely aware of the importance of language and words and made her "conscious of the *necessity* of writing" (Milligan 35). While living in the Middle East helped solidify her "Americanness," it also contributed to the rich tapestry of images, stories, and sensibilities that appear in her poetry, prose, and essays. It was also during her stay in Palestine that Nye began to sing, play guitar, and write songs. Her background in music and her particular interest in the oral storytelling tradition of the Middle East have contributed to her unique style—articulated in her poetry through her use of longer, rhythmic lines.

Nye returned to the United States with her family in 1967 and completed her high school education in San Antonio, Texas, where she later attended Trinity College and received her BA in English. While Nye never formally studied poetry writing in college, she did attend workshops and continuously sought the feedback and support of other writers, editors, and poets. Nye was especially influenced by the American poets W. S. Merwin and William Stafford. After graduating from college, Nye remained in San Antonio, with her husband Michael Nye and her son Madison. Although she travels extensively throughout the United States, Nye also teaches workshops and actively works with the Poetry in the Schools program in Texas. Nye has received numerous awards for her work including the Texas Institute of Letters Award; the Carity Randall Prize; the Peter I. B. Lavan Younger Poets Award; and the International Poetry Forum. She has twice traveled to the Middle East and Asia for the United States Information Agency (USIA), working to promote international understanding through the arts. Nye received a Guggenheim Fellowship in 1997–98 and has appeared on two Public Broadcasting System poetry specials: *The Language of Life with Bill Moyers* (1995) and *The United States of Poetry* (1996).

MAJOR WORKS AND THEMES

Nye's three early volumes of poetry, *Different Ways to Pray* (1980), *Hugging the Jukebox* (1982), and *Yellow Glove* (1986) established her reputation as a humanistic poet who captures the sense of the "dignity of daily life" (Moyers 326). Although the poetry in these first three volumes, from which some selections were later included in the collection *Words under Words* (1995), has often been cited as the work most clearly distinguishing Nye as a Palestinian American poet, the range of themes is far greater than this title affords. While Nye has shown a great concern with the landscape and feeling of the Palestinian exile, her early work shows just as much, if not more of a preoccupation with the Hispanic Southwest and her travels in Latin America as it does with her Arab and Palestinian heritage. This sense of a disparate geography, of home and exile, and the travels of the spirit and soul come together in Nye's poems as a kind of spiritual reconciliation. In her work, Nye celebrates the daily and mundane, such as in images of onions, figs, and buttonholes, and the capacity that objects and moments have to experience a kind of transcendence. Some of her most anthologized poems of this early period include "Kindness," "The Art of Disappearing," "My Father and the Figtree," "Making a Fist," "Arabic Coffee," "Yellow Glove," and "No One Thinks of Tegucigalpa."

While her attention to her local surroundings in Texas, with its proximity to Mexico and Central America, and the imposing sense of borders loom large in these earlier volumes, Nye also presents the grave subject of the plight of the Palestinian people with grace. Rather than being polemical or overtly political, Nye's sense of protest is depicted in the quiet and subtle images of everyday life in the face of the indignities of Israeli occupation. One of her better-known poems, "The Man Who Makes Brooms" (*Yellow Glove*) pays homage to a Palestinian broommaker, who carries on the simple task of making brooms from straw while the world around him erupts in the violence of war and occupation.

Nye's attention to detail, to making the small and invisible visible, are equally present in her 1994 volume, *Red Suitcase*. Like her earlier work, which names the strangeness we all feel at being, in her own words, "in a kind of exile, an exile from the part of ourselves where poems come from" (Moyers PBS), her later poems reach into those places that suggest both the necessity of conversation with the world and her own sense of responsibility as a poet to name what is in the world. This rapt attention to the details of everyday life and our longing for meaning is found in "From Here to There" where Nye writes of the thing in us that wants order such as "pillows lined across the head of the bed," swept porches, and raised window shades (17).

The poems in *Red Suitcase* and *Fuel* (1998) reflect Nye's acute sense of loss brought on by two watershed events in the Middle East: the intifada (the Palestinian uprising against the Israeli occupation) and the Gulf War of 1991. Both these collections have an urgency in them that speaks to the unspeakable pain of loss, whether it is the human recognition of a woman seeing her baby growing up and entering the world of school where he/she sharpens pencils as in "What Is Supposed to Happen" or in the more public losses of Palestinians who endure the injustices of an occupation that persists until it distorts their humanity as in "The Palestinians Have Given Up Parties."

In the same way that Nye seems preoccupied with naming the silent, small gestures of human life, she is also concerned in her more recent work with helping to give voice to others. Since 1992, Nye has been a prolific editor of anthologies, the two most recent dedicated to children's and younger poets' work: *Salting the Ocean: 100 Poems by Young Poets* (2000) and *Come with Me: Poems for a Journey*, an anthology of children's poems (2000). She has also written several fictional children's books including *Sitti's Secrets* (1994), *Benito's Dream Bottle*, illustrated by Yu Cha Pak, (1995), *Lullaby Raft* (1997), and *Habibi* (1997). Nye has also published a collection of essays, *Never in a Hurry: Essays on People and Places* (1996), and collaborated on an English translation of the Palestinian writer Fadwa Tuqan's autobiography.

CRITICAL RECEPTION

Given Nye's prolific output over the past ten years, it is surprising that her work has not received more critical attention in both poetry and scholarly journals. The reception of her work has to a large degree been a symptom of her terrific range and the seeming disparateness of her themes that perhaps make it difficult for her work to be discussed and critically assessed in traditional critical circles. Critics take two general approaches in viewing her work. Philip Booth's 1989 reading of Nye's *Yellow Glove* reveals the first of these approaches as he reads this collection as part of a trend represented in the works of three other female poets: C. D. Wright, Marianne Boruch, and Margaret Gibson. Booth identifies these poets as possessing strong voices, unique visions, and who, he suggests, are "woefully under-reviewed . . . especially by men" (162). Booth's essay focuses on the ways that Nye "brings the strange home" and captures both the familiar and unfamiliar in a "gracefully conversational" style (164).

Other critics adhere to a narrower understanding of Nye as a Palestinian American poet and focus on the themes of exile and alienation, as well as on her humane representation of the Palestinian people in a contrast to the popularly evoked media image of Arabs as terrorists. This critical reception celebrates Nye as an emerging generation of Arab American poets, along with other poets such as Elmaz Abinader and Gregory Orfalea, who also grapple with the dissonance between the humanity of their cultures and the generally negative stereotypes promulgated in newspaper and television headlines about the Middle East.

A significant assessment of Nye's work, for example, appeared in a 1991 issue of *Paintbrush: A Journal of Poetry, Translations, and Letters*. This issue of the journal, published just after the 1991 Gulf War, features an interview with the poet that reveals the personal, political, and writerly influences of her work (see Milligan). Gregory Orfalea in the same issue of *Paintbrush* offers an extensive commentary on her work and reflects more specifically on the Arab and Palestinian sources in Nye's work. Like other critics, Orfalea pays tribute to Nye's tremendous courage in tackling difficult political subjects and in her desire to "hear out the speech of others, as they strain for meaning" (61). Orfalea, like others, notes the attention that Nye gives not just to her Palestinian heritage, but also to the heritage of her own sense of place as a resident of Texas. As Orfalea and other reviewers remind us, her location is indicative of Nye's understanding of what it means to straddle geography, maps, and language and to inhabit more than one place. Newspaper reviews of the various poetry anthologies that Nye has edited and of her more recent collection of essays, *Never in a Hurry*, focus attention on the theme of wandering, not just as subject matter in much of her work, but also as a reflection of the many genres in which she chooses to write.

BIBLIOGRAPHY

Works by Naomi Shihab Nye

Different Ways to Pray. Portland, OR: Breitenbush Books, 1980.

Hugging the Jukebox. New York: Dutton, 1982.

Yellow Glove. Portland, OR: Breitenbush Books, 1986.

A Mountainous Journey: A Poet's Autobiography: Fadwa Tuqan. Trans. Olive E. Kenney and Naomi Shihab Nye. London: Women's Press, 1990.

This Same Sky: A Collection of Poems from around the World. New York: Four Winds Press, 1992.

Red Suitcase: Poems. Brockport, NY: BOA Editions, 1994.

Sitti's Secrets. New York: Four Winds Press, 1994. (children's book)

Benito's Dream Bottle. New York: Simon and Schuster, 1995. (children's book)

The Tree Is Older than You Are: A Bilingual Gathering of Poems and Stories from Mexico with Paintings by Mexican Artists. New York: Simon and Schuster, 1995.

Words under Words: Selected Poems. Portland, OR: Breitenbush Books, 1995.

Never in a Hurry: Essays on People and Places. Columbia: University of South Carolina Press, 1996.

Habibi. New York: Simon and Schuster, 1997. (children's book)

Lullaby Raft. New York: Simon and Schuster, 1997. (children's book and song)

Fuel: Poems. Rochester, NY: BOA Editions, 1998.

The Space between our Footsteps: Poems and Paintings from the Middle East. New York: Simon and Schuster, 1998.

Come with Me: Poems for a Journey. New York: Greenwillow, 2000. (children's book)

Salting the Ocean: 100 Poems by Young Poets. New York: Greenwillow, 2000.

Mint Snowball. Tallahassee, FL: Anhinga Press, 2001.

19 Varieties of Gazelle: Poems of the Middle East. New York: HarperCollins Juvenile Books, 2002. (children's book)

Studies of Naomi Shihab Nye

Booth, Philip. "Loners Whose Voices Move." *Georgia Review* 43.1 (1989): 161–78.

Collof, Pamela. "The Texas Twenty." *Texas Monthly*, 26 Sept. 1998, 111+.

Milligan, Bruce. "Writing to Save Our Lives: An Interview with Naomi Shihab Nye." *Paintbrush* 18.35 (1991): 31–52.

Moyers. Bill. *The Language of Life: A Festival of Poets*. New York: Doubleday, 1995. 319–34.

———. *The Language of Life: A Festival of Poets*. Directed by Bill Moyers and David Grubin. PBS, 1995.

Orfalea, Gregory. "Doomed by Our Blood to Care: The Poetry of Naomi Shihab Nye." *Paintbrush* 18.35 (1991): 56–66.

Schliesman, Megan. "Naomi Shihab Nye: People! People! My Heart Cried Out." *Book Links* 7.6 (1998): 40–43.

United States of Poetry, Parts 1–3. Directed by Mark Pellington. Washington Square Films, 1996 (videocassette)

SHARON OLDS (1942–)

Cassandra A. Van Zandt

BIOGRAPHY

Publisher of six volumes of poetry, Sharon Olds was born in 1942 in San Francisco, California. She grew up in a distinctly religious home. Olds and her siblings were subjected to physical abuse by both parents. When she was in her forties, her father died from cancer. These events, as well as others such as the births of her children, serve as a generative source for much of her work.

Olds attended Stanford where she received her BA in 1964, and she earned her PhD from Columbia University in 1972. In 1976 she joined the faculty of the Theodor Herzl Institute, in New York City. Two years later, she won the Madeline Sadin Award from the *New York Quarterly* for her poem "The Death of Marilyn Monroe," included in the collection *The Dead and the Living* (1984). In 1980, at the age of thirty-seven, Olds published her first volume of poetry and has since garnered multiple awards for her writing, including the National Book Critics' Circle Award, the Lamont Award, and the San Francisco Poetry Center Award. She was named the New York State poet laureate for 1998–2000.

The former director of the New York University Creative Writing Program, Olds is currently an associate professor of English at New York University where she teaches poetry workshops. Her work, however, does not revolve solely around academia; she also has discovered a way in which to use her talents to benefit the community around her. Olds founded and continues to teach in a program at Goldwater Memorial Hospital in New York, which provides writing workshops for severely physically challenged individuals.

MAJOR WORKS AND THEMES

In her first collection, *Satan Says* (1980), Olds introduces some of the themes that recur throughout her work: sex, human intimacy, parent-child relationships, motherhood, abuse, and religion. *The Dead and the Living* (1984) and *The Gold Cell* (1987) continue in this vein. Olds wrote the poems contained in the latter volume in 1980, 1981, and 1982. With this collection, she began a pattern of publishing poems written several years before their publication date, which has allowed her the opportunity to revise the poems as she selects them for the collection. In fact, *The Wellspring,* published in 1996, contains work written more than a decade earlier. With poems written through 1982, it picks up where *The Gold Cell* stops. Olds's collections are "literally dozens of short poems" that function as "snapshots" (Dillon 108). She formerly described herself as a "salvation addict" because she realized that she consistently wanted poems to have happy endings ("The Simple Acts of Life"). One may surmise, then, that her ability to write poems that do not conclude on a forced positive note signals growth in her writing. "Letter to My Father from 40,000 Feet" (*The Father* 63) is such a poem. It terminates not with reconciliation nor an affirmation of love but rather with her arm wrestling a man who reminds her of her father and slamming his arm to the ground "long after he cries out" (64).

Her work is full of vivid images remarkable for their corporeality. Often, these visceral metaphors take the form of bodily excretions: mucus, urine, excrement, semen, breast milk, menstrual blood, and sweat. Alicia Ostriker places Olds's work in context with other post-1960s women poets and explains that many seem to see "the body as a source essentially of pain, not pleasure: "The damaged bodies of war victims, the hungry bodies of famine victims are acutely important images in the work of . . . Sharon Olds," as well as many others (98). The "bodies" in Olds's poems menstruate, masturbate, neck, have sex, give birth, are sexually violated and physically abused, eat, vomit, and die. Yes, Olds writes of pain, but she also writes of pleasure. The physical pleasure of sex manifests as the most often occurring representation of pleasure. "I Love It When" serves as just one instance in which these pleasures are extolled. One reviewer determined that Olds "writes about sexuality in a way that no other poet does" (*Economist* 91). One of her often anthologized poems, "Sex Without Love" (*The Dead and the Living* 57), uses multiple sexual puns, "insistent rhythm," repetition of the words "come to the," and strategically placed spaces to mimic "the rhythmic thrusting and heavy breathing" of the partners whom the poem critiques: sexual partners who would eschew emotional attachment (Sutton 179).

Commonly referred to as confessional poetry, Olds's work is frequently described as analogous to writing by Sylvia Plath and Anne Sexton. Sandra Gilbert cites these two poets, as well as Allen Ginsberg and Robert Lowell, as pioneers of the "tradition of frank, sometimes brutally explicit familial analysis and self-analysis" to which she says Olds is "a crucial heir" (50). The family is central to Olds's poetry. The speaker in the poems typically identifies herself in terms of her familial relationships; she is a daughter, sister, wife, and mother. Indeed, she seems to endeavor "to define herself within the context of the family into which she was born as well as the family she herself has made" (Lesser 748). Olds's poems reflect the multiple facets of these relationships. "Killing My Sister's Fish" tells of a young child's pouring ammonia into the tank that held her sister's goldfish "just because they were alive, and she liked them" (*The Wellspring* 15). "The Elder Sister" (*The Dead and the Living* 48) marks a transformation in this sibling relationship and represents it from a changed point of view: adulthood. The speaker reflects upon their childhood as she recalls her sister's urinating on her in bed but also speaks of her sister's wrinkles as the "dents" on the speaker's "shield" because her elder sister functioned as a buffer that protected the speaker and enabled her to "escape" from a traumatizing home life. Numerous other poems continue this theme of abuse. *Blood, Tin, Straw*'s "The Day They Tied Me Up" describes a child's being tied to a chair and told that she would not be untied until she apologizes. Marking a shift in the power structure, the still-bound child determines that she will never apologize and is unsurprised when her mother kneels before her and spoon-feeds alphabet soup to her. Throughout, the poem repeatedly links the speaker to images of reading and deciphering that underscore this changing power dynamic. She reads the blot of ink that she has poured onto her parents' bed as she does a Nancy Drew book; she reads with her tongue the letters of the soup and exhibits a new kind of power through her access to knowledge. At the close of the poem, her mother feeds the child this "discordant fuel" that she wants her daughter "to decipher" so that she will "thrive" (41–42).

Other poems suggest erotic parent-child relationships. Indeed, Ostriker refers to Olds as "among our most eloquent celebrants of the erotic mother-child relation" and points to "Young Mothers V" from *Satan Says* as an example in which the women are depicted as "alert animals" (182). Olds's work eroticizes the father-child relationship as well. Fraught with sexual energy, the speaker's gaze in "Looking at My Father" in *The Gold Cell* is likened to an animal gazing at water and then proceeding to imbibe until contented and able to sleep. The poem recounts the father's body in detail, and the speaker affirms that her body thinks his is perfect.

Mirroring this relationship, "My Father Speaks to Me from the Dead," the poem that concludes the collection *The Father*, illustrates the father's "love" for the daughter by articulating his love for her body. Peter Scheponik comments, however, that though "love" is used as a "refrain" in this poem, there is "little evidence of any emotional connection" (60). Unlike the other poems in this volume, the father (rather than the daughter) is the speaker; his description begins at her feet and rises up the length of her body as "the lines of the poem move past her legs with slow deliberation, producing a taut chord of sexual intimacy" (60). Indeed, even her brain is likened to labia (*The Father* 78). While *The Father* returns to many of the themes visited in Olds's other works, it proves unique as the collection is devoted entirely to poems that address her father's dying of cancer. The collection opens with poems that depict her return home to visit him, moves through the process of his dying, and touches upon moments after his death. Discussing this poem, Laura E. Tanner uses theories regarding the gaze in order to explain that "the intimacy of the gaze" is not solely a means of "negotiating sexual difference," but also "a way of establishing connection between a healthy subject and a person with terminal illness" (104). Tanner's reading would seem to be supported by Ostriker's contention that Olds's poems illustrate "self-integration through visionary integration with both parents" (194). In several of the poems throughout Olds's work, the speaker not only compares herself to her father, but also describes herself *as* him. "Why My Mother Made Me" (*The Gold Cell*) asserts that the reason is that the speaker is what her mother always wanted: the speaker's father "as a woman" (33).

CRITICAL RECEPTION

The responses to Olds's work vary, ranging from high praise to strong criticism. One reviewer describes *Blood, Tin, Straw* (1999) as "poetry as memoir, mined from the very core of her being" (Seaman 339). Another declares that, in her narcissism, Olds "casually annex[es] the Holocaust as a symbol for her antipathy to her father"

(Kirsch 40). In light of Gilbert's paralleling Olds and Plath, it is worthy of note that this criticism is one that has been leveled at both poets. Olds has been lauded as a "legitimate daughter of Whitman" (Lesser 750) and censured for what is perceived as the limited focus of the subject of her work: "The major subject—almost the only subject—of Olds's poetry is the fierce and unrelenting fight with a childhood of Calvinism" (Kirsch 38). This critic, as well as many others, picks up on the religious tenor of many of the poems. Often the critics seem to follow Olds's lead as their word choice echoes the religious typology of her poetic terrain. She writes "Psalm" (*The Father*), and her poems are described as "psalms in praise of sex, holy matrimony, and motherhood" (Seaman 339). Olds pens "Satan Says," and the commentator discusses the speaker's "blaspheming" her parents in the piece (Kirsch 38). Along this vein, Lesser contends that "Prayer," the final poem in *Satan Says*, "can be seen as Olds's credo; the articles of her faith, the 'central meanings' she splendidly celebrates, are sex and birth. It is one of many erotic poems in which she convincingly incarnates a sexual consciousness that is male and female at once" (748). *The Father* has been called "tasteless" (Logan 60) and "easily one of the oddest [books of poems] ever published" (Bedient 169). Yet, Gilbert contends that "despite Olds's failures," it is "ultimately an exemplary text in the late Twentieth Century . . . history of 'family values' as poetic, *topos*, theme, plot, preoccupation" (52–53).

BIBLIOGRAPHY

Works by Sharon Olds

Satan Says. Pittsburgh, PA: University of Pittsburgh Press, 1980.
The Dead and the Living. New York: Knopf, 1984.
The Gold Cell. New York: Knopf, 1987.
The Father. New York: Knopf, 1992.
The Wellspring. New York: Knopf, 1995.
Blood, Tin, Straw. New York: Knopf, 1999.

Studies of Sharon Olds

Bedient, Calvin. Review of *The Father*, by Sharon Olds. *Salmagundi* (1993): 169–81.
Brown-Davidson, Terri. "The Belabored Scene, The Subtlest Detail: How Craft Affects Heat in the Poetry of Sharon Olds and Sandra McPherson." *The Hollins-Critic* 29.1 (1992): 1–10.
Christian, Graham. Review of *Blood, Tin, Straw*, by Sharon Olds. *Library Journal* 124.20 (1999): 142.
Dillon, Brian. " 'Never Having Had You, I Cannot Let You Go': Sharon Olds' Poems of a Father-Daughter Relationship." *Literary Review* 37.1 (1993): 108–18.
Gilbert, Sandra M. "Family Values." Review of *The Father*, by Sharon Olds. *Poetry* 164.1 (1994): 39–53.
Kirsch, Adam. "The Exhibitionist." Review of *Blood, Tin, Straw*, by Sharon Olds. *New Republic*, 27 Dec. 1999, 38.
Lesser, Rika. Review of *The Father*, by Sharon Olds. *Nation* 255.20 (1993): 748–50.
Lindgren, Kristin. "Birthing Death: Sharon Olds's *The Father* and the Poetics of the Body." In *Teaching Literature and Medicine*, edited by Anne Hunsaker Hawkins and Marilyn Chandler McEntyre. New York: Modern Language Association, 2000. 260–66.
Logan, William. "No Mercy." *The New Criterion* 18.4 (1998): 60–67.

Matson, Suzanne. "Talking to Our Father: The Political and Mythical Appropriations of Adrienne Rich and Sharon Olds." *American Poetry Review* 18.6 (1989): 35–41.

McGiveron, Rafeeq O. "Olds's 'Sex Without Love.' " *Explicator* 58.1 (1999): 60–62.

Oldfield, Sybil. "The News from the Confessional—Some Reflections on Recent Autobiographical Writing by Women and Its Areas of Taboo." *Critical Survey* 8.3 (1990): 296–305.

Ostriker, Alicia Suskin. "I Am (Not) This: Erotic Discourse in Bishop, Olds, and Stevens." *The Wallace Stevens Journal* 19 (1995): 234–54.

———. *Stealing the Language: The Emergence of Women's Poetry in America*. Boston: Beacon Press, 1986.

Review of *Blood, Tin, Straw*, by Sharon Olds. *Booklist,* 1 Jan. 2000, 815.

Review of *Blood, Tin, Straw*, by Sharon Olds. *Publishers Weekly*, 27 Sept. 1999, 98.

Review of *The Wellspring*, by Sharon Olds. *Economist* 13 July 1996, 91.

Scheponik, Peter C. "Olds's 'My Father Speaks to Me from the Dead.' " *Explicator* 57.1 (1991): 59–62.

Seaman, Donna. Review of *Blood, Tin, Straw*, by Sharon Olds. *Booklist,* 1 Oct. 1999, 339.

"The Simple Acts of Life." *The Power of the Word with Bill Moyers*. Vol. 1. Directed by David Grubin. Produced by WNET, New York, and New Jersey Network. Video recording, 1989.

Sutton, Brian. "Olds's 'Sex Without Love.' " *Explicator* 55.3 (1997): 177–80.

Tanner, Laura. "Death Watch: Terminal Illness and the Gaze in Sharon Olds's *The Father*." *Mosaic* 29.1 (1996): 103–21.

MARY OLIVER (1935–)

Roxanne Harde

BIOGRAPHY

Born September 10, 1935, in Cleveland, Ohio, to schoolteacher Edward William Oliver and Helen Vlasak Oliver, Mary Oliver studied at Ohio State University and Vassar. Oliver worked for a time as secretary to Edna St. Vincent Millay's sister, and her early work is frequently compared to that of Millay. Oliver's first academic posting was the Mather Visiting Professorship at Case Western Reserve, Cleveland (1980). She has taught at Bucknell, the University of Cincinnati, and has been writer-in-residence at Sweet Briar College, Virginia. She has been a William Blackburn Visiting Professor in Creative Writing at Duke University and, since 1996, has held the Katharine Osgood Foster Chair for Distinguished Teaching at Bennington College in Vermont. She divides her time between Bennington and her permanent home in Provincetown, Massachusetts.

The title poem from Oliver's first book, *No Voyage and Other Poems* (1963), won first prize from the Poetry Society of America in 1963. Oliver's other books of poetry include *The River Styx, Ohio and Other Poems* (1972); *American Primitive* (1983); *Twelve Moons* (1979); *Dream Work* (1986); *House of Light* (1990), which won the Christopher and L. L. Winship Awards; *New and Selected Poems* (1992), which won the National Book Award for Poetry; and *West Wind* (1997); and two chapbooks: *The Night Traveler* (1978) and *Sleeping in the Forest* (1978). Oliver's *oeuvre* also includes two prosody handbooks and an essay collection: *A Poetry Handbook* (1994), *Rules for the Dance* (1998), and *Blue Pastures* (1995), and *Winter Hours* (1999) is a collection of essays, poems, and prose poems.

In 1984 Oliver won the Pulitzer Prize for Poetry, and she has received the Devil's Advocate Award from the Poetry Society of America (1968); a National Endowment for the Arts Creative Writing Fellowship (1972–73); the Alice Fay di Castagnola Award (1973); the Ohioana Book Award (1973); the Journalism Award from *Commonweal* (1978); the Cleveland Arts Prize for Literature (1979); the Shelley Memorial

Award (1980); and a Guggenheim Fellowship (1980). In 1992, as she accepted the National Book Award for *New and Selected Poems*, Oliver identified herself as a lesbian in a public acknowledgment of the woman to whom she dedicates her books, Molly Malone Cook.

As she approaches retirement, having polished her formidable powers as a worker in words, Oliver seems as comfortable in writing her own life as she has any other genre in which she has worked. With her new volume of poetry, *The Leaf and the Cloud* (2000), Oliver's career clearly is nowhere near the golden years.

MAJOR WORKS AND THEMES

In the title essay of *Winter Hours*, Oliver states that she "could not be a poet without the natural world" (98), a contention clear from her first book. In *No Voyage* and her second book, *The River Styx, Ohio*, Oliver sets lyrical nature poems that utilize mastery of image and form against poems that roam across Ohio and New England landscapes to England and Scotland. However, nowhere else in her body of work does Oliver place her speakers indoors to this extent. At the same time, these speakers look repeatedly to the natural world. In "No Voyage" the wounded speaker lies "on a cot by an open window" remembering past voyages (1). In "Spring in the Classroom" from *The River Styx, Ohio*, a volume in which memory and myth re-create the past, the speaker tells the story of a woman who seems dead indoors but is proven living, "furry and blooming" once outside (5). Critics note that as Oliver relates the tensions between humans and the natural world, she posits contemporary humans as more caring and sensitive as they participate in their environment (Alford, Oates). Oliver explains that she writes an elemental poetry that figures itself as organically out of doors (*Winter Hours* 102).

American Primitive, Oliver's Pulitzer winning book, is defined as both spare and rich, its themes set forth with uncomplicated syntax and diction. Critics agree that in *American Primitive*, Oliver takes her readers past the superfluous concerns of postmodern culture to focus "on man's most elemental concerns, those involving his own physical nature in the here-and-now, in the cycle of time, and in relation to the 'other' in his universe" (Mellard 67). Alford posits that Oliver finds in accepting the hard truths of mortal existence the essential meaning of life (287), but that this acceptance comes through a heightened sensual perception (288). "August," the opening poem of the volume, makes clear that as Oliver's speaker fills her senses with ripe blackberries, she comes very close to the life of the bear with "this thick paw . . . this happy tongue" (3). Vicki Graham reads the mimetic power of "August" and the rest of the volume as a primitive magic that allows an exchange between things that have come together (371). In its entirety, *American Primitive* encourages a blurring of boundaries and sets forth a fusion of self and nature that leads to an enriched understanding of the human and natural worlds.

Like *American Primitive*, *Dream Work* and *Twelve Moons*, the volumes that precede and come after it, situate their themes in the relations between human and nonhuman nature. Lisa M. Steinman finds these volumes unconnected with any past but feels history "loitering under the surface of many of the poems" and deeply moving in their mixture of statement and image and avoidance of sentimentality (436). Similarly, Sandra Gilbert sees in *Dream Work* the earthiness of Marianne Moore and Elizabeth Bishop as Oliver celebrates "the intransigent otherness of birds, beasts, and flowers

. . . in order to learn the lessons of survival" (113). Part of Oliver's strategy of survival comes as she looks to "the god of dirt" to find poetic inspiration in "One or Two Things" (52). Alford suggests *Twelve Moons*, with its celebration of natural cycles and the companion dreams that motivate human existence, involves constructing a subjectivity that does not depend on separation from nonhuman nature (72). This theme is clear from the opening poem, "Sleeping in the Forest," in which the speaker draws on all senses to be absorbed by so many "small kingdoms," that in the morning she has "vanished at least a dozen times into something better" (3).

Oliver's work in the 1990s articulates her continuous themes with the same organic subtlety. *House of Light* and *West Wind* explore the rewards of solitude in nature, but the self-reflexivity of *Dream Work* becomes a recurrent theme. Oliver's turning to works of prose and prosody enhances this addition. She articulates in essays both the pedagogical and the personal, and her use of female-centered language becomes more frequent in her poetry. For example, "The Waterfall," dedicated to May Swenson, takes the female element through the many changes of a woman's life, beginning with "its lace legs and womanly arms" (*New and Selected Poems* 19). Her final book of the decade, *Winter Hours*, explores the themes of her life, with essays on the poets she admires, essays on how she spends her days, and poetry about what and whom she loves. These works brim with the promise of further examinations of a woman's experience.

Oliver has set forth both her poetics and pedagogy in handbooks and essays that teach both reader and writer how to scan metrical verse, how to read it fully through an understanding of diction, rhythm, and metrics. Oliver's prosodic tactics place scansion as necessary even in nonmetric verse, and she argues throughout the Introduction to *Rules for the Dance* and in "Some Thoughts on the Line" that the foundation of every poem is its formality of motion, whether or not it is wholly metrical poetry. In *Rules for the Dance*, Oliver's thorough discussion of rhythm, pattern, rhyme, diction, and meter is meant for writers of poetry, as much as for its readers. In "The Place of Poetry," Oliver explains that her poetry is for the nonliterary as well as the literary audience, ruminates on the present separation in America between literature and life, and admonishes poets to "have the feel and smell of the world on them to battle back across the separation if the audience is to be restored" (733). In "Some Thoughts on the Line," Oliver discusses the use of vernacular language as connected to the ambiguous but restless desire of poets to speak on behalf of the "people entire" (45). She writes that as the poem comes into its careful existence, "the poet these days may thrill us still with finery, but just as likely with the simple cloth of plain speech which, in the conflagration of the poem, has also caught fire" (46). In prose and verse, through poems of interiority and nature, Oliver purposefully tailors this simple cloth to catch imagination's fire.

CRITICAL RECEPTION

Like many of Oliver's critics, Anthony Manousos describes her as a nature poet whose investigations of the natural world elicit themes most attached to human experience (114). Alford also writes of union and connectedness in Oliver's work and its "theme of revitalization" (283). In his reading of "Going to Walden," John Chamberlain notes that Oliver uses the language of reason to point out what it means to go into the natural world and take from it what understanding one can (225). Recent readings of Oliver as a nature poet have moved past criticism oriented toward the romantic nature lyric to place Oliver's work in a more sociopolitical perspective. In a postcolonial reading of the Native American presence in Oliver's poetry, Robin Riley Fast points out that Oliver offers Euro-American readers a way of responding to Native Americans and our common past "that both acknowledges that history and consequences of colonization and uses that knowledge to start moving beyond the limits of cultural bias" ("The Native American Presence" 59). Fast concludes that Native Americans "suggest to Oliver an alternative model of relationship to nature" (66). Focusing on Oliver's reworking of that "stereotypically female genre, the nature poem," Russell finds the sexual and sensual in such poems as "Rain" and "White Flowers" as "embody[ing] certain aspects of lesbian sexuality while at the same time refusing the label" (22).

Other recent scholarship on Oliver addresses feminist concerns. Fast discusses the feminine voice in Oliver's poetry as connected to Moore and Bishop, finding "clear indications . . . that Oliver conceives of her own poetic voice as a woman's voice" ("Moore, Bishop and Oliver" 364). Janet McNew questions the inability of contemporary criticism in the romantic tradition to appreciate Oliver's nature poetry, and she argues that the poetic strategies of women such as Oliver "are less bound by patriarchal strictures than is the literary criticism which evaluates them" (60). McNew contends that Oliver is not a programmatic feminist, but insists that "her dreams of reunion with female creatures and maternal nature receive validation in feminist terms" (65). Diane S. Bonds suggests that the lack of feminist appreciation of Oliver's poetry "derive[s] from skepticism that identification with nature can empower women to speak or to write" (1). Bonds reads Oliver's use of the language of nature and her assertion of the material validity of nature as valid feminist strategies, particularly in Oliver's presupposition of a connectivity with nature, rather than the quest for a lost unity (3, 10). Like Bonds and McNew, Vicki Graham argues that Oliver's nature poetry holds a valid feminine voice (353). Oliver's recent claims in *Winter Hours* about the importance of both nature and women's experience to her work will quite likely suggest to her audience new and enriched ways of reading her work.

BIBLIOGRAPHY

Works by Mary Oliver

No Voyage and Other Poems. Boston: Houghton, 1963.
The River Styx, Ohio and Other Poems. New York: Harcourt, 1972.
The Night Traveler. Cleveland, OH: Bits Press, 1978. (chapbook).
Sleeping in the Forest. Athens: *Ohio Review Chapbook*, 1978.
Twelve Moons. Boston: Little, Brown, 1979.
"The Place of Poetry: Symposium Responses." *Georgia Review* 35.4 (1981): 715–56.
American Primitive. Boston: Little, Brown, 1983.
Dream Work. Boston: Atlantic Monthly Press, 1986.
"Some Thoughts on the Line." *Ohio Review* 38 (1987): 41–46. (essay)
House of Light. Boston: Beacon Press, 1990.
New and Selected Poems. Boston: Beacon Press, 1992.
A Poetry Handbook. San Diego, CA: Harcourt, 1994.
White Pine: Poems and Prose Poems. San Diego, CA: Harcourt, 1994.
Blue Pastures. New York: Harcourt, 1995. (essays).

West Wind. Boston: Houghton, 1997.
Rules for the Dance: A Handbook for Writing and Reading Metrical Verse. Boston: Houghton, 1998.
Winter Hours: Prose, Prose Poems, and Poems. Boston: Houghton, 1999.
The Leaf and the Cloud: A Poem. New York: Da Capo Press, 2000.

Studies of Mary Oliver

Alford, Jean B. "The Poetry of Mary Oliver: Modern Renewal Through Mortal Acceptance." *Pembroke Magazine* 20 (1988): 283–88.
Bonds, Diane S. "The Language of Nature in the Poetry of Mary Oliver." *Women's Studies* 21.1 (1992): 1–15.
Burton-Christie, Douglas. "Nature, Spirit, and Imagination in the Poetry of Mary Oliver." *Cross Currents* 46.1 (1996): 77–87.
Chamberlain, John. "Hurry Up or Wait: Oliver's 'Going to Walden.' " *Thoreau Society Bulletin* (Fall 1998): 225.
Fast, Robin Riley. "Moore, Bishop, and Oliver: Thinking Back, Re-Seeing the Sea." *Twentieth Century Literature* 39.3 (1993): 364–79.
———. "The Native American Presence in Mary Oliver's Poetry." *The Kentucky Review* 12.1–2 (1993): 59–68.
Gilbert, Sandra. Review of *Dream Work*, by Mary Oliver. *Poetry* 148 (1987): 113–16.
Graham, Vicki. " 'Into the Body of Another': Mary Oliver and the Politics of Becoming Other." *Papers on Language and Literature* 30.4 (1994): 352–72.
Gregerson, Linda. Review of *American Primitive*, by Mary Oliver. *Poetry* 145 (1984): 38–39.
Manousos, Anthony. "Mary Oliver." *Dictionary of Literary Biography: American Poets since World War II*, edited by Donald J. Griener. Detroit, MI: Gale, 1980. 112–14.
McNew, Janet. "Mary Oliver and the Tradition of Romantic Nature Poetry." *Contemporary Literature* 30.1 (1989): 59–77.
Mellard, Joan. "Mary Oliver, Poetic Iconographer." *Language and Literature* 16 (1991): 65–73.
Oates, Joyce Carol. Review of *The Night Traveler*, by Mary Oliver. *New Republic*, 9 Dec. 1978, 28–29.
Russell, Sue. "Mary Oliver: The Poet and the Persona." *Harvard Gay and Lesbian Review* 4.4 (1997): 21–22.
Steinman, Lisa M. "Dialogues Between History and Dream." *Michigan Quarterly Review* 26.2 (1987): 428–38.

GRACE PALEY (1922–)

Austin Booth

BIOGRAPHY

Poet, short-story writer, antiwar activist, antinuclear activist, environmentalist, teacher, and feminist, Grace Paley is one of the most important American short-story writers of the twentieth century, as well as a key figure in postmodern feminist and Jewish writing. Her short stories and poems establish Paley as an innovative stylist, a writer with a unique voice who captures the everyday lives of the working-class men and women who populate her works. Paley was born December 11, 1922, in the Bronx; many of her short stories and poems are set in New York City, where Paley has lived most of her life. She attended Hunter College and New York University and has taught at Columbia University, Syracuse University, and Sarah Lawrence College.

Paley came from a family of Russian Jewish immigrants, Zionists, and leftist political activists. She grew up speaking Russian and Yiddish, as well as English. Paley's political activist upbringing had a great influence on her writing, as did her family and community. Surrounded by stories told by family members and neighbors, Paley began writing at age five. Her Russian Jewish heritage and the experiences of New Yorkers are pervasive themes in her work. As Paley has commented, "Whatever I say comes from what I hear. It comes from the speech of my city. But that has to go through my American-Jewish ear" (Hulley 19).

Paley entered Hunter College at age sixteen, later dropped out, and returned to school at the New School for Social Research in the 1940s, where she studied under poet W. H. Auden. Paley married at nineteen (she was divorced in 1971), and from 1942–44 lived with her husband in U.S. Army camps. During these years, Paley developed a "woman's consciousness," or a sense of the importance of the individual and collective voices of women: "I won't say feminist consciousness, because I didn't know enough, but a certain female or feminine or woman's consciousness. . . . Just feeling that I was a part of this bunch of women, that our lives were common and important" (Lidoff 6–7).

Until Paley was in her midthirties, she wrote poetry exclusively; in the 1950s she began to write stories, later gathered into the collection *The Little Disturbances of Man* (1959). A group of ten stories concentrated on an urban neighborhood, the stories in *The Little Disturbances of Man* focus on ordinary people, particularly women, the "little disturbances" in their lives and how they deal with them. As a mother of two children, Nora (born 1949) and Danny (born 1951), Paley was committed to writing about the quotidian concerns of women in their daily lives as mothers, wives, and workers, particularly the ways in which women negotiate a world in which they and their children experience discrimination.

Paley was actively involved in a number of political movements in the 1960s, including the women's liberation movement and the antiwar movement. She went to North Vietnam in 1969 and to Chile in 1972; in 1973 she was a delegate of the War Resisters League to the World Peace Congress in Moscow, and in 1981, Paley was one of the organizers of the Women's Pentagon Action.

Enormous Changes at the Last Minute, Paley's second collection of short stories, appeared in 1974, and like *The Little Disturbances of Man*, focuses on everyday people (including some of the characters from her earlier collection). In *Enormous Changes at the Last Minute* storytelling, and the ethics and politics of writing emerged as important themes in Paley's writing. *Enormous Changes at the Last Minute* led to critical recognition of Paley as a major force in twentieth-century American short-story writing.

Paley's poetry, like her fiction, is concerned with voice, politics, and family. Even more than her fiction, however, Paley's poetry collections *Leaning Forward* (1985), *Long Walks and Intimate Talks* (1991), and *New and Collected Poems* (1992), focus on exploring Jewish traditions and how Jewish Americans think about their personal and cultural histories. Paley won a Guggenheim Fellowship in fiction in 1961; a National Council on the Arts Grant and a National Institute of Arts and Letters Award for short-story writing in 1970; a Rea Award for the short story and a Vermont Governor's Award for Excellence in the Arts in 1993; and a Lannan Foundation Literary Award for fiction in 1997. *The Collected Stories* (1994) was both a National Book Award nominee and a Pulitzer Prize finalist.

MAJOR WORKS AND THEMES

Paley's work is known for its attention to storytelling; storytelling in Jewish communities and stories about the daily experiences of women are major themes in both her poetry and fiction. A related theme in Paley's work is the ethical responsibility of remembering and repeating others' stories, a responsibility that has its roots in both Judaism and feminism. Her poetry, like her fiction, challenges political, social, and narrative authority through romantic irony, or humor. Paley's work, personal and political, exemplifies second-wave feminism's tenet that "the personal is political." In Paley's works, politics, community, Judaism, and family are all inextricably linked.

Paley's Russian Jewish heritage is an important theme in her work. Much of her fiction and poetry is concerned with Jewish characters or speakers who negotiate both their cultural heritage and their present-day cultural identities. Her work examines Jewish traditions from the viewpoint of second-generation American Jews and asks how Jewish Americans write about their histories. Writing as an act of remembering is crucial to Paley's vision. The notion of remembering through storytelling comes from a Jewish oral tradition that has a strong influence on Paley's style. The narrator in her short story "Debts," for example, claims that writing continues the oral telling of stories of one's ancestors. Here storytelling is crucial to the integrity of family and community as well as the preservation of cultural history. Paley, following the Jewish belief in the saving power of narrative and memory, imagines storytelling as an act of bearing witness, which can "save a few lives" as her character Faith Darwin puts it (*The Collected Stories* 133). At the same time, Paley's poetry explicitly addresses second-generation American Jewish contradictory attitudes toward Judaism. Several poems in *Leaning Forward*, for example, explore anxieties over "forgetting Jerusalem," or not "keeping one's mind on Jerusalem" (24, 43), while other poems express the importance of knowing and telling one's family histories. In "Song Stanzas of Private Luck," Paley tells her own family history of her uncle Grisha's exile and her own birth (*New and Collected Poems* 81).

One of the stories Paley's short fiction and poetry tells is of the political, indeed ethical, importance of the act of storytelling. Listening to different people's voices can create a community of storytellers in which differences are heard, respected, and celebrated. In "Responsibility," Paley writes of the responsibility of the poet to go outside academia into "two-room apartments on Avenue C and buckwheat fields and army camps" to hear others tell their stories, and then to pass those stories on (*New and Collected Poems* 56). In Paley's work, a careful attention to the voices of others is a highly valued attribute.

Storytelling is as crucial to individual development as it is to communal understanding in Paley's works; it is the way in which both the speakers of her poems and the narrators of her stories express themselves and become themselves. The way in which Paley's characters, narrators, and speakers express themselves through language, particularly dialogue, is again, a tradition in Jewish fiction. Like many twentieth-century Yiddish Eastern-European authors, Paley uses ordinary, everyday, oral language to express history and establish community, both with other characters and with the reader. In Paley's work, however, this everyday language emerges as crucial to self-invention, a function that allows for "enormous changes" to occur. Paley's poetry begins with language—with the ordinary voice of everyday people, either alone or in dialogue. Much of her poetry echoes the orality of Jewish literature, including Yiddish cadence, oral history narrative forms (such as including the history of the telling of a tale along with the tale), biblical speech, a chant-like rhythm, or the exchange of gossip.

Paley populates her poetry with ordinary people, telling of the "little disturbances" in their lives and how they deal with those disruptions. Her work focuses on the everyday lives of women, their children, their resourcefulness in face of poverty, their sexual desires, and their relationships with men. One of Paley's central themes is the experience of American women fighting back against oppressive authorities, both in their personal and political relationships. A sense of place also permeates Paley's poetry as it does her fiction, from descriptions of the gingko trees on Jane Street in "An Arboreal Mystery" to mothers taking their children to school in "20th Street Spring" (*New and Collected Poems* 16, *Leaning Forward* 25).

Stories told by parents, aunts, uncles, cousins, and grandparents appear throughout Paley's poetry. Similarly, poems to her family appear. In "note to grandparents" and "For Danny," for example, Paley tells her family about what her children are doing (*Leaning Forward*). Indeed, like her fiction, Paley's poetry is semi-autobiographical.

Several of her poems detail her relationship with her father. An untitled poem in *Leaning Forward* tells of her identification with her father (41), and the poems "My Father at 85" and "My Father at 89" tell of what her father regrets he will miss seeing—the end of the Vietnam War—and what he remembers seeing: his dog Mars greeting him when he returned home from prison (*Leaning Forward* 69, 70). While Paley's fiction deals more with the sense of release that accompanied her father's death, her poetry—for example, "on Mother's Day" (*Leaning Forward* 34)—expresses her sorrow over his passing.

CRITICAL RECEPTION

Paley's work has been uniformly well received and has been the subject of many scholarly articles and books; she also has granted many interviews to literary and political periodicals. Reviews and scholarly treatments of Paley's work emphasize the realistic, humorous voice of her stories and poetry as well as her experiments with narrative technique. Although Paley's stories have attracted more critical attention than her poetry, both her short fiction and her poetry have been treated from similar critical and theoretical perspectives. Criticism of Paley's work can be divided among the following (overlapping) categories: critical and theoretical work on feminism and women's literature, ethnicity and ethnic literature, humor, narrative experimentation, and voice.

As previously mentioned, Paley's writing follows the feminist maxim that the personal is political. Many critical works and reviews have remarked on Paley's ability to capture the voices of ordinary women telling their stories. Her work has also been read as an examination of the formation and strength of communities among women. Paley's emphasis on women's voices, some critics argue, work not only to undermine sociopolitical systems that deny women's experiences as valid, but literary codes and conventions that do so as well. Like her stories, Paley's poems are political precisely because of her unrelenting attention to the concerns of daily life.

Paley's work has also been read as a celebration of ethnic difference. Her stories and poems rely on voice (especially conversational voices) to establish the Jewish, black, Irish, and other characters featured in her works. Paley's use of oral traditions places her firmly within a tradition of Jewish literature. Paley has been an especially important contributor to Jewish fiction because of her re-creation of a specifically second-generation American Jewish voice within her stories and poems.

Paley's use of metafictional techniques as well as the lack of closure and minimalist style of her writing has made her an exemplary figure among writers of postmodern short fiction. Although her poetry has not been read as innovative generically, it exhibits the same oral storytelling qualities, ironic humor, and frankness of her short-fiction writing. What links all of Paley's work, and, indeed, all of the criticism of Paley's works, is her attention to voice, to the everyday language that people speak about their worlds, a language that, in turn, shapes their worlds as well.

BIBLIOGRAPHY

Works by Grace Paley

The Little Disturbances of Man. New York: Doubleday, 1959. (short stories)
Enormous Changes at the Last Minute. New York: Farrar, 1974. (short stories)

Later the Same Day. New York: Farrar, 1985. (short stories)
Leaning Forward. Penobscot, ME: Granite Press, 1985. (poetry)
Long Walks and Intimate Talks. New York: Feminist Press at The City University of New York, 1991. (short stories and poetry)
New and Collected Poems. Gardiner, ME: Tilbury House, 1992.
The Collected Stories. New York: Farrar, 1994.
Just as I Thought. NewYork: Farrar, 1998. (nonfiction miscellany)
Begin Again: The Collected Poems of Grace Paley. New York: Farrar, 2000.

Studies of Grace Paley

Aarons, Victoria. "A Perfect Marginality: Public and Private Telling in the Stories of Grace Paley." *Studies in Short Fiction* 27 (1990): 35–43.
———. "Talking Lives: Storytelling and Renewal in Grace Paley's Short Fiction." *Studies in American Jewish Literature* 9 (1990): 20–35.
Arcana, Judith. *Grace Paley's Life Stories: A Literary Biography*. Urbana: University of Illinois Press, 1993.
Bach, Gerard, and Blaine H. Hall, eds. *Conversations with Grace Paley*. Jackson: University Press of Mississippi, 1997.
Clark, LaVerne Harrell. "A Matter of Voice: Grace Paley and the Oral Tradition." *Women and Language* 23 (2000): 18–32.
DeKoven, Marianne. "Mrs. Hegel-Shtein's Tears." *Partisan Review* 48 (1981): 217–23.
Delta, 14 May 1982. Special issue devoted to Paley.
Friebert, Stuart. "Kinswomen." *Field* 34 (1986): 93–102.
Gardner, Joann. "Grace Paley: An Interview." *American Poetry Review* 23 (1994): 19–24.
Halfmann, Ulrich, and Philipp Gerlach. "Grace Paley: A Bibliography." *Tulsa Studies in Women's Literature* 8 (1989): 339–54.
Hulley, Kathleen. "Interview with Grace Paley." *Delta*, 14 May 1982,19–40.
Iannone, Carol. "A Dissent on Grace Paley." *Commentary* 80 (1985): 54–58.
Lidoff, Joan. "Clearing Her Throat: An Interview with Grace Paley." *Shenandoah* 32 (1981): 3–26.
Mandel, Dena. "Keeping up with Faith: Grace Paley's Sturdy American Jewess." *Studies in American Jewish Literature* 3 (1983): 85–98.
Perry, Ruth. "Grace Paley. Interviewed by Ruth Perry." In *Women Writers Talking*, edited by Janet Todd. New York: Holmes & Meier, 1983. 35–56.
Rosen, Norma. *Accidents of Influence: Writing as a Woman and a Jew in America*. Albany: State University of New York Press, 1992.
Taylor, Jacqueline. *Grace Paley: Illuminating the Dark Lives*. Austin: University of Texas Press, 1990.

LINDA PASTAN (1932–)

Andrea Adolph

BIOGRAPHY

A native New Yorker, Linda Pastan was raised in the Bronx, an only child who began writing at the age of twelve or thirteen. "Books were my main companions," she recalls of her childhood, "and writing became my way of talking to the characters in those books and to the authors of those poems" (Adelman 29). Pastan went on to study the literature that kept her company during her youth, eventually earning degrees from Radcliffe (1954) and from Brandeis (MA 1957). In 1953 she married Ira Pastan and, as the roles of wife and mother of three children became important to her, she put writing and literature on hold for more than a decade. Once she returned to poetry, however, she apparently never looked back.

Her many books have earned her critical praise and several of the literary world's more notable prizes. *The Five Stages of Grief* (1978) was recognized by the Poetry Society of America with their Di Castagnola Award, and *Carnival Evening: New and Selected Poems 1968–1998* (1998) became a finalist for the National Book Award. Pastan has also received a fellowship from the National Endowment for the Arts, as well as the Dylan Thomas Award, a Pushcart Prize, and *Poetry* magazine's Beth Hokin Prize.

From 1991–95, Pastan served as the poet laureate of Maryland. During her term, she worked to bring poetry to people who might otherwise not come into contact with it, visiting hospitals and a prison, as well as schools, in order to demystify the genre. Paston asserts that "poetry is not a matter of knowledge but of emotional experience" (Adelman 29).

Pastan lives with her husband in Potomac, Maryland, and, though she has taught at The American University and at the Breadloaf Writer's Conference for more than twenty years, she is one of a rare breed of "professional poets" who does not typically divide herself between writing and teaching or other work. Pastan writes as part of her daily routine, a routine that finds its way into her poems on occasion. Her essay

"Writing about Writing" (1991) suggests that while it might be against some of the rules of poetry to write about the creative act itself, any writing is better than no writing. As her lengthy publication history attests, Pastan has been both prolific and successful in her endeavors.

MAJOR WORKS AND THEMES

Pastan's poetry is strewn with the remnants of life, with the objects and geographies of what some might call the "everyday" and of what others might simply term a "woman's world." Such a domestic environment encapsulates much of her work, especially the poems of her earlier collections. Pastan's mostly lyric pieces, often philosophical in nature, are anchored firmly to earth by the regular appearance of the quotidian: "books and bread and firewood" ("Letter" in *Carnival Evening*). The familiar aspects of home and of the kitchen are signposts through her poetry that otherwise contains much more difficult themes, such as illness, death, and mortality. Liz Rosenberg sees Pastan's attention to detail as "unmasking the seeming simplicity of complex things" (F1). Since much of the time Pastan writes from the distinctly female standpoints of daughter, mother, and wife, the domestic world is an expected backdrop and provides a necessary method for a poet who illuminates both the tedium and the exuberance hidden amidst the materiality of the everyday world. The juxtaposition of this world, however, against more serious matters allows for Pastan to avoid falling into any rigid definition of "female" or of "domestic." Her emphasis on the physical realm helps her to underscore a connection central to her poetry, a link between the sensual world and the more ephemeral life of the mind suggested in her poem "The War Between Desire and Dailiness," where "all order disappears" unless the minutiae of life are present (*Waiting for My Life* 41).

Pastan's work, even when it is marked by grief or by some other sadness, is filled with a distinctly female sensuality. Her poems' speakers address lovers and husbands shamelessly, openly, and the female body is presented as integral to sensual experiences, both sexual and otherwise. Because Pastan's first collection appeared when she was approaching forty years of age, the sexuality throughout her work is one of maturity and is expressed deliberately, without coyness or hesitance. Along with the domestic qualities of the home, this sensuality brings an important texture to Pastan's poems. The world of married domesticity, when enriched by the appearance of mature female desire, becomes more than a traditional setting for a woman's existence. Instead, the home resonates with the life force of conception and reproduction and with validation of a woman's role beyond the realm of nurturing and caretaking. At once domesticated and wild, uninhibited, the female presence in Pastan's poems mends the rift between the too typical versions of woman: saintly or sexualized. Pastan aptly unifies the feminine and the female.

When her gaze turns from the dailiness within the home, Pastan becomes a keen observer of the natural world that surrounds the domestic one. None of her poetry collections avoids contact with the natural environment, but her later works become more concerned with the natural world as the prominence of a domestic world fades. *A Fraction of Darkness* (1985) includes a number of poems concerned with not simply what is external, but with the connections of that outer world to an inner life. As with her use of the everyday in earlier works, Pastan here uses the idea of nature to convey a psychic interior and to explore the ways in which the intellectual and the natural are not always mutually exclusive realms. In "Domestic Animals," cat and dog with "dream claws and teeth" are as aligned with the external world as with the safer, sleep-induced one, and images such as these work to remind readers how blurred the divisions of inner and outer worlds can become (*Heroes in Disguise* 46). In these works, too, the female body, though still a vehicle for sensuality, also becomes more fragile, thus reinforcing the human form as a part of the natural world. As the poems explore loss through death (often of parental figures), they further remind both narrator and reader of the fragility and ultimate mortality of the body; Pastan's poems reflect a respect not only for the natural world, but also for its inevitable cycles and rhythms.

The domestic and natural worlds are also mirrored in Pastan's representations of interpersonal relationships, which, even when presented as satisfying, are never beyond precarious. Some early poems, such as "Distances" (*A Perfect Circle of Sun*), invoke the potential of any relationship to end. In *The Five Stages of Grief*, as well, Pastan imagines the multiple distances between the living; when placed in the framework of grieving, each small loss becomes a personal death. If domestic and natural environments provide the scenery for Pastan's work then personal relationships are what give her poems substance and resonance. These poems present what transpires, good and bad, between individuals as important, as necessary, but they do so without falling into overtly personal or sentimental territory. Her poetry avoids a confessional mode but instead reaches out to readers on the level of experience. Grief and loss, even imagined loss, and the pain that an unresolved argument can cause, are extended as common human experiences. Pastan's later work continues this theme of concern for relationships, for the grieving of losses, but does so more subtly. The cycle of life and death, integrated as it is into the natural imagery of these later texts, appears as less threatening and more as something to be accepted.

Relationships within the family structure are the most prominent interpersonal connections in Pastan's poetry. Figures of parents, husband, and children appear in every collection. These relationships, as they are both celebrated and mourned, become part of the "mythology" of her canon. With each collection of poems, familial relationships grow and shift; they become individual themes to trace in tandem with the more pronounced themes of home or nature. The idea of this "realistic" myth is strengthened by the actual mythological references Pastan weaves into most of her collections. An entire section of *The Imperfect Paradise* (1988) makes use of *The Odyssey*, and "This Enchanted Forest" (*Carnival Evening*) retells the tales of Rumpelstiltskin and of Gretel, among others. The dominant mythological presence, though, is religious rather than secular. The figure of Eve cycles through several collections, appearing more as archetypal woman and mother than as biblical icon. As an image of woman that encompasses many aspects of female experience, this Eve bridges the gap between shared mythologies and the more immediate and personal drama of the family as it unfolds. Sandra Gilbert suggests that Pastan "mythologizes those powers of the household whose magic she consistently tries to spell out" (153). Pastan's work illuminates the ways in which the daily worlds of home and of family become the stories that we tell, the contemporary myths that bind us together.

CRITICAL RECEPTION

Reviewers have most often written favorably about Pastan's poetry—especially her later work—but have occasionally questioned her poetic style. Her spare lines and "audacity in juxtaposing pure image with pure statement" (Pitchford 105) have impressed Gilbert, whose appreciation of Pastan's avoidance of literary extravagance overrides her distrust of moments of "cleverness" in the work (155). Gilbert addresses Pastan's interest in the everyday world and suggests that such an interest might stem from the fact that Pastan "is quite self-consciously a *woman* poet" (150). Peter Stitt reduces Pastan's focus on the domestic and on interpersonal relationships to "readily accessible" and "seldom inviting . . . intellectual illumination," but he also praises her technique (208). Though reactions to her poetry are not unified, critics do recognize Pastan as an important contemporary voice.

Although regularly and respectfully reviewed, Pastan's work has not yet been the subject of much literary criticism. Both Harriet Parmet and Sanford Pinsker write about Pastan as a distinctly Jewish poet. Pinsker connects Pastan's Jewishness with the family and domestic issues so central to her poems: "She is acutely conscious that families are generational and, moreover, that the ghosts of the heart abide" (200). While Gilbert presents the "feminine" focus of Pastan's poetry, Pinsker understands the family as important to Jewish culture and tradition. He also points out everyday objects in Pastan's work that represent her ethnic heritage. Whether examining her work through religious or domestic lenses, readers and critics are drawn to the stuff of everyday life so central to Pastan's poetry.

BIBLIOGRAPHY

Works by Linda Pastan

A Perfect Circle of Sun. Chicago: Swallow Press, 1971.
Aspects of Eve. New York: Liveright, 1975.
On the Way to the Zoo. Washington, D.C.: Dryad Press, 1975.
The Five Stages of Grief. New York: Norton, 1978.
Setting the Table. Washington, D.C.: Dryad Press, 1980.
Waiting for My Life. New York: Norton, 1981.
PM/AM: New and Selected Poems. New York: Norton, 1982.
A Fraction of Darkness. New York: Norton, 1985.
The Imperfect Paradise. New York: Norton, 1988.
Heroes in Disguise. New York: Norton, 1991.
"Writing about Writing." In *Writers on Writing*, edited by Robert Pack and Jay Parini. Hanover, NH: University Press of New England, 1991. 207–20.
An Early Afterlife. New York: Norton, 1995.
Carnival Evening: New and Selected Poems 1968–1998. New York: Norton, 1998.

Studies of Linda Pastan

Adelman, Kenneth L. "Word Perfect." *Washingtonian*, 31 May 1996, 29–30+.
Franklin, Benjamin V. "Theme and Structure in Linda Pastan's Poetry." *Poet Lore* 75 (1983): 234–41.
Gilbert, Sandra M. "The Melody of the Quotidian." Review of *Waiting for My Life*, by Linda Pastan. *Parnassus* 11.1 (1983): 147–67.
Parmet, Harriet L. "Jewish Voices and Themes: Rose Drachler, Julia Vinograd and Linda Pastan." *Studies in American Jewish Literature* 13 (1994): 52–58.
Pinsker, Sanford. "Family Values and the Jewishness of Linda Pastan's Poetic Vision." In

Women Poets of the Americas: Toward a Pan-American Gathering, edited by Jacqueline Vaught Brogan and Cordelia Chávez Candelaria. Notre Dame, IN : University of Notre Dame Press, 1999. 199–209.

Pitchford, Kenneth. "Metaphor as Illness: A Meditation on Recent Poetry." Review of *The Five Stages of Grief*, by Linda Pastan. *New England Review* 1 (1978): 96–119.

Rosenberg, Liz. "A Poet of Wholeness." Review of *Carnival Evening: New and Selected Poems 1968–1998*, by Linda Pastan. *The Boston Globe*, 30 Aug. 1998, F1+.

Stitt, Peter. "Stages of Reality: The Mind/Body Problem in Contemporary Poetry." Review of *PM/AM: New and Selected Poems*, by Linda Pastan. *Georgia Review* 37.1 (1983): 201–10.

MARGE PIERCY (1936–)

Maureen Langdon Shaiman

BIOGRAPHY

Marge Piercy was born March 31, 1936, to Robert, a Welsh and a nonpracticing Presbyterian, and Bert Bernice Bunnin Piercy, Jewish of Russian/Lithuanian descent, in Detroit, Michigan. The maternal side of Piercy's staunchly union, working-class family was very political; her paternal grandfather, a union organizer, was killed while organizing bakery workers. Piercy was particularly close to her maternal grandmother, who raised her as Jewish and told marvelous family stories. Piercy credits her mother, who taught her to observe sharply and remember what she observed, with making her a poet.

Prolonged illness taught Piercy to take refuge in books, and at age fifteen, she wrote her first poem and decided to become a writer. Piercy won a scholarship to the University of Michigan, and she received the university's Hopwood Award for poetry. However, she struggled with classism and the elitist, alienated, opaque literary ideal in vogue at the time. Coming of age in the stultifying 1950s, when the only choices for women were "conformity or exile," Piercy felt she had to "marry or die" (*Parti-Colored Blocks for a Quilt* 114, 116). She married a French Jewish physicist, got her MA in one year from Northwestern University, and then left school to support her husband. Piercy left her husband at age twenty-two, holding a series of part-time jobs in Chicago while trying to write. She wrote six novels she considered too political and too feminist for publication although she did publish poems occasionally.

In 1962 she remarried and relocated with her husband to New York, becoming deeply involved in the civil rights and antiwar movements. Piercy started an adult chapter of Students for a Democratic Society and found in the Left what she had been searching for all her life, a movement against class structures and the methods used by men in power to maintain dominance over women, minorities, and the poor. The movement, however, offered no support for her writing, considering it self-indulgent. Disillusionment with the movement set in when Piercy realized that the men in the movement dominated women, treating them like domestic and sexual servants. She then became heavily involved with the women's movement, finding political and emotional support for her writing. Her first book of poetry, *Breaking Camp*, was published in 1968 and her first novel, *Going Down Fast*, in 1969.

In 1970 Piercy and her husband moved to Wellfleet, Cape Cod, and she quickly felt a connection to the land and by extension to all living things. After divorce in the late 1970s, Piercy married her third husband, Ira Wood, in 1982. Piercy has taught at many universities but prefers to give readings and workshops and so travels a good deal. Piercy has been involved with the Writer's Guild, National Organization of Women, arts councils, women's centers, public policy boards, Israel Center for the Arts and Literature, and the National Endowment for the Arts.

MAJOR WORKS AND THEMES

Marge Piercy's primary goal as a poet is "to be of use" (the title of her fourth book of poetry). Her work, characterized by the use of her own voice, intimate subject matter, honesty of expression, and directness of style, often seems at first reading to be confessionally written for emotional catharsis. However, she makes abundantly clear in interviews and essays that her poems are art, not therapy; they are for others.

Beginning with her second collection *Hard Loving* (1969), Piercy's style has been simple and direct, usually with complete sentences rich with metaphor and passion, and written deliberately against her esoteric training. While not discounting the fact that Piercy's poems are often very complex in imagery, emotions, and range, critic Judson Jerome praises Piercy's poems for being "readable . . . moving, engaging, amusing, entertaining, insightful" (56). Although sometimes criticized for her unruliness and lack of restraint, Piercy controls her anger and exuberance, her tone, and lines, and most poems are short.

Piercy's feminist and socialist political commitment is strong in all her work; she is concerned with all ways in which the rich and powerful oppress, dominate, damage, and kill others. The majority of poems in her first two volumes, *Breaking Camp* and *Hard Loving*, comprise political concerns, particularly protests against the Vietnam war and the corporate fat cat, described as a "federal reserve of food" with "ramparts of flesh" (*Breaking Camp* 29). The section in a later collection, *To Be of Use* (1973), entitled "A Just Anger" is the first to deal at length with women's issues, a concern seen in much of Piercy's work over the years. She compares women to bonsai trees, which must be pruned, crippled, dwarfed from the beginning to contain their growth ("A work of artifice" 3), and she writes with sarcasm about "inconvenient" women easily traded for beasts of burden ("The nuisance" 12). She exhorts women to unlearn silence.

In the much anthologized "Barbie doll," a healthy, strong girl is told she is ugly and unacceptable, nothing but "a fat nose on thick legs," so she cuts off her nose and legs. In the casket with a small putty nose, she is called pretty at last, which is, says Piercy with vicious irony, "a happy ending" (*To Be of Use* 26). Twenty-five years later, Piercy still writes about this enslavement to appearance. With mocking irony, she claims superiority over the women of the past with their corsets, huge wigs and metal cages, proclaiming that we only starve and exercise ourselves to death (title poem, *What Are Big Girls Made Of?* 25). Many poems celebrate individual women's contributions and celebrations of women's laughter and work: abortion clinic workers, girlhood friends now dead from poverty, current friends, an elegy for Audre Lorde, and an offering "For strong women" (*The Moon Is Always Female*).

A common theme in Piercy's work is the relationships between men and women, illustrating the feminist battle slogan of the 1970s, "the personal is political." At first, she characterizes love only as manipulation and betrayal; later the view is more mature—open, joyful, deliberate, as well as painful. She charts the difficulty of "learning to love differently," to let go rather than to possess, and the agony of the "homely war," the end of a very long intimate relationship. Her violent imagery does justice to this kind of pain.

Jubilant love poems become more and more frequent in *Stone, Paper, Knife* (1983) and *My Mother's Body* (1985), after the beginning of her third and current marriage. The latter contains a beautiful series of wedding poems called "The Chuppah," the canopy used in Jewish wedding ceremonies. The chuppah symbolizes a roof open to the seasons, a home but not a prison or a box. These poems chart the daily ups and downs of love, the common traps in otherwise good love. "Why marry at all?" signals a shift in political methods as well: Rather than the revolutionary attitude of much of her earlier poetry, here Piercy acknowledges that we "cannot invent a language of new grunts" but must begin where we are and shape our own meanings and destinations (43).

Although many think of Piercy only as an angry feminist writing about toxic waste and betrayed love, she is also one of the funniest poets around. "The back pockets of love," a goofy ode to her lover's toes, acknowledges that love is concerned not only with the lover's grand and profound attributes but also with the small, daily things we do and are, including the body in its entirety (*Stone, Paper, Knife* 90–91). She must leave bushels of zucchini on the neighbor's doorstop, ring the bell and run ("Attack of the squash people," *The Moon Is Aways Female*). Her lover's broken leg in a cast becomes a "moby prick" ("The damn cast" *The Moon Is Always Female*). She imagines that "The world in year 2000" will be buried to seven inches with those styrofoam peanuts that come with every mail-order (*Stone, Paper, Knife*). Attention to the detail of everyday life yields the rich humor in quotidian frustrations.

The examination and celebration of the natural world emerge as another primary theme in Piercy's poetry. *Living in the Open* (1976) marks a shift in Piercy's work from urban to rural settings and concerns. In *The Twelve-Spoked Wheel Flashing* (1978), Piercy structures the book for the first time not by theme but by season. Piercy, an avid gardener, feels strongly her own connection to the earth. Sometimes nature will symbolize a fact about humans or provide a useful metaphor. Often she takes this connection to nature to a much more profound level as in "September afternoon at four o'clock." By comparing both moments in time and people to pears, Piercy illustrates a philosophy of living that appreciates what is ripe in the present while knowing that both decay and rebirth await in the future. Often, a poem that begins by focusing on the natural world will end by illuminating the connections between nature and humans. More importantly, Piercy's poetry demonstrates that everything we do affects the earth and the state of the earth affects us: Oil companies bribe senators to look the other way from their leaks and waste, which then kill the local crabs that she eats.

The Moon Is Always Female (1980) contains Piercy's longest and most ambitious poem cycle, "The Lunar Cycle," with one poem for each of the thirteen lunar months. These poems explore the meanings and experiences of being a woman in a woman's body and illuminate the many ways of knowing with the body as well as with the brain. This epistemology of the body "enacts Piercy's vision of contemporary women's poetry": a confrontation of convention and the healing of the psyche by the integration of the body, mind and emotions (Piper 1). She bears witness to the limitations and mutilation women's bodies have long endured and still suffer, while reclaiming the experience of the lived body for the self. "Right to life," for example, indicts politicians who lay the same claim to women's bodies as they do to the land they want to mine or animals they wish to breed.

My Mother's Body (1985), *Available Light* (1988), *Mars and Her Children* (1992) and *What Are Big Girls Made Of?* (1997) contain Piercy's usual concerns, but in these volumes, she also begins to explore death: her own aging and death and the deaths of her mother, father, half-brother, and family members interred in Nazi death camps. These works mark the beginning of a serious exploration in her poetry of her Jewish identity and history, and her attempt to reconcile it with her embrace of the earth goddess. Piercy's most recent collection, *The Art of Blessing the Day* (1999), is a collection of poems on a Jewish theme; many of them previously collected in her other books.

Piercy consistently demonstrates her belief that the world can change for the better, that despite all of the damage that the powerful can do to people and to the earth, hope exists that we will come together, by ones and twos, to bring ourselves and "other loving travelers" "to a new land" (*The Moon Is Always Female* 31). "Nishmat," (*Available Light* 122–23), a prayer for Jewish liturgy, lists all of the gifts we are given every day so that we may do what needs to be done joyously, a fitting culmination of the Piercy's work to date.

CRITICAL RECEPTION

Piercy is better known as a novelist than a poet, in particular for *Woman on the Edge of Time* (1976), a feminist science-fiction classic, and about which more has been written than on all the rest of her work combined. Nevertheless, Piercy's poems have been included in over 150 anthologies, and she has won several awards, including the National Endowment for the Arts Award in 1978, and the Golden Rose for poetry in 1990. For most of her career, Piercy has been classified in the subcategory "activist poet," and as Nan Nowik points out, "While [Piercy, Walker and Rich] sell well and are sought after for campus visits and get taught in women's and ethnic studies courses, they are not frequently taught in the standard contemporary literature classes, nor do they usually appear on English Department reading lists" (217).

As a challenger of the patriarchal politics in poetic convention, it is not surprising that most feminist poets and critics laud Piercy and that the male literary establishment has excoriated her work as polemical, offensive, and inferior. Most critics, especially for the first fifteen or so years of her career, tended to divide along political lines: those for and against the political in art. The first two critical studies of Piercy, appearing together in 1977 in *Modern Poetry Studies*, reflect this division. Jean Rosenbaum explores Piercy's "vision of integrity," her desire for "a world of wholeness and completeness" and does not censure her challenge to traditionally gendered poetics (194). Victor Contoski pronounces her poetry a failure because its meaning overshadows its form, finding it "emotional, righteous, and often clever, lacking, by and large, the subtle insights and revelations of wisdom" (216).

Many during these years offered qualified praise, believing her work to be didactic and polemic but also emotionally affecting. When discussing principally Piercy's style, Margaret Atwood applauded her "surge and flux," her "courage, gut energy and verbal fecundity" ("Unfashionable" 602). Keith Harrison, however, enjoyed her "cryptic and fanciful" poems but believed she often "overwrites"; that "the proliferation of her often very powerful images sometimes works against her" (239).

There have been few serious critical studies of her poetry. In 1985 Edith Wynne published a study of Piercy's imagistic technique and its sometimes metaphysical results. The collection of critical essays on Piercy, entitled *Ways of Knowing*, edited by Sue Walker and Eugenie Hamner, contains an overview of her work, an interview, six essays on her novels and four on her poetry, which are the kind of thorough explications not found in reviews.

As Piercy's poetry has matured, focusing more on self-discovery and family exploration and becoming more complex and more successful at integrating the personal and political, the criticism has tended to run more favorably. Atwood now calls her "wide open and fully controlled, flexible, tender, clear-sighted and compassionate" ("Strong" 22). Walker affirms that "Piercy's marriage and the death of her mother have marked a period of growth and development in her work" and that "by 1983 the discipline of art has relegated any polemic to secondary significance" (142, 141). However, in 1985, Sandra Gilbert maintained that Piercy "prefer[s] politics to poetics" and "lapses into clumsiness, . . . and sloganeering" (159). Some still consider her poetry uneven, raw, and unedited. Most critics, despite their political and aesthetic leanings, appreciate her passion, courage, and affecting honesty.

BIBLIOGRAPHY

Works By Marge Piercy

Breaking Camp. Middletown, CT: Wesleyan University Press, 1968.
Going Down Fast. Roseville, MN: Trident, 1969. (novel)
Hard Loving. Middletown, CT: Wesleyan University Press, 1969.
Dance the Eagle to Sleep. New York: Doubleday, 1970. (novel)
The Grand Coolie Damn. Somerville, MA: New England Free Press, 1970. (essays)
Small Changes. New York: Doubleday, 1973. (novel)
To Be of Use. New York: Doubleday, 1973.
Living in the Open. New York: Knopf, 1976.
Woman on the Edge of Time. New York: Knopf, 1976. (novel)
The High Cost of Living. New York: Harper, 1978. (novel)
The Twelve-Spoked Wheel Flashing. New York: Knopf, 1978.
The Moon Is Always Female. New York: Knopf, 1980.
Vida. New York: Summit, 1980. (novel)
Braided Lives. New York: Summit, 1982. (essays)
Circles on the Water: Selected Poems of Marge Piercy. New York: Knopf, 1982.
Parti-Colored Blocks for a Quilt: Poets on Poetry. Ann Arbor: University of Michigan Press, 1982. (essays)
Stone, Paper, Knife. New York: Knopf, 1983.
Fly Away Home. New York: Summit, 1984. (novel)
My Mother's Body. New York: Knopf, 1985.
Gone to Soldiers. New York: Summit, 1987. (novel)
Available Light. New York: Knopf, 1988.

Early Ripening: American Women Poets Now, ed. Winchester, MA: Pandora, 1988. (anthology)
The Earth Shines Secretly: A Book of Days. Cambridge, MA: Zoland Books, 1990. (daybook calendar)
He, She and It. New York: Knopf, 1991. Published as *Body of Glass*, London: Michael Joseph, 1992. (novel)
Mars and Her Children. New York: Knopf, 1992.
The Longings of Women. New York: Fawcett Columbine, 1994. (novel)
The Eight Chambers of the Heart: Selected Poems. London: Penguin, 1995.
City of Darkness, City of Light: A Novel. New York: Fawcett, 1996.
What Are Big Girls Made Of? New York: Knopf, 1997.
Storm Tide. With Ira Wood. New York: Fawcett, 1998. (novel)
The Art of Blessing the Day: Poems with a Jewish Theme. New York: Knopf, 1999.
Early Grrrl: The Early Poems of Marge Piercy. Wellfleet, MA: Leapfrog, 1999. Published as *Written in Bone: The Early Poems of Marge Piercy*, Nottingham, England: Five Leaves Publications, 1998.
Three Women. New York: Morrow, 1999. (novel)
So You Want to Write. Wellfleet, MA: Leapfrog, 2001. (non-fiction)
Sleeping with Cats. New York: Morrow, 2002. (memoir)

Studies of Marge Piercy

Atwood, Margaret. "Strong Woman." *New York Times Book Review*, 8 Aug. 1982, 10+.
———. "An Unfashionable Sensibility." *The Nation* 223.19 (1976): 601–02.
Contoski, Victor. "Marge Piercy: A Vision of the Peaceable Kingdom." *Modern Poetry Studies* 8 (1977): 205–16.
Gilbert, Sandra. Review of *My Mother's Body*, by Marge Piercy. *Poetry* 147.3 (1985): 159–61.
Guttman, Naomi. " 'Rooms Without Walls': Marge Piercy's Ecofeminist Garden Poetry." *Proteus* 15.2 (1998): 10–18.
Harris, Marie. "Let Me See that Book." *Parnassus* 3.1 (1973): 149–58.
Harrison, Keith. "A Round of Poets." *The Carleton Miscellany* 17.2–3 (1979): 234–43.
Jerome, Judson. "Grabbing the Gusto: Marge Piercy's Poetry." *Writer's Digest* 61 (1981): 56+.
Jordan, June. "The Black Poet Speaks of Poetry." *American Poetry Review* 3 (July-Aug. 1974): 62–63.
Mazzaro, Jerome. "At the Start of the Eighties." *Hudson Review* 33 (1980): 455–68.
Mitchell, Felicia. "Marge Piercy's *The Moon Is Always Female*: Feminist Text, Great Books Context." *Virginia English Bulletin* 40.2 (1990): 34–45.
Nowik, Nan. "Mixing Art and Politics: The Writings of Adrienne Rich, Marge Piercy, and Alice Walker." *Centennial Review* 30 (1986): 208–18.
Piercy, Marge. "Interview with Michelle Gerise Godwin." *The Progressive* 65.1 (2001): 27–30.
Piper, Deborah Marie. " 'All One Vision': The Poetry of Marge Piercy." Thesis. University of Maryland, 1990.
Rodden, John. "A Harsh Day's Light: An Interview with Marge Piercy." *Kenyon Review* (Spring 1988): 132–43.
Rosenbaum, Jean. "You Are Your Own Magician: A Vision of the Integrity in the Poetry of Marge Piercy." *Modern Poetry Studies* 8 (1977): 198–205.
Schreiber, Ron. Review of *The Moon Is Always Female*, by Marge Piercy. *American Book Review* 4.3 (1982): 10.
Walker, Sue, and Eugenie Hamner, eds. *Ways of Knowing: Essays on Marge Piercy*. Mobile, AL: Negative Capability Press, 1991.
Wynne, Edith J. "Imagery of Association in the Poetry of Marge Piercy." *Publications of the Missouri Philological Association* 10 (1985): 57–73.

SYLVIA PLATH (1932–1963)

Kimberly Orlijan

BIOGRAPHY

Perhaps best known for the poems she wrote in the last few months of her short life, Sylvia Plath was a prolific writer from a very early age, publishing her first poem at age eight. Plath was born in Boston, Massachusetts, on October 27, 1932, to parents who valued and encouraged educational pursuits in Sylvia and her younger brother Warren. Her father, Otto Plath, a German immigrant and professor of entomology and German at Boston University, was an often-times overbearing figure in the family who, according to her mother Aurelia Plath, was a workaholic whose workspace the family felt the need to map if they had to move his books. When Sylvia was eight years old, her father died of gangrene caused by untreated diabetes. His incessant presence in Sylvia's psyche and corpus proved colossal.

After Otto's death, Aurelia struggled, with the help of her parents, to maintain a middle-class lifestyle for her children, providing them with a multitude of lessons and instilling in them a love for learning. This love, coupled with her drive to succeed at everything she attempted, led Sylvia Plath to be a high achiever at Wellesley High School and Smith College, which she attended on a scholarship funded by the popular novelist Olive Higgins Prouty. At Smith she continued to publish short stories and poetry in newspapers and in magazines, garnering several prizes and doing exemplary work in her courses. Her hard work won her a spot as a guest editor at *Mademoiselle* during the summer of 1953, the summer of a breakdown during which Plath attempted suicide by ingesting a bottle of sleeping pills. These events form the bases for her "autobiographical novel," *The Bell Jar* (1963).

Sent to the private psychiatric hospital McLean's (thanks to the generous financial help of Prouty) and given six months of intensive treatment with the psychiatrist Ruth Beuscher, with whom Plath maintained a lifelong correspondence, Plath emerged "patched" and "retreaded" (*The Bell Jar*). She returned to Smith, wrote an honors thesis on Dostoyevski's use of the double figure, graduated summa cum laude, and won a Fulbright scholarship to study English at Newnham College in Cambridge University. While at Cambridge, Plath was again a successful student, but she also cultivated an active social and dating life. She believed that women had as much right to a sexual life as men, bemoaning the double standard that society held for men and women. Her ideal was to find a sexually magnetic and intellectually gifted man. When she met the poet Ted Hughes at a Cambridge party in 1956, she felt that she had found her consummate partner. The two married in London in June 1956.

In 1957 Hughes and Plath moved to the United States where Plath taught English Composition for a year at her alma mater Smith. She did not enjoy teaching and felt that she wanted to devote all of her time to writing. For the next couple of years, the pair lived in Boston and wrote. Plath took a course at Boston University from the poet Robert Lowell and came to know her classmate Anne Sexton, whose work became an inspiration to her (as well as a touchstone and source of competition). During this time, Plath held secretarial jobs, including one in the psychiatric unit of Massachusetts General Hospital transcribing patients' histories and dreams, in order to support herself and Hughes. She also was active in typing and submitting Hughes's poems for publication.

After an autumn at the famous writers' colony Yaddo, Hughes and Plath returned to London in 1959. In 1960 Plath's first collection of poems, *The Colossus and Other Poems*, was published, and the couple's first child, Frieda, was born. Soon thereafter, the family began to look for a cottage in the English countryside. They found what seemed the ideal manor house in Devon, and Plath continued to write poetry and *The Bell Jar*. After a miscarriage, Plath gave birth to their son Nicholas in January 1962. Plath's marriage had been shaky for some time, and five months after Nicholas was born, Plath discovered Hughes's affair with Assia Guttman. Hughes left her soon thereafter.

Plath and her children moved to a flat in London's Primrose Hill in order to escape the solitude of Devon and to start a new life. In October 1962, she wrote the poems that she knew would make her name. She composed these "October poems" early in the morning, before the children awoke, at a pace of about one a day. They include such famous pieces as "Daddy," "Lady Lazarus," and "Ariel." Despite her successful writing, Plath sunk deeper into a clinical depression and, in the worst London winter in one hundred years, had trouble making ends meet. Two weeks after *The Bell Jar* was published (under the pseudonym Victoria Lucas) and a few days before divorce proceedings were to begin—on February 11, 1963—Plath committed suicide by gassing herself in her oven.

MAJOR WORKS AND THEMES

Despite the publication of one well-received volume of poetry (*The Colossus and Other Poems*) and one novel (*The Bell Jar*) before her death, Sylvia Plath's reputation as one of the most powerful women poets of the twentieth century rests mainly on her posthumous publications. Indeed, the poems written in the last few months of her life—collected in *Ariel* (1965)—have, arguably, made her name and are certainly the most anthologized. These poems include her most well known, and arguably her most puissant, poem "Daddy."

Although often thought to deal solely with her actual father and the overwhelming influence he had in her life and life's work, "Daddy" also addresses Plath's continual struggles with "daddy poetry," the male (as well as female) poetic precursors that haunt much of Plath's writings. Certainly, this poem encapsulates many of the repeated themes and motifs in Plath's *oeuvre*. Many of Plath's texts deal with the poetics of subjectivity and focus on memory—often childhood memory and, more specifically, conflict with one or both parents. In "Daddy," the speaker characterizes the daddy figure—as well as a husband figure who becomes inseparable from the daddy figure—as a Nazi and herself as a Jew. However, the speaker does not play the helpless victim; instead, she wreaks revenge on the father/husband figure by plunging a "stake" in his "fat, black heart." As is typical of many of Plath's poems, the ending is highly ambiguous: "I'm through" could be a positive statement of renunciation of the father figure as a burdensome and threatening force or a statement of self-annihilation.

Although Marjorie Perloff and other critics have assailed Plath's texts for being too personal and not political, "Daddy" and other works demonstrate that Plath interweaves the personal and the political. Indeed, by positioning the speaker as a Jew and the daddy figure as a Nazi, Plath presents the self, representative of larger social and political forces, compelled to struggle with the events of history and the constraints of culture. Furthermore, Plath's poetry is often critical of past or present injustices, whether having to do with race, class, or gender.

Indeed, gender inequality emerges as one of Plath's most prominent themes. Plath often laments in her *Journals* (1982) that she was born a woman without the freedoms and rights that American and British cultures grant men. At times, though, she seems to embrace her role as woman and, especially, the role of mother. For Plath, motherhood is a burden and a barrier to her ability to devote her self to writing ("Metaphors" *Crossing the Water* and "Morning Song" *Ariel*), but it also serves as a trope that she uses to represent her creative potency ("By Candlelight" *Winter Trees* and her powerful radio play *Three Women*). Her changing and complex expressions concerning childbirth, as well as marriage and womanhood, represent the multiple personae in her texts.

Several Plath poems speak to the trope of doubling and the concomitant fear that such doubling causes throughout Plath's textual discourse. Steven Axelrod argues that "doubling was Plath's fundamental way of ordering all aspects of her world" (*Sylvia Plath* 195). Connected to images of doubling in Plath's texts are representations of mirror images, "true" and "false" selves, and death and rebirth. Indeed, one can argue that two of Plath's collections demonstrate a split in her textual personality—*Letters Home* (1975) and *Journals of Sylvia Plath* (1982). At times, the letters (written mainly to and edited by her mother) seem almost sickeningly sweet and therefore disingenuous, whereas the journals writhe with pain and seethe with anger.

A number of Plath's poems grapple with the true self versus false self-dichotomy vis-à-vis the process of death and rebirth. Her 1961 poem "Face Lift" deals with the transformation and apparent rebirth of the subject through a face lift operation, from which the speaker emerges as a baby. Such a rebirth, however, proves as ambiguous as the ending of "Daddy," for one must wonder how positive the renewal can be when the speaker ends up in the rather powerless position of an infant. Perhaps more potent an ending is that of another of Plath's most anthologized poems, "Lady Lazarus," which, as the title indicates, takes as its topic the death and rebirth of a female figure. Instead of emerging as a baby, red-haired Lady Lazarus declares at the end of the poem that she rises from the ashes and "eat[s] men like air" (*Collected Poems* 247).

CRITICAL RECEPTION

Just as there are various personae within Plath's texts, so too do multiple and often warring factions within Plath studies exist. Certainly, Plath's work, as well as her life, has garnered a great deal of critical attention. One of the major players in determining the trajectory of Plath studies has been the poet's husband, Ted Hughes. Although estranged at her death, Hughes gained control of Plath's literary estate. One might well thank him for publishing much of Plath's *oeuvre*, for *The Bell Jar* and *The Colossus and Other Poems* were Plath's only extant publications (outside of the many uncollected stories and poems) at the time of her death at age thirty.

However, while publishing many of Plath's texts after her death, Hughes also destroyed and "lost" others, including a journal that Plath wrote in until just days before her suicide, and an almost completed novel. Moreover, critics wishing to quote from Plath's texts have had to gain permission from the Hughes-appointed literary executor (formerly Olwyn Hughes, Ted's sister, who has been reluctant to grant permission to studies deemed disagreeable to Hughes). How much of this inaccessibility to Plath's writings has, and will change, since Hughes's death in 1998 remains to be seen fully.

Plath's published work has been edited with heavy and invested hands (*Letters Home*, edited by Plath's mother Aurelia). Moreover, Hughes, when publishing Plath's most celebrated collection, *Ariel*, left out poems such as "The Jailer" and "The Rabbit Catcher," poems that Plath, who at least tentatively arranged her proposed collection prior to her death, included. When publishing Plath's collection of stories and memoirs, *Johnny Panic and the Bible of Dreams* (1979), Hughes all but dismisses their value and strength by asserting in the introduction that Plath's reputation rests on the poems of the last six months of her life (9). This insistence, along with his statement in his influential essay "Notes on the Chronological Order of Sylvia Plath's Poems" that Plath's early poems were written "very slowly, Thesaurus open on her knee . . . as if she were working out a mathematical problem" (188) have been difficult assessments for Plath critics to shake. Such assertions led to many critics' employment of the thesaurus theory and claims that the early poems in *The Colossus* are overly academic, crafted, and, in Pamela Smith's words, "controlled—straight-jacketed, possibly" (124). Critics such as Marjorie Perloff and Mary Lynn Broe have also ascribed to this theory and have all but dismissed the early poems.

In the mid- to late-1990s, critics began to examine the earlier poems and to reject the thesaurus theory (Axelrod and Dorsey). This move marks a change in the evaluation of Plath's corpus. Another significant shift in Plath criticism has been Lynda Bundtzen's inauguration of a feminist movement in Plath studies with the 1983 publication of *Plath's Incarnations*. Before Bundtzen, critics had for the most part rejected *The Bell Jar*, as well as many poems, as merely autobiographical. Bundtzen argues that many of Plath's texts are actually allegories about femininity.

More recently, critics have focused on the linguistically self-reflexive moves in Plath's texts. For example, Axelrod has expanded and complicated the representational spectrum of *The Bell Jar* by arguing for an intertextual reading that considers the novel in light of Virginia Woolf's *Mrs. Dalloway*. He also considers poems such as "Three Women" and "Words" as central to the Plath *oeuvre* and discusses the ways that they examine textual production and words (*Sylvia Plath*). Jacqueline Rose's text *The Haunting of Sylvia Plath* has significantly altered Plath studies by discussing Plath in the light of postmodern methods of criticism. Rose denies the thesaurus theory and argues that we cannot read Plath's texts in a linear, progressive way. Rose also asserts that Plath is "neither one identity nor multiple identities simply dispersing themselves. She writes at the point of tension" (10). Even further, Rose deconstructs the role of the Plathean critic and analyzes the Plath archive and the editing of Plath's texts. In extending her analysis to include the archive and the editing process, Rose opens up Plath studies to readings that move beyond and challenge the confines of the material thus far available to scholars. Indeed, the October 2000 publication of an unabridged edition of Plath's *Journals* may prove to help further challenge Plath scholars and propel critical discussions of this poet's work.

BIBLIOGRAPHY

Works by Sylvia Plath

The Colossus and Other Poems. London: Heinemann, 1960.

The Bell Jar. London: Heinemann, 1963; New York: Harper, 1971. (novel)

Ariel. London: Faber & Faber, 1965.

Three Women: A monologue for three voices. Londen: Turret Books, 1968. (play)

Crossing the Water. London: Faber & Faber, 1971.

Winter Trees. London: Faber & Faber, 1971.

Letters Home: Correspondence, 1950–1963, edited by Aurelia Schober Plath. New York: Harper, 1975.

Johnny Panic and the Bible of Dreams: Short Stories, Prose, and Diary Excerpts. New York: Harper, 1979.

Collected Poems, edited by Ted Hughes. New York: Harper, 1981.

Journals of Sylvia Plath, edited by Frances McCullough and Ted Hughes. New York: Dial, 1982.

The Journals of Sylvia Plath, 1950–1962, edited by Karen V. Kukil. London: Faber and Faber, 2000.

Studies of Sylvia Plath

Aird, Eileen M. *Sylvia Plath: Her Life and Work.* New York: Harper, 1973.

Alexander, Paul, ed. *Ariel Ascending.* New York: Harper, 1985.

Annas, Pamela J. *A Disturbance in Mirrors: The Poetry of Sylvia Plath.* Westport, CT: Greenwood, 1988.

Axelrod, Steven Gould. "Plath's Literary Relations: An Essay and an Index to the *Journals* and *Letters Home.*" *Resources for American Literary Study* 14.2–3 (1984): 59–84.

———. *Sylvia Plath: The Wound and the Cure of the Words.* Baltimore, MD: The Johns Hopkins University Press, 1990.

———and Nan Dorsey. "The Drama of Creativity in Sylvia Plath's Early Poems." *Pacific Coast Philology* 32.1 (1997): 76–86.

Broe, Mary Lynn. *Protean Poetic: The Poetry of Sylvia Plath.* Columbia: University of Missouri Press, 1980.

Bundtzen, Lynda K. *Plath's Incarnations: Women and the Creative Process.* Ann Arbor: University of Michigan Press, 1983.

Butscher, Edward. *Sylvia Plath: Method and Madness.* New York: Seabury Press, 1976.

———. *Sylvia Plath: The Woman and the Work.* New York: Dodd, 1977.

Gilbert, Sandra M. "A Fine, White Flying Myth: The Life/Work of Sylvia Plath." In *Shake-*

speare's Sisters: Feminist Essays on Women Poets, edited by Sandra M. Gilbert and Susan Gubar. Bloomington: Indiana University Press, 1979. 245–60.

Holbrook, David. *Sylvia Plath: Poetry and Existence*. London: Athlone, 1976.

Hughes, Ted. "Notes on the Chronological Order of Sylvia Plath's Poems." In *The Art of Sylvia Plath*, edited by Charles Newman. London: Indiana University Press, 1970. 187–95.

Hunter Steiner, Nancy. *A Closer Look at Ariel: A Memory of Sylvia Plath*. New York: Harper's Magazine Press, 1973.

Kroll, Judith. *Chapters in a Mythology: The Poetry of Sylvia Plath*. New York: Harper, 1976.

Lane, Gary, ed. *Sylvia Plath: New Views on the Poetry*. Baltimore, MD: Johns Hopkins University Press, 1979.

Newman, Charles, ed. *The Art of Sylvia Plath*. London: Indiana University Press, 1970.

Perloff, Marjorie. "Extremist Poetry: Some Versions of the Sylvia Plath Myth." *Journal of Modern Literature* 2 (1972): 581–88.

———. "The Two *Ariels*: The (Re)Making of the Sylvia Plath Canon." *American Poetry Review* 13 (1984): 10–18.

Rose, Jacqueline. *The Haunting of Sylvia Plath*. Cambridge: Harvard University Press, 1992.

Smith, Pamela. "Architectonics: Sylvia Plath's *Colossus*." In *Sylvia Plath: Method and Madness*, edited by Edward Butscher. New York: Seabury Press, 1976. 111–24.

Stevenson, Anne. *Bitter Fame: A Life of Sylvia Plath*. Boston: Houghton, 1989.

Uroff, Margaret Dickie. *Sylvia Plath and Ted Hughes*. Urbana: University of Illinois Press, 1979.

Wagner, Linda W., ed. *Critical Essays on Sylvia Plath*. Boston: Hall, 1984.

———. *Sylvia Plath: A Biography*. New York: Simon, 1987.

MINNIE BRUCE PRATT (1946–)

Tenea D. Johnson

BIOGRAPHY

The acclaimed poet, activist, and essayist, Minnie Bruce Pratt, was born in Selma, Alabama, on September 12, 1946. She was raised in nearby Centreville "by older parents in a rural area where the Victorian segregation of the sexes was still maintained, and where a separate women's culture was still real" (*Rebellion* 19). She pursued her education in Tuscaloosa at the University of Alabama. Working at the school's literary magazine, she met a poet who soon became her husband. Her poetry stopped when her marriage began. Pratt pursued her graduate career at the University of North Carolina; her real education also began during this period, doing grassroots organization with the women of Fayetteville. This work initiated a lifelong dedication to activism that would help to sustain the poet in her oncoming tribulations. During this time she gave birth to two sons.

Pratt's life changed drastically when she began to claim her lesbian identity. She went through a miserable divorce in which she lost custody of her sons because she was a lesbian. Her relationship with her sons and with the social system that had taken them away from her became a prominent theme in her work. During and after the loss of her children, Pratt continued to fight for social justice with various activist groups and causes ranging from feminist and lesbian causes to racial equality. Shortly after starting her professorial career, Pratt founded Woman Writes: A Southeastern Lesbian Writers Conference. This collective in which the participants taught one another served as the nest from which her style of writing and self-discovery originated. Shortly after she became a founding member of *Feminary: A Feminist Journal for the South, Emphasizing Lesbian Visions* and later LIPS, a lesbian-feminist action group.

In concert with her activism, Pratt taught as a professor of woman's studies, creative writing, and feminist theory at various institutions including several historically black universities in the South and Northeast. Currently, she teaches at The Union Institute, an alternative PhD-granting institution, and lives in Jersey City, New Jersey, with lover and transgender activist Leslie Feinberg.

MAJOR WORKS AND THEMES

Minnie Bruce Pratt has built her career on analyzing the world through her own experience. In poetry, prose, and essays, she relates the stories and impressions of her transformation from a "good" Southern white mother to a political lesbian poet. She uses the knowledge gained from this complex experience to look at the world with new eyes trained on searching out and speaking out against oppression. Pratt has said that "coming out" did not make her return to poetry, but rather the same honesty that led her to come out demanded honesty and analysis in all aspects of her life. Thus Pratt infuses all her work with both an autobiographical impulse and social commentary. For Pratt, the personal is always political and vice versa. Also, the various negative reactions to her new social identity prompted Pratt to further her political efforts in the field of writing. The themes she presents in her work reflect this commitment: identity politics, lesbian life/love, the South, crossing social boundaries, and motherhood.

The identity politics surrounding sexual orientation, feminism, women's liberation, and race figure prominently in all of Pratt's writing. When Pratt claimed her lesbian identity in 1975, she became privy to a new perspective: that of the oppressed. She chronicles her introduction to lesbian life in *The Sound of One Fork* (1981) and *We Say We Love Each Other* (1985). These works clearly show that when one claims a homosexual identity, one's relationship with his or herself and the world significantly changes. In *The Sound of One Fork*, Pratt shows that reclaiming her sexual identity includes claiming her sexuality, the right and desire for sex and sexual play. This returned power causes the work's narrator to notice and speak out against all the obstacles to women's liberation, including, biased upbringing, sexist social norms, and strict gender boundaries that keep the feminine trussed up in other people's expectations. *We Say We Love Each Other*, in turn, celebrates lesbian identity. Yet, the love poetry collection also critiques the South of Pratt's childhood in its treatment of women. Instead of relying on the greater society's relationship, she finds her joy in the separate women's cultures inhabiting everyday life in the South. In fact, *The Sound of One Fork*, Pratt's first book, is a direct product of just such a culture. The Feminary Collective, inspired by the Women-in-Print movement, taught members all the aspects of book production from page layout to actual printing. Pratt, with help from other members, did all the production and sales for the volume.

Minnie Bruce Pratt's work is in constant play with social boundaries. By writing through her own experiences as a Southern white mother and lesbian, Pratt shares a poetic and personal means of social commentary that attempts not only to enlighten the reader, but also to move one toward a greater consciousness of the contradictions around every corner. Pratt's recently published *Walking Back Up Depot Street* (1999) exemplifies this trend not just in content but also in the narrative structure of the work. The protagonist, Beatrice, visits the corners of memory and experience to flesh out and re-assess the true character of the South—the one behind the convenient mythos created by the hegemony of her childhood—before she leaves for the postindustrial North. The protagonist's journey leads the reader through many of Pratt's major themes: the South, the complicated racial history and reality of the United States, living as a lesbian, and the ever-rich process of personal transformation that fuels both the author and her work. These multivocal narrative poems relay the rhythm and cadence of the segregated South from Bible-belt preachers to share croppers. Unlike the rest of Pratt's poetry collections to date, *The Walk Back Up Depot Street* is not explicitly autobiographical; rather, it is heavily informed by Pratt's own experience growing up as a member of a privileged social group in the segregated South.

The entirely autobiographical *Crime Against Nature* (1990) also presents themes of segregation, separation, and multivocality. It too plays with the notion of time reflecting on the past that shapes the present. The collection narrates the author's separation from her sons, and its main theme is motherhood. Because of the circumstances in which she lost custody of her children—because she was lesbian—identity politics also inform the work. The titles of the poems in the collection—"The Child Taken from the Mother," "Justice Come Down," "Declared Not Fit," "My Life You're Talking About"—illustrate the stops along the journey that Pratt takes to express outrage at her situation, meditate on the concept of mother, and tell the pain and the clarity that only comes with pain.

CRITICAL RECEPTION

During the late 1980s and the 1990s, Minnie Bruce Pratt's work has been widely rewarded and acclaimed. *Crime Against Nature* received the 1989 Lamont Poetry Selection from the Academy of American Poets; the 1991 American Library Association Gay and Lesbian Book Award for Literature; a nomination for the Pulitzer Prize in Poetry; and prompted the National Endowment for the Arts to grant her a Creative Writing Fellowship in 1990. After right-wing reactionaries protested this award because Pratt wrote about lesbian themes, the Fund for Free Expression gave her the Lillian Hellmann-Dashiel Award for the political persecution that she, along with fellow recipients Audre Lorde and Chrystos, endured. Also, this collection on multiple identities and interrupted motherhood has become a seminal work of gay and lesbian studies precisely because "Pratt's poems deal directly and explicitly with issues of anger, shame, sexuality and injustice," addressing some of the most prominent themes in the field (Kaganoff 78).

Many critics (Griffin, Gordon) analyze Pratt's work primarily through the lens of sexual orientation and gender. Using this framework, they consider her work emblematic of a new era in identity formation, one in which dyadic categories such as gender and sexuality are problematized by the reality of multiple identity and gender performance. A few critics, such as Arlene Richards, go so far as to use Pratt's writing as a central case study in the nature of lesbianism, attempting to translate her "psychic journey" into a map upon which sexual identity transformation can be followed. This application of Pratt's autobiographics wanders a bit out of poetic territory but suggests the extent to which critics are concerned with the power of the connection between the personal and political characteristics of her work.

BIBLIOGRAPHY

Works by Minnie Bruce Pratt

The Sound of One Fork. Durham, NC: Night Heron Press, 1981.

We Say We Love Each Other. Minneapolis, MN: Spinsters/Aunt Lute, 1985.

Yours in Struggle: Three Feminist Perspectives on Anti-Semitism and Racism. With Elly Bulkin and Barbara Smith. Ithaca, NY: Firebrand Books, 1988.
Crime Against Nature. Ithaca, NY: Firebrand Books, 1990.
Rebellion: Essays 1980–1991. Ithaca, NY: Firebrand Books, 1991.
Walking Back Up Depot Street. Pittsburgh, PA: University of Pittsburgh Press, 1999.

Studies of Minnie Bruce Pratt

Gordon, Leonore. "Tongues of Ice." *American Book Review* 13.1 (1991): 21–22.
Griffin, Connie D. "Ex-Centricities: Multi-Cultural Self-Representation in Contemporary American Women's Autobiographies." *Style* 35:2 (2001): 321–40.
Kaganoff, Penny. "Crimes of Nature." *Publisher's Weekly*, 2 March 1990, 77–79.
Martin, Biddy, and Chandra Talpade Mohanty. "Feminist Politics: What's Home Got to Do With It?" In *Feminisms: Anthology of Literary Theory and Criticism*, edited by Diane Pierce Herndl and Robyn R. Warhol. New Brunswick, NJ: Rutgers University Press, 1997. 293–310.
Richards, Arlene. "Talking about Lesbians: Minnie Bruce Pratt and Her Psychic Journey." *Psychoanalysis and Psychotherapy* 13: 2 (1996): 109–21.
Richardson, Valerie. "National Endowment for the Arts Helps Fund Porn Stars Stage Show." *Washington Times*, 5 Feb. 1990, natl. ed: A1.
Sarles, Patricia A. Review of *Rebellion: Essays 1980–1991*, by Minnie Bruce Pratt. *Library Journal* 116.21 (1991): 178–80.
Whitehead, Kim. "Walking from the Tombigbee." *Southern Changes* 17: 1 (1995): 23–24.

ADRIENNE RICH (1929–)

Kathleen Moore

BIOGRAPHY

Adrienne Rich, a poet and essayist of remarkable distinction, was born in Baltimore, Maryland, to parents Arnold Rich, a physician and professor at Johns Hopkins Medical School, and Helen (maiden name Jones) Rich, a pianist and composer. Rich's father was Jewish and grew up in Birmingham, Alabama; her mother was a white southern Protestant. With the encouragement and guidance of her parents, Rich learned music and read extensively from her father's library. Her style was formed by the poets she found there, such as Robert Frost, John Donne, Wallace Stevens, and William Butler Yeats, and she later claimed to have learned her craft from them ("When We Dead Awaken" *On Lies, Secrets, and Silence* 171). Rich graduated Phi Beta Kappa from Radcliffe College in 1951, and that same year, she was chosen by W. H. Auden as the winner of the Yale Series of Younger Poets Award for her first published collection of poems, *A Change of World* (1951). In 1952 she was awarded a Guggenheim Fellowship and traveled for a time in Europe.

Rich married Alfred Conrad, a Harvard University economist, in 1953, and gave birth to three sons within five years and while still in her twenties. In 1955, the year of her first son's birth, she published a second collection of poetry titled *The Diamond Cutters,* but eight years spent with the duties of children and household passed before Rich found the time to publish another. While not the most brilliant phase of Rich's career, these years provided a period of incubation for the radical poetry that eventually formed her reputation. Although the demands of motherhood conflicted with her work as a poet, she later claimed that it was the experience that finally "radicalized" her. The publication of *Snapshots of a Daughter-in-Law* in 1963 marked Rich's rise to national prominence. This volume along with her third, *Necessities of Life,* published in 1966, began Rich's treatment of women's themes.

Rich and her husband moved from Cambridge, Massachusetts, to New York City in 1966 and became increasingly involved in radical politics, especially the antiwar and civil rights movements. During this time, she developed a strong belief in the importance of social action leading to change. She later said that James Baldwin and Simone de Beauvoir significantly influenced her political views in the 1950s and 1960s ("Split at the Root" *Blood, Bread, and Poetry* 237). In 1970, Rich left her marriage of seventeen years and identified herself with the Women's Liberation movement. Her husband committed suicide the following year.

Rich carried on her interest in women's issues in her next two volumes, *Leaflets* (1969), and *The Will to Change* (1971). In 1974 she won the National Book Award for *Diving into the Wreck* (1973), thought by many to be her most widely read volume of poetry. In the late 1970s, she identified herself as a feminist and began advocating a radical feminism. Her political views informed her subsequent poetry collections—*Twenty One Love Poems* (1976), *The Dream of a Common Language* (1978), *A Wild Patience Has Taken Me This Far* (1981), *The Fact of a Doorframe* (1984)—and her essay collections—*Of Woman Born: Motherhood as Experience and Institution* (1976) and *On Lies, Secrets, and Silence, Selected Prose* (1979). Rich experimented with poetic form, moving away from formalism in search of ways to more clearly explore the experience of women, and published *Your Native Land, Your Life* (1986), *Blood, Bread and Poetry: Selected Prose, 1966–1978* (1986), and *Time's Power: Poems, 1985–1988* (1988).

Throughout her writing career, Rich gained wide attention by lecturing at American universities, most notably as professor of English at Stanford University from 1986–93. She has held positions as visiting professor and adjunct lecturer at schools such as Swarthmore College, Columbia University Graduate School for the Arts, City College of New York, Brandeis University, Bryn Mawr College, Rutgers University, Cornell University, and Scripps College. Rich has received numerous accolades, such as the National Book Award (1974); the Ruth Lilly Poetry Prize by the Modern Poetry Association and American Council for the Arts (1986); the Robert Frost Silver Medal for Lifetime Achievement in Poetry, Poetry Society of America (1992); the William Whitehead Award of the Gay and Lesbian Publishing Triangle for Lifetime Achievement in Letters (1992); and the *Los Angeles Times* Book Award in Poetry (1992). She was awarded the 1997 National Medal of the Arts, but she declined it.

Rich's literary career, long and illustrious, continued in the last decade of the twentieth century without breaking stride, publishing: *An Atlas of the Difficult World* (1991), *Dark Fields of the Republic* (1995), and *Midnight Salvage* (1999). Rich and her partner Michelle Cliff moved to the California coast in 1984, where she resides today.

MAJOR WORKS AND THEMES

Adrienne Rich's political poetry, as Charles Altieri notes, must be read in two ways, as an exploration of the life of women in contemporary culture and as an exploration of "general human concerns for identity and community ("Self Reflection as Action" 344). Her themes take shape around two poles: the power and potential of language to determine consciousness and our lived reality, and the importance of personal experience and reflection in creating social community. Her writing presumes that in understanding ourselves through the past and through the language we share about that past we can come to break free of the powerful, oppressive, and misguided cultural constructs that have such power over us. Language detached from personal experience brings deception and the space for abusive power, blockades to the politics to which Rich's poetry is committed. For Rich, vision must have an affinity for action. Poetry has the responsibility to transform, and to that end, it must cultivate unease, be ever vigilant, and work to overcome passivity, stagnation, and blind acceptance.

Rich has been deeply engaged with history and the poetic tradition in an attempt to retrieve the lost history of women and their experience. Rich writes in "When We Dead Awaken": "Revision—the act of looking back, of seeing with fresh eyes, of entering an old text from a new critical direction—is for women more than a chapter in cultural history: it is an act of survival. Until we can understand the assumptions in which we are drenched we cannot know ourselves" (167). A major theme of her work is to retrieve and expand the fragments of the lives of past and present women, both anonymous and known. According to Jan Montefiore, Rich's poetry emphasizes the network of influence between women, the links between past and present poets, between the "foremothers" from whom we inherited our thoughts and our inheritance (7). This focus evolved tentatively at first, moving her poetic voice from a somewhat frustrated conformity to the political order, to a resolute relocation of power within the self. This voice is the source of energy and vision within Rich's work and the means by which self-creation becomes the catalyst for social transformation. Her poetry works with tradition and the experience of women not to validate tradition, but rather to break its hold over us.

In Rich's first two volumes, *A Change of World* and *The Diamond Cutters*, her imitation of the poetic forms of the poets she grew up reading demonstrates her skill and breadth of knowledge. This early work manifests primarily a traditional poetics with a covert feminism, unrecognized at the time. Although well received at the time of publication, recent critical assessment holds that these early works contain only a small number of the seeds of Rich's future power. According to Montefiore, the poems are "well-mannered and passive on the surface and content with restraint," and they use images that subtly communicate the power that the woman artist feels but dares not express overtly in America in the 1950s (72). Rich claims in "When We Dead Awaken" that looking back at her early poems she is "startled because beneath the conscious craft are glimpses of the split I even then experienced between the girl who wrote poems, who defined herself in writing poems, and the girl who was to define herself by her relationships with men" (171). A reader can discern beneath the surface formalism of Rich's early work a characteristic tension in the recurring images of passivity, estrangement, and stifled silence.

Snapshots of a Daughter-in-Law is considered a transitional book in Rich's development as a poet. In this volume, the voice of the poet is personal and female, a stance Rich deliberately adopted for the first time as she attempted to move away from the constrictions of formalism and experiment with poetic form in order to find ways to express the fragmentation and confusion she felt as a woman living in American culture in the 1960s. In Albert Gelpi's words, "The verbal and metaphorical compression and the formal symmetry of the poems from the fifties had given way in the sixties to an unmetered, unrhymed line and an open form which allowed for a searching of her experience on psychological and political terms" (297). In one of her best-known essays, "When We Dead Awaken: Writing as Re-Vision" in *On Lies, Secrets, and Silence*, Rich claims that the title poem of *Snapshots* was "an extraordinary relief to write" (175) because there she was able to write for the first time directly about experiencing herself as a woman. Her self-consciousness puts irony and anger in the service of the reconstruction of the self, the female reader, and all human culture. As Alice Templeton writes, "Rich clearly condemns androcentric culture as she creates a context in which historical and literary texts from high culture actually indict the culture they are meant to serve" (13). Poems in *Snapshots* capture images of women, known and unknown, situated within an oppressive cultural space that denies them full subjectivity. For example, the volume's title poem presents an image of Emily Dickinson finding time to write poetry as she goes about her tedious domestic chores (10).

In *Snapshots*, themes such as the burden of history, the separateness of individuals, and the need for meaningful human relationships carry an added sensibility regarding gender and its express impact on one's life. The volume's title sets this group of poems within a frame of woman as daughter-in-law, wife, and mother bound into a set role within traditional social patterns and an awakening sense of identity. The adoption of this personal, exploratory voice carries a perspective that calls into question assumptions about identity and gender relations and debates throwing over these assumptions versus living within their structures. In the last poem of *Snapshots*, titled "The Roofwalker," the poet speaks in the voice of a worker who has built a "roof [she] can't live under" (16). She can risk change or continue to practice her misguided craft. Although still working within conventional poetic forms, *Snapshots* begins Rich's overt expression of her feminist vision and her indictment of patriarchal society that will take another decade to surface in more overt and strategic ways.

Rich's next three volumes, *Necessities of Life*, *Leaflets*, and *The Will to Change*, expand and develop her idea of the relationship between private and public life. They openly confront patriarchal culture and language and develop a voice deeply dissatisfied with contemporary society. Wendy Martin remarks that the poems in these volumes reaffirmed Rich's commitment to linking the power of poetry to revolutionary change (185). Imagination is tied to the renovation of culture, and images that affect political consciousness are used to move poetry from aesthetic icon to revolutionary force. The voice of the poems asserts the inseparability between public and private affairs.

Rich experimented with alternatives to traditional poetic forms so as to find the language to reflect the deep connection she believed exists between consciousness and social structure. She relied on her poetic form to reflect the unrest and discordance of the world she wanted to capture, making use of techniques such as counterpoint and large spaces between words, and incorporating the details of daily urban life, informal syntax, and political slogans to convey a sense of cultural fragmentation (Martin 187). Claire Keyes points out that the title poem of *Leaflets*, "Shooting Script," is paradigmatic of the experiment with form at this time, having five sections, each part taking a different approach through lineation and narrative as Rich attempts to capture "the fluctuations of a mind . . . confronted by the stark impassivity of the universe" (100). The poem appears formless: clusters of lines replace the stanza, punctuation disappears and then reappears; images and allusions lack connections; ambiguities dominate. Yet, more than simply asserting the imminent destruction of everything, the open form and spontaneity of these poems offer tentative visions of possibilities within the ruins of what is, as the poet exhorts the importance of imagining how we can use what we have to create what we need. "Shooting Script" urges the reader along the path to discovery. Alienation is ultimately transcended as the poet reminds the reader of the potential for change through imagination, consciousness, and language.

Diving into the Wreck is thought by many to be Rich's most distinguished work. According to Martin, its unusual combination of aesthetics and activism not only won the volume considerable praise, it also merited it the National Book Award in 1974 (169). In *Diving into the Wreck,* Rich continues her work of exploring the frustration and anger of a thinking woman in a culture that has denied essential aspects of her experience. Rich achieves a profound exploration of her consciousness as a woman, defining that experience for herself as a way to encourage other women to do the same so as to build a community of women. *Diving into the Wreck* constitutes a radical feminist critique of modern society—critics have used words such as "fierce" (Walker 228) and "visionary anger" (Keyes 137) to describe the poetry in this volume—hence, it can be seen as a major transitional work in Rich's corpus. The volume continues Rich's work of reinventing cultural standards and asserting the need for self-exploration and self-determination. In the title poem, "Diving into the Wreck," the poet/explorer sorts through the pieces of history to recover the history of women: "the thing itself and not the myth" (54). Another poem,"The Phenomenology of Anger," relies on an extended metaphor of fire as both a destructive force (of human life in war, of one's self in moments of passivity, of human relationships through apathy) and a force of purification (of the aggression of war, of patriarchy, of oppression) and regeneration (the fire of anger and a new form of consciousness that can make new, a move away from rigidity). Templeton writes, "The hope for cultural regeneration and personal renewal in *Diving into the Wreck* comes from two possibilities: connecting with other women and communicating an alternative feminist ethics, especially through poetry and writing" (53–54), themes found most succinctly in the poem "For a Sister" written about the political activist Natalya Gorbanevskaya's arrest and eventual release, and Gorbanevskaya's turn to writing her story as a way to redress the skewed view of accounts sanctioned by the establishment.

Rich's hope in a woman's community as the potential source for positive change is central to her next volume, *The Dream of a Common Language.* Here Rich begins the process of revision, which informs her poetics from this point. She attempts to provide women with mythic structures that will affirm the identity and experiences of women and make known female interdependence. The volume is divided into three parts: "Power" (which traces the achievements and difficulties of women from history such as Elvira Shatayev and Emily Dickinson), "Twenty-One Love Poems" (which explores human, and especially female, sexuality), and "Not Somewhere Else, but Here" (which explores the possibilities for positive action and human connection in the present). The volume's major theme is that language is the conduit for the human connection, and the dialogic model shapes much of the volume's work. Like dialogue, revisioning women's identity is shaped by a give and take process where ideas are built through exploration and constant revision.

In *A Wild Patience Has Taken Me This Far,* Rich continues to reenvision history in order to celebrate the achievements of women, achievements often sketched through endurance and success. *Of Woman Born* is a collection of prose pieces that explore the concept of motherhood in modern culture. *On Lies, Secrets, and Silence* continues Rich's vision for female self-determination, and *Blood, Bread, and Poetry* examines issues such as female relationships, racial identity, and racism. Rich considers her major work of the last decade of the twentieth century—*An Atlas of the Difficult World, Dark Fields of the Republic,* and *Midnight Salvage*—as a trilogy, each book containing "a long poem which is a kind of theater of struggle with forces that are hostile to art and to human dignity overall" (Bulkin 2); the final poem of *Midnight Salvage*, "A Long Conversation," examines a three-century conversation about human freedom, revolution, and art among people such as William Blake, Samuel Taylor Coleridge, Che Guevara, Karl Marx, and Richard Nixon. Rich said of this poem that she "wanted to show how many-voiced that conversation has been, and goes on being" and "to salvage something both truthful and beautiful from all that" (Bulkin 2). Rich's treatment in her latest volume of subjects such as politics, ecology, and poetics continues her commitment to social activism.

CRITICAL RECEPTION

Adrienne Rich has had a long and distinguished career as a poet and essayist. Critics often refer to a development or evolution in her work that moves from imitation to personal discovery. Recent critics consider her career to have really begun with *Snapshots of a Daughter-in-Law* when she stepped outside the shadow of influence and began speaking from her own experience and in her own style. Her extensive body of work has merited wide critical attention, and she has left a legacy to the feminist movement that will be long lasting. Since the publication of *Diving into the Wreck*, critics have taken Rich's poetry and prose as constituting a radical feminist politics that has made a significant contribution to women's quest in challenging a dominant, male-oriented culture. While many of her views have generated debate—for example, by feminist critics who question the possibility of a feminist poetics—she writes as a woman of her time who is deeply invested in challenging cultural assumptions.

Critics generally agree on Rich's technical skills—her powers of expression, rhetorical energy, keenness of observation, and knowledge of poetic tradition—however, her straightforward political position has generated protest from critics who disagree with her views. Some find fault with what they perceive as an antimale bias in Rich's work, and others disparage what they see as a didactic tone in her work. Her politics and her visionary anger have engendered a great deal of debate about the place of ideology in poetry. Some critics find that the combination of ideology and traditional poetics has given Rich the space for experimentation—"the combination that has always produced the strongest literature" (Cooper 272). Templeton assesses that "Adrienne Rich's poetry has always raised profound questions about the cultural uses of poetry. For over forty years her work has moved critics to comment on the nature of poetic art, its political significance, the character of poetic tradition, and the value of poetry as a cultural and political activity" (1).

Rich's poetry, though appealing to women drawn to the feminist movement, has circulated extensively among general audiences. Writer Margaret Atwood, in a *New York Times* review of Rich's *Diving into the Wreck*, writes, "If Adrienne Rich were not a good poet, it would be easy to classify her as just another vocal Women's Libber, substituting polemic for poetry, simplistic messages for complex meanings. But she *is* a good poet, and her book is not a manifesto, though it subsumes manifestoes; nor is it a proclamation, though it makes proclamations"(1). Rich's focus on women's issues has not limited critical appreciation to women. Helen Vendler writes about *Diving into the Wreck* that Rich "forsakes distinctions between men and women, for the most part, and sees us all as crippled creatures, scarred by that process of socialization and nurture" (310). Charles Altieri finds that Rich's voice incorporates a concern for identity and community that is not necessarily gender specific ("Self-Reflection as Action"

344). Terrence Des Pres writes, "One doesn't have to be a woman to see the decency of feminist concerns. . . . Being female is not in itself the criterion for valuing Rich's poems" (358). Poet Ruthann Robson has recently written in her review of *Midnight Salvage*, "Looking back at Rich's work, there were also always the voices of men—of men who were poets and resisters of fascism. Just as there has always been an unstinting political context into which the language of poetry intercedes" (2). As in earlier work, Rich's latest volume is political, positing human desire in all its forms as resistance: to death, stagnation, oppression, and totalitarianism.

BIBLIOGRAPHY

Works by Adrienne Rich

Ariadne: A Play in Three Acts and Poems. Baltimore, MD: J. H. Furst, 1939.
Not I, But Death, A Play in One Act. Baltimore, MD: J. H. Furst, 1941.
A Change of World. New Haven, CT: Yale University Press, 1951.
The Diamond Cutters and Other Poems. New York: Harper, 1955.
Snapshots of a Daughter-in-Law: Poems, 1954–1962. New York: Harper, 1963; New York: Norton, 1967; London: Chatto & Windus, 1970.
Necessities of Life: Poems, 1962–1965. New York: Norton, 1966.
Selected Poems. London: Chatto & Windus, 1967.
Leaflets: Poems, 1965–1968. New York: Norton, 1969; London: Chatto & Windus, 1972.
The Will to Change: Poems, 1968–1970. New York: Norton, 1971; London: Chatto & Windus, 1973.
Diving into the Wreck: Poems, 1971–1972. New York: Norton, 1973.
Poems: Selected and New, 1950–1974. New York: Norton, 1975.
Of Woman Born: Motherhood as Experience and Institution. New York: Norton, 1976. (prose)
Twenty-One Love Poems. Emeryville, CA: Effie's Press, 1976.
Women and Honor: Some Notes on Lying. Pittsburgh, PA: Motheroot Publications, 1977. Reprinted in *On Lies, Secrets and Silence*. 185–194. (monograph)
The Dream of a Common Language: Poems, 1974–1977. New York: Norton, 1978.
On Lies, Secrets, and Silence: Selected Prose, 1966–1978. New York: Norton, 1979.
Compulsory Heterosexuality and Lesbian Existence. Denver, CO: Antelope Publications, 1980. (prose; pamphlet)
A Wild Patience Has Taken Me This Far: Poems, 1978–1981. New York: Norton, 1981.
Sources. Woodside, CA: Heyeck Press, 1983.
The Fact of a Doorframe: Poems Selected and New, 1950–1984. New York: Norton, 1984.
Blood, Bread, and Poetry: Selected Prose, 1979–1986. New York: Norton, 1986.
Your Native Land, Your Life: Poems. New York: Norton, 1986.
Time's Power: Poems, 1985–1988. New York: Norton, 1989.
An Atlas of the Difficult World: Poems, 1988–1991. New York: Norton, 1991.
Collected Early Poems, 1950–1970. New York: Norton, 1993.
What Is Found There: Notebooks on Poetry and Politics. New York: Norton, 1993.
Dark Fields of the Republic, 1991–1995. New York: Norton, 1995.
Selected Poems, 1950–1995. Knockeven, Ireland: Salmon, 1996.
Midnight Salvage: Poems, 1995–1998. New York: Norton, 1999.

Studies of Adrienne Rich

Altieri, Charles. *Self and Sensibility in Contemporary American Poetry*. Cambridge: Cambridge University Press, 1984.

———. "Self Reflection as Action." In *Adrienne Rich's Poetry and Prose: Poems, Prose, Reviews and Criticism,* edited by Barbara and Albert Gelpi. New York: Norton, 1993. 342–56.

Atwood, Margaret. Review of *Diving into the Wreck,* by Adrienne Rich. In *Adrienne Rich's Poetry and Prose: Poems, Prose, Reviews and Criticism,* edited by Barbara and Albert Gelpi. New York: Norton, 1993. 277.

Auden, W. H. Foreword to *A Change of World,* by Adrienne Rich. New Haven, CT: Yale University Press, 1951. 7–11. Reprinted in *Adrienne Rich's Poetry and Prose: Poems, Prose, Reviews and Criticism,* edited by Barbara and Albert Gelpi. New York: Norton, 1993. 277.

Bulkin, Elly. "Poet(ry) for a Dissenting Movement: An Interview with Poet Adrienne Rich." *Sojourner* 24.11 (1999): 21+.

Cooper, Jane Roberta, ed. *Reading Adrienne Rich: Reviews and ReVisions, 1951–1981.* Ann Arbor: University of Michigan Press, 1984.

Des Pres, Terrence. "Adrienne Rich, North America East." In *Adrienne Rich's Poetry and Prose: Poems, Prose, Reviews and Criticism,* edited by Barbara and Albert Gelpi. New York: Norton, 1993. 357–68.

Felski, Rita. *Beyond Feminist Aesthetics: Feminist Literature and Social Change.* Cambridge: Harvard University Press, 1989.

Gelpi, Barbara, and Albert, eds. *Adrienne Rich's Poetry and Prose: Poems, Prose, Reviews and Criticism.* New York: Norton, 1993.

Keyes, Claire. *The Aesthetics of Power: The Poetry of Adrienne Rich.* Athens: University of Georgia Press, 1986.

Martin, Wendy. *An American Triptych: Anne Bradstreet, Emily Dickinson, Adrienne Rich.* Chapel Hill: University of North Carolina Press, 1984.

McDaniel, Judith. *Reconstituting the World: The Poetry and Vision of Adrienne Rich.* Argyle, NY: Spinsters Ink, 1979.

Montefiore, Jan. *Feminism and Poetry: Language, Experience, Identity in Women's Writing.* New York: Pandora Press, 1987.

Oakes, Elizabeth. "To 'Hold them in Solution Unsolved': The Ethics of Wholeness in Four Contemporary Poems." *Real* 25.1 (2000): 49–59.

Robson, Ruthann. "Intimate Resistance." Review of *Midnight Salvage,* by Adrienne Rich. *Lambda Book Report* 7.9 (1999): 14.

Templeton, Alice. *The Dream and the Dialogue: Adrienne Rich's Feminist Poetics.* Knoxville: University of Tennessee Press, 1994.

Vendler, Helen. "Ghostlier Demarcations, Keener Sounds." In *Adrienne Rich's Poetry and Prose: Poems, Prose, Reviews and Criticism,* edited by Barbara and Albert Gelpi. New York: Norton, 1993. 299–309.

Walker, Cheryl. "Trying to Save the Skein." In *Reading Adrienne Rich: Reviews and ReVisions, 1951–1981,* edited by Jane Roberta Cooper. Ann Arbor: University of Michigan Press, 1984. 226–31.

MURIEL RUKEYSER (1913–1980)

Kathleen Carlton Johnson and
Catherine Cucinella

BIOGRAPHY

Muriel Rukeyser was born on December 15, 1913, in New York City, the daughter of Lawrence B. and Myra (Lyons) Rukeyser. Although her parents were Jewish, Rukeyser did not spend her early childhood in an overtly Jewish home, yet her Jewish heritage heavily influenced her poetry. She received religious training and attended the Manhattan School of Ethical Culture, the Feldstone School, Vassar College, and Columbia University. Rukeyser's brief stay at the Roosevelt Aviation School became the basis for her first book of poetry, *Theory of Flight* (1935), which won the prestigious Yale Younger Poets prize of 1935. Rukeyser's work, however, reflects a much wider influence than her formal education. The sources of her poetry and intellectualism generated from her reading of history, anthropology, the arts, her study of physics and the science of the Elizabethan era, as well as from her own personal experiences.

In 1933 she went to Alabama as a journalist for *Student Review* to cover the trial of nine African American youths accused of raping two white girls; Rukeyser's experiences covering the Scottsboro trial resulted in her poem "The Trial" and began her lifelong involvement as a political and socialist activist. Never content with the role of passive observer, Rukeyser traveled to Spain in 1936 (arriving on the day that the civil war broke out) and became involved in the Spanish cause. Also in 1936 she went to West Virginia to investigate the deaths of workers mining silica; in the 1970s Rukeyser journeyed to Vietnam to protest American involvement in that country and to Seoul, South Korea, in support of the radical poet Kim Chi-Ha, who faced execution. All of these incidents made their way into Rukeyser's poetry.

In 1943 Rukeyser worked in the poster division of the Office of War Information drawn there by the opportunity to work with other artists and writers; however, she quit after six months because of resistance to the political messages that found their way into her designs. Although initially seeking teaching fellowships in traditional academic settings, Rukeyser "began to teach in alternative places" (Kertesz 369). In 1945 she became a lecturer at California Labor School where she met painter Glynn Collins to whom she was briefly married (the marriage was annulled). However, she did have a child with a man whom she never married, choosing instead single motherhood. Her son, William, was born in 1947, and the same year, Rukeyser received a yearly income from an anonymous benefactor. Rukeyser refused the yearly income when she began teaching at Sarah Lawrence College in New York City in 1954. Never wanting more than part-time teaching jobs, she left Sarah Lawrence College in 1967 when they granted her tenure. Rukeyser explains, "I couldn't be a tenured professor at any college; it would make me very nervous" (Kertesz 372). Making ends meet with a variety of part-time teaching jobs, poetry readings, and help from friends, Rukeyser continued to write and raise her son.

Rukeyser not only wrote poetry, but she also wrote biography (on such people as physicist Willard Gibbs, Wendell Wilkie, and Thomas Hariot), translated the works of Mexican poet Octavio Paz and the Swedish poet Gunnar Ekelof, lectured, and authored children's books, plays, and stories. Her awards include the Oscar Blumenthal Prize for poetry, 1940; the Harriet Monroe Poetry Award, 1941; a grant from the National Institute of Arts and Letters, 1942; a Guggenheim Fellowship, 1943; the Levinson Prize for poetry, 1947; an honorary doctorate in literature from Rutgers University, 1961; an American Council of Learned Societies Fellowship, 1963; voted president of PEN American Center, 1975; the Copernicus Award (for recognition of lifetime contribution to poetry) and the Shelley Memorial Award, 1977.

Rukeyser suffered her first stroke in 1964 and her second in 1977. In 1978 she agreed to speak on the "Lesbians and Literature" panel at the 1978 meeting of the Modern Language Association; however, illness prevented her from attending. Muriel Rukeyser died in New York City on February 12, 1980.

MAJOR WORKS AND THEMES

Because Rukeyser's work defies a single classification, it proves difficult to confine Rukeyser to one type or period of poetry. Her subjects range from such diverse topics as poverty and injustice in the South, as witnessed by her at the Scottsboro Nine trial in Alabama, to pregnancy and motherhood as expressed in the poems written to her unborn child in the "Nine Poems." In *The Gates* (1976), she protests both in poetry and in person the imprisonment and death sentence of fellow poet Kim Chi-Ha. The volume's title poem, "The Gate," uses metaphor to question how can we remove that which separates us as humans from our more transcending humanity.

Rukeyser's work, intense from the start, attempts to draw new forces out of the old, to question science, history, indeed the world, and in so doing, sees life worthy of poetry's concern. One finds in Rukeyser a generous and passionate voice like no other American poet, and this passion emerges in her first book of poetry, *Theory of Flight*. This volume expresses a belief in the possibilities of the machine age as it sees a need for human connections. If Rukeyser's work has a hallmark, it is her optimism, her confidence, and her commitment not only to her poetry, but also to the ideals that drive her words: her concern for others, her deep respect for personal and individual humanity, and an undying confidence in what poetry could accomplish.

Rukeyser's understanding of poetry's ability to touch the personal in order to move outward emerges as the prevailing and unifying thread throughout her work. While addressing many thematic concerns—the construction of romantic love, the necessity of engagement in political and social causes, the importance of the imagination in social engagement, the connection between the body and history, the politics of sexuality, and the conviction that both science and art held promise for humanity—Rukeyser always wrote about the value and responsibility of poetry.

Rukeyser had from the very start of her poetic career articulated her philosophy of poetry. In "Poem out of Childhood," she writes, "Breathe-in experience, breathe-out poetry" (*Theory of Flight*). Her style reflects her philosophy: short constructions of experiences clothed in simple yet powerful words, placed on the page with the care of a master craftsman utilizing a wide variety of poetic forms: elegies and odes, lyrics and ballads, dramatic monologues and biographical narratives, epigrams and documentary poems. Certainly, one can discern Rukeyser's attitude toward poetry throughout her work. However, *The Life of Poetry* (1949), a collection of lectures and talks that Rukeyser presented at Vassar, the California Labor School, Columbia, and various other venues in the 1940s, testifies most clearly to her understanding of, commitment to, and use of poetry. Rukeyser defines poetry as something that outlasts monuments, something "passed between the generations"(3), "an approach to the truth of feeling" (7); poetry is brief, compact, and complex; it both invites one to feel and requires a response (8). Poetry concerns itself with "the crisis of our spirit" and leads us "to the emotional meanings at every moment" (19). Poetry demands an exchange—an exchange of human energy that initiates meetings and dislodges "false barriers" (185, 19). Ultimately, Rukeyser argues for the connection of poetry to every aspect of humanity.

This connection propels and underwrites all of her work, and Rukeyser sees in poetry an obligation to address the issues of the world and to move one to act regarding these issues. Therefore, Rukeyser's poetry always speaks of the political, and as Adrienne Rich writes in the introduction to *A Muriel Rukeyser Reader*, Rukeyser "was beyond her time—and seems, at the edge of the twenty-first century, to have grasped resources that we are only now beginning to reach for: connections between history and the body, memory and politics, sexuality and public space, poetry and physical science, and much else" (xi). "The Book of the Dead," a hybrid, multivoiced poem detailing the gruesome deaths of miners from silicosis (a lung disease caused by breathing silica), seeks to encapsulate a given incident and situate it within in a larger political and social framework (*U.S. 1*). "The Book of the Dead" challenges the systems that perpetuate inequality and injustice through networks of power. Through its incorporation of letters, interviews, testimony from congressional hearings, and Stock Exchange printouts, this poem indicts capitalism, redefines boundaries between document and poem, and challenges all documentary conventions, finally emerging as a poetry of witness. "The Book of the Dead" demands response—if only a personal reaction of compassion, sadness, horror, outrage, and anger. Yet like the volumes that follow *U.S. 1* (1938), this volume sees possibility in poetry, a hope in the telling of events.

A Turning Wind continues Rukeyser's insistence that imagination and social action remain inseparable. Published in 1939, *A Turning Wind* seeks to establish relationships between joy, fear, madness, and destruction through a dizzying array of poems: in particular, the biographical poems included in this volume take on a filmic quality as images seem to jump from line to line and from page to page suggesting a cinematic montage. This movement reinforces a desire for connection, and in its blurring of boundaries, this movement denies human isolation. In *Beast in View* (1944), the denial of disengagement takes on a darker and more somber tone than it does in Rukeyser's previous work. This volume addresses both her contemporaries' dwindling involvement in social causes and her own negotiations with her private battles as well as her attempt to situate herself in relation to the social and political wars in the world. In poems such as "Anjanta," Rukeyser accesses the landscapes of the imagination to depict a growing disinterest in broad social concerns and to offer a renewed connection between the individual and the social; in "Who in One Lifetime," she asks, "Who in one lifetime sees all causes lost?" (*Muriel Rukeyser Reader* 99); in "Suicide Blues," the speaker begs for "real" voice, knowing that "real" voice offers salvation (*Muriel Rukeyser Reader* 107); and in "Eighth Elegy, Children's Elegy," the speaker yearns to grow up in order to return to love (*Muriel Rukeyser Reader* 106). These personal desires, however, reach beyond the individual as each poem makes clear that through knowledge, experience, integration, voice, and love poetry as well as the individual can move toward political and social action.

Always drawing on her own experiences and always making them political, Rukeyser introduces the themes of childbirth and motherhood in *The Green Wave* (1948), published the year following her son's birth. However, these themes do not define the entire volume as the inclusion of Rukeyser's translations of Octavio Paz's poems makes clear. Paz's poems also infuse *The Green Wave* with his political and artistic frameworks. In subsequent volumes, Rukeyser begins to show more concern with the body (*Body of Waking* [1958] and *Waterlily Fire* [1962]), and her first volume after her 1964 stroke, *The Speed of Darkness* (1968), details her struggles to reclaim language. However, Rukeyser's personal struggle exemplifies all women's attempts to speak and to be heard. This volume contains the lines that now resonate within feminist literary studies: "No more masks! No more mythologies!" ("The Poem as Mask"). While continuing this search for voice—unmasked and demythologized—Rukeyser returns to a more overtly political message in *Breaking Open* (1973) and *The Gates* (1976). The former generates from and includes Rukeyser's experiences in Hanoi and Washington, D.C., as an antiwar protester; the latter from her visit to South Korea, and her heightened awareness of the limitations of the body due to her failing health also influences both volumes. These two works also include themes of growth, of childhood, and the ever-present demand for social awareness and political engagement.

CRITICAL RECEPTION

Kenneth Rexroth writes that "Muriel Rukeyser is the best poet of her exact generation," and he identifies her as "one of the most important writers of the Left of her time." However, Rexroth also points out that "the Left alternately embraced and damned her" ("Foreword" xi-xii). This ambivalence about Rukeyser's position within the tradition of poetry of the Left resonates in discussions of both her poetry and her place within an American tradition of letters. Early on, Louise Bogan expressed her disapproval of Rukeyser's poetic voice, finding that it did not sound appropriately "female" (Kertesz 3). In addition, Rukeyser's insistence upon linking poetry with the emotional, the social, the political, and the cultural alienated her from the New Critics of the 1940s. Adrienne Rich summarizes and explains Rukeyser's critical reception: "She was sometimes the target of extraordinary hostility and ridicule, based on a critic's failure to read her well or even try to understand her methods: . . . because she was too complicated and too independent to follow any political 'line,' or because she would not trim her sails to a vogue of poetic irony and wit, . . . an idea of what a women's poetry should look like" ("Beginners" 16). Although misunderstood or dismissed by reviewers and critics, Rukeyser's poetry has long been appreciated by poets, and today, critical attention to Rukeyser, her life and her work, focuses on the visionary aspects of her poetics, her influence within an American poetic tradition, and her place within a canon of women poets.

Louise Kertesz begins this study with the 1980 publication of *The Poetic Vision of Muriel Rukeyser*, a work that traces the themes and images in Rukeyser's work and situates the poet within poetic traditions and in relation to her contemporaries. The publication of *Out of Silences: Selected Poems* (1992) and *A Muriel Rukeyser Reader* (1994) provide new access to Rukeyser's work as most of it had long been out of print. The appearance of these volumes along with the republication of Rukeyser's *The Life of Poetry* in 1996 brought new critical attention to Rukeyser. In her review of *The Life of Poetry*, Priscilla Long acknowledges the relevancy of Rukeyser's material, pointing specifically to Rukeyser's use of "truth" and "meaning" and the poet's refusal to "define the content of truth or the meaning of meaning" (15). Although she focuses specifically on "The Book of the Dead," Shoshana Wechsler also finds Rukeyser's poetry relevant to contemporary literary concerns identifying in "The Book of the Dead" an objectivity that suggests "the whole terrain of postmodernity" (121). This critical scrutiny of Rukeyser's work adds this poet's voice to the ongoing dialogue regarding the place, purpose, and use of poetry today.

The latest critical collection on Rukeyser's work, *"How Shall We Tell Each Other of the Poet?": The Life and Writing of Muriel Rukeyser*, edited by Anne Herzog and Janet Kaufman, contains analysis of the poet's work as well as reminiscences about her life, and it also includes poems written by poets influenced by Rukeyser's work. The topics of the analytical essays range from contextualizing autobiographical elements within a critical framework, theorizing Rukeyser's use and understanding of form, examining Rukeyser's poetry of witness through the lens of her Jewish heritage, exploring the relationship of Rukeyser's experiences as a woman writer within a larger political context, analyzing how a woman writer represents the lives of other women, and finally, to addressing the critical neglect of Muriel Rukeyser. This collection begins to answer the questions put forth by Rich in her 1993 essay, "Beginners": "What happens when a woman, drawing on every political breakthrough gained by women since Dickinson's death in 1886, assumes the scope of her own living to be at least as large as Whitman's." Whereas Rich answers, "She falls between the cracks" (15), new scholarship responds (to paraphrase lines from Rukeyser's "Käthe Kollwitz"), "She splits the world open by telling the truth about her life."

BIBLIOGRAPHY

Works by Muriel Rukeyser

Theory of Flight. New Haven, CT: Yale University Press, 1935.
U.S. 1. New York: Covici, Friede, 1938.
A Turning Wind: Poems. New York: Viking, 1939.
The Soul and Body of John Brown. New York: privately printed, 1940.
Wake Island. Garden City, NY: Doubleday, 1942.

Willard Gibbs. Garden City, NY: Doubleday, 1942. (biography)
Beast in View. Garden City, NY: Doubleday, 1944.
The Green Wave. Garden City, NY: Doubleday, 1948.
Elegies. Norfolk, CT: New Directions, 1949.
The Life of Poetry. New York: Current Books, 1949. Reprinted in Ashfield, MA: Paris Press, 1996. (lectures)
Orpheus. San Francisco: Centaur Press, 1949.
Selected Poems. New York: New Directions, 1951.
One Life. New York: Simon & Schuster, 1957. (biography of Wendell Wilkie)
Body of Waking. New York: Harper, 1958.
Waterlily Fire: Poems 1935–1962. New York: Macmillan, 1962.
The Orgy. New York: Coward McCann, 1965. (novel)
The Outer Banks. Santa Barbara, CA: Unicorn Press, 1967.
The Speed of Darkness. New York: Random House, 1968.
Mazes. New York: Simon & Schuster, 1970.
The Traces of Thomas Hariot. New York: Random House, 1971. (biography)
Twenty-Nine Poems. London: Rapp & Whiting, 1972.
Breaking Open: New Poems. New York: Random House, 1973.
The Gates: Poems. New York: McGraw-Hill, 1976.
The Collected Poems of Muriel Rukeyser. New York: McGraw-Hill, 1978.
Out of Silences: Selected Poems, edited by Kate Daniels. Evanston, IL: Triquarterly Books, 1992.
A Muriel Rukeyser Reader, edited by Jan Haller Levi. New York: Norton, 1994.

Studies of Muriel Rukeyser

Cooper, Jane. " 'Meeting Places': On Muriel Rukeyser." *American Poetry Review* 25.5 (1996): 11–16.
Daniels, Kate. "Muriel Rukeyser and Her Literary Critics." In *Gendered Modernisms: American Women Poets and Their Readers*, edited by Margaret Dickie and Thomas Travisano. Philadelphia: University of Pennsylvania Press, 1996. 247–63.
Flynn, Richard. " 'The Buried Life and the Body of Walking': Muriel Rukeyser and the Politics of Literary History." In *Gendered Modernisms: American Women Poets and Their Readers*, edited by Margaret Dickie and Thomas Travisano. Philadelphia: University of Pennsylvania Press, 1996. 264–79.
Gardinier, Suzanne. " 'A World that Will Hold All the People': On Muriel Rukeyser." *Kenyon Review* 14.3 (1992): 88–105.
Goldensohn, Lorrie. "Muriel Rukeyser's Body Politic and Poetic." In *Freedom and Form: Essays in Contemporary American Poetry*, edited by Esther Giger and Agnieszka Salska. Lodz, Poland: Wydawnictwo Uniwesytetu Lodzkiego, 1998. 67–78.
Herzog, Anne F., and Janet E. Kaufman, eds. *"How Shall We Tell Each Other of the Poet?": The Life and Writing of Muriel Rukeyser*. New York: St. Martin's, 1999.
Kadlec, David. "X-Ray Testimonials in Muriel Rukeyser." *Modernism/Modernity* 5.1 (1998): 23–47.
Kalaidjian, Walter. "Muriel Rukeyser and the Poetics of Specific Critique: Rereading 'The Book of the Dead.' " *Cultural Critique* 20 (1991–92): 65–88.
Kertesz, Louise. *The Poetic Vision of Muriel Rukeyser*. Baton Rouge: Louisiana State University Press, 1980.
Long, Priscilla. "The Poetics of Passion." Review of *The Life of Poetry*, by Muriel Rukeyser. *Women's Review of Books* 14.5 (1997): 10–15.
Rexroth, Kenneth. Foreword to *The Poetic Vision of Muriel Rukeyser*, Louise Kertesz. Baton Rouge: Louisiana State University Press, 1980. xi-xii.

Rich, Adrienne. "Beginners." *Kenyon Review* 15.3 (1993): 12–17.

———. Introduction to *A Muriel Rukeyser Reader*, edited by Jan Haller Levi. New York: Norton, 1994. xi-xv.

Thurston, Michael. "Documentary Modernism as Popular Front Poetics: Muriel Rukeyser's 'Book of the Dead.' " *Modern Language Quarterly* 60.1 (1999): 59–83.

Wechsler, Shoshana. "A Ma(t)ter of Fact and Vision: The Objectivity Question and Muriel Rukeyser's 'Book of the Dead.' " *Twentieth Century Literature* 45.2 (1999): 121–37.

Wright, Andrea Rohlfs. "Masks Uncovered: (Fe)male Language in the Poetry of Muriel Rukeyser." *College Teachers of English Studies* 60 (1996): 34–40.

NATASHA SAJÉ (1955–)

Renée R. Curry

BIOGRAPHY

Natasha Sajé was born in Munich, Germany, and grew up in New York City and New Jersey. She has earned three degrees: a BA from the University of Virginia, an MA from Johns Hopkins, and a PhD from the University of Maryland at College Park. This poet has received numerous honors including the Bannister Writer-in-Residence at Sweet Briar College, the Robert Winner Award from the Poetry Society of America, and grants from the states of Maryland and Utah and from Baltimore City. Sajé was also a poet-in-the-schools from 1989–98. Her book of poetry, *Red under the Skin* (1994), was chosen from among nine hundred manuscripts to win the 1993 Agnes Lynch Starrett Poetry Prize; the book also won the Towson State Prize in Literature that year, and it was awarded publication in the Pitt Poetry series of 1994.

Sajé is currently working on her second book of poetry. Sajé teaches at Westminster College in Salt Lake City, Utah, and in the Vermont College, Montpelier, VT, MFA in Writing Program.

MAJOR WORKS AND THEMES

In *Red under the Skin*, Sajé's sole published book to date, the most apparent and delectable theme is that of hunger: sexual hunger, literary hunger, as well as hunger for food and knowledge. The book opens with a prelude poem that mischievously discusses reading the works of the late Henry James. In this poem, Sajé likens such reading to the trust that sado-masochistic sex involves. With James, a reader never knows what is to come, just as in "S&M," one also never knows. However, Sajé points out that reading James is ultimately disappointing because one is never quite satisfied: Although the sex is good and the length of the activity is pleasing, one never climaxes emotionally from the experience.

Such graphic sexuality is depicted throughout this poetry, always under the guise of a hungering that the body, mind, and soul experience in life. In "Creation Story," the poet discusses vanilla and its aphrodisiacal uses throughout time: Variously it cured male impotence and served to make lovers "*cunt-struck*" when smelling a woman. In "Reeling," Sajé luxuriates in writing about the particular hunger of females lusting for males. She describes the throbbing and movement of her ovaries as she feasts her eyes upon the male body; the desire to nestle into male skin; the fantasy of grabbing a male thigh; the images of males undressing in front of her; and, the desire to whisper to men regarding how she wants them to have sex with her. This poem makes it perfectly clear that heterosexual women hunger physically and passionately for men and debunks the myth that straight women mostly desire men for emotional comfort. In "Tongues," the sexual hunger makes itself evident in the narrator's admission that she loves to lick another's body.

Sexual hunger is not the only hunger about which Natasha Sajé writes. In *Red under the Skin*, the intricate and numerous activities of the tongue become a signifier of the body's need to taste the specificity and specialties of life. In "Creation Story," the tongue is powerless to move some words toward their root meanings. In "Things," the tongue only occasionally discovers ways of articulating the things that have registered in the mind.

In "Tongues," Sajé analyzes the tongue from a biological standpoint, describing the mechanisms of its ability to taste. She examines the tongue from a historical perspective, discussing periods when God removed the tongues of disbelievers and when rapists cut out their victims' tongues. The poem depicts the quiet of a professor's tongue while awaiting student responses to a question as well as gypsy killings by tongue licking. The close of the poem delivers a postmodern climax in which a food-loving friend refuses to eat tongue because of the excess of hunger it implies. In this poem, the poet makes clear that the appetites signified by the tongue are often more than sensual; frequently, the tongue is the most activist and political signifier of the entire body. In "Leningrad," the roasted tongues of the poem come from a father's boots. Even though these tongues do not signify an activism of the body, they still represent the politics of a particular war. In "Chocolates," the tongue measures the precise dissolution of chocolate as well as the warring words of anger and the seductive words of love.

The food represented in Natasha Sajé's work calls forth not only the nature of human bodily hunger, but also the care and detail that development of an appetite as well as satisfaction of an appetite can incur. This poet details the process by which we prepare and cook foods in order to draw a complex analogy between the social construction of the various arts of cooking and the social construction of human understanding of the different bodies we occupy. In "Creation Story," Sajé savors the curing, slicing, and preparing of the sweet vanilla bean while comparing this process to the inability of our language systems to extract certain words from their origins. "Spring Rolls" features a young Saigon wife who fries, pounds, and spices the foods of her country for her foreign husband while she contemplates the story and the war that brought her to her current situation. The poem "Mussels" depicts the bubbling, breathing, iridescent, savory, marshmallow-like and bunching mussels as signifiers of the seeming outward and inward likeness in species harboring the occasional immeasurable and invaluable pearl inside our beings. In "Consommé," the poet suggests that the construction of soup is like the assimilative practices of peoples; however, she claims that the particulars that make a distinct consommé are always discernible in their parts.

The pivotal poem of the book is the title poem "Red under the Skin," which encapsulates the relationship between different forms of hungering and the fact that all peoples hunger differently. Sajé uses autobiography to amplify the intricacies of hunger that revolve about and within and that construct the self. The poem reveals the history of the Serbs and Croats and her father's particular pride in being Slovene, even in exile. It details the problems of particularizing an identity in that the poet's father was Serbian Orthodox, her mother Bosnian Muslim, and her husband Croatian Catholic. Sajé ponders with the reader whether such combinations afford healing or further dissent among peoples. She chronicles the distancing that occurs in her family and the loss of certain friends as well as the constant onslaught of questions aimed at encouraging her to choose from among the varied parts of her identity. Through an exploration of the numerous historic events that mark her family, Sajé reveals the exacting measure and mismeasure of an identity—and one person's life—formed out of the complex combinations of such events. The poet also makes clear the origin of the late twentieth-century passion and hunger for identity politics.

The more recent poems, the ones that Sajé plans to incorporate into her second book of poetry, still employ images of sexuality, the tongue, literary references, and self-reflexivity about language, but hunger will not be the driving force of these poems. Although it is difficult to imagine the themes of a book not yet published, certain commonalities do emerge and promise another intriguing journey through experiences elemental to human existence. In "A Minor Riot at the Mint," published in *Ploughshares*, 1998, water emerges as the guiding element of the poem as is true in "Channel," in *New Republic*, 2000; "Wonders of the Invisible World," in *Paris Review*, 2001; "Bend," in *Kenyon Review*, 2001; and in all the new poems, "We Saw No Caribou," "Parabola," "Marble Steps," and "Cinemania."

CRITICAL RECEPTION

Natasha Sajé's poems have been well received. Poets such as Alicia Ostriker, Gregory Orr, and Stanley Plumly have found her work to be intelligent, compassionate, precise, lovely, carnal, mortal and filled with ironic music. Angela Sorby from *The Chicago Review* praises *Red under the Skin* because it is consistent in its bodily-based voice and substantial in its content. Sorby revels in Sajé's ability to keep from straining any of her points, calling the work "smart" and "sexy" (99).

Judith Vollmer, in her review essay for *Poet Lore*, also praises Sajé's content for its particulars. Vollmer writes that even though so many writers of late have taken race, class, and/or gender as their topics and even though so many critics have seen these topics too many times, Sajé has a way of making this subject matter wild again (72). Vollmer views *Red under the Skin* as a book with tremendous range and a provocative sense of the relentless (73).

Sajé is clearly a poet to watch as she explores further what it means to exist and to desire while in the particular bodies we each inhabit.

BIBLIOGRAPHY

Works by Natasha Sajé

Red under the Skin. Pittsburgh, PA: University of Pittsburgh Press, 1994.
"A Minor Riot at the Mint." *Ploughshares* 24.4 (1998–99).

"Channel." *New Republic* 15 Sept. 2000.
"Wonders of the Invisible World." *Paris Review* 160 (2001).
"Bend." *Kenyon Review* 22.3–4 (2001).

Studies of Natasha Sajé

"Poetry: Adele Slaughter, Michael Jay McClure, Natasha Sajé, Jane Hilberry." *The Virginia Quarterly Review* 70.4 (1994): 663.
Sorby, Angela. Review of *Red under the Skin*, by Natasha Sajé. *Chicago Review* 41.1 (1995): 97–99.
Vollmer, Judith. "Delicious Abandon Its Sustenance, and Nerve." *Poet Lore* 91.31 (1996): 70–73.

MARY JO SALTER (1954–)

Isaac Cates

BIOGRAPHY

Mary Jo Salter, one of the most artful and accomplished poets identified with "The New Formalism," has at this writing published four books of poems and currently serves as one of the editors of *The Norton Anthology of Poetry*. She was born August 15, 1954, in Grand Rapids, Michigan, and grew up there, in Detroit, Michigan, and in Baltimore, Maryland. Her mother, the painter Lormina Paradise Salter, appears frequently in her poems; her father Albert Gregory Salter, an advertising executive, manifests as a tense and abstracted figure in her recent "Home Movies: A Sort of Ode," and as a palpable absence in "Libretto" (*A Kiss in Space*).

Salter attended Harvard University, studying under Robert Fitzgerald and Elizabeth Bishop and earning her BA in 1976. At Harvard she also encountered the poet Brad Leithauser, who later—in 1980, two years after Salter returned from her MA at New Hall, Cambridge—became her husband. After her return from England, while Leithauser was earning his JD, Salter worked at Harvard as an instructor in expository writing and as a staff editor at the *Atlantic Monthly*.

Shortly after their marriage, the couple left for a three-year stay in Kyoto, Japan, where Salter taught English as a foreign language. In 1983, on her return from Japan, Salter won the Discovery/*The Nation* Prize and a National Endowment for the Arts Fellowship. Details from her time in Kyoto provide the final section of her first book of poems, *Henry Purcell in Japan* (1985).

In 1984 she and Leithauser joined the faculty at Mount Holyoke College, Massachusetts, where they continue to teach, with frequent years abroad. They have resided in Rome (1985), London (1986), and Reykjavik (1989, with an Ingram Merrill Fellowship)—and twice in Paris (1992–94, with a Guggenheim Fellowship; 1996–97, with the Amy Lowell Traveling Fellowship). Salter's next three books describe these foreign locales: Rome and London in *Unfinished Painting* (1989), Reykjavik in *Sunday Skaters* (1994), and Paris in the most recent, *A Kiss in Space* (1999). From 1992–

95, she was the poetry editor for *The New Republic*, and she served as the the editor for nineteenth- and twentieth-century American and Canadian poets in *The Norton Anthology of Poetry* (fourth edition, 1996). She continues to live in South Hadley, Massachusetts, with Leithauser and their daughters Emily and Hilary.

MAJOR WORKS AND THEMES

Salter organizes her books so that each centers on a recurring motif or image, but she also returns in each book to a handful of central questions and themes. *Henry Purcell in Japan*, for example, is uniquely concerned with reading the unfamiliar: from parsing another culture's constellations or gradually understanding kanji ideographs, characters that carry ideas not words, in "Japanese Characters," to watching a snowfall transform or distort a familiar landscape in "Inch by Inch." In "On Reading a Writer's Letters," the unnamed deceased writer leaves her readers only "lines of a character nobody knew" completely except the writer herself, and often in *Henry Purcell*, the text—whether a postcard, a display at the Hiroshima museum in "Welcome to Hiroshima," or the vertical grave markers of the gorgeous title poem—cannot be read or interpreted entirely.

In *Unfinished Painting*, the partiality of interpretation is more often the fault of the text or artifact. In the opening piece, "The Rebirth of Venus," as in the title poem, we are faced with an unfinished painting, a work of art that will never be finished. The earlier poem describes a sidewalk chalk artist copying Botticelli's *Birth of Venus*. Salter praises the anonymous artist's care, which leads him to work deliberately despite the threat of rain, and his vision, which shows him faces on the sidewalk among the future's black umbrellas. The title poem describes a painting (which appears on the book's dust jacket) of Salter's brother as a boy, painted by her mother. Her mother seems to have left the piece unfinished partly because motherhood demanded too much of her time (raising "the real boy" takes time away from the portrait) and partly because she was (unlike the anonymous sidewalk artist) doubtful of having an audience for such a domestic work. Salter, in retrospect, provides that sensitive audience; one of the book's two sequences is a heartfelt elegy for her mother. Another section is a nine-part elegy for a Japanese friend who committed suicide, a sequence of remembrances for a life that tragically echoes the unfinishedness of the painting or the chalk drawing.

Sunday Skaters in its turn has a particular concern for time—clock-faces appear in "Lines Written on Your Face," "The Twelfth Year," and the title poem; several of the other poems treat time in retrospect ("Inside the Midget") or in historical span ("The Hand of Thomas Jefferson"). *A Kiss in Space* has as a central motif brief but consequential contact, whether between the astronaut Norman Thagard and the cosmonaut Yelena Kondakova in the title poem, between the *Titanic* and the iceberg in "A Leak Somewhere," or among Alexander Graham Bell, Helen Keller, and Arthur Conan Doyle in the book's central sequence, "Alternating Currents."

Focusing on these themes, however, or on the longer poetic sequences that announce them, evades or ignores one of Salter's recurring questions, which is almost a condition of her peripatetic life: a tension between the foreign and the domestic. This tension is felt strongly in each of her books and may be analogous to the contrary claims, for a poet, of description and emotion. Here Salter owes much to her teacher Elizabeth Bishop, though Bishop allowed relatively little of her private life into her poems. Salter has acknowledged this debt, pointing to unconscious borrowings even in her BA thesis (which was titled, as if in tribute, "The Map Collector"). When Salter describes Japanese grammar reversing like the nap of velvet, its "shade of meaning" changing when she touches it ("Japanese Characters" *Henry Purcell*), or a tall joey nursing from its mother's pouch as someone rummaging in a purse ("Kangaroo," *A Kiss in Space*), we can feel Bishop's gift for apt metaphor, for careful observation of the genuinely foreign. When Salter, mysteriously alone in a New Hampshire coffee shop in "Collage," finally asks the surprising ultimate question of travel—who Salter the traveler truly *is*—we hear Bishop in the query if not, perhaps, in the answer Salter finds (*A Kiss in Space*).

While each of Salter's books narrates another segment of her two-decade travelogue, each also holds (often in a central section) poems of pure domesticity. We are reminded that she travels as a resident and, unlike Bishop, with a growing family. *Henry Purcell in Japan* shows us her trip with Leithauser to secure a marriage license ("At City Hall"); *Sunday Skaters* then reveals tension in their developing marriage ("The Twelfth Year"). Their daughter Emily has grown, through the books, from an unborn child ("Expectancy," *Henry Purcell*) to a vocal infant ("Emily Wants to Play," *Unfinished Painting*), to a teen alive and separate enough to surprise her mother's expectations ("A Fracture," *Sunday Skaters*). Hilary, five years Emily's junior, also appears as a teething child ("Hilary in Her Glory," *Sunday Skaters*) and, later, as a girl old enough to read to herself, so her mother cannot know the contents of her book ("Marco Polo," *A Kiss in Space*). These domestic poems usually give little hint at location, involved instead with Salter's sentiments as a wife or mother, using household details sometimes as quotidian as a refrigerator magnet made by her daughter ("Up and Down," *A Kiss in Space*) to evoke, for example, the complex of love and nostalgia a parent feels for a growing child. The magnet is the outline of her daughter's hand; Salter wonders when she started to see the magnet as waving goodbye.

Salter thus presents a double persona in each of her books: she is at once a careful, detached observer of details abroad and a caring, devoted mother and wife. By the standards of contemporary magazine verse, the domestic poems (generally shorter, less detailed, less ironic) may seem minor by comparison, but they complicate Salter's descriptive poems in a necessary way. The almost reliquary child's wristwatch in "Welcome to Hiroshima" is all the more unsettling—and the splendid dolls in "Among the *Ningyo*," all the more charming—when we recall that their observer is an expectant mother (*Henry Purcell*); the restaurant interior in "Hail in Honfleur" (*A Kiss in Space*) seems to gain a quick romantic charge from the earlier "Inside the Midget" (*Sunday Skaters*), which describes a deli that had been a site of courtship for Salter and Leithauser.

There is another tension between the domestic and the descriptive, however, palpable in "Unfinished Painting" and informing the conclusion of Salter's essay "A Poem of One's Own" (1991): the danger (implied, perhaps, in the slow but steady pace of Salter's publication) that motherhood and marriage may steal time from art. She notes that "the list of the best poets in our language" can be seen as "a nearly unbroken catalog of childlessness" (34)—that almost none of our major poets have been mothers—and wonders whether there is a necessary relation here.

Salter announces, earlier in this essay, that she is uneasy with the label "woman poet," that she wishes it were possible to write (or read) without owning a limited identity, "and yet, and yet. (Whenever we take up the slippery question of gender, there must be another 'and yet.')" (30). The double demands on her attention, from the domestic and the artistic, from the personal and the foreign, shape her poems both in theme and in the process of their production. The desire to be merely the poetic eye, like Keats's dream of the chameleon poet, may finally be unattainable. As she admits lightly in "A Benediction" (*Sunday Skaters*), Salter had to pay a sitter for the time to write the very verses we're reading.

CRITICAL RECEPTION

Salter's reviewers inevitably focus first on her technical proficiency. Even a cursory glance at her books reveals Salter's dedication to form, and her work has appeared in the New Formalist anthologies *Rebel Angels: 25 Poets of the New Formalism* (edited by Mark Jarman and David Mason 1996) and *A Formal Feeling Comes: Poems in Form by Contemporary Women* (edited by Annie Finch 1994). However, Salter is not entirely comfortable with value placed on form for form's sake. Although her stanzas are often strictly metered, and although she has published three villanelles and two sonnets, she does not seem to share the dedication to traditional forms visible in such poets as Molly Peacock or Marilyn Hacker. Salter prefers more open forms: blank verse, nonce-stanzas, or quatrains with shifting rhyme-schemes. Henry Taylor has written that she favors a form that "is pleasantly difficult to pin down" (13). In the introduction to her selection in *A Formal Feeling Comes*, Salter writes that a true poet "seeks a finish that may employ, but goes beyond, the conventional tools" (190); that is, rhyme or meter may help to create the "beautiful surface" she advocates, but they are by no means sufficient as the only tools. Salter's essay on Emily Dickinson's wordplay, "Puns and Accordions" (1990), announces a few subtler tricks of "finishing" that surface, and we can see Salter using similar techniques when we see the *hail halt* (in "Hail in Honfleur," *A Kiss in Space*)—or when, floating over Chartres in a hot-air balloon in "Fire-Breathing Dragon" (*A Kiss in Space*), she speaks of the cathedral as "a towering flamboyance." (In *flamboyance* we hear both the French *flambeau* and the *buoyancy* that keeps the balloon aloft.)

A handful of Salter's critics have faulted her for being too adept, or at times *merely* adept: David Lehman has noted a "tendency to slide into gentility" (143), and Langdon Hammer has written that in her work "the intelligence is so wry, . . . the tone so unfailingly polite, it can feel like the 1950s all over again" (132). However, if Salter is susceptible to this criticism, it should also recall the poets she names, in her brief essay "Poets and Parents" (1995), as ideal and actual audiences for her work: James Merrill and Amy Clampitt. She praises neither for mere formal brilliance but singles out Merrill for his "high standards for metaphor and mischief" and Clampitt for, among other virtues, her "microscopically detailed vision" (46). Both of these praises could also be offered to Salter's teacher Elizabeth Bishop. Salter's careful, clever, rigorous forms aspire to the virtues of all three senior poets; Merrill, Clampitt, or Bishop might wear Lehman's derisive "gentility," in perhaps a different sense, as a compliment.

BIBLIOGRAPHY

Works by Mary Jo Salter

Henry Purcell in Japan. New York: Knopf, 1985.
The Moon Comes Home. New York: Random House, 1989. (children's book)

Unfinished Painting. New York: Knopf, 1989.
"Puns and Accordions: Emily Dickinson and the Unsaid." *Yale Review* 79 (1990): 188–221. (criticism)
"A Poem of One's Own." *New Republic*, 4 March 1991, 30–34. (essay)
"Thick-Skinned." *New Republic*, 6 July 1992, 42. (essay)
Sunday Skaters. New York: Knopf, 1994.
"Poets and Parents." *New Republic*, 6 March 1995, 46. (essay)
A Kiss in Space. New York: Knopf, 1999; Lancashire, UK: Arc Publications, 2000.

Studies of Mary Jo Salter

Benfey, Christopher. "Dickinson's Children." Review of *Unfinished Painting*, by Mary Jo Salter. *New Republic*, 17–24 July 1989, 31–32.
Hammer, Langdon. Review of *A Formal Feeling Comes*, ed. Annie Finch, and *Sunday Skaters*, by Mary Jo Salter. *Yale Review* 83.1 (1995): 126–36.
Lehman, David. "The Not-So-New Formalism." Review of *Unfinished Painting*, by Mary Jo Salter. *Michigan Quarterly Review* 29 (1990): 140–44.
Phillips, Robert. "Utterly Unlike." Review of *A Kiss in Space*, by Mary Jo Salter. *Hudson Review* 52 (2000): 689–90.
Shaw, Robert B. Review of *Sunday Skaters*, by Mary Jo Salter. *Poetry* 166 (1995): 109.
Taylor, Henry. "Faith and Practice: The Poems of Mary Jo Salter." *The Hollins Critic* 37.1 (2000): 1–18.
Walzer, Kevin. *The Ghost of Tradition: Expansive Poetry and Postmodernism*. Ashland, OR: Story Line Press, 1998. 72–84.

SONIA SANCHEZ (1934–)

Sister Shiree Sarana and Catherine Cucinella

BIOGRAPHY

Sonia Sanchez, "protest" poet, playwright, essayist, educator, and author of short stories and children's books, was born on September 9, 1934, in Birmingham, Alabama, to Wilson L. Driver and Lena Jones Driver, who died in childbirth when Sonia was a year old. After her mother's death, Sonia and her older sister lived with their paternal grandmother, Elizabeth "Mama" Driver. When her grandmother died, six-year-old Sonia lived with several people until 1943 when her father took the girls to live in Harlem with him and his third wife. Sanchez says that she began writing poetry after the death of her grandmother because the loss "made [her] begin that whole process of writing things down" (Kelly 680).

Sanchez attended and graduated in 1955 from Hunter College in New York with a BA in political science, and she studied writing at New York University under Louise Brogan, who taught Sanchez craft and form. During this time, Sanchez, along with Haki R. Madhubuti (Don L. Lee), Amiri Baraka (LeRoi Jones), and others, participated in weekly poetry workshops. This early workshop experience informs Sanchez's view of poetry as craft—a craft that one has to learn—a craft that depends on discipline. When asked about her early literary and cultural influences, Sanchez points to the "ordinary" people who made up her everyday life: the person who gave her her first book to read; the bookstore owner who introduced her to books about blacks in the Caribbean; the man who taught her about African American history; the black woman librarian who gave Sanchez African American poetry to read. Sanchez read Langston Hughes, Countee Cullen, Paul Laurence Dunbar, Margaret Walker, and Gwendolyn Brooks. Sanchez also acknowledges the influence of Martin Luther King, Jr., and Malcolm X on both her politics and her poetry (Kelly 680–81).

In the 1960s, Sanchez worked in the civil rights movement, held integrationist ideas, aligned with the Congress of Racial Equality (CORE), and published her first poems in various journals. By the end of the 1960s, influenced by the separatist views of

Malcolm X, Sanchez moved away from her integrationist stance, and her first book of poetry, *Homecoming* (1969), reflects her social activism and black militancy. During this time, Sanchez taught at Downtown Community School (1965–67), New York, San Francisco State College (1967–68), and at the University of Pittsburgh (1969–70). She also developed curricula for black studies programs, helped to establish one of the first black studies programs in the country at San Francisco State, and was the first professor to offer a seminar on African American women writers and poets ("The Black Woman" in 1969 at the University of Pittsburgh). Sanchez married and divorced Albert Sanchez, and in 1968, she married poet Etheridge Knight whom she later divorced in the 1970s. Sanchez has three children, Anita, Morani Neusi, and Nungu Neusi.

The 1970s proved a time of broadened vision for Sanchez. She converted to Islam in 1971, traveled to China and the Caribbean in 1973 and to Cuba in 1979. Sanchez left the Nation of Islam in 1975 because of women's inferior status and, as she told Susan Kelly in a 2000 interview, it saw her as a revolutionary pan-Africanist and socialist (683). She also taught at Rutgers University, Manhattan Community College, and Amherst College during the 1970s. In 1977 Shanchez moved to Philadelphia and began teaching at Temple University where she is the Laura H. Cornell Professor of English. Besides the publication of *We BaddDDD People* in 1970, this decade also saw the publication of *Love Poems* and *A Blues Book for Blue Black Magical Women* (1973), and *I've Been a Woman: New and Selected Poems* (1978). Deeply committed to her belief that black people must understand their black cultural identity, Sanchez began writing fiction and poetry for children during this time.

Sanchez's other volumes of poetry include *Homegirls & Handgrenades* (1984), winner of the American Book award in 1985; *Under a Soprano Sky* (1987); *Does Your House Have Lions?* (1995), nominated for both the NAACP Image Award and National Book Critics Award; *Wounded in the House of a Friend* (1995); *Like the Singing Coming Off the Drum: Love Poems* (1998); and *Shake Loose My Skin: New and Selected Poems* (1999). Sanchez's list of honors attests to her literary and academic successes: a PEN Writing Award, 1969; a National Institute of the Arts and Letters grant, 1970; a National Endowment for the Arts Award, 1978–79; a Tribute to Black Women Award (Smith College), 1982; a Lucretia Mott Award, 1984; an International Women's Award from the Mayor's Commission for Women, Philadelphia, 1987; an Oni Award from the International Black Women's Congress, 1992; a Roots Award from the Pan-African Studies Community Education Program, 1993; a PEN Fellowship in the arts, 1993–94, and a Legacy Award from Jomandi Productions, 1995.

MAJOR WORKS AND THEMES

Sonia Sanchez deals consistently and unwaveringly in her work and in her activism with being female and black in a society structured by racism, sexism, and classism. In her essay "The Blue/Black Poetics of Sonia Sanchez," Regina B. Jennings provides a concise list of Sanchez's thematic concerns: "love, harmony, race, unification, myth, and history," and according to Jennings, "[Sanchez's] poetic personas are diverse, incorporating themes from China, to Nicaragua, to Africa" (120). These thematic concerns also include a return to and understanding of blackness, the importance of family, blacks' commitment to struggle, and the politics of language.

This concern with the politics of language marks *Homecoming*, as the poems in this volume begin the legitimatization of Black English by taking "Black speech and put[ting] it in the context of world literature" (Madhubuti 421). Sanchez uses this urban black speech to underscore the homecoming to which the title refers: "the act of returning home as a rejection of fantasy and an acceptance of involvement" (Williams 432). This involvement demands a return to "things" black—speech, music, rhythm—and a rejection of the values of white America. Because *Homecoming* and *We a BaddDDD People* emerge out of the Black Arts movement, they respond to the political and social unrest of the 1960s.

Much of the anger, conflict, and revolution of the 1960s reconfigures into a sense of black empowerment in the 1970s, although blacks remained disenfranchised and marginalized within white America. However, Sanchez's work during the 1970s manifests this tone of empowerment as well as reflecting on a personal, emotional, and spiritual journey: *A Blues Book for Blue Black Magical Women*, *Love Poems*, and *I've Been a Woman*. Each volume continues the themes and concerns of Sanchez's earlier work, yet these volumes demonstrate the range and maturity of the poet's craft. In *Love Poems* Sanchez evokes a lyricism that speaks movingly of passages, changes, and transformations in her life. Yet Madhubuti rightly notes that while much of Sanchez's work is autobiographical, the autobiographical does not limit as it is not "only about Sonia Sanchez" (420). Thus, Sanchez can write about an ex-husband, a troubled marriage, a vexed father-daughter relationship in such poems as "Father and Daughter" and "Poem No. 2" from *Love Poems* without limiting a reader's experience.

The connections that Sanchez seeks within and across her poetry resound in *Love Poems* as they do in *A Blues Book for Blue Black Magical Women* and *I've Been a Woman*. *A Blues Book* encapsulates Sanchez's spiritual autobiography. Presented in five parts, this volume moves from birth to rebirth. Sanchez points to *A Blues Book* as "about a woman who has been in the struggle" (Tate 140), and in the essay "Ruminations/Reflections" (1984), she writes, "In *A Blues Book for Blue Black Magical Women*, I attempt to show a Black woman moving/loving/living in America and the consequences of that movement" (417). Completed during her years in the Nation of Islam, this volume bespeaks her commitment to it; however, *A Blues Book*'s dominant theme remains the spiritual and emotional journey of a black woman.

In *I've Been a Woman*, Sanchez begins her use of haiku and tanka, forms that appear consistently in her later works. The poems in the section entitled "Haikus/Tankas & Other Syllables," according to David Williams, "are an accumulation of moments that define love, age sorrow, and pride in terms of action" (466). In this volume, Sanchez transforms the haiku through her "conscious decision to imbue [it] with Afrocentric motifs" (De Lancey "Refusing" 23). Sometimes Sanchez uses conjunction, simile, and metaphor to alter the structure of the haiku, but more often, the poet textualizes the form through an inclusion of " 'African' ideas," as well as a black and feminine ethic (Melham 89). Thus, this volume continues Sanchez's concern with a poetics that keeps the political in plain view.

Homegirls & Handgrenades, one of Sanchez's most acclaimed volumes, contains both fiction and poetry. The titles of its four sections—"The Power of Love," "Blues Is Bullets," "Beyond the Fallout," and "Grenades Are Not Free"—indicate the thematic concerns of *Homegirls*. This mixed genre collection opens with poems affirming love's enduring force: poems not only about lovers or for lovers, but rather poems about the existence of love. "The Power of Love" begins with "Poem No. 10," which asks if love will stay in the reality of the speaker's presence, and ends with " 'Just Don't Never Give Up on Love,' " a prose piece that relates a conversation between an old woman and a young mother. The affirmations of this first section give way in "Blues Is Bullets" to the pain, betrayals, and disappointments of love. As with all her poetry, Sanchez uses stylistic precision and cutting language to particularize experiences while simultaneously equating the particular to the social, writing in "Poem Written after Reading Wright's 'American Hunger,' " about a man's "easy desire/to ride" "a simple woman" dismissing her as callously as does the society who casts away blackness and femaleness (17). In "After Saturday Night Comes Sunday," another prose piece, a woman, finding both her junkie husband and all her money gone, stands naked on her porch, vulnerable in her nakedness as both female and black (35). The power of Sanchez's poetics emerges at these moments when the personal and the political merge, and this merger propels the rest of *Homegirls & Handgrenades*, finding final articulation in the last section "Grenades Are Not Free." This section opens with a prose piece "Bubba," which tells of Harlem, of the South, and finally of dreams unrealized. Sanchez closes "Grenades Are Not Free" with two very powerful pieces: "A Letter to Dr. Martin Luther King" and "MIA's." The former details the decade after King's assassination, ending with a note of hope for the coming day. The latter addresses those missing in action in Atlanta, Johannesburg, and El Salvador, widening the political scope of suffering and oppression.

The poetry volumes that follow Homegirls—*Under a Soprano Sky*, *Does Your House Have Lions?*, *Wounded in the House of a Friend*, *Like the Singing Coming Off the Drum*, and *Shake Loose My Skin*—expand many of Sanchez's earlier themes, emphasize her focus on form and precision of language, and introduce new themes and techniques. *Under a Soprano Sky* utilizes haikus, tankas, blues, as well as more prosaic forms, and this volume exhibits a womanist aspect in its elegies for and tributes to a wide range of persons: her Grandmother Driver, her brother, victims of Hiroshima, a Vietnam vet, a black man, members of MOVE (a back-to-nature movement) killed by police in Philadelphia, John Brown, and Paul Robeson. The introspective woman's voice that emerges in this text carries a tone of political and social activism so prevalent in all Sanchez's work. In *Does Your House Have Lions?* (a telling of Sanchez's brother's life, his battle with AIDS, and his death), Sanchez utilizes a jazzlike structure, introducing four different voices that correspond with each of the four sections of the book.

Sanchez dedicates her next collection *Wounded in the House of a Friend* to Alice Walker (Aliciacita) and Robert Allen (Roberto), and in this volume, she once again utilizes a variety of poetic forms and blurs generic boundaries. For example, "Wounded in the House of a Friend," the only poem in Part I, includes poetry, prose, and drama as it articulates the wounding of and wounds caused by love through deceit, rejection, and betrayal. The poem's structure relies on sets, with each set corresponding to the various lovers as well as to the poet's voice. This volume, however, does not focus exclusively on the issue of "wounded" love. Joyce Ann Joyce writes in her review of the poem, "This collection contains more poems that highlight and comment positively on the accomplishments of famous contemporary African Americans than any of Sanchez's previous volumes" (377). These famous African Americans include Bill Cosby, Susan Taylor, Johnnetta Cole, Bernice Reagan, and Toni Morrison, and her celebration of these people serves a dual purpose: through them she celebrates black life and history as well as black women, and through these poems she condemns the effects of slavery (drug abuse, abuse of children and of women, black self-hatred, and black-on-black crime) (Joyce 377).

Sanchez's body of work reflects her continued perfection of form as it reconfigures and revitalizes ongoing thematic concerns. Although her most recent collection, *Shake Loose My Skin*, contains Sanchez's new poems only in section VII, these new poems recontextualize the poet's concerns with black political, social, and personal life in the terms of the contemporary. The section opens with "Mrs. Benita Jones Speaks," a prose piece, that asks, "Why?": Why a black woman, mother of three, with a decent job cannot live in a white neighborhood? Why must she live always "trailed by myths that this country has invented about her?" (141). Mrs. Benita Jones demands an answer, and she offers one, amazed at the disappearance of God. Mrs. Benita Jones does not let her listeners off the hook, nor does Sonia Sanchez.

CRITICAL RECEPTION

Most reviewers and scholars of Sanchez's work acknowledge her contributions to and influence upon African American literature, and they identify her as a political poet deeply concerned with the issues that face black people and especially those facing black women. Scholarship on Sanchez focuses on her womanist voice, her use of form, African influences in her work, and her unwavering commitment to address systems of oppression. In her review of *Wounded in the House of a Friend*, Joyce Ann Joyce captures the consensus of most reviewers of Sanchez's poetry: "Even a cursory glance at her poetry from *Homecoming* to this new collection reveals that [Sanchez] has always written about the most personal of issues and confirms her idea that the personal is political" (377).

Reviewers of Sanchez's poetry find it "complex, disturbing, challenging," often negotiating between "awakening political consciousness and . . . imagination to order or shape words and create sounds that represent the highest degree of poetic art" (Asim 27, Joyce 376). Melham finds *Love Poems* "marked by simplicity and delicacy, and the poems mov[ing] in clear images that swirl about the reader" (88). These reviewers and critics react to Sanchez's success at melding form and content and at presenting the political in images and languages that startle and disturb while simultaneously evoking a sense of the aesthetic that comforts and promises.

Ultimately, her works recognize the reaffirming aspects of valuing a black heritage and of claiming subjectivity as a black man or woman. Thus, Sonia Sanchez writes to, about, and for black people, while simultaneously reaching beyond the constraints of particularized experiences. Acknowledging her white audience, Sanchez tells Claudia Tate, "I've always known that if you write from a black experience, you're writing from a universal experience as well. . . . I know what being universal means. I know you don't have to whitewash yourself to be universal" (142). Sonia Sanchez does not whitewash herself, her language, her politics, or her poetics.

BIBLIOGRAPHY

Works by Sonia Sanchez

Homecoming. Highland Park, MI: Broadside Press, 1969.
We a BaddDDD People. Highland Park, MI: Broadside Press, 1970.

It's a New Day: Poems for Young Brothas and Sistuhs. Highland Park, MI: Broadside Press, 1971.

The Adventures of Fat Head, Small Head, and Square Head. New York: Third Press, 1973. (juvenile)

A Blues Book for Blue Black Magical Women. Highland Park, MI: Broadside Press, 1973.

Love Poems. New York: Third Press, 1973.

I've Been a Woman: New and Selected Poems. San Francisco: Black Scholar Press, 1978.

A Sound Investment and Other Stories. San Francisco: Black Scholar Press, 1979.

Homegirls & Handgrenades. New York: Thunder's Mouth Press, 1984.

"Ruminations/Reflections." In *Black Women Writers (1950–1980): A Critical Evaluation*, edited by Mari Evans. Garden City, NY: Anchor-Doubleday, 1984. 415–18. (essay)

Under a Soprano Sky. Trenton, NJ: Africa World Press, 1987.

Does Your House Have Lions? Boston: Beacon Press, 1995.

Wounded in the House of a Friend. Boston: Beacon Press, 1995.

Like the Singing Coming Off the Drum: Love Poems. Boston: Beacon Press, 1998.

Shake Loose My Skin: New and Selected Poems. Boston: Beacon Press, 1999.

Studies of Sonia Sanchez

Alim, H. Samy. "360 Degreez of Black Art Comin at You: Sista Sonia Sanchez and the Dimensions of a Black Arts Continuum." *BMA* 6.1 (2000): 15–33.

Asim, Jabari. Review of *Does Your House Have Lions?* by Sonia Sanchez. *American Visions* 15.1 (1998): 27–28.

Badejo, Diedre L. "Birthing Orality in Mother Tongue Eubonics: Sistah Sonia Speaks." *Literary Griot* 10.2 (1998): 85–94.

Baker, Houston A., Jr. "Our Lady Sonia Sanchez and the Writing of a Black Renaissance." In *Black Feminist Criticism and Critical Theory*, edited by Joe Weixlmann and Houston A. Baker, Jr. Greenwood, FL: Penkevill, 1988. 169–202.

Crown, Kathleen. "A Collector of Shouts: Black Spirit, Black Arts, and the Poetry of Sonia Sanchez." *BMA* 3.2 (1998): 25–60.

De Lancey, Frenzella Elaine. "Beauty Practiced as the Tree: Of Scrupulous Trees and Poets and Legends and Legacies: Sonia Sanchez and Patricia A. Johnson." *BMA* 5.1 (1999): 25–57.

———. "Refusing to Be Boxed In: Sonia Sanchez's Transformation of the Hiaku Form." In *Language and Literature in the African Imagination*, edited by Carol Aisha Blackshire-Belay. Westport, CT: Greenwood, 1992. 21–36.

———. "Sonia Sanchez's *Blues Book for Blue Black Magical Women* and Sister Souljah's *The Coldest Winter Ever*: Progressive Phases amid Modernist Shadows and Postmodernist Acts." *BMA* 6.1 (2000): 123–44.

Evans, Mari, ed. *Black Women Writers (1950–1980): A Critical Evaluation*. Garden City, NY: Anchor, 1984.

Gabbin, Joanne Veal. "The Southern Imagination of Sonia Sanchez." In *Southern Women Writers: The New Generation*, edited by Tonette Bond Inge. Tuscaloosa: University of Alabama Press, 1990. 180–203.

Gray, Cecil Conteen. "To Change the World, to Change the Self: Social Transformation, Love and More Love, and Subterranean Spiritual Threads within the Work of Sonia Sanchez." *BMA* 3.2 (1998): 1–24.

Jennings, Regina. "The Blue/Black Poetics of Sonia Sanchez." In *Language and Literature in the African Imagination*, edited by Carol Aisha Blackshire-Belay. Westport, CT: Greenwood, 1992. 119–32.

Joyce, Joyce Ann. Review of *Wounded in the House of Friend*, by Sonia Sanchez. *African American Review* 31 (1997): 376–78.

Kelly, Susan. "Discipline and Craft: An Interview with Sonia Sanchez." *African American Review* 4 (2000): 679–87.

Madhubuti, Haki. "Sonia Sanchez: The Bringer of Memories." In *Black Women Writers (1950–1980): A Critical Evaluation,* edited by Mari Evans. Garden City, NY: Anchor-Doubleday, 1984. 419–32.

Melham, D. H. "Sonia Sanchez: Will and Spirit." *MELUS* 12.3 (1985): 73–98.

Rome, Danielle Alyce. "An Interview with Sonia Sanchez." In *Speaking of the Short Story: Interviews with Contemporary Writers*, edited by Farhat Iftekharuddin, Mary Rohrberger, and Maurice Lee. Jackson: University Press of Mississippi, 1997. 229–36.

Salaam, Kalamu ya. "Love and Liberation: Sonia Sanchez's Literary Uses of the Personal." *BMA* 3.1 (1997): 57–120.

Saunders, James Robert. "Sonia Sanchez's *Homegirls and Handgrenades*: Recalling Toomer's Cane." *MELUS* 15.1 (1988): 73–82.

Spady, James. "The Centrality of Black Language in the Discourse Strategies and Poetic Force of Sonia Sanchez and Rap Artists." *BMA* 6.1 (2000): 47–72.

———. "Sonia Sanchez: The Consummate Teacher." *BMA* 3.1 (1997): 14–23.

Springer, Glenda. "Sonia Sanchez Represents the Black Woman as a Divine Spiritual Expression." *BMA* 3.2 (1998): 61–69.

Tate, Claudia. "Sonia Sanchez." In *Black Women Writers at Work*, edited by Claudia Tate. New York: Continuum, 1983. 132–48.

Williams, David. "The Poetry of Sonia Sanchez." In *Black Women Writers (1950–1980): A Critical Evaluation*, edited by Mari Evans. Garden City, NY: Anchor-Doubleday, 1984. 433–48.

LESLIE SCALAPINO (1947–)

David Clippinger

BIOGRAPHY

Leslie Scalapino long has been regarded as a central figure in the West Coast Language poetry movement that emerged in the late 1970s. Nearly all of her life, Scalapino has lived on the West Coast, and except for brief stints, she has lived and worked in the greater San Francisco Bay area.

Born on July 25, 1947, in Santa Barbara, California, to Robert Anthony (a professor) and Dee Scalapino (a singer), Leslie Scalapino was raised in Berkeley, California. After graduating from Berkeley High School, Scalapino left the area to attend Reed College, Portland, Oregon, only to return to the University of California, Berkeley, where she earned an MA—an experience, she remarks, that was "so awful that it has not yet been erased from memory" (*How Phenomena Appear to Unfold*, back page, author's biography).

In June 1968, Scalapino married Wesley St. John; their marriage lasted roughly five years, and they were divorced in 1973. During the early 1970s, Scalapino divided her time between various part-time jobs and her poetry. Her first book of poetry, *O and Other Poems*, was first published in 1975, which was followed by *The Woman Who Could Read the Minds of Dogs* (1976) and *Instead of an Animal* (1977). In 1976 Scalapino was awarded her first (of two) National Endowment for the Arts fellowships, and her position within the West Coast Language movement that included Lyn Hejinian and Barrett Watten, as well as older San Francisco-based writers such as Philip Whalen, was established. Scalapino co-edited the journal *Foot* in 1979, which featured many of the West Coast Language poets, and that experience led to the establishment in 1986 of her own press, O Books, which is still in operation and is dedicated to publishing younger, emerging experimental poets.

During the 1980s, Scalapino's reputation was cemented by a list of substantial awards, including her second National Endowment for the Arts Fellowship as a Senior Fellow (1986); the Before Columbus Foundation Award (1988); the Lawrence Lipton

Award (1988); San Francisco State University Poetry Center Award (1988); and a Woodrow Wilson Fellowship. During that same time period, she was affiliated with various colleges and universities—most notably the New College of California; the San Francisco State University; University of California, San Diego; and Bard College, Annandale-on-Hudson, New York. Throughout the 1980s, Scalapino wrote and published four of her major works: *Considering How Exaggerated Music Is* (1982), *That They Were at the Beach—Aelotropic Series* (1985), *Way* (1988), and *How Phenomena Appear to Unfold* (1990).

In May 1987, Scalapino married Tom White, a biochemist, whom she met in 1974. They currently live in Oakland, California. Scalapino has continued to publish books of essays, poems, plays, novels, and collaborations and is regarded by many as one of the foremost avant-garde contemporary women poets.

MAJOR WORKS AND THEMES

Scalapino is a distinctively postmodern poet in that her work blurs the boundaries between genres—especially poetry and fiction—and has as its locus the hierarchy of social values and subjectivities. Furthermore, her work is process-centered, a theory in practice that refuses to privilege content over form. As she explains in her essay "How Phenomena Appear to Unfold" (from the book of the same title), "I am concerned in my own work with the sense that phenomena appear to unfold. (What it is or) how is it that the viewer sees the impression of history created, created by oneself though it's occurring outside" (119). The poems document the impression of sensory data, therefore, eschewing form and plot as a means of containing and definitively rendering the world. Plot, Scalapino remarks in her introduction to *The Front Matter, Dead Souls* (1996), is a "continual series of actions" (1), and the poems often emphasize the panoramic via the observations and reflections of her narrators as they meander through city streets observing the "continual" action of reality. The challenge for the reader is the act of confronting a text where the patterns of meaning mirror reality and have not been narrowed into a prescribed form—an "ordered" poetic rendering/condensation of reality. Such poetry is extremely challenging both linguistically and semantically and places Scalapino within a lineage of poetically innovative poets that stretches from Emily Dickinson to Gertrude Stein and H.D., and into the postmodern present with Lyn Hejinian, with whom Scalapino has collaborated.

From her first book, *O and Other Poems* (1975), to her most recent, *New Time* (1999), Scalapino's poetic project has been the consistent and sustained interrogation of the relationships between the world of phenomena and a narrator's consciousness of those events. In this sense, the works investigate the matrix of personal subjectivity and cultural discourse, which is presented as the integration of the narrativity of the novel with the elliptical and associatively loaded language of poetry. For example, "The Woman Who Could Read the Minds of Dogs," first published in 1976 and collected in *Considering How Exaggerated Music Is* (1982), highlights the memories and narratives of various men as they reflect upon their relationships with women, wives, fathers, and mothers. While the poem is "objective" in tone and focus—thereby avoiding a politically oriented didacticism—it brings into relief the impact of social and cultural values upon gender and subjectivity. In this sense, Scalapino's poetry emphasizes political issues without assuming an overtly political stance. Her poetry is a heightened socio-political consciousness that does not resort to telling the reader what to think.

Subsequently, at the heart of Scalapino's poetry is a social consciousness explicit in the act of seeing, and the poems refuse to be blind to social injustices that are often submerged in cultural consciousness and absent in so-called works of art. The book-length poem, *Way*, for example, focuses upon the economic imbalances of the Reagan era. Through the eyes and minds of a person who has been mugged, a waitress in a department store restaurant, a school-age child, and others, the poem presents images of homelessness against the backdrop of economic affluence, with housing projects juxtaposed with expensive cars and imported goods. *The Return of Painting, the Pearl, and Orion: A Trilogy* (1991), a novel, continues the exploration of the social and economic aspects of the American landscape, including the marginalized fringes of society—AIDS victims and the homeless. The portrait of America that Scalapino offers is a society constructed upon hypocrisy, lies, oppression, and a lack of human compassion.

Later works such as *New Time* and her collaborative works with Lyn Hejinian continue to push at what constitutes reality and consciousness. These poems and novels employ a language that is not constrained by the rules of syntax and therefore emphasizing how the real is constructed by social conventions, rules, and ideological beliefs that attempt to mediate the world. By disrupting language, Scalapino's poetry seeks to deconstruct the hierarchies of oppressive social values. In this regard, Scalapino's poetry is driven by an explicit socio-ethical agenda that has been the mainstay of the linguistically innovative and socially minded tradition of feminist Language Poetry.

CRITICAL RECEPTION

Critical attention to the work of Leslie Scalapino began about ten years after her first published book of poetry. Edith Jarolim's "No Satisfaction: The Poetry of Leslie Scalapino" was the first published essay devoted to Scalapino, which rightfully situated her poetry with that of the linguistically and socially charged agendas of the so-called Language Poets.

In 1991 Marjorie Perloff included extended discussions of Scalapino in *Radical Artifice: Writing Poetry in the Age of Media*. Perloff located Scalapino with a visually centered avant-garde poetry tradition including Gertrude Stein, John Cage, David Antin, and others. This linkage with such visually innovative poets emphasizes the predominance of sight in Scalapino's work and how visual images affect the form of her poetry. As such, Perloff locates Scalapino within the postmodern landscape that privileges the visual in billboards, advertisements, and television, and her scholarship traces how Scalapino's work is both a response to such visual data as well as a critique of contemporary culture dominated by surfaces.

Scalapino began to receive more critical attention in the 1990s, and essays including Joseph Conte's "Seriality and the Contemporary Long Poem" have reified Scalapino's place within an avant-garde/language-based poetry tradition. In 1992 the journal *Talisman* devoted a special issue to Scalapino, which includes many of the major critical readings of Scalapino's works, an engaging interview with Scalapino, as well as Scalapino's own essays and poems. Elisabeth Frost's important essay "Signifyin(g) on Stein: The Revisionist Poetics of Harryette Mullen and Leslie Scalapino" (1995) further reinforced Scalapino's place within a feminist poetic history that has its roots in Gertrude Stein.

While critical attention to Scalapino includes only fifteen or so essays in relation to over twenty-five years' worth of poetry, Scalapino has entered into the parlance of mainstream poetry, and her poetry and essays have appeared in such canonical magazines as the *American Poetry Review*. Her readership continues to grow, and one might expect that in the near future more scholarly works will be devoted to Scalapino's place within the American poetry landscape.

BIBLIOGRAPHY

Works by Leslie Scalapino

O and Other Poems. Berkeley, CA: Sandollar Press, 1975.

The Woman Who Could Read the Minds of Dogs. Berkeley, CA: Sandollar Press, 1976.

Instead of an Animal. Berkeley, CA: Poltroon Press, 1977.

This Eating and Walking at the Same Time Is Associated All Right. Bolinas, CA: Tombouctou Books, 1979.

Considering How Exaggerated Music Is. Berkeley, CA: North Point Press, 1982.

That They Were at the Beach—Aelotropic Series. Berkeley, CA: North Point Press, 1985.

Way. Berkeley, CA: North Point Press, 1988.

Crowd and Not Evening or Light. Oakland, CA: O Books/Sun & Moon Press, 1990.

How Phenomena Appear to Unfold. Elmwood, CT: Poets and Poets Press, 1990. (essays and plays)

The Return of Painting, The Pearl, and Orion: A Trilogy. Berkeley, CA: North Point Press, 1991. (novel)

Objects in the Terrifying Tense/Longing from Taking Place. New York: Roof Books, 1993. (essays)

Defoe. Los Angeles: Sun & Moon Press, 1994. (novel)

The Front Matter, Dead Souls. Hanover, NH: Wesleyan/University Press of New England, 1996.

Green and Black: Selected Poems. Jersey City, NJ: Talisman House Publishers, 1996.

New Time. Hanover, NH: Wesleyan/University Press of New England, 1999.

The Public World/ Syntactically Impermanence. Hanover, NH: Wesleyan/University Press of New England, 1999. (essays)

Sight. With Lyn Hejinian. Washington, D.C.: Edge, 1999.

Studies of Leslie Scalapino

Campbell, Bruce. "Neither In Nor Out: The Poetry of Leslie Scalapino." *Talisman* 8 (1992): 53–60.

Conte, Joseph M. "Seriality and the Contemporary Long Poem." *Sagetrieb* 11 (1992): 35–45.

Ellis, Stephen. "Lock-Step Chaos: Leslie Scalapino's Multiples of Time." *Talisman* 8 (1992): 63–66.

Frost, Elisabeth A. "Signifyin(g) on Stein: The Revisionist Poetics of Harryette Mullen and Leslie Scalapino." *Postmodern Culture* 5 (May 1995), n.p.

Hinton, Laura. "Formalism, Feminism, and Genre Slipping in the Poetic Writings of Leslie Scalapino." In *Women Poets of the Americas: Toward a Pan-American Gathering*, edited by Jacqueline Vaught Brogan and Cordelia Chávez Candelaria. Notre Dame, IN: University of Notre Dame Press, 1999. 130–45.

Jarolim, Edith. "No Satisfaction: The Poetry of Leslie Scalapino." *North Dakota Quarterly* 55 (1987): 268–275.

Nash, Susan Smith. "Magic and Mystery in Poetic Language: A Response to the Writings of Leslie Scalapino." *Talisman* 14 (1995): 90–100.

Perloff, Marjorie. *Radical Artifice: Writing Poetry in the Age of Media.* Chicago: University of Chicago Press, 1991. 49–51.

Ratcliffe, Stephen. "Listening to Reading." *Talisman* 8 (1992): 61–62.

Watten, Barrett. "The Political Economy and the Avant-Garde: A Note on Haim Steinbach and Leslie Scalapino." *Talisman* 8 (1992): 49–52.

ANNE GRAY HARVEY SEXTON (1928–1974)

Kathleen L. Nichols

BIOGRAPHY

The Pulitzer Prize-winning poet Anne Gray Harvey Sexton was born in Newton, Massachusetts, and raised in an affluent home in the Boston suburbs. However, the young Sexton felt unwanted by her parents, Mary Gray Staples and Ralph Churchill Harvey, who drank heavily. She did form a close attachment with her great-aunt ("Nana" in her poetry), but when the elderly woman had a breakdown and was institutionalized, Sexton blamed herself for causing her aunt's "madness." Diane Middlebrook's biography documents sexual abuse or, at the very least, highly inappropriate encounters between Sexton and several family members, behavior that Sexton later would act out in relation to her elder daughter, according to this daughter's Linda Gray Sexton, autobiography. The guilt and pervasive sense of loss stemming from these troubled family relationships form major themes in Sexton's confessional poetry.

The nineteen-year-old Sexton eloped with Alfred Muller Sexton II ("Kayo") who would eventually work in the Sexton woolen business. With the birth of their daughters in 1953 and 1955, Sexton became overwhelmed with the responsibilities of motherhood and marriage and was hospitalized several times for emotional problems and the first of her many suicide attempts. The emergence of the poet began when Sexton's psychiatrist ("Dr. Sidney Martin" in her poetry) encouraged her to write poetry as part of her therapy. By 1957 she had enrolled in John Holmes's poetry workshop at the Boston Center for Adult Education where she met poet Maxine Kumin, who became her lifelong friend and collaborator on several children's books. The following year she studied briefly with W. D. Snodgrass and enrolled in Robert Lowell's poetry seminar at Boston University, where she met Sylvia Plath and George Starbuck.

Sexton's first volume of poetry, *To Bedlam and Part Way Back* (1960), drew heavily on her psychiatric experiences. Her second volume, *All My Pretty Ones* (1962), was nominated for a National Book Award, and she won the Pulitzer Prize in 1967 for her third volume, *Live or Die* (1966). Despite her meteoric rise to fame, Sexton continued to need periodic hospitalization for mental problems, but in the productive years that followed, she formed a rock group; taught poetry writing at several colleges; worked on an autobiographical play produced off-Broadway, but never published, as *Mercy Street* in 1969; and published *Love Poems* (1969). *Transformations* (1971) gave a contemporary twist to the Brothers Grimm fairy tales and an operatic version was produced by the Minnesota Opera Company in 1973. Her last three prepared volumes of poetry—*The Book of Folly* (1972), *The Death Notebooks* (1974), and *The Awful Rowing toward God* (1975)—revealed a new emphasis on religious themes.

After Sexton divorced her husband in 1973, her life quickly fell apart, and she committed suicide in 1974. The official cause of death was carbon monoxide poisoning, but years of excessive drinking and prescription drug addiction probably played a significant role in her demise. Published posthumously, *45 Mercy Street* (1975) and *Words for Dr. Y* (1978) were compiled by her daughter from Sexton's drafts.

MAJOR WORKS AND THEMES

Sexton's first three volumes of poetry contain many of the autobiographical themes that preoccupied her throughout her poetic career: mental breakdown and recovery, parent-daughter relationships, and women's roles and identities. Repetitious stanza structures with complex rhyme patterns and meter are common in these early volumes, but Sexton experimented with a looser, more prosaic line, as well as a variety of voices ranging from the colloquial to the prophetic, in her later poetry, which includes critiques of cultural myths and her spiritual quests. Throughout her poetry, the highly original—even startlingly bizarre or surreal—metaphor is her forte.

Sexton's first volume of poetry, *To Bedlam and Part Way Back*, introduced the themes of madness and suicide that would become familiar staples to her readers over the years. "You, Dr. Martin," the opening poem, contrasts her god-like therapist moving freely through the mental institution with Sexton and the other inmates psychologically immobilized like a "row of moccasins" on a "silent shelf" (4). She confesses to the "father-doctor" in "Cripples and Other Stories" that her madness causes her to see "dead rats in toilets" (*Live or Die* 80), and she hears the siren voices of the spring leaves outside her window singing a death call to her in "Leaves that Talk" (*45 Mercy Street*). The conflicting impulses informing much of Sexton's poetry are succinctly summarized in the title of her third volume, *Live or Die*. She chooses life—"the excitable gift"—"Live" (90), but two other titles in the same collection are "For the Year of the Insane" and "Wanting to Die," while "The Addict" lovingly recounts her bedtime ritual for taking the sleeping pills that will kill her "in small amounts" (86). In the remarkable "Death Baby" sequence in *The Death Notebooks*, death is a frozen baby she carries within her. On the other hand, her journey toward death in her last prepared volume of poetry is characterized, according to the title, as *The Awful Rowing toward God*. This volume contains numerous animal and scatological metaphors, as did her earlier poems, expressing at times a suicidal self-loathing.

These themes closely link to the problematic family relationships Sexton explores in her poetry. One of her strongest poems, "The Double Image" (*To Bedlam*), painfully probes her relationship both with her mother and with her daughter Joy. This double relationship is brilliantly captured in the metaphor of the two portraits of Sexton and her mother hanging across the hall from each other, mirroring each other, just as her mother's cancer mirrors Sexton's suicidal impulses "as if death were catching" (56).

As Margaret Honton notes in "The Double Image and the Division of Parts," the key words describing the mother-daughter relationship here are "blame," "debt," and "guilt" (100). So that Sexton's own daughter will not be reduced to a passive reflection of her guilty mother, Sexton gives her permission to "love your self's self" (54). These themes, dealing with some form of guilt, often reappear in poems such as "Operation" in *All My Pretty Ones*, yet some of Sexton's most optimistic poems, such as "Little Girl, My String Bean, My Lovely Woman" in *Live or Die*, are moving love poems to her own daughters.

Other themes of guilt also surface in Sexton's poetry. Although Sexton was never completely sure if her incest memories were accurate, her biographer, Middlebrook, concludes that "Sexton's symptoms and behavior—in particular, [her] dissociative states . . . , her tendency to sexualize significant relationships, and the fluidity of the boundaries she experienced between herself and other people—fit the clinical picture of a woman who has undergone sexual trauma" (57). At any rate, disturbing variations on the midnight image of "fat, white-bellied men" nakedly "lurching" over her bed in "Ghosts" (*All My Pretty Ones* 27) intrude into a number of Sexton's poems and, in "Briar Rose" (*Transformations*), cast a new light, according to Diane Hume George, on the heroine who is seduced and left "permanently infantilized by her earlier relationship to an idolatrously loving father" (George, *Oedipus* 39). Fuller treatments of this seduction-betrayal theme emerge in the poetic sequence "The Death of the Fathers" in *The Book of Folly* and in her unpublished one-act play *Mercy Street*.

In a number of poems, Sexton celebrates female fertility and sexuality ("In Celebration of My Uterus" in *Love Poems*), but her poetry more often expresses the suspicion that being born female in a society that restricts women's options to housewife and mother is the real problem she shares with other women. An early poem such as "Farmer's Wife" in *To Bedlam* portrays a woman suffering from what Betty Friedan diagnosed a few years later in her book *The Feminine Mystique* as the housewife's "problem with no name." In "Her Kind," another *To Bedlam* poem (which Sexton always used to open her poetry readings), the persona is a "possessed witch" (21)—presumably the kind of woman in "The Black Art" (*All My Pretty Ones*) who writes poetry and, according to Caroline Hall, "pays for her imaginative powers with her sanity" (105). Even though this witch-poet knows that society has traditionally burned such women at the stake, the speaker's rueful refrain in the previous poem concedes that she "is not a woman, quite" (21), at least not from society's viewpoint.

Sexton's most notable storytelling witch, however, is probably the witty narrator in *Transformations* whose revised fairy tales constitute a cultural critique of sex-role stereotyping. The witch-narrator, for example, satirically transforms the good Cinderella and her colorless Prince into "two dolls in a museum case" (56) and characterizes the eldest daughter in "Twelve Dancing Princesses" as "the pick of the litter" on the marriage commodity market (89). This narrator interprets "The Maiden without Hands" in the poem by that name as the ideal desired by men because, maimed, she epitomizes the helpless and dependent woman, and most shockingly in "Briar Rose," suggests that incest is the underlying model for romantic love and marriage in Western society. Through her dark humor, the witch-narrator reveals how trapped these heroines are in their prescribed gender roles.

This kind of revisionary mythmaking becomes an increasingly important tool employed by the later Sexton who also dismantles the religious myths found in Genesis, the Psalms, and the Gospels in her attempts to deconstruct the divine masculine "power over" model that subordinates women. An outstanding example is the sequence called "The Jesus Papers" in *The Book of Folly*. In the opening poem, "Jesus Suckles," Sexton transforms traditional Madonna and Child iconography into a Freudian narrative told from the perspective of the infant Jesus who quickly moves beyond the pre-Oedipal relationship of blissful union with his nursing mother to a post-Oedipal (and misogynistic) rejection of his mother. Later, Jesus will "save" Mary Magdalene by "lancing" her breasts so that she will renounce her sexuality that could destroy his celibacy (96). To Alicia Ostriker in "That Story," these poems reveal the Christian "split between Flesh and Logos," a division that privileges the masculine "will to control" over the feminine "will to nurture" (278). On the other hand, Sexton's dream visions and prayers in poems such as "Somewhere in Africa" (*Live or Die*), "Rats Live on No Evil Star" (*Death Notebooks*), and especially "The Consecrating Mother" (*45 Mercy Street*) explore the possibilities of beneficent nature goddesses who, as Estella Lauter puts it, unite the splits between "nursing and copulation, child and adult, love and power, life and death, soul and body" (42). However, Ostriker notes that these ecstatic images cannot finally compete with "the child-woman's ferocious need for cosmic love" ("That Story" 281) in *The Awful Rowing toward God*, even though it requires the daughter's submission to a duplicitous father-god. Despite this disappointing ending, George declares in her introduction to her book on Sexton that Sexton is "one of our most important religious poets" (*Criticism* xx).

CRITICAL RECEPTION

In her introduction to *The Complete Poems* (1981), Maxine Kumin contends that "women poets in particular owe a debt to Anne Sexton, who broke new ground, shattered taboos, and endured a barrage of attacks along the way because of the flamboyance of her subject matter (xxxiv). She adds that from the beginning, Sexton's reviewers and critics were "enchanted or repelled with equal passion" (xxi). The critical distaste can be seen, for instance, in the reviews of James Dickey (Colburn 63–64; 106). The more ambivalent Robert Lowell praised the "power" of her early books but expressed embarrassment at what he viewed as her later excesses (Colburn 24). However, many critics, including women reviewers such as Louise Bogan, Muriel Rukseyer, and Joyce Carol Oates, found much to praise, including Sexton's feminine themes, wit, and skill (Wagner-Martin 5–9).

Initially, Sexton was classified as a confessional poet, a label that to some implied self-indulgent narcissism, but which elicited thoughtful major studies by M. L. Rosenthal, Robert Phillip, and others in the late 1960s and early 1970s. However, this label, increasingly viewed as a strait jacket, obscured "the range of her themes, the territory of her poetics, and the radical nature of her vision" (George, *Criticism* xvii). Scholars continue to wrestle with Sexton's confessional label.

Renewed interest in Sexton's poetry and reputation became apparent in the late 1980s with the publication of four excellent collections of new and reprinted articles (Bixler; Colburn; George; and Wagner-Martin) representing a variety of approaches. However, most are feminist, an approach Ostriker's fine book-length study takes in defining the place of Sexton, among others, in the tradition of women's poetry, while Lauter uses a feminist-Jungian approach to study goddess archetypes in the literature and art of Sexton and others. More recently, Middlebrook's discussion of the sexual abuse revealed in her excellent biography of Sexton, supplemented by the moving autobiography by Sexton's daughter, Linda Gray Sexton, expands upon the incest themes that George addresses through a psychoanalytical framework in *Oedipus Anne*.

BIBLIOGRAPHY

Works by Anne Gray Harvey Sexton

To Bedlam and Part Way Back. Boston: Houghton, 1960.
All My Pretty Ones. Boston: Houghton, 1962.
Selected Poems. London: Oxford University Press, 1964.
Live or Die. Boston: Houghton, 1966.
Love Poems. Boston: Houghton, 1969.
Transformations. Boston: Houghton, 1971.
The Book of Folly. Boston: Houghton, 1972.
The Death Notebooks. Boston: Houghton, 1974.
The Awful Rowing toward God. Boston: Houghton, 1975.
45 Mercy Street, edited by Linda Gray Sexton. Boston: Houghton, 1975.
Anne Sexton: A Self-Portrait in Letters, edited by Linda Gray Sexton and Lois Ames. Boston: Houghton, 1977.
The Words of Dr. Y: Uncollected Poems with Three Stories, edited by Linda Gray Sexton. Boston: Houghton, 1978.
The Complete Poems, edited by Linda Gray Sexton. Boston: Houghton, 1981.
No Evil Star: Selected Essays, Interviews, and Prose, edited by Steven E. Colburn. Ann Arbor: University of Michigan Press, 1985.
The Selected Poems of Anne Sexton, edited by Diane Wood Middlebrook and Diana Hume George. Boston: Houghton, 1988.

Studies of Anne Gray Harvey Sexton

Bixler, Frances, ed. *Original Essays on the Poetry of Anne Sexton*. Fayetteville: University of Arkansas Press, 1988.
Clark, Hilary. "Depression, Shame, and Reparation: The Case of Anne Sexton." In *Scenes of Shame: Psychoanalysis, Shame, and Writing*, edited by Joseph Adamson and Hilary Clark. Albany: State University of New York Press, 1999. 189–206.
Colburn, Steven E., ed. *Anne Sexton: Telling the Tale*. Ann Arbor: University of Michigan Press, 1988.
George, Diana Hume. *Oedipus Anne: The Poetry of Anne Sexton*. Urbana: University of Illinois Press, 1987.
———, ed. *Sexton: Selected Criticism*. Urbana: University of Illinois Press, 1988.
Hall, Caroline King Barnard. *Anne Sexton*. Boston: Twayne, 1989.
Honton, Margaret. "The Double Image and the Division of Parts: A Study of Mother-Daughter Relationships in the Poetry of Anne Sexton." In *Sexton: Selected Criticism*, edited by Diana Hume George. Urbana: University of Illinois Press, 1988. 99–116.
Lauter, Estella. "Anne Sexton's Radical Discontent." In *Women as Mythmakers: Poetry and Visual Art by Twentieth-Century Women*. Bloomington: Indiana University Press, 1984. 23–46.
Middlebrook, Diane Wood. *Anne Sexton: A Biography*. Boston: Houghton, 1991.
Ostriker, Alicia Suskin. *Stealing the Language: The Emergence of Women's Poetry in America*. Boston: Beacon, 1986.
———. "That Story: The Changes of Anne Sexton." In *Anne Sexton: Telling the Tale*, edited by Steven E. Colburn. Ann Arbor: University of Michigan Press, 1988. 3–87.

Phillip, Robert. "Anne Sexton: The Blooming Mouth and the Bleeding Rose." In *The Confessional Poets*. Carbondale: Southern Illinois University Press, 1973. 73–91.

Rees-Jones, Deryn. "Consorting with Angels: Anne Sexton and the Art of Confession." *Women: A Cultural Review* 10 (1999): 283–96.

Rosenthal, M. L. "Other Confessional Poets." In *The New Poets: American and British Poetry since World War II*. New York: Oxford University Press, 1967. 131–38.

Sexton, Linda Gray. *Searching for Mercy Street: My Journey Back to My Mother, Anne Sexton*. Boston: Little, Brown, 1994.

Wagner-Martin, Linda, ed. *Anne Sexton: Critical Essays*. Boston: G. K. Hall, 1989.

NTOZAKE SHANGE (1948–)

Sister Shiree Sarana and Catherine Cucinella

BIOGRAPHY

Ntozake Shange, poet, playwright, and novelist, was born October 18, 1948, as Paulette Williams into an upper-middle-class family in Trenton, New Jersey. Her father, Paul T. Williams, a surgeon, and her mother, Eloise Williams, a psychiatric social worker, encouraged Shange's and her siblings' interest in music, literature, and art. Great artists and intellectuals, the likes of Dizzy Gillespie, Miles Davis, Charlie Parker, Chuck Berry, Josephine Baker, and W.E.B. Du Bois often visited the Williams family, thus providing the Williams children with a particularly rich cultural experience.

At age eighteen, Shange attended Barnard College in New York, graduating in 1970. During these years, she both married and separated from her law school husband. Shange also attempted suicide several times during this period as she internalized an anger resulting from her awareness of and frustration with the limitations she felt as an African American woman. As she began to recover from her suicide attempts, Shange focused her rage outward—directing it against society and its treatment of women. She attended the University of Southern California where, in 1973, she earned an MA in American Studies. While in graduate school, Shange formalized her name change: Ntozake ("she who brings her own things") and Shange ("she who walks like a lion").

Known as a "woman writer" and a "feminist writer," Shange's works manifest blatantly feminist themes as well as expressing racial and sexual anger. In 1975 she won fame and critical acclaim with the production of her choreopoem, *For Colored Girls Who Have Considered Suicide/When the Rainbow Is Enuf*, which deals with black women's survival in the face of loneliness, rejection, pain, and rape.

By the late 1970s and the early 1980s, Shange began to focus on writing novels and poetry. Her collections of poetry include *Melissa & Smith* (1976), *Natural Disasters and Other Festive Occasions* (1977), *Nappy Edges* (1978), *A Daughter's Ge-*

ography (1983), *From Okra to Greens: Poems* (1984), *Ridin' the Moon in Texas: Word Paintings* (1987), and *The Love Space Demands: A Continuous Saga* (1991). Her novels include *Sassafrass, Cypress & Indigo: A Novel* (1982), *Betsey Brown* (1985), and *Liliane: Resurrection of the Daughter* (1994). Besides the publication *For Colored Girls Who Have Considered Suicide/When the Rainbow Is Enuf* (1977), Shange's other plays include *A Photograph: Lovers in Motion: A Drama* (1981), *Three Pieces: Spell #7, A Photograph: Lovers in Motion, Boogie Woogie Landscapes* (1981), and *From Okra to Greens/A Different Kinda Love Story* (1983). In addition, Shange has published a collection of essays, a children's book, and a cookbook: *See No Evil: Prefaces, Essays & Accounts, 1976–1983* (1984), *I Live in Music* (1994), and *If I Can Cook You Know God Can* (1998).

Shange studied dance and performed with the Third World Collective, Raymond Sawyer's Afrikan American Dance Company; Sounds and Motion; and West Coast Dance Works, as well as with her own dance company then called Colored Girls Who Have Considered Suicide. She has taught, read, and lectured at various colleges, including Sonoma State University, Mills College, Detroit Art Institute, Howard University, New York University, and Yale University. Shange also was the Mellon Distinguished Professor of Literature at Rice University, and she taught drama in the Creative Writing Program at the University of Houston.

Ntozake Shange has garnered distinction as an educator, performer, director, and writer, winning two Obie awards (*For Colored Girls Who Have Considered Suicide When the Rainbow Is Enuf*) and the adaptation of Bertolt Brecht's *Mother Courage and Her Children* (1981). She was nominated for the 1981 Tony, Grammy, and Emmy awards for *For Colored Girls*. Shange has also been awarded National Endowment of the Arts and Guggenheim Foundation fellowships. She has received the Outer Circle Critics Award; the Adelco Award; the *Los Angeles Times* Book Prize for Poetry; Lila Wallace-Reader's Digest Fund annual writer's award; Paul Robeson Achievement Award; Living Legend Award, National Black Theatre Festival; and a Pushcart Prize.

MAJOR WORKS AND THEMES

In all her writing, but specifically in her poetry, Shange uses innovative language and language familiar to black people to develop her major thematic concerns: the realities of being black and female in America, racial and sexual anger, and oppression and survival within a racist and sexist society. Shange disregards standard rules of grammar and punctuation; she loves using lower case letters, slashes, and unique spellings. This technique is replete throughout her work. Shange uses the dialect and speech patterns of Black English, which provides her poetry with a flow and coherence that also enhances her entire body of work. However, her work does not rely only on black dialect as Shange also uses standard English. She often uses a juxtaposition of these two "Englishes" to exemplify the cultural struggle of black people in the United States.

Shange's work seldom separates issues of race and gender. As she elaborates, "I couldn't side with a racist or a sexist. I'm a feminist. I never had any choice between black women and children. I would side with whatever would be best for women and children of color. Some people have elaborate distinctions. I don't have them" (Brown 40). Thus Shange's work continually presents black people, particularly black women and children, negotiating their lives and building individual identities within a society that devalues both femaleness and blackness. Shange introduces this theme in her first major work, *For Colored Girls*, and it remains in her subsequent writings. A mixed genre piece—poetry, music, dance, and drama—*For Colored Girls* reveals the anger of black women confined and limited by the mandates of white patriarchy, and it makes clear that these black women suffer both from a white racist/sexist culture and from a black sexist culture.

Shange does more, however, than chronicle a history of abuse, frustration, and oppression. Her poetry, plays, and novels celebrate the survival of black women under any circumstances. In *For Colored Girls*, the women look toward a promising future as they come to realize, both collectively and individually, a self-love for their blackness and their femaleness. As many critics and reviewers of Shange's work point out, Shange praises black women who experience loneliness and rejection and who suffer emotional and physical pain but refuse to despair. So her work exposes anger while simultaneously depicting the resilience of black people, especially black women. The theme of black women's abilities to adapt and overcome "in spite of" recurs consistently throughout Shange's works.

Shange pulls on her own personal experiences of a failed marriage and multiple suicide attempts to present the injustice that black women endure. However, in an interview with Edward K. Brown, Shange makes clear that her work is not "Black Fiction as autobiography" (38). While acknowledging that some of what she writes comes from what she knows, Shange views her work as fiction, as intellectual work, and at times fanciful. Shange identifies one of her major concerns as the "imaginings" of women of color, and these imaginings arise from denied hopes and dreams within a racist and sexist society (Brown 45). For Shange the imaginings of black women provide a means of survival in the face of constant struggle.

Shange, however, presents all aspects of black women's experiences including joy, optimism, and playfulness. Her poetry and prose depict one's journey to create a selfhood through a range of conflicting and alternating emotions; therefore, her work takes on the characteristics of a collage, favoring fragments, yet also including sentences, presenting fleeting images while sustaining complete thoughts, moving forward, yet rejecting lineality while embracing circularity. Both stylistically and thematically, Ntozake Shange questions what it means to be human, the need for relationships, the relationship between the body and the self, and she searches for the answer to these questions through the experiences of the black woman about whom she writes, through her experimentation with language, and through her intricate blending of genres.

CRITICAL RECEPTION

Although Ntozake Shange seems more well known for her plays and novels, her critics praise her poetry for its originality, musicality, passion, honesty, and mastery of words. Critics also agree that her works often defy categorization as Shange constantly blurs generic boundaries, thus creating startling new pieces. Critical treatments of her work recognize Shange's political stance, her feminism, and her innovative language, as well as the poetry's musicality and performative aspects. While some reviewers of Shange's work find her use of nonstandard spelling and punctuation distracting, Shange sees her lower case letters, slashes, and spellings as "ways to accentuate very subtle ideas and emotions so that the reader is not in control of the process" (Tate 163). Shange constructs her poems to convey a sense of dance, of movement, and of music, which invite and lead her readers through the nuances and meanings of the poetry.

In her reading of "serious lessons learned," in *Nappy Edges*, Helen Kidd identifies Shange's "writing as one of process rather than an end product, finished, static, fixed to the page. The intersection of different creative forms becomes the poem itself . . . [which] exists in a further dimension, as a performance, which constitutes further opening and exploration" (200). Specifically, Kidd addresses Shange's poetry, but most critics find this same fluidity and play of possibilities in Shange's plays and novels. In many ways, this movement emerges from Shange's feminism as she rejects the category of woman and insists on the particularity of woman and the multiplicity of women.

Although Shange's poetry volumes have been reviewed, few in-depth critical treatments of her poetry exist. The essays of Helen Kidd and P. Jane Splawn begin a necessary critical conversation regarding Shange's poetry, and both these scholars situate Shange's poetry within a feminist context. Kidd views the poet's emphasis on the "heterogeneity of women's emotional and physical needs and experiences . . . [as] a profoundly political statement" (201). Splawn echoes Kidd's assessment as she argues for Shange's contribution to a New World consciousness that links the victimization of black women with "the perpetuation of racist and expansionist regimes" (418). Splawn finds in the work of Shange a rejection of essentialist notions and a connection between the expression of feminist issues in Shange's poetry and the global concerns of a New World aesthetic (430). Splawn's reading of Shange's work makes clear the importance of Ntozke Shange as a feminist, poet, playwright, and novelist who blurs generic boundaries in an attempt to deny limitations, categories, and complacency.

BIBLIOGRAPHY

Works by Ntozake Shange

Melissa & Smith. New York: St. Martin's, 1976.

For Colored Girls Who Have Considered Suicide/When the Rainbow Is Enuf. New York: Macmillan, 1977. (play)

Natural Disasters and Other Festive Occasions. San Francisco: Heirs International, 1977.

Nappy Edges. New York: St. Martin's, 1978.

A Photograph: Lovers in Motion: A Drama. New York: Samuel French, 1981.

Three Pieces: Spell #7, A Photograph: Lovers in Motion, Boogie Woogie Landscapes. New York: St. Martin's, 1981. (play)

Sassafrass, Cypress & Indigo: A Novel. New York: St. Martin's, 1982.

A Daughter's Geography. New York: St. Martin's, 1983.

From Okra to Greens/A Different Kinda Love Story. New York: Samuel French, 1983. (play)

From Okra to Greens: Poems. St. Paul, MN: Coffeehouse Press, 1984.

See No Evil: Prefaces, Essays & Accounts, 1976–1983. San Francisco: Momo's Press, 1984.

Betsey Brown. New York: St. Martin's, 1985. (novel)

Ridin' the Moon in Texas: Word Paintings. New York: St. Martin's, 1987.

The Love Space Demands: A Continuous Saga. New York: St. Martin's, 1991.

I Live in Music. New York: Steward, Tabori and Chang, 1994. (poem; children's book)

Liliane: Resurrection of the Daughter. New York: St. Martin's 1994. (novel)
If I Can Cook You Know God Can. New York: Beacon Press 1998.

Studies of Ntozake Shange

Brown, Edward K., II. "An Interview with Ntozake Shange." *Poets and Writers* 21.3 (1993): 38–47.

Bush, Glen. "Creative Orality: Writing Orality into African American Literature." *Publications of the Mississippi Philological Association* 94 (1994): 8–14.

Huse, Nancy. "Because the Rainbow Is Not Enuf." *Paradoxa* 2 (1996): 490–93.

Johnson, Maria. "Shange and Her Three Sisters 'Sing a Liberation Song': Variations on the Orphic Theme." In *Black Orpheus: Music in African American Fiction from the Harlem Renaissance to Toni Morrison*, edited by Saadi Simawe. New York: Garland, 2000.

Kidd, Helen. " '. . . If It's a Statistic, It's Not a Woman': A Look at 'Serious Lessons Learned,' by Ntozake Shange." In *Contemporary Poetry Meets Modern Theory*, edited by Antony Easthope and John O. Thompson. Toronto, Canada: University of Toronto Press, 1991. 195–207.

Kim, Jeongho. "Shange's Writing: Discourse of the 'Other.' " *Journal of English Language and Literature* 40.1 (1994): 99–118.

Lester, Neal. "An Interview with Ntozake Shange." *Studies in American Drama* 4 (1990): 42–66.

———. "Ntozake Shange." In *Speaking on Stage: Interviews with Contemporary American Playwrights*, edited by Phillip Kolin and Colby H. Kullman. Tuscaloosa: University of Alabama Press, 1996.

———. *Ntozake Shange: A Critical Study of the Plays*. New York: Garland, 1995.

Lyons, Brenda. "Interview with Ntozake Shange." *Massachusetts Review* 28 (1987): 687–96.

Peters, Erskine. "Some Tragic Propensities of Ourselves: The Occasion of Ntozake Shange *For Colored Girls Who Have Considered Suicide/ When the Rainbow is Enuf*." *Journal of Ethnic Studies* 6.1 (1978): 79–85.

Splawn, P. Jane. " 'Change the Joke(r) and Slip the Yoke': Boal's 'Joker' System in Ntozake Shange's *For Colored Girls Who Have Considered Suicide/When the Rainbow Is Enuf* and *Spell #7*." *Modern Drama* 41 (1998): 386–98.

———. "New World Consciousness in the Poetry of Ntozake Shange and June Jordan: Two African-American Women's Responses to Expansionism in the Third World." *College Language Association Journal* 4 (1996): 417–32.

Tate, Claudia, ed. *Black Women Writers at Work*. New York: Continuum, 1983. 149–74.

Timpane, John. " 'The Poetry of a Moment': Politics and the Open Form in the Drama of Ntozake Shange." In *Modern American Drama: The Female Canon*, edited by June Schlueter. Madison, NJ: Fairleigh Dickinson University Press, 1990.

Waxman, Barbara Frey. "Dancing out of Form: Dancing into Self: Genre and Metaphor in Marshall, Shange, and Walker." *MELUS* 19.3 (1994): 91–106.

Wheliss, Sarah, and Emmanuel S. Nelson. "Ntozake Shange." In *Contemporary African American Novelists: A Bio-Bibliographical Critical Sourcebook*, edited by Emmanuel S. Nelson. Westport, CT: Greenwood, 1999.

JANE SHORE (1947–)

Renée R. Curry

BIOGRAPHY

Jane Shore was born in North Bergen, New Jersey, to Essie and George Shore. She and her younger sister spent their childhood living in an apartment atop a dress shop, Corduroy Village, owned and run by the Shores. The poet features her North Bergen life throughout her four published books of poetry to date: *Eye Level* (1977), *The Minute Hand* (1987), *Music Minus One* (1996), and *Happy Family* (1999). In the last two books, Shore's work also includes mention of her husband, novelist Howard Norman, and their daughter, Emma. Shore has received many awards for her work including the Lamont Poetry Prize, the Juniper Prize, and the National Book Critics Circle Finalist Award; as well, she has received numerous grants and fellowships, including a John Simon Guggenheim Foundation grant and two grants from the National Endowment for the Arts. She is currently a professor at The George Washington University in Washington, D.C.

MAJOR WORKS AND THEMES

All four of Jane Shore's books of poetry exhibit an ardent interest in family structure, identity, history, peculiarities, psychology, emotions, religion, and rituals. Reading through all four books chronologically provides the reader with the sense of acute curiosity and compassion that exudes from one adult (not unlike ourselves) who continuously struggles to remember her past as a child but also struggles honestly with resituating the events of her past into an adult framework. As a result, we witness in Shore's work a process of moving from criticism and judgment of one's parents to the thorough understanding of extremely intimate motivations at work in the same parents as well as in the self.

In *Eye Level*, Shore is most interested in the self, the body, and the resilience of the flesh. By the time of her second book, *The Minute Hand*, however, Shore becomes the poet familiar to us for her understanding of family. In "Eighth Notes," from *The Minute Hand,* a poem dedicated to George Shore, the poet reveals the knowledge that her father might have become a musician had it not been for his marriage to Essie and the birth of Jane. In 1996, in *Music Minus One*, Shore entitles the entire book to honor the man who always played his music solo at home. By the time this book was published, Shore's father has passed away, and she remembers thinking as a child in the poem "Monday" that no matter how many times he nicked and cut himself shaving as a young man, nothing seemed to diminish his power and strength. She still sees remnants of his musical power and strength exhibited in her sister's singing voice, which she addresses in "Workout." However, by the end of the book, Shore reaches a fuller understanding of the speed at which George Shore's life—however strong, however nicked and cut—had passed.

In the superb poem "The Combination," Shore funnels all the feelings regarding her father's death and life into the revelation of the safe combination that she has memorized for twenty years. During all this time, she and her father ritualized the opening of the safe should anything happen to him or her mother. The combination takes on the effect of a dramatic revelation in the poem as Shore meticulously chronicles each turn of the dial and the ultimate opening of the door after George Shore has died. What she finds is not astounding in any way except that the safe reveals nothing scandalous. Jane Shore never overwrites the dramatic moments in poetry, nor does she use understatement to make precious the delicate moments of story; she just lets the language tell what it honestly must tell. Thus, the profundity revealed in the moment that Shore's hands open the safe in "The Combination" is simple: a father loved a wife and two daughters and left everything he had from his life's long labors in the dress shop to his children. To the poet, this moment validates that she had been right all along; they had been a family unit dedicated to one another—"everything on the up and up" (101).

In the hands of a less skilled and less attentive poet, such revelations might sound the voice of a too-privileged normalcy, or of a clichéd Norman Rockwell depiction, or of a daughter steeped in denial, but Shore's adherence to detail in the poetry and her humility even in wondering whether something might not be on the up and up assures us that she is simply telling us—not smugly informing us—the truth of her family life.

Another aspect of themes about family life captured in Shore's poetry is the impeccable way she has of embedding worldly tragedies in the web of mundane family activity. The family is what makes tragedy, if not acceptable, then, at least, bearable. In an early poem, but still one of her most compelling, "Young Woman on the Flying Trapeze," Shore memorializes the death of a trapeze artist that she and her family witnessed and caught on film (*The Minute Hand*). The trauma of seeing such an event when she was merely five years old is told from the safe distance of viewing the film repeatedly with the family. At times, the family would rewind the film and bring the woman back to "reel" life from her fall, all the time fathoming themselves her rescuers. Shore nestles this tragedy beside stanzas that describe other footage of her family living room, her refrigerator, and herself learning to walk as a baby. The tragedy is made palatable as long as the family continues in its everyday setting and activities.

In "Best Friend," a poem from *Music Minus One*, Shore tells the story of a friend's father who, after a horrific plane crash in their neighborhood, finds a severed hand still wearing its diamond engagement ring. The trauma experienced in the neighborhood and especially between the two girlfriends is tucked once again among images of family ordinariness: family men smoking and playing cards together, sausages cooking on the stove, children's photos around the house, quiet afternoon play among kids, and the girlfriend's average-looking father. In Jane Shore's poetry, the commonplace family mitigates the potential long-term trauma of such events and emphasizes the anomaly of such tragedies.

Related to this theme of embedded tragedy is the sense which Jane Shore portrays, as she ages and becomes a parent herself, that tragedy can seem often only inches or seconds away from one's cherished family members. In "Happy Family," from her most recent book of the same name, Shore describes a quiet evening at a Chinese restaurant. The poem includes images of domestic ordinariness swirling around her husband and daughter. As the meal ends, Shore describes her young daughter reaching to eat the last item left on the plate. The garnish, perhaps a vegetable, perhaps a fruit, is both aesthetically pleasing and appetizing: as the daughter touches the food, a waiter rushes over to their table exclaiming that the food is poisonous. Shore, once again, does not overdramatize the moment or understate it. She just tells the end of the story: The family pays the bill and eats their fortune cookies, ironically looking to small slips of paper to read the fates that they now, since their child side-stepped poisoning, may envision, albeit with an unwitting sense of fragility.

Jane Shore, for all the ways in which she enlarges family intricacies, does understand that each family exists in a larger cosmos. Reflections of this cosmos occur in the early books of poetry, but they materialize much more forcefully in *Happy Family.* In her early poetry, numerous mentions of the planets, stars, and comets serve to give dimension to earthly happenings. She also frequently questions the power of language in terms relational to that of galaxies and universes. The Milky Way swirls around events at school, and family members participate in parallel events, each "orbiting" in their own small worlds. However, in "Buying a Star," "Science Fair," and "Fairbanks Museum and Planetarium," as well as in many other of the poems throughout *Happy Family,* cosmological language plays a significant role. For Shore, this language represents that which blankets and safeguards the romantic event, human death, and family unification. Life under the stars in a Shore poem is always ultimately "happy": Friends teach games to the children, birds make music even in the dark, babies sleep, husbands work, and life—even after the painful deaths of two beloved parents—goes on as does the poet's ability to write poetry: the "syllables of pure pleasure" ("Happiness" 82).

Jewishness also plays a large thematic role in Shore's poetry. She depicts throughout her work the importance of Jewish holy rituals and employs the detailed language particular to her religion in lyrical lines. She describes tenderly the yarmulke that covers her father's head and the voice of the cantor in *The Minute Hand* ("High Holy Days" 21). In *Music Minus One*, she explores from a child's point of view the differences between Gentiles and Jews: One believes in Christ and one believes in God ("The Holiday Season" 25); the variances in emotional capacities of rabbis ("Last Breath" 38); and the dominance of Christian images in the world and their effect on young Jewish girls ("A Vision" 54–56).

In her most recent book of poetry, *Happy Family*, Shore designs a complex interweaving of her multiple heritages as she sees them: her Jewish heritage, her heritage as an American raised in the 1950s, and her heritage as a poet. In "The Second Coming," all of these influences synchronize to define the complex existence that the poet claims for herself. In "God," Shore reveals the significance of her friendships with Gentile girls and the effects that knick-knack representations of God had on her as a child. Of course, being Jewish causes great consternation in regard to Hitler and the Holocaust. In "Mrs. Hitler," Shore bravely explores the way she played a game about concentration camp as a girl, a game that permitted her to make sense of the fragmented information and opinions, which adults in her family espoused, throughout her childhood. Shore also handles generational issues regarding folkloric attributes of Jewishness in her poetry. In "Evil Eye," she chastises her mother for believing that spitting three times on her newborn child's head and naming the child something ugly will ward off the evil eye. Shore lovingly jokes in "Shit Soup" about the way in which the Yiddish word "*shit-arein*," which means "to pour in," all too awkwardly sounds like one is adding shit to the household food. This joke epitomizes much of what Shore finds most pleasing about language: the play of it, especially when the play is about creating a story.

CRITICAL RECEPTION

Jane Shore's poems have been well received. Poets such as W. S. Merwin, David St. John, and Stuart Dybeck have found her work to be quiet, graceful, exact, evocative of delicate mysteries, and capable of calling needed attention to the minute. Reviewers from the *New York Times*, the *Boston Sunday Globe*, the *Vermont Times*, and the *Detroit Free Press* have repeatedly discussed her work positively in terms of its seamless personal history, domestic landscapes, ability to instigate memory, and authenticity. Poetry critic Doris Lynch writes in *Library Journal* that Shore's power lies in her "storytelling" and in her "eye for detail." (96). Like her mentor, Elizabeth Bishop, Lynch claims that Shore always looks to enliven the dimension of her visions. She makes the joys and the painful topics of childhood large and more completely visible. Rachel Hadas, poetry critic for *Kenyon Review*, agrees that Shore's poems are powerful in their domestic storytelling and in their ability to make the "invisible visible" (176). Hadas also makes note of Elizabeth Bishop's mentorship; however, she finds yet another unique aspect of Jane Shore's work: She describes Shore as "tactful" (157), by which Hadas means that Shore does not feel the need to discover family skeletons or scandals in order to write authentically about the family.

Lorrie Goldensohn, poet, literary critic, biographer of Elizabeth Bishop, and longtime friend of Shore's, tells us that Jane Shore knew poetry would be her life's work from quite a young age (209). Goldensohn claims that this self-knowledge was not conceit, but rather quite well founded. This critic revels in Shore's attention to "craft and formal cunning" (210) and in her ability to explore a self on the page that is always "part comedienne, part chameleon, and alert, wise, curious, and acquisitive" (211). From a critical standpoint, Shore is a poet for us to watch. She promises to keep us informed and to keep us humble regarding our roles as members of families.

BIBLIOGRAPHY

Works by Jane Shore

Eye Level. Amherst: The University of Massachusetts Press, 1977.
The Minute Hand. Amherst: The University of Massachusetts Press, 1987.

Music Minus One. New York: Picador, 1996.
Happy Family. New York: Picador, 1999.

Studies of Jane Shore

Atlas, James. *Ten American Poets*. Cheadle, Cheshire, England: Carcanet. 1973.
Goldensohn, Lorrie. "About Jane Shore." *Ploughshares* 23.4 (1997–98): 209–14.
Hadas, Rachel. "Four Voices Thinking Out Loud: 'Through One Tear,' by Edward Nobles; 'Falling Water,' by John Koethe; 'Music Minus One,' by Jane Shore; 'Now,' by Judith Baunel. *Kenyon Review* 30.3–4 (1998): 157–74.
Lynch, Doris. "Book Reviews: Arts & Humanities." *Library Journal* 124 (1999): 96–102.

LESLIE MARMON SILKO (1948–)

Rebecca Tillett

BIOGRAPHY

One of the most powerful political voices of contemporary Native America, Leslie Marmon Silko was born in Albuquerque, New Mexico, on March 5, 1948, of mixed Mexican, Indian, and Anglo American ancestry. Raised at Laguna Pueblo, Silko was educated first at the Bureau of Indian Affairs reservation school, then at schools in Albuquerque. In 1969 Silko's first short story, "The Man to Send Rain Clouds," was published by *The New Mexico Quarterly*, the same year in which she graduated from the University of New Mexico with an honors degree in English. Influenced by her childhood memories of the lawsuit undertaken by the Pueblo of Laguna against the State of New Mexico, Silko enrolled in law school at the University of New Mexico. Her time there coincided with the disappointing resolution of the Laguna legal case and became representative of what Silko acknowledges to be a "breaking point" in her life: the realization that "injustice is built into the Anglo-American legal system" (*Yellow Woman and a Beauty of the Spirit* 19–20).

Rejecting a career in law, Silko enrolled in a graduate program in creative writing in 1971, influenced by her firm belief that stories, told well, can actively change the world. Silko began to establish her writing career in 1974, contributing seven stories, including the titular one, to the anthology *The Man to Send Rain Clouds*, and publishing her first volume of poetry, *Laguna Woman*. Both received instant critical recognition. In the mid-1970s, Silko moved to Alaska where, partially funded by a Rosewater Foundation grant, she wrote her first novel *Ceremony* (1977). As her popular success increased, Silko moved back to the Southwest, taking teaching posts at the University of New Mexico and the University of Arizona. In 1981 Silko established her interest in mixed genres with the publication of the multigenre *Storyteller*, followed by a second multigenre text, *Sacred Water: Narratives and Pictures*, in 1993. This interest culminated in the publication of *Rain* (1996), a collaboration with Silko's photographer father, Lee Marmon. In receipt of a MacArthur Foundation Award, Silko spent ten years writing the highly political and controversial novel *Almanac of the Dead* (1991), which in turn influenced her 1996 collection of political essays, *Yellow Woman and a Beauty of the Spirit*. Her most recent work is the 1999 novel, *Gardens in the Dunes*. Silko has quite rightfully established herself as a major voice of the Americas, winning numerous prizes, awards, and critical recognition. She currently resides on an isolated ranch on the outskirts of Tucson, Arizona.

MAJOR WORKS AND THEMES

While Silko has published only one volume of poetry, she is nonetheless devoted to multigenre works, which blend the poem, short story, novel, essay, autobiography, and photography in a way that actively subverts the rigidity of conventional literary genres. Through all her work, Silko develops two primary foci: Laguna and its oral storytelling tradition and a compelling, ironic, and often controversial, critique of Anglo American politics and culture. In an interview in 1980, Silko emphasized her intense identification with her Laguna heritage: "This place I am from is everything I am as a writer and a human being" (Fisher 18). This assertion is supported by the title of Silko's only volume of poetry, *Laguna Woman*, and by poems such as "Indian Song: Survival" and "Toe'osh: A Laguna Coyote Story," both of which recognize story as a vehicle for identity and for cultural continuity. Notably, Silko's notion of survival embraces and transcends death: The two poems that open and close the volume ("Poem for Myself and Mei-Mei" and "Preparations") focus upon death as merely one aspect of a much larger cycle. In *Laguna Woman*, Silko stresses what critics Louise Barnett and James Thorson identify as her "formative influence" (2): the significance of traditional Laguna belief and its inseparability from the land. In "Where Mountainlion Lay Down with Deer," the protagonist detects his ancestors in the "smell" of the wind (4); in "Love Poem," stories are remembered in "cottonwood leaves" (23); and, in "Sun Children," the returning foliage is "born out of song" (18). Significantly, the form of Silko's poems actively emulates the oral tradition by reproducing the natural hesitations, repetitions, and ellipses of speech and by asserting polyvocality through a variety of complimentary, sometimes competing, voices.

Silko's interest in the concept of a written "oral" form is equally evident in *Storyteller*, a work that amalgamates poetry with short stories, photography, and autobiography. Silko's concerns are given immediate visual emphasis: The text is produced in an unusual and striking "landscape" format. *Storyteller*, highly intertextual, incorporates poems from *Laguna Woman* and *Ceremony* and short stories from *The Man to Send Rain Clouds*. The volume also establishes an internal dialogue between individual pieces and voices. Silko attempts to replicate not just the dynamics of Laguna culture, but also the dynamics of the storytelling tradition, as stories and poems blend with, contradict, and re-create each other. In *Storyteller*, Silko continues to analyze what it means to be a Laguna Woman. Central to her analysis is the Laguna belief system, the mythic figures of Yellow Woman and Coyote evident in the stories "Yellow Woman," "A Geronimo Story," and "Coyote Holds a Full House in His Hand," and the poems "Cottonwood" and "Storytelling." Of equal significance are Silko's descriptions of cultural practices in poems such as "Deer Song" and "Deer Dance / For Your Return." These poems act both to reject popular misconceptions of Native cultures and to reinstate ritual as the center of the Laguna worldview. The cyclic return of the necessities of life is emphasized: the "swirling" snow elk ("In Cold Storm

Light" 12); the deer that "come home" with the hunters that show them "reverence and appreciation" ("Deer Dance" prose epilogue); and the rain clouds sent to the people as a "gift from ocean" ("Prayer to the Pacific" 30). The overwhelming significance of rain to the Southwest has led to Silko's subsequent multigenre works, *Sacred Water* and *Rain*, both of which blend short, sometimes political, statements and essays with photography.

Silko's experimentation with form continues from her novel *Ceremony*, which seamlessly blends poetry with a prose narrative. The nonchronological structure of the text is emphasized through the insertion of poetic mythic sequences that, echoing and exposing the nature and direction of the prose action, are crucial to an understanding of the text. For example, the text is framed by the lines "Sunrise" to suggest a cyclic motion and expose the ceremonial nature of the story. The poem that opens the novel describes the Laguna creatrix Thought-Woman who brings the world into being through the power of imagination. Thought-Woman illustrates Silko's own narrative beliefs that the narrator tells the reader or listener what "she [Thought-woman] is thinking" (17).

Perhaps the most anthologized poem from *Ceremony*, also included in *Storyteller*, is the powerful "Long Time Ago," which tells of the creation of "white skin people," into a world "already complete" by Native American witches. The power is evident in Silko's terminology: The white people do not see life, and they fear both the world and themselves, and ultimately "destroy what they fear." Silko's analysis of Anglo-Indian relations refuses absolutely any idea of the Indian as "victim," insisting that the ultimate evil is not whites, but "witchery": exploitation and oppression in every form. Silko lists the destruction to come in the Americas: starvation, "drought," "slaughter," "terrible diseases," and finally, the discovery of uranium on reserved lands, the "final pattern" that will "explode everything." Perhaps the most alarming and paradoxically exhilarating aspect of the poem is Silko's calm assertion of the transformative power of story that, once released into the world, "*can't be called back*" (original emphasis) (191).

Silko's own favorite story, the titular "Storyteller," clearly exposes her political response to Anglo-Indian relations in the United States. Centering upon a young Yupik woman imprisoned for killing a white trader, the story refuses the "easy" route offered by lies of accidental death and insists that, regardless of personal cost, the story "must be told as it is" (*Storyteller* 31). Silko's belief that "truth will out" is evident in her novels and essays, rooted even more firmly in political critique. Driven by her own homesickness for Laguna, Silko's novel *Ceremony* successfully illustrates the importance of the land, designating landscape as a primary character. The importance is emphasized throughout the novel by the insertion of mythic creation and, more specifically, "emergence" poems stressing the relation between people and land. Silko pursues this theme far more controversially in her powerful and bleak novel *Almanac of the Dead*, which unsettles Anglo American perceptions by presenting a revision of five hundred years of genocide in the Americas on the very quincentennary of Columbus's "discovery." Silko's vision of the Americas is full of "furious, bitter spirits" who refuse to remain silent and will "never stop until justice had been done" (424). In this context, the "Indian Wars have never ended in the Americas" (17).

This more political theme is also evident in Silko's collection of essays, *Yellow Woman and a Beauty of the Spirit*, and in her most recent novel *Gardens in the Dunes*, which analyzes the relationship between gardens, gardening, collecting, and imperialism, in the context of the treatment of Native peoples in the Americas. Less bleak than *Almanac of the Dead*, the novel remains equally dedicated to a truthful depiction of Anglo-Indian relations, evoking the dead in the context of the Ghost Dance phenomenon that culminated in the Wounded Knee massacre of 1890. Translating the gladiolus bulbs of Anglo American display into a useful Native American staple foodstuff, *Gardens in the Dunes* furthers the healing begun in *Ceremony*, employing horticulture to illustrate the cross-pollination that is essential for all healthy cultures.

CRITICAL RECEPTION

Silko received immediate critical recognition for her poetry and her prose, presented in 1974 with both a poetry award from the *Chicago Review* for *Laguna Woman*, and a National Endowment for the Humanities Discovery Grant for "The Man to Send Rain Clouds." Silko also received a Rosewater Foundation Grant for the writing of *Ceremony*, was awarded the Pushcart Prize for Poetry (1977) and the Boston Globe, and was the youngest writer to be included in *The Norton Anthology of Women's Literature* with her short story "Lullaby." Having been awarded the Native Writers' Circle of the Americas lifetime achievement award in 1994, she was recently named a "Living Cultural Treasure" by the New Mexico Humanities Council.

Early comment on Silko established her reputation as a powerful Native American voice. For Alan Velie, Silko's continual defiance and evasion of traditional literary conventions has ensured her classification, in the title of his study, as a "literary master." The majority of critical commentary has focused upon Silko's adherence to Laguna traditions, in particular the oral storytelling tradition. Thus, Kenneth Lincoln argues that Silko writes "the concept of a true, living story, the personal inflection embodied and embraced in communal history" (224), and Bernard Hirsch notes that Silko "expresses with grace and power" Laguna life that is "timeless and ongoing, changing and evolving, contradictory and continuous" (25). Quite rightfully, the unusual blend of poetry and prose and the simplicity and beauty of Silko's writing ensured that *Ceremony* achieved enormous popular success, to the extent that the novel is today included on school syllabi across the United States. This critical recognition was strengthened by Silko's *Storyteller*, which "confirmed Silko's determination to alter Euro-American literary forms to accommodate her own heritage" (Barnett and Thorson 1).

While Silko was critically feted in the 1970s and 1980s, the highly political and controversial nature of her second novel *Almanac of the Dead* created an essentially hostile critical backlash. As Barnett and Thorson comment, the novel is "more complex, more shocking, more apocalyptic than any other novel of the latter part of the century" (1). The starkness of the contrast in tone and content with *Ceremony* has ensured that *Almanac*, after being derided, has been largely ignored by the critics. The first full-scale study appeared nearly a decade after the novel's publication. For Barnett and Thorson, the critical neglect suggests that Silko's "powerful vision of cultural decadence, racial conflict, and fearful retribution has been so unpalatable . . . that it obscured the novel's achievement" (2). As a result, Silko's most recent work, *Gardens in the Dunes*, received a more wary reception and has, as yet, produced little extensive critical response.

Recent scholarship on Silko (Barnett and Thorson, Rand, Stein) argues for a reevaluation of Silko's most recent work. These critics suggest that Silko's work be read as an extended experiment in the Laguna storytelling tradition, in which stories continue to be told and to evolve. Thus, all find that the overt political challenge in Silko's later novels can be traced to a more covert, but unarguably present, political subtext in her earlier canonized works.

BIBLIOGRAPHY

Works by Leslie Marmon Silko

Laguna Woman: Poems. New York: Greenfield Review Press, 1974.

The Man to Send Rain Clouds: Contemporary Stories by American Indians, edited by Kenneth Rosen, New York: Viking Press, 1974.

Ceremony. New York: Viking Press, 1977. (novel)

Storyteller. New York: Arcade Publishing, 1981. (multigenre)

Almanac of the Dead: A Novel. New York: Simon and Schuster, 1991.

Sacred Water: Narratives and Pictures. Tucson, AZ: Flood Plain Press, 1993. (multigenre)

Rain. With Lee Marmon. New York: Library Fellows of the Whitney Museum of American Art, 1996. (essays)

Yellow Woman and a Beauty of the Spirit: Essays on Native American Life Today. New York: Simon and Schuster, 1996.

Gardens in the Dunes: A Novel. New York: Simon and Schuster, 1999.

Studies of Leslie Marmon Silko

Barnett, Louise, and James Thorson, eds. *Leslie Marmon Silko: A Collection of Critical Essays.* Albuquerque: University of New Mexico Press, 1999.

Coltelli, Laura. *Winged Words: American Indian Writers Speak.* Lincoln: University of Nebraska Press, 1990.

Fisher, Dexter, ed. *The Third Woman: Minority Women Writers in the United States.* Boston: Houghton, 1980. 18–23.

Graulich, Melody, ed. *Yellow Woman.* New Brunswick, NJ: Rutgers University Press, 1993.

Hirsch, Bernard A. "The Telling Which Continues: Oral Tradition and the Written Word in Leslie Marmon Silko's *Storyteller.*" *American Indian Quarterly* 12.1 (1988): 1–26.

Jaskoski, Helen. *Leslie Marmon Silko: A Study of the Short Fiction.* New York: Twayne, 1998.

Krumholz, Linda J. "To Understand This World Differently: Reading and Subversion in Leslie Marmon Silko's *Storyteller.*" *ARIEL* 25.1 (1994): 89–113.

Lincoln, Kenneth. *Native American Renaissance.* Berkeley: University of California Press, 1983.

Nelson, Robert M. *Place and Vision: The Function of Landscape in Native American Fiction.* New York: Peter Lang, 1993.

Owens, Louis. *Other Destinies: Understanding the American Indian Novel.* Norman: University of Oklahoma Press, 1992.

Rand, Naomi. *Silko, Morrison, and Roth: Studies in Survival.* New York: Peter Lang, 1999.

Ruoff, A. LaVonne. "Ritual and Renewal: Keres Traditions in the Short Fiction of Leslie Silko." *MELUS* 5.4 (1978): 2–17.

St. Andrews, B. A. "Healing the Witchery: Medicine in Silko's *Ceremony.*" *Arizona Quarterly* 44 (1988): 86–94.

Salyer, Gregory. *Leslie Marmon Silko.* New York: Twayne, 1997.

Seyersted, Per. *Leslie Marmon Silko.* Boise, ID: Boise State University, 1980.

Stein, Rachel. *Shifting the Ground: American Women Writers' Revisions of Nature, Gender, and Race.* Charlottesville: University Press of Virginia, 1997.

Velie, Alan. *Four American Indian Literary Masters: N. Scott Momaday, James Welch, Leslie Marmon Silko, and Gerald Vizenor.* Norman: University of Oklahoma Press, 1982. 104–21.

Wright, Anne, ed. *The Delicacy and Strength of Lace: Letters Between Leslie Marmon Silko and James Wright.* St. Paul, MN: Graywolf Press, 1986.

CATHY SONG (1955–)

Nikolas Huot

BIOGRAPHY

Born in Honolulu, Hawaii, on August 20, 1955, to a Chinese mother and a Korean father, Cathy Song grew up in Wahiawa, a small plantation town, and in the Waialae Kahala (upper middle-class) section of Honolulu. She graduated from Kalani High School in Honolulu, where she started to write poetry, and attended the University of Hawaii at Manoa for two years, where she worked with poet-critic John Unterecker. She completed her bachelor's degree in English at Wellesley College in 1977 and enrolled at Boston University for her master's degree in creative writing. Only a year after earning her MA, her first collection of poetry, *Picture Bride*, was selected by Richard Hugo as the 1982 winner of the Yale Series of Younger Poets competition and was published by Yale University Press the following year.

Since her return to Hawaii from the mainland in 1987, Song has worked for the Bamboo Ridge study group, which encourages local Hawaiian writers to pursue their crafts, and Bamboo Ridge Press, which gives Hawaiian writers an outlet for publication. Besides furthering the careers of others, Song has also brought forward her own by publishing two more collections of poetry, *Frameless Windows, Squares of Light* (1988) and *School Figures* (1994), and by co-editing an anthology of fiction and poetry by women writers, *Sister Stew* (1991). Cathy Song and her husband currently reside in Honolulu, where they are both teaching and raising their three children.

MAJOR WORKS AND THEMES

In her poetry, Cathy Song usually examines the everyday world that touches and affects her. As such, possible topics for Song's poetry include the lives of her grandparents in Hawaii following their immigration from China and Korea, the resistance of third-generation Asian Americans to the traditional Asian ways and their paradoxical needs to embrace their Asian ancestry, and the more mundane aspect of her life as a daughter, mother, and wife. Using mostly women voices, as well as her own, Song writes about what she or the speaker knows and understands of the world surrounding her. As Patricia Wallace notes, Cathy Song's poems "transform what seems simple or ordinary—including words themselves—by lifting things out of their ordinary settings" (11). Even though Song solely explores her family's past and her everyday life in her poems, the overall portrayal she depicts in her poetry is not that dissimilar from the general Asian American experience.

In *Picture Bride*, Song takes the reader on a journey from a time where her grandparents toiled on a sugar cane plantation to present-day Hawaii. She portrays her grandmother's arrival as a picture bride in Hawaii, her loneliness, her suffering, and her sorrow. She also depicts the difficult struggle between assimilation and tradition for Asian immigrants, as Hawaii becomes a state. Furthermore, Song portrays the alienation felt by Asian Americans, as they are a part yet apart from the East and the West. She also explores quite frequently the "hidden but relentless desire for escape" (Hugo xiii): escape from a life of traditional obligations, escape from a life of hard labor, escape from the physical location, escape from a life that thwarts individuals. Among the noteworthy poems found in *Picture Bride* are "The Youngest Daughter," which talks about filial obligations and the desire to flee those responsibilities; "Easter: Wahiawa, 1959," which looks at Americanization and the pursuit of a better life for immigrants; "The White Porch," which describes the stifling life of a young woman and her only moments of escape; "Lost Sister," which talks about a young woman who flees repressive China only to find more restrictions in the United States; and "The Seamstress," which shows the suppressed life of an older woman. Overall, in *Picture Bride*, Song manages to combine the different poems in the collection and generate a remarkable, collective picture of the lives of Asian women in Hawaii.

Frameless Windows, Squares of Light further explores the themes introduced in her first collection of poetry, but she also includes new ones such as childbirth and art. In this volume, Song continues to frame specific moments of her past, real or imagined. Most memorable in this collection are "A Mehinaku Girl in Seclusion," about the three-year isolation a young girl must endure after her first menstruation and her apprenticeship of female subjugation; "Humble Jar," which is about the "useful yet undervalued" life of the mother who keeps buttons in a jar as mementoes of her scattered life; and "Heaven," which concerns connections with the past.

Song's third collection of verse, *School Figures*, continues to portray subjects that grow out of her personal experiences. Still voicing thoughts of others and of herself in her poetry, Song brings the reader of her third volume to such places as a karaoke bar, a piano lesson, a tennis court, and her kitchen. Less concerned with ethnicity in this volume (although seemingly more in touch with it), Song explores further than before relationships between husband and wife, mother and son, and mother and daughter. "A Conservative View" examines stereotypes between cultures inside the Asian American community; "The Grammar of Silk" explores how a mother wishes a better life and an escape for her daughter; "Forever Yours" denounces conformity and falsity; and "Wednesday Night, Karaoke Bar" shows how one must create one's own "music" in order to recapture an earlier, happier time.

CRITICAL RECEPTION

Cathy Song's poetry has been very well received over the years. Not only did she win the Yale Series of Younger Poets competition in 1982, but she was also awarded the Elliot Cades Award for Literature in 1988 for her second volume of poetry, the Hawai'i Award for Literature in 1993, and the Shelley Memorial Award from the Poetry Society of America in 1994. In 1997 Song was awarded one of the few Literature Fellowships for Poetry from the National Endowment for the Arts. Other than awards, Song receives many accolades from academics and publishers as more and more of her poems are studied in college courses and anthologized in such significant volumes as *The Norton Anthology of American Literature*, *The Heath Anthology of American Literature*, and *The Open Boat: Poems from Asian America*. Song's poems have such an appeal that jazz saxophonist Andrew Rathbun even composed a song cycle for octet, entitled "Jade," based on her poetry.

Critics have been slightly more inconsistent when reading Song's work. Most critics consent, for example, that Song's strengths lie in her "startlingly clear description," in her "talent for unfolding the layers of memory and capturing the innocence of childhood," and in the "marvelous organic nature of her imagery and in complete fusion of form, image, occasion, and emotion" (Chou 430, Yogi 159, Lim 99). However, not all critics approve of Song's approach to her subjects. In her review of *Picture Bride*, Shirley Lim is probably the most critical about Song's "strained, mechanical, and unconvincing" uses of Asian cultural fragments (99). In fact, Lim believes that Song is most effective as a poet when she "gives up her concern with surface ethnic-coloristic effects and concentrates on the details of her world, her vision" (99). On the other hand, Susan Schultz believes that, as an Asian American poet, Song is not concerned enough with "the fascinating world in which she lives, one fraught with gender, ethnic, and class tensions"; rather, she asserts that the main reason for Song's success is her "conservatism, for her poetry does not directly challenge the dominant cultural attitudes" (274). That same passivity is what Richard Hugo praised in his foreword to Song's award winning collection, where he describes Song's strength in her "quietude": "In her receptivity, passive as it seems, lies passion, a passion that is expressed in deceptive quiet and an even tone" (ix).

The same criticisms and praises come forth in the reviews of *Frameless Windows, Squares of Light* and of *School Figures*. In his study of Song's poetry, Zhou Xiaojing applauds Song's ability to "recreate multiple voices and perspectives in one poem, enriching the visual details with narrative and dramatic details, without losing the emotional intensity and philosophical abstraction of lyricism" (209). Jessica Greenbaum, on the other hand, feels that when Song uses other people's voices to tell their stories, it "often results in a stiff, unlived-in feel that stymies this otherwise lithe poet" (19). Greenbaum also criticizes Song's use of "too many metaphors and unwieldy biographical information" (19). Ironically, Jerome Chou praises Song's "characteristic straightforward diction," and Anne-Elizabeth Green comments on Song's "distinct view of those instants of time . . . [from] a real/imagined past" (Chou 430, Green 324). Overall, though, critics see in Cathy Song a remarkable talent in describing fleeting moments and making ordinary situations into noteworthy poems.

BIBLIOGRAPHY

Works by Cathy Song

"Beginnings (For Bok Pil)." *Hawaii Review* 6 (1976): 55–65. (short story)
Picture Bride. New Haven, CT: Yale University Press, 1983.

Frameless Windows, Squares of Light. New York: Norton, 1988.
Sister Stew: Fiction and Poetry by Women, edited with Juliet S. Kono. Honolulu, HI: Bamboo Ridge Press, 1991.
School Figures. Pittsburgh, PA: University of Pittsburgh Press, 1994.

Studies of Cathy Song

Bloyd, Rebekah. "Cultural Convergences in Cathy Song's Poetry." *Peace Review* 10 (1998): 393–400.
Choo, David. "Cathy's Song: Interview with Cathy Song." *Honolulu Weekly*, 15 June 1994, 6–8.
Chou, Jerome. "Cathy Song." In *American Women Writers*, edited by Carol Huard Green and Mary Grimley Mason. New York: Continuum, 1994. 429–30.
Fujita-Sato, Gayle K. " 'Third World' as Place and Paradigm in Cathy Song's *Picture Bride*." *MELUS* 15.1 (1988): 49–72.
Green, Anne-Elizabeth. "Cathy Song." In *Contemporary Women Poets*, edited by Pamela L. Shelton. Detroit, MI: St. James Press, 1998. 322–24.
Greenbaum, Jessica. "Family Albums." Review of *Frameless Windows, Squares of Light*, by Cathy Song. *Women's Review of Books* 6.1 (1988): 19.
Hugo, Richard. Foreword to *Picture Bride*. New Haven, CT: Yale University Press, 1983. ix-xiv.
Johnson, Don. Review of *School Figures*, by Cathy Song. *Southern Humanities Review* 30 (1996): 297–99.
Kallet, Marilyn. "Illuminating Kinship." Review of *Frameless Windows, Squares of Light*, by Cathy Song. *Belles Lettres* 6.1 (1990): 31.
Kim, Elaine. "Asian American Writers: A Bibliographical Review." *American Studies International* 22.2 (1984): 41–78.
Kyhan, Lee. "Korean-American Literature: The Next Generation." *Korea Journal* 34.1 (1994): 20–35.
Lim, Shirley. "A Review of *Picture Bride*, by Cathy Song." *MELUS* 10.3 (1983): 95–99.
Nomaguchi, Debbie Murakami. "Cathy Song: 'I'm a Poet Who Happens to Be Asian American.' " *International Examiner*, 2 May 1984, 9.
Schultz, Susan M. "Cathy Song." *Dictionary of Literary Biography* 169. Detroit, MI: Gale, 1996. 267–74.
Shaw, Robert B. Review of *Frameless Windows, Squares of Light*, by Cathy Song. *Poetry* 154.5 (1989): 289–90.
Sumida, Stephen. *And the View from the Shore: Literary Traditions of Hawaii*. Seattle: University of Washington Press, 1991.
Townsend, Alison. "Women in the Middle." Review of *School Figures*, by Cathy Song. *Women's Review of Books* 13.10–11 (1996): 40–41.
Usui, Masami. "Women Disclosed: Cathy Song's Poetry and Kitagawa Ukiyoe." *Studies in Culture and the Humanities* (1995): 1–19.
Wallace, Patricia. "Divided Loyalties: Literal and Literary in the Poetry of Lorna Dee Cervantes, Cathy Song and Rita Dove." *MELUS* 18.3 (1993): 3–19.
Xiaojing, Zhou. "Breaking from Tradition: Experimental Poems by Four Asian American Women Poets." *Revista Canaria de Estudios Ingleses* 37 (1998): 199–218.
Yogi, Stan. Review of *Picture Bride*, by Cathy Song. *Amerasia Journal* 14.1 (1988): 157–60.

ELIZABETH SPIRES (1952–)

Natalie Stillman-Webb

BIOGRAPHY

Although she grew up in the Midwest, Elizabeth Spires remembers of her childhood that "the most charged, romantic, physical image in my imagination was the ocean"; now, settled on the East Coast as an adult, it is an image prevalent in her poetry (Christie 37). Born in Lancaster, Ohio, Spires was raised in Circleville. She attended Catholic school, an experience she has written about (most notably in a prose poem in the center of her volume *Annonciade*, entitled "Falling Away"). She graduated from Vassar College in 1974. For several years, Spires worked as a freelance writer and editor for a publishing company in Columbus, Ohio, before returning to school to pursue an MA from The Johns Hopkins University, in Baltimore, Maryland. In 1981 her master's thesis was published as the collection *Globe*. Her first volume of poetry was followed by *Swan's Island* (1985), which contains fewer childhood reminiscences but continues some of *Globe*'s spiritual themes. Spires married novelist Madison Smartt Bell in 1985, at the Ladew Topiary Gardens in Monkton, Maryland, the setting of the final poem in *Swan's Island*.

In 1986–87 Spires was named the Amy Lowell Travelling Poetry Scholar, and she lived for a time in London. The "Author's Note" from *Annonciade* (1989) observes that many of its poems were written while Spires was in London. This volume, more so than her others, emphasizes place, whether London, France, or New England. *Annonciade* received Wellesley College's Sara Teasdale Poetry Award. Throughout her career, Spires has won many awards, including a Guggenheim Fellowship and a grant from the Whiting Foundation.

In 1991 Spires gave birth to a daughter, Celia; her experience of motherhood is the subject of many of the poems in her latest volume, *Worldling*, published in 1995. Currently, she teaches at Goucher College, in Baltimore, where she and Bell are writers in residence; she also teaches in the Writing Seminars at Johns Hopkins. In addition to poetry, Spires has written many works of juvenile literature in the past two decades, and she has published essays on and interviews with other writers, most notably W. D. Snodgrass, Josephine Jacobsen, Philip Larkin, Mary Swanders, and Elizabeth Bishop.

MAJOR WORKS AND THEMES

Like the poetry of Elizabeth Bishop, for whom Spires expresses great admiration and was fortunate enough to interview shortly before Bishop's death, Spires's early poetry is not confessional or preoccupied with the personal, but instead demonstrates a certain restraint of emotion and an attention to form. Spires's work evinces a preoccupation with art, specifically with art objects or relics. *Globe* contains many meditations on works of visual art. For instance, "After Three Japanese Drawings," a set of narratives, describes individuals in each of the paintings. *Swan's Island* continues this trend, with a focus on others' art works, from sculpture to photographs, quilts, and gardens. The back cover of the volume observes of this tendency that "the scenery of artifice is more than a posed attitude: it is the living surface through which the poet confronts our precarious existence in the world, driven by a moral, even spiritual, need to find love, faith, and even redemption." In addition, in her emphasis on artifice, Spires is careful to present her artifacts as not static objects but as an "Ever-Changing Landscape," as she titles her poem about a visit to the Ladew Topiary Gardens. Though carefully manicured during the summer months, the topiary have all winter to grow how they will.

This tension between form and freedom seems to reflect Spires's own poetic style, since she alternates between structured form and free verse. As she has commented in her piece "Some Notes on Form" included in the anthology *A Formal Feeling Comes: Poems in Form by Contemporary Women* (1994), the form of her poems grows organically out of the subject matter she is treating: "To limit ourselves as poets to either form or free verse exclusively is to narrow our expressive possibilities both in terms of what subjects we will write about and how that subject matter will be treated" (212).

Spires's emphasis on artifice relates thematically in her poems to an emphasis on human disconnection. This emphasis is evident in several poems in *Swan's Island.* For instance, in "Waving Goodbye," the speaker and her lover are both distorted by their reflections in a gazing ball standing in a garden. In "Mascara," two sisters putting on makeup observe their faces in reflection, which seems to emphasize and distort certain aspects of their relationship. While the speaker is given a vision of "my own face, unmasked," the reflection at the same time calls attention to differences between the sisters, the "ten years apart" (13). Attempts to apprehend the other in these poems often fail, and human connection proves elusive, underscored by Spires's frequent use of words such as "shadows" and "ghosts," repeated particularly in poems about the relationship between lovers in this volume. In the poems of *Annonciade*, a focus on relics widens the distance between individuals temporally, rather than bringing them together. In this collection, poems such as "Faberge's Egg," "Victoriana: Gold Mourning Pendant with an Eye Painted on Ivory," and "Mutoscope" present a historical object that provides impetus for meditation. Yet none brings connection: For instance, the mutoscope, a historical entertainment device, offers the modern viewer a glimpse of the past (namely images of a woman undressing) while at the same time implying that the promise of knowing or connecting proves illusory, since the glimpse the device provides is "so small, so faraway and fragmentary" (18).

In addition to her focus on art and artifice, another method that Spires uses to explore the past and different perspectives is her use of different personae. In an interview with A. V. Christie, Spires recalls first experimenting with voice—in what she calls "dramatic monologues"—after hearing Anthony Hecht read his poem "Behold the Lilies of the Field." She observes, "Amazingly enough the idea of writing in a voice had never occurred to me" (Christie 39). In *Globe*, especially section II, Spires presents many diverse personae, speaking in soliloquies that often remind one of Robert Browning: She writes in the voice of a sea captain's wife in "Widow's Walk" and as Irish tinkers in "The Travellers." Elsewhere she has written from the point of view of actual historical people, such as Elizabeth Siddall in "Exhumation," as well as mythic creatures, such as the mermaid in "The Comb and the Mirror." Though she employs a male persona in poems such as "Seven Gough Square," written in the form of a letter from Samuel Johnson to his wife, Spires focuses largely on women's voices and experiences with her personae. With a feminist impulse, Spires documents historical injustices, for instance, in poems such as "Salem, Massachusetts: 1692," which treats a "true" witch's revenge against a witch-hunter. In this poem, the speaker wonders of the hunter, "How you could disregard the terrible shrieks" of the innocent (*Globe* 32). Spires also often critiques the idea of women as art objects, employing the voice of a young woman in "Courtesan with Fan" and an artist's model in "Blue Nude."

In her latest work, Spires focuses on women's experience in a more personal way, one that places an emphasis on connection, rather than disjunction, between self and other and perhaps strives for some kind of balance between the two. In much of *Worldling*, Spires relates her own journey through motherhood, from "Letter in July" and "The Summer of Celia," chronicling her pregnancy, to "Theatre of Pain," about her experience of childbirth. "Celia Dreaming" and "Childhood" are reveries on her new motherhood, and in "The Awakening," the speaker ponders when it was that she herself changed from child to mother. These are poems about transformation and about the tension between unity and separation. In "The Summer of Celia," the poet revels in her communion with her unborn daughter, fearing the moment of disconnection that must come at the moment of birth, when both mother and child will waken from a dream, "shocked and surprised, in our separate bodies" (7).

In light of her focus in her latest poetry on the experience of both having been a child and now parenting one, Spires's authorship of children's literature seems fitting. Her works for children encompass diverse genres, including a pop-up book—*Simon's Adventure* (1982)—as well as a board book for small children, entitled *The Falling Star* (1981). Some of her children's works integrate poetry into narrative. For example, her two books of riddles, *Riddle Road* (1999) and *With One White Wing* (1995), which contain many riddles in verse form, prompt children to see everyday objects in a new way. In addition, Spires has penned works for older children. One of these, *I Am Arachne* (2001), retells in first person the stories of different characters from Greek and Roman myths. Another work, *The Mouse of Amherst* (1999), features a mouse named Emmaline, who lives in a wall of Emily Dickinson's bedroom and exchanges poems with the poet. Appropriately, Spires has chosen Dickinson as the focus for her story, since Spires's poetry bears similarities to Dickinson's, with its frequent employment of formal structure and attention to subjects that might be perceived by others as small or hidden.

CRITICAL RECEPTION

Reviews of Spires's poetry have focused on its lyricism, its use of form and image, as well as its religious aspects. Tony Whedon, for instance, touches upon all of these elements in his extensive discussion of *Annonciade*, which focuses on the eloquent, long title poem. Whedon asserts that Spires "writes with craft and stateliness, her grand balancing of thematic and linguistic opposites, tempered by a classical reserve, is never permitted to overmaster her poem. That reserve is also kept in check—lest it anesthetize the poem—by her sustained vision of a faith forged by suffering" (107). Spires, he observes, "explor[es] the ramifications of faith in an incredulous age" (119).

Critics of Spires's earlier poetry have attended to Spires's use of art works as subject matter and to her preoccupation with detail. While expressing admiration for the language of the poetry and its controlled form, some reviewers have critiqued what they see as a distance between art and life in her poems. One critic notes of *Swan's Island* that a focus on art in Spires's lyric poetry distances the reader from actual experience (Jarman 338). Disagreement exists over Spires's attention to detail in her poems, especially those that deal with artistic subjects. The poems of *Annonciade* have been compared to jewels: says one scholar, "Each poem is placed carefully like a jewel in a setting" (Muske 33). Yet some see this close observation and specific subject matter as potentially limiting and have termed Spires a "miniaturist." Pheobe Pettingell asserts, "The reader's eye and ear finally tire peering at so many infinitesimal jewels" (16).

Yet reviews of Spires's later volume, *Worldling,* emphasize a balance between her employment of portraiture and engagement of experience and life. This engagement is largely seen in Spires's poems about her own experience of motherhood, but also in poems such as "Two Watchers," "The Rock," "Fisher Beach," and "The Great Sea," which draw upon ocean imagery in both narrating a scene and exploring the inner life of the speaker. The poems in *Worldling* have been called "models of grace, of patient articulation, of balance" (Baker, "Line" 202). As David Baker observes, through these poems Spires "creates an almost mythic contest between steadfastness and the fluid, uncontrollable movements of time" (204). In her latest work, critics seem to view Spires as effectively inviting a sense of wonder as she combines weighty subjects and emotions with delicate imagery.

BIBLIOGRAPHY

Works by Elizabeth Spires

Boardwalk. Cleveland, OH: Bits Press, 1977.

Count with Me. Columbus, OH: Merrill, 1981. (juvenile literature)

The Falling Star. Illustrated by Carlo A. Michelini. New York: Grosset & Dunlap, 1981. (juvenile literature)

Globe. Middletown, CT: Wesleyan University Press; Irvington, NY: Distributed by Columbia University Press, 1981.

Simon's Adventure: With 34 Pop-Open Doors. Illustrated by Judy Hand. Yellow Springs, OH: Antioch, 1982. (juvenile literature)

Swan's Island: Poems. New York: Holt, Rinehart and Winston, 1985.

Annonciade. New York: Viking, 1989.

"Some Notes on Form." In *A Formal Feeling Comes: Poems in Form by Contemporary Women*, edited by Annie Finch. Brownsville, OR: Story Line Press, 1994. 211–12. (essay)

With One White Wing: Puzzles in Poems and Pictures. Illustrated by Erik Blegvad. New York: Margaret K. McElderry Books, 1995. (juvenile literature)

Worldling. New York: Norton, 1995.

The Mouse of Amherst. Illustrated by Claire Nivola. New York: Frances Foster Books, 1999. (juvenile literature)

Riddle Road: Puzzles in Poems and Pictures. Illustrated by Erik Blegvad. New York: Margaret K. McElderry Books, 1999. (juvenile literature)

I Am Arachne: Fifteen Greek and Roman Myths. Illustrated by Mordicai Gerstein. New York: Farrar, 2001. (juvenile literature)

Studies of Elizabeth Spires

Baker, David. "Earthly Quires." Review of *Annonciade*, by Elizabeth Spires. *Kenyon Review* 13.3 (1991): 161–81.

————. "Line by Line." Review of *Worldling*, by Elizabeth Spires. *Kenyon Review* 18.3–4 (1996): 191–205.

Chappell, Fred. "Book Reviews." Review of *Annonciade*, by Elizabeth Spires. *Georgia Review* 53 (1989): 385–94.

Christie, A. V. "The Power of the Visible Is the Invisible." *Southwest Review* 80.1 (1995): 35–57.

Collins, Floyd. "A Fine Excess." Review of *Worldling*, by Elizabeth Spires. *Gettysburg Review* 9 (1996): 331–52.

Jarman, Mark. "Singers and Storytellers." Review of *Swan's Island*, by Elizabeth Spires. *Hudson Review* 39 (1986): 334–47.

Muske, Carol. "Go Be a King in a Field of Weeds." Review of *Annonciade*, by Elizabeth Spires. *New York Times Book Review*, 5 Nov. 1989, 32–33.

Pettingell, Pheobe. "Writers and Writing: Tales of Eros in Verse." Review of *Annonciade*, by Elizabeth Spires. *New Leader*, 6 March 1989, 15–16.

Taylor, John. "Short Reviews." Review of *Worldling*, by Elizabeth Spires. *Poetry* (1997): 295–98.

Whedon, Tony. "Post-American Style." *Iowa Review* 23.1 (1993): 101–19.

RUTH STONE (1915–)

Vanessa Warne

BIOGRAPHY

Ruth Stone was born in Roanoke, Virginia, in 1915 and raised in Indiana. After attending the University of Illinois, Stone married her second husband, the poet and novelist Walter B. Stone, with whom she had three daughters. In 1959 Stone's husband took a sabbatical from Vassar College and the family moved to England. While in England, Walter Stone committed suicide. Returning to the United States with her daughters, Stone struggled with the loss of her husband and with the necessity of supporting her young family. In 1963 she was awarded a two-year fellowship by the Radcliffe Institute. Stone went on to hold a series of creative writing teaching positions at such universities as the University of Wisconsin, Madison; Indiana University, Bloomington; and the University of California, Davis.

Stone published her first collection of poems, *In an Iridescent Time*, in 1959, several months before the death of her husband. The poems in this collection are notable for their lyricism and their syntactic complexity. Stone's second volume, *Topography and Other Poems*, was published in 1971. In this volume, the influence of Stone's experience of widowhood is apparent in numerous poems devoted to explorations of grief. *Cheap: New Poems and Ballads* was published in 1975. As its title suggests, images of commerce and consumption dominate the volume.

Twelve years passed between the publication of *Cheap* and Stone's fourth book, *Second-Hand Coat: Poems New and Selected* (1987), a volume notable for its humor. In 1990, at the age of seventy-five, Stone was appointed to her first tenured position as professor of English and creative writing at State University of New York, Binghamton. In 1991 she published *Who Is the Widow's Muse?* a sequence of fifty-three poems devoted to the relationship between widowhood and authorship. In 1995 Stone published *Simplicity*, a collection characterized by thematic variety and by rapid shifts between a humorous and a serious tone. The same degree of variety is apparent in Stone's most recent collection, *Ordinary Words* (1999). In this collection Stone brings together poems on aging, language, and contemporary American culture. She also continues to experiment with a variety of poetic forms, adding a prose poem entitled "In the Arboretum" to her already varied repertoire of monologues, dialogues, elegies, ballads, and lyrics.

In addition to her six collections, Stone has published four chapbooks: *Unknown Messages* (1973), *American Milk* (1986), *The Solution* (1989), and *Nursery Rhymes from Mother Stone* (1992). She has also been a contributor to such periodicals as the *Iowa Review*, the *Kenyon Review*, *Ploughshares*, *Prairie Schooner*, and the *Massachusetts Review*. Her work has been anthologized in a number of different collections including *No More Masks* (1973), *The Norton Anthology of Literature by Women* (1985), and *The Oxford Book of Women's Writing in the United States* (1995). Stone has also received numerous awards and honors, including the Bess Hokin Prize from *Poetry* magazine (1954); the Kenyon Review Fellowship in Poetry (1956); a Radcliffe Institute Fellowship from Harvard University (1963–65); the Shelley Memorial Award from the Poetry Society of America (1964); a grant from the Academy of Arts and Letters (1970); two Guggenheim Fellowships (1971 and 1975); the Delmore Schwartz Award (1983); the Whiting Writer's Award (1986); and the Paterson Poetry Prize (1988).

MAJOR WORKS AND THEMES

Since publishing her first book at the age of forty-four, Stone has demonstrated a steady interest in the patterns and rhythms of family life. This interest is well represented by one of her most frequently anthologized pieces, the title poem of *In an Iridescent Time*. In this poem, a speaker envisions her mother and aunts as young girls washing clothes by hand together. In *Topography* Stone pays particular attention to relationships existing between children and their parents. "Last Lullaby," addressed to the poet's youngest daughter, explores the close but constantly evolving nature of the bond that exists between mother and child. *Topography* also contains "I Have Three Daughters," a poem that uses folk song rhythms to explore intergenerational tensions. Stone's most recent book, dedicated to her three daughters, contains several poems about family life, including "The Ways of Daughters" and "A Movement."

An appreciation of the natural world is also a prominent feature of Stone's poetry. "Snow," from *In an Iridescent Time*, opens with the simple but evocative statement, "Plentiful snow deepens the path to the woods" (1). In *Topography* poems such as "Poles" and "The Winnowing" examine the relation of rural life to seasonal rhythms. In a similar vein, the title poem of *Simplicity* describes the experience of gathering water from a stream in winter. *Simplicity* also contains ample evidence of Stone's interest in science. In poems such as "Love and Money" and "Things I Say to Myself While Hanging Laundry," physics and biology provide Stone with both imagery and subject matter.

Descriptions of the natural world also make an important contribution to the travel poems about long-distance bus and train trips. These poems make much of the opportunities that travel presents for the poet's voyeuristic observation of fellow passengers. Stone's experimentation with travel poems achieves a kind of climax in *Cheap*, with poems such as "Bored on a Greyhound" and "En Route." One of Stone's most memorable poems in this mode is from *Simplicity* and is entitled "Nuns at Lunch on the Bus." The poem combines detailed descriptions of the appearance and actions of two nuns with reflections on their inner lives, both physical and emotional. To some extent, a poem such as "Nuns at Lunch on the Bus" can be seen as one manifestation of Stone's larger fascination with the private lives of everyday people. In a poem from *In an Iridescent Time* entitled "From the Window," a speaker describes her observations of a painfully narcissistic moment in another woman's life; in "Apprentice to the Dance," from *Topography*, the hidden passions of an awkward pubescent girl catch and hold the speaker's attention.

In the course of her career, Stone's emotional life has proven her most important source of subject matter. Again and again, Stone returns to the subject of her husband's death and the impact that it had and continues to have on her life. In this sense, Stone's poetry can be seen as a profound and sustained study in grief. In *Topography*, Stone gives voice to emotions about her loss which range from despondency to anger. For instance, in "Poles," a speaker describes the experience of viewing a picture of the deceased loved one and finding herself "shaking [her] head at the shame that lies down and dies" (9). Similar sentiments find expression in *Cheap*, a volume in which Stone continues to recall and reflect on daily life with her husband. "Sabbatical Love" and "Mist at the University of Illinois" pay close attention to the role of memory in the grieving process. The poem "Habit," also from *Cheap*, is structured on a powerful comparison between the speaker's production of elegiac poems and the disinterment of the decaying body of her deceased lover. Stone's understanding of the connection between grieving and writing finds its most thorough expression in *Who Is the Widow's Muse?*. The poems in this sequence trace the evolution of a relationship between a widowed poet figure and her muse. In the sequence's final poem, the muse places a prohibition on the production of more grieving poems, explaining to the poet: "Once and for all . . . he is forever dead" (14). The influence of such a prohibition is not, however, apparent in Stone's own work. *Simplicity* contains a number of elegiac poems, including "That Day" and "Coffee and Sweet Rolls." Similarly, *Ordinary Words* contains "Then," a poem in which the speaker addresses the dead loved ones, remembering an earlier stage in her grieving and reaching the conclusion that "My trouble was I could not keep you dead" (6).

Stone also discusses the production of poetry in a number of nonelegiac, self-reflexive pieces. In "My Son," from *Topography*, Stone compares a lost and unfinished poem to a son who never had the chance to be born. *Cheap* continues in this vein, seeing Stone refer in "In No Time" to boxes of old poems as "abortions that I could not love" (6). In *Second-Hand Coat*, she writes about the "Po-Biz" and life at the "poetry factory" (6). "Flash," from *Simplicity*, also explores the industrial and commercial potential of authorship, once again equating the production of poetry with factory work. Much of Stone's work in this area involves considerations of the relationship of gender and authorship. In "Words," a poem from her most recent collection, Stone engages with a statement made by Wallace Stevens in order to explore the gendered nature of a poet's gaze. This poem emerges as the latest manifestation of a poetic career characterized by a commitment to feminist politics and poetics.

CRITICAL RECEPTION

In 1982, Tillie Olsen describes Ruth Stone as "one of the major poets of her time" (Gilbert et al. 327). A number of critics have echoed Olsen's assessment of Stone's work. For example, Frances Mayes calls Stone "wise and abundantly gifted" (24), and Willis Barnstone refers to her as "the major poet in our language" (96). Critics have also noted Stone's lack of widespread recognition. In a 1972 review, Harvey Gross laments that "although she has been widely honored . . . , she is not, given her excellence, widely known" (95). Similarly, Julie Fay explains that Stone has "lived on a tributary rather than the main stream of poetry" and expresses the hope that *Second-Hand Coat* will "bring her the attention that her work merits" (18). More recently, in an article from 1996, Roger Gilbert comments on Stone's "relative obscurity" (179). Similar assessments of Stone's status have been made by Sandra Gilbert, one of Stone's most vocal supporters. Writing in 1982, Gilbert describes Stone as "largely unknown," identifying her as a "paradigm of the 'lost' woman writer" (Gilbert et al. 323). In an earlier review, Gilbert discusses the dispossession and marginalization of female poets such as Stone. In this review, Gilbert also reads the cranky, tenacious elderly woman in Stone's poem "The Song of Absinthe Granny" as a figure for the female poet, "an emblem both of the female artist's rage and of her survival" (299).

A desire to put an end to Stone's obscurity was one of the primary motivations informing the 1996 publication of *The House Is Made of Poetry: The Art of Ruth Stone*, a collection of essays dedicated to Stone's work. In this book, Wendy Barker and her coeditor, Gilbert, bring together a diverse array of responses to Stone's work. In addition to critical discussions of Stone's poetry, the book contains memoirs of Stone written by friends and colleagues. In "Ruth Stone and Her Poems," Sharon Olds remembers her first meeting with Stone and describes the poet as "a place where life turned into art" (5). In "Like a Laser Beam," Martha Nell Smith locates Stone's work in a literary genealogy of women poets by focusing on connections between Stone's poetry and that of Emily Dickinson. The collection also contains important essays by Janet Lowry, Aliki Barnstone, and Kandace Brill Lombart on Stone's representation of widowhood. In the final piece in the volume, Gilbert explores the prominent role played by compassion and charity in Stone's poetry and describes Stone's poems as "definitions of love" (201). These essays, along with numerous others, make *The House Is Made of Poetry* a collection that contributes to the appreciation and renown of Ruth Stone's work.

BIBLIOGRAPHY

Works by Ruth Stone

In an Iridescent Time. New York: Harcourt, 1959.
Topography and Other Poems. New York: Harcourt, 1971.
Unknown Messages. Hinsboro, IL: Nemesis Press, 1973.
Cheap: New Poems and Ballads. New York: Harcourt, 1975.
American Milk. Fanwood, NJ: From Here Press, 1986.
Second-Hand Coat: Poems New and Selected. Boston: Godine, 1987; Cambridge, MA: Yellow Moon, 1991.
The Solution. Baltimore, MD: Alembic Press, 1989.
Who Is the Widow's Muse? Cambridge, MA: Yellow Moon, 1991.
Nursery Rhymes from Mother Stone. Binghamton, NY: Mbira Press, 1992.
Simplicity. Northhampton, MA: Paris Press, 1995.
Ordinary Words. Ashfield, MA: Paris Press, 1999.

Studies of Ruth Stone

Barker, Wendy, and Sandra M. Gilbert, eds. *The House Is Made of Poetry: The Art of Ruth Stone*. Carbondale: Southern Illinois University Press, 1996.

Barnstone, Willis. "Poet in the Mountains" In *The House Is Made of Poetry: The Art of Ruth Stone,* edited by Wendy Barker and Sandra M. Gilbert. Carbondale: Southern Illinois University Press, 1996. 78–100.

Fay, Julie. "Art in Obscurity." *Women's Review of Books* 6 (1989): 18.

Gilbert, Roger. "Ruth Stone's Intricate Simplicities." *Iowa Review* 26 (1996): 179–93.

Gilbert, Sandra M., et al. "On Ruth Stone." In *Extended Outlooks: The Iowa Review Collection of Contemporary Women Writers*, edited by Jane Cooper et al. New York: Collier, 1982. 323–30.

Gross, Harvey. "On the Poetry of Ruth Stone: Selections and Commentary." *Iowa Review* 3 (1972): 94–106.

Hartman, Geoffrey. "Six Women Poets." In *Easy Pieces*. New York: Columbia University Press, 1985. 108–21.

Howe, Florence. "Fragile Strengths, Complex Simplicities." *Women's Review of Books*, 13 Dec. 1995, 11–12.

Kessler, Jascha. "The Inner World Where Poets Wander." *Poetry Quarter*, 2 Oct. 1971, 50.

Lattimore, Richard. "Poetry Chronicle." *Hudson Review* 23 (1976): 119–20.

Mayes, Frances. Review of *Second-Hand Coat: Poems New and Selected*, by Ruth Stone. *San Jose Mercury News*, 10 July 1988, 24.

Olds, Sharon. "Ruth Stone and Her Poems." In *The House Is Made of Poetry: The Art of Ruth Stone*, edited by Wendy Barker and Sandra M. Gilbert. Carbondale: Southern Illinois University Press, 1996. 5–8.

Pettingell, Phoebe. "Plurality of Words." *Poetry* 119 (1972): 234–39.

Smith, Martha Nell. "Like a Laser Beam." In *The House Is Made of Poetry: The Art of Ruth Stone,* edited by Wendy Barker and Sandra M. Gilbert. Carbondale: Southern Illinois University Press, 1996. 17–29.

KAREN SWENSON (1936–)

Marlene D. Allen

BIOGRAPHY

Karen Swenson was born on July 29, 1936, in New York City, the daughter of Howard and Dorothy Swenson. In 1958 she married Michael Shuter, with whom she had a son, Michael, Jr. She attended Barnard College, where she received her BA degree in 1959, and then earned an MA from New York University in 1971. Subsequently, she began work on a doctorate degree in Old English and began teaching at the City College of New York in Harlem in 1969, but due to a New York City budget crisis, she lost her job in 1976. As a result, Swenson began traveling across the United States to fill various positions as a poet-in-residence in various universities, including Clark University, Skidmore College, Denver University, and the University of Idaho. She also gave readings and taught as poet-in-the-schools in Nebraska, Montana, Oregon, California, Colorado, Idaho, and Washington. Her various travels, as itinerant poet, forced her eventually to give up her pursuit of her PhD and, as Swenson said in an interview in *Belles Lettres*, caused her son to "feel abandoned, but it gained me a new sense of self and an intimate knowledge of parts of my country I would not otherwise have seen" (Davidson 53). During this time, she also experienced two other major changes in her life that affected her poetry: the deaths of her mother and her father.

Swenson began writing poetry in high school but says she ceased when she had her son at age twenty-five. She then resumed writing after his birth after an argument with her husband, who complained, "You always talk about writing but you never do it," a spur for which she says she is now grateful (Nelson 132). Her first collection of poems, *An Attic of Ideals*, was published in 1974, her chapbook, *East-West*, in 1980, and her second volume of poetry, *A Sense of Direction*, was published in 1989. Her next collection, *The Landlady in Bangkok*, was inspired by her years of travel in Southeast Asia. The book was chosen by Maxine Kumin as a National Poetry series winner in 1993 and was subsequently published by Copper Canyon Press in 1994. In addition to writing poetry during her years in Southeast Asia, Swenson also wrote articles on her travel experiences for periodicals such as the *New York Times* and the *Wall Street Journal.* Her latest work, *A Daughter's Latitude* (1999), is a collection of selected poems from her earlier books as well as other poems she wrote from the 1960s to the 1990s previously uncollected in book form.

In 1973 Swenson received a *Transatlantic Review* Poetry Fellowship at Breadloaf Writers' Conference; furthermore, in 1987 and 1989, she was a Yaddo fellow and an Albee Foundation fellow from 1990 to 1991. In addition to winning the National Poetry series competition in 1993, she received an Honorable Mention from the Arvon Foundation in England for her poem "The Ice-Cream Sandwich" in 1988 and was a runner-up for the Ann Stanford Poetry Award that same year. Her poems have been published widely in journals such as *The New Yorker, Poetry, Paris Review,* and *Prairie Schooner.*

MAJOR WORKS AND THEMES

Unsurprisingly, since Karen Swenson has spent such a significant portion of her life on the road, travel emerges as one of the major themes in her poetry. In her work, she represents her various journeys as physical quests and as emotional and intellectual searches for meaning. Her travels allowed her the opportunity not only to speculate on the landscapes she encountered but also on her own life, on her sense of self, and on how others around her have affected her worldview. Her five collections of poetry reflect Swenson's progression toward finding meaning in her life.

An Attic of Ideals provides the beginning of the emotional and spiritual journey Swenson makes. The poems betray Swenson's feminist sensibilities and ideals as she ruminates in the collection upon what it means to be a woman in a male-dominated and male-centered world. In an interview in *Belles Lettres,* she expresses, "Being a woman is for me being an alien in the world" (Davidson 52). Various poems in the work illustrate this viewpoint, including "The Heroines," which presents the inspiration for *An Attic of Ideals*'s title. The poem reveals how women, being preoccupied with the "shelved principles" of the men in their lives, in essence are relegated to an "attic of ideals," thereby cutting themselves off from the world around them. Swenson uses domestic images associated with housework to illustrate her point: The women in the poem must dust "broken bowls of justice, honor," thereby implicitly participating in the destruction of their dreams. She further depicts the stagnation and inactivity of the lives to which most women are designated in her use of images such as "quiet reservoir" and "still lake" (*Daughter's Latitude* 11).

In poems such as "The Moon" (*Attic*), Swenson mixes the personal and the cultural by using a national event, the landing of American astronauts on the moon, to reflect on gender roles and the nature of men. Although many at the time of the landing saw the event as a monumental and proverbial "giant step" ahead for mankind, Swenson depicts the event as a "public deflowering" of the feminized moon, a masculine enterprise gleefully embarked upon by men who cannot stand the moon's "openness." Other poems in *Attic* that illustrate the feminist sensibilities of the work include "The Price of Women," "The Portrait," "Virginia," and "Dear Elizabeth." Further themes present in the collection include the relationships between men and women, death, and memory.

The collection also introduces a theme Swenson would later explore more intensely in *A Sense of Direction*: her dysfunctional relationship with her mother. For instance, in "Hooks and Eyes" Swenson uses sewing imagery to depict how her mother, in making dresses for the most important occasions in Swenson's life, her first communion and her wedding, in fact attempted to fit her into certain molds (or modes) of behavior and living.

Swenson's chapbook *East-West* and her collection *A Sense of Direction* begin the theme of travel that eventually culminated in the award-winning *The Landlady in Bangkok.* She wrote both books during periods of intense crises in her life: her divorce from her husband in 1970; the loss of her teaching position at City College; her series of visiting appointments as poet-in-residence or poet-in-the-schools throughout the United States; and the death of her mother. As a result, a sense of fluctuation and change pervades the two collections, in which she reminisces on her personal relationships as well as her relationships to the landscapes she visits. In "Moving," from *East-West,* Swenson uses the occasion of packing to move to ponder her newly broken marriage. In boxing up the accoutrements of her and her husband's shared household, the persona of the poem encounters the emptiness of the newly vacated spaces in their former home, which in turn emphasizes the barrenness of the years she spent with a husband who was indifferent to their marriage.

In *A Sense of Direction,* Swenson begins by reflecting upon her relationship with her now-deceased mother that she had first contemplated in *An Attic of Ideals,* then focuses upon her travels across the United States. The latter section of the collection deals with her father, who died in the early 1980s. In poems such as "Selling Her Engagement Ring," "My Mother Left Me," "The White Rabbit," and "Like a Henry Moore Statue," Swenson explores the lack of communication between herself and her mother and the emptiness of their relationship, which, sadly, ultimately becomes the only tangible item left after her mother's death. The rabbit of "The White Rabbit" that the young persona of the poem beats to death emblematizes her mother's abusiveness, as her mother beats her because she kills the animal in misplaced anger at her mother. The unhealable "zero" in the middle of the persona in "Like a Henry Moore Statue" becomes a synonym for the incurable nothingness of her relationship with her mother.

Interspersed with the poems about her mother are travel poems such as "Dinosaur National," "The State of Wyoming," and "The Itinerant Poet's Road Song," a delightful ballad recounting her driving experiences out West, with her cat vomiting on her tapes as she leaves Lolo Pass, on the border between Montana and Idaho, her car spinning out because of black ice near Livingston, Montana, and a semitruck "trailin' [her] Honda's ass" as she makes her way toward Denver (*Daughter's Latitude* 112–13). The latter section of the collection focuses upon her relationship with her father in poems such "Spring Walk," in which Swenson uses images such as "old derelict road," "dead-ends," "gone," "broken," and repetitions of various forms of the word "rotted" to foreshadow her father's impending death as the persona and her father embark upon a spring walk.

The Landlady in Bangkok also deals with the idea of travel, but in this collection, Swenson moves geographically beyond the United States to focus upon her encounters in Southeast Asia. Accompanying this territorial shift is a resulting metaphorical and thematic shift from dealing with the self and the personal to a focusing on the global and the universal. Thus, for instance, Swenson takes her concerns such as those about the roles of women in Western society to a higher level in poems such as "What Does a Woman Want?" which opens the collection. A play on Sigmund Freud's famous question about women's motives, Swenson once again explores how women's lives are endlessly "delayed" while men are allowed to progress with theirs without hindrance. The men the persona of the poem encounters in Southeast Asia view her, a single, middle-aged woman who travels by herself without the accompaniment of a man, suspiciously. They see her, as she says in "Medias Res," as a new breed of woman who emerges, like a fungus, from the women who fulfill more traditional roles.

The commonalities of Eastern and Western culture provide another theme that becomes apparent in poems such as "The Beast," in which Swenson ingeniously works the Western Oedipal myth of the son who slays the father to protect the mother into an Eastern exotic tale (itself reminiscent of the Greek myth of Cupid and Psyche) of a king's daughter who, seized by an eagle, unknowingly marries a beast who rescues her. The beast is later slain by their son, from whom the beast cannot hide his true nature. In "Background and Design," the persona watches a Michael Jackson video on a television shop window in Bangkok and becomes intensely aware of the ironies of her situation as a white woman mingling with young Asian children as they all watch an American who is brown like the children but is "normalized" because of his fame. The uncollected poems in Swenson's *A Daughter's Latitude* also illustrate many of the themes of her earlier works, such as the connections between Eastern and Western cultures and the lost dreams and hopes of women in poems such as "Plato's Cave," "The Strapless," and "The Lovers."

CRITICAL RECEPTION

Though Swenson has been writing poetry since the 1960s, has won prizes and appointments as a result of her work, and has published five collections of poetry, her work suffers largely from disregard by literary scholars. The reviews that are available cite Swenson as a gifted poet whose use of imagery is original and remarkable. In his assessment of *The Landlady in Bangkok*, Philip K. Jason expresses, "Her greatest tool is the intelligent eye that produces [a] quality of heightened awareness. She gives us an attractive mind at play" (197). Jason further notes that Swenson's *Landlady* encompasses the best aspects of the tradition of the travel book as a recording of the exploration of new landscapes and terrains and the resulting inquiries that formulate in the mind of the traveler about both that which is familiar and that which is new (200).

In her interview with Swenson published by *Belles Lettres*, Phebe Davidson calls *Landlady* most important "for what it says and how—both elements uniquely Swenson's, both an outgrowth of her own life and her poetic consciousness" (51). Robert Phillips, in reviewing *A Daughter's Latitude*, observes, "If a good poet, in the oft-quoted remark by Randall Jerrell, is someone who manages, in a lifetime of standing out in thunderstorms, to be struck by lightning five or six times, Karen Swenson seems to have been struck with at least as much frequency, and her big collection . . . reveals her to be a poet to whom attention must be paid" (696). Swenson certainly is a poet who has wrestled with many of the major philosophical and ideological issues of our time in verse that is both imaginative and skillful. Hopefully, future literary scholars will study Swenson's work more closely, for it has much to reveal about how the inner psychological struggles of the poet become synecdoches of the vastly changing world around her.

BIBLIOGRAPHY

Works by Karen Swenson

An Attic of Ideals. Garden City, NY: Doubleday, 1974.
East-West. Lewiston, ID: Confluence Press, 1980.
A Sense of Direction. New York: The Smith Publishers, 1989.
The Landlady in Bangkok. Port Townsend, WA: Copper Canyon Press, 1994.
A Daughter's Latitude. Port Townsend, WA: Copper Canyon Press, 1999.

Studies of Karen Swenson

Davidson, Phebe. "Karen Swenson." *Belles Lettres* 10.3 (1995): 51–53, 59.
Jason, Philip K. Review of *The Landlady in Bangkok*, by Karen Swenson. *Prairie Schooner* 70.3 (1996): 197–200.
Kuzuma, Greg. "The Outward Path: An Interview with Karen Swenson." *New Letters* 60.2 (1994): 95–104.
Nelson, Ronald J. "An Interview with Karen Swenson." *Denver Quarterly* 24.1 (1989): 132–41.
Phillips, Robert. "Utterly Unlike." *Hudson Review* 52.4 (2000): 689–96.

CHASE TWICHELL (1950–)

Marlene D. Allen

BIOGRAPHY

Chase Twichell was born on August 20, 1950, in New Haven, Connecticut, the daughter of Charles P. and Ann Chase Twichell. Her father Charles, a teacher at Choate boys' preparatory school, taught Latin, and her mother, a homemaker, later worked in a bookstore. The family spent their summer vacations in Keene, New York, a town located in the Adirondack Mountains below Montreal. The natural setting in Keene would later have a great effect on Twichell's worldview and would serve as an inspiration for her poetic art. Twichell says her New Haven hometown, in contrast, had little discernible effect upon her except as a contrast to Keene (Daniel 214).

As a young child, Twichell was intensely fascinated with painting, a near-obsession that drove her parents, fearful that she was becoming, as she expresses, "socially abnormal," to extreme measures. When at age fourteen she entered St. Timothy's, a boarding school for girls in Maryland, her parents laid down the mandate that she was forbidden to take art classes for at least a year. As a form of revenge, Twichell, who had begun reading poetry early in her life, then began to write poetry seriously.

During her college years, Twichell took classes at Mills, Reed, Wesleyan, and Trinity colleges. At Wesleyan she studied with the poet Richard Wilbur and with the poet Hugh Ogden at Trinity. In 1973 Twichell graduated with honors in English from Trinity and a year later enrolled at the University of Iowa's Workshop, where she held a writing and teaching fellowship. While at Iowa studying writing, she simultaneously minored in typography and design and apprenticed at Windover Press for a year. After receiving her MFA degree in 1976, she went to work for Pennyroyal Press, in West Hatfield, Massachusetts, for nine years. During this time, she also wrote two collections of poetry, *Northern Spy* (1981) and *The Odds* (1986), while also teaching occasionally at Hampshire College. Twichell left Pennyroyal in 1985 to take a teaching position in the MFA program at the University of Alabama in Tuscaloosa, where she co-edited the Alabama Poetry series. During her tenure at Alabama, she met the novelist Russell Banks, a visiting professor, whom she later married. Twichell taught for three years at Alabama then left in 1988 with Banks to eventually settle at Princeton University, where Banks held an endowed chair and she taught in the creative writing program. The couple stayed in Princeton for nine years, during which time Twichell published two additional collections of poetry, *Perdido* (1991) and *The Ghost of Eden* (1995). She also edited, along with Robin Behn, *The Practice of Poetry* (1992), a collection of creative writing exercises she and Robin Behn gathered from various contemporary poets.

In 1998 Twichell and Banks left Princeton and retired to the Adirondacks permanently. In that same year, her latest book, *The Snow Watcher*, was published. Twichell has started her own publishing company, Ausable Press, which she operates from her home. The press publishes both poetry and regional interest books.

MAJOR WORKS AND THEMES

Because Twichell has spent such a large portion of her life in the Adirondack mountain area, it is not surprising that natural themes and imagery abound in her writings. Instead of capturing the beauties of nature on the canvas, as she undoubtedly would have done had she been allowed to live out her childhood ambitions to become a painter, Twichell instead has chosen to do so using the medium of words. Upon reading her poetry, the reader is struck by one recurring visual image: snow. Her poems often feature snowy landscapes that Twichell uses as a source for her poetic ruminations on many themes and issues: the inherent beauty and divinity of nature, death and mortality, intellectual reflections upon the artistic process, and the search for self in the midst of an earth becoming extinct before our very eyes. For instance, in poems such as "Snow Light," from her first book, *Northern Spy*, Twichell uses a snowy winter day as her setting to ponder upon the uniqueness of nature. The trees the persona espies when stopping during a nature walk is both burdened yet paradoxically "lightened" by the snow on its branches. The lightness and heaviness of the snow becomes a metaphor for the oxymoronic "unearthliness" of earth, a divinity existing ironically along with the materiality of earth. This spirituality of earth and nature forms the well-spring of Twichell's poetic inspiration.

In "The First Snow," also from *Northern Spy*, Twichell intermingles her preoccupations with nature with another common feature of her poems: sexuality. She sets the poem on a crisp autumn day, where geese fly in the air embarked presumably upon their annual pilgrimages down south for the winter. The beauties of this autumn day arouse an emotion in the speaker similar to a sexual arousal. In a highly original reversal of traditional metaphorical associations, Twichell portrays autumn, rather than springtime, as a time of burgeoning sexual energy instead of connecting it with the usual decay that leads to the death commonly affiliated with winter. She uses potent imagery to link various forms of autumn sexuality, human, animal, heavenly, and natural, in the poem. The "V's" of Canada geese "contract and relax" as they float through a northern heavenly sky that is "liquid and stroking," and snowflakes build up "tensile strength" in a sky full only with "moisture and temperature"(*Northern Spy* 50). The poem finally ends the building sense of tension in the final two lines, where all of this sexual activity eventually climaxes into "the slow upheaval of your body in mine" (50). Other poems in this collection that merge nature and sexual energy include "The Iris, That Sexual Flower" and "Physics," which depicts female sexual gratification as "a tiny engine" that builds up from "separate sparks" and comes apart like a "fractured atom" (32).

Twichell also uses nature in her poems to speculate on the process of creating poetic art. For instance, in "Meteor Showers, August 1968," from her second collection *The Odds*, the persona of the poems compares a remembered meteor shower from her childhood to the process of writing poetry. Words fall out onto the page in a manner similar to how meteors fall from the sky. They are "a paradigm" that regulates the mind, and, therefore, to be truly creative the mind has to "renounce" the form of words, or stand firm before the form like a "stockade or a dam," in order to free itself from the ordering words impose upon it. Only by doing so can a writer truly tap into the creative process. In "Japanese Weeping Cherry," also from *The Odds*, the form of the tree, the subject of the poem, enters the form of the poem in the process of its creation, thereby corrupting the tree to create a "new pureness" (27). The "reality" of the tree becomes transformed by artistry into crumbling corsages in a drawer, a metaphor for time. The beauty of this transformation of reality into poetry, like the beauty of the Japanese Weeping Cherry, becomes unending, as it spreads beyond the poet's own consciousness when the poem is read by another person. Thus, Twichell makes a powerful assertion on the nature of art with this poem. She makes us realize the communality of art, in the sense that it is a shared experience between the reader and the poet. The meaning that a poet places in a poem at the moment of its creation is only one facet of its meaning, as a poem gathers even more substance when it is read by another. Therefore, the artistry of poetry is interminable and self-perpetuating.

Twichell also explores the theme of mortality in her poetry. In her fourth book, *The Ghost of Eden*, Twichell's meditation on this subject culminates in a brilliant collection of poems that merge her focus on both her own individual mortality and the dying of the earth. She says the work grew out of her preoccupations with the changes in the environment that have greatly affected the planet, but upon writing the poems in the collection, she found an inherent irony in the work: "The ghost of Eden is the remnant world, on one hand . . . but the real ghost turns out to be me. I'm the one who's wandering around weightless, and that made fighting through these poems emotionally and intellectually difficult" (Daniel 216). The struggles she experienced, as a person who grew up surrounded by nature, while writing these poems are apparent as the reader comes to realize Twichell both grieves for humankind's loss of its connection to nature and grapples with finding a sense of self in face of this loss. In poems such as "Girl with Sad Face," this disconnection is evident as the persona of the poem, gazing at a picture of herself as a child, sees her former self as a girl whose "chosen music" was "silence" and who spoke only the language of animals. Because she has subsequently been shut off from that girl-self who was close to nature, the persona is now alone, and a sense of sadness resulting from her knowledge of her solitary state pervades the poem. In "The Devil I Don't Know," Twichell moves from grieving for the self to anguish for the dead animals, emblematic of a dying earth, that the speaker views while strolling through a supermarket.

In Twichell's work, one also discerns the influence of her study of Zen Buddhism, most notably in her latest collection, *The Snow Watcher*. The sparse and minimalistic poems of this work, which Greg Johnson notes display a "haikulike brevity," (575) reflect in form that of Twichell's freeing herself from the concerns of the material world. They also illustrate the opening up of herself to a heightened consciousness she undoubtedly gained from her study of the religion, which perhaps gave her the wherewithal to deal with her emotions. As a result, the poems are quieter in tone and less angry than those of *The Ghost of Eden* and demonstrate her sense that a true knowledge and sense of self can be gained through monastic seclusion. In poems such as "Weightless, Like a River," the persona goes to a monastery to search for a teacher with whom she can study and while there engages in a "dawn zazen." Twichell states in the notes to the book that a *zazen* is a form of meditation to achieve enlightenment whose "purpose is to observe and ultimately to still the habitual activity of what we call the 'self' so that we can perceive its true nature" (*Snow Watcher* 101). The diminutiveness of "The Year I Got Rid of Everything" (it is only five lines long) echoes the enlightenment and divinity the speaker, lifted up to the heavens by a "huge invisible magnet," achieves upon freeing herself from her material goods. In essence, *The Snow Watcher* is Twichell's definitive work, as she ably and intelligently portrays her thematic, metaphorical, and philosophical shifts in thinking, resulting in a collection that displays a poetic mind finally at peace with itself and with the world around it.

CRITICAL RECEPTION

In general, critics have praised Twichell's work and find that it displays an original and noteworthy poetic skill. Though there are no full-length literary studies of her poems, most reviewers feel her work shows great promise and intellect. In reviewing *The Snow Watcher,* Greg Johnson expresses, "Chase Twichell has developed through five published collections an instantly recognizable voice: soft-spoken, economical to the point of austerity, yet graced by flashes of wit and passion" (575). Other readers have noted that Twichell's poems succeed well in merging her intellectual and artistic sides to the side of her that champions natural and environmental causes. David Daniel relates that her poems "marr[y] an urbane intellectual vigor—a classical grace and distance—to the passion of one who loves the world outside the window" (214). Twichell's poems are innovative and impressive expressions of her concerns about our world. Undoubtedly, as readers search for new voices that articulate the environmental crises facing the earth and express how one can deal with these crises, they will stumble upon Twichell's work and realize how one such voice has found resolution through her artistry.

BIBLIOGRAPHY

Works by Chase Twichell

Northern Spy: Poems by Chase Twichell. Pittsburgh, PA: University of Pittsburgh Press, 1981.

The Odds. Pittsburgh, PA: University of Pittsburgh Press, 1986.

Perdido. New York: Farrar, 1991.

The Practice of Poetry: Writing Exercises from Poets Who Teach, edited with Robin Behn. New York: Harper's, 1992.

The Ghost of Eden. Princeton, NJ: Ontario Review Press, 1995.

The Snow Watcher. Princeton, NJ: Ontario Review Press, 1998.

Studies of Chase Twichell

Burt, Stephen. Review of *The Ghost of Eden,* by Chase Twichell. *Times Literary Supplement,* 7 July 1995, 14.

Daniel, David. "About Chase Twichell." *Ploughshares* 19.4 (1994): 214–17.
Johnson, Greg. "On Their Own Premises." *Georgia Review* 53 (1999): 566–79.
Samson, Ian. Review of *The Ghost of Eden*, by Chase Twichell. *London Review of Books* 18 (1996): 26–27.
Skipper, Louie. "The One Clear Unspoken Sign: Four Young Poets." *Black Warrior Review* 12 (1986): 103–20.
Tyrell, Michael. Review of *The Snow Watcher*, by Chase Twichell. *Boston Review* 24.2 (1999): N.p.
Wunderlich, Mark. Review of *The Ghost of Eden*, by Chase Twichell. *Boston Review* 21.3 (1996): N.p.

MONA JANE VAN DUYN (1921–)

J. Elizabeth Clark

BIOGRAPHY

The first woman poet laureate for the United States, Mona Van Duyn, was born in Waterloo, Iowa, on May 9, 1921. This poet, educator, and essayist has played a key role in defining and advocating American poetry since the 1970s through her positions as chancellor of the American Academy of Poets (1985-present) and then as the sixth poet laureate in 1992. Her poetry has appeared in leading magazines such as *The New Yorker*, *The Kenyon Review*, and *The Atlantic*.

Van Duyn received a BA from the Iowa State Teachers College in 1942 (now the University of Northern Iowa). In 1943 she received an MA from the University of Iowa and married Jarvis Thurston. She began her teaching career at the prestigious Iowa Writers' Workshop from 1943–46 and moved on to teach at the University of Louisville (1946–50). Since 1950, Van Duyn has lived in St. Louis where she taught at Washington University, first as an adjunct lecturer in the University College adult education program and later as the Visiting Hurst Professor in the Department of English, until she retired in 1990. Throughout her career, she has been an active teacher in many writers' workshops such as Breadloaf. Her fame has spread internationally, affording her the opportunity to teach at the Salzburg, Austria, Seminar in American Studies.

In 1947 she co-founded *Perspective: A Quarterly of Literature and the Arts* with her husband and continued to co-edit the periodical until 1970. Her first volume of poetry, *Valentines to the Wide World*, was published in 1958; her second book, *A Time of Bees*, was published a few years later (1964). Van Duyn received critical acclaim and attention after the publication of her third book, *To See, To Take* (1970), for which she received a National Book Award (1971). Based on the success of her first three books, Van Duyn also won the Bollingen Prize, an unusual and triumphal recognition after only a few volumes of poetry. Van Duyn maintained her distinguished career with the publication of *Letters from a Father, and Other Poems* (1982), the 1991 Pulitzer Prize winning *Near Changes* (1990), *Firefall* (1993), and *If It Be Not I: Collected Poems 1959–1982* (1993).

MAJOR WORKS AND THEMES

Van Duyn, noted for her lyrical poetry and quirky rhyme schemes, has been compared to Robert Lowell, Elizabeth Bishop, Marianne Moore, and W. H. Auden for her style and themes. She uses humor, personal experience, observation, and irony to make everyday life seem extraordinary; as such, she set a thematic precedent for many contemporary women poets writing after the 1970s. Known for this examination of the quotidian, Van Duyn is sometimes called a "domestic poet" for her celebration of married life and love. Much of what would become her defining poetic project began with her first book, *Valentines to the Wide World* in which Van Duyn theorizes that art and love have a particular power to redeem ordinary moments. Through her poems, Van Duyn captures the odd, ordinary moments, preserving them against the loss of time. *Valentines* also contains the first of the marriage poems, "Toward a Definition of Marriage," which have become a defining theme in all of her work.

To See, To Take continues this theme, exploring it through everyday moments and Van Duyn's use of literary characters, such as W. B. Yeats's "Leda and the Swan" revisited in Van Duyn's "Leda Reconsidered." In this collection, as in *Merciful Disguises: Published and Unpublished Poems* (1973) containing selections written from 1965 to 1973, Van Duyn is the quintessential married poet. The answer to all problems lies in domestic love and art; she looks to her own life, her parents' relationship, and the relationships of friends to demonstrate this theme. Both collections also represent a new exploration of metaphors for the female life. In *Merciful Disguises*, Van Duyn uses the image of flight, as Lorrie Goldensohn notes, "to make a place for the visionary and idealistic imagination in a female life, and accomplish their difficult ascent" (43).

Near Changes, *Firefall*, and *If It Be Not I* similarly engage the world of daily life. *Near Changes*, while still a volume of "domestic" verse, expands Van Duyn's poetic consideration with poems that address the world in which she lives. Coyly beginning with "Glad Heart at the Supermarket" and "First Trip through an Automatic Carwash," Van Duyn moves from the household world to the everyday world outside of the family. She ends, however, with less humorous observations, making her first extensive foray into socio-political issues. "Tears" explores the sorrow of tears containing an AIDS-related virus.

Firefall and *If It Be Not I* are Van Duyn's newest collections; Robyn Selman notes that in these newest poems, Van Duyn continues to write about women's everyday lives. She is, according to Selman, the poet of all women, "their poet. Her lines are born out of that disappearing mid-century klatsch. Though her language and forms are flawless and her references ornately classical, the meanings of her poems translate readily into a universal suburbanese" (60). Van Duyn brings grace and wonder to themes of washing machines and marriage.

Some of Van Duyn's most interesting and divergent work comes in *A Time of Bees* and *Bedtime Stories* (1972). These two collections feature "characters" through whom Van Duyn explores the world. While some of her conclusions remain the same, that strong relationships provide the foundation to solve difficult problems, she experiments with radically different approaches to that theme. *Bees* focuses on a couple's attempt to kill bees living in their home. Here, the relationship held up for inspection is not that of the human couple, but rather that of the bees.' Despite the imminent danger to their lives, or perhaps because of it, the bees reproduce, thereby extending their lives and heritage. In *Bees*, as in her other works, Van Duyn explores the idea of marriage and relationships through the female; she finds her inspiration in a particularly feminine sensibility. Similarly, *Bedtime Stories* explores women and their roles in relationships through Van Duyn's grandmother's experiences as a first-generation American. Van Duyn departs from her usual voice to imitate her grandmother's voice, one markedly different from the poet's voice in accent, class, and agrarian background.

CRITICAL RECEPTION

In addition to the Bollingen, National Book Award, and Pulitzer Prize, Van Duyn has also been awarded *Poetry*'s Eunice Tietjens Memorial Prize; the Harriet Monroe Award; *Poetry Northwest*'s Helen Bullis Prize two times; the Hart Crane Memorial Award; the Ruth Lilly Prize; the Loines Prize of the National Institute of Arts and Letters; the Shelley Memorial Prize; and fellowships from The Academy of American Poets, the American Academy of Arts and Sciences, the Guggenheim Foundation, and the National Endowment for the Arts.

Through these awards, among the most prestigious in the American poetry world, and her positions as poet laureate and chancellor of the American Academy of Poets, Van Duyn has enjoyed consistently warm critical reception since the beginning of her career. Her verse has been celebrated for its language and style. Many critics also lauded her aesthetic commitment to formal verse.

However, amid the glowing receptions, a small group of critics have consistently critiqued Van Duyn for her subject matter. In a review entitled "Late Callings," William Logan observes that Van Duyn's poetry is like W. H. Auden's because she turns the ordinary poetic through her "intelligent talk" and her "sociable and even chatty" poems (318). Despite his praise in comparing Van Duyn to Auden, however, Logan uses the comparison to demonstrate how Van Duyn falls short of the mark set by master-poet Auden: "She lacks his intelligent ear: Her poems slouch off toward prose without some formal obligation to attend to, and her early experiments with rhyme sound like earnest low-paid doggerel" (318). Logan's comments typify much of the criticism against women's poetry in general; her love of the quotidian is compared to Auden and then disparaged; her work is unintelligent, according to this review. She is incapable—primarily because of her subject matter—of inspiring the intellect.

Harvey Shapiro's "As Three Poets See Reality" echoes many of these same sentiments: "She writes as . . . a housewife, putting up poems as another good woman might put up peaches. . . . Her poems describe vacation trips to the mountains or the shore. She writes about female friends, children, relatives. All of this is patently unfashionable. Unfashionable also is the fact that her poems have subjects. More damning than that, there is the basic assumption in her work that it is possible to elicit meaning from the world" (22). Despite these two examples, representative of the grounds on which critics oppose Van Duyn's success, she has received critical acclaim as one of the most celebrated American contemporary women poets. Through her dedication to her subject material, she provides a lyric and inspiring example of new avenues for American poetry.

BIBLIOGRAPHY

Works by Mona Jane Van Duyn

Valentines to the Wide World. Iowa City, IA: Cummington Press, 1958.
A Time of Bees. Chapel Hill: University of North Carolina Press, 1964.
To See, To Take. New York: Atheneum, 1970.
Bedtime Stories. Champaign, IL: Ceres Press, 1972.
Merciful Disguises: Published and Unpublished Poems. New York: Atheneum, 1973.
Letters from a Father, and Other Poems. New York: Atheneum, 1982.
Near Changes. New York: Knopf, 1990.
Firefall. New York: Knopf, 1993.
If It Be Not I: Collected Poems 1959–1982. New York: Knopf, 1993.

Studies of Mona Jane Van Duyn

Abel, Marianne. "Conversations with Pulitzer Prize Winners Jane Schorer and Mona Van Duyn." *Iowa–Woman* 11.3 (1991): 18–23.
Burns, Michael. *Discovery and Reminiscence: Essays on the Poetry of Mona Van Duyn.* Fayetteville: University of Arkansas Press, 1998.
Corn, Alfred. Review of *Near Changes,* by Mona Van Duyn. *Poetry* 157.1 (1990): 47–50.
Earnshaw, Doris. Review of *Firefall,* by Mona Van Duyn. *World Literature Today* 68.2 (1994): 376.
———. Review of *If It Be Not I: Collected Poems 1959–1982,* by Mona Van Duyn. *World Literature Today* 68.2 (1994): 135.
Goldensohn, Lorrie. "Mona Van Duyn and the Politics of Love." *Ploughshares* 4.3 (1978): 31–44.
Hall, Judith. "Strangers May Run: The Nation's First Woman Poet Laureate." *Antioch Review* 52.1 (1994): 141–46.
Hass, Robert. Review of *Letters from a Father, and Other Poems,* by Mona Van Duyn. *Washington Post Book World* 12.36 (1982): 6–7.
Hirsch, Edward. "Violent Desires." *New York Times Book Review,* 19 Nov. 1990, 24.
Hunting, Constance. "Methods of Transport." *Parnassus* 16.2 (1991): 377–89.
Logan, William. "Late Callings." *Parnassus* 18.2 (1992): 317–27.
Rizza, Peggy. "Another Side of this Life: Women as Poets." In *American Poetry since 1960: Some Critical Perspectives,* edited by Robert B. Shaw. Chester Springs, PA: Dufour, 1974. 167–80.
Rosenthal, M. L. "A Common Sadness." *New York Times Book Review,* 13 March 1983, 6.
Selman, Robyn. "Housekeeping." *The Village Voice,* 1 June 1993, 60–61.
Shapiro, Harvey. "As Three Poets See Reality." *New York Times,* 22 Sept. 1973, 22.
Shaw, Robert B. "Life Work." *Shenandoah: The Washington and Lee University Review* 44.1 (1994): 38–48.
Woods, John. "The Teeming Catalogue." *Poetry* 96.1 (1960): 47–51.

DIANE WAKOSKI (1937–)

Susan R. Bowers

BIOGRAPHY

Diane Wakoski was born August 3, 1937, in Whittier, California, the daughter of John Joseph and Marie (Mengel) Wakoski. Her father was often absent because of his career in the U.S. Navy, so her mother was the primary parent for Diane and her younger sister. Wakoski's experiences as a gifted child in a Polish working-class family figure prominently in her poetry. She attended high school in Fullerton, California, and entered the University of California, Berkeley, in the fall of 1956 after one year at Fullerton Junior College. Wakoski won first prize in a poetry contest at the end of her junior year and graduated from Berkeley in 1960. Her first book of poetry, *Coins and Coffins*, was published by Hawk's Well Press in 1962.

The fact that Wakoski gave birth to two children whom she had to give up for adoption has had a profound influence on her poetry. She became pregnant the first time during her year at Fullerton and gave birth on June 11, 1956, to a son. Less than four years later, in her last semester at Berkeley, she discovered that she was pregnant again, and her second child, a daughter, was born on September 5, 1960.

In the San Francisco area, she was loosely connected with Beatnik poets. Her move to New York City in the fall of 1960 brought her in contact with avant-garde artists and writers there, especially Deep Image poets. She got a job as a bookstore clerk for the British Book Centre. She gave a reading in the spring of 1961 in a new poets' series at the YM-YWCA Poetry Center at 92nd and Lexington and soon became active in the coffeehouse circuit of poetry readings. In 1963 she became an English teacher at Junior High School 22 in Manhattan, where she remained until February 1966.

Wakoski's relationships with men have been intense and often turbulent. On October 22, 1965, she married her first husband, S. Shepard Sherbell, a magazine editor. They were divorced two years later, and on February 22, 1973, she married Michael Watterlond, another poet, from whom she was divorced in 1975. She married Robert J. Turney, to whom she remains married, on February 14, 1982. Her husbands and lovers often appear in her poems with little or no disguise.

Her poetry has been recognized by some of the nation's most prestigious prizes, including the Robert Frost Fellowship in Poetry from Bread Loaf Writers Conference in 1966; the Cassandra Foundation award in 1970; a 1984 Fulbright Grant; and the William Carlos Williams Prize in 1989. Wakoski has lived in East Lansing, Michigan, since 1976, where she teaches at Michigan State University, which awarded her the university's Distinguished Professor Award in 1990.

MAJOR WORKS AND THEMES

Diane Wakoski occupies a niche of her own in American poetry. She has focused on being a woman in American society, using her own experiences as the foundation for a personal mythology that challenges the culture's repression of the female and the creative. Wakoski, extremely prolific, has published more than fifty books, including three books of critical essays in addition to the poetry and is a regular contributor to numerous periodicals. As a critic, she has a strong feel for what she and her fellow poets are doing: "Those of us writing poetry today are doing so on a series of formal premises which may be different from anything in the past. One of those premises is that the work must organically come out of the writer's life" (*Toward a New Poetry* 11).

Wakoski avoids traditional and fixed forms, striving, instead, for a natural and often conversational voice. She nonetheless maintains tight artistic control. Hayden Carruth has noted, "Wakoski has a way of beginning her poems with the most unpromising materials imaginable, then carrying them on, often on and on and on, talkily, until at the end they come into surprising focus" (311). Her early association with the Deep Imagists produced an emphasis on the image, especially the surrealist image, as a primary organizing structure in her poems. Her sixteen years of musical training are evident in her use of digression as a musical structure, the repetition of images and words, and her performance poems.

Wakoski's poetry often carries intense personal emotional weight at the same time that it satirizes public icons. In *The George Washington Poems* (1967), she calls Washington her "mythical father-lover" and through him addresses several men in her own life. But the satirism can mask what Alicia Ostriker has called the "forceful emotionality" of these poems (" 'What Are Patterns For?' " 488). Ostriker points to how the central poem, "The Father of My Country," re-creates Wakoski's own "desperate love and need of the absent, indifferent father who has both created her identity and betrayed her" (489).

Wakoski's poetry is deliberately not confessional, as Taffy Wynne Martin emphasizes, "Wakoski's poetry acknowledges loss—of children, of love, of sustaining myths—and develops out of that a coherent body of work in which desire functions as an enabling drive" ("Diane Wakoski's Personal Mythology" 157). For example, Wakoski often plays with the mythic connotations of her own name: Diana as moon goddess. Wakoski's transmutation of the facts of her own life into a personal mythology is epitomized by the poetry of *Smudging* (1972). Wakoski considers the title poem one of her best: It describes her own transformation from a frightened little girl growing up in the orange groves to "the one who steps magically out" of the orange peels. Yet Wakoski refuses to heroicize herself. For several decades, she has been publishing parts of her epic poem *Greed* (1968), (1969), (1971), (1973), (1984), defining greed as the feeling that one is "above having to bow down" to the kinds of compromises that humans must make (*Greed/Parts 8, 9, 11* 19).

Wakoski has been influenced by the work of Walt Whitman, Wallace Stevens, Lorca, D. H. Lawrence, Charles Olson, and William Carlos Williams. Williams's epic poem *Paterson* serves as Wakoski's model for her 1991 volume *Medea the Sorceress*. In this long poem, she integrates fragments of letters to friends, short poems, pieces of prose by others, and thoughts on a variety of topics. Her work on the contemporary long poem is one of her most important legacies as a poet.

Wakoski, a complex poet, is a narrative poet attracted to the lyric and dramatic, and she is an extremely intellectual poet with a deep knowledge of music, science, and mythology. Ultimately, she defies classification: "My poetry is an attempt to define the world in humanitarian terms; to embrace both the honest and the compassionate." Wakoski finds salvation in love and truth and insists that neither alone can save us (*Greed/ Parts 8, 9, 11* 19–20).

CRITICAL RECEPTION

Wakoski does not identify herself as a feminist poet, and some feminist critics have taken her to task for her emphasis on traditional female roles in relationships with men and on heterosexuality. Even so, Wakoski's emphasis on discovering who she is as a woman in American society has resulted in her inclusion in a number of feminist anthologies and critical texts. Since her earliest poetry, she has been seen by many critics as a confessional poet, although she disavows the label. Early in her career, Wakoski shocked many of her readers and some critics with the intensity of her anger in such volumes as *The Motorcycle Betrayal Poems* (1971). Some critics have complained that her prolific production has led to an uneven *oeuvre*.

Although Wakoski has attracted a number of reviews and short critical pieces, her work has not garnered any long critical studies. Taffy Wynne Martin, who has written on her more than any other critic, argues that Wakoski's poetry "remains—as it should—in search of a critical method" (171).

BIBLIOGRAPHY

Works by Diane Wakoski

Coins & Coffins. New York: Hawk's Well Press, 1962.

Dream Sheet. New York: Software Press, 1965.

Discrepancies and Apparitions. Garden City, NY: Doubleday, 1966.

The George Washington Poems. New York: Riverrun Press, 1967.

The Diamond Merchant. Cambridge, MA: Sans Souci Press, 1968.

Greed Parts One and Two. Los Angeles: Black Sparrow Press, 1968.

Inside the Blood Factory. Garden City, NY: Doubleday, 1968.

A Play and Two Poems. With Robert Kelly and Ron Loewinsohn. Los Angeles: Black Sparrow Press, 1968.

Greed Parts 3 and 4. Los Angeles: Black Sparrow Press, 1969.

The Lament of the Lady Bank Dick. Cambridge, MA: Sans Souci Press, 1969.

The Moon Has a Complicated Geography. Palo Alto, CA: Odda Tala Press, 1969.

Thanking My Mother for Piano Lessons. Mount Horeb, WI: Perishable Press, 1969.

Black Dream Ditty for Billy "The Kid" Seen in Dr. Generosity's Bar Recruiting for Hell's Angels and Black Mafia. Los Angeles: Black Sparrow Press, 1970.
Love, You Big Fat Snail. San Francisco: Tenth Muse, 1970.
Exorcism. Boston: My Dukes, 1971.
Greed: Parts 5–7. Los Angeles: Black Sparrow Press, 1971.
The Motorcycle Betrayal Poems. New York: Simon and Schuster, 1971.
On Barbara's Shore. Los Angeles: Black Sparrow Press, 1971.
This Water Baby: For Tony. Santa Barbara, CA: Unicorn Press, 1971.
The Pumpkin Pie, Or Reassurances Are Always False, Tho We Love Them, Only Physics Counts. Los Angeles: Black Sparrow Press, 1972.
The Purple Finch Song. Mount Horeb, WI: Perishable Press, 1972.
Smudging. Los Angeles: Black Sparrow Press, 1972.
Sometimes a Poet Will Hijack the Moon. Providence, RI: Burning Deck, 1972.
Dancing on the Grave of a Son of a Bitch. Los Angeles: Black Sparrow Press, 1973.
Greed: Parts 8, 9, 11. Los Angeles: Black Sparrow Press, 1973.
The Owl and the Snake: A Fable. Mount Horeb, WI: Perishable Press, 1973.
Stilllife: Michael, Silver Flute and Violets. Storrs: University of Connecticut, 1973.
Winter Sequences. Los Angeles: Black Sparrow Press, 1973.
The Magellanic Clouds. Los Angeles: Black Sparrow Press, 1974.
Trilogy: Coins and Coffins; Discrepancies and Apparitions; The George Washington Poems. Garden City, NY: Doubleday, 1974.
Creating a Personal Mythology. Los Angeles: Black Sparrow Press, 1975.
Fable of the Lion and the Scorpion. Milwaukee, WI: Pentagram Press, 1975.
Virtuoso Literature for Two and Four Hands. Garden City, NY: Doubleday, 1975.
George Washington's Camp Cups. Madison, WI: Red Ozier Press, 1976.
The Laguna Contract of Diane Wakoski. Madison, WI: Crepuscular Press, 1976.
Waiting for the King of Spain. Santa Barbara, CA: Black Sparrow Press, 1976.
Overnight Projects with Wood. Madison, WI: Red Ozier Press, 1977.
The Ring. Santa Barbara, CA: Black Sparrow Press, 1977.
Spending Christmas with the Man from Receiving at Sears. Santa Barbara, CA: Black Sparrow Press, 1977.
The Man Who Shook Hands. Garden City, NY: Doubleday, 1978.
Pachelbel's Canon. Santa Barbara, CA: Black Sparrow Press, 1978.
Trophies. Santa Barbara, CA: Black Sparrow Press, 1979.
Cap of Darkness; Including Looking for the King of Spain and Pachelbel's Canon. Santa Barbara, CA: Black Sparrow Press, 1980.
Toward a New Poetry. Ann Arbor: University of Michigan Press, 1980. (essays)
Making a Sacher Torte: Nine Poems, Twelve Illustrations. With Ellen Lanyon. Mount Horeb, WI: Perishable Press, 1981.
Divers. N.p.: Barbarian Press, 1982.
The Lady Who Drove Me to the Airport. Worcester, MA: Metacom Press, 1982.
The Magician's Feastletters. Santa Barbara, CA: Black Sparrow Press, 1982.
Saturn's Rings. New York: Targ, 1982.
Looking for Beethoven in Las Vegas. New York: Red Ozier Press, 1983.
The Collected Greed, Parts 1–13. Los Angeles: Black Sparrow Press, 1984.
The Managed World. New York: Red Ozier Press, 1985.
Why My Mother Likes Liberace: A Musical Selection. Tucson, AZ: Sun-Gemini Press, 1985.
The Rings of Saturn. Santa Rosa, CA: Black Sparrow Press, 1986.
Celebration of the Rose: For Norman on Christmas Day. Montclair, NJ: Caliban Press, 1987.
Roses. Montclair, NJ: Caliban Press, 1987.
Emerald Ice: Selected Poems, 1962–1987. Santa Rosa, CA: Black Sparrow Press, 1988.
Medea the Sorceress. Santa Rosa, CA: Black Sparrow Press, 1991.

Jason the Sailor. Santa Rosa, CA: Black Sparrow Press, 1993.
The Ice Queen. Tuscaloosa, AL: Parallel Editions, 1994.
The Emerald City of Las Vegas. Santa Rosa, CA: Black Sparrow Press, 1995.
Argonaut Rose. Santa Rosa, CA: Black Sparrow Press, 1998.
The Butcher's Apron: New & Selected Poems Including "Greed Part 14." Santa Rosa, CA: Black Sparrow Press, 2000.

Studies of Diane Wakoski

Allred, Joanne. "Diane Wakoski." In *Updating the Literary West,* edited by Max Westbrook and Dan Flores. Fort Worth, TX: Christian University Press, 1997. 367–78.
Bartlett, Lee. "Diane Wakoski." In *Talking Poetry: Conversations in the Workshop with Contemporary Poets,* edited by Lee Bartlett. Albuquerque: University of New Mexico Press, 1987. 235–54.
Buschendorf, Christa. "Gods and Heroes Revised: Mythological Concepts of Masculinity in Contemporary Women's Poetry." *Amerikastudien/American Studies* 43.4 (1998): 599–617.
Carruth, Hayden. Review. *Hudson Review* 27.2 (1974): 311–12.
Cooley, John R. *Earthly Words: Essays on Contemporary American Nature and Environmental Writers.* Ann Arbor: University of Michigan Press, 1994.
Hoy, Jody. *The Power to Dream: Interviews with Women in the Creative Arts.* New York: Global City Press, 1995.
Lammon, Martin. "Diane Wakoski—The Greatest English Lyric?" In *Written in Water, Written in Stone: Twenty Years of Poets on Poetry.* Ann Arbor: University of Michigan Press, 1996.
Martin, Taffy Wynne. "Diane Wakoski's Personal Mythology: Dionysian Music, Created Presence." *Boundary 2* 10.3 (1982): 155–72.
———. "An Interview with Diane Wakoski." *Dalhousie Review* 61.3 (1981): 476–96.
Newton, Robert. *Diane Wakoski: A Descriptive Bibliography.* Jefferson, NC: McFarland, 1987.
Olson, Toby, ed. "Symposium on Diane Wakoski." *Margins* 28–30 (1976): 90–129.
Ostriker, Alicia. "In Mind: The Divided Self and Women's Poetry." *Midwest Quarterly* 24.1 (1983): 351–56.
———. " 'What Are Patterns For?' Anger and Polarization in Women's Poetry." *Feminist Studies* 10.3 (1984): 485–503.
Packard, William. *The Poet's Craft: Interviews from the New York Quarterly.* New York: Paragon House, 1987.
Wagner, Linda. "Wakoski and Rukeyser." *American Modern Essays in Fiction and Poetry.* Port Washington, NY: National University Publications/ Kennikat Press, 1980. 235–37.
————. "Wakoski's Early Poems: Moving Past Confession." In *Still the Frame Holds: Essays on Women Poets and Writers,* edited by Sheila Roberts and Yvonne Pacheco Tevis. San Bernardino, CA: Borgo, 1993.

MITSUYE YAMADA (1923–)

Karen L. Polster

BIOGRAPHY

Poet, short-story writer, essayist, editor, teacher, and human rights activist, Mitsuye Yamada is a pioneer of Asian American poetry and a leading advocate for multicultural feminism. She was born in Kyushu, Japan, and raised in Seattle, Washington. Her father, Jack Yasutake, was founder and president of a Japanese poetry society that met regularly at his home. In 1942 Yamada was sent to the barren desert of Minidoka, Idaho, one of ten internment camps established by the U.S. government to incarcerate Japanese and Japanese Americans after the bombing of Pearl Harbor. While in camp, Yamada wrote snippets of verse and prose that would become the source for her later poetry. After signing the infamous "loyalty oath," Yamada was allowed to leave the camp in 1944. She attended the University of Cincinnati and then moved to New York where she received a BA from New York University in 1947. She earned her MA from the University of Chicago in 1953. Yamada has taught ethnic and children's literature and creative writing at several universities and colleges. She and her husband, Yoshikazu Yamada, a research chemist, raised two children and live in Irvine, California.

Throughout her teaching career, Yamada has also been involved in a number of activist organizations. She served on the board of MELUS (Multi-Ethnic Literatures of the United States) and Amnesty International USA. She is the founder of the Multicultural Women Writers of Orange County and has organized a variety of Asian Pacific Women's conferences. Realizing the lack of awareness regarding Asian American history, she salvaged her Minidoka writings "out of mothballs" and published her first collection, *Camp Notes and Other Poems* in 1976. The difficulty of developing a language specific to Japanese American women's historical and cultural experiences led to her identification with all colonized people, particularly women. She contributed two essays to the groundbreaking multicultural feminist work *This Bridge Called My Back* in 1981. "Invisibility as an Unnatural Disaster" reflects the "double invisibility" of being both Asian and a woman while "Asian Pacific American Women and Feminism" urges women of color to develop a feminist agenda that addresses their particular concerns. That same year, she and Chinese American poet Nellie Wong were the subjects of the Public Broadcasting System documentary *Mitsuye and Nellie: Asian American Poets*. This film uses their poetry to present Asian American history and the complications of biculturalism.

Awarded a writer's residency from Yaddo in 1984, Yamada co-edited two volumes of poetry by Orange County artists: *The Webs We Weave* (1986) and *Sowing Ti Leaves* (1990). Her second poetry collection, *Desert Run: Poems and Stories* (1988), portrays the search for her cultural heritage as she returns to Minidoka forty years after the internment and travels to Japan. She has noted *Desert Run* is about our constant revising of the past. "The title poem expresses my coming to see the desert with new eyes," she said, and "about returning to my roots in Japan and finding new meanings within myself" (Jaskoski 107).

MAJOR WORKS AND THEMES

The taut, spare poetry of *Camp Notes* focuses on the narrator's interior reaction to a specific event. While their compact intensity is reminiscent of haiku, Yamada's verse is more free form and her subjects more personal than the typical haiku abstractions of nature. She notes the influence of her father's Japanese *senryu* poems and the work of feminist writers such as Tillie Olsen, Carolyn Kizer, and Marge Piercy on the immediacy of her style and her subject matter. Her complex word play satirizes the trumped up accusations of espionage and racism behind the internment. The *Desert Run* poems are longer and more stylistically elaborate, as Yamada analyzes the influences of internment and Japan upon her life. These poems are more reflective and thus lose some of the immediacy and emotional charge of her earlier work.

Yamada's poems meld personal stories with political concerns and decenter the national narratives of immigration and World War II to focus on the experiences of Japanese American women. The first section of *Camp Notes* relates the immigration of her grandmother and mother. Their stories are expanded in the *Desert Run* poem "I Learned to Sew" and short story, "Mrs. Higashi Is Dead." "Through understanding the nature of my mother's experience," she writes, "I have become more sensitive to the needs of Third World women throughout the world" ("Asian" 74). The most famous section of *Camp Notes* fights the silence of both Japanese Americans and national history accounts regarding the internment. These poems document the evacuation, the armed guards and barbed wire fences, the endless lines for the showers and meals, the forced "loyalty oath," the boredom, the humiliation, the crude barracks, and the fierce desert storms of Minidoka. "Recruiting Team" presents the irony of the army's call for volunteers from the camps to fight for a country that has denied or rescinded their citizenship and incarcerated their families without charge. The need for the Japanese and Japanese Americans to relate their own experiences is expressed in "Evacuation," as an Anglo newspaper photographer poses a young child as she is leaving for the camps and writes his own caption of her situation as "a lesson" to Japan.

Yamada's work blurs the boundaries between sexism and racism as she writes about gender bias in the Japanese culture and the danger of both racial oppression and rape within the Anglo world. She recalls how her parents were incensed that she might marry a pacifist, but indifferent that she was one herself. Her brother, Mike, was expelled from the University of Cincinnati for his political views, while she was not. "As a Japanese national and a 'girl,' " she notes, her politics *"didn't make any difference to anyone"* ("Invisibility" 38). The standards of femininity within the Japanese community takes a violent turn in the *Desert Run* poem "The Club" in which a husband uses the statue of a geisha to beat his wife. In the *Camp Notes* poem "The Night Before Goodbye," what begins as a quiet moment with her mother ends with the admonition that Yamada keep her underwear mended so as not to shame the family if she is involved in an accident. This responsibility of modesty expected from Japanese women is answered by the next poem "Cincinnati," where mended underwear or no, she is spat upon because of her race. The poem is marked with threats of sexual violation as well that are expanded in the poem "Freedom in Manhattan." After being released from Minidoka, she is held hostage in her New York apartment as rapists try to break down the door.

The double consciousness of dual cultures is expressed in the poems "Here" and "There" in which she is taunted for being Japanese in America and for being American when she visits her father's family in Japan (*Camp Notes and Other Poems*). In the *Desert Run* short story "Returning," a young Japanese American tries to "pass" for a native Japanese, and in the poem "Guilty on Both Counts" she is blamed for Pearl Harbor in America and for Hiroshima in Japan. The *Desert Run* poem "Lichens" examines the symbiotic relationship between cultures within multiracial subjects.

Yamada's work challenges the so-called Asian silence regarding internment. Although the incarceration was through no fault of their own, some Japanese Americans were embarrassed to discuss the camps. More often, they were stymied by a resistance from mainstream America to truly "hear" the reality of their experiences. In "A Bedtime Story" and "Enryo" the young daughter is ignored when she tries to protest her father's traditional stories of patriarchal heroism. In "Dialogue," she is silent in front of him, knowing he will not understand her need for independence. Yamada extends this situation to all minorities in "The Speech," in which a Zambian speaker stands silently weeping in the face of an Anglo audience breathless to hear about hardship and exotica, rather than his country's actual needs and experiences (*Camp Notes and Other Poems*). In "Desert Run," Yamada admits she was originally oblivious to the sounds of silence within the Idaho desert of her internment (*Desert Run*).

Her poems also present the apparent silence of women who have been traditionally excluded from the dominant discourse. In *Silences* (1978), Tillie Olsen enumerated the many barriers to female literary expression, such as the conflicting demands of a household, rejection by the literary establishment, a lack of models, imposed repression and self-censorship. Yamada expands upon Olsen's list in her essay "The Cult of the 'Perfect' Language" as she notes that bicultural writers are silenced by themselves and the mainstream for not being proficient in the "proper style" of English. "We must let them know there is a down side to being 'perfect,' " Yamada claims. "Those of us who have been around long enough know about the 'model minority' syndrome" (142). This conviction is also expressed in the *Desert Run* poem "Drowning in My Own Language," which presents the classic feminist water motif from an Asian American perspective.

In *Desert Run*'s "Another Model," Yamada exhorts African and Third World women not to relegate the fight for feminism to a second-class status in favor of ethnic justice, insisting that these struggles must be conducted simultaneously. The *Camp*

Notes poem "To a Lady" criticizes not only the refusal of Americans at large to protest the internment, but also feminists who ignore the connections between racism and sexism. "Our white sisters [should] see," she insists, "why being a feminist activist is more dangerous for women of color" ("Asian" 74). In her quest for an inclusive feminism, she identifies with victims of the Jewish Holocaust in the *Desert Run* poems "For Laura Who Still Hears the Geese," and "For Priscilla." She also presents the oppression of ethnic men within an Anglo patriarchy in poems such as "American Son" and "My Cousin" (*Desert Run*). "I am still hopeful," she writes, "that the women of color in our country will be the link to Third World women throughout the world, and that we can help each other broaden our visions" ("Asian" 75).

CRITICAL RECEPTION

Even if they do not make an extensive evaluation of her poetry, many studies of Asian American literature mention *Camp Notes* as a pioneering work. Stan Yogi notes that her work "crosses generational boundaries," since she was born in Japan, was part of the internment, and deals with the contemporary activist concerns of feminism and racism against Asian Americans and the melding of the private and the political (139–40). Shirley Geok-Lin Lim notes the double consciousness of her work as an Asian American woman as well as the social and historical importance of *Camp Notes* in U.S. "memory and history" (292). Phillipa Kafka in her feminist study of Asian American writers, *(Un)Doing the Missionary Position* (1997), notes that Yamada made substantial contributions in ending the "gender assymetry" of literature (156).

In the extended studies of her poetry, Anita Patterson points out that Yamada forces readers to reconsider the ideas of national obligation and citizenship. Susan Schweik notes that internment camp poems are unique in their representation of a woman's first-hand experiences of war. By "substituting the camp for the battlefield as an arena of critical experience," she explains, these poems "remap the boundaries of the American canon of war poetry" as an exclusively male soldier's realm. She also notes that Yamada's poetry forms "a significant means of resistance" (*Gulf* 174, 176).

Through her life and work, Yamada claims she has "tried to contribute towards making our society a truly multicultural one" that reflects "the experiences of women . . . the working class and ethnic minorities of both sexes" (Jaskoski 97).

BIBLIOGRAPHY

Works by Mitsuye Yamada

Camp Notes and Other Poems. San Lorenzo, CA: Shameless Hussy Press, 1976.

"Asian Pacific American Women and Feminism." In *This Bridge Called My Back: Writings by Radical Women of Color*, edited by Cherríe Moraga and Gloria Anzaldúa. Watertown, MA: Persephone Press, 1981. 71–75.

"Invisibility Is an Unnatural Disaster: Reflections of an Asian American Woman." In *This Bridge Called My Back: Writings by Radical Women of Color*, edited by Cherríe Moraga and Gloria Anzaldúa. Watertown, MA: Persephone Press, 1981. 35–40.

The Webs We Weave: Orange County Poetry Anthology, edited with John Brander. Laguna Beach, CA: Literary Arts Press, 1986.

Desert Run: Poems and Stories. Latham, NY: Kitchen Table Women of Color Press, 1988.

"The Cult of the 'Perfect' Language; Censorship by Class Gender and Race." In *Sowing Ti Leaves: Writings by Multicultural Women*, edited by Mitsuye Yamada and Sarie Sachie Hylkema. Irvine, CA: MCWW Press, 1990. 127–46.

Studies of Mitsuye Yamada

Geok-Lin Lim, Shirley. "Immigration and Diaspora." In *An Interethnic Companion to Asian American Literature*, edited by King-Kok Cheung. New York: Cambridge University Press, 1997.

Jaskoski, Helen. "A MELUS Interview: Mitsuye Yamada." *MELUS* 15:1 (Spring 1988): 97–107.

Kafka, Phillipa. *(Un)Doing the Missionary Position: Gender Asymmetry in Contemporary Asian American Woman's Writing*. Westport, CT: Greenwood Press, 1997.

Mitsuye and Nellie: Two Asian-American Women Poets. Produced by Allie Light and Irving Saraf. San Francisco: Light-Saraf Films, 1981.

Olsen, Tillie. *Silences*. New York: Delacorte Press/Seymour Lawrence, 1978.

Patterson, Anita Haya. "Resistance to Images of the Internment: Mitsuye Yamada's *Camp Notes*." *MELUS* 23.3 (1998): 103–15.

Schweik, Susan. *A Gulf So Deeply Cut: American Women Poets and the Second World War*. Madison: University of Wisconsin Press, 1991. 192–209

———. "A Needle with Mama's Voice: Mitsuye Yamada's *Camp Notes* and the American Canon of War Poetry." In *Arms and the Woman: War, Gender and Literary Representation*, edited by Helen M. Cooper, et al. Chapel Hill: University of North Carolina Press, 1989. 225–43.

Yogi, Stan. "Japanese American Literature." In *An Interethnic Companion to Asian American Literature*, edited by King-Kok Cheung. New York: Cambridge University Press, 1997.

SELECTED BIBLIOGRAPHY

Bennet, Paula. *My Life, A Loaded Gun: Female Creativity and Feminist Poetics*. Boston: Beacon Press, 1986.

Bloom, Harold, ed. *American Women Poets*. New York: Chelsea, 1986.

Candelaria, Cordelia. *Chicana Poetry: A Critical Introduction*. New York: Greenwood, 1986.

Curry, Renée R. *White Women Writing White: H.D., Elizabeth Bishop, Sylvia Platn, and Whiteness*. Westport, CT: Greenwood Press, 2000.

Davidson, Phebe. *Conversations with the World: American Women Poets and Their Work*. Pasadena, CA: Trilogy, 1998.

DeShazer, Mary K. *Inspiring Women: Reimagining the Muse*. New York: Pergamon Press, 1986.

Dickie, Margaret, and Thomas Travisano, eds. *Gendered Modernisms: American Women Poets and Their Readers*. Philadelphia: University of Pennsylvania Press, 1996.

Evans, Mari, ed. *Black Women Writers (1950–1980): A Critical Evaluation*. Garden City, NY: Anchor, 1984.

Finch, Annie, ed. *A Formal Feeling Comes: Poems in Form by Contemporary Women*. Brownsville, OR: Story Line Press, 1994.

Ford, Karen Jackson. *Gender and the Poetics of Excess: Moments of Brocade*. Jackson: University Press of Mississippi, 1997.

Freedman, Diane P. *An Alchemy of Genres: Cross-Genre Writing by American Feminist Poet-Critics*. Charlottesville: University Press of Virginia, 1992.

Friedman, Ellen G., and Miriam Fuchs, eds. *Breaking the Sequence: Women's Experimental Fiction*. Princeton, NJ: University of Princeton Press 1989.

Gabbin, Joanne V., ed. *The Furious Flowering of African American Poetry*. Charlottesville: University Press of Virginia, 1999.

Horno-Delgado, Asunción, et al., eds. *Breaking Boundaries: Latina Writing and Critical Readings*. Amherst: University of Massachusetts Press, 1989.

Keller, Lynn. *Forms of Expansion: Recent Long Poems by Women*. Chicago: University of Chicago Press, 1997.

———, and Cristanne Miller, eds. *Feminist Measures: Soundings in Poetry and Theory*. Ann Arbor: University of Michigan Press, 1994.

Mark, Alison, and Deryn Rees-Jones, eds. *Contemporary Women's Poetry: Reading, Writing, Practice*. New York: St. Martin's Press, 2000.

Middlebrook, Diane Wood, and Marilyn Yalom, eds. *Coming to Light: American Women Poets in the Twentieth Century*. Ann Arbor: University of Michigan Press, 1985.

Miller, R. Baxter, ed. *Black American Poets Between Worlds, 1940–1960*. Knoxville: University of Tennessee Press, 1986.

Montefiore, Jan. *Feminism and Poetry: Language, Experience, Identity in Women's Writing*. New York: Pandora, 1987.

Muske, Carol. *Women and Poetry: Truth, Autobiography, and the Shape of the Self*. Ann Arbor: University of Michigan Press, 1997.

Nielsen, Aldon Lynn. *Black Chant: Languages of African-American Postmodernism*. Cambridge: Cambridge University Press, 1997.

———, ed. *Reading Race in American Poetry: "An Area of Act."* Urbana: University of Illinois Press, 2000.

Ostriker, Alicia. *Stealing the Language: The Emergence of Women's Poetry in America*. Boston: Beacon Press, 1986.

Pérez-Torres, Rafael. *Movements in Chicano Poetry: Against Myths, Against Margins*. Cambridge: Cambridge University Press, 1995.

Prins, Yopie, and Maeer Shreiber, eds. *Dwelling in Possibility: Women Poets and Critics on Poetry*. Ithaca, NY: Cornell University Press, 1997.

Robelledo, Tey Diana. *Women Singing in the Snow: A Cultural Analysis of Chicana Literature*. Albuquerque: University of New Mexico Press, 1995.

Sánchez, Marta Ester. *Contemporary Chicana Poetry: A Critical Approach to an Emerging Literature*. Berkeley: University of California Press, 1985.

Schweik, Susan. *A Gulf So Deeply Cut: American Women Poets and the Second World War*. Madison: University of Wisconsin Press, 1991.

Simpson, Megan. *Poetic Epistemologies: Gender and Knowing in Women's Language-Oriented Writing*. Albany: State University of New York Press, 2000.

Smethurst, James Edward. *The New Red Negro: The Literary Left and African American Poetry, 1930–1946*. New York: Oxford University Press, 1999.

Steele, Cassie Premo. *We Heal from Memory: Sexton, Lorde, Anzaldúa, and the Poetry of Witness*. New York: Palgrave, 2000.

Sullivan, James D. *On the Walls and in the Streets: American Poetry Broadsides from the 1960s*. Urbana: University of Illinois Press, 1997.

Vendler, Helen Hennessy. *The Given and the Made: Strategies of Poetic Redefinition*. Cambridge: Harvard University Press, 1995.

———. *The Music of What Happens: Poems, Poets, Critics*. Cambridge: Harvard University Press, 1988.

Vickery, Ann. *Leaving Lines of Gender: A Feminist Genealogy of Language Writing*. Hanover, NH: Wesleyan University Press, 2000.

Viramontes, Helen María, and María Herrera-Sobek, eds. *Chicana Creativity and Criticism: New Frontiers on American Literature*. Albuquerque: University of New Mexico Press, 1996.

Walker, Cheryl. *Masks Outrageous and Austere: Culture, Psyche, and Persona in Modern Women Poets*. Bloomington: Indiana University Press, 1991.

Whitehead, Kim. *The Feminist Poetry Movement*. Jackson: University Press of Mississippi, 1996.

Yorke, Liz. *Impertinent Voices: Subversive Strategies in Contemporary Women's Poetry*. New York: Routledge, 1991.

INDEX

Page numbers in **bold** indicate the location of the main entry

ABOUT THE EDITOR AND CONTRIBUTORS

ANDREA ADOLPH, a doctoral candidate at Louisiana State University, is currently completing a dissertation on representations of food and eating in twentieth-century British women's fiction. She holds degrees from California State University, Fresno, and Mills College. She co-edited *Bite to Eat Place: An Anthology of Contemporary Food Poetry and Poetic Prose* (1995), and she has published poems and essays in various journals.

JESSICA ALLEN is a graduate student in the English department at the University of Washington. Her scholarly interests include contemporary American poetry and women's studies. She lives in Seattle.

MARLENE D. ALLEN is a PhD candidate in the Department of English at the University of Georgia. Her research and teaching interests include African American literature, twentieth-century American literature, multicultural American literature, and women's literature. Her dissertation focuses upon African American women's science fiction literature.

ROBERT ARCHAMBEAU teaches at Lake Forest College where he specializes in nineteenth- and twentieth-century poetry. He has published *Word Play Place: Essays on the Poetry of John Matthias* (1998) and has articles in a variety of journals.

SHARON L. BARNES is an assistant professor of English at the Tuscarawas campus of Kent State University and the author of a dissertation on the poetry and prose of Audre Lorde.

KATHLYN A. BARROS is currently finishing up the last part of her dissertation on Pat Mora, Sandra Maria Esteves, and Coco Fusco entitled "Writing Out Loud: U.S. Latina/o Poets and the Re-Formation of American Literature." She has taught English at various institutions in Southern California and is currently teaching Chicana/o literature at California State University, San Bernardino.

SAMIYA A. BASHIR, co-editor of *Role Call: A Generational Anthology of Social & Political Black Art & Literature* (2001), is a poet, writer, and editor currently serving as a contributing editor for *Black Issues Book Review* and *Curve* magazines and *NiaOnline.com*. Her work has appeared in journals, anthologies, and online publications. Bashir is a graduate of the University of California, at Berkeley, where she was honored as poet laureate of the nine-campus university, and studied and taught with the Poetry for the People program. She continues to teach creative writing and poetry to adults and children through affiliations with universities, public schools, and city/state agencies.

TARA BETTS teaches creative writing with Young Chicago Authors and is working on a book of nonfiction about Ida B. Wells. Betts won the Guild Complex's 1999 Gwendolyn Brooks Open Mic Award, received a Ragdale Foundation Fellowship and a 1999 *Poets & Writers* grant. She has published a chapbook, and her poetry has appeared in numerous journals.

JOELLE BIELE received her BA from Tufts University and her MFA in poetry and PhD in English from the University of Maryland, College Park. She is the recipient of a Fulbright Senior Scholarship Award to Germany, where she taught at the University of Oldenburg. Her poetry appears in *Antioch Review*, *The Iowa Review*, and *Nimrod*. She teaches at the University of Maryland, College Park.

BENAY BLEND received her doctorate in American studies from the University of New Mexico. She currently lives in Albuquerque, New Mexico, where she is revising her manuscript on Mary Austin for the University of Iowa Press. Her research interests include Latina writers, women and nature, and environmental issues of the American Southwest.

AUSTIN BOOTH is humanities specialist at State University of New York, Buffalo. Her present work concerns women and cyberculture.

SUSAN R. BOWERS is an associate professor of English at Susquehanna University, Pennsylvania. She has published on Toni Morrison, Theodore Roethke, and Anne Sexton, and is completing a book on contemporary American women's love poetry. She holds a PhD in English from the University of Oregon.

JANA EVANS BRAZIEL teaches African, African diasporic, and Caribbean literatures at the University of Wisconsin, La Crosse. She has published articles on postcolonial writers such as Flora Balzano, Assia Djebar, Out El Kouloub, and Jamaica Kincaid. She has co-edited *Theorizing Diaspora: A Reader* (2002). Braziel has also published on Janis Joplin, Bessie Smith, and David Lynch (forthcoming and co-edited with Kathleen Le Besco *Bodies Out of Bounds: Fat and Transgression* (2001).

MARIA ELENA CABALLERO-ROBB is a doctoral candidate at the University of California, Santa Cruz. Her dissertation "Poetry and the Public Sphere: Politics, Participation, and Uncommon Speech" is on nineteenth- and twentieth-century poetries and poetics.

ISAAC CATES is a PhD candidate at Yale University, where he coordinates the graduate colloquium on contemporary poetry. His dissertation "Nature Poetry after Darwin" treats the confluence of science and poetry in the twentieth century. His poems have appeared in *Schuylkill* and *The Southwest Review*.

LAURIE CHAMPION, associate professor of English at San Diego State University, Imperial Valley, specializes in twentieth-century American writers, especially women and minorities. Her work has appeared in several journals, including the *Southern Quarterly* and *Short Story Journal*. She is co-editor of *Blacks in the West: A Century of Short Stories* (1998) and *Contemporary American Women Fiction Writers: An A-to-Z Guide* (2002) and editor of *The Critical Response to Mark Twain's Huckleberry Finn* (1991), *The Critical Response to Eudora Welty's Fiction* (1994), and *American Women Writers, 1900–1945: A Bio-Bibliographical Sourcebook* (2000).

J. ELIZABETH CLARK is an assistant professor of English at Fiorello H. LaGuardia Community College in New York City. She received her PhD in American Literature from Binghamton University in 2000. Her primary research interests include the poetry of AIDS, twentieth-century American political poetry, Latina/o Literature, and pedagogy. She serves as part of the editorial collective for the magazine *Radical Teacher*. Her poetry has appeared in various journals. She is currently working on a critical manuscript about post-protease AIDS poetry.

DAVID CLIPPINGER is an assistant professor of English and American studies at Pennsylvania State University. His essays on twentieth-century American poetry have been published in various journals, encyclopedias, and books. He recently edited *The Body of This Life: Reading William Bronk* (2001) as well as an expanded edition of *Life Supports: William Bronk's Collected Poetry* (1997). *The Mind's Landscape: William Bronk and American Poetry* and *Accumulating Position: The Selected Letters of William Bronk* are both forthcoming.

DARLENE COHN received her BA in English in 1994, her MA in English and her MA in Teaching English in 1998 from State University of New York, Binghamton. She has taught high school English in St. Louis, Missouri, from 1998–2000. Presently she is writing articles and poetry from her home in Valparaiso, Indiana. She lives with her husband, Jesse, and two cats, Thisbe and Ed.

CATHERINE CUCINELLA received her PhD from the University of California, Riverside, and is a special lecturer at Oakland University, Rochester, Michigan. She has published articles on women poets and writers in various journals and reference books.

RENÉE R. CURRY is a professor and director of the Institute for Human Communication at California State University, Monterey Bay. She is the author of *White Women Writing White: H.D., Elizabeth Bishop, Sylvia Plath* (2000), and *Whiteness*; coeditor of *States of Rage: Emotional Eruption, Violence, and Social Change* (1996);

and editor of *Perspectives on Woody Allen* (1996). She has published numerous articles on twentieth-century poets, fiction writers, and filmmakers.

LISA B. DAY is a visiting assistant professor in the Department of English and Theatre at Eastern Kentucky University. Her publications, research interests, and editing projects focus on nineteenth-century American literature and multiethnic literature.

MICHAEL DITTMAN teaches at Butler Community College, Pennsylvania. He has published *Weapons As Necessary As Arms* (2001) and articles on poets in several collections and journals.

LYNN DOMINA is an associate professor of English at the State University of New York, Delhi. Her books include a collection of poetry, *Corporal Works* (1998), and a reference book, *Understanding a Raisin in the Sun* (1998). Her poetry has appeared in several journals.

SHANNA FLASCHKA is a graduate student at the University of Mississippi, specializing in gothic literature. She unearthed her penchant for poetry as a college freshman in a course entitled "Contemporary American Women Poets." She currently teaches in the freshmen English program at the university.

MONIKA GIACOPPE received her PhD in comparative literature from Pennsylvania State University and is an assistant professor of world and comparative literature at Ramapo College of New Jersey.

TIMOTHY GRAY, assistant professor of English at the College of Staten Island, City University of New York, teaches American literature. He has written and published on Frank O'Hara, James Schuuler, and Gary Snyder; he also has book reviews in *American Literature* and *Postmodern Culture*. His current projects include an article on Griel Marcus and a book on Gary Snyder and the San Francisco Renaissance.

ROXANNE HARDE, a doctoral candidate in English at Queen's University, Ontario, Canada, has published on both contemporary and early American and Canadian women's poetry. She is currently completing a dissertation on early American women's poetry as feminist theology, which includes a section on the ecofeminist leanings of Mary Oliver and Emily Dickinson as read in light of contemporary feminist theologians.

NIKOLAS HUOT is a doctoral candidate in English at Georgia State University. His research interests include Asian American and African American literatures.

ANETT JESSOP earned her MA in creative writing (poetry) and completed course work for the PhD at the University of Minnesota, Twin Cities. She has taught literature, creative writing, and composition classes at the University of Minnesota and Hamline University in Minnesota. Currently, she coordinates the graduate program in English at the University of California, Davis.

KATHLEEN CARLTON JOHNSON holds a BA from the College of William and Mary and two MAs from Villanova University and is pursuing further graduate studies in literature at Dalhousie University, Halifax, Nova Scotia. She has a long-standing interest in Elizabeth Bishop and is currently writing a book on American women poets of the 1950s.

TENEA D. JOHNSON, a native of Kentucky, is a scholar, writer, and musician living in New York City. She received her BA in humanities at New College in Sarasota, Florida and completed an MA at New York University's Gallatin School, where she focused on poetics and politics of the African diaspora. In the spring of 2002, her literary history of the Great Migrations and their effect on the South's image in black literature will be included in the journal, *Humanities in the South*. She also writes fiction, poetry, essays, profiles, and feature articles.

PERSIS M. KARIM is an assistant professor at San Jose State University where she teaches comparative literature and ethnic American literature. She is co-editor of *A World Between: Poems, Short Stories, and Essays by Iranian Americans* (1999).

MONIFA A. LOVE received her PhD from Florida State University; she is the author of *Provisions* (1989) and *Freedom in the Dismal* (1998). She co-authored *"... my magic pours secret libations"* (1996). She has recently completed her second novel, a new collection of poetry, and a children's book. She is currently working on *After the Rain: Life with an Extraordinary Man* about her late husband, visual artist Ed Love. In addition, Love is collaborating with artist Charles Mills on the cultural memoir *Romancing Harlem.*

CHRISTINA J. MAR is a doctoral student in the English Department at the University of California, Riverside. She received her BA in English and women's studies from the University of California, Los Angeles. She specializes in minority discourse, feminist theory, and twentieth-century American literature.

JACQUELINE A. K. MCLEAN earned her PhD in English literature from New York University in 1996. She teaches literature and creative writing at Texas Tech University, where she is also on the adjunct faculty of the Honors College and Women's Studies. Her poems have appeared in several journals. She is co-editing an anthology of poetry of the Southwest and has published three biographies for young adults.

CLAUDIA MILSTEAD is an assistant professor of English at Missouri Valley College. She earned her MA and PhD degrees at the University of Tennessee. She teaches poetry and American literature.

ROBERT MILTNER, assistant professor at Kent State University, Stark Campus, teaches creative writing, composition, and contemporary American and Irish literature. He earned his PhD from Kent State University in 1998. Miltner has published three poetry chapbooks: *On the Off-Ramp* (1996), *The Seamless Serial House* (1993), and *Against the Simple* (1995). His poems, book reviews, and articles have appeared in several journals and periodicals. Additionally, he has written several biographical entries.

DEBORAH M. MIX is visiting assistant professor of English at Kalamazoo College in Michigan. Her articles on modern and contemporary women poets have appeared in *Contemporary Literature*, *Sagetrieb*, and *How2*. She has recently completed work on her book manuscript *"A Vocabulary of Thinking": Gertrude Stein and Contemporary American Women's Experimental Writing*.

KATHLEEN MOORE is a lecturer in the English department at the University of California, Riverside. She has published scholarly articles on Elizabeth Bishop and William Faulkner and co-authored *Techniques for the Thesis-Bound Essay: A Guide to Writing*, forthcoming.

KATHLEEN L. NICHOLS, professor of English and coordinator of women's studies at Pittsburg State University in Kansas, teaches women's literature, American literature, and American drama. Her publications include essays on Anne Sexton, Gwendolyn Brooks, Muriel Rukeyser, Willa Cather, Agnes Smedley, Ernest Hemingway, and earlier American women dramatists and novelists. She is currently working on a study of Emily Dickinson.

ORATHAI NORTHERN is a graduate student at the University of California, Riverside. Her fields of interest include contemporary African American and Asian American literature, critical race and gender theory, and performance studies. She passionately attends theater events and local poetry readings.

KIMBERLY ORLIJAN received her doctorate in English literature from the University of California, Riverside in 1999. Her dissertation deals with the function of food and consumption in twentieth-century literature and culture and includes a chapter on Sylvia Plath. She is currently a lecturer at the university, having taught a variety of courses, including one on twentieth-century women poets and one on Sylvia Plath.

MARIE C. PARETTI received her PhD from the University of Wisconsin, Madison. She has published on both contemporary poetry and composition pedagogy. Her conference papers include work on American poets Louise Glück and Jorie Graham and Afra-Caribbean writer M. Nourbese Philip. Paretti currently teaches literature, technical writing, and composition at Virginia Tech.

DEBORAH PHELPS is an associate professor of English at Sam Houston State University in Huntsville, Texas, where she teaches Victorian literature and women's studies. She has published essays on Elizabeth Barrett Browning, women in academe, and gender and professional writing. Her poetry has most recently appeared in *Southern Poetry Review* and *Parnassus*.

KAREN L. POLSTER received her doctorate in English from the University of California, Riverside, in 2000. She has contributed an entry on Tillie Olsen to *Contemporary Jewish American Novelists* (1997) and has an essay in the upcoming book *The Magical Worlds of Bernard Malamud*. Her articles have appeared in *Modern Jewish Studies* and *Studies in American Jewish Literature*.

RICHARD QUINN holds a PhD in English from the University of Iowa and is currently a scholar and writer living in Chapel Hill, North Carolina. He has published articles and reviews on poetry, jazz, and critical theory in *Callaloo*, *The Iowa Review*,

Postmodern Culture, and other journals. He is currently writing a book on improvisation in contemporary American culture.

AMY MOORMAN ROBBINS has an MA in literature from Portland State University and is currently a PhD candidate in American literature at the University of California, Riverside. Her work focuses on twentieth-century American women poets; she has written and presented papers on Mary Oliver, Anne Sexton, Cherríe Moraga, and playwright Suzan-Lori Parks.

CHRIS RUÍZ-VELASCO is an assistant professor of English at California State University, Fullerton. His work focuses on twentieth-century American literature, Chicano/a literature, and contemporary American culture, especially the place of the text in current culture.

SISTER SHIREE SARANA has published her poetry in several anthologies, has two poetry collections, and writes for community newspapers. She believes that writing is a tool that should be used to enlighten, challenge, inspire, and uplift the human condition.

MAUREEN LANGDON SHAIMAN is currently finishing her PhD in English at the State University of New York, Stony Brook. She teaches contemporary literature, composition and women's studies and writes primarily on contemporary fiction by North American women and on American popular culture.

ERNEST J. SMITH is an associate professor in English at the University of Central Florida. He is the author of several essays on modern American poetry, as well as a book on Hart Crane's *White Buildings* (1990). His current project explores the intersections of American poetry, history, and issues of social concern in relation to gender, ethnicity, and poetic form.

NATALIE STILLMAN-WEBB earned her PhD in English from Purdue University in 2000. She has presented her work on writers such as Toni Morrison, Carole Maso, and Marilynne Robinson at several conferences. She is currently a lecturer in the writing program at the University of Utah, where she teaches professional writing and introductory composition.

REBECCA TILLETT, a research student at the University of Essex in the United Kingdom, studies contemporary Native American literatures of the American Southwest, with the support of the Arts and Humanities Research Board (formerly the British Academy). Her primary area of interest is Leslie Marmon Silko and her controversial novel *Almanac of the Dead* (1991), alongside authors such as Esther Belin, Aaron Carr, Irvin Morris, Simon Ortiz, Luci Tapahonso, and Anna Lee Walters.

CASSANDRA A. VAN ZANDT is a doctoral candidate at the University of California, Riverside. She specializes in modernism, women writers, and poets.

KATHRINE VARNES teaches at the University of Missouri, Columbia. She is co-editor of *An Exaltation of Forms: Contemporary Poets Celebrate the Diversity of Their Art* (2002) and the author of several critical essays on poetry.

BARBARA SCHWARZ WACHAL earned a BS in accounting in 1981; BAs in biology and English in 1997 from Greenville College in Illinois; an MA in English from St. Louis University in 2001, and currently she is a PhD candidate in American studies at St. Louis University. Her interests include American literature, specifically the American Renaissance and antebellum periods, abolitionism, and American culture between the world wars. She has contributed essays to a number of literary and historical collections.

VANESSA WARNE is a fourth-year PhD student in the department of English at Queen's University in Canada. She has presented papers on Romantic and Victorian literature in Scotland and the United States. She has also been published in *Canadian Poetry*.

SANDRA L. WEST teaches African American literature at Virginia Commonwealth University and is co-author of *The Encyclopedia of the Harlem Renaissance* (2002).

SERETHA D. WILLIAMS is an assistant professor of English and world humanities at Augusta State University in Georgia. Her specialization is African and African diaspora women's literature. She has presented and published numerous papers on women's literature. She earned her doctoral degree in comparative literature from the University of Georgia in 1998.